Dramatic Texts and Records of Britain:
A Chronological Topography to 1558

In 1800 entries this valuable reference work covers texts and records of dramatic activity for about 400 sites in Britain from Roman times to 1558. Grouped in sections – Texts listed chronologically; Records of England, Wales, Scotland, Ireland, and Other, classified by county, site, and date; and Doubtful Texts and Records – the entries summarize the contents of each record and give bibliographic information.

Professor Lancashire presents a comprehensive survey of almost every type of literary and historical record, document, and work: civic, church, guild, monastic, and royal court minutes and financial accounts; national records – Chancery, Parliament, Privy Council, Exchequer; royal proclamations; wills; local court rolls; jest-books, poems, prose treatises, sermons; archaeological remains, artifacts, illustrations. He brings together works in several normally unrelated fields: Roman theatre in Britain; medieval drama as such, including the Corpus Christi play and the moral play; court revels of the Tudors, and of their predecessors in England and Scotland; and finally Latin and Greek drama as played in Oxford and Cambridge colleges.

An introduction outlines the history of early drama in Britain. Appendixes include indexes of about 335 towns or patrons with travelling players, complete with rough itineraries; about 180 playwrights; and about 320 playing places and buildings. There are illustrations, four maps, and a large general subject and name index.

IAN LANCASHIRE is Professor of English at the University of Toronto.

IAN LANCASHIRE

Dramatic Texts and Records of Britain: A Chronological Topography to 1558

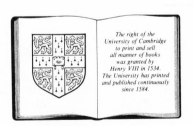

The right of the
University of Cambridge
to print and sell
all manner of books
was granted by
Henry VIII in 1534.
The University has printed
and published continuously
since 1584.

CAMBRIDGE UNIVERSITY PRESS

Cambridge
London   Melbourne   Sydney

Published by the Press Syndicate of the University of Cambridge
The Pitt Building, Trumpington Street, Cambridge CB2 1RP
296 Beaconsfield Parade, Middle Park, Melbourne 3206, Australia

© University of Toronto Press 1984

First published in Great Britain 1984 by Cambridge University Press

Printed in Canada at
the University of Toronto Press

British Library Cataloguing in Publication Data

Lancashire, Ian
Dramatic texts and records of Britain.
1. Theater – Great Britain – History
I. Title
792'.0941   PN2582.S/

ISBN 0 521 26295 X

For A.C. Cawley

Contents

viii Contents

Introduction

FORM AND SCOPE

1 This topographical guide to British dramatic texts and records up to the accession of Elizabeth I is less than a full descriptive calendar and more than a finding list. Each entry has four parts: (1) a reference number; (2) a date or chronological limits; (3) the name of a text; or the record of a dramatic representation or show, a playing place, a playwright, visits of acting troupes, an official act of control over playing, or other evidence relating to plays and their production; and (4) a brief bibliographical reference to the most reliable published editions of the text or the record, or – lacking these – to manuscript sources. I have tried to be complete up to 1558. For isolated records, my entries are fuller than for bulky, complex records, from which, rather than attempting a full descriptive summary, I have gleaned essential facts, useful for indexing purposes, and directed students to the edited materials themselves, which tend to resist simplification or paraphrase.

2 The known body of dramatic texts and records reveals intense, varied, and widespread dramatic activity in these island kingdoms both in the Roman occupation from the first to fifth centuries and in the Middle Ages and early Renaissance from the tenth century onward. Up to the reign of Elizabeth there are about 160 existing dramatic texts or fragments, evidence of dramatic activity or interest from about 395 sites or dioceses, and additional documentation for 334 itinerant playing troupes, of which 205 are identified by their home site and 129 by their patron or principal player. E.K. Chambers, who last collected this evidence – in appendixes W and X of his *Mediaeval Stage* (II, 329-461), published eighty years ago – has less than seventy sites. Since then, theatre

historians and records' editors have been hampered and sometimes mis-led because so much information lay scattered and obscure. This guide thus exists to collect systematically the known historical evidence; the task of providing the interpretation necessary to make of it a proper history has mainly had to be left to others. Already a great deal may be said in assessing the patterns and character of British medieval drama, and yet there is some reason to believe that our present understanding is neither entirely true nor final. The loss and destruction of early local records have been massive; the very nature of plays and pageants was often such as to leave behind no record; the topographical distribution of surviving materials is uneven; some records exist only in unreliable editions or antiquarian works; and a considerable amount of previously obscure or unpublished information is continually being collected or brought to light. What we now have in hand, however, by no means amounts to an interim report. Editors, antiquarians, local historians, and students of our early drama and theatre for over two hundred years have been enthusiastically assembling and preserving a large body of materials for which we must be increasingly grateful as we learn how much of what they were able to see is no longer extant.

A BRIEF HISTORY

3 Accounts of early drama in Britain have relied heavily on existing play-texts, some of them (especially before 1300) Continental, some unrepresentative of their time. Theatre historians have also not been able to look at the sum of dramatic evidence, the texts and records of Romano-British theatre, of medieval scriptural, moral, and folk plays, of neo-classical Latin and Greek drama, and of court spectacle, in order to see if a unified picture of early drama is possible. Glynne Wickham's *Early English Stages* (*118*) and *Medieval Theatre* (*422*) give our most thorough and up-to-date overview at present. A.P. Rossiter's survey (*341*) is a somewhat old-fashioned but still delightful introduction to the subject. For the best specialized works, students should read Hardison (*159*) and Axton (*24*) for drama to ca 1400, Kahrl (*198*) and Tydeman (*396*) for scriptural and moral plays to ca 1550, and Wilson-Hunter (*428*) and the Revels history for sixteenth-century drama (*335*), supplemented by Anglo for court revels (*7*), by Boas for university drama (*48*), and by Craik and Southern (*85, 362*) for the interlude. This short introduction, which presents a new and tentative overview, first through the Roman

period, then by reign, helps guide the user through this guide and suggests some new lines of inquiry.

4 During the Roman occupation, until the late fourth century at least, Britain had large theatres of the sort that were not built again there until 1576. Six towns, Brough-on-Humber, Canterbury, Catterick, Cirencester, Colchester, and St Albans, had conventional Roman theatres with raised stage and sometimes with proscenium arch and curtain slot. Apart from a single allusion in Tacitus' *Annals*, all evidence for this sophisticated tradition, which lasted as long as did medieval drama on these islands, has been archaeological. The performances are unrecorded for which eight tragic or comic masks (these were found at Baldock, Caerleon, Catterick, Harlow, London, and Wilderspool) may have been worn, and in which our first known player ('ludia'), Verecunda, perhaps acted – her name was scratched, graffito-like, on a piece of pottery found at Leicester. Recent scholarship suggests that the proximity of these civic theatres to temples implies a religious drama; and Romano-British drama was indeed homogeneous, urban, and widespread. It had no dominant centre but ranged from Yorkshire to Kent. If amphitheatres were also used for shows, as seems likely, another twelve widely dispersed towns or military centres should be added to an already impressive theatrical network.

5 Dramatic activity in Anglo-Saxon England up to the reign of Edgar (959-73) is obscure, although Edwin's palace at Yeavering in the early seventh century had a partial outdoor theatre suitable for entertainments, and an order from the Council of Rome in 679 that English bishops and clerics should cease countenancing 'jocos vel ludos' before them suggests a very early base for playing in the church. The 'deofles 3amena' condemned by Wulfstan's canons ca 1005-7 may also allude to these, although outside the Old English glosses of (mainly) Continental Latin literature the vernacular lacks any references to what we would call dramatic plays. Yet Jeff Opland (*281*:243-5) has argued from glossaries that the *gleoman* is associated with 'wandering theatrical entertainers' from the late tenth century. One doubtful gloss, ca 1000, is striking: 'Istriones sunt gestuosi qui se uertunt, dicarum feminarum exprimebant qui imitantur ominem rem facere i., imitatores gliwmen.' By about 965-75, with the appearance of the 'Quem quaeritis' liturgical representation at Winchester, however, there was certainly a clerical and monastic dramatic tradition, and its subject was the life of Christ. Another dramatic trope, occurring about a century later at Canterbury, deals with Ascensiontide. (In the eleventh century, when an interlinear gloss was made of

the Winchester liturgical piece, there was in effect a 'Quem quaeritis' in Old English.) Such texts, as Young and others have shown, resemble many tropes on the Continent.

6 Records and texts from the twelfth century reveal a new and possibly unrelated drama developing alongside liturgical representations: extra-liturgical scriptural plays in Anglo-Norman and Latin, performed sometimes outside the church building. The first record of a play of this sort is the St Catherine presented by Geoffrey (shortly to be abbot) of St Albans, formerly of Le Mans, at monastic Dunstable, probably before Henry I (1100-35) at his nearby palace. Under Stephen (1135-54) our first known playwright, Laurentius, prior of Durham, wrote an extant Latin 'peregrinus' dialogue that seems to be a liturgical representation. In the reign of Henry II (1154-89) both liturgical and extra-liturgical drama appears: there are miracle and saints' plays at London (ca 1170-82), and resurrection plays, probably done within the ritual, at the ecclesiastical centres of Lichfield (ca 1188-98) and Eynsham (1196). Our first two vernacular texts are the Anglo-Norman *Mystère d'Adam* and *La Seinte Resurrecion* (ca 1146-74, ca 1180), the latter possibly with auspices at Beverley or Canterbury. During the next century, in the long reign of Henry III (1216-72), the network of monastic and cathedral towns presenting religious plays expands to include Beverley (ca 1220), York (ca 1220-5), Salisbury (1222), Norwich (ca 1260), and Wells (ca 1270). To these can be added the diocese of Lincoln (ca 1235-53). Generally, liturgical representations are indicated, sometimes with masks (as at Beverley and Wells). There must have been a strong dramatic influence from the Continent, for England's kings were truly European princes at this period.

7 Studies of these early texts until recently have derived the vernacular non-liturgical plays from those performed within church ritual. E.K. Chambers (263) and Karl Young (444), followed by Hardin Craig (83) and others, ordered the texts in an achronological way to support a thesis that drama descended in an evolutionary chain of development from trope to Elizabethan tragedy. A.P. Rossiter described these as 'cultural continuities' (341:7). In 1965 O.B. Hardison first collapsed this neat critical superstructure by showing how complex dramatic forms within liturgical drama often predated, and for centuries co-existed with, simpler, supposedly prior forms; and since then liturgists, musicologists (notably William Smoldon [358]), and drama historians have preferred to treat the beginnings of the various play-types separately. Such dramatic traditions, as David Bevington (39) has said, are really discontinu-

ities. Clifford Flanigan (137) gives a particularly helpful synopsis of recent theories of the literary genesis of this drama.

8 E.K. Chambers, followed by R.J.E. Tiddy (388), Charles R. Baskervill (31), Alan Brody (50), and Richard Axton, has also stressed the influence of Germanic cult rites on medieval drama. Folk plays and games must have existed, but we know little of their character. To judge from the number of ecclesiastical prohibitions of 'ludi' in sacred places at this time, however, the church and churchyard often provided the auspices; and these celebrations clearly had play kings and queens and were known by several names: king plays, games, or revels from Surrey west to Somerset, and north to Leicester and Shropshire, summer games in Yorkshire and on both east and west coasts, and perhaps (later) Mays in the midlands and along the east coast. The Lateran Council of 1215 led to many diocesan prohibitions in England in the following decades, but clerical hostility went back at least to Alcuin. Attempts to reconstruct these plays, generally thought to be pre-literate 'ludi' with plots of hero combat, death, and resurrection, have relied on very late folk plays, the earliest of which, the Revesby text of 1779, unfortunately appears to have had the early Tudor interlude, *Youth* (ca 1513), as a direct source. The earliest datable record of a 'mummers' play' of this kind, a St George 'pastime' at Cork no earlier than 1660, is ca 1685 (162:7). Two sixteenth-century Robin Hood plays evidently descend from late medieval ballads rather than games; and, as F.L. Utley and Barry Ward (237) show, the only texts illustrating the St George plays are also ballads. (To what extent the many early records of St George plays, often clearly a saint's play, may bear on the folk play one finds at Cork is also unclear.) Folk 'ludi,' as in pre-Norman England, may have been spectator sports like wrestling, and thus related to tourneying and courtly feats at arms. These may have been the secular plays rewarded by John (1199-1216) at Stogursey in 1210, our first sign of court revels, and prohibited by Alexander II of Scotland ca 1214-15 out of mourning for his late father. (On the other hand, just before, in 1207, the first recorded use of civic pageantry for a royal entry arises in London.)

9 Another factor in the genesis of early British drama is what E.K. Chambers has said it owes nothing to, 'the tragedy and comedy of insolent Greece and haughty Rome' (61:1). Yet by the thirteenth century we find the same pattern of dramatic activity as existed under Roman rule: homogeneous, probably religious plays performed through the provinces in towns with major religious buildings. Early book-catalogues, in addition, testify to English knowledge of profane secular plays. Lists of

holdings record copies of Terence at many sites in the twelfth century, such as monasteries at Canterbury, Durham, and St Albans – the last, interestingly, with ink-drawings of masked actors. Wearing of masks characterizes the early non-liturgical religious drama, as at Beverley (where the practice is termed usual) and Wells. Richard Axton has reasonably argued from Hroswitha's imitations of Terencian comedy at Gandersheim in Saxony, and from Latin farces like *Babio*, that Roman mimicry had from a very early period penetrated clerical plays and that frequent twelfth-century attacks on these suggest their 'contamination ... by secular tradition' (24:31). Recent editions of *Babio*, the composition of which we can now date ca 1150-85 in England, possibly by Walter Map at court, firmly point to a tradition of this kind of profane drama here as well as on the Continent. Theiner (*386*) has also argued that medieval churchmen were generally knowledgeable about Terence's plays. Learned clerics who undertook play productions outside the rigid ritual of the Roman liturgy might well have been inclined to look through a copy of an ancient Roman playwright's works. Then, as today, scholars must have relied on book-learning occasionally to see them through unscholarly problems.

10 Records suggest that the reigns of Edward I (1272-1307), Edward II (1307-27), and Edward III (1327-77) were a transitional period when secular drama was legitimized by court practice. Edward I introduced semi-dramatic personification into his Arthurian 'spel' of 1299, and a long and vigorous tradition of tournaments with participants dressed as dramatic figures began under him at Boston in 1288. Edward III brought this kind of secular play to some sophistication, to judge from his elaborate revels costumes for the Christmas 1347-8 tournies and from his choice of Tartars and of the seven deadly sins as themes for the royal challengers at Cheapside in 1331 and 1362. The text of our first extant secular play, the *Interludium de Clerico et Puella*, dates from the early thirteenth century; perhaps it belonged to the 'ludis theatralibus' at Edward II's court. Disguisings at Christmas had begun in London by 1334, and even provincial towns like Exeter in 1352 presented secular plays. A single instance of private household revels, perhaps dramatic, appeared at Hereford in 1286.

11 Yet the royal court had no great effect then on the homogeneous, church-based drama of the previous century. Kings continued to patronize local plays. Edward I rewarded a St Nicholas play performed by clerks at Gloucester in 1283, his queen witnessed miracle plays put on by the king's own minstrels at Lanercost Priory in 1307, their troubled son had

four clerks play interludes before him at Cowick in 1323, and his son in turn kept Christmas with 'multa mirabilia' at Wells in 1331-2. The court was still too movable to be a serious rival in play-making at Westminster or elsewhere. For these performances, and for the miracles that Lanchester vicars were forbidden to see in 1293, that occurred at Clerkenwell Priory outside London about 1300-1, and that Robert of Brunne condemns in 1303 as being made by clerks, we may justifiably use a poet's phrase ca 1330, 'clerkes plei.' (This phrase was also used to describe religious drama in Scotland throughout the sixteenth century.) A good example of this form is the miracle play performed by clerks in the Carlisle market place in July 1345. The fragmentary *Pride of Life* (ca 1350) may be a clerks' play; and a long history of cathedral drama at Lincoln from 1317 belongs in this tradition. Some of these plays must have been the work of religious guilds led by local chaplains.

12 By about 1335-50, however, the monastic and clerical base for the religious drama seems to be changing. Robert Holcot then refers to a new season for plays, Corpus Christi – a feast that began to be generally observed in England about 1318 – and not long thereafter, in 1353, a religious guild, the Cambridge Corpus Christi Guild, is recorded as having a single play, 'ludo filiorum Israel.' This new feast did not take the religious drama of Christ's Passion and Resurrection out of the churches and into the towns, as some have said. The 'clerk's play' at Beverley and Carlisle had already occurred outdoors in mid-summer. Neither did clerics avoid participating in Corpus Christi plays, some of which, until well into the Reformation, were single interludes or scriptural plays – as at King's Lynn in 1384-5, Bury St Edmunds in 1389 (also by a Corpus Christi Guild), and as late as the 1530s at Tamworth – quite suitable for religious guilds and their clergy. For some time clerks' plays would have appeared quite indistinguishable from plays on Corpus Christi. The new feast did, however, attract plays to a time of year that allowed a wider range of auspices for performance. Winter weather had made Christmas and most Easter plays indoors affairs for which the church was frequently the only available place and the clergy were the inevitable patrons. A production on Corpus Christi, falling between 21 May and 24 June, made increasingly possible play-sponsorship and play-performance by secular authorities, civic officials, and craft guilds, in the streets and market-places of the community. Exeter and (probably) Cambridge used their own market-places as a 'theatre' by 1338 and 1348, and the henge at Castilly in Cornwall was reworked ca 1275-1325 to make a 'Plain an gwarry' for an audience of up to two thousand persons, per-

haps to see an early lost version of the *Ordinalia* (ca 1375). The most striking example of this change in auspices is of course the development of the great Corpus Christi pageant cycles in the important towns of the north, and (perhaps more slowly) in towns in the midlands, East Anglia, and the south (Coventry by 1392, Ipswich by ca 1400, and Exeter before 1413). Here the control over the play-text and the actual production and financing of the plays lay with city officials and the craft guilds. A good instance of the co-existence of the old clerks' play and the new lay drama occurs at York in 1376. In the very year when its great Corpus Christi cycle, a product of civic guilds (not the minster), is first recorded, one town cleric wills his play-books to a fellow churchman.

13 It is tempting to see in the old clerks' plays the nucleus of the repertory of itinerant town players who begin to be noticed in town accounts about this time. We meet the first such troupe in 1360 in Oxford. The financial accounts of Reading (from 1382) and New Romney (from 1387) reveal many parish troupes. The dispute about playing garments at Everton in 1418 probably involves one. Even parishes without the financial resources of guilds moved to perform plays, and although we do not find explicit evidence of motive at this early date it seems likely that, as at Pulloxhill ca 1486-93, parishes put on plays to raise money for maintaining the church fabric and for other community ends. Much of this local parish activity, however, is bound to have been secular and folk; Robert of Brunne had, some fifty-five years before, condemned summer games along with miracles.

14 The reign of Richard II (1377-99) witnessed the first serious attack on the old 'clerks' play.' The threat did not come from the court, although at this time in the king's mummings at Eltham and London, for which he relied on (it seems) a regular troupe of mummers, a distinctive kind of revels developed that would be almost lost after his death until the rise of the Tudors. Neither did the success of the crafts' Corpus Christi play in itself reduce the impulse of clerks to put on plays. If I am right in making out *The Castle of Perseverance* in its original form to be the Lincoln Pater Noster (and a clerks') play, first recorded in 1397, then York's own Pater Noster (1385) was also this kind of piece, belonging to a different tradition from the civic pageants. Such moral dramatizations of the conflict between trumping, wailing vices and virtues intent on saying their 'pitter-patter' ('as men seyen' in the York play, according to a Lollard ca 1385-95) must have pre-dated the Cheapside tournament of 1362 in which the challengers were the seven sins. The two playbooks of both the Pater Noster and Creed plays of York, sponsored by religious guilds

(not the crafts) until the dissolution, were owned by chaplains, who willed them at death as if they were private property. Clerical drama can also be glimpsed at Bicester Priory (ca 1377-99), Hedon (1390), Whitby Abbey (ca 1394-6), Selby Abbey (1398), and Wells (1407). The new stumbling block for this old ecclesiastical drama was Lollard hostility to miracle plays, especially when *performed* by churchmen. Clerics were vulnerable to such criticism in a way lay folk were not. Previous criticism had been restricted to 'ludi' inappropriately done on consecrated ground, and even Robert of Brunne had defended both the Nativity and the Resurrection plays. Wyclif and his followers, however, in the 'treatise of miracles' playing' ca 1380-1410 and elsewhere, attacked miracle plays on principle as false images. Merely by having the Miller's clerk Absolon participate in miracles, Chaucer also satirized them.

15 Under this assault the civic and guild plays did not fall, but the religious drama of London did, for alone of all the great towns of England it tried to realize the form of the Corpus Christi play within what were exclusively ecclesiastical or parish auspices. Under Richard II the London miracle plays briefly flourished. St Paul's School was perhaps performing Old Testament history plays at Christmas in 1378, and the Clerkenwell Old and New Testament plays acted generally in August – and still, it seems, the work of the city clerks – appeared several times between 1384 and 1391, and on two occasions the king himself and his nobility, sharing anti-Lollard views, attended. As far as we know, no other London guild supported these plays, and the only other civic dramatic activity then relates to royal entries.

16 Under Henry IV (1399-1413), Henry V (1413-22), and Henry VI (1422-61) the old drama of London crumbled, and with it went the attempt of the City – which had grown to be the country's financial centre – to host and perhaps to dominate in play-making. The Roman model, a homogeneous decentralized network of individual provincial play-making towns, remained intact. The great Clerkenwell plays were revived briefly in 1409-11, at which time Henry IV witnessed them from a special scaffold, but thereafter the London clerks lost their importance. The record of four London clerks hired by the Brewers to put on a play in 1435 shows how they had fallen to the status of one of many competing playing troupes, and by 1464, when taking part in a pageant for Elizabeth Woodville's coronation, they performed as singers only. Until the clerks moved their play-making across the river onto Bankside and into the London seats of the nobility and the bishops their influence on drama would be small. The next monarch who to our knowledge wit-

nessed a Corpus Christi play was Margaret, queen of Henry VI, in 1457, and she had to travel to Coventry to see one. Reginald Pecock, who came to court from Oxford under Humphrey, duke of Gloucester, the first known patron of a playwright, and who should thus have known something about drama, wrote about 1449 in an anti-Lollard work that plays showing Christ's death occur 'ful seelde and in fewe placis and cuntrees.' One wealthy lay Londoner's extremely strict memoranda to himself, ca 1425-35, on his religious devotions and moral self-criticism firmly reject any frequenting of 'spectacula,' and his apparently Lollard principles must have been representative of his fellow citizens' views. These are telling expressions of the isolation of London and the home counties from the rest of the island.

17 After 1400, Corpus Christi plays by craft guilds, generally still written (one imagines) but now infrequently acted by clerks (as at Fountains Abbey ca 1456-9 and Lincoln from 1472), emerged in many other provincial centres: Durham (1403), Exeter (before 1413), Ipswich, Chester (by 1422), Worcester (probably from 1424), and Newcastle (1426). Under James II (1437-60), Scotland's first recorded Corpus Christi plays start up at Aberdeen (1440) and Dundee (ca 1450). Our major play-texts from this period, including the York, N-town, and Towneley cycles (by about 1450), are not from the London area but from East Anglia or the north, where productions by clerics were more secure, if not immune, from Lollard persecution. The revised ending of *The Castle of Perseverance* (ca 1425-40), in which a debate among the Four Daughters of God replaces a miraculous intercession by the Virgin Mary (an image?), is one possible example of the reactionary effects of the Lollard movement. The N-town cycle, written and compiled by a cleric, monk, or friar, may be another. It is a manuscript 'edition' of a base cycle of Old and New Testament pageants, a two-part passion play acted in alternate years, a Marian cycle of ecclesiastical origin, and several individual plays including an Assumption of the Virgin that must have been performed in a large cathedral or collegiate church. Did this Norfolk clerk-compiler incorporate texts with such different auspices in order to preserve ecclesiastical plays that were no longer being performed?

18 Early criticism on the scriptural cycles and the moral plays (and on two other traditions, the saint's play and the miracle play, surviving only in a fragment, 'Dux Moraud') identifies them as the third stage in the evolutionary secularization of church drama. Such analysis, as by A.P. Rossiter, vividly portrays Gothic 'contemporaneity' in the cycles, espe-

cially in pageants dealing with the marital woes of Noah, of Joseph, and of Gyb and Mak in the Wakefield 'Second Shepherds' Play,' and 'carnal reverence' in the moral plays (pp 71, 89), as in the scatology in *Mankind*. This approach stresses, various students now believe, certain 'realistic' or 'comic' pageants at the expense of more representative plays in which legitimate devotional motives outweigh the playwright's 'secular commitment.' Arnold Williams' fine study of the characterization of the Towneley Pilate (426) also belongs in a long tradition of critical emphasis on elements in these cycles that seem most at odds with religious devotion. Likewise, existing moral plays, thought to have grown out of Prudentius' *Psychomachia* and the Pater Noster play, seemed 'degraded' (A.W. Pollard's term for *Mankind* [234]) in their satire on social and political vices. The most complete statement of this approach is by Robert L. Ramsay in his introduction to Skelton's *Magnificence* (1908).

19 Yet the truth is probably nearer Richard Axton's shrewd guess that the cycles, far from being an advance in secular entertainment, 'were in some ways a *reaction* on the part of orthodoxy to a long and flourishing tradition of miracle plays performed for popular audiences by preaching friars and enterprising worldly clerks' (25:39). Assessing the cycles' original literary character, let alone showing that it was reactionary in its time, proves difficult because most play texts date from the second half of the fifteenth century (Chester's may date from the early Tudor period) and all show signs of multiple authorship and varying dates of composition. Even where the textual strata are ignored, however, a variety of recent approaches has demonstrated that the cycles are essentially devotional, not secular, plays. In 1946 Harold Gardiner (146) even attributed the demise of the cycles almost solely to religious conviction, that is, to Protestant censorship. Critics have since proposed a variety of unifying principles for the cycles, all devotional: typological foreshadowing (V.A. Kolve [211]); Christ's own works in the world, that is, the meaning of the Feast of Corpus Christi (Jerome Taylor [380]); and the structure of the creed, as well as iconographical cycles of medieval religious art (Rosemary Woolf [436]). Recent complete books devoted to one cycle (three on Wakefield, and several on N-town and York), Clifford Davidson's EDAM series, and many scholars publishing article-length studies in journals such as Davidson's own *Comparative Drama*, and in anthologies edited by Taylor-Nelson (381) and Denny (99), have all furthered this approach. And, after the books by Mary P. Coogan (1947) and John J. Molloy (1952) on *Mankind* and *Wisdom* and their devotional sources,

critics such as Merle Fifield (*136*) and Robert Potter (*307*) have taken an approach to the form, as suggested by G.R. Owst (*282*) in 1961, through the didactic sermon.

20 While play-making in the counties boomed, the only dramatic activity in Lancastrian London – what is surely the key to the city's future dominance in that respect – was the growth of a commercial audience for players. London guilds, lacking a tradition of drama themselves, sought out plays for their annual feasts: the Drapers (1404), the Brewers (1425), the Blacksmiths (1426), the Cutlers (1442), and the Carpenters (1454) all hired players in this century. This market attracted provincial players (as from Gloucester in 1432) and also probably helped create the very early acting troupes patronized by noblemen, the earliest of which in this guide is four boys of Thomas Beaufort, duke of Exeter (whose seat was at Greenwich), that played interludes before Henry VI at Eltham in Christmas 1426. One such troupe, that of Jack Travaill – which also performed then (and in the following year) – was evidently from London. Did this, the country's first recorded professional troupe, arrive from the Continent in the wake of the Lancastrian victory at Agincourt a decade before? The play of a knight called 'fflorence' performed at Bermondsey in 1444, and the clerks' plays in neighbouring Southwark from 1444 to 1459, however, probably are not by semi-professional playing troupes acting before guild audiences in this period. Like Elizabethan players avoiding a puritan City citizenry, these clerks may have settled on the south bank to avoid the repressive, Lollard-minded authorities of London.

21 The Lollard sentiments that curtailed scriptural plays in London also undermined court revels under the Lancastrian kings. Henry IV and his son both uncovered Lollard assassination plots that were to have disguised the traitors as Christmas mummers (in 1400 and 1415), and so it is not surprising that, apart from a special Eltham mumming for the emperor of Constantinople, mummings are not recorded in either reign. During the protectorship of John, duke of Bedford, 1422-9, John Lydgate wrote seven extant mummings for Henry VI, and his council probably ordered playing troupes for the Christmas celebrations of 1426-7, but as soon as this contemplative king could govern for himself these revels appear to have ceased. He rewarded 'lusores' on St George's feast at Windsor the next year (a garter ceremony? and in 1449-50?); yet in other respects (apart from an ambiguous reference to those who are probably his minstrels in 1451 at Canterbury) Henry's piety, in later years compounded by a depression and a stupor severe enough to sug-

gest madness, abhorred entertainments. Although his play-loving queen, Margaret of Anjou, kept traditional Christmas disguisings in 1452-3, Henry's attitude to them can be surmised from a remarkable anecdote by John Blacman about the king and his shock at a Christmas show of bare-breasted young women. In contrast, court revels in Scotland are well documented from 1446 on.

22 Edward IV, who might have taken part in the show that offended Henry, nonetheless shared Lancastrian indifference to court drama. In his reign (1461-83) there are no records of any court drama whatsoever, aside from a doubtful troupe of players who may be minstrels, and a few coronation pageants; and London plays were limited to guild feasts and an embryonic Midsummer Watch (1477, cancelled in 1481). This state of affairs is hard to explain, because in court ceremonial and in jousting Edward shared the Burgundian taste for splendour. Whatever the cause, the result was that, as the provincial towns provided auspices for the great cycles rejected by London, wealthy noble patrons and educational or monastic institutions – not the king's court – had to meet the demand for sophisticated secular plays.

23 The nobility led the way. Tito Livio Frulovisi had come to England from Italy at the invitation of Humphrey, duke of Gloucester, and had written two Latin comedies there for him in 1437-8. Elizabeth Berkeley, countess of Warwick, is the first noble figure whom we know to have had household disguisings during Christmas (1420-1). Humphrey Stafford, duke of Buckingham, had a special disguising chamber at Writtle by 1442-3; and he evidently allowed his players to tour in 1451. In this decade various patrons, from the earl of Westmorland (1457) to country gentry like Sir Thomas Brews (1454) and Sir William Plumpton (1456), sponsored troupes. At the beginning of Edward's reign, in 1463, there were enough interluders with access to expensive clothes customarily worn by men of high rank – and thus probably with the backing of a noble patron – to receive a special exemption from a statute governing apparel. Henry Bourchier, earl of Essex and lord treasurer in 1460-2, may have urged this protection, since he is known to have had a troupe (by 1469); and powerful noblemen like the earls of Arundel (1477) and Oxford (1490) followed suit. From this period a larger number of household accounts of noblemen and wealthy gentry survive, and they reveal a taste for plays similar to that of the London guilds and – a new development? – of provincial town mayors and councils. Among places rewarding players or having disguisings are the seats of Lady Morley in Norfolk (before 1459), Sir John Howard at Stoke-by-Nayland (from

1465), John Arundell at Lanherne (1466-7), and Sir William Stonor at Stonor (1481-2).

24 The surviving non-civic play-texts have been linked, however, not with patrons or even towns but with what we might call the provincial courts: Cambridge, Oxford, schools like Eton, and monastic centres. Thomas Chaundler had written the extant closet morality, *Liber Apologeticus*, at Oxford about 1457-61, and players were received at New College, Oxford, from 1461, and at King's Hall, Cambridge, from at least 1457. The Winchester interlude *Occupation and Idleness* seems to have been written for presentation at Winchester School, *Mankind* has strong links with the Cambridge area, and *Wisdom* has features that have suggested ecclesiastical auspices near London. All are moral interludes written ca 1460-80 with a vigorous secular element. In Scotland this university drama began at Glasgow in 1462 with an interlude on St Nicholas's day. England's first two known secular playwrights came from precisely this breeding ground. Sir Thomas More's comedy of Solomon was probably written ca 1492-4 at Oxford's Magdalen College, which had a tradition of drama – both the secular (?) play with 'le capp mayntenaunce' in 1486-7 and an Easter play by 1495. As Alan Nelson has shown, Henry Medwall had been exposed to King's College (Cambridge) disguisings in the 1480s, just before he produced the remarkable *Fulgens & Lucres* and *Nature* for the court in the next decade. For the first time, the old Roman model is threatened by the emergence of a 'national' theatre in the south, homogeneous but narrow, the product of a closely knit elite of university fellows and clerks.

25 Our interest in reading these texts as products of individual troupes, patrons, and courts (that is, of particular auspices) has a long history. Its beginnings lay in the isolation of certain pageants of the Towneley cycle as belonging to the small town of Wakefield – or to auspices in its vicinity – and to Hardin Craig's fruitless attempts to locate the N-town cycle at Lincoln (following a suggestion by C.M. Gayley in 1908). Craig's work in Lincoln local archives led to the first Malone Society edition of medieval play records, that for Lincolnshire by Stanley J. Kahrl (*196*) in 1974. Independently, Renaissance theatre historians of the last century searching for evidence of visits by Shakespeare's company to provincial towns drew attention to richly detailed borough accounts, and in 1965 Giles Dawson's edition of the Kent dramatic records (*96*) was published by the Malone Society. The climate of interest in both the sites of medieval play-texts and the itinerant companies that carried performances to them led to Richard Southern's seminal book on the staging site of *The*

Castle of Perseverance (*361*) and David Bevington's equally important *From 'Mankind' to Marlowe* (*40*), which showed how most sixteenth-century moral interludes were composed with a given (restrictive) troupe-size in mind. In 1959 the first volume of Glynne Wickham's *Early English Stages* explored the highly varied kinds of staging available to medieval players, a theme central to Alan Nelson's attack on the 'true-processional' performance of the York cycle as technically unfeasible (*273*) and to Stanley J. Kahrl's analysis of existing texts as examples of 'station to station' or 'place and scaffold' plays (*198*). By this time a knowledge of dramatic auspices had become an essential prerequisite for interpretation of a text. Aided by Jacob Bennett's studies of the dialects of early play-texts, and by record series such as REED and the Malone Society, the work of giving plays 'a local habitation' continues to occupy many minds.

26 Our regnal history continues with Richard III, the last Yorkist (1483-5), who was probably not unlike his brother in his attitude to court revels. Richard lived much in the north, and its love for pageantry comes out in his progress of 1483, and in his attendance on the Coventry Corpus Christi play only weeks before his defeat at Bosworth. Yet Richard, his playing troupe while duke of Gloucester notwithstanding, left no sign of having wanted drama at court.

27 Henry VII (1485-1509) also attended the Coventry Corpus Christi play in 1487 and 1493, but unlike Richard he had a shrewd appreciation of the political advantages that court revels would give a monarch whose claim to the throne was derived almost entirely from his victory under the God of Battles. Under Henry and his second son and namesake (1509-47) we see the triumph of a new centralized 'clerks' play' over local citizen drama. The court at Greenwich, Richmond, and West-minster, and – for the first time – London (by the efforts of its guilds) made the capital eminent in English drama. The royal court created a year-round industry in revels – well documented by Sydney Anglo (*7*) – that employed the royal chapel, the king's interluders, and a busy circle of craftsmen (to judge from Richard Gibson's revels accounts) in putting on disguisings and plays by first-rate secular clerks: playwrights such as Henry Medwall, William Cornyshe (father and son), John Skelton, John Heywood, and John Redford. The first play performance known to have occurred before Henry VII was clerical drama: York welcomed him in June 1486 with a play by four clerks (only on his second visit to the city in 1487 did he see the Corpus Christi play). No company toured the provincial cities more frequently than the king's players, insight into the

workings of which can be gained by looking at Chancery suits involving members George Maller and John Young. The market for players' services that the guild feasts had helped to create now brought more companies into being, probably encouraged playwright John Rastell – a Coventry man who significantly moved from that great Corpus Christi city into London to try his fortune in drama – to build, about 1524-6, the first London public theatre, in Finsbury Fields, and turned the presses of Wynkyn de Worde, Richard Pynson, and the Rastells themselves to printing play-texts for public consumption. At the same time the London parishes began putting on plays, St Mary at Hill (1485), St Andrews, Holborn (1503), St Stephen Walbrook (1519), St Peter Cheap (1519), St Andrew Hubbard (1526), All Hallows in the Wall (1528), and St Katharine's (1529). Their plays joined the guilds' magnificent Midsummer Show, held twice annually on the eves of 23 and 28 June and offering many different religious and historical pageants each year.

28 London and the court in the early Tudor period gave auspices for a national drama, but what fed that enterprise were the universities, the county seats of the nobility, and schools in the large towns and in the monasteries: that is, the above-mentioned provincial courts. Cambridge and Oxford trained those clerks who administered the courts, royal and noble, and filled their chapels; and their texts were changing with the spread of Italian humanism. Isolated bequests of Terence, Plautus, Seneca, and Euripides in the mid-fifteenth century imply that these university fellows did not much read such works, but the publication of a Terence at London ca 1495-7 coincided with his appearance on the Cambridge curriculum by 1502, weighted equally with Aristotle. Oxford taught Terence from ca 1505-15 (and Greek drama from 1517), to such an extent that John Dorne's book sales there in 1520 included many copies of both Terence and Aristophanes. Within a decade of introducing Roman comedies as texts the colleges began staging them: at Cambridge, a Terence in 1510-11 and a Plautus in 1522-3; and at Oxford, a comedy at Wolsey's Cardinal's College in 1529. In turn, the students who acted in them became schoolmasters who had, by statute, to use Terence daily as a text in Latin conversation: St Paul's (1518), Ipswich (1528), Cuckfield (1528), Eton (1529), and Winchester (ca 1529-31). At Wressle a chapel performed scriptural plays for the fifth earl of Northumberland; its clerks' educational background may explain why comedies and tragedies are mentioned in his Twelfth Night ceremonial ca 1515. Then the schools truly became play-grounds, and the school master a *ludimagister*. Paul's boys gave Terence's *Phormio* before Wolsey at court in 1528 (a year after

Wolsey's own men did the *Menaechmei* there), and by the 1540s even as small a school as Hitchin had a large dramatic repertory. Although the accommodation of education to drama was not always easy – Vives removed Terence and Plautus from the Princess Mary's programme of studies in 1523, Edward VI cancelled the Terence lecture at Cambridge in 1549, and Bury school in 1550 taught only the 'chaster' plays – the university and school curricula came to be dominated by drama texts. By the 1550s both Oxford and Cambridge were staging Greek and Latin comedies and tragedies by all the major authors. Few educated Englishmen, no matter where they lived in these islands, could for long avoid seeing or hearing of the drama of the humanist clerks.

29 Although academic players did not travel, noblemen's interluders visited college towns, as well as provincial cities, priories, and other noblemen's seats from Sheriff Hutton in the north to Belvoir and Hunstanton in the midlands and Wulfhall and Tiverton in the south. The fifth earl of Northumberland had interluders too, as did – in Henry VIII's reign – four dukes, three marquesses, eleven other earls, and a dozen or so lords, not to omit the members of the king's family. The number of players in over 55% of these troupes (whether sponsored by towns or by patrons) was four, to judge from figures that survive for sixty troupes in all. Only a little over 10% had five players, that is, the 'ffoure men and a boy' who appear in *Sir Thomas More* in the early 1590s (40:68-85). Reciprocal visits by these troupes over many years led to the development of a common repertory of plays, which became the political cutting edge of these bustling, ambitious patrons. The printed plays of this period, that is, moral interludes, seem to make up this repertory; an anonymous letter about 1500, in a collection with Oxford associations, implies that the owners of English interludes and comedies were persons whose co-operation was difficult to get. Were they patrons with wealth or high rank? On the other hand, most scriptural, Corpus Christi, and saints' plays, and Robin Hood or king plays and games, probably belonged to troupes sponsored by towns.

30 Critical studies on these play-texts have also, unsurprisingly, been affected by the same evolutionary theories that complicated research on earlier plays. The closer to Shakespeare's plays in time, the more scholars have assumed the obvious lines of influence. Historical surveys have covered the London-Oxbridge centres of performance of the early Tudor period. Sydney Anglo (7) and Gordon Kipling (206) have examined court revels; C.C. Stopes (373) and H.N. Hillebrand (168) the royal chapel children; Albert Feuillerat, the documents of the Revels Office (an

edition [131]); F.S. Boas (48) and G.C.M. Smith the university drama; T.H. Vail Motter (261) the school drama; A.W. Reed (328) and Pearl Hogrefe (172) the humanist circle of playwrights, Medwall, Rastell, and Heywood; J.H. Smith and Ruth H. Blackburn (46) the Biblical drama, mainly non-civic; and in the past few years full scholarly editions of the works of the most important Tudor playwrights by Barry Adams, Richard Proudfoot, Richard Axton, and Alan Nelson have been added to the biographical monographs done by scholars of the previous generation. Books on special themes cover most of these play-texts: B.J. Whiting on proverbs (420); J.E. Bernard, Jr (37), on metre; T.W. Craik (85) on staging and costumes; Richard Southern (362) on hall staging; and David Bevington (41) on political and social context. Some of this scholarship has allowed a hidden 'evolutionary' assumption that 'new' forms like the moral interlude had replaced the older drama. Three extraordinary bibliographical tools, STC (370); W.W. Greg's *Bibliography of the English Printed Drama* (153); and Alfred Harbage's *Annals* (11), revised by S. Schoenbaum, have indirectly countenanced this assumption. So (justly) influenced have scholars been by STC and Greg that playwrights like John Redford, whose work survives only in manuscript, have been neglected. More important, because none of the dozens of provincial scriptural or folk plays from this period was, to our knowledge, printed, our history of early Tudor drama has been heavily biased in favour of moral interludes, which tended to be published not only because they were topical but because printers had good reason to court the noble patrons of the troupes responsible for performing them. The play-text most often cited as representative of the period is one that was printed four times, more than any other such play: yet *Everyman*, a moral translated from the Dutch, is quite atypical of English drama up to its publication. No book on the town drama of Tudor England has so far been written.

31 Yet the provincial civic and guild plays grew unchecked. Corpus Christi plays or pageants, at times in cycle form, spread to – or are recorded first at – Salisbury (1461), Stamford (1465), Lincoln (1472), Great Yarmouth (1473), Plymouth (1479), Ashburton (1492), Canterbury (before 1494), Bristol (1499), Glastonbury (1500), and about ten other towns by 1535. Records in Scotland show apparently new plays at Perth (1485), Lanark (1488), and Edinburgh (1503); Dublin had its Corpus Christi play before 1498; our first documented performance of a Cornish miracle play relates to Sancreed about 1500; and Welsh scriptural play-texts crop up in this period, some of which may have been

performed by touring Abergavenny parishioners in 1537. There is no sign of waning inspiration in the repertory either: striking saints' plays appear in many towns, a St Meriasek at Camborne (1495-1501), a Mary Magdalen at Taunton (1504), a St Christian at Coventry (1505), a St Christina at Bethersden (1519), and Feliciana and Sabina at Shrewsbury (1515-16), to name a few. A will of 1499 mentions a 'ludo de Mankynd' at East Retford, just over twenty miles west of Lincoln, and this seems to be a version of what is likely the old Pater Noster play of Lincoln, *The Castle of Perseverance*. Some older forms, such as the Robin Hood play (first mentioned here at Exeter in 1427, and rarely found, until the late Tudor period, anywhere on the east coast from Kent to Yorkshire, although a text survives from the Norwich area about 1475), experience a sudden growth in popularity. Between 1490 and 1530 at least fourteen towns first record this play or game. The St George pageant or play, first recorded at Chester in 1431, grows in a dozen towns, from Lydd (1456) to Stratford (1541) and throughout England, except for Lincolnshire and Yorkshire.

32 Only occasionally does one find evidence that at this early date the new national (London-based) clerks' drama is beginning to affect its town counterpart. When Beverley needed to have its Corpus Christi play 'transposed' in 1519-20, the town governors turned to William Pyers, a poet and clerical retainer in the household of the fifth earl of Northumberland at Wressle, a seat that rivalled the royal court in both scriptural plays and interludes. In the south, perhaps because of pressure from the Lord Warden of the Cinque Ports, the town of Lydd hired Richard Gibson, the yeoman of the king's revels and a former king's interluder, to revise its own St George play in 1526-7 and 1530-2; and New Romney was forced to get, also through Gibson (it appears), the king's permission in 1517 and 1532-3 to put on its Passion play. The 'property player' that Boxford, Suffolk, brought to town, with players from other towns, to put on a local play in 1535 was probably educated enough to be called, in the loose contemporary way, a clerk. John Coldewey (71) has discussed the work of this professional, whose role in modifying the old tradition of provincial civic drama must have been considerable.

33 Up to the mid-1530s, however, the crown did little to regiment drama in the network of provincial towns. The king's 'matter' and the Reformation changed all that. Plays at court had long served political expediency – for example, Medwall's *Fulgens and Lucres* issued a stinging rebuke to nobility whose suppression was in the interest of Henry VII and of Medwall's patron Archbishop Morton; and Anne Boleyn's rela-

tion, Thomas, earl of Wiltshire, had a good pragmatic reason to depict Wolsey sent down to hell in a farce of 1531 – but it remained for Henry VIII to formulate a wide-ranging rationale and programme for national drama. At first, action was haphazard. London and the court mocked cardinals in plays and games in 1533. One play intended at Gloucester College, Oxford, 'a place of monks,' was put down by Cromwell in 1534. Then Richard Morison proposed to the king in 1535-6 that the popular Robin Hood plays be suppressed in favour of anti-papist propaganda. The former survived, as Bishop Latimer found to his indignation in 1549; but papist pageants such as the St Thomas at Canterbury (in 1538) were purged, and the latter thrived. About that time John de Vere, earl of Oxford and Great Chamberlain, harnessed John Bale's considerable energies to the task, and soon Thomas Cromwell had Bale, John Heywood, and Nicholas Udall all hard at work. We would give much to have Bale's play on the king's two marriages, Heywood's masque of Arthur's knights, Udall's 'Ezechias,' and even plays such as the *Rex Diabole* that Lady Lisle's London agent found in 1538 among the 'new scripture matters' waiting for a buyer. In the late 1530s Thomas Wylley of Yoxford and Robert Radcliffe of Cambridge offered Cromwell and the king various plays or dialogues. From 1536 to 1540 Cromwell's players acted at Cambridge, Shrewsbury, Leicester, Oxford, Thetford, Barnstaple, Maldon, and York, and Bale's troupe made a sensation by playing anti-Becket matter at Canterbury in 1538-9. By 1539 these anti-papal 'sports and follies' had reached the common village feast, according to a French diplomat. Not all this change in direction was simply the will of the king and his ministers. In Scotland at the same time anti-papist plays by Friar Kyllour at Stirling (ca 1535-6), James Wedderburne at Dundee (ca 1540-5), and Sir David Lindsay at Linlithgow (1540) were competing with more traditional 'clerk plays.'

34 In England, what Henry VIII had done was to unleash forces not even he could control, and a period of retrenchment set in. Cromwell's fall was bad news for many playing companies as well: attacks on propagandistic religious plays started up in London in 1541, and the first statute prohibiting unorthodox plays was passed in 1543. This was a brief respite for the established town drama.

35 The reigns of Edward VI (1547-53) and Mary (1553-8) were a study in contrast in their attitude to drama, as in many other things. Edward's government relaxed control on itinerant playing companies sympathetic to the Protestant cause. The only record I have seen of a nobleman's troupe performing a *scriptural* play turns up in Norwich in 1551-2 when

the marquess of (?) Dorset's gameplayers did the play of 'zacheus,' the New Testament rich man of Luke 19 who gave away half his goods to the poor. The crown, in contrast, increasingly acted to suppress and restrict local playing in the network of provincial towns. The Feast of Corpus Christi was suppressed in 1548. Any play counter to the Act of Uniformity was subject to penalty by a statute of 1549. As a central authority took grip, elitist drama at court, at schools like Hitchin, and at the universities prospered. Young Edward had his own 'Comediam de meretrice Babylonica' performed at Hampton Court revels in Christmas 1548, and John Bale, returning from exile abroad for, as it turned out, a brief stay, outraged one Bishopstoke conservative in religion by putting on his *Three Laws* for the town at Christmas 1551. When the citizen unwisely suggested that the king was but a poor child in the hands of heretical elements, Bale retaliated by publishing a pamphlet ridiculing this citizen for his mad fits. Very few new provincial town plays were undertaken, and even in London the once-thriving parish plays virtually ceased after 1540. Coventry's semi-dramatic Corpus Christi procession ended in 1546. By 1550, when Henry Bullinger presented to the king his *Decades*, which attacked all Passion plays, York had removed the Marian pageants from its cycle, and Chester both the clergy's Corpus Christi play and the Last Supper pageant. Reacting to the Wymondham rebellion of July 1549, which had been set off at the time of the annual town play, the Council prohibited all plays in English throughout the realm for the next three months. By 1552 the Council had taken to jailing in the Tower of London a cooper who had been guilty of making plays.

36 The tables were turned when Edward's sister came to the throne the next year. Mary had much more to fear from itinerant playing troupes than from the town drama, and her control of these companies tightened: in 1555 she ordered heretical books (including Bale's) burned, and the next year she forbad performances by these troupes throughout the kingdom. London in 1554 and 1557, Hatfield Broad Oak in 1556, and Canterbury in 1557 felt special acts of repression. One incident illustrates her attitude. In 1553, some months after Mary came to the throne, certain players from Coventry were jailed, apparently on religious grounds, but one of the most stubborn of these, John Careless, was let out briefly so that he could take part in the town's own play, after which he returned himself into custody. Other towns too benefited from Mary's decentralizing of controls on their activities. Canterbury briefly revived its St Thomas pageant in 1554-5, New Romney planned to revive its pre-Reformation Passion play in 1556, Wakefield's Corpus Christi play

appeared (first?) in 1555, Southwark brought back its Palm Sunday prophets in 1555, and for the first time in perhaps 150 years London was
able to see a Passion play, at the Grey Friars, in 1557. Even at court and
college play-making seems to have shed some of its earlier responsibili-
ties. William Baldwin's winsome and sadly lost 'discourse of the hole
worlde' in sixty-two natural and allegorical characters whose names begin with 'L,' and *Gammer Gurton's Needle* by Master W.S., lack overt signs
of dogma or political will. Even *Respublica*, dramatizing the politics of
the time, applies its whip lightly.

37 At Elizabeth's accession, Mary's tolerant policy towards town
drama at least, although not her politics, was continued. Sir William
Cecil immediately moved to use plays against Catholics, but an early
proclamation of 1559 banning plays was recalled, and shortly afterwards
Elizabeth acted to protect the Catholic religion from attack in plays. She
also did little to prevent towns from enjoying their old drama. The Scottish Kirk tried to crush, by statute, Robin Hood plays in 1555 and all
scriptural or clerk plays in 1574, but Elizabeth, as the head of the English
church, apparently preferred if at all possible to let local opinion decide
the fate of local plays. In general Corpus Christi plays continued until
the ecclesiastical authorities – who were unquestionably opposed to
them – had attracted local popular opinion to their side, or until the
towns wanted to spend their money on other things: Sherborne lasted
until 1574, Wakefield until 1576, and York until 1580 (although Archbishop Grindal had managed to silence the Creed play in 1568 and the
Pater Noster play in 1575). St Ives had a six-day play with a structure for
Heaven in 1575; Salisbury presented Thomas Ashton's Passion play at
least until 1569; Tewkesbury abbey rented out garments for a Christ as
late as 1578; and Boston planned a Passion play in 1579. Sometimes the
towns turned to Old Testament subjects: Lincoln acted Tobias in 1564,
Derby did Holofernes in 1572, and Coventry abandoned, if reluctantly,
its Corpus Christi play in 1580 for the Destruction of Jerusalem in 1584.

38 Some recent scholarship argues that these scriptural plays were
harried off their pageant wagons by puritan scruples, but there is evidence that puritans were ready to use plays for their own purposes and
that the decline of the local scriptural play also had economic causes.
John Coldewey (70) has shown that in Essex, at least, the play-motive
was profit and the heavy expense of costumes alone discouraged towns
from providing what, to judge from Willis' description of a performance
by a travelling professional company in Gloucester ca 1565-75, was more
cheaply available from troupes originating in London. One wonders

whether ecclesiastical authorities would have had the success they did in suppressing scriptural plays at York, Coventry, Chester, and Wakefield if these towns had not been facing financial collapse and if their civic officials had not been vulnerable to local pressure to cut, drastically, public expenditure. Other weaknesses in the 'suppression theory' have been discussed by Bills (43). Certainly Henslowe's diary shows that Old and New Testament plays, including ones on Judas and Pontius Pilate, were staged in the professional theatres as late as from 1591 to 1602. Even in the reign of James, by 1612, two towns, Kendal and Manning-tree, regularly set out, respectively, a Corpus Christi play and a moral play as a requisite of their charter to have their fairs. The early history of the British drama concludes, ironically, with the break-down of decentralized town-drama (introduced by Rome) just as a playhouse not unlike the old Roman theatre and plays deeply influenced by Seneca and written by a new generation of clerks, the university wits, were about to revolutionize the production and writing of drama.

AREAS FOR FURTHER RESEARCH

39 This field is a very active one already. In text editing we look forward to revised editions of the cycles from EETS, to new editions of the Winchester interludes and of Bale's plays from the Cambridge series edited by Richard and Marie Axton, and to further beautifully printed facsimile editions from Leeds. Several years ago (213) I suggested that a scholarly old-spelling play-series was needed for separable sections of cycles and for other texts of no great length. The Cambridge series of interludes has developed in response to that need; one hopes that we will soon also have new editions of John Lydgate's mummings, the small group of Welsh scriptural and moral plays, and the works of John Redford and Nicholas Udall. The PLS Performance Texts have also developed recently to meet a demand for well-edited modern-spelling editions suitable for preparing productions of these plays.

40 The search for records of performance and performers has developed impressively, at first under the sponsorship of the Malone Society, and since 1976 under REED. An international team of editors is now combing through provincial record offices in Britain; its progress can be followed in REEDN (the project newsletter). Some important classes of records yet to be searched lie in the PRO in London. The more promising of these are materials in Exchequer Accounts Various, the state papers of the reigns of Edward VI and Mary, and the complaints and bills to be

found in the Court of Chancery (late 14th century to 1640), and in the Courts of Star Chamber and Requests (both from the early Tudor period to about 1625). Outside the PRO, the largest neglected classes of records not linked with any one city or county appear to be personal and household accounts and papers, wills (from the fifteenth century), the cause papers and *acta* from the ecclesiastical courts, and possibly year books, notes of a legal nature about cases heard in court (from the early fourteenth century). Another area in which as yet there are unedited materials is court revels. While scholars are editing the early Tudor revels accounts and dramatic and musical references in the household and personal accounts of Henry VII and Henry VIII, there is much to be gleaned, concerning minstrelsy and mumming, from crown records of earlier reigns, especially from household and wardrobe documents from the time of John-Edward I. To judge from the materials used by Constance Bullock-Davies (53) in her eye-opening study of revels in 1307 at a royal feast of Edward I, similar studies might be written of court spectacle in the reigns of Edward III, Richard II, and the Lancastrians, Henry IV-VI. Excellent guides to these complex bodies of documents are by G.R. Elton (1969), R. Ian Jack (1972), and Bruce Webster (1975); and the *Handbook for REED Editors* (329) gives detailed bibliography for use in searching provincial archives.

41 Another neglected area of records' research is the surviving evidence of early material culture related to playing: archaeological remains of buildings or sites, existing illustrations or plans of those that have been totally lost, and early artifacts or wearing apparel. Archaeologists have worked in detail on some Roman theatres, and local historians have examined certain Cornish 'plain an gwarry,' but we are still far from taking advantage of the surviving evidence for outdoor playing places and for the many great halls, inns, and churches that we know provided auspices for plays. We have also applied little of what we know about early technology to playing materials such as masks, garments, wagons, fireworks, and scaffolding. Richard Hosley's study of Henry VIII's banqueting house at Calais in 1520, Meg Twycross' and Sarah Carpenter's work on masks (395), and several scholarly reconstructions of the York Mercers' Doomsday pageant wagon show what can be made of this rich vein of information.

42 The most important work to be done surely lies in the interpretation of texts and records, particularly in the application of the latter to the former. There are dozens of play-texts whose dates and auspices we cannot guess, let alone confidently state. Yet sometimes a play's myster-

ies melt away when it can be fixed in an historical matrix of place and time. A better understanding of records will also make the quality of medieval play-performance better appreciated by all those students who read the play-texts. Peter Meredith's discussions of the Chester plays and of the York Mercers' pageant (1979) offer instructive examples of what this new criticism will offer us.

DATING

43 Texts are dated according to their known or estimated period of composition or first performance. Record entries are dated according to whether they seem to (1) concern a *performance* (noted by the suffix *p*); (2) give a *record* of a play, pageant, troupe, or other aspect of dramatic activity in a way that does not necessarily indicate an actual performance (noted by the suffix *r*); or (3) deal with performances and allusions together over a long period (expressed generally by year-limits without suffix). Dates are normally rendered according to the modern calendar year. Many records are of course dated by regnal, mayoral, or financial years that begin in one calendar year and end in the following one. Complex sets of records that concern the same play over a long time are often conflated into a single entry here, dated by limits: these do not imply continuous activity, and the first and the last years also need not mark the start and the end of actual performance history. Negative evidence for any place or time cannot be assumed to mean negative dramatic activity. A painstaking reading of the total array of original documents for a locality will sometimes permit one to put an exact value on many dates in this guide. Only too often, on the other hand, as a look at REED's *Handbook for Editors* and any of its editions will show, many records have dates that are uncertain or ambiguous.

LIST OF PLAY-TEXTS

44 The chronological list of plays, dramatic fragments, and pageants (with speeches) up to 1558 includes both published and unpublished pieces. Sometimes what is and what is not dramatic is not obvious. Chaucer and Lydgate evidently read or performed their works in public, the latter (at least) with the help of court spectacle; many literary dialogues, despite a lack of stage directions, are ripe for dramatic performance; and even intermittent third-person narrative does not rule out performance by mimes. As a result, a few doubtful pieces are allowed a

place here. I have also included some genuinely dramatic Continental texts in contemporary English translations, and scriptural and moral plays traditionally of interest to students of medieval and early Tudor drama where these appear up to about 1580, and sometimes well into the seventeenth century. Each entry directs the student to good editions, translations, facsimile editions, bibliographical information in standard reference works, and important critical books. Entries also indicate what we know of the geographical provenance of texts; and where one location has a strong claim, the main entry for the text has been put under that city or town in the topographical schedule of dramatic records, a cross-reference to which is given in the chronological list of texts. For further help in questions of dialect, auspices, and staging – as well as of authorship, date, sources, and literary and theatrical analysis – students should turn to the *Manual*, Stratman, and *CBEL*.

TOPOGRAPHICAL SURVEY OF RECORDS

45 The topographical list of dramatic records, extending to 1558 (and to about 1580, and rarely later, where survivals of scriptural plays, moral interludes, and Robin Hood plays occur), also includes both published and unpublished evidence. Again the distinction between dramatic and non-dramatic is hard to draw in practice. With plays, pageants, interludes, comedies, and tragedies there is no doubt. Less-well-understood, but closely related, are 'steraclis' or 'staracles'; the Abbots of Unreason, Bonaccord, and Marham, linked with Robin Hood plays; representations with vices, dizzards, Jake-of-Lent, and the king of Christmas; and those court and household revels, feats at arms, and tournaments that exhibit persons in semi-dramatic disguise, or that offer mummings, disguisings proper, and masques, dances often accompanied by elaborate pageant devices. Other records are not obviously dramatic ones. Roman amphitheatres were places for military sports, baitings, and public executions, but on occasion shows and plays must surely have occurred there (as the discovery of a tragic mask at Caerleon implies). Spectacular pageants with speeches often shade into 'sights' and shows lacking in words and action, into *tableaux vivants* or movable representations sometimes peopled with scriptural, historical, and allegorical figures. Pageants recorded at Dublin, Hereford, Ipswich, Lincoln, and London (the Midsummer Show) appear to have at times spoken drama; on other occasions these seem to be just spectacular movable images. Dumbshows will also have included many early 'ludi' and 'spectacula,' May, King, and summer

games, Robin Hood gatherings, and Palm Sunday prophets (to what extent these do more than read the Passion in public is unclear, but a dramatic speech survives from one at Wells ca 1270).

46 Then there are references to 'players' and 'lusores.' No doubt some 'players' were minstrels, and some 'lusores' players at competitive games or gamblers, just as the occasional 'pley' may have been a legal plea. The terminology for entertainers is in general shifting and unclear. I have followed Chambers (263:II, 230-3), Anna J. Mill (251:44), Giles Dawson (96:x-xv), and David Galloway and John Wasson (145:xvi-xvii) in accepting, as probably dramatic players, all those called 'players,' '(inter)ludentes,' '(inter)lusores,' 'ludatores,' 'disguisers,' 'interluders,' 'banncriers,' and 'game players,' and in excluding from this guide 'histriones,' 'mimi,' 'ministrelli,' and the like as minstrels (but see Alton [5:35]). A few times local usage is exceptional: at Thetford, for example, actors were certainly called 'iocatori.' Evidence from Old English glosses and medieval and Tudor English-French and English-Latin word-lists often conforms to this usage.

47 I have excluded records of minstrelsy, church ales, tournaments, boy bishop or St Nicholas ceremonies, lords of misrule, kings and queens of the May, summer lords and ladies, animal wards, and other miscellaneous entertainers, except where these may be related to a play or show. These activities appear to belong to a very broad spectrum of medieval entertainments only infrequently 'dramatic.' Where they do give rise to drama, however, they also raise questions about the adequacy of our present understanding of medieval 'play.' Minstrels performed plays and pageants as early as 1307 at Lanercost Priory and as late as 1556 in Norwich; perhaps the Oxford Council had such acting in mind when it referred to the 'ludi' of 'histriones' as being both seen and heard. Henry VIII in 1512 and 1522 put the mock battle to allegorical uses recalling *The Castle of Perseverance*; and the young men of York may have done the same in 1555 when they assaulted a fort for a Shrove Tuesday pastime. Only the editing and analysis of further records collections will enable us to refine the distinctions on which this list must rely.

48 Students interested in ceremonial and musical entertainments on the periphery of drama will find them documented in editions of dramatic records. Good specialized surveys are also available: Andrew Hughes on liturgical offices (178), Charles R. Baskervill (31) and Roscoe Parker (283) on folk activities; Violet Alford (3) and E.C. Cawte (59) on animal disguisings; Lawrence Blair (113) on church ales and their activities; Enid Welsford (418) on fools; Noël Denholm-Young (98) and

Anglo (9) on tournaments; Andrew Hughes (177), Richard Rastall (319), and Constance Bullock-Davies (53) on minstrelsy; F.J.E. Raby (318) on the Latin 'comoediae' of England (II, 126-32); and Francis L. Utley (397) on literary dialogues.

49 Most entries in this list describe one play or representation and place it chronologically among similar dramatic records set under the name of the town in which the performances took place. Where plays lack titles, an entry may include enough details of characters or properties or costume materials to indicate the dramatic subject. The existence of a playbook shows that a site had more than a still pageant or a spectacle without speeches. For these reasons, I include such details in my entries. There is often no more information than that the town enjoyed plays, had playing places, and received visits from itinerant acting troupes; in these instances a general entry, often dated by broad limits, has been preferred to no entry at all. What E.K. Chambers aptly called documents of control and of criticism are also included: ecclesiastical prohibitions, crown proclamations and statutes, and a wide variety of homiletic and utilitarian allusions to playing. Finally, literary references help document contemporary usage of playing terms; allusions probably reflecting British experience have thus found a place here.

BIBLIOGRAPHICAL SOURCES

50 Citations are to the best printed edition or extracts of the original documents, except where I have drawn from manuscript materials directly or where researchers have allowed me access to their yet unprinted collections. Any work not examined at first hand is described as 'not seen.' Occasionally, as for instance in describing pageants for a royal entry that has been noticed in many contemporary chronicles, I give the most important references and refer to an authority that notices the others. Works such as E.K. Chambers' *The Mediaeval Stage* (1903), John T. Murray's *English Dramatic Companies, 1558-1642* (1910), Robert Withington's *English Pageantry* (1918-20), Anna J. Mill's *Mediaeval Plays in Scotland* (1927), William S. Clark's *The Early Irish Stage* (1955), the Harbage-Schoenbaum *Annals* (1964), *The English Drama 1485-1585* (1969) by F.P. Wilson and G.K. Hunter, and Alan H. Nelson's *The Medieval English Stage* (1974) have already drawn attention to many of these records. My debt to these reference works, the history of which I have elsewhere discussed (together with that of the gradual recovery and republication of our play-texts [213]), is a large one. Since their publication, however, new materials have been printed and earlier neglected information has

been renoticed. My aim has been to gather scattered materials together from our best sources of knowledge about theatre history (the Malone Society Collections, the Records of Early English Drama series, and the individual publications of many scholars working in many countries), from government publications such as the reports of the Historical Manuscripts Commission, the Rolls Series, and the letters and papers of the English monarchs, and from (in some respects) the most useful product of British historical scholarship, the many general and local history record series, periodicals, and studies, including the Victoria County Histories. My search through this vast literature has not been exhaustive – to keep up with current developments in the expanding field of British local history is difficult enough – but I hope that it has produced a representative survey and an improved map for future explorers.

DOUBTFUL TEXTS AND RECORDS

51 In this section I have gathered those legitimate records about the meaning or relevance of which there is some doubt, scholars' innocent misrepresentations of what a record says, and fabricated references by three rascals, Thomas Warton, William Ireland, and John Payne Collier. I have not, however, set down minor points of disagreement with others or gone as far as I might have in reducing the contributions of Warton and Collier. Some otherwise unsubstantiated records by them appear throughout this guide; *caveat lector*.

APPENDIXES

52 Information in dramatic records has sometimes been too bulky and miscellaneous to appear in my entries: the names of visiting playing troupes sponsored by their home city, town, or parish, or by a noble patron, knight, or gentleman, or simply identified by the name of a principal player; the names of playwrights or men responsible for writing out texts for performance; and an account of playing places 'theatres,' and buildings in which plays were known to have been performed. This evidence appears in Appendixes I-III. Information there has been derived from materials described in the main entries, and its source may be traced by the citation or entry-reference number.

53 In Appendix I, playing troupes to 1558 are listed according to name, whether (a) the city, town, or region from which they came, or (b) a patron (identified by surname, alphabetically, to which a cross-reference is given from his or her title) or principal player. I have given some

biographical information about patrons (seats, and main titles) and, where possible, about the players themselves. Under each troupe appear, organized chronologically by year, the places it visited and the terms that were used to describe it. This rough index to the relative importance of each troupe among its fellows, and to the extent and habitual stages of its travels, may be used as a supplement to Murray's *English Dramatic Companies*. The uncertain dating of many local references to these troupes, in part owing to inadequate records editions, makes a detailed itinerary hard to construct at present. A patrons' calendar by Mary A. Blackstone (47) is in progress.

54 Appendix II, on playwrights, must include some persons who did not actually compose play-texts but only acted as scribes or production personnel. Individuals questionably identified as playwrights of extant texts have also found a place here. Where possible, I have given life dates and biographical references.

55 Appendix III lists playing places and buildings to 1558. Although there are not many 'theatres' mentioned in this guide, plays were performed indoors and outdoors almost everywhere: in church naves, chapels, and choirs, churchyards, and church houses; in guild halls, court halls, great or manor halls, private houses (especially belonging to prominent citizens such as the mayor), inns, alehouses, and schools; in inn yards, hall yards, gardens, streets, gateways, and market places; in fields, pits, rounds, quarries, and playing grounds; and on wagons, scaffolds, bridges, and boats. 'Theatra' can be almost any place to which one comes to see something, although at court, and in schools and universities, they are almost certainly scaffolds or stages, often for the audience to sit on, as erected at Westminster Hall in 1494, and as mentioned in the *Vulgaria* of Eton fellow William Horman in 1519. This appendix lists what appear to be playing sites and buildings chronologically, notes whether (or to what extent) they have survived, and gives some bibliographical references to printed descriptions, plans, and illustrations that may help in reconstructing how plays were staged there.

56 Appendix IV is a list of reference numbers for entries in this guide, sorted chronologically, with salient dates from British history and Continental dramatic history.

HOW TO USE THIS GUIDE

57 The structure of this guide is topographical. Dramatic texts and records from a given site are entered under the name of that site, and sites are organized into four kingdoms or principalities. This arrange-

ment may offer some difficulties to users who are interested (1) in dramatic subjects, (2) in all evidence *about* a county or a site, and (3) in a straightforward chronological account of the development of drama in Britain.

58 Users interested in (1) particular subjects should begin with the index: this gives not only authors, place names, and proper names, but also types of plays, playing sites, and stages, play-characters, play-titles or subjects, and properties. The itinerant revels of the royal court take place mainly at Eltham, Greenwich, Hampton Court, London and Westminster, Richmond and Windsor; for other sites, see under the monarch's name in the index.

59 To find (2) all evidence relating to any one site, the user should go, not just to the site heading in the topographical list, but to Appendix I(a), where the activities of a site's players away from home are noticed; to GENERAL under England, where entries document government statutes and policies affecting local authorities; and to the index, which collects any stray references, such as patrons who have seats near, texts with possible auspices at, and doubtful records associated with, that site.

60 The chronological list of play-texts is the most important source of information we have. A user who collates that list with GENERAL records under England, and with LONDON AND WESTMINSTER, will find (3) a representative overview of performance history. Regional differences between the theatre history of London and that of the provinces will emerge in a comparison of the capital and York (for the north), Coventry (the midlands), Chester (the northwest), Norwich (East Anglia), Exeter (the southwest), and Canterbury (the southeast). There is little evidence from Wales, but sections on Edinburgh and Dublin are representative of Scotland and Ireland. Appendix IV directs one to most entries for a given year or span of years throughout the guide.

GENERAL INDEX

61 This includes place names, proper names, and subjects. All these appear in the body of this book, with one exception: the names of characters who have speeches in surviving play-texts (except for those in plays that are doubtful and in editions or translations of classical drama) appear with a citation number followed by an asterisk.

ACKNOWLEDGMENTS

62 I began compiling this guide at the invitation of A.C. Cawley to revise a brief handlist of towns with recorded performances of religious plays

that he wished to append to his essay in the volume on medieval drama edited by Lois Potter in the Revels History of English Drama series. That handlist would not have grown into this sizable undertaking without his encouragement, wisdom, and help. He has read, several times, early versions of this guide, and saved me from both mistakes and oversights. As bibliographer for Records of Early English Drama from 1976, on the Advisory Board of which Professor Cawley has served from its start, I have also had the generous support of my colleague Alexandra F. Johnston, General Editor of REED, of its editors and staff – especially my research associates in bibliography, Dr Mary Blackstone and Dr Theodore De Welles – and of its sponsors, the Social Sciences and Humanities Research Council of Canada and the University of Toronto. Much of this work was finished while on research leave during 1979-80, for which I am grateful to the REED Executive and sponsors, and to my own teaching home within the university, Erindale College.

63 Although the research and selection of materials for, and the organization and writing of, this guide are mine, I have been blessed with much help from friends and colleagues. John Leyerle, who taught me medieval drama, has been a counsellor and friend in need for over fifteen years. My work on behalf of REED and its editors, from which I have freely drawn here, has been rewarded in kind. Dr Blackstone helped me survey Berkshire, Buckinghamshire, and Kent materials; at a late stage Dr De Welles gave me various important records I had not found; Dr Audrey Douglas undertook to survey the reports of the Historical Manuscripts Commission; and Suzanne Westfall and Willard McCarty assisted me in scanning certain government publications. My own research assistant, Susan Burch, gave useful help in England. Working independently of REED's editors, as we had planned, I collected information from published materials and several years ago passed on my findings to them.

64 Editors including JoAnna Dutka and David Galloway (Norwich), Anne Lancashire (London corporation and guilds), Audrey Douglas (Cumbria), John Anderson (Newcastle), J.A.B. Somerset (Shropshire), John Wasson (Devon), David George (Lancashire), John Elliott (Oxford), Peter H. Greenfield (Gloucestershire), Meredith McMunn (the Scottish court), and Christopher Dean (the East Riding) have since drawn my attention to some errors and omissions. At an earlier stage editors including A.F. Johnston (York), L.M. Clopper (Chester), R.I. Ingram (Coventry), Alice Hamilton (Leicestershire), David Klausner (Hereford and Worcester), and Diana Wyatt (Beverley) enlightened my ignorance with grace as I tried to carry out the bibliographical work outlined in my

'REED Research Guide.' JoAnna Dutka, our newsletter editor, has published various bibliographical lists and surveys that have contributed to this guide. David Galloway and John Wasson, who have edited the records of Norfolk and Suffolk for the Malone Society, kindly let me see their materials, first in typescript and then in page proofs; for their courtesy, and that of Richard Proudfoot, the General Editor of the Malone Society, I am grateful indeed. John Coldewey, who is editing the Essex records for the Malone Society, also offered me help. For advice on individual points I am grateful to John Astington, David Bromwich (Local History Library, Taunton), Angus Cameron, Roger Custance (Winchester College), J.F.J. Collett-White (Bedford County Record Office), Dr Robert Dunning, Daniel Hows (National Library of Wales), Jill Levenson, Peter Meredith, Ann Quick, Richard Reid (Company of Merchant Adventurers, York), M.M. Rowe (Devon Record Office), W.R. Streitberger, John Wacher, Edward Wilson, D.R. Wilson (Curator in Aerial Photography, University of Cambridge), and Abigail Young. Indebtedness for specific items is indicated in the text at the appropriate point, but none of these people should be held accountable for my errors, omissions, and interpretation of evidence. I will be grateful to learn of any corrections or additions to the materials in this book.

65 I owe special thanks to many libraries and librarians. For a dozen summers I have relied on the unrivaled collections and dedicated staff of the British Library, the Institute of Historical Research, and the University of London Senate House Library. To have worked in that magic Bloomsbury triangle has been a rich privilege. I have also been very fortunate to have had the full resources of the University of Toronto libraries, particularly the Robarts, Fisher Rare Book, and Pontifical Institute of Mediaeval Studies collections; and I owe a special debt of gratitude to the Interlibrary Loan staff at the Robarts Library.

66 I have been lucky also in my publishers, the University of Toronto Press. Prudence Tracy and Ian Montagnes have steered this book home with friendly advice and good humour, and without the two readers whose reports the Press obtained for me this book would lack some most useful things. For help at an earlier stage I should like to thank Jane Armstrong of Methuen publishers.

67 My wife and colleague Anne has done more than anyone, not only to encourage and help my work, but to give me the time, in our young family of five, that enabled me to complete it.

68 This book has been computer-assisted at various stages. For the DECsystem-10 and its text-editing and formating programs SOS, TECO, and RUNOFF by which I have written and stored this work. I am indebted

to the helpful, able staff of the University of Toronto Computing Services and to the support of Erindale College, especially Dean R.W. Van Fossen. In particular, John Bradley produced a concordance of an early text that helped me to compile the index. To my colleague Willard McCarty at the REED office I owe the elegant programs by which reference numbers were assigned to my entries and to the citations to them in the appendices and index. My student, Irene Dutton, with cheerful efficiency, entered into storage much of the index. Would that I had taken fuller advantage of the technology that my predecessors lacked to have made a better book than this, for omissions and errors surely remain. They would have been worse had I not had in mind the example of our first theatrical records collector, William Prynne, who for his pains in *Histrio-Mastix* (1633) was jailed, fined, and deprived of both his Oxford degree and his ears!

Bibliographical Abbreviations

AA   *Archaeologia Aeliana.* 1

AASRP   *Associated Architectural Societies' Reports and Papers.* 2

Alford   Violet Alford. *The Hobby Horse and Other Animal Masks.* Ed
Margaret Dean-Smith. 1978. 3

ALHTS   *Accounts of the Lord High Treasurer of Scotland.* Vol I. Ed Thomas
Dickson. 1877. Vols II-IX. Ed James B. Paul. 1900-11. 4

Alton   'The Academic Drama in Oxford: Extracts from the Records of
Four Colleges.' Ed R.E. Alton. *Collections Volume V.* MalS. 1959
(1960). 5

Anderson   M.D. Anderson. *Drama and Imagery in English Medieval
Churches.* 1963. 6

Anglo   Sydney Anglo. *Spectacle, Pageantry, and Early Tudor Poetry.*
1969. 7

Anglo, 'Cornish'   Sydney Anglo. 'William Cornish in a Play,
Pageants, Prison, and Politics.' *RES*, NS 10 (1959), 348-60. 8

Anglo, 'Records'   Sydney Anglo. 'Financial and Heraldic Records of
the English Tournament.' *Journal of the Society of Archivists*, 2 (1962),
183-95. 9

Annales Monastici   *Annales Monastici.* Ed Henry R. Luard. RS 36. I.
1864. 10

Annals   Alfred Harbage, and rev S. Schoenbaum. *Annals of English
Drama 975-1700: An Analytical Record of All Plays, Extant or Lost,
Chronologically Arranged and Indexed by Authors, Titles, Dramatic Companies, &c.* 2nd edn 1964. Supplements by S. Schoenbaum. 1966.
1970. 11

Anonimalle Chron.   *The Anonimalle Chronicle 1333 to 1381.* Ed V.H.
Galbraith. Publs of the Univ. of Manchester, 175. 1927. 12

Anonymous Plays   *Anonymous Plays.* 3rd ser. Ed John S. Farmer. EED. 1906. *13*

AntiqJ   *The Antiquaries Journal.* *14*

Antiquary   *Tribute to an Antiquary.* Ed Frederick Emmison and Roy Stephens. 1976. *15*

APC   *Acts of the Privy Council of England.* NS. Ed J.R. Dasent and others, 46 vols. 1890-1964. *16*

AR   *The Antiquarian Repertory.* Comp Francis Grose and Thomas Astle. New edn. 4 vols. 1807-9. *17*

Arber   *A Transcript of the Registers of the Company of Stationers of London; 1554-1640 A.D.* Ed Edward Arber. 1875-94. *18*

Arch   *Archaeologia.* *19*

Arch. Cant.   *Archaeologia Cantiana.* *20*

Ascham   *The Whole Works of Roger Ascham.* Ed J.A. Giles. 3 vols. 1864-5. *21*

A to Z   *The A to Z of Elizabethan London.* Comp Adrian Prockter and Robert Taylor. Intro John Fisher. 1979. *22*

Aveling   Hugh Aveling. *Northern Catholics: The Catholic Recusants of the North Riding of Yorkshire 1558-1790.* 1966. *23*

Axton   Richard Axton. *European Drama of the Early Middle Ages.* 1974. *24*

Axton, 'Modes'   Richard Axton. 'Popular Modes in the Earliest Plays.' In Denny, pp 13-39. *25*

Bakere   Jane A. Bakere. *The Cornish Ordinalia: A Critical Study.* 1980. *26*

Baldwin 1   T.W. Baldwin. *William Shakspere's Small Latine & Lesse Greeke.* 2 vols. 1944. *27*

Baldwin 2   T.W. Baldwin. *Shakspere's Five-Act Structure: Shakspere's Early Plays on the Background of Renaissance Theories of Five-Act Structure from 1470.* 1947. *28*

'Bale's Chronicle'   'Robert Bale's Chronicle.' In *Six Town Chronicles of England.* Ed Ralph Flenley. 1911. *29*

BanC   Bannatyne Club. *30*

Baskervill   Charles R. Baskervill. 'Dramatic Aspects of Medieval Folk Festivals in England.' SP, 17 (1920), 19-87. *31*

Beadle   H. Richard L. Beadle. 'The Medieval Drama of East Anglia: Studies in Dialect, Documentary Records and Stagecraft in Two Volumes.' PhD diss Univ. of York. 1977. *32*

Beal   *Index of English Literary Manuscripts.* Vol I, pts I-II. Comp Peter Beal. 1980. *33*

Bellenden *The Chronicles of Scotland Compiled by Hector Boece.* Trans
John Bellenden (1531). Ed Edith C. Batho and H.W. Husbands. Vol
II. STS 3rd ser, 15. 1941. *34*

Benbow W. Wager. *The Longer Thou Livest and Enough Is as Good as a
Feast.* Ed R. Mark Benbow. Regents Renaissance Drama Series.
1967. *35*

Bentham James Bentham. *The History and Antiquities of the Conventual
& Cathedral Church of Ely.* 2nd edn 1812. William Stevenson. *A Supplement.* 1817. *36*

Bernard J.E. Bernard, Jr. *The Prosody of the Tudor Interlude.* Yale
Studies in English 90. 1939. *37*

Bevington *Medieval Drama.* Ed David Bevington. 1975. *38*

Bevington, 'Acting' David Bevington. 'Discontinuity in Medieval Acting Traditions.' In *The Elizabethan Theatre 5.* Ed G.R. Hibbard. 1975,
pp 1-16. *39*

Bevington, MM David M. Bevington. *From 'Mankind' to Marlowe:
Growth of Structure in the Popular Drama of Tudor England.* 1962. *40*

Bevington, TDP David Bevington. *Tudor Drama and Politics: A Critical
Approach to Topical Meaning.* 1968. *41*

BIHR *Bulletin of the Institute of Historical Research.* *42*

Bills Bing D. Bills. 'The "Suppression Theory" and the English Corpus Christi Play: A Re-Examination.' *Theatre Journal,* 32 (1980),
157-68. *43*

BJRL *Bulletin of the John Rylands Library.* *44*

BL British Library, London. *45*

Blackburn Ruth H. Blackburn. *Biblical Drama under the Tudors.* 1971. *46*

Blackstone Mary A. Blackstone. 'Notes towards a Patrons Calendar.'
REEDN, 1981:1, pp 1-11. *47*

Boas Frederick S. Boas. *University Drama in the Tudor Age.* 1914. *48*

BrMag *The British Magazine.* *49*

Brodyc Alan Brody. *The English Mummers and their Plays: Traces of
Ancient Mystery.* 1970. *50*

Brooke Iris Brooke. *Medieval Theatre Costume: A Practical Guide to the
Construction of Garments.* 1967. *51*

Buchanan George Buchanan. *Rervm Scoticarvm Historia.* 1582. *52*

Bullock-Davies Constance Bullock-Davies. *Menestrellorum Multitudo:
Minstrels at a Royal Feast.* 1978. *53*

CA *Cornish Archaeology.* *54*

Calderwood David Calderwood. *The History of the Kirk of Scotland.* Ed
Thomas Thomson. 8 vols. Wodrow Society. 1842-9. *55*

Cal. Inq. Misc.   *Calendar of Inquisitions Miscellaneous (Chancery) Preserved in the Public Record Office.* 7 vols. 1916-69. *56*

Campbell   Lily B. Campbell. *Divine Poetry and Drama in Sixteenth-Century England.* 1959. *57*

CAS   Cambridge Antiquarian Society. *58*

Cawte   E.C. Cawte. *Ritual Animal Disguise: A Historical and Geographical Study of Animal Costume in the British Isles.* The Folklore Society. 1978. *59*

Chambers, EF-P   Sir Edmund Chambers. *The English Folk-Play.* 1933. *60*

Chambers, ELCMA   E.K. Chambers. 'Medieval Drama.' *English Literature at the Close of the Middle Ages.* OHEL II.2. 1947, pp 1-65. *61*

Chaucer   *The Works of Geoffrey Chaucer.* Ed F.N. Robinson. 2nd edn 1957. *62*

ChauR   *The Chaucer Review. 63*

Chronicle   *A Chronicle of London, from 1089 to 1483.* [Ed Edward Tyrrell and Nicholas H. Nicolas]. 1827. *64*

Chronicles   *Chronicles of the Reigns of Edward I. and Edward II.* Ed William Stubbs. RS 76. 2 vols. 1882-3. *65*

Clark   William S. Clark. *The Early Irish Stage: The Beginnings to 1720.* 1955. *66*

Cobb   Gerald Cobb. *London City Churches.* Rev edn 1977. *67*

Coffman   G.R. Coffman. 'The Miracle Play in England: Some Records of Presentation, and Notes on Preserved Plays.' *SP*, 16 (1919), 56-66. *68*

Coldewey   John C. Coldewey. *Early Essex Drama: A History of its Rise and Fall, and a Theory Concerning the Digby Plays.* PhD diss Univ. of Colorado. 1972 (publ 1973). *69*

Coldewey, 'Demise'   John C. Coldewey. 'The Last Rise and Final Demise of Essex Town Drama.' *MLQ*, 36 (1975), 239-60. *70*

Coldewey, 'Player'   John C. Coldewey. 'That Enterprising Property Player: Semi-Professional Drama in Sixteenth-Century England.' *TN*, 31 (1977), 5-12. *71*

Collier   J.P. Collier. *The History of English Dramatic Poetry to the Time of Shakespeare: and Annals of the Stage to the Restoration.* 3 vols. 1831. 2nd edn 1879. *72*

Collins   Fletcher Collins, Jr. *The Production of Medieval Church Music-Drama.* 1972. *73*

CompD   *Comparative Drama. 74*

Concilia   David Wilkins. *Concilia Magnae Britanniae et Hiberniae, a Synodo Verolamiensi A.D. CCCC XLVI. ad Londinensem A.D. M DCC XVII.* 4 vols. 1737. *75*

Concilia Scotiae   *Concilia Scotiae. Ecclesiae Scoticanae Statuta tam Provincialia quam Synodalia quae Supersunt MCCXXV-MDLIX.* Ed Joseph Robertson. BanC. 2 vols. 1866. *Statutes of the Scottish Church 1225-1559 Being a Translation of Concilia Scotiae.* Ed David Patrick. SHS, 54. 1907. *76*

Cooper   Charles H. and Thompson Cooper. *Athenae Cantabrigienses.* Vol I. 1858. *77*

Cornish   J.B. Cornish. 'Ancient Earthworks and Defensive Enclosures.' In *The Victoria History of the County of Cornwall.* Vol I. Ed William Page. 1906, pp 451-73. *78*

Councils & Synods   *Councils & Synods with Other Documents Relating to the English Church.* II: A.D. *1205-1313.* Ed F.M. Powicke and C.R. Cheney. 1964. *79*

'Court Festivals'   Sydney Anglo. 'The Court Festivals of Henry VII: A Study Based upon the Account Books of John Heron, Treasurer of the Chamber.' *BJRL*, 43 (1960-1), 12-45. *80*

Cox   J.C. Cox. *Churchwardens' Accounts from the Fourteenth Century to the Close of the Seventeenth Century.* 1913. *81*

CP   G.E. C[okayne]. *The Complete Peerage.* New edn. Ed V. Gibbs and others. 13 vols. 1910-59. *82*

Craig   Hardin Craig. *English Religious Drama of the Middle Ages.* 1955. *83*

Craik   T.W. Craik. 'The Political Interpretation of Two Tudor Interludes: *Temperance and Humility* and *Wealth and Health.*' RES, NS 4 (1953), 98-108. *84*

Craik, TI   T.W. Craik. *The Tudor Interlude: Stage, Costume, and Acting.* 1967. *85*

CS   Camden Society. *86*

CSP   *Calendar of State Papers, Domestic Series, of the Reigns of Edward VI. Mary, Elizabeth 1547-1580.* Ed Robert Lemon. 1856. *87*

CUL   Cambridge University Library. *88*

CYS   Canterbury and York Society. *89*

Davey   Richard Davey. *The Nine Days' Queen: Lady Jane Grey and her Times.* Ed Martin Hume. 1909. *90*

Davidson   Charles Davidson. *Studies in the English Mystery Plays.* 1892. *91*

Davidson, DA   Clifford Davidson. *Drama and Art: An Introduction to the Use of Evidence from the Visual Arts for the Study of Early Drama.* EDAM Monograph Series, 1. 1977. *92*

Davies   W.T. Davies. *A Bibliography of John Bale.* OBS Proceedings and Papers, V. 1940, for 1936-9. Supplement in NS 1.i. 1948, for 1947, pp 44-5. *93*

Davis 1   *Non-Cycle Plays and Fragments.* Ed Norman Davis. EETS SS 1. 1970. *94*

Davis 2   *Non-Cycle Plays and the Winchester Dialogues: Facsimiles of Plays and Fragments in Various Manuscripts and the Dialogues in Winchester College MS 33.* With Introductions and a Transcript of the Dialogues by Norman Davis. LeedsTMMDF V. The University of Leeds, School of English, 1979. *95*

Dawson   *Collections Volume VII. Records of Plays and Players in Kent 1450-1642.* Ed Giles E. Dawson. MalS 1965. *96*

De Lafontaine   *The King's Musick: a Transcript of Records Relating to Music and Musicians (1460-1700).* Ed Henry C. De Lafontaine. [1909]. *97*

Denholm-Young   Nöel Denholm-Young. 'The Tournament in the Thirteenth Century.' In *Studies in Medieval History Presented to Frederick Maurice Powicke.* Ed R.W. Hunt, W.A. Pantin, and R.W. Southern. 1948, pp 240-68. *98*

Denny   *Medieval Drama.* Ed Neville Denny. Stratford-upon-Avon Studies 16. 1973. *99*

De Selve   *Correspondance Politique de Odet de Selve Ambassadeur de France en Angleterre (1546-1549).* Ed Germain Lefèvre-Pontalis. Inventaire Analytique des Archives du Ministère des Affaires Étrangères. 1888. *100*

Dew   *Diocese of Hereford. Extracts from the Cathedral Registers. A.D. 1275-1535.* Trans E.N. Dew. Cantilupe Society. 1932. *101*

Digby Plays   *The Late Medieval Religious Plays of Bodleian MSS Digby 133 and E Museo 160.* Ed Donald C. Baker, John L. Murphy, and Louis B. Hall, Jr. EETS ES 283. 1982. *102*

Diller   Hans-Jürgen Diller. *Redeformen des englischen Misterienspiels.* 1973. *103*

DME   *The Drama of Medieval Europe.* Proceedings of the Colloquium held at the University of Leeds 10-13 September 1974. Leeds Medieval Studies 1. 1975. *104*

DNB   *The Dictionary of National Biography.* Ed Sir Leslie Stephen and Sir Sidney Lee. 22 vols. 1921-2. *105*

Duff   E. Gordon Duff. *Fifteenth Century English Books: A Bibliography of Books and Documents Printed in England and of Books for the English Market Printed Abroad.* Bibliographical Society Illustrated Monographs 18. 1917. *106*

Dugdale   Sir William Dugdale. *Monasticon Anglicanum.* New edn. 8 vols. Ed John Caley, Sir Henry Ellis, and Bulkeley Bandinel. 1846. *107*

Dunbar   The Poems of William Dunbar. Ed James Kinsley. 1979. *108*

Dunn   *The Medieval Drama and its Claudelian Revival.* Ed E. Catherine Dunn, Tatiana Fotitch, and Bernard M. Peebles. 1970. *109*

Durkan-Ross   John Durkan and Anthony Ross. 'Early Scottish Libraries.' *The Innes Review*, 9 (1958), 3-167. *110*

Dust-Wolf   Philip Dust and William D. Wolf. 'Recent Studies in Early Tudor Drama: *Gorboduc, Ralph Roister Doister, Gammer Gurton's Needle,* and *Cambises.' ELR*, 8 (1978), 107-18. *111*

Dutka   JoAnna Dutka. *Music in the English Mystery Plays.* EDAM Reference Series 2. 1980. *112*

ECA   Lawrence Blair. *English Church Ales.* 1940. *113*

EDAM   Early Drama, Art, and Music Series. *114*

Edgerton   William L. Edgerton. *Nicholas Udall.* 1965. *115*

Edinburgh Records   Edinburgh Records. The Burgh Accounts. Ed Robert Adam. I. 1899. *116*

EED   Early English Dramatists. Ser ed John S. Farmer. *117*

EES   Glynne Wickham. *Early English Stages 1300 to 1660.* 2 vols in 3. 1959-72. *118*

EETS OS, ES, SS   Early English Text Society, Original Series, Extra Series, Supplementary Series. *119*

EHR   English Historical Review. 120

ELN   English Language Notes. 121

ELR   English Literary Renaissance. 122

Elton   G.R. Elton. *England, 1200-1640.* The Sources of History: Studies in the Uses of Historical Evidence. 1969. *123*

Emden 1   A.B. Emden. *A Biographical Register of the University of Oxford to A.D. 1500.* 3 vols. 1957-9. *124*

Emden 2   A.B. Emden. *A Biographical Register of the University of Oxford A.D. 1501 to 1540.* 1974. *125*

ERBE   Extracts from the Records of the Burgh of Edinburgh. A.D. 1403-1528. Ed J.D. Marwick. Scottish Burgh Records Society. 1869. *A.D. 1528-1557.* 1871. *126*

ES   E.K. Chambers. *The Elizabethan Stage.* 4 vols. 1923. *127*

EssR   Essex Review. 128

ETJ   *Educational Theatre Journal.* 129

Farnham   Willard Farnham. *The Medieval Heritage of Elizabethan Tragedy.* 1936. *130*

Feuillerat 1   *Documents Relating to the Revels at Court in the Time of King Edward VI and Queen Mary.* Ed Albert Feuillerat. MKAED 44. 1914. *131*

Feuillerat 2   *Documents Relating to the Office of the Revels in the Time of Queen Elizabeth.* Ed Albert Feuillerat. MKAED 21. 1908. *132*

Fichte   Jörg O. Fichte. *Expository Voices in Medieval Drama: Essays on the Mode and Function of Dramatic Exposition.* Erlanger Beiträge zur Sprach- und Kunstwissenschaft 53. 1975. *133*

Fifield   Merle Fifield. *The Castle in the Circle.* 1967. *134*

Fifield, 'Chaucer'   Merle Fifield. 'Chaucer the Theatre-goer.' *PLL,* 3, Supplement (1967), 63-70. *135*

Fifield, RFW   Merle Fifield. *The Rhetoric of Free Will: The Five-action Structure of the English Morality Play.* Leeds Texts and Monographs NS 5. 1974. *136*

Flanigan   C. Clifford Flanigan. 'The Liturgical Drama and its Tradition: A Review of Scholarship 1965-1975.' *RORD,* 18 (1975), 81-102; 19 (1976), 109-36. *137*

Folger   *Catalog of Manuscripts of the Folger Shakespeare Library.* 3 vols. 1971. *138*

Folie   Erasmus. *The Praise of Folie.* Trans Sir Thomas Chaloner. Ed Clarence H. Miller. EETS OS 257. 1965. *139*

Foxe   *The Acts and Monuments of John Foxe,* with a Life of the Martyrologist, and Vindication of the Work, by the Rev George Townsend. 8 vols. [Ed S.R. Cattley]. [1843-9: rpt] 1965. *140*

Frank   Grace Frank. *The Medieval French Drama.* 1954. *141*

Friars' Chronicle   *Chronicle of the Grey Friars of London.* Ed J.G. Nichols. CS 53. 1852. *142*

Fricker   Robert Fricker, *Das Ältere englische Schauspiel.* Band I: Von den Geistlichen Autoren bis zu den 'University Wits.' 1975. *143*

Fritz Saxl   *Fritz Saxl 1890-1948: A Volume of Memorial Essays from his Friends in England.* Ed D.J. Gordon. 1957. *144*

Galloway-Wasson   *Records of Plays and Players in Norfolk and Suffolk, 1330-1642.* Ed David Galloway (Great Yarmouth and Wymondham) and John Wasson. MalS Collections XI. 1980/1. *145*

Gardiner   Harold C. Gardiner, S.J. *Mysteries' End. An Investigation of the Last Days of the Medieval Religious Stage.* 1946. *146*

GBRC   Great Britain Record Commission. *147*

Geritz   Albert J. Geritz. 'Recent Studies in John Rastell.' *ELR*, 8 (1978), 341-50. *148*

Gesta Abbatum   *Gesta Abbatum Monasterii Sancti Albani a Thoma Walsingham.* Ed H.T. Riley. 3 vols. RS 28. 1867-9. *149*

Giles   *Incerti Scriptoris Chronicon Angliae de Regnis Trium Regum Lancastrensium, Henrici IV, Henrici V, et Henrici VI.* Ed Joannes A. Giles. 1848. *150*

Great Chronicle   *The Great Chronicle of London.* Ed A.H. Thomas and I.D. Thornley. 1938. *151*

Greene   *The Early English Carols.* Ed Richard L. Greene. 2nd edn. 1977. *152*

Greg   W.W. Greg. *A Bibliography of the English Printed Drama to the Restoration.* 4 vols. The Bibliographical Society, Illustrated Monographs, 24. 1939-59. *153*

Gregory's Chronicle   'Gregory's Chronicle,' in *The Historical Collections of a Citizen of London in the Fifteenth Century.* Ed J. Gairdner. CS NS 17. 1876, pp 55-239. *154*

Habicht   Werner Habicht. *Studien zur Dramenform von Shakespeare: Moralität, Interlude, romaneskes Drama.* Anglistische Forschungen 96. 1968. *155*

Halle   Edward Halle. *The Union of the Two Noble Families of Lancaster and York: 1550.* Scolar Press facs. 1970. *156*

Halliwell-Phillipps   *Halliwell-Phillipps Scrapbooks: An Index.* Comp J.A.B. Somerset. REED. [1979.] *157*

Hampson   Charles P. Hampson. *The Book of the Radclyffes: Being an Account of the Main Descents of this Illustrious Family from its Origin to the Present Day.* 1940. *158*

Hardison   O.B. Hardison, Jr. *Christian Rite and Christian Drama in the Middle Ages: Essays in the Origin and Early History of Modern Drama.* 1965. *159*

Harvey-Dietrich   Nancy Lenz Harvey and Julia C. Dietrich. 'Recent Studies in the Corpus Christi Mystery Plays.' *ELR*, 5 (1975), 396-415. *160*

HBC   Henry Bradshaw Society. *161*

Helm   Alex Helm. *The English Mummers' Play.* Foreword by N. Peacock and E.C. Cawte. Folklore Society Mistletoe Ser 14. 1981. *162*

HEP   Thomas Warton. *History of English Poetry from the Twelfth to the Close of the Sixteenth Century.* Ed W.C. Hazlitt. 4 vols. 1871. *163*

Herbert   William Herbert. *The History of the Twelve Great Livery Companies of London.* 2 vols. 1834-7. *164*

Heywood   *The Dramatic Writings of John Heywood.* Ed John S. Farmer. 1905. *165*

Heywood, *Apology*   *An Apology for Actors (1612) by Thomas Heywood. A Refutation of the Apology for Actors (1615) by I.G.* Intro Richardson H. Perkinson. Facs edn 1941. (Also pref Arthur Freeman. Facs edn 1973.) *166*

Hill   Sir Francis Hill. *Medieval Lincoln.* 1965. *167*

Hillebrand   Harold N. Hillebrand. *The Child Actors.* 1926. *168*

HLQ   *Huntington Library Quarterly. 169*

HMC   Historical Manuscripts Commission. *170*

Hobhouse   *Church-Wardens' Accounts of Croscombe, Pilton, Yatton, Tintinhull, Morebath, and St. Michael's, Bath, Ranging from A.D. 1349 to 1560.* Ed Bishop Hobhouse. SomRS [4]. 1890. *171*

Hogrefe   Pearl Hogrefe. *The Sir Thomas More Circle: A Program of Ideas and their Impact on Secular Drama.* 1959. *172*

Holden   William Baldwin. *'Beware the Cat' and 'The Funerals of King Edward The Sixth.'* Ed William P. Holden. Connecticut College Monographs, 8. 1963. STC 1243-4. *173*

Holinshed   *Holinshed's Chronicles of England, Scotland, and Ireland.* 6 vols. 1807-8. *174*

Houle   Peter J. Houle. *The English Morality and Related Drama: A Bibliographical Survey.* 1972. *175*

Household Books   *Household Books of John Duke of Norfolk, and Thomas Earl of Surrey; Temp. 1481-1490.* Ed J.P. Collier. Roxburghe Club. 1844. *176*

Hughes   Andrew Hughes. *Medieval Music: the Sixth Liberal Art.* Rev edn. 1980. *177*

Hughes, MMMO   Andrew Hughes. *Medieval Manuscripts for Mass and Office: A Guide to their Organization and Terminology.* 1981. *178*

Hutchins   John Hutchins. *The History and Antiquities of the County of Dorset.* 3rd edn. Ed W. Shipp and J.W. Hodson. 1861-74; rpt 1973. *179*

Illustrations   [John Nichols]. *Illustrations of the Manners and Expences of Antient Times in England, in the Fifteenth, Sixteenth, and Seventeenth Centuries.* 1797. *180*

Illvstrivm   John Bale. *Illvstrivm Maioris Britanniae Scriptorvm.* 1548. STC 1295. *181*

IMEV   Carleton Brown and Rossell H. Robbins. *The Index of Middle English Verse.* The Index Society 1943. And Rossell H. Robbins and John L. Cutler. *Supplement to the Index of Middle English Verse.* 1965. *182*

Index *Index Britanniae Scriptorum Quos ex Variis Bibliothecis non Parvo Labore Collegit Ioannes Baleus, cum Aliis. John Bale's Index of British and Other Writers.* Ed R.L. Poole and M. Bateson. Anecdota Oxoniensia, Mediaeval and Modern Series, 9. 1902. *183*

ISSMT International Society for the Study of Medieval Theatre. *184*

Issues *Issues of the Exchequer; Being a Collection of Payments Made out of his Majesty's Revenue from King Henry III. to King Henry VI. Inclusive.* Ed Frederick Devon. 1837. *185*

Jack R. Ian Jack. *Medieval Wales.* The Sources of History: Studies in the Uses of Historical Evidence. 1972. *186*

James Montague Rhodes James. *The Ancient Libraries of Canterbury and Dover.* 1903. *187*

JBAA *The Journal of the British Archaeological Association. 188*

JCS Gerald Eades Bentley. *The Jacobean and Caroline Stage.* 7 vols. 1941-68. *189*

Jeaffreson John C. Jeaffreson. 'The Manuscripts of William More Molyneux, Esq., of Loseley Park, Guildford, Co. Surrey.' *7th Report.* HMC. App, pt I. 1879, pp. 596-681. *190*

JEFDSS *Journal of the English Folk Dance and Song Society. 191*

Jones Gwenan Jones. *A Study of Three Welsh Religious Plays.* 1939. *192*

JRCI *Journal of the Royal Institution of Cornwall. 193*

JTS *Journal of Theological Studies. 194*

JWCI *Journal of the Warburg and Courtauld Institutes. 195*

Kahrl *Collections Volume VIII. Records of Plays and Players in Lincolnshire 1300-1585.* Ed Stanley J. Kahrl. MalS, 1969 (1974). *196*

Kahrl, 'Review' Stanley J. Kahrl. 'The Civic Religious Drama of Medieval England: A Review of Recent Scholarship.' *Renaissance Drama,* NS 6 (1973), 237-48. *197*

Kahrl, TMED Stanley J. Kahrl. *Traditions of Medieval English Drama.* 1974. *198*

Kantrowitz Joanne S. Kantrowitz. *Dramatic Allegory: Lindsay's 'Ane Satyre of the Thrie Estaitis.'* 1975. *199*

Kelley Michael R. Kelley. *Flamboyant Drama: A Study of 'The Castle of Perseverance,' 'Mankind,' and 'Wisdom.'* 1979. *200*

Kelly William Kelly. *Notices Illustrative of the Drama, and Other Popular Amusements, Chiefly in the Sixteenth and Seventeenth Centuries, Incidentally Illustrating Shakespeare and his Cotemporaries; Extracted from the Chamberlains' Accounts and Other Manuscripts of the Borough of Leicester.* 1865. *201*

Kempe *The Loseley Manuscripts.* Ed A.J. Kempe. 1836. *202*

Ker   N.R. Ker. *Medieval Libraries of Great Britain: A List of Surviving Books.* 1941. *203*

Kinghorn   A.M. Kinghorn. *Mediaeval Drama.* 1968. *204*

King's Works   The History of the King's Works. Ed H.M. Colvin. Vols I-III; Plans. 1963-75. *205*

Kipling   Gordon Kipling. *The Triumph of Honour: Burgundian Origins of the Elizabethan Renaissance.* 1977. *206*

Kirk of Scotland   Acts and Proceedings of the General Assemblies of the Kirk of Scotland, from the Year M.D.LX. 3 vols. Ed Thomas Thomson. BanC. 1839-45. *207*

Klausner   David Klausner. '[Research in Progress].' REEDN, 1979.1, pp 20-4. *208*

Knighton   *Chronicon Henrici Knighton, vel Cnitthon, Monachi Leycestrensis.* Ed Joseph R. Lumby. RS 92. 2 vols. 1889-95. *209*

Knox   *The Works of John Knox.* Ed David Laing. 2 vols. Wodrow Society. 1846-8. *210*

Kolve   V.A. Kolve. *The Play Called Corpus Christi.* 1966. *211*

L. & P. Hen. VIII   *Letters and Papers, Foreign and Domestic, of the Reign of Henry* VIII. Ed J.S. Brewer, J. Gairdner, and R.H. Brodie. 21 vols. 1862-1918. Vol I, rev R.H. Brodie. 1920. *Addenda.* 2 vols. 1929-32. *212*

Lancashire   Ian Lancashire. 'Medieval Drama.' In *Editing Medieval Texts English, French, and Latin Written in England.* Ed A.G. Rigg. 1977, pp 58-85. *213*

Lancashire, 'Guide'   Ian Lancashire. 'REED Research Guide.' REEDN, 1976:1, pp 10-23. *214*

Laneham   Robert Laneham: A Letter [1575]. Scolar Press facs. 1969. *215*

Leach   Arthur F. Leach. *Educational Charters and Documents 598 to 1909.* 1911. *216*

LeedsSE   Leeds Studies in English. 217

LeedsTMMDF   Leeds Texts and Monographs, Medieval Drama Facsimiles. *218*

Legge   M. Dominica Legge. 'The Anglo-Norman Drama.' In her *Anglo-Norman Literature and its Background.* 1963, pp 311-31. *219*

Leland   *Joannis Lelandi Antiquarii de Rebvs Britannicis Collectanea.* Ed Thomas Hearne. 1774. 6 vols. *220*

Leland, *Itin.   The Itinerary of John Leland in or about the Years 1535-1543.* Ed Lucy T. Smith. 11 parts. 5 vols. 1907-10. *221*

Lesley   John Lesley, Bishop of Ross. *The History of Scotland, from the Death of King James I. in the Year M.CCCC.XXXVI, to the Year M.D.LXI.* BanC 38. 1830. [Translated and printed later as his] *De Origine Moribus & Rebus Gestis Scotorum.* 1578. See also *The Historie of Scotland Wrytten First in Latin by ... Jhone Leslie ... and Translated in Scottish by Father James Dalrymple ... 1596.* Ed E.G. Cody and William Murison. STS 19, 34. 1889-95. *222*

Letter-Books   Calendar of Letter-Books Preserved among the Archives of the Corporation of the City of London at the Guildhall. 11 vols. [Letter-Books A-I, K-L.] Ed Reginald R. Sharpe. 1899-1912. *223*

Lipphardt   Walther Lipphardt. *Lateinische Osterfeiern und Osterspiele.* 5 vols. 1975-6. *224*

Lisle Letters   The Lisle Letters. Ed Muriel St Clare Byrne. 6 vols. 1981. *225*

Literary Remains   Literary Remains of King Edward the Sixth. Ed John G. Nichols. 2 vols. Roxburghe Club. 1857. See also *The Chronicles and Political Papers of King Edward VI.* Ed W.K. Jordan. 1966. *226*

LN&Q   Lincolnshire Notes & Queries. 227

'London Chronicle'   'A London Chronicle 1523-1555.' In *Two London Chronicles from the Collections of John Stow.* Ed C.L. Kingsford. *Camden Miscellany Vol. XII.* CS 3rd ser 18. 1910, pp 1-43. *227.5*

Loseley mss   Loseley MSS Reproduced by the Historical Manuscripts Commission, National Register of Archives, from Originals Prepared by the Archivist, Guildford Muniment Room, Castle Arch, Guildford, Surrey. [ca 1950]. *228*

LRS   Lincoln Record Society. *229*

Lupton   J.H. Lupton. *A Life of John Colet, D.D., Dean of St. Paul's, and Founder of St. Paul's School.* New edn. 1909. *230*

MaC   Maitland Club. *231*

Machyn   *The Diary of Henry Machyn, Citizen and Merchant-Taylor of London, from A.D. 1550 to A.D. 1563.* Ed John G. Nichols. CS 42. 1848. *232*

Mackenzie   W. Roy Mackenzie. *The English Moralities from the Point of View of Allegory.* Harvard Studies in English 2. 1914. *233*

Macro Plays   The Macro Plays. Ed Mark Eccles. EETS OS 262. 1969. This supercedes ES 91, ed F.J. Furnivall and A.W. Pollard (1904). *234*

MalS   The Malone Society. *235*

Malverne   *Polychronicon Ranulphi Higden Monachi Cestrensis.* Ed J.R. Lumby. Vol IX (containing a continuation of the Polychronicon by Johannes Malverne). RS 41. 1886. *236*

Manual   Anna J. Mill, Sheila Lindenbaum, and Francis L. Utley and Barry Ward. 'XII. Dramatic Pieces.' In *A Manual of the Writings in Middle English 1050-1500.* Vol V. Ed Albert E. Hartung. Connecticut Academy of Arts and Sciences. 1975, pp 1315-84. (Numbers following this abbreviation are reference numbers given to dramatic texts in *A Manual.*) *237*

Margeson   J.M.R. Margeson. *The Origins of English Tragedy.* 1967. *238*

Marprelate   *The Marprelate Tracts 1588, 1589.* Ed William Pierce. 1911. *239*

Marshall   Mary H. Marshall. '*Theatre* in the Middle Ages: Evidence from Dictionaries and Glosses.' *Symposium,* 4 (1950), 1-39, 366-89. *240*

Materials Hen. VII   *Materials for a History of the Reign of Henry VII.* Ed W. Campbell. RS 60. Vol II. 1877. *241*

MCD   Institute of Cornish Studies. *The Medieval Cornish Drama.* Special Bibliography No 2. 1973. *242*

McGee-Meagher   C.E. McGee and John C. Meagher. 'Preliminary Checklist of Tudor and Stuart Entertainments: 1588 [ie 1558]-1603.' *RORD,* 24 (1981), 51-155. 'Preliminary Checklist ... 1485-1558.' *RORD,* 25 (1982), 31-114. *243*

MedS   Mediaeval Studies. 244

Medwall   *The Plays of Henry Medwall.* Ed Alan H. Nelson. 1980. See also *The Plays of Henry Medwall: A Critical Edition.* Ed M.E. Moeslein. 1981. *245*

Memorials   *Memorials of London and London Life, in the XIIIth, XIVth, and XVth Centuries. Being a Series of Extracts, Local, Social, and Political, from the Early Archives of the City of London.* A.D. *1276-1419.* Ed Henry T. Riley. 1868. *246*

Memorials Hen. VII   *Memorials of King Henry the Seventh.* Ed James Gairdner. RS 10. 1858. *247*

Meredith   Peter Meredith. '"Item for a grone – iij d" – Records and Performance.' In *REED Proc,* pp 26-60. *248*

Mery Tales   Shakespeare's Jest Book. A Hundred Mery Tales. Ed Herman Oesterley. 1866. *249*

MET   *Medieval English Theatre. 250*

Mill   Mill, Anna J. *Mediaeval Plays in Scotland.* St Andrews University Publs, 24. 1927. *251*

Mill (PMLA)   A.J. Mill. 'Representations of Lyndsay's *Satyre of the Thrie Estaitis,*' PMLA, 47 (1932), 636-51; [Corrigenda] 48 [1933], 315-16. *252*

Mill-Chambers 'Dramatic Records of the City of London: The Repertories, Journals, and Letter Books.' Ed Anna J. Mill and E.K. Chambers. In *Collections Vol. II. Part III.* Ed W.W. Greg. MalS, 1931, pp 285-320. *253*

Minor Poems *The Minor Poems of John Lydgate.* Ed Henry N. MacCracken. 2 vols. EETS ES 107 and OS 192. 1910, 1934. *254*

MKAED Materialien zur Kunde des älteren Englischen Dramas. *255*

MLN *Modern Language Notes.* *256*

MLQ *Modern Language Quarterly.* *257*

MLR *Modern Language Review.* *258*

More *Journal of Prior William More.* Ed Ethel S. Fegan. WorcsHS. 1914. *259*

Morris Richard Morris. *Cathedrals and Abbeys of England and Wales: The Building Church, 600-1540.* 1979. *260*

Motter T.H. Vail Motter. *The School Drama in England.* 1929. *261*

MP *Modern Philology.* *262*

MS E.K. Chambers. *The Mediaeval Stage.* 2 vols. 1903. *263*

MSS Wells W.H.B. Bird and W.P. Baildon. *Calendar of the Manuscripts of the Dean and Chapter of Wells.* HMC. 2 vols. 1907, 1914. *264*

MSS Welsh J.G. Evans. *Report on Manuscripts in the Welsh Language.* HMC. 7 vols. 1898-1901. *265*

Murimuth *Adae Murimuth Continuatio Chronicarum ...* Ed Edward M. Thompson. RS 93. 1889. *266*

Murray John T. Murray. *English Dramatic Companies 1558-1642.* 2 vols. 1910. *267*

Music & Poetry John Stevens. *Music & Poetry in the Early Tudor Court.* 1961. *268*

N&Q *Notes & Queries.* *269*

NA *Norfolk Archaeology.* *270*

Nagler A.M. Nagler. *The Medieval Religious Stage: Shapes and Phantoms.* 1976. *271*

Nance R.M. Nance. 'The Plen an Gwary or Cornish Playing Place.' JRIC, 24 (1933-36), 190-211. *272*

Nelson Alan H. Nelson. *The Medieval English Stage: Corpus Christi Pageants and Plays.* 1974. *273*

Nicolas Sir Nicholas Harris Nicolas. 'Observations on the Institution of the Most Noble Order of the Garter.' *Arch*, 31 (1846), 1-163. *274*

Nicoll Allardyce Nicoll. *Masks Mimes and Miracles: Studies in the Popular Theatre.* 1931. *275*

Nungezer   Edwin Nungezer. *A Dictionary of Actors and of Other Persons Associated with the Public Representation of Plays in England before 1642*. 1929. *276*

NYorkCROJ   *North Yorkshire County Record Office Journal*. *277*

OBS   Oxford Bibliographical Society. *278*

OHEL   Oxford History of English Literature. *279*

OHS   Oxford Historical Society. *280*

Opland   Jeff Opland. *Anglo-Saxon Oral Poetry: A Study of the Traditions*. 1980. *281*

Owst   G.R. Owst. *Literature and Pulpit in Medieval England*. 1961. *282*

Parker   Roscoe E. Parker. 'Some Records of the "Somyr Play."' In *Studies in Honor of John C. Hodges and Alvin Thaler*. Ed Richard B. Davis and John L. Lievsay. 1961, pp 19-26. *283*

Parsons   *Tenth-Century Studies: Essays in Commemoration of the Millennium of the Council of Winchester and 'Regularis Concordia.'* Ed David Parsons. 1975. *284*

Paston   *Paston Letters and Papers of the Fifteenth Century*. Ed Norman Davis. 2 vols. 1971, 1976. *285*

PBSA   *Publications of the Bibliographical Society of America*. *286*

Peacock   *English Church Furniture, Ornaments and Decorations, at the Period of the Reformation*. Ed Edward Peacock. 1866. *287*

Pevsner, *Corn*   Nikolaus Pevsner. *Cornwall*. 2nd edn. Rev Enid Radcliffe. 1970. *288*

Pevsner, *Cumb*   Nikolaus Pevsner. *Cumberland and Westmorland*. 1967. *289*

Pevsner, *Dorset*   John Newman and Nikolaus Pevsner. *Dorset*. 1972. *290*

Pevsner, *Hants*   Nikolaus Pevsner and David Lloyd. *Hampshire and the Isle of Wight*. 1967. *291*

Pevsner, *Leics*   Nikolaus Pevsner. *Leicestershire and Rutland*. 1960. *292*

Pevsner, *Lincs*   Nikolaus Pevsner and John Harris. *Lincolnshire*. 1964. *293*

Pevsner, *London*   Nikolaus Pevsner. *London*. I. The Cities of London and Westminster. 3rd edn. Rev Bridget Cherry. 1973. [II] *London except the Cities of London and Westminster*. 1952. *294*

Pevsner, *Norf*   Nikolaus Pevsner. *North-West and South Norfolk*. 1962. *295*

Pevsner, *Norwich*   Nikolaus Pevsner. *North-East Norfolk and Norwich*. 1962. *296*

Pevsner, *S-Devon*   Nikolaus Pevsner. *South Devon.* 1952. *297*

Pevsner, *Suff*   Nikolaus Pevsner. *Suffolk.* 2nd edn. Rev Enid Radcliffe. 1974. *298*

Pevsner, *YorksER*   Nikolaus Pevsner. *Yorkshire: York and the East Riding.* Contributions by John Hutchinson. 1972. *299*

Pevsner, *YorksWR*   Nikolaus Pevsner. *Yorkshire: The West Riding.* 1959. *300*

Pineas   Rainer Pineas. *Tudor and Early Stuart Anti-Catholic Drama.* Bibliotheca Humanistica et Reformatorica 5. 1972. *301*

Pitcairn   *Criminal Trials in Scotland, from A.D. M.CCCC.LXXXVIII to A.D. M.DC.XXIV ...* Comp Robert Pitcairn. 3 vols. *1833. 302*

Pitscottie   Robert Lindesay of Pitscottie. *The Historie and Cronicles of Scotland.* Ed Æ. J.G. Mackay. 3 vols. STS 42-3, 60. 1899, 1911. *303*

Plomer   Henry R. Plomer. 'An Inventory of Wynkyn de Worde's House "The Sun in Fleet Street" in 1553.' *The Library*, 3rd ser, 6 (1915), 228-34. *304*

PlyIDCNHS   *Annual Reports and Transactions of the Plymouth Institution and Devon and Cornwall Natural History Society. 305*

PMLA   *Publications of the Modern Language Association of America. 306*

Potter   Robert Potter. *The English Morality Play: Origins, History and Influence of a Dramatic Tradition.* 1975. *307*

PPL   *Papers on Language & Literature. 308*

PQ   *Philological Quarterly. 309*

Price   David C. Price. *Patrons and Musicians of the English Renaissance.* 1981. *310*

PRO   Public Record Office, London. *311*

Proclamations   *Tudor Royal Proclamations.* Ed P.L. Hughes and J.F. Larkin. Vols I-II. 1964-9. *312*

Prosser   Eleanor Prosser. *Drama and Religion in the English Mystery Plays: A Re-evaluation.* Stanford Studies in Language and Literature 23. 1961. *313*

PS   Parker Society. *314*

PSomANHS   *Proceedings of the Somersetshire Archaeological & Natural History Society. 315*

PSuffIANH   *Proceedings of the Suffolk Institute of Archaeology and Natural History. 316*

PWCornFC   *Proceedings of the West Cornwall Field Club. 317*

Raby   F.J.E. Raby. *A History of Secular Latin Poetry in the Middle Ages.* 2 vols. 1934. *318*

Rastall   Richard Rastall. 'The Minstrels of the English Royal House-
holds, 25 Edward I – 1 Henry VIII: An Inventory.' *R.M.A. Research
Chronicle*, 4 (1964), 1-41. *319*

Rastell   *Three Rastell Plays: 'Four Elements,' 'Calisto and Melebea,'
'Gentleness and Nobility.'* Ed Richard Axton. 1979. *320*

Rawcliffe   Carole Rawcliffe. *The Staffords, Earls of Stafford and Dukes of
Buckingham 1394-1521.* 1978. *321*

RCHM *Cambridge*   Royal Commission on Historical Monuments. *An
Inventory of the Historical Monuments in the City of Cambridge.* 2 parts.
1959. *322*

RCHM *Dorset*   Royal Commission on Historical Monuments. *An Inventory of the Historical Monuments in Dorset.* Vols I, II.3. 1952, 1970. *323*

RCHM *Essex*   Royal Commission on Historical Monuments. *An Inventory of the Historical Monvments in Essex.* 4 vols. 1916-23. *324*

RCHM *Herts*   Royal Commission on Historical Monuments. *An Inventory of the Historical Monvments in Hertsfordshire.* 1911. *325*

RCHM *London*   Royal Commission on Historical Monuments. *An
Inventory of the Historical Monuments in London.* 5 vols. 1924-30. *326*

RCHM *Oxford*   Royal Commission on Historical Monuments. *An Inventory of the Historical Monuments in the City of Oxford.* 1939. *327*

Reed   A.W. Reed. *Early Tudor Drama: Medwall, the Rastells, Heywood,
and the More Circle.* 1926. *328*

REEDH   Records of Early English Drama. *Handbook for Editors.* Comp
A.F. Johnston and S.B. Maclean, with contributions by M. Blackstone and C. Louis. 1980. *329*

REEDN   Records of Early English Drama. *Newsletter.* *330*

REED *Proc.*   *Records of Early English Drama: Proceedings of the First
Colloquium.* Ed JoAnna Dutka. REED. 1979. *331*

Reliquiae   *Reliquiae Antiquae.* Eds Thomas Wright and James O.
Halliwell. 2 vols. 1841-3. *332*

RenQ   *Renaissance Quarterly.* *333*

RES   *The Review of English Studies.* *334*

Revels 2   Norman Sanders, Richard Southern, T.W. Craik, and Lois
Potter. *The Revels History of Drama in English. Volume II: 1500-1576.*
1980. *335*

Roberts   R.J. Roberts. 'John Rastell's Inventory of 1538.' *The Library*,
6th ser, 1 (1979), 34-42. *336*

Robertson-Gordon   *Collections Volume III. A Calendar of Dramatic
Records in the Books of the Livery Companies of London 1485-1640.* Ed
Jean Robertson and D.J. Gordon. MalS, 1954. *337*

Robinson   John W. Robinson. 'On the Evidence for Puppets in Late Medieval England.' *Theatre Survey*, 14 (1973), 112-17. *338*

Robyn Hood   R.B. Dobson and J. Taylor. *Rymes of Robyn Hood: An Introduction to the English Outlaw*. 1976. *339*

RORD   *Research Opportunities in Renaissance Drama*. *340*

Rossiter   A.P. Rossiter. *English Drama from Early Times to the Elizabethans: Its Background, Origins and Developments*. 1950. *341*

RRCSAL   Reports of the Research Committee of the Society of Antiquaries of London. *342*

RRDS   Regents Renaissance Drama Series. *343*

RSARTS   Renaissance Society of America, Renaissance Text Series. *344*

RTDevA   *Report and Transactions of the Devonshire Association*. *345*

Rubel   Helen F. Rubel. 'Chabham's *Penitential* and its Influence in the Thirteenth Century.' PMLA, 40 (1925), 225-39. *346*

Scheurweghs   *Nicholas Udall's Roister Doister*. Ed G. Scheurweghs. MKAED NS 16. 1939. *347*

Schirmer   Walter F. Schirmer. *John Lydgate: A Study in the Culture of the XVth Century*. Trans Ann E. Keep. 1961. *348*

Schmitt   Natalie C. Schmitt. 'Was There a Medieval Theatre in the Round? A Re-examination of the Evidence.' In Taylor-Nelson, pp 292-315. *349*

School Book   *A Fifteenth Century School Book from a Manuscript in the British Museum (MS. Arundel 249)*. Ed William Nelson. 1956. *350*

Scriptorum   John Bale. *Scriptorum Illustrium Maioris Brytanniae Catalogus*. 2 vols. Basle, 1557, 1559. Gregg International Publishers Ltd, 1971. *351*

Secular Lyrics   *Secular Lyrics of the XIVth and XVth Centuries*. Ed Rossell H. Robbins. 2nd edn. 1955. *352*

SHS   Scottish History Society. *353*

ShS   *Shakespeare Survey*. *354*

Simancas   *Calendar of Letters and State Papers Relating to English Affairs, Preserved Principally in the Archives of Simancas*. Ed M.A.S. Hume. 4 vols. 1892-9. *355*

SJ   *Jahrbuch der Deutschen Shakespeare-Gesellschaft*. *356*

Smith   *English Gilds*. Ed Toulmin Smith. EETS OS 40. 1870. *357*

Smoldon   William L. Smoldon. *The Music of the Medieval Church Dramas*. Ed Cynthia Bourgeault. 1980. *358*

Somerset   *Four Tudor Interludes*. Ed J.A.B. Somerset. 1974. *359*

SomRS   Somerset Record Society. *360*

Southern 1   Richard Southern. *The Medieval Theatre in the Round: A Study of the Staging of 'The Castle of Perseverance' and Related Matters.* 2nd edn. 1975. *361*

Southern 2   Richard Southern. *The Staging of Plays before Shakespeare.* 1973. *362*

SP   *Studies in Philology. 363*

Spain   *Calendar of Letters, Dispatches, and State Papers, Relating to the Negotiations between England and Spain, Preserved in the Archives at Vienna, Brussels, Simancas and Elsewhere.* Ed G.A. Bergenroth, Don Pascual de Gayangos, and others. 13 vols. 1862-1954. *364*

SpaldC   Spalding Club. *365*

Spivack   Bernard Spivack. *Shakespeare and the Allegory of Evil: The History of a Metaphor in Relation to his Major Villains.* 1958. *366*

SQ   *Shakespeare Quarterly. 367*

SS   Surtees Society. *368*

Statutes   *The Statutes of the Realm.* Ed A. Luders, T.E. Tomlins, J. Raithby, and others. Vols II-IV. 1816-19. *369*

STC   *A Short-Title Catalogue of Books Printed in England, Scotland, & Ireland ... 1475-1640.* Ed A.W. Pollard and G.R. Redgrave. 1926. 2nd edn, begun by W.A. Jackson and F.S. Ferguson, and completed by K.F. Pantzer. Vol 2, I-Z. 1976. *370*

Stemmler   Theo Stemmler. *Liturgische Feiern und Geistliche Spiele: Studien zu Erscheinungsformen des Dramatischen im Mittelalter.* Buchreihe der Anglia 15. 1970. *371*

Sticca   *The Medieval Drama.* Ed Sandro Sticca. 1972. *372*

Stopes, *Hunnis*   C.C. Stopes. *William Hunnis and the Revels of the Chapel Royal.* MKAED 29. 1910. *373*

Stow, *Chronicles*   John Stow. *The Chronicles of England.* 1580. STC 23333. *374*

Stow, *Survey*   *A Survey of London by John Stow Reprinted from the Text of 1603.* Ed C.L. Kingsford. 2 vols. 1908. *375*

Stratman   Carl J. Stratman. *Bibliography of Medieval Drama.* 2nd edn. 2 vols. 1972. *376*

STS   Scottish Text Society. *377*

TAASDurN   *Transactions of the Architectural and Archaeological Society of Durham and Northumberland. 378*

Tanner   Lawrence E. Tanner. *Westminster School.* 1934. *379*

Taylor   Jerome Taylor. 'The Dramatic Structure of the Middle English Corpus Christi, or Cycle, Plays.' In Taylor-Nelson, pp 148-56. *380*

Taylor-Nelson   *Medieval English Drama: Essays Critical and Contextual.* Ed Jerome Taylor and Alan H. Nelson. 1972. *381*

TBGAS   *Transactions of the Bristol and Gloucestershire Archaeological Society. 382*

TCBS   *Transactions of the Cambridge Bibliographical Society. 383*

Test. Ebor.   Testamenta Eboracensia. Ed James Raine. 5 vols. SS 4, 30, 45, 53, 79. 1836-84. *384*

TFT   The Tudor Facsimile Texts. A series of facs editions ed by John S. Farmer. 146 vols. 1907-14. *385*

Theiner   Paul Theiner. 'The Medieval Terence.' In *The Learned and the Lewed: Studies in Chaucer and Medieval Literature.* Ed Larry D. Benson. Harvard English Studies 5. 1974, pp 231-47. *386*

Thompson   Elbert N.S. Thompson. *The English Moral Plays.* 1910. *387*

Tiddy   R.J.E. Tiddy. *The Mummers' Play.* Ed D.R. Pye. 1923. *388*

TN   Theatre Notebook. 389

Trevelyan   Trevelyan Papers Prior to A.D. 1558. Ed J.P. Collier. CS 67. 1857. *390*

TRHS   Transactions of the Royal Historical Society. 391

TShropANHS   Transactions of the Shropshire Archaeological and Natural History Society. 392

TSPES   Transactions of the St. Paul's Ecclesiological Society. 393

TTCS   Three Tudor Classical Interludes: Thersites, Jacke Jugeler, Horestes. Ed Marie Axton. 1982. *393.5*

Two Latin Comedies   Two Latin Comedies by John Foxe the Martyrologist. Ed John H. Smith. RSARTS IV. 1973. *394*

Twycross-Carpenter   Meg Twycross and Sarah Carpenter. 'Masks in Medieval English Theatre: The Mystery Plays.' *MET*, 3 (1981), 7-44, 69-113 (to be concluded). *395*

Tydeman   William Tydeman. *The Theatre in the Middle Ages: Western European Stage Conditions, c.800-1576.* 1978. *396*

Utley   Francis Lee Utley. 'VII. Dialogues, Debates, and Catechisms.' In *A Manual of the Writings in Middle English 1050-1500.* Vol III. Ed Albert E. Hartung. 1972, pp 669-745. *397*

VCH   The Victoria County Histories. *398*

VCHBucks   The Victoria History of the County of Buckingham. II. Ed William Page. 1908. *399*

VCHCamb   The Victoria History of the County of Cambridge and the Isle of Ely. Vol III. Ed J.P.C. Roach. 1967. Vol IV. Ed R.B. Pugh. 1953. *400*

VCHEssex   The Victoria History of the County of Essex. Vol II. Ed W. Page and J.H. Round. 1907. *401*

VCHHants   The Victoria History of Hampshire and the Isle of Wight. Vols III, V. Ed William Page. 1908, 1912. *402*

VCHOxford   *The Victoria History of the County of Oxford.* Vol III. Ed
 H.E. Salter and Mary D. Lobel. 1954. *403*

VCHSuffolk   *The Victoria History of the County of Suffolk.* Vol II. Ed
 William Page. 1907. *404*

VCHSurrey   *The Victoria History of the County of Surrey.* Vols III-IV. Ed
 H.E. Malden. 1911-12. *405*

VCHWarw   *The Victoria History of the County of Warwick.* Vol IV. Ed
 L.F. Salzman. 1947. *406*

VCHWorc   *The Victoria History of the County of Worcester.* Vol III. Vol
 IV. Ed William Page and J.W. Willis-Bund. 1924. *407*

*Venice   State Papers and Manuscripts Relating to English Affairs, Existing
 in the Archives and Collections of Venice, and in Other Libraries of
 Northern Italy.* Vols I-VII. Ed Rawdon Brown and G. Cavendish-
 Bentinck. 1864-90. *408*

Venn   *Alumni Cantabrigionses: A Biographical List of All Known Students, Graduates and Holders of Office at the University of Cambridge,
 from the Earliest Times to 1900.* Comps John Venn and J.A. Venn.
 Part I. 4 vols. 1922-7. *409*

*Visitations   Visitation Articles and Injunctions of the Period of the Refor-
 mation.* Ed W.H. Frere. Alcuin Club, 14-16. 1910. *410*

Wacher, *Towns*   John Wacher. *The Towns of Roman Britain.* 1974. *411*

Wallace   Charles W. Wallace. *The Evolution of the English Drama up to
 Shakespeare.* 1912. *412*

Walsingham   Thomas Walsingham. *Historia Anglicana.* Ed Henry T.
 Riley. RS 28. 2 vols. 1863-4. *413*

Wasson   John Wasson. 'The *St. George* and *Robin Hood Plays* in
 Devon.' MET, 2 (1980), 66-9. *414*

Wasson, 'Guide'   John Wasson. 'How to Read Medieval Manuscripts:
 A Guide for EDAM and Other Researchers.' *The EDAM Newsletter,* 5
 (1983), 47-84. *414.5*

Webster   Bruce Webster. *Scotland from the Eleventh Century to 1603.* The
 Sources of History: Studies in the Uses of Historical Evidence.
 1975. *415*

Wells   *English Drama (Excluding Shakespeare): Select Bibliographical
 Guides.* Ed Stanley Wells. 1975. See chapters by John Leyerle and
 T.W. Craik. *416*

Weeuer   John Weeuer. *Ancient Fvnerall Monvments.* 1631. *417*

Welsford   Enid Welsford. *The Fool: His Social and Literary History.*
 1935. *418*

Wenzel   Siegfried Wenzel. 'An Early Reference to a Corpus Christi
 Play.' MP, 74 (1977), 390-4. *419*

Whiting   Bartlett J. Whiting. *Proverbs in the Earlier English Drama with Illustrations from Contemporary French Plays.* Harvard Studies in Comparative Literature 14. 1938. *420*

Wickham   *English Moral Interludes.* Ed Glynne Wickham. 1976. *421*

Wickham, MT   Glynne Wickham. *The Medieval Theatre.* 1974. *422*

Wickham, SDH   Glynne Wickham. *Shakespeare's Dramatic Heritage: Collected Studies in Mediaeval, Tudor and Shakespearean Drama.* 1969. *423*

Wiles   David Wiles. *The Early Plays of Robin Hood.* 1981. *424*

Williams   T.W. Williams. 'Gloucestershire Mediaeval Libraries.' *TBGAS,* 31 (1908), 78-195. *425*

Williams, DME   Arnold Williams. *The Drama of Medieval England.* 1961. See also his 'The English Moral Play before 1500.' *Annuale Mediaevale,* 4 (1963), 5-22. *426*

Wilson   R.M. Wilson. 'Drama.' In his *The Lost Literature of Medieval England.* 2nd edn 1970, pp 209-33. *427*

Wilson-Hunter   F.P. Wilson. *The English Drama 1485-1585.* Ed G.K. Hunter. Oxford History of English Literature IV.i. 1969. *428*

WiltANHM   The Wiltshire Archaeological and Natural History Magazine. 429

WiltANHSRB Wiltshire Archaeological and Natural History Society Records Branch. *430*

Wing   Donald Wing, comp. *Short-Title Catalogue of Books Printed in England, Scotland, Ireland, Wales, and British America and of English Books Printed in Other Countries 1641-1700.* 3 vols. 1945-51. 2nd edn. Vol I. 1972. *431*

Withington   Robert Withington. *English Pageantry: An Historical Outline.* 2 vols. 1918. *432*

Wolffe   Bertram Wolffe. *Henry VI.* 1981. *433*

Wood   Anthony a Wood. *Athenae Oxonienses.* Ed P. Bliss. 4 vols. 1813-20. *434*

Wood, *House*   Margaret Wood. *The English Mediaeval House.* 1965. *435*

Woolf   Rosemary Woolf. *The English Mystery Plays.* 1972. *436*

WorcsHS   Worcestershire Historical Society. *437*

Workman   Herbert B. Workman. *John Wyclif.* 2 vols. 1926. *438*

Wright   Thomas Wright. *Anglo-Saxon and Old English Vocabularies.* 2nd edn. 2 vols. Ed Richard P. Wülcker. 1968. *439*

Wriothesley   Charles Wriothesley. *A Chronicle of England during the Reigns of the Tudors, from A.D. 1485 to 1559.* Ed William D. Hamilton. 2 vols. CS NS 11, 20. 1875-7. *440*

Wyclif   The English Works of Wyclif Hitherto Unprinted. Ed F.D. Matthew. EETS OS 74. 2nd edn. 1902. *441*

ILLUSTRATIONS AND MAPS

Captions

1 Celtic type of face mask found at Catterick (photograph by F.M.B. Cooke; reconstruction by Miss Pat O'Halloran). Crown copyright: reproduced by permission of John Wacher and the Controller of Her Majesty's Stationery Office.

2 Plan of St Albans and its Roman theatre (from *The Roman Theatre of Verulamium* by S.S. Frere and K.M. Kenyon). Reproduced by permission of S.S. Frere.

3 The Roman theatre, St Albans (18 June 1948). Reproduced by permission of the Director in Aerial Photography, University of Cambridge.

4 A page of text of the 'Visitatio Sepulchri' from *Regularis Concordia*, with Old English glosses (BL Cotton ms Tiberius A.III, fol 21v). Reproduced by permission of the British Library.

5 Ink-drawing of masks from a twelfth-century Terence from St Albans (Bodleian Library ms Auct. F.2.13, fol 3r). Reproduced by permission of the Bodleian Library.

6 Ink-drawing of masked actors in a scene from Terence's *Andria* (Bodleian Library ms Auct. F.2.13, fol 30v). Reproduced by permission of the Bodleian Library.

7 William Borlase's reconstruction of the 'Plain an Gwarry' at Perran Round (*The Natural History of Cornwall* [1758], pl XXIX, fig III). Reproduced by permission of the British Library.

8 Maumbury Rings, Dorchester (6 July 1967). Reproduced by permission of the Director in Aerial Photography, University of Cambridge.

9 A proclamation of 1418 by the mayor of London against the playing of interludes (Letter Book I, fol 223). Reproduced by permission of the Corporation of London Records Office.

10 Indenture between the pageant masters and the Mercers of York listing the properties of their Doomsday pageant on 11 June 1433. Reproduced by the permission of the Company of Merchant Adventurers of the City of York.

11 Stage diagram of *The Castle of Perseverance* (Folger Shakespeare Library ms V.A.354, fol 191v). Reproduced by permission of the Folger Shakespeare Library.

12 The end of the Towneley *Prima Pastorum* and the start of the *Secunda Pastorum* (Huntington Library ms HM 1, fol 38r). Reproduced by permission of the Huntington Library, San Marino, California.

13 The Hall, Winchester College (1982). Reproduced by the permission of the Warden and Fellows of Winchester College.

14 The beginning of Richard Pynson's edition of Terence's *Phormio* ca 1495-7 (Bodleian Library ms Fairfax 18.P.1 [printed part]). Reproduced by permission of the Bodleian Library.

15 The chancel of the church of St Mary Magdalene, Taunton, drawn by F.T. Dollman (from *Some Account of the Church of St. Mary Magdalene* [1845]).

16 The household accounts of Henry VIII for Epiphany 1510 (BL Add. ms 21481, fol 22r). Reproduced by permission of the British Library.

17 Plan of the second storey of Wressle Castle ca 1600, including the chapel, the dining chamber, and the hall (Petworth House Archives, 3544, West Sussex Record Office). Reproduced by permission of Lord Egremont.

18 Ceremonial orders for Twelfth Night ca 1515 in the Wressle household of Henry Algernon Percy, 5th earl of Northumberland (Bodleian Library ms Eng. hist. b.208, fol 40r). Reproduced by permission of the Bodleian Library.

19 Opening of Richard Gibson's revels accounts for Henry VIII concerning John Ritwise's tragedy or 'farsa' about the Pope, presented 10 November 1527 at Greenwich (BL Egerton ms 2605, fol 37v). Reproduced by permission of the British Library).

20 William Stukeley's plan of 14 June 1718 of the ruins of the great hall at York Place (later Whitehall), erected by Cardinal Wolsey. Reproduced by permission of the British Library.

21 A page from John Bale's holograph copy of *King Johan*, with the scene of Sedition's entrapment by Imperial Majesty (Huntington Library ms HM 3, fol 32r). Reproduced by permission of the Huntington Library, San Marino, California.

22 A water-colour by W.H. Redfern in 1875 of the Falcon Yard, Cambridge. Reproduced by permission of the Syndics of the Fitzwilliam Museum, Cambridge.

23 John Carter's plan and elevation of Trinity Hall, Aldersgate Street, London, in 1782 (Guildhall Library Portfolio 591/TRI). Reproduced by permission of the Guildhall Library, City of London.

24 Map of Great Britain, showing county and diocesan boundaries and Scottish places occurring in this guide.

25 Map of England, showing places occurring in this guide.

26 Map of London, based on an original c 1558.

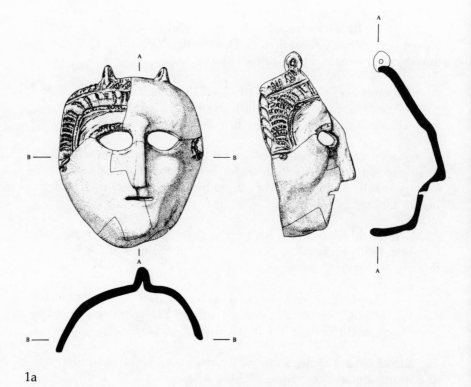

1a

1b

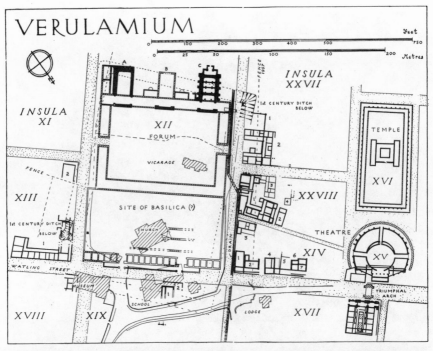

2

3

cantare. Quem queritis. Quo decantato fine tenus. respondeatur.

hi tres uno ore. Ihm nazarenum. Quibus ille. Non est hic surrexit

sicut predixerat. Ite nuntiate quia surrexit a mortuis. Cuius

iussimus uoce uertant se illi tres ad chorum dicentes. Att. resurrexit

dns. Dicto hoc rursus ille residens. uelut reuocans illos. dicat antiph

Venite & uidete locum. Hec uero dicens. surgat & erigat uelum.

ostendatq eis locum cruce nudatum. Sed tantum linteamina

posita. quibus crux inuoluta. erat. Quo uiso. deponant turribula

que gestauerant in eodem sepulchro. Sumantq; linteum. & exten

dant contur clerum. ac uelut ostendentes quod surrexerit dns

etiam non sit illo inuolutus. hanc canant antiph. Surrexit

dns desepulchro. Super ponantq; linteum altari. finita anaph.

prior congaudens protriumpho regis nri. quod deuicta morte

surrexit. incipiat hymnum. Te dm laudamus. Quo incepto;

una pulsentur omnia signa. post cuius finem. dicat sacerdos

uersum. In resurrectione tua xpe. uerbotenus & mitig matu

tinas dicens. Ds madiutorium meum intende. & a cantore. ilico

inchoetur antiph cum psalmo. Dns regnauit quia ds misereatur

nri. hoc non cantatur in loco. Sed tantum ds ds nr adte deluce con

iuncam canonicorum more. Quinque psalmi iure peractis

cum antiphonis sibi rite peranentibus capitulo. exam apres

bicero uersuq; surrexit dns desepulchro. ut mos est apuero

dicto iniecetur antiph in eauangelia. Qua peracta. dicatur

coll. De omnibus scis more solito his septem diebus non cantamus

5

Tibi pater me dedo · quid uis oneris impone · impera.
Uis me uxorem ducere · hanc suis amittere? ut potero feram.
hoc modo te obsecro · ut ne credas a me ad legatum hunc senem ·
Sine me expurgem · atq; illum huc coram adducam.
    Sim Adducas. pa a) Sine pater.
Equum postulat · da ueniam. paa) Sine te uxorem. Sino Sino
Quid uis cupio dum ne abhoc me falli comperiar chremes.
Pro peccato magno paululum supplicii satis est patri.

Mihi orare · una harum quæ uis causa me ut faci
    am monet.
Uel tu uel quod uerum est · uel quod ipsi cupio glycerio.
Andrium ego cineonem uideo · certe is est. Salutus
    sis chreme.

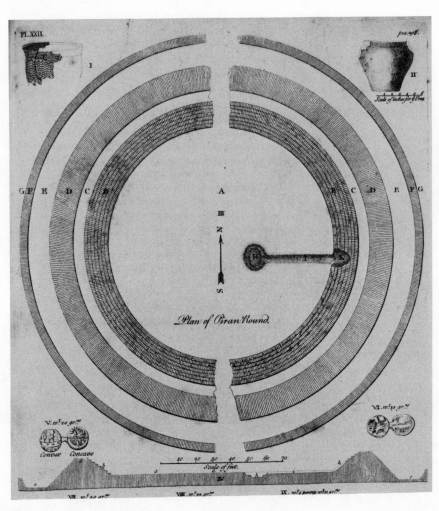

PL. XXIX.   p.248.

I   II

Scale of inches for 2 Urns

G F E D C B   A   B C D E F G
                                               III
                                                N

                                                S

Plan of Piran Round.

V. mᵗ 20 grᵗⁱ   VI. mᵗ 40 grᵗⁱ

Convex Concave

          10   20   30   40   50   60   70
                  Scale of feet.
                       IV

VII. mᵗ 20 grᵗⁱ   VIII. mᵗ 22 grᵗⁱ   IX. mᵗ 4 penny wᵗ 21 grᵗⁱ

7

8

9

10a

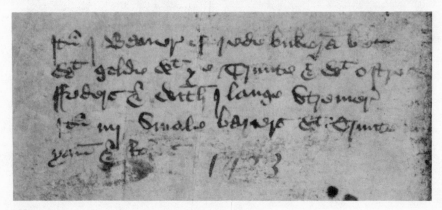

10b

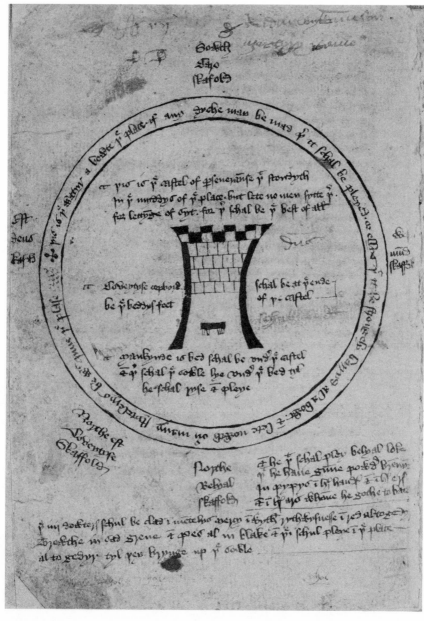

11

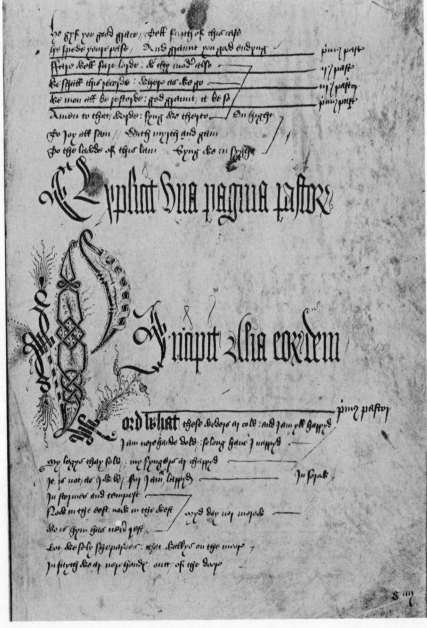

he gyf you good grace // doth knoth of this wyse
he spede your pesse : And grawnt you gud endyng —————— primꝰ past
stryfe doth sese lorde : & thy worde also —————— ij past
he shall this prowde : whoys tru to go —————— iij pastor
he mon all be restoryde : god grawnt it be so —————— iiij pastor
Amen to that lorde : syng we therto —————— Du hyght

No joy all sam // hath myrth and gam
No the ladde of this lam : syng we in fayth

Explicit vna pagina pastorum

Incipit alia corundem

Lord what these weders ar cold : and I am ylt happyd —————— primꝰ pastor
I am nere hande dold : so long haue I nappyd
my legys thay fold : my fyngers ar chappyd
It is not as I wold : for I am al lappyd —————— In sorak
In sorowe and tempest
Now in the est, nock in the west : wyd day ney mopak
wo is hym has nerd rest
Lot kee soly shepardes : that hatkys on the morp
In stryth kee ar nere hande : out of the dorp

ꝼ iiij

13

¶ Comedia quinta Phormio.

¶ Argumentum familiarissimum.

Chremes et Demipho duo fuerunt fratres
athenis. Demipho filiu habebat antipho/
nem. ipe amauit phaniu chremetis patrui
filiam naturalē. abſente et chremete, et demipho=
ne. Chremes preterea habebat filium phedriam.
is meretricem amabat. chremes duas habebat vx
ores. vnam athenis. ex ea ſuſceperat phedriam fi/
lium. alteram lemni. ideſt in iſula lemnos. ex ea
habuit phanium filiam. vocabatur athenis chre=
mes: et lemni ſtilpho. Uxor. e. lemno venit athe=
nas. maritum non inuenit. ppt. mutatum nomē
interea moritur. Phanium plorat: & ſepulturam
procurat. cam antipho vidit. et vxorem duxit. pa=
tres reuerſi irati ſūt. Sed per dolum phormionis
paraſiti viginti minas patres ſoluerunt: vt phor=
mio cam phanium vxorem duceret. cū ea pecunia
emerunt meretricem Phedrie. et antipho phaniū
vxorem retinuit. ¶) Con

Phormionis argumentum.

Chremetis ft aberat peregre demipho relicto
athenis antiphone filio. chremes habebat
ttam lemni vxorem ac filiā: athenis aliam coniugē
et amantē vnice natum fidicinam. mater. e. lemno
ai

15

Sonday the vijth day of Cristemmes

Anno p^{mo} h^{ij}
Die Januar^{ij}

Item for offrin…s vpon this Sonday ye vijth daye ___ ccc̄iij^s iiij^d

Item to Wontamps. petie John. Cokorell and
Haltazer mynstrelles for their rewardes _____ xl^s

Item to Alisaunder goldsmyth vpon his bill
for diuse partie of Iuelle and plate _____ iiij m̄li

Item to thurroldes at armes for their labor ___ xl^s

Item to my lorde of mysrule in full payment
of xl^{li} for his bysynes in Cristemmes ___ xl^{li}

Item to Corneles vandestrete vpon his warunt
for ye Tappette made for Wyndowes at yᵗ to… ___ xl^{li}

Item to the gentelmen of ye kinge Chapell in Ro… xl^{li} vij^s vj^d

Item to the gentelmen of the kinge Chapell
that playd in thall vpon yeth myght in Ro ___ x^{li}

Item to the kinge players in Rewardes _____ liij^s iiij^d

Item for a carte from Richemonde to grene
wiche wᵗ a standerde wᵗ the garde Iaquette ___ iiij^s

Item to S̄ John Digby knyght vpon a warunt in
full content for his expense at Calais __ cccxx^{li} xiiij^s iiij^d

Item to Emott de hensd vpon a warunt for his
half yeres ffes due at Cristemmes last passed ___ cc^{li}

Sonday at Grenewyche

Anno p^{mo} ɥ^{ij}
Die Januar^{ij}

Item for offringes vpon this Sonday _____ vj^s viij^d

Item for the wage of the yomen of the chaber
for the moneth of december last passed __ iiij^{xx} iij^{li} vj^s viij^d

Item for John Phice wage for the same moneth __ ccc^{li}

Item for S̄ott edwarde wage for yᵉ same moneth __ ccc^{li}

Sonday at Westmynster

Anno p^{mo} ɥ^{ij}
Die Januar^{ij}

Item for offringes vpon this Sonday _____ vj^s viij^d

Item for offringes vpon monday at masse of ye holyghost _ vj^s viij^d

Item to Crystas Browne for takinge of deres
to enstore Grenewyche parke _____ vij^s vj^d

Sū̄ pagi̅n _____ xviij^c xxx vij^{li} v^s

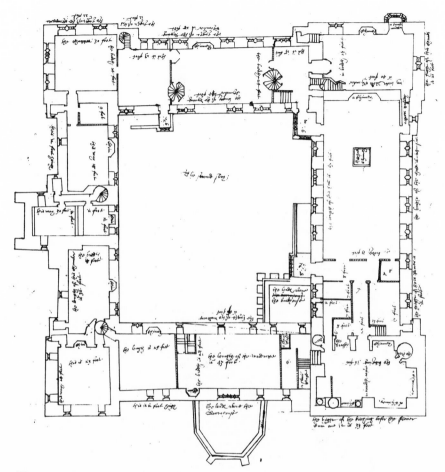

17

Item That it be ordeined the said night That there be a third play as an
enterlude a comody or tregidy to be played whil the lord and the lady
after the disguysing cum into the said Hall

In euche time both Monkes & Friers
Were Sodomits & Sortiers

Charles Wrellesthorpe

The disguysers and in after this
Maiours following noth in torchlight to be
but befor them at their riding in to the
hall noth in ye moost moodest sorte as
shalbe appointed by the marshalles to do it no then alister

Nicolas Chauncelie

Furst ij or men boarders to beir ij torchet to light them into the hall
and when the said disguysers cum into the hall then the
said partenus that bereth the said torchet to make their decenme and
kud noth at that tyme thar to stond in fede and the iij Minstrealles singe at the
disguysers and kind noth as they be comyng into the hall befor the said
Minstrelles to stond a fede and play and than the disguysers to make
their deceome altogether and damne furst damne as they be
appointed And when the said disguysers hath damne then said adiuyng
John half of them to stond sppn the one syde and half sppn the other
fede if their be no moomey promised avaunce that if there be moomey
disguysed than they to cum in furst kud if their be no moomey disguysed they
half of the Minstrealles left behind to see in the other disguysers coming
the second after they have decenght in the moomey and they have damned
and their decenme made and stand a fede And they to do as the
other did befor and then they to stonde sppn the other side Nicolas

To see oselesien

Charles Chauncelie

18

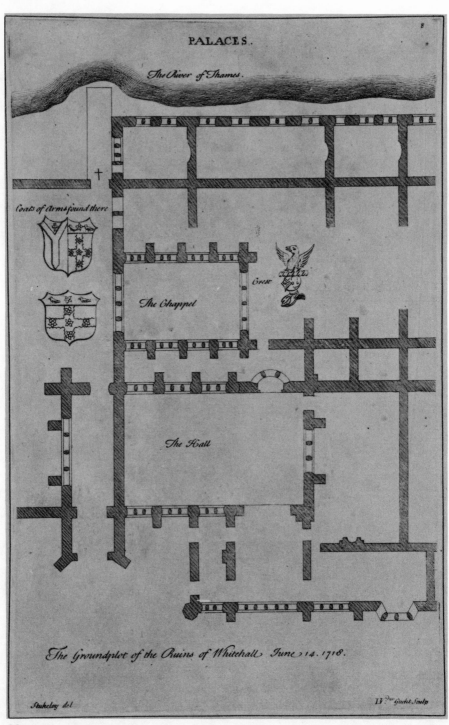

The River of Thames.

Coats of Arms found there

Crest

The Chappel

The Hall

The Groundplot of the Ruins of Whitehall June 14. 1718.

Stukeley del.

B. Van Gucht Sculp.

20

take vertue wyth ye, for euery acte ye doo ⸺
so shall ye be sure, not out of the waye to goo ⸺

Sedicyon in hat

where I see ye, I am glad I haue spyed ye .

Nobylyte theye is Sedicyon, stande yow asyde a whyle ⸺
ye shall see how we, shall catche hym by a wyle ⸺

Sedicyon No noyse amonge ye, where is the mery chere ⸺
that was wont to be, with quaffyng of double bere ⸺
the worlde is not yet, as some men woulde it haue ⸺
I haue bene abroade, and I thynke I haue playde the knaue ⸺

Cyvyle order thou canst do none other, except thou change thy mode ⸺

Sedicyon what myschiefe ayle ye, that ye are to me so blunt ⸺
I haue sene the daye, ye haue fauoryed me perfectyon ⸺

Pleasure thy selfe is not so, thu art of any other complectyon ⸺
for thys is the thiefe, that fyrst subdued kynge Iohn ⸺
vexynge other prynces, that sens haue ruled thys ye graye ⸺
And now he doth saye, he hath so played the knaue ⸺
that the worlde is not yet, as some men woulde it haue ⸺
It woulde be knowne syr, what he hath done of late ⸺

Imp. Ma what is thy name syrde, to vs here intymate ⸺

Sedicyon A faytwayy, a faytwayy, for tode dey passyd, a faytwayy ⸺
is thys none wyll holde me, and I haue made so manye ⸺

Imp. Ma tell me what thy name is, thys playeth ye knaue I trowe ⸺

Sedicyon I am wyndelesse good man, I haue muche payne to blowe ⸺

Imp. Ma I saye, tell thy name, or the sacke shall the costrayne ⸺

Sedicyon Holy perfectyon, my godmother called me playne ⸺

Nobylyte yt is Sedicyon, God gyue hym a very myschiefe ⸺

Cyvyle order a verye beaste is not, a more detestable thiefe ⸺

Sedicyon by the messe ye lye, I see wele ye do not knowe me ⸺

Imp. Ma as brother, art thu come? I am right glad we haue the ⸺

Sedicyon

21

22

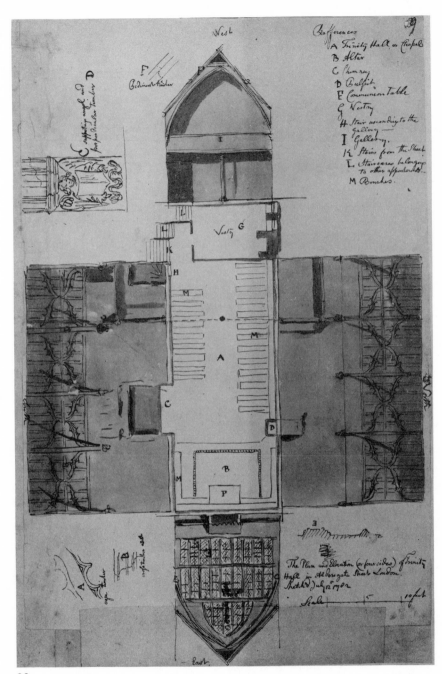

23

32 St John's Town of Dalry
20 Samuelston
11 Stirling
7   Strageath
43 Tomen-y-mur
42 Wrexham
28 Yeavering

DIOCESE
COUNTY

Map continues on p 98

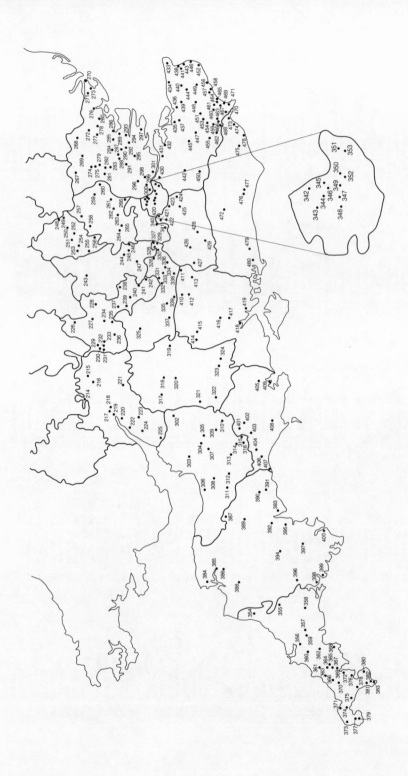

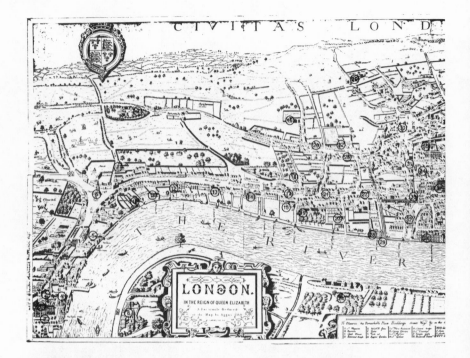

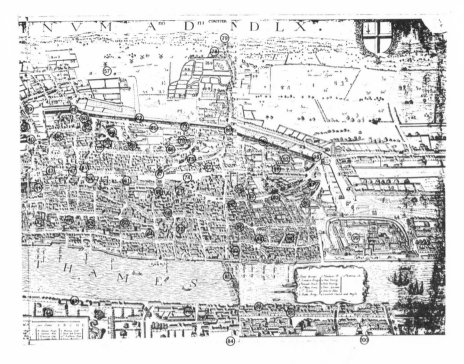

NVM A⁰ Dⁿⁱ CIRCITER N D L X.

CHRONOLOGICAL LIST OF DRAMATIC TEXTS

Chronological List of
Dramatic Texts

721/24-40?
1 A fragmentary Harrowing of Hell dialogue in the Book of Cerne. See under DOUBTFUL TEXTS.

9th century
2 A dialogue of Joseph and Mary in the seventh Advent lyric of the Exeter Book. See under DOUBTFUL TEXTS.

965-75
3 'Visitatio Sepulchri.' See under WINCHESTER.

978-80
4 'Quem Quaeritis.' See under WINCHESTER.

ca 1075-1100
5 Ascensiontide trope, 'Quem cernitis ascendisse super astra, o Christicolae?' (copied late 11th century, probably at Christchurch, Canterbury; text ed W.H. Frere, *The Winchester Troper from MSS. of the Xth and XIth Centuries*, HBS 8 [1894], p 110).

ca 1080-1120
6 Fragmentary Anglo-Norman life of St Catherine with extensive dialogue, possibly mimed in performance by one or two clerics (E.C. Fawtier-Jones, 'Les Vies de Sainte Catherine d'Alexandrie en Ancien Français,' *Romania*, 56 [1930], 80-104; Legge, pp 311-12; cf under DUNSTABLE ca 1100-19).

ca 1130
7 Three Latin plays, with some French refrains, by Hilarius, 'Suscitacio Lazari,' 'Ludus super Iconia Sancti Nicolai,' and 'Historia de Daniel Representanda.' See under DOUBTFUL TEXTS.

ca 1146-74
8 *Le Mystère d'Adam*, possibly written and acted in England (text ed W. Noomen [1971]; facs ed L. Sletsjoe, Bibliothèque Française et Romane, Serie D, 2 [1968]; ed and trans, Bevington, pp 78-121; also trans Lynette R. Muir, 'Adam,' *Proceedings of the Leeds Philosophical and Literary Society, Literary and Historical Section*, 13 [1970], 153-204; Stratman 3272-3303, 7333-44).

ca 1149-54
9 'Rithmus Laurentii de Christo et eius Discipulis,' a Latin 'peregrinus' dramatic dialogue by Laurentius, prior of Durham. See under DURHAM.

ca 1160-85
10 *Babio*, a 'comedia' possibly by Walter Map, to whom Henry II was patron (text in *Three Latin Comedies*, ed Keith Bate, Toronto Medieval Latin Texts 6 [1976], pp 35-60, from the earliest ms, probably compiled at court in the 1190s; trans Malcolm M. Brennan, Citadel Monograph Ser 7 [1968]).

ca 1180
11 *La Seinte Resureccion*, written in England; revised ca 1275, possibly with Canterbury auspices (text ed T.A. Jenkins, J.M. Manly, M.K. Pope, and J.G. Wright, Anglo-Norman Text Society, 4 [1943]; ed and trans, Bevington, pp 122-36; also trans Richard Axton and John Stevens, in *Medieval French Plays* [1971], pp 45-69; Stratman 7369-75; Chambers, ELCMA, p 11, suggests auspices at Bury St Edmunds, and see also below under BEVERLEY [ca 1220]).

ca 1188-98
12 'The Shrewsbury Fragments.' See under LICHFIELD.

ca 1200-30
13 Two supposed Anglo-Norman dramatic versions of the four daughters of God by Guillaume Herman and Stephen Langton. See under DOUBTFUL TEXTS.

5 Dramatic Texts

ca 1225
14 Public letters or proclamations by 'Genius of Christmas'? Discretion, and 'Transaetherius' before Robert Grosseteste as King of Christmas. See under OXFORD.

ca 1250
15 'The Harrowing of Hell,' a poem with dialogue. See under DOUBTFUL TEXTS.

before ca 1272-83
16 'Dame Sirith' (East Midland dialogue with narrative links, possibly mimed by a minstrel, according to J.A.W. Bennett and G.V. Smithers, eds, *Early Middle English Verse and Prose* [1966], pp 77-95; IMEV 342; dated by George H. McKnight, ed, *Middle English Humorous Tales in Verse* [1913], pp xxi-xliii).

ca 1275-1300
17 'The Cambridge Prologue,' a 'game' with an emperor (text ed Davis 1, pp 114-15; facs edn, Davis 2, pp 1-5; auspices possibly in Ireland; *Manual* 4).

ca 1300-25
18 Caiphas in a Palm Sunday procession. See under WELLS ca 1270.

ca 1300-25
19 'Interludium de Clerico et Puella' (text in *Early Middle English Verse and Prose*, pp 196-200; facs edn, Davis 2, pp 7-11; Northern provenance; Stratman 3991-9; *Manual* 6; IMEV 668).

ca 1300-25
20 'The Rickinghall (Bury St Edmunds) Fragment' of a king and his messenger (text ed Davis 1, pp 116-17; facs edn, Davis 2, pp 13-17; East Midland dialect; *Manual* 5; auspices possibly at Bury).

ca 1325-50
21 Fragment of speech by Diabolus, possibly dramatic, in sermon notes compiled at Oxford (text: Carleton Brown, 'Sermons and Miracle Plays,' *MLN*, 49 [1934], 394-6).

ca 1350
22 *The Pride of Life* (text ed Davis 1, pp 90-105; facs edn, Davis 2, pp 19-23; auspices in Ireland are suggested; Stratman 6207-18; *Manual* 26; Houle 43).

1363-76
23 Liturgical representation of the harrowing of hell; and a 'Visitatio Sepulchri.' See under BARKING ABBEY.

ca 1375
24 The Cornish *Origo Mundi, Passio Domini Nostri,* and *Resurrexio Domini Nostri.* See under PENRYN.

1376-1580
25 The York Corpus Christi play. See under YORK.

ca 1380-1420
26 'The Durham Prologue' (text ed Davis 1, pp 118-19; facs edn, Davis 2, pp 25-9; a north-eastern dialect; *Manual* 7).

1392-1580
27 The Coventry 'Shearmen and Taylors' Pageant' and 'Weavers' Pageant.' See under COVENTRY.

1397-1440
28 *The Castle of Perseverance.* See under LINCOLN.

15th century
29 'A Dramatic Monologue by Law,' ie, the Law of Moses (text in *Secular Lyrics,* pp 113-14; IMEV 3376).

15th century
30 'A Mumming of the Seven Philosophers,' for Christmas; the Nuncius of Senek, and seven philosophers, greeting the king of Christmas (text in *Secular Lyrics,* pp 110-13; IMEV 3807).

15th century
31 'A Nine Worthies Pageant' (text in *The Commonplace Book of Robert Reynes of Acle,* ed Cameron Louis [1980], pp 236, 436-7; IMEV 3666).

7 Dramatic Texts

15th century
32 Fragment of a supposed Passion play in English. See under DOUBT-
FUL TEXTS.

15th century
33 'Stanzas on Three Worthies' (the third stanza, by David, being in
the first person; text in *The Commonplace Book of Robert Reynes*, pp 235,
432-5; IMEV 1929.5).

ca 1400
34 Actor's part in a Cornish play, advice to a man to take a girl as his
wife, and to the girl to control him in marriage (text ed and trans,
Henry Jenner, 'Descriptions of Cornish Manuscripts – II. The Four-
teenth-Century Charter Endorsement, Brit. Mus. Add. Ch. 19491,' JRIC,
20 [1915-21], 41-8; the best edition is by R.M.N[ance]., 'New Light on
Cornish,' *Old Cornwall*, 4 [1943-51], 214-16).

ca 1400?
35 'Visitatio Sepulchri.' See under DUBLIN.

1421-1575
36 Chester Corpus Christi play and Whitsun pageants. See under
CHESTER.

1424
37 Lydgate's 'Mumming at Eltham.' See under ELTHAM.

ca 1424-30
38 Lydgate's 'Bycorne and Chychevache.' See under LONDON.

ca 1424-30
39 Lydgate's 'Mumming at Bishopswood.' See under STEPNEY (Bishop's
Wood in).

ca 1425
40 'Dux Moraud' (text of the duke's part only, ed Davis 1, pp 106-13;
facs edn, Davis 2, pp 67-71; auspices probably in Norfolk or Suffolk;
Stratman 3912-16; *Manual* 8; evidently a miracle of the Virgin, for
which see Constance B. Hieatt, 'A Case for *Duk Moraud* as a Play of
the Miracles of the Virgin,' *MedS*, 32 [1970], 345-51).

ca 1425-50
41 Possibly dramatic fragments (text ed Diana Wyatt, 'Two Yorkshire Fragments: Perhaps Dramatic?' REEDN, 1978.1, pp 17-21; from near Beverley and Hull?).

1426-31
42 John Lydgate's translation, from the French, of the 'Danse Macabre,' a poem-dialogue between Death and men of all degrees, from Pope to Hermit (such dances on the Continent were acted publicly; text in *The Dance of Death*, ed Florence Warren, EETS OS 181 [1931]; reprinted first by William Dugdale, *The History of St. Pauls Cathedral* [1658], pp 289-96; IMEV 2590-1).

ca 1427
43 Lydgate's 'A Mumming at London.' See under LONDON.

1427
44 Lydgate's 'Mumming at Hertford.' See under HERTFORD.

1427-1589
45 The Newcastle play of Noah's ark. See under NEWCASTLE UPON TYNE ([2]).

1429
46 Lydgate's 'Mumming for the Mercers of London.' See under LONDON.

1429
47 Lydgate's 'Mumming for the Goldsmiths of London.' See under LONDON.

ca 1430
48 Lydgate's 'Mumming at Windsor.' See under WINDSOR.

1432 21 February
49 Pageants for the entry of Henry VI into London. See under LONDON.

1437-8
50 Tito Livio Frulovisi's two Latin comedies *Peregrinatio* and *Eugenius*, written in the household of Humphrey, duke of Gloucester, probably at his manor of Bella Court in East Greenwich (texts: *Opera Hactenus*

Inedita T. Livii de Frulovisiis de Ferraria, ed C.W. Previté-Orton [1932], pp xiii-xiv, xvi-xviii, xxviii-xxix, 185-286; R. Weiss, *Humanism in England during the Fifteenth Century,* 3rd edn [1967], pp 42, 188, and 'Humphrey Duke of Gloucester and Tito Livio Frulovisi,' in *Fritz Saxl,* pp 218-27).

ca 1440-50
51 *Occupation and Idleness* and *Lucidus and Dubius,* two interludes in Winchester College ms 33A. See under WINCHESTER.

ca 1440-83?
52 Christmas game with God's speeches to his apostles and how each was 'baptiste and none knewe of other,' by Benedict Burgh, of Sandon, Essex (1440), Colchester (1466), Bridgnorth (1470), St Paul's (1472) and St Stephen's, Westminster (1476; text ed Max Förster, 'Über Benedict Burghs Leben und Werke,' *Archiv,* 101 [1898], 53-5; *IMEV* 2749).

1445 28 May
53 Pageants for Queen Margaret's entry into London. See under LONDON.

ca 1450? or 1520?
54 *Christ's Burial and Christ's Resurrection* (texts in *Digby Plays,* pp lxxiv-xcix, 141-93, where the editors date these texts as having been written by a Carthusian in Yorkshire about 1520, probably at Kingston-on-Hull [a stratum of North Midlands and East Anglian dialect, however, also appears]; facs, intro D.C. Baker and J.L. Murphy, LeedsTMMDF III [1976]; for performance on Good Friday afternoon and Easter morning; Stratman 3383-93; *Manual* 3).

ca 1450-75
55 The N-town or Hegge plays (text: *Ludus Coventriae or The Plaie called Corpus Christi,* ed K.S. Block, EETS ES 120 [1922], and facs, *The N-Town Plays,* intro Peter Meredith and Stanley J. Kahrl, LeedsTMMDF IV [1977]; Stratman 4058-286; *Manual* 12; Harvey-Dietrich, pp 402-3; uncertain auspices, but from Norfolk, and probably from Norwich [not at Lincoln], for which see Jacob Bennett, 'The Language and the Home of the "Ludus Coventriae,"' *Orbis,* 22 [1973], 43-63; Mark Eccles, '*Ludus Coventriae* Lincoln or Norfolk?' *Medium Ævum,* 40 [1971], 135-41; and Alan H. Nelson, 'On Recovering the Lost Norwich Cor-

pus Christi Cycle,' *CompD*, 4 [1970-1], 246-50; and less probably from Bury St Edmunds, for which see Gail M. Gibson, 'Bury St. Edmunds, Lydgate, and the *N-Town Cycle*,' *Speculum*, 56 [1981], 56-90; see also Claude Gauvin, *Un Cycle du Théâtre Religieux anglais du Moyen Âge: Le Jeu de la Ville de 'N'* [1973], and Patrick J. Collins, *The N-Town Plays and Medieval Picture Cycles*, EDAM Monograph Ser, 2 [1979]). The play has the following pageants:

1 / the creation of heaven and the angels, and the fall of Lucifer;
2 / the creation of the world and man, and the fall of man;
3 / Cain and Abel;
4 / Noah and the death of Lamech;
5 / Abraham and Isaac;
6 / Moses;
7 / the prophets;
8 / the conception of Mary (barrenness of Anna);
9 / Mary in the temple;
10 / the betrothal of Mary;
11 / the parliament of heaven, and the salutation and conception;
12 / Joseph's return;
13 / the visit to Elizabeth;
14 / the trial of Joseph and Mary;
15 / the birth of Christ;
16 / the adoration of the shepherds;
17 / the adoration of the magi;
18 / the purification;
19 / the massacre of the innocents, and the death of Herod;
20 / Christ and the doctors;
21 / the baptism;
22 / the temptation;
23 / the woman taken in adultery;
24 / the raising of Lazarus;
25 / the council of the Jews, and the entry into Jerusalem;
26 / the last supper, and the conspiracy of the Jews and Judas;
27 / the betrayal;
28 / King Herod, the trial of Christ before Annas and Caiphas, and Peter's denial;
29 / the death of Judas, the trial of Christ before Pilate, and the trial of Christ before Herod;
30 / Pilate's wife's dream, the trial of Christ and the thieves before Pilate, and the condemnation and scourging;

31 / the procession to Calvary, and the crucifixion;

32 / the descent into Hell of Anima Christi;

33 / the embassy to Pilate of Joseph of Arimathea, the episode of Longeus, the descent from the cross and burial, and the guarding of the sepulchre;

34 / the harrowing of hell, the resurrection and appearance to the Virgin, and the compact of the soldiers and Pilate;

35 / the announcement to the three Maries;

36 / the appearance to Mary Magdalene;

37 / the appearance on the way to Emmaus, and the appearance to Thomas;

38 / the ascension, and the choice of Matthias;

39 / the day of Pentecost;

40 / the Assumption of the Virgin; and

41 / doomsday.

ca 1450-99

56 An Irish prose version of the harrowing of hell. See under DOUBT-FUL TEXTS.

ca 1450-1520

57 'Y Tri Brenin o Gwlen' or 'The Three Kings of Cologne'; and 'Y Dioddefaint' or 'The Passion,' including a harrowing of hell and a resurrection, possibly by Iorwerth Fynglwyd, fl 1490, a Glamorgan-shire poet (texts ed and trans by Jones, pp 128-51, and 152-237, and cf pp 10-99).

ca 1450-?1576

58 The Towneley cycle, with the Wakefield pageants (text: *The Towneley Plays*, ed George England, intro Alfred W. Pollard, EETS ES 71 [1897]; and *The Towneley Cycle: A Facsimile of Huntington MS HM 1*, intro A.C. Cawley and Martin Stevens, LeedsTMMDF II [1976]), with the following pageants (starred numbers belong to plays in *The Wakefield Pageants in the Towneley Cycle*, ed A.C. Cawley [1958]; Strat-man 4443-837; *Manual* 11; Harvey-Dietrich, pp 403-7; and for three critical books on these plays, see Arnold Williams, *The Characterization of Pilate in the Towneley Plays* [1950], John Gardner, *The Construction of the Wakefield Cycle* [1974], Walter E. Meyers, *A Figure Given: Typology in the Wakefield Plays* [1978], and Jeffrey Helterman, *Symbolic Action in the Plays of the Wakefield Master* [1981]; and see also under WAKEFIELD):

1 / the creation (Barkers);
2* / the killing of Abel (Glovers);
3* / Noah and the ark;
4 / Abraham;
5 / Isaac;
6 / Jacob;
7 / the prophets;
8 / Pharaoh (Litsters);
9 / Caesar Augustus;
10 / the annunciation;
11 / the salutation of Elizabeth;
12* / the first shepherds' play (see PLATE 12);
13* / the second shepherds' play (see PLATE 12);
14 / the offering of the magi;
15 / the flight into Egypt;
16* / Herod the great;
17 / the purification of Mary;
18 / the play of the doctors;
19 / John the Baptist;
20 / the conspiracy;
21* / the buffeting;
22 / the scourging;
23 / the crucifixion;
24 / the talents;
25 / the deliverance of souls;
26 / the resurrection of the Lord;
27 / the pilgrims (Fishers);
28 / Thomas of India;
29 / the Lord's ascension;
30 / the judgment;
31 / Lazarus;
32 / the hanging of Judas.

ca 1451
59 The ceremony and part of the prophet in the Palm Sunday procession, played by a boy dressed as a prophet, together with three clerics (*Processionale ad Usum Insignis ac Praeclarae Ecclesiae Sarum*, ed W.G. Henderson [1882], pp vi, 50-1; the text of this ceremony exists only in the editions of 1508 and 1517, and sometime before 1528 it was dropped until its brief reappearance in the 1555 edition under Mary;

STC 16233-4; see also Nigel Davison, 'So Which Way Round Did They Go? The Palm Sunday Procession at Salisbury,' *Music and Letters*, 61 [1980], 11-12; for the probable date of the introduction of the ceremony, see LONDON under 1451).

ca 1454-99
60 'The Brome Play of *Abraham and Isaac*.' See under BROME.

ca 1457-61
61 Thomas Chaundler's *Liber Apologeticus de Omni Statu Humanae Naturae*. See under OXFORD.

ca 1460-70
62 *Wisdom* (text in *Macro Plays*, pp 113-52, and *Digby Plays*, pp lxiii-lxxii, 116-40; facs ed David Bevington, Folger Facsimiles 1 [1972], and in *The Digby Plays*, intro Donald C. Baker and J.L. Murphy, LeedsTMMDF III [1976]; Stratman 6014-18, 6468-87; *Manual* 28; Houle 57; the only full critical book on the play is by John J. Molloy, *A Theological Interpretation of the Moral Play, 'Wisdom, Who Is Christ'* [1952]; Milton McC. Gatch, 'Mysticism and Satire in the Morality of *Wisdom*,' *PQ*, 53 [1974], 342-62, locates the play in the London palace of the bishop of Ely, then William Grey, in Holborn).

1461
63 Abraham and Isaac play. See under NORTHAMPTON.

1461
64 Pageant of William the Conqueror for Edward IV's entry into Bristol. See under BRISTOL.

1461-1520
65 *The Play of the Sacrament*. See under CROXTON.

1464
66 *Mankind* (text in *Macro Plays*, pp 153-84; Bevington, pp 901-38; facs ed David Bevington, Folger Facsimiles 1 [1972]; auspices in or near Cambridge, possibly collegiate, for which see Walter K. Smart, 'Some Notes on *Mankind*,' *MP*, 14 [1916-17], 45-58, 293-313; and Thomas J. Jambeck and Reuben R. Lee, '"Pope Pokett" and the Date of *Mankind*,' *MS*, 39 [1977], 511-13; Stratman 6014-40; *Manual* 29; Houle

32; and Sister Mary P. Coogan, *An Interpretation of the Moral Play, 'Mankind'* [1947]).

ca 1470-90?
67 'A Speech of "Delight,"' and 'An Epilogue' (texts ed Davis 1, pp 121-2; facs edn, Davis 2, pp 85-90; probably East Anglian; *Manual* 21, 32; *IMEV* 1927).

1475
68 'Robin Hood and the Sheriff of Nottingham.' See under NORWICH (1473).

ca 1475?
69 'A Pageant of Knowledge,' attributed to Lydgate, a presentation of the seven estates (with a one-line speech each), the seven ladies of sapience, the founders of the seven artificial sciences, the authors of the seven liberal sciences, the seven planets, the twelve signs of the zodiac, the four elements, the four complexions, the four seasons, and the world (*Minor Poems*, II, 724-38; *IMEV* 3503-4, 3651).

ca 1475-1500?
70 'The Ashmole Fragment,' actor's part for Secundus Miles (text ed Davis 1, p 120; facs edn, Davis 2, pp 79-83; unknown provenance; *Manual* 20).

1479 29 August
71 Subtlety of 'Pastor Bonus,' the Bishop, and St Andrew, probably performed on this date at the installation of John Morton, bishop of Ely. See under ELY.

ca 1480
72 Seven stanzas spoken in the first person by Faith, Charity, Temperance, Justice, Force, Hope, and Prudence, for a pageant? (BL blockbook broadside, damaged text ed W.L. Schreiber, *Handbuch der Holz- und Metallschnitte*, VI [1928], no 2984, pp 51-4; cf T.O. Mabbott, 'The Text of the English Xylographic Poem on the Seven Virtues,' *MLN*, 65 [1950], 545; STC 17037 [publ 1500?]; *IMEV* 338.5).

1480-1510?
73 'The Maner of the Crying of ane Playe,' formerly attributed to William Dunbar. See under EDINBURGH.

15 Dramatic Texts

1480-1520
74 *The Conversion of St. Paul,* an East Midlands text, originally from
Cambridgeshire and East Anglia (*Digby Plays,* pp xv-xxx, 1-23 [lines
412-515, an inserted scene of Belyall and Mercury, probably dates from
the 1550s]; Bevington, pp 664-86; facs intro Donald C. Baker and J.L.
Murphy, LeedsTMMDF III [1976]; Stratman 3828-40, 3855-79; *Manual*
19; for possible auspices in 1562, see under CHELMSFORD).

1480-1520
75 *Mary Magdalen* (an East Anglian text, with Norfolk features, in
Digby Plays, pp xxx-lii, 24-95; Bevington, pp 687-753; facs, intro
Donald C. Baker and J.L. Murphy, LeedsTMMDF III [1976]; auspices at
King's Lynn, Norfolk, suggested, on linguistic evidence, by Jacob
Bennett, 'The *Mary Magdalene* of Bishop's Lynn,' *SP,* 75 [1978], 1-9;
Stratman 3828-32, 3841-7, 3855-79; *Manual* 19; Houle 35; for possible
auspices in 1562, see under CHELMSFORD).

1485
76 William Ireland's fabricated play-text, 'The Divill and Rychard.'
See under DOUBTFUL TEXTS.

1486
77 Pageants for the entry of Henry VII. See under BRISTOL, HEREFORD,
WORCESTER, and YORK.

ca 1490-1500
78 Henry Medwall's *Nature* (text in *Medwall,* pp 91-161; 'The Play of
Lucrece: A Fragment of an Interlude Printed c. 1530,' ed W.W. Greg,
in *Collections Part II,* MalS [1908], pp 137-42; auspices in Cardinal
Morton's household, probably at Lambeth or at Knole, Kent; TFT 17;
Greg 17-18; *Index,* p 166; *Scriptorum,* II, 71; STC 17779 [publ 1530-4];
Stratman 6057-62, 6078-88; *Manual* 31; Houle 38; for 'Thenterlude of
Nature' in a printer's inventory of 1553, see Plomer, p 233).

1495-7
79 Six comedies by Terence, *Andria, Eunuchus, Heauton Timorumenos,*
Adelphoe, Phormio, and *Hecyra,* printed separately by Richard Pynson
(STC 23885 [publ 1495-7]; Duff, pp 108-9; for two later editions by
Wynkyn de Worde, in 1504 [printed in Paris] and ca 1510, see STC
23885.3-5.5; see PLATE 14).

ca 1495-1501
80 *The Life of St. Meriasek.* See under CAMBORNE.

ca 1496-7
81 Henry Medwall's *Fulgens and Lucrece* (text in *Medwall*, pp 31-89, and cf pp 17-18; auspices in Cardinal Morton's household? Greg 1-2; STC 17778 [publ 1512-16]; Stratman 6003-5, 6057-77).

1498
82 John Skelton's 'The Bowge of Courte.' See under DOUBTFUL TEXTS.

16th century
83 Fragment of a Welsh religious interlude or moral play, beginning 'Dechryad part 'r offeiriad' (not seen; Bodl. ms Welsh f.9 [R]; Summary Catalogue 30820).

16th century
84 'Ymddiddan ryng yr effeiriad ar gwr bonheddig,' or 'The Play of [or conversations between] the Priest and the Gentleman,' a moral play (partial text transcr in *MSS Welsh*, I, ii [1899], pp 428, 454; II, i [1902], pp 106-7; Jones, pp 13, 100; and, entitled 'The Strong Man,' a brief English plot summary in Thomas Parry's *A History of Welsh Literature*, trans H.I. Bell [1955], pp 186-7).

ca 1500
85 'Llyma Ymddiddan yr Enaid ar Korff' or 'Dialogue of the Soul and Body' (text ed and trans Jones, pp 238-59, and cf 100-20).

ca 1500?
86 Three-part Scots song by the leader of a Plough Monday pastime (a text of 1666 is given by H.M. Shire and K. Elliott, 'Pleugh Song and Plough Play,' *Saltire Review*, 2.vi [Winter 1955], 39-44).

1501 12 November
87 Pageants for the entry of Catherine of Aragon. See under LONDON.

ca 1507-8
88 *Mundus et Infans*, otherwise titled *The World and the Child* (text in *Specimens of the Pre-Shaksperean Drama*, ed J.M. Manly, I [1897], 353-85; TFT 6; Greg 5; STC 25982 [publ 1522]; Stratman 6504-18; Houle 37; auspices at Ampthill, Beds., the seat of Richard Grey, 13th earl of Kent,

suggested by Ian Lancashire, 'The Auspices of *The World and the Child*,' *Renaissance and Reformation*, 12 [1976], 96-105).

ca 1510-19?

89 *Everyman*, probably a translation of the Dutch *Elckerlijk* (text: *Everyman*, ed A.C. Cawley [1961]; and ed Bevington, pp 939-63, and John Astington, PLS Performance Text 2 [1980]; TFT 5; Greg 4; STC 10603-6 [publ 1510?]; Stratman 5501-655; *Manual* 30; Houle 12).

1512

90 *The Killing of the Children*, an East Midlands play (text in *Digby Plays*, pp lii-lxiii, 96-115; Poeta's prologue mentions a shepherds' play and a three kings' play as acted in the previous year, and promises a non-extant play of Mary's purification in the temple preceding a play of Herod and the slaughter of the Innocents; facs intro Donald C. Baker and J.L. Murphy, LeedsTMMDF III [1976]; Stratman 3828-32, 3848-79; *Manual* 19; written by John Parfre, of Thetford? for whom see D.C. Baker and J.L. Murphy, 'The Late Medieval Plays of MS. Digby 133: Scribes, Dates, and Early History,' RORD, 10 [1967], 155; for possible auspices in 1562, see under CHELMSFORD).

1512-13

91 *Palamedes*, by Remaclus Arduenne, a Latin comedy dedicated and printed in London (not seen; H.S., 'An Early Latin Comedy Written in London,' *The British Museum Quarterly*, 8 [1933-4], 34-5 [publ 1512-13]; and Strickland Gibson, 'Fragments from Bindings at the Queen's College, Oxford,' *The Library*, 4th ser, 12 [1931-2], 432-3).

ca 1513

92 *The Interlude of Youth* (text in *Two Tudor Interludes*, ed Ian Lancashire, The Revels Plays [1980]; TFT 19; Greg 20; STC 14111-12 [publ 1532-3]; Arber, I, 75 ['youghte charyte and humylyte,' ca 1557-8]; Stratman 6519-38; Houle 59; Lancashire suggests auspices at Wressle or Leconfield, Yorks., E.R., seats of Henry Algernon Percy, 5th earl of Northumberland; for 'Thenterlude of Youth' in a printer's inventory of 1553, see Plomer, p 233; see also under WRESSLE).

ca 1513-21

93 *The Pardoner and the Friar*, attributed to John Heywood (text in *Heywood*, pp 1-25; TFT 13; Greg 14; STC 13299 [publ 1533]; Stratman 5709-19, 5768-80).

1514 6 January
94 Dr D. Cooper's song, 'I have bene a foster,' possibly belongs in an interlude with a moresque including Venus, Beauty, and a fool. See under RICHMOND.

ca 1514
95 *Hick Scorner* (in *Two Tudor Interludes*, ed Ian Lancashire, The Revels Plays [1980]; TFT 4; Greg 3; STC 14039-40 [publ 1515-16]; Stratman 5876-87; Houle 16; suggested auspices at Suffolk Place, Southwark, seat of Charles Brandon, duke of Suffolk; for 16th-century references to the character of Hick Scorner and the play, see Lancashire, App 2).

1517-20
96 John Rastell's *The Nature of the Four Elements* (text in *Rastell*, pp 29-68; TFT 7; titled 'Naturam naturatam' in *Illvstrivm*, fol 222r, and *Scriptorum*, I, 660; Greg 6; STC 20722 [publ 1520?]; Stratman 6225-48; Houle 39; Geritz, p 343).

ca 1519-20
97 John Skelton's *Magnificence* (text ed Paula Neuss, The Revels Plays [1980]; TFT 11; *Scriptorum*, I, 652; 'The Garland of Laurel,' *The Complete Poems of John Skelton Laureate*, 3rd edn, ed Philip Henderson [1959], p 386; Greg 11; STC 22607 [publ 1530?]; Stratman 6287-333; Houle 31; possibly about the purge of the king's 'minions' in May 1519, the 'all Frenche' Nicholas Carew, John Peachy, and Francis Bryan, the king's liberality to whom had become a scandal [Halle, fols 67v-8v; J.J. Scarisbrick, *Henry VIII* (1968), pp 117-18]; Neuss, dating the play ca 1520-2, tentatively suggests performance at the London Merchant Tailors' guild hall [pp 42-3]; for twelve copies of 'thenterlude of magnifycence' in a 1553 printer's inventory, see Plomer p 233).

ca 1519-28
98 *Gentleness and Nobility*, attributed to John Heywood (and to Rastell, less surely; text in *Rastell*, pp 97-124; TFT 8; termed 'the play of gentilnes & nobilite' in 1538 [Roberts, p 38]; Greg 8-9; STC 20723 [publ 1533]; Stratman 5675-89; Geritz, p 344).

ca 1519-28
99 John Heywood's *The Play of the Weather* (text ed T.N.S. Lennam, MalS [1971 (1977)]; and Bevington, pp 990-1028; TFT 14-15; *Index*, p

217; *Scriptorum*, II, 110; Greg 15 and IV, 1651 [copy of John Dudley, lord Lisle, 1547-51r]; STC 13305-7a [publ 1533]; Stratman 5709-19, 5793-815; Houle 56).

before 1520
100 *The Interlude of Johan the Evangelist* (text ed W.W. Greg, MalS [1907]; TFT 24; Greg 26; STC 14643 [publ ca 1550]; Stratman 5942-9; Houle 20).

ca 1520
101 *Terens in Englysh*, an anonymous English translation of Terence's *Andria* published in Paris (STC 23894 [publ ca 1520]; Greg 12; cf Alexander H. Brodie, 'Terens in Englysh: Towards the Solution of a Literary Puzzle,' *Classica et Mediaevalia*, 27 [1966], 397-416, which disposes of the attribution to John Rastell).

ca 1520-2
102 John Heywood's *The Four P.P.* (text in *Heywood*, pp 26-64; TFT 20; *Index*, p 217; *Scriptorum*, II, 110; Greg 21 and IV, 1651 [copy of John Dudley, lord Lisle, 1547-51r, 'a play called ye 4 pees']; STC 13300-2 [publ 1545?]; Stratman 5709-45).

ca 1520-33
103 John Heywood's *Witty and Witless* (text in *Heywood*, pp 191-217; TFT 9; Greg II, 962; Stratman 5709-19, 5816-25).

1522 4 March
104 William Cornyshe's carol 'Yow and I and Amyas,' possibly for the pageant 'Chateau Vert' at Wolsey's York House. See under LONDON.

1522 6 June
105 Pageants for Charles V's entry into London. See under LONDON.

ca 1523-5?
106 *Calisto and Melebea* (text, anonymously adapted from *La Tragicomedia de Calisto y Melibea* by Fernando de Rojas, in *Rastell*, pp 69-96; sometimes attributed to Rastell; TFT 10; termed 'the play of melebea' in 1538 [Roberts, p 36]; Greg 10; STC 20721 [publ ca 1525]; Stratman 5407-20; Geritz, pp 343-4).

1528-33
107 *Johan Johan the Husband*, probably by John Heywood, a translation of *Farce nouvelle tres bonne et fort joyeuse du Paste* (text ed G.R. Proudfoot, MalS [1967 (1972)]; and Bevington, pp 970-89; TFT 12; Greg 13; STC 13298 [publ 1533]; Stratman 5709-19, 5746-67).

1528-33
108 John Heywood's *A Play of Love* (text ed J.A.B. Somerset, MalS [1977 (1978)]; also his *Four Tudor Interludes*, pp 52-96; TFT 16; *Index*, p 217; *Scriptorum*, II, 110; Greg 16 and IV, 1651 [copy of John Dudley, lord Lisle, 1547-51r]; STC 13303-4 [publ 1534]; Stratman 5709-19, 5781-92; Houle 28).

ca 1528
109 'Temperance and Humility: A Fragment of a Morality Printed c. 1530' (text ed W.W. Greg in *Collections Part III*, MalS [1909], pp 243-6; Greg 7; STC 14109.5 [publ ca 1528]; Stratman 6336-8; Houle 47; written 1534-6, according to Craik, pp 98-101).

ca 1530
110 'The Prodigal Son. A Fragment of an Interlude Printed c. 1530' (text ed W.W. Greg, in *Collections Part I*, MalS [1907], pp 27-30; Greg 19; STC 20765.5 [publ 1530?]; Stratman 6139-40).

ca 1530-43?
111 Fragment of a pageant text (text ed Elizabeth D. Adams, 'A Fragment of a Lord Mayor's Pageant,' MLN, 32 [1917], 285-9, suggesting London auspices; R. Withington, 'A Note on "A Fragment of a Lord Mayor's Pageant,"' MLN, 34 [1919], 501-3, suggests a provincial royal entry *temp.* Henry VII; IMEV 575, 1547.5).

1530-60?
112 *The Resurrection of Our Lord* (sometimes dated 1580-1630? text ed J.D. Wilson and B. Dobell, MalS [1912]; *Manual* 22).

ca 1531-47?
113 Fragmentary interlude possibly by John Redford, of Courage, Kindness, Cleanness, and Concupiscence (text ed A. Brown, W.W. Greg, and F.P. Wilson, MalS [1951], p 51).

ca 1531-47
114 John Redford's fragmentary interlude of D, G, I, and Tom (text ed
Arthur Brown, W.W. Greg, and F.P. Wilson, MalS [1951], p 47).

1533 31 May
115 Coronation pageants for Anne Boleyn, with verses by Nicholas
Udall. See under LONDON.

1533
116 'Old Christmas *Or* Good Order: A Fragment of a Morality Printed
by William Rastell in 1533' (text ed W.W. Greg, in *Collections Volume
IV*, MalS [1956], pp 33-9; Greg 14.5; STC 18793.5, as 'Not by J. Skelton'
[publ 1533]; Stratman 5706-8; Houle 15; listed among Skelton 'Apocrypha' by Maurice Pollet, *John Skelton: Poet of Tudor England*, trans
John Warrington [1971], pp 260-1; termed 'the play of good order' in
1538 [Roberts, p 36] and 1553 [Plomer, p 233]).

ca 1533-51
117 A moral 'playlet'? (text ed David Galloway, '"The Seven Deadly
Sins": Some Verses from an Archdeacon's Visitation Book (1533-51),'
REEDN, 1979.1, pp 9-13).

1533-65
118 'The Story of the Creation of Eve, with the Expelling of Adam and
Eve out of Paradise.' See under NORWICH (ca 1530-65).

ca 1536-9?
119 Three dialogues by Robert (=Ralph?) Radcliffe, 'A Governance of
the Church,' 'Between the Poor Man and Fortune,' and 'Between
Death and the Goer by the Way.' See under CAMBRIDGE.

1536-44
120 *Absalom*, by Thomas Watson. See under CAMBRIDGE.

1537 12-24 October
121 *Thersites*, an adaptation of Ravisius Textor's dialogue, possibly
with auspices at Oxford (text: TTCS, pp 5-15, 37-63, and *Six Anonymous
Plays: First Series (c. 1510-1537)*, ed J.S. Farmer, EED [1905], pp 194-226;
TFT 31; cf Boas, pp 20-1; Greg 37; STC 23949 [publ 1562?]; Stratman
6339-53; Edgerton suggests performance also at court [pp 34-5]).

1537?-65
122 'Albion Knight: A Fragment of a Morality' (text ed W.W. Greg, in *Collections Part III*, MalS [1909], pp 229-42; Greg 38; STC 275 [publ 1566?]; Stratman 5315-22; Houle 1; dated in the winter of 1537-8 according to Madeleine H. Dodds, 'The Date of "Albion, Knight,"' *The Library*, 3rd ser, 4 [1913], 157-70).

1538
123 John Bale's *Three Laws, The Chief Promises of God, John Baptist's Preaching*, and *The Temptation of Our Lord*; see under BISHOPSTOKE, and KILKENNY (1553 20 August); and for Bale's *King Johan*, see under CANTERBURY (1539 2 January).

1540
124 Sir David Lindsay's *Satyre of the Thrie Estaitis*. See under SCOTLAND; LINLITHGOW (and CUPAR, EDINBURGH, and PERTH).

ca 1540
125 *Acolastus*, by William Gnaphaeus (Fullonius), ed and trans by John Palsgrave for the teaching of Latin grammar (text: *The Comedy of Acolastus*, ed P.L. Carver, EETS OS 202 [1937 (for 1935)]; STC 11470 [publ 1540]).

1540-60
126 'Love Feigned and Unfeigned,' a fragmentary morality (text ed Arundell Esdaile in *Collections Part I*, MalS [1907], pp 17-25; Stratman 6000-2; Houle 29).

1541
127 Nicholas Grimald's *Christus Redivivus*. See under OXFORD.

ca 1541-2
128 *Godly Queene Hester* (text ed W.W. Greg, MKAED 5 [1904]; Greg 33; STC 13251 [publ 1561]; Stratman 5697-705; Houle 14; doubtfully attributed to William Hunnis by Stopes, *Hunnis*, pp 263-4; a post-reformation play probably complimenting Queen Catherine Howard [Hester] and her uncle Thomas, duke of Norfolk [Mardocheus], Roman Catholic sympathizers, at their overthrow of Thomas Cromwell [Aman; a suggestion that I owe to my student Kathy Pearl]; Greg argues that Aman is Wolsey).

ca 1541-6
129 Nicholas Grimald's *Archipropheta*. See under OXFORD.

1541-7
130 'The Four Cardinal Virtues: A Fragment of a Morality' (text ed
W.W. Greg, in *Collections Volume IV*, MalS [1956], pp 41-54; Greg 21.5;
STC 14109.7 [publ ca 1545]; Stratman 5656-7).

ca 1543
131 A one-line fragment (?) in English of Roger Ascham's lost translation of Sophocles' *Philoctetes* into Latin (in a letter to Archbishop Lee,
Ascham asks if this piece, written in imitation of Seneca, may appear
addressed to Lee; *Ascham*, I, 32; the single line appears in Ascham's
'Toxophilus' [separately paginated in II, p 59]; STC 837-9 [publ 1545];
cf L.V. Ryan, *Roger Ascham* [1963], p 300).

ca 1544
132 *Jephthah*, a play in Greek by John Christopherson. See under
CAMBRIDGE.

1544-5
133 John Foxe's *Titus et Gesippus*. See under OXFORD.

ca 1544-7
134 John Redford's *Wit and Science* (text ed Arthur Brown, W.W. Greg,
and F.P. Wilson, MalS [1951]; and Bevington, pp 1029-61; TFT 18;
Stratman 6249-69; Houle 58; probably acted at court by the almonry
boys of St Paul's, at which Redford was almoner and master of the
song school, for the young Prince Edward while his father was married to Catherine Parr; Linda Beamer, 'A Critical Edition of John Redford's Play, *Wyt and Science*,' Ph D diss [Univ. of Toronto, 1973], pp
122-3, suggests autumn 1546, a time of re-opened negotiations for
Edward's proposed marriage to Mary Stuart).

1544-7
135 Alexander Nowell's prologues to Terence's *Adelphi* and *Eunuchus*,
and Seneca's *Hippolytus*. See under LONDON.

ca 1545-9
136 Prose fragment of a verse comedy, interlude, or play on the parts
of man, with Reason and Will, made by John Heywood at the request

of Thomas Cranmer, archbishop of Canterbury (text in *The Autobiography of Thomas Whythorne*, ed J.M. Osborn [1961], pp 13-14, 74).

1547 19 February
137 Pageants for Edward VI's procession through London to Westminster for his coronation. See under LONDON.

ca 1547-8
138 Nicholas Udall's *Ralph Roister Doister* (text: *Roister Doister*, ed W.W. Greg, MalS [1934 (1935)]; Scheurweghs; Greg 46; STC 24508 [publ 1566?]; Arber, I, 331; Dust-Wolf, pp 110-12; Edgerton argues for auspices at Windsor in September [pp 89-94]).

1547?
139 *A Newe Dialog betwene Thangell of God, & the Shepherdes in the Felde*, by Thomas Becon. See under RICHMOND.

ca 1547-50?
140 'Somebody and Others' (text ed W.W. Greg, in *Collections Vol. II. Part III*, MalS [1931], pp 251-7; Greg 25; STC 14109.3 [publ ca 1550]; Stratman 6334-5; Houle 46; a translation from the French 'La Vérité Cachée,' for which see Peter J. Houle, 'A Reconstruction of the English Morality Fragment *Somebody and Others*,' PBSA 71 [1977], 259-77).

1547-53
141 *Nice Wanton* (text in Wickham, pp 143-62; also ed David Parry and Kathy Pearl, PLS Performance Text [1] [1978]; TFT 28; Greg 31; STC 25016-17 [publ 1560]; Stratman 6126-35; Houle 41).

1547-53?
142 *July and Julian* (text ed Giles Dawson, MalS [1955]; ms dated ca 1559-71, but see lines 133-4, 929, 1123; performed after 'learned devisis' by certain men, probably by a schoolmaster and his boys in or near London [see line 895], perhaps Paul's boys, as the play includes a couplet by John Redford).

1547-66
143 *The Life and Repentaunce of Marie Magdalene*, by Lewis Wager (text ed F.I. Carpenter, new edn, Univ. of Chicago Decennial Publs, 2nd ser, 1 [1904]; TFT 36; Greg 47; STC 24932-2a [publ 1566]; Stratman 6373-81; Houle 24).

ca 1550?
144 An English translation of Euripides' *Iphigenia at Aulis* by Lady
Jane Lumley, possibly at Nonsuch, home for most of her married life
(text: *Iphigenia at Aulis Translated by Lady Lumley*, ed H.H. Child, MalS
[1909]; cf CP, VIII, 278-9; Lumley obtained Nonsuch in 1556 [ES I, 11, n
4]; and David H. Greene, 'Lady Lumley and Greek Tragedy,' *Classical
Journal*, 36 [1940-1], 537-47).

ca 1550?
145 *The Disobedient Child* by Thomas Ingelend of Cambridge (text: *The
Dramatic Writings of Richard Wever and Thomas Ingelend*, ed John S.
Farmer [1905], pp 43-92; usually dated ca 1559-70, mainly on the
basis of a very doubtful reference in the *Stationers' Register* in 1569
[Arber, I, 398]; but see Farmer, pp 122-3, for pre-Elizabethan allusions;
evidently a school play; Venn, I.ii, 448, places Ingelend as 'probably of
Christ's [College, Cambridge], c. 1520'; TFT 42; Greg 54; STC 14085
[publ 1570?]; Stratman 5898-908).

ca 1550
146 Interlude of Detraction, Light Judgment, Verity, and Justice; fragmentary text, published in London ca 1550 (STC 14109.2, p 489 [publ
ca 1550]).

ca 1550
147 'Parte of a Play<e>' (text in 'Five Dramatic Fragments,' ed G.R.
Proudfoot, *Collections Volume IX*, MalS [1971 (1977)], pp 52-7; L.A.
Cummings, '"Parte of a Play": a Possible Dramatic Fragment (c 1550)
from the Office of the Master of the Revels,' REEDN, 1977.2, pp 2-15,
with facs).

ca 1550-3
148 *Lusty Juventus* by R. Wever (text ed J.M. Nosworthy, MalS [1966
(1971)]; Somerset, pp 97-127; TFT 35; Greg 41; STC 25148-9.5 [publ
1550?]; Stratman 6413-24; Houle 30).

ca 1550-70
149 Richard Kaye's verses on the nine worthies, possibly at Oxford (a
text with only eight speakers: J.G. Milne and Elizabeth Sweeting, 'Mar-
ginalia in a Copy of Bartholomaeus Anglicus' "De Proprietatibus
Rerum." A New Version of the Nine Worthies,' MLR, 40 [1945], 85-89;
IMEV 1322.5).

ca 1551-4
150 *Gammer Gurton's Needle*, by Mr S., Mr of Art, probably William Stevenson. See under CAMBRIDGE.

1553
151 *Respublica*, attributed to Nicholas Udall. See under LONDON.

1553-8
152 *Impatient Poverty* (text ed R.B. McKerrow, MKAED 33 [1911]; TFT 27; Greg 30; STC 14112.5-13 [publ 1560]; Stratman 5888-97; Houle 18).

1553-8
153 *Jack Juggler*, an adaptation of Plautus' *Amphitruo* (text ed E.L. Smart and W.W. Greg, MalS [1933]; *Jack Juggler (Third Edition)*, ed B.I. Evans and W.W. Greg, MalS [1936 (1937)]; and TTCI, pp 15-24, 64-93; a doubtful attribution to Nicholas Udall appears in *Jacke Jugeler*, ed W.H. Williams [1914], pp viii-xvii; TFT 30; Greg 35; STC 14837-7a.5 [publ 1562?]; Stratman 5910-30; Houle 19).

ca 1554-5
154 *The Interlude of Wealth and Health* (text ed W.W. Greg, MalS [1907]; TFT 26; Greg 27; Arber, I, 75; STC 14110 [publ 1565?]; Stratman 6400-12; Houle 55; probably written for winter performance by the Queen's interluders before Queen Mary, according to Craik, pp 101-8).

1555
155 Ralph Worsley's *Synedrii Id Est Concessus Animalium*, a verse paraphrase of William Caxton's *History of Renart the Fox*, evidently intended for acting (text not seen: Trinity College, Cambridge, ms O.3.25, with an incomplete prose version, *Synedrium Id Est Concessus Animalium*, both unprinted; described by M.R. James, *The Western Manuscripts in the Library of Trinity College, Cambridge*, III [1902], no 1197, pp 209-10; and analysed by Boas, pp 366-82).

1556
156 John Foxe's *Christus Triumphans* (text: *Two Latin Comedies*, pp 199-371).

1556
157 Norwich waits' pageant of Time for the mayor's installation. See under NORWICH.

ca 1557-8
158 *Jacob and Esau* (text ed J. Crow and F.P. Wilson, MalS [1956]; TFT
40; Greg 51; STC 14326.5-27 [publ 1557, 1568]; and see Paul Morgan,
'Fragments of Three Lost Works from the Stationers' Registers Recently Found in Bindings in College Libraries,' *Bodleian Library Record*,
7 [1962-7], 300-2 and pl XXIV, for the fragment of 1557 [not in Greg?];
Arber, I, 77; Stratman 5931-41; attributed to William Hunnis by
Stopes, *Hunnis*, pp 265-70).

1558
159 Jasper Heywood's English translation of Seneca's *Troas*. See under
OXFORD.

1559 14 January
160 Pageants for Elizabeth's coronation. See under LONDON.

ca 1560
161 'A Play of Robin Hood for May-Games from the Edition by William Copland, c. 1560,' actually two plays, 'Robin Hood and the Friar'
(lines 1-150) and 'Robin Hood and the Potter' (lines 151-251; text ed
W.W. Greg in *Collections Part II*, MalS [1908], pp 125-36; and *Robin
Hood and the Friar*, ed Mary A. Blackstone, PLS Performance Text 3
[1981]; TFT 29; Greg 32; STC 13691 [publ 1560?]; Stratman 6540-53,
6566-661; *Manual* 37).

ca 1560-9
162 'Troilus and Cressida, a Welsh interlude,' translated in part from
Chaucer (text in *Troelus a Chresyd O Lawysgrif Peniarth 106*, ed W.B.
Davies [1976]; frequently dated ca 1602-12, just before the period
when the play was transcribed, 1613-22, but for the earlier date see
R.I. Stephens Jones, 'The Date of *Troelus a Chresyd* (Peniarth 106),' *The
Bulletin of the Board of Celtic Studies*, 26 [1976], 430-9; John S.P. Tatlock,
'The Welsh "Troilus and Cressida" and its Relation to the Elizabethan
Drama,' *MLR*, 10 [1915], 265-82, summarizes the play and translates
the first two scenes into English).

1561
163 Lord Mayor's Show of David, Orpheus, Amphion, Arion, and
Topas. See under LONDON (1504-68 [28]).

ca 1562
164 *The Most Virtuous & Godly Susanna* by Thomas Garter (text ed B. Ifor Evans and W.W. Greg, MalS [1936 (1937)]; Arber, I, 210, 383; Greg 76.5 [publ 1578]; Stratman 5670-4; Houle 54).

ca 1563
165 *Tom Tyler and His Wife* (text ed G.C. Moore Smith and W.W. Greg, MalS [1910]; TFT 144; Arber, I, 210; Greg 820; Wing 1792-1792A [publ 1661]; Stratman 6354-9; Houle 52).

1564-5
166 'Crying Christmas.' See under LINCOLN.

ca 1564-5
167 *King Darius* (text: *Anonymous Plays*, pp 41-92; TFT 34; Arber, I, 298; Greg 40; STC 6277-8 [publ 1565]; Houle 21).

ca 1564-5
168 *The Play of Patient Grissell* by John Phillip (text ed Ronald B. McKerrow and W.W. Greg, MalS [1909]; Arber, I, 309, 385; Greg 52; STC 19865 [publ 1566?]; Stratman 6153-66; Houle 42).

ca 1565
169 *The Cruel Debtor*, attributed to William Wager (text: 'The Cruel Debtor: A Fragment of a Morality Printed by Colwell, c. 1566,' ed W.W. Greg, in *Collections Parts IV & V*, MalS [1911], pp 315-23, and for Wager's first name, see Greg's comment, pp 324-7; 'The Cruel Debtor: A Further Fragment,' ed W.W. Greg, in *Collections Vol. II. Part II*, MalS [1923], pp 142-4; Arber, I, 307 [by 'Wager']; Greg 43; STC 24934 [publ 1566]; Stratman 5470-2; Houle 10).

ca 1566
170 *The Trial of Treasure*, attributed to Lewis Wager or William Wager (text: *Anonymous Plays*, pp 203-46; TFT 38; Greg 49; STC 24271 [publ 1567]; Stratman 6360-72; Houle 53; Leslie M. Oliver, 'William Wager and *The Trial of Treasure*,' HLQ, 9 [1945-6], 419-29, discusses the authorship question).

ca 1567
171 *Apius and Virginia* by R.B. (text ed Ronald B. McKerrow and W.W. Greg, MalS [1911]; TFT 47; Arber, I, 357, ?400; Greg 65; STC 1059 [publ

1575]; Houle 3; sometimes attributed to Richard Bower, master of the boys at Westminster, for which see ES, II, 31; III, 236; IV, 3).

ca 1567-8
172 *The Contention between Liberality and Prodigality*. See under LONDON.

ca 1567-8
173 *Like Will to Like* by Ulpian Fulwell (text: Somerset, pp 128-64; TFT 39; Arber, I, 379; Greg 50; STC 11473-4 [publ 1568]; Stratman 5659-69; Houle 25).

ca 1567-8
174 *The Marriage of Wit and Science*. See under LONDON.

1568
175 Lord Mayor's show of John the Baptist. See under LONDON (1504-68 [13]).

ca 1568
176 *Enough Is as Good as a Feast* by William Wager (text ed R. Mark Benbow, RRDS [1967]; type-facs ed Seymour De Ricci [1920]; Greg 57; STC 24933 [publ 1570?]; Stratman 6382-6; Houle 11).

ca 1568
177 *The Longer Thou Livest the More Fool Thou Art* by William Wager (text ed R. Mark Benbow, RRDS [1967]; TFT 41; Arber, I, 386; Greg 53; STC 24935 [publ 1569]; Stratman 6387-93; Houle 26).

ca 1570-2
178 Riding of Yule, Yule's wife, and children. See under YORK.

ca 1570-3
179 *New Custom* (text: *Anonymous Plays*, pp 157-202; TFT 46; Greg 59; STC 6150 [publ 1573]; Stratman 6114-25; Houle 40; for the date of composition, see Leslie M. Oliver, 'John Foxe and the Drama *New Custom*,' HLQ, 10 [1946-7], 407-10).

ca 1570-80
180 'Processus Satanae.' See under LIMEBROOK.

ca 1571
181 *Misogonus*. See under CAMBRIDGE.

ca 1571-5
182 *The Tide Tarrieth No Man* by George Wapull (text: 'The Tide Taryeth No Man. Ein Moralspiel aus Shakespeares Jugendzeit,' ed Ernst Rühl, *SJ*, 43 [1907], 1-52; TFT 50; Arber, II, 303; Greg 70; STC 25018 [publ 1576]; Stratman 6394-9; Houle 51).

ca 1571-7
183 *The Marriage between Wit and Wisdom* by Francis Merbury, possibly at Christ's College, Cambridge (text ed Trevor N.S. Lennam, MalS [1966 (1971)]; TFT 53; Arber, II, 586; Greg, II, 963-4 [ms dated 1579 and possibly copied from a printed edition]; Stratman 6089-103; Houle 34).

ca 1572-7
184 *All for Money* by Thomas Lupton (text: 'All for Money. Ein Moralspiel aus der Zeit Shakespeares,' ed Ernst Vogel, *SJ*, 40 [1904], 129-86; TFT 51; Arber, II, 321; Greg 72; STC 16949 [publ 1578]; Stratman 6006-13; Houle 2; for the date of composition, see ES, III, 411).

ca 1572-80
185 *The Conflict of Conscience* by Nathaniel Woodes (text ed Herbert Davis and F.P. Wilson, MalS [1952]; TFT 54; Greg 78; STC 25966-6.5 [publ 1581]; Stratman 6488-503; Houle 9; for possible auspices at Cambridge in 1572-4, or at Norwich in 1574-80, where Woodes was vicar of St Mary's, South Walsham, see Celesta Wine, 'Nathaniel Wood's *Conflict of Conscience*,' PMLA, 50 [1935], 661-78).

1582
186 Fragment of a Welsh interlude, copied by Thomas Aspull (last leaf only of the first of ?several plays: text in Peniarth ms 98, part of which is transcribed in *MSS Welsh*, I, ii [1899], p 467, and trans by Jones, p 8).

1588-91
187 Richard Tarlton's *Seven Deadly Sins* (theatrical plot). See under LONDON.

1610-25
188 A fragmentary cycle of 18 Old Testament pageants from Lancashire (text: *The Stonyhurst Pageants*, ed C. Brown [1920]; Stratman
4418-36; *Manual* 23): 1 / Jacob; 2 / Joseph; 3 / Moses; 4 / Josue
[Joshua]; 5 / Gedeon; 6 / Jephte; 7 / Samson; 8 / Saul; 9 / David;
10 / Solomon; 11 / Elias; and 12 / Naaman.

1611 12 August
189 'the Creacion of the worlde with noyes flude,' by William Jordan,
the 'conveyor' (text ed and trans Whitney Stokes, 'Gwreans an Bys.
The Creation of the World, a Cornish Mystery,' *Trans. of the Philological
Society* [1864]; for the title and authorship, see p 196 and Paula Neuss,
'The Staging of the "Creacion of the World,"' *TN*, 33 [1979], 116-25;
and generally her *The Creacion of the World: A Critical Edition and Translation* [1983]).

ca 1620-50?
190 An ms play in Latin, 'Sanctus Tewdricus sive Pastor bonus, Rex et
Martyr.' See under DOUBTFUL TEXTS.

TOPOGRAPHICAL LISTS OF DRAMATIC RECORDS

List of Sites

All these sites appear in the topographical list with the exception of (1) those marked by a delimiter‡, which are found in Appendix I(a) – sites marked by an asterisk* appear in both the list and this appendix – and (2) those in square brackets, which identify provincial seats of patrons who had playing troupes but whose houses, manors, or castles do not appear in this book as having evidence of dramatic activities.

ENGLAND

BEDFORDSHIRE
Dunstable
Eversholt
Everton
Leighton Buzzard‡
Little Barford
Northill
Pulloxhill
[Woburn Abbey]

BERKSHIRE
Aldermaston‡
Bray
Datchet‡
Ditton Park
Easthampstead
Eton*
Finchampstead‡

Reading*
Sindlesham‡
Sonning‡
Thatcham
Wantage
Windsor
Wokingham‡

BUCKINGHAMSHIRE
Amersham
[Chenies]
High Wycombe‡
Missenden Abbey
Winslow

CAMBRIDGESHIRE
Bassingbourn
Cambridge*

Downham
Ely Priory
Isleham‡
Leverington
Madingley‡
Stetchworth

CHESHIRE*
Chester
Wilderspool
Witton

CINQUE PORTS*

CORNWALL*
Bodmin
Camborne
Castilly
Dunheved otherwise
  Launceston*
Lanherne
Liskeard‡
Mount Edgcumbe
Penryn
St Breock
St Columb Major
St Ives
Sancreed
Stratton
Truro

CUMBERLAND
Carlisle
Lanercost Priory

DERBYSHIRE*
Derby
[South Wingfield Manor]

DEVON
Ashburton
Barnstaple
Braunton
Chagford
Chudleigh
Colyton‡
Dartmouth
Exeter*
Farway
Honiton
Morebath
Plymouth*
Plymstock
Tavistock
[Tawstock]
Tiverton
Torrington‡
Woodbury

DORSET
Beaminster
Bishop's Caundle‡
Dorchester
Lyme Regis
Netherbury
Poole
Sherborne*
Wimborne Minster*
Yetminster‡

DURHAM
Bishop Auckland‡
Durham
Gateshead
Lanchester

ESSEX*
Aveley
Barking Abbey

Billericay*
Braintree
Castle Hedingham
Chelmsford*
Coggeshall‡
Colchester
Dunmow
[Earls Colne]
Easton‡
Finchingfield
[Gaynes Park]
Halstead
Harlow
Harwich
Hatfield Broad Oak
Havering
Heybridge
Hornchurch
Ingatestone Hall
Kelvedon‡
Latchingdon‡
Maldon
Manningtree
Margaret Roding‡
New Hall (or Beaulieu)
Rayleigh
Roding‡
Saffron Walden
Sandon*
Stow Maries‡
Tilty Abbey
Ulting‡
West Ham
Wix Priory
Woodham Ferrers‡
Writtle*

GLOUCESTERSHIRE
Berkeley Castle
Bristol
Cirencester

Gloucester*
Hailes Abbey
Lanthony Abbey
Slimbridge‡
[Sudeley Castle]
Tewkesbury
Thornbury
Wotton‡
Wotton under Edge,
    Wortley in

HAMPSHIRE
Andover
[Basing]
Bishopstoke
Crondall
Silchester
Southampton
[Thruxton]
Titchfield
Winchester
Yateley‡

HEREFORDSHIRE
Hereford
Leominster
Limebrook

HERTFORDSHIRE
Baldock
Bishop's Stortford
Braughing‡
Cheshunt
Hatfield
Hertford
Hitchin
St Albans*
St Mary de Pré
Stanstead Abbots and St
    Margaret‡

HUNTINGDONSHIRE
Hinchingbrooke
Ramsey Abbey

KENT
Appledore‡
Ash‡
Benenden‡
Bethersden*
Boughton Street*
Brookland‡
Canterbury*
[Cowling Castle]
Cranbrook‡
Deal‡
Deptford
Dover*
Dymchurch‡
Elham‡
Eltham
Faversham*
Folkestone*
Fordwich
Great Chart‡
Greenwich
Hadley?‡
Ham Street‡
Herne‡
High Halden‡
Hythe*
Ivychurch‡
Linstead
Lydd*
Lympne‡
Maidstone*
Moatenden
New Romney*
Otford
Penshurst

Richborough
Rochester*
Ruckinge‡
St Mary in the Marsh‡
Sandwich*
Shooters Hill
Sittingbourne‡
Stone‡
Tenterden‡
Thanet, Isle of‡
Wittersham‡
Wye*

LANCASHIRE*
Burnley
[Knowsley]
Lancaster
[Lathom House]
Manchester
Preston
Wigan‡

LEICESTERSHIRE
Arnesby
Belvoir Castle
[Bradgate Old Manor]
Cranoe
Leicester
Melton Mowbray

LINCOLNSHIRE
Addlethorpe Ingoldmells
Bardney
Barton-upon-Humber‡
Boston
Crowland‡
Cumberworth
Deeping‡

Donington on Bain*
Frampton‡
Frieston‡
Grimoldby‡
Grimsby*
[Grimsthorpe]
Hagworthingham
Holbeach
Holland, parts of‡
Horbling
Kirton‡
Leverton
Lincoln*
Long Sutton
Louth
Marsh Chapel‡
Nun Coton
Sleaford*
South Kyme
Spalding*
Stallingborough*
Stamford*
Stone Rochford, or North and
    South Stoke‡
Sutterton
Swineshead‡
Tattershall
Thornton Abbey
Thorpe St Peter
Waddingham
Welby‡
Welton iuxta Louth
Whaplode‡
Wigtoft
Witham on the Hill
Withern‡

LONDON AND WESTMINSTER*

MIDDLESEX
Clerkenwell
[Hackney]
Hampton Court
Hoxton
Islington
Mile End‡
Shoreditch
Stepney
Syon Abbey

NORFOLK
[Attleburgh]
Caister
Croxton
Dereham
Dersingham‡
Docking‡
East Harling
[Framlingham]
Fring‡
Garboldisham‡
Great Bircham‡
Great Yarmouth*
Heacham‡
Hickling Priory
Horning‡
Hunstanton Hall
Kenninghall‡
King's Lynn*
Loddon
Lopham‡
Middleton
Northrepps‡
North Walsham‡
Norwich*
Ringstead‡
St Benet of Hulme
Sedgeford‡
Shelfanger‡

Shernborne‡
Shipdham
Snettisham
Swaffam
Thetford Priory
Tilney
[Topcroft]
Walsoken‡
Wymondham*

NORTHAMPTONSHIRE
Culworth
Daventry‡
Kingsthorpe
Northampton
Peterborough

NORTHUMBERLAND
Morpeth
Newcastle upon Tyne

NOTTINGHAMSHIRE
East Retford
Lenton
Newark-on-Trent‡
Norwell
Nottingham*
Southwell
Upper Broughton‡
Wollaton Hall

OXFORDSHIRE*
Abingdon*
Banbury
Bicester Priory
Duns Tew
Eynsham
Frilford
Henley on Thames*
Oxford

Stonor
Thame
West Wittenham‡
Witney

RUTLAND
[*None*]

SHROPSHIRE
Bridgnorth
Ludlow
Shrewsbury
Worfield
Wroxeter

SOMERSET
Axbridge
Bath
[Bridgwater]
Castle Cary‡
Croscombe
Glastonbury
Montacute‡
Muchelney
North Curry
Stogursey
Taunton*
Tintinhull
Wells
Wincanton‡
Yeovil

STAFFORDSHIRE
Cannock‡
[Chartley]
Heighley Castle
Lichfield*
Tamworth*
Walsall
Willenhall

SUFFOLK*
Aldeburgh
Bardwell‡
Beccles‡
Blythburgh‡
Boxford
Bramfield‡
Brome
Bungay*
Bury St Edmunds
Dunwich‡
Eye
Gislingham‡
Hadleigh*
Haughley
Ipswich
Ixworth‡
Lavenham‡
Long Melford*
Metfield
Mettingham College
Mildenhall*
[Nettlestead]
South Elmham‡
Stoke-by-Nayland*
Thorndon
Thorington‡
Walsham-le-Willows*
Walberswick
Wenhaston‡
[Westhorpe Hall]
Woodbridge
Yoxford

SURREY*
Bermondsey
[Bletchingley]
Guildford
Hascombe
Kingston on Thames*

Merton
Nonsuch
Putney
Richmond
Seale
Shere

SUSSEX
[Arundel]
Battle Abbey
Chichester
Cuckfield
Hastings‡
Lewes*
[Offington]
Rye*
South Malling‡
Steyning
Winchelsea‡

WARWICKSHIRE
Atherstone upon Stour‡
Coleshill‡
Coventry*
Kenilworth
Long Itchington‡
Maxstoke Priory*
Middleton‡
Solihull‡
Stratford upon Avon
Warwick
[Weston]

WESTMORLAND
Kendal

WILTSHIRE
Calne
Devizes
Easton

Longleat
Mere
Salisbury
Wilton Abbey
Wulfhall

WORCESTERSHIRE
Battenhall
Bewdley
Cleeve Prior‡
Crowle
Evesham*
Grimley
Henwick
Martley‡
Ombersley‡
Worcester*

YORK (CITY OF)*

YORKSHIRE, EAST RIDING
Beverley
Brough-on-Humber
Burstwick‡
Burton Pidsea‡
Cottingham‡
Dunnington‡
Hedon
Hessle‡
Howden‡
Hull, or Kingston upon Hull
[Leconfield]
Long Riston‡
Riccall‡
Wressle

YORKSHIRE, NORTH RIDING
[Bolton Castle]
Brandsby
Catterick

Healaugh
Masham
[Middleham]
Sheriff Hutton
Thirsk‡
Topcliffe*
Whitby

YORKSHIRE, WEST RIDING
Chevet
Cowick
Doncaster
Fountains Abbey
Kirk Deighton
Leeds‡
Nidderdale
Pontefract
Ripon*
Rossington
Rotherham
Selby Abbey
[Sheffield Lodge]
Sherburn in Elmet
Snaith‡
Wakefield*
Wistow

DIOCESES
Bath and Wells
Canterbury
Chichester
Coventry and Lichfield
Durham
Ely
Exeter
Gloucester
Hereford
Lincoln
London
Norwich

43 Sites

Salisbury
Winchester
Worcester
York

WALES

CLWYD
Rhuddlan
Wrexham‡

DYFED
Carmarthen

GWENT
Abergavenny
Caerleon
Caerwent
[Raglan Castle]

GWYNED
Tomen-y-Mur

DIOCESES
St Asaph

SCOTLAND

BORDERS
Jedburgh Abbey
Peebles

CENTRAL
Fintry
St John's Town of Dalry
Stirling

DUMFRIES AND GALLOWAY
Dumfies

FIFE
Cupar
Dunfermline
St Andrews

GRAMPIAN
Aberdeen
Arbuthnott

HIGHLAND
Inverness

LOTHIAN
Borthwick
Cranston
Dalkeith
Dirleton
Edinburgh*
Haddington
Lasswade
Leith
Linlithgow*
Samuelston

STRATHCLYDE
Ayr
Dumbarton
Glasgow
Lanark

TAYSIDE
Arbroath
Craigie
Dundee
Muthill
Perth*
Strageath

DIOCESES
Aberdeen
St Andrews

IRELAND

Dublin
Kilkenny

DIOCESES
Dublin

OTHER

Ardres
Calais*
France‡
Guines
Picardy‡

England

679 October r
191 The Council of Rome, treating of the English church, orders bishops and clerics not to allow 'jocos vel ludos' before them (*Councils and Ecclesiastical Documents Relating to Great Britain and Ireland*, ed Arthur W. Haddan and William Stubbs, III [1871], p 133).

799 before 10 July r
192 Alcuin refers to 'spectacula et diabolica figmenta' in citing Augustine's attack on 'histriones et mimos et saltatores' (*Epistolae Karolini Aevi*, II, ed Ernestvs Dvemmler, Monvmenta Germaniae Historica, Epistolae, IV [1895], letter no 175, p 290).

9th-10th centuries r
193 'Jocationes, et saltationes, et circum, vel cantica turpia et luxuriosa, vel lusa diabolica' should not be made because they are pagan practices (from the 'Penitential' [cap 38, item 9] of Pseudo-Theodore, a 9th-century Frankish compilation used in the late Old English period; *Ancient Laws and Institutes of England*, ed B. Thorpe, Gt. Brit. Rec. Com., 28 [1840], p 298, and cf p 300 and Thomas P. Oakley, *English Penitential Discipline and Anglo-Saxon Law in their Joint Influence*, Columbia Univ. Stud. in Hist., Econ., and Public Law, 107, no 2 [1923], pp 31-2).

10th century r
194 Aelfric's vocabulary (Wright, I) includes various words for playing, including the following: '*Theatrum*, wafungstede' (col 145; 'place

for shows'); 'Amphitheatrum, syneweald wafungstede' (col 145; 'circular place for shows'); 'Spectacula, uel ludicra, yppe, uel weardsteal' (col 150; 'stage'? or 'watch-tower'?); 'orcestra, uel pulpitus, gligmanna yppe' (col 150; 'player's? stage'); and 'Histriones, truðas' (col 150; 'trumpeters? actors?'). The somewhat later supplementary vocabulary also has 'Spectaculum, waefð, uel waefersyn, uel wafung' (col 180; 'spectacle, or sight, or display').

10th-12th centuries r
195 Old English glosses on various Latin texts regularly concerned terms for playing (*Old English Glosses Chiefly Unpublished*, ed Arthur S. Napier, Anecdota Oxoniensia, Mediaeval and Modern Ser, XI [1900]; cf *The Old English Glosses of MS. Brussels, Royal Library, 1650*, ed Louis Goossens [1974]; for a guide to these and other such terms, see *A Microfiche Concordance to Old English*, comp Richard L. Venezky and Antonette diPaolo Healey [1981], and Angus Cameron, Allison Kingsmill, and Ashley C. Amos, *Old English Word Studies: A Preliminary Author and Word Index* [1983]). The most important words seem to be the following:

1 / 10th century: 'on wafungstowe' (for 'in circi spectaculo'; Napier, 4/59);

2 / 11th century: 'aewiscu,' or 'shameful thing' ('ludicra ... inhonesta'; 21/6); 'bismergleow' or 'shameful lust' ('ludicra'; 17/17); 'emwlaetung' or 'sight' ('spectaculum'; 1/1124); 'faeðelas' or 'play-actors'? ('histriones, mimarii ᵹrece'; 39/2); 'gamenlic' ('theatrales'; 1/4369); 'gamen' ('ludorum ... iocorum,' 'ioco'; 1/2871, 2886-7); 'gliw' or 'mirth or play' ('ludorum'; 1/3173); 'plega' ('ludorum'; 7/199); 'pleghuses' ('theatri'; 1/1752); 'sceawung' or 'show' ('spectaculum'; 11/11); 'waeferlic' ('theatrales'; 1/62); 'waefersolor' or 'stage' ('pulpito'; 1/3458); 'waefersyn' or 'show' ('spectaculum,' 'theatri ... spectaculi'; 1/234, 1124, 2758, 4044, 4370, 5134, 7/252, 8/189; and 1/3457); 'waefiendre' ('theatrali ... uisibili'; 1/233); 'wafung' or 'display' ('spectaculum'; 1/3511, 4425); 'wafungstowe' or 'place for shows' ('circi'; 7/251, 8/188); 'witehus' or 'place of torture' ('amphitheatrum'; 1/3333, 3558); and 'wundrung' or 'wonder' ('spectaculum'; 1/4370);

3 / 12th century: 'plegstowe' ('palaestra,' ie 'wrestling place'; 2/146).

11th century r
196 Two groups of glosses (Wright, I) concern playing terms:

1 / 'Theatrales, ða pleglican' (col 486); and

2 / 'Ludorum, plegena' (col 431); 'Ludicra, plegan, [i]ustas' (col 436); 'Ludo, ic plege' (col 438); and 'Amphitheatri, plegstowe' (col 342).

1005-7 r
197 Regulations for the secular clergy by Wulfstan, bishop of Worcester and archbishop of York, require abstinence from heathen songs and 'deofles amena' on feast days (*Wulfstan's Canons of Edgar*, ed Roger Fowler, EETS OS 266 [1972], pp 6-7, no 18; the source is Pseudo-Theodore [p 28]).

mid-11th century r
198 The Old English interlinear translation of the pseudo-Daniel dream book states that, in dreaming, 'To be waiting in a theatre or amphitheatre ['on plegstow odde on wafungstowe'] betokens some agitation' (from BL Cotton ms Tiberius A.III; *Leechdoms, Wortcunning, and Starcraft of Early England*, ed Oswald Cockayne, RS 35, III [1866], pp 206-7; cf Max Förster, 'Beiträge zur mittelalterlichen Volkskunde. IV,' *Archiv*, 125 [1910], 39-70).

ca 1150-66 r
199 Aelred, abbot of Rievaulx, condemns English singing men in choirs for their histrionic gestures and way of singing, performed as if the layfolk came 'ad theatrum' instead of to a house of prayer ('Speculum Charitatis,' II, 33, in PL, CXCV, 571; Young, I, 548; trans G.G. Coulton, *Five Centuries of Religion*, I [1929], p 530, as 'playhouse').

1159 r
200 John of Salisbury, secretary to Theobald of Bec, archbishop of Canterbury, distinguishes between respectable 'histriones' who by gesture, language, and voice did comedy and tragedy and were contemporaries of Plautus, Menander, and Terence, and current 'histriones' and 'mimi' who, by their 'spectacula inhonesta,' earn excommunication from the church and deserve extermination by their prince (*Ioannis Saresberiensis Episcopi Carnotensis Policratici*, ed Clemens C.I. Webb [1909], I, 46-9, and II, 309, trans Joseph B. Pike, *Frivolities of Courtiers and Footprints of Philosophers* [1938], pp 36-9, 367; and I, 245, trans John Dickinson, *The Statesman's Book of John of Salisbury* [1927; rpt 1963], p 16; and cf I, 190-6, 199; II, 233, 236-42, 310-13, 316).

ca 1179-1206 r
201 Gerald of Wales, dining with the monks at Canterbury, observed
that their sign language and hissing or whistling resembled what went
on 'ad ludos scenicos aut inter histriones et joculatores' (*Giraldi Cambrensis Opera*, RS 21, I, ed J.S. Brewer [1861], p 51, and IV [1873], pp
40-1; cf Urban T. Holmes, Jr, '*Ludos Scenicos* in Giraldus,' MLN, 57
[1942], 188-9).

1206 r
202 Thurkill, a farmer who lived in Stisted, Essex, had a vision of hell,
'De theatrali ludo daemonum et cruciatu animarum,' in which sinners
were forced to act out their sins in *platea* within a round *domus* with
seats about the walls for the demons, who watched as if at a merry
show ('ad laetum spectaculum'; H.L.D. Ward, 'The Vision of Thurkill,
Probably by Ralph of Coggeshall,' *JBAA*, 31 [1875], 433-5, 449-54).

1215-30 r
203 Thomas Chabham, subdean of Salisbury, in his *Penitential* condemns 'histriones' as entertainers who perform with masks and present indecent, abusive songs and music, and also 'qui ludunt in
ymaginibus inhonestis' (Rubel, pp 232-3).

ca 1220-8 r
204 'Actiones' (glossed as 'miracle-plays') of Fyfield and Idbury are to
belong to the canon of Brixworth, Northamptonshire, and those of
Milton and Langley to the canon of Shipton, Oxfordshire, while those
of Lyneham are to be equally divided (*Charters and Documents Illustrating the History of the Cathedral, City, and Diocese of Salisbury*, ed W.R.
Jones and W.D. Macray, RS 97 [1891], pp xi-xii, 104; Shipton under
Wychwood had 'games' ca 1247 according to *Crown Pleas of the Wiltshire Eyre, 1249*, ed C.A.F. Meekings, WiltANHSRB 16 [1961], p 59).

1225-30 r?
205 Statutes of an unidentified bishop prohibit 'inhonesti ludi qui ad
lasciviam invitant in cimiteriis agantur' (*Councils & Synods*, p 195).

ca 1225-30r
206 A woman is instructed to state during confession the place of her
sin, as 'Sire þus ich ... eode on ring. biheold hit oðer wrestlung. o er fol
gomenes' (*The English Text of the Ancrene Riwle*, ed E.J. Dobson, EETS OS

267 [1972], p 236; cf EETS OS 216 [1944], p 121 ['scurriles ludos']; OS 219 [1944], pp 225-6; OS 225 [1952], p 143; OS 240 [1958], p 73; OS 249 [1962], p 163; OS 252 [1963], p 112; and OS 274 [1976], p 135).

ca 1250 r
207 A play about a virtuous king whose wishes were granted through the help of St Nicholas (mentioned in an English verse homily that precedes the play; Carleton Brown, 'An Early Mention of a St. Nicholas Play in England,' *SP*, 28 [1931], 594-601).

1253 r
208 Among articles of inquiry concerning the clergy and laity throughout England is a question about whether 'ludos' by the laity are done in consecrated places (*Annales Monastici*, I, 307).

1259 r
209 The Oxford Council, in articles of inquiry for monasteries, says of the 'ludi' of 'histriones': 'eorum ludi non videantur, vel audiantur, vel permittantur fieri coram abbate vel monachis' (*Annales Monastici*, I, 485).

ca 1275-99 r
210 Any priest ought to avoid going to a 'spectaculum' (*Le Speculum Laicorum*, ed J. Th. Welter, Thesaurus Exemplorum, 5 [1914], p 25).

ca 1283 r
211 John of Wales warns clergy especially against vain 'ludi' and 'spectacula,' some of them 'a theatro' (*Communiloquium*, The Phoenix Ser [1964], pt I, dist X, cap 7).

14th-16th centuries r
212 'Plain an Gwarry' or playing places, from place-name or archaeological evidence, are found at the following sites (H.M. Whitley, 'Cornish Rounds or Playing Places,' *Devon & Cornwall Notes & Queries*, 7 [1912-13], 172-4; Nance, pp 190-211; and various compilers, 'Parochial Check-Lists of Antiquities,' *PWCornFC*, 2 [1956-61], and its successor, *CA*, 1 [1962]–; Bakere, pp 23-7, sensibly comments that these rounds would have been wrestling rings as well as earthwork theatres; for a sceptical discussion of Cornish rounds as playing places, see Schmitt, pp 307-9):

1 / parish of Constantine, at Trebah and Lower Treglidgwith (Edith Dowson, CA, 5 [1966], 81);

2 / parish of Grade-Ruan, at Ruan Major and Ruan Minor (Whitley, p 173; Nance, p 194; E. Dowson, CA, 6 [1967], 104);

3 / parish of Kea (Whitley, p 173; Richard Warner, CA, 3 [1964], 97);

4 / parish of Landewednack? (Cornish, p 472; E. Dowson, CA, 9 [1970], 156);

5 / parish of Ludgvan (Vivian Russell, CA, 8 [1969], 119);

6 / Newlyn East (Nance, p 194, but modern according to Cornish, p 472);

7 / parish of Perranzabuloe, at Perran Round, about 130 feet in diameter (William Borlase, *The Natural History of Cornwall* [1758], pp 297-8 and pl XXIX, fig III; see PLATE 7; R. Warner, CA, 2 [1963], 72);

8 / parish of Redruth (Cornish, p 472; Whitley, pp 172-3; Nance, p 194; Michael Tangye, CA, 6 [1967], 92);

9 / parish of St Allen? (R. Warner, CA, 3 [1964], 99);

10 / parish of St Buryan (V. Russell, PWCornFC, 2 [1956-61], 142);

11 / parish of St Erme (Whitley, p 173);

12 / parish of St Ewe (Peter Sheppard, CA, 6 [1967], 100);

13 / parish of St Goran (P. Sheppard, CA, 5 [1966], 76);

14 / St Hilary (Nance, p 194);

15 / parish of St Just in Penwith, a site about 126 feet in diameter, badly restored in the mid-19th-century, by which time it was only 'a low ruinous ring mound' (William Borlase, *Antiquities, Historical and Monumental, of the County of Cornwall*, 2nd edn [1769], pp 207-8 and pl XVIII; A. Guthrie, 'The Plain-an-gwarry, St. Just, Cornwall. Report on an Exploratory Excavation,' PWCornFC, 2 [1956-61], 3-7; V. Russell, *ibid*, p 101; and, for a sceptical account, Treve Holman, 'Cornish Plays and Playing Places,' TN, 4 [1950], 52-4);

16 / parish of St Keverne, at Laddenvean and Tregoning? (E. Dowson, CA, 7 [1968], 105);

17 / parish of St Stephen-in-Brannel, at Churchtown? (P. Sheppard, CA, 9 [1970], 147); and

18 / parish of Sithney (Cornish, p 473; Whitley, p 173).

1303 r

213 Clerks should not make or see summer games, or miracles (where faces are disguised by visors), although they may play, in the church, the resurrection or (Robert's addition) the nativity (*Robert of Brunne's 'Handlyng Synne,' A.D. 1303, with those Parts of the Anglo-French Treatise*

on Which it Was Founded, William of Wadington's 'Manuel des Pechiez,' ed Frederick J. Furnivall, EETS OS 119 [1901], pp 155-6).

ca 1307-27 r
214 Edward II fraternized with ';scurris, cantoribus, tragedis ...' (trans by John Trevisa as 'harlottes ... syngers and ... gestoures ...'; *Polychronicon Ranulphi Higden Monachi Cestrensis*, ed Joseph R. Lumby, VIII, RS 41 [1882], pp 298-9).

before 1313
215 Walter Reynolds, newly made archbishop of Canterbury, ultimately owed his preferment to his excelling 'in ludis theatralibus,' by which he got the king's favour (*Vita Edwardi Secundi Monachi Cuiusdam Malmesberiensis*, ed and trans Noël Denholm-Young [1957], p 45).

ca 1325-50 r
216 Business keeps many from sermons but few from 'novis spectaculis' or plays called 'Miracles,' done by 'foolish clerics' and acted by players with masks; the Devil leads men away to pageants, as at Easter (John Bromyard's *Summa Predicantium*, cited from an unedited manuscript by Owst, pp 395-6, 480-1; 393, 466, 595; partly translated by G.G. Coulton, *Five Centuries of Religion*, I [1929], p 535).

ca 1330 r
217 Squires dress proudly; 'Hii ben degised as turmentours that comen from clerkes plei' ('Poem on the Evil Times of Edward II,' *The Political Songs of England*, ed and trans Thomas Wright, CS 6 [1839], p 336; *IMEV* 4165).

ca 1335-49 r
218 Robert Holcot, in his *Super Sapientiam Salomonis*, refers to 'ludus deuocionis et gaudij spiritalis, qualem faciunt Christiani in die corporis Christi' (Rubel, p 239; Wenzel, pp 390-4).

ca 1337-49 r
219 Those persons surrounding Christ hanging on the cross are 'as foles *that* gedirs til a somere gamen' (commentary on Psalms xvi.12; Richard Rolle, *The Psalter or Psalms of David*, ed H.R. Bramley [1884], p 57).

ca 1340 r
220 An East Anglian illustration of a wheeled dragon, a pageant?
(Peter Meredith and John Marshall, 'The Wheeled Dragon in the *Luttrell Psalter*,' MET, 2 [1980], 70-3).

ca 1370-90 r
221 'Wel bycommes such craft vpon Cristmasse, / Laykyng of enterludez, to laȝe and to syng, / Among þise kynde caroles of knyȝtez and ladyez' (*Sir Gawain and the Green Knight*, ed J.R.R. Tolkien and E.V. Gordon, 2nd edn, rev Norman Davis [1967], p 14, lines 471-3).

1372 r
222 Some priests care more for public shows ('publicis spectaculis') than for the sacraments (from a sermon by the chancellor of the University of Oxford; Robert O'Brien, 'Two Sermons at York Synod of William Rymyngton 1372 and 1373,' *Cîteaux Commentarii Cisterciensis*, 19 [1968], 49; cf Owst, p 274).

ca 1376-9 r
223 Sloth confesses that he would rather hear 'a somer game of souteres' than the gospels (William Langland, *The Vision of William concerning Piers the Plowman*, ed Walter W. Skeat, EETS OS 38 [1869], Passus V, line 413).

ca 1377-99 r
224 Richard II excludes 'mommers and our mynstrels' from an article that London citizens cannot go to law with one another outside the city walls, excepting for pleas of freehold beyond the City liberties (from a royal charter; [Richard Arnold] *The Customs of London, Otherwise Called Arnold's Chronicle* [1811], p 17, art 8 [publ 1503?]; STC 782-3).

ca 1377-1400 r
225 Some lords, influenced by ladies, would present 'a wilde pleiere of someres gamenes' to a benefice (from a tract probably by a follower of Wyclif; *Wyclif*, p 246; cf Workman, II, 201).

ca 1380-1400 r
226 Lamenting the exile of moral virtues, without which no saint can be, a preacher observes, 'ȝiff þis world be an enterludie, as doctors

ymagynne, I wote neu*er* who shall pley þe seynte in our*e* ent*e*rludie'
(*Middle English Sermons*, ed W.O. Ross, EETS OS 209 [1940 for 1938], pp
xxxv, 252, 254).

ca 1380-1410
227 A 'treatise of miracles' playing,' a tract attacking plays or interludes about Christ's miracles and works, about his Passion and that
of his saints, and about Antichrist and doomsday (text in *A Middle
English Treatise on the Playing of Miracles*, ed Clifford Davidson [1981];
and *Reliquiae*, II, 42-57; see also *Selections from English Wycliffite Writings*, ed Anne Hudson [1978], pp 97-104, 187-9, with notes on analo-
gous writings).

ca 1383 r
228 The religious spend their hours in 'veyn pleies & corioustees' ('Of
the Leaven of Pharisees,' *Wyclif*, pp 6, 23; by John Purvey according
to Workman, I, 331).

before 1385 r
229 To 'pleie a pagyn of þe deuyl' is to sing songs of lechery, battles,
and lies, to shout like a madman, to despise God, and to swear blas-
phemously in Christmas celebrations ('The Ave Maria,' *Wyclif*, p 206;
by Wyclif himself according to Workman, I, 331).

ca 1387-90? r
230 John Purvey's last sermon in his series of twelve attributes to a lax
'fool' the wish to live as his forefathers did, 'well loved of theaters
[players?], wrestlers, buckler-players, of dancers and singers' (Margaret Deanesly, *The Lollard Bible and Other Medieval Biblical Versions*
[1920], p 274; cf p 271).

ca 1387-1400 r
231 Chaucer's probable allusions to plays and theatres include the
following:
    1 / Theseus' round 'noble theatre ... / Walled of stoon, and dyched al
withoute,' for the 'game' or tournament in the central grassy 'place'
('The Knight's Tale,' *Chaucer*, lines A1885-92, A1901, A2091, A2585;
and Christopher Dean, 'The "Place" in "The Knight's Tale,"' *N&Q*, 211
[1966], 90-2);

2 / the Wife of Bath went to 'pleyes of myracles,' and her last husband Jankin told her of a Roman who left his wife because she was 'at a someres game' without his knowledge (*Chaucer*, lines D558, D648);

3 / Venus dancing with a firebrand before the bride and the crowd at the wedding feast of January and May (a disguising; 'The Merchant's Tale,' *Chaucer*, lines E1727-8, E1777-8; and Fifield, 'Chaucer');

4 / an Orleans clerk describes hall feasts where 'subtile tregetoures pleye' by bringing in a barge on water, a flowered meadow, a vine, and a castle, and then by suddenly making them disappear ('The Franklin's Tale,' *Chaucer*, lines F1139-51; probably French practice, for which see Laura H. Loomis, 'Secular Dramatics in the Royal Palace, Paris, 1378, 1389, and Chaucer's "Tregetoures,"' *Medieval English Drama*, ed Jerome Taylor and Alan H. Nelson [1972], pp 98-115);

5 / see under OXFORD (ca 1387-1400 r); and

6 / see under DOUBTFUL RECORDS (ca 1397-1400r).

ca 1392-93? r
232 The *Florarium Bartholomei* of John of Mirfield forbids attendance at 'spectacula' on feast days (Owst, p 274).

1394 r
233 Tournament where the twelve challengers dressed as monks, an abbot, and his convent (location unknown; 'Annales Ricardi Secundi et Henrici Quarti, Regum Angliae,' *Chronica Monasterii S. Albani*, ed Henry T. Riley, RS 28, III [1866], p 165).

ca 1394-99 r
234 A Minorite friar claims that members of his order never mix at 'marketts & myracles' (*Pierce the Ploughmans Crede*, ed Walter W. Skeat, EETS OS 30 [1867], p 5, l 107; IMEV 663).

15th century r
235 A Latin homily condemning men for frequenting taverns, dances, and pageants; and an English one against 'pleyng veyn pleys with all rybawdry and all harlotry' at Christmas (Owst, pp 481, 483, citing BL Add. ms 21253 and a Gloucester Cathedral ms).

15th century r
236 BL Harleian ms 2345, no 99, a product of Winchcomb Abbey (Glos.), refers to celebrations on St John Baptist's nativity (Midsummer

day, 24 June) with 'turpibus & illicitis Ludis' (*A Catalogue of the Harleian Manuscripts*, GBRC 4, II [1808], p 661; cited by Baskervill, p 51).

15th century r
237 'It [money] maket justynges, pleys, dysguysynges, / Ladys to synge and daunce' (Greene, p 231, no 393, stanza 4; IMEV 113).

15th century r
238 Terms about playing in three Latin-English vocabularies (Wright, I) include the following:
    1 / 'a game or a pleye' (for 'Ludus'; col 594); and 'a spectacle' ('Spectaculum ... Item est instrumentum iuvans visum'; col 612);
    2 / a section termed 'Nomina ludorum' including 'entyrlute' (for 'interludium'; col 666); and
    3 / 'a spectakylle' (for 'spectaculum'); and a similar section including 'a play' (for 'ludus'; col 737).

ca 1400-15 r
239 Men sin at Christmas in reveling and 'playes of vanyte' (*Mirk's Festial: A Collection of Homilies, by Johannes Mirkus*, ed Theodor Erbe, pt 1, EETS ES 96 [1905], p 63).

ca 1400-20 r
240 A comparison of a procession of singing children, each holding a green branch, through a wood with the child Jesus, to a 'somyr play' (*The Middle English Stanzaic Versions of the Life of Saint Anne*, ed Roscoe E. Parker, EETS OS 174 [1928], p 67, line 2592).

1405-10 r
241 'to representyn in pleyynge at Cristemesse Heroudis & þe thre kyngis & oþer proces of þe gospel boþin þan & at Estryn and in oþir tymes,' all 'steraclis [miracles] & pleyys' done principally for devotion and honest mirth to teach men to love God, are lawful; plays for ribaldry, lies, and lechery, and against the faith of holy church, are never lawful (*Dives and Pauper*, ed Priscilla H. Barnum, EETS OS 275 [1976], pp 293-4, and see collation for 'steraclis' as a variant for 'miracles'; Chambers, ELCMA, p 15, thinks the word is a moralists' parody of 'spectacle').

1407 r

242 Master William Thorpe, on trial for heresy, describes good pilgrims as people who approve when the virtuous absent themselves
'fro spectacles of veyne seyngis and hearingis' (William Thorpe,
Examinacions: Thorpe and Oldcastell (Antwerp 1530), The English
Experience [facs], 766 [1975], sig D7v; STC 24045).

ca 1410 r

243 Boston of Bury (fl 1410), an Augustinian monk at Bury St
Edmunds, lists among books he has seen in his travels in England:
Plautus' *Amphitruo, Asinaria, Aulularia, Captiui, Casina, Cistellaria, Cur-
culio,* and *Epidicus;* Terence's *Adelphi, Andria, Eunuchus, Heauton
Timorumenos, Hecyra,* and *Phormio;* and Seneca's tragedies (R.A.B.
Mynors, 'The Latin Classics Known to Boston of Bury,' *Fritz Saxl*, pp
201, 207).

ca 1422-45 r

244 A certain great lord brought before young Henry VI at Christmas
a dance or show ('choreas, vel spectaculum') of young women with
bare breasts, but he angrily averted his eyes, turned his back to them,
and went out to his chamber with the words, 'Fy fy, for shame, for-
sothe ye be to blame' (a disguising; *Henry the Sixth: A Reprint of John
Blacman's Memoir,* ed and trans M.R. James [1919], pp 8, 30; STC 3123
[written after 1471; published ca 1510]; cited without source by Stow,
Chronicles, p 730; for John Blackman, see A.B. Emden, *A Biographical
Register of the University of Cambridge to 1500* [1963], pp 670-1; and
Wolffe, pp 5-14).

ca 1424-30? r

245 John Lydgate's 'Tragoedias quoque ac Comoedias, aliaque non
iniucunda edidit' (*Illvstrivm,* fol 203r; *Scriptorum,* I, 587).

ca 1429

246 Among amusements bad for the clergy are those of 'perverse
mockery' by 'actors'; and among ones to be avoided by perfect men
are 'wanton, vain, and voluptuous ... interludes, and other theatrical
shows' (G.R. Owst, *The Destructorium Viciorum of Alexander Carpenter*
[1952], p 28).

ca 1445 r
247 Idleness is 'to gon to wakys & to wrestlyng*es*, to dau*n*synges & to steraclys ...,' to run off on holy days 'to wrestelynges, markettys, & feyris, to steraclys & dau*n*cys ...' (*Jacob's Well, an Englisht Treatise on the Cleansing of Man's Conscience*, ed Arthur Brandeis, EETS OS 115 [1900], pp 105, 291, and cf pp viii, xiii).

before 1449? r
248 Wives like 'At grete gaderyng*es* to walken vpon the playne, / And at staracles to sitte on hie stages' ('The Pain and Sorrow of Evil Marriage,' *Minor Poems*, II, 459-60, lines 101-2; attributed to Lydgate; *IMEV* 919).

ca 1449
249 No Christian man is as good an image of Christ as a wooden or stone crucifix 'except whanne a quyk man is sett in a pley to be hangid nakid on a cros and to be in semyng woundid and scourgid. And this bifallith ful seelde and in fewe placis and cuntrees'; secular men, unlike clerics, spend money in 'reueling' and 'in wantowne and nyse disgisingis of araies' (Reginald Pecock, *The Repressor of Over Much Blaming of the Clergy*, ed Churchill Babington, RS 19 [1860], I, 221, II, 371).

ca 1450-64 r
250 John Capgrave of King's Lynn notes that among places to see plays in England some are called 'ampheatrum,' ie 'a place all rou*n*d swech as we haue her in þis lond'; Roman 'theatra' were half circles 'in whech men stand to se pleyis or wrestiling*is*' (Richard Beadle, 'The East Anglian "Game-place": a Possibility for Further Research,' *REEDN*, 1978.1, pp 2-4, citing Capgrave's *Ye Solace of Pilgrimes: A Description of Rome*, circa A.D. 1450, ed C.A. Mills [1911], pp 17-18).

1459? 24 December r
251 Lady Morley forbids 'sportys' such as disguisings and music in her household during the Christmas after her husband's death (*Paston*, I, 257).

1463 29 April r
252 'Pleyers in their Enterludes' are excepted from restrictions in the statute concerning apparel (*Rotuli Parliamentorum* [1783], V, 505; *Statutes*, II, 402, 3 Edw. IV c 5; act repealed in 1482-3, II, 668-70, 22 Edw. IV c 1).

1478 20 May r
253 No one acting Herod in 'Corpus Crysty play' played 'better *and* more agreable to hys pageaunt' than did John de la Pole, duke of Suffolk, in railing against Sir John Paston at Hellesdon in Whitsun week (letter written to Sir John from Norwich on the eve of Corpus Christi; *Paston*, II, 426).

1483 23 August r
254 Richard III is received with pageants everywhere on his progress, which passed through Reading, Oxford, Woodstock, Gloucester, Worcester, Warwick, Coventry, Leicester, and on to Nottingham and York (letter of his secretary John Kendale from Nottingham, now lost, but in Robert Davies, *Extracts from the Municipal Records of ... York* [1843], pp 163-4, and earlier in Francis Drake's *Eboracum: or the History and Antiquities of the City of York* [1736], p 116; and cf James Gairdner, *History of the Life and Reign of Richard the Third*, 2nd edn [1879], pp 142-5).

1483 r
255 'a Bane of a play' (translating 'preludium, proludium'); 'a Game' (for 'ludicrum, ludus, & cetera; vbi a play'); 'a Paiande' (for 'lusorium'); 'A Play' (for 'Iocus, Ioculus, ludus, ludicrum, ludiolus'); 'to Play' (for 'iocari, ioculari, ludere, di-, lusare, lusitare'; 'a Player' (for 'iocista, lusor'); and 'a Playnge place' (for 'diludium'; *Catholicon Anglicum*, ed Sidney J.H. Herrtage, EETS OS 75 [1881], pp 20, 149, 266, 282).

ca 1483-1523
256 Lost works by John Skelton, supposed to be plays, include the following ('The Garland of Laurel,' *The Complete Poems of John Skelton Laureate*, ed Philip Henderson, 3rd edn [1959], pp 385-6, 389; *Index*, pp 254-5; *Scriptorum*, I, 651-2):
  1 / 'Of Virtue ... the sovereign interlude'; 'De virtute comediam';
  2 / 'His comedy, Achademios'; 'Transtulit ex Tullio Achademion' (Cicero's *Academica*);
  3 / 'Of pageants that were played in Joyous Guard' (a poem about feats at arms? according to Alexander Dyce, ed, *Poetical Works* [1843], II, 330);
  4 / 'Theatrales ludos' (Bale's translation of the previous work?);
  5 / 'De bono ordine, comoediam' (only in *Scriptorum*; sometimes identified with 'Old Christmas *Or* Good Order'; see under TEXTS [1533]); and

6 / *The Nigramansir*, probably a fabrication by Warton (see under DOUBTFUL RECORDS [1504? 31 March p]).

1489 after 13 January r
257 Justices of the Peace are to enforce existing statutes, as in controlling 'unlawful plays' (*Proclamations*, I, 18-19).

before 1490 r
258 Young Thomas More, a member of Cardinal Morton's household, would step in among the players at Christmas to act extemporaneously (William Roper, 'The Life of Sir Thomas More,' in *Two Early Tudor Lives*, ed Richard S. Sylvester and Davis P. Harding [1962], p 198).

1500 r
259 *Ortus Vocabulorum*, of unknown authorship and date but published by Wynkyn de Worde in London in this year (STC 13829; facs edn, Scolar Press [1968]), has some references to players and playing: 'Amphiteatrum' (for 'a iustyng place'; sig B7v); 'Diludium' (for 'a playnge place'; sig L3v); 'historio' (for 'ioculator,' performing 'ludos ... in theatro or a mynstrall'; sig R2v); 'Ludus' (for 'a playe'; sig V8r); 'Lusor' (for 'a player'; sig X1r); 'Lusus' (for 'a playnge'; sig X1r); and 'Theatrum' (for 'a comyne place to loke in'; sig Oo3r).

ca 1500 r
260 An unknown letter-writer acquires privately-owned interludes or comedies in English – despite their rarity and the difficulty of gaining the co-operation of such owners – for his correspondent to copy and then return (Oxford auspices, by a member of the More circle? trans in *School Book*, p xxix).

ca 1500-35
261 Henry Parker, eighth Lord Morley, writes 'comedias ac tragedias plures' (*Index*, p 166; *Scriptorum*, II, 103).

ca 1501 November r
262 Thomas More makes additions 'to the comedy about Solomon' (*St. Thomas More: Selected Letters*, ed Elizabeth F. Rogers [1961], pp 1-2; for its possible performance at Magdalen College, Oxford, see under that heading ca 1495-9; in 1519 Erasmus writes of More, 'Adolescens

comoediolas et scripsit et egit' [*Opvs Epistolarvm Des. Erasmi Rotero-dami*, ed P.S. and H.M. Allen, IV (1922), p 16; *L. & P. Hen. VIII*, III.i, no 394, p 138]; Bale's *Illvstrivm*, fol 220r, and *Scriptorum*, I, 655, mention 'Comoedias iuueniles').

1504 r
263 On the night before the wedding of King Oriant and Beatrice there were 'made moriskes, comedies, daunces, interludes, & al maner of Ioyous sportes' in his palace (*The Knight of the Swanne* [London: R. Copland, 1504], sig B1r; STC 7571; a prose romance translated from the French for Edward Stafford, 3rd duke of Buckingham).

1510 21 January r
264 'Players in enterludes' are excepted from restrictions in the stat-utes concerning apparel (*Statutes*, III, 8-9, 1 Hen. VIII c 14; re-enacted 5 February 1515, for which see III, 179-82, 7 Hen. VIII c 6).

1511 r
265 Priests give themselves to 'sportes and playes,' although rules of the church fathers forbid a clerk being a 'common player' ('The Ser-mon of Doctor Colete, Made to the Conuocation at Paulis,' in Lupton, App C, pp 295, 300-1; STC 5550).

1512 4 February r
266 Statute prohibits persons owning or selling visors or disguising themselves as mummers (*Statutes*, III, 30, 3 Hen. VIII c 9).

ca 1514-33 r
267 Sir Thomas More's allusions to drama (see R.J. Schoeck, 'Sir Tho-mas More and Lincoln's Inn Revels,' *PQ*, 29 [1950], 426-30, for a pro-posal that Sir Thomas was the 'More' named as alternate Master of the Revels at Lincoln's Inn in 1528) include the following:
1 / a soldan, acted by a souter (cobbler), in a stage play on a scaffold with tormentors who might strike someone addressing the soldan by his actor's real name (ca 1514-18; *The Complete Works of St. Thomas More. Volume 2. The History of King Richard III*, ed Richard S. Sylvester [1963], pp 80-1, 258-9);
2 / a comedy of Plautus (with household slaves) spoiled by an actor in philosopher's attire who recites 'the passage from the *Octavia* where Seneca is disputing with Nero' (1516; *The Complete Works of St. Thomas*

More. Volume 4. Utopia, ed Edward Surtz, SJ, and J.H. Hexter [1965], pp 98-9, 372-3);

3 / a 'lorel' who, playing 'the lord' in a stage play or interlude, is proud of his 'gay golden gown' despite his knave's old coat worn after the play is done (ca 1522; his *The Four Last Things*, ed D. O'Connor [1935], pp 42, 49);

4 / heretical writers are like friars, following an abbot of misrule in a Christmas 'game,' who preach a 'mowynge sermon' on a stool; and a soldan in a stage play making bragging boasts and running out in frantic rages (1532-3; *The Complete Works of St. Thomas More. Volume 8. The Confutation of Tyndale's Answer*, ed Louis A. Schuster, Richard C. Marius, James P. Lusardi, and Richard J. Schoeck [1973], pt I, p 42; pt 2, p 919); and

5 / a man 'playeth as though he came in in a mummary' for any word he says; inasmuch as he is not answerable for it (1533; *The Workes of Sir Thomas More* [1557], p 975; STC 18076).

1518 5 April r
268 Richard Pace writes Erasmus that he has read the comedies and tragedies that Erasmus sent to Sir Thomas More (*L. & P. Hen. VIII*, II.ii, no 4059, p 1257).

1520 22 March r
269 Thomas Wolsey's statutes for monasteries of regular Augustinian canons require them not to mix in 'ludis ... inhonestis' or to be 'lusores' (*Concilia*, III, 687).

1523 r
270 Juan Luis Vives in his *De Ratione Studii Puerilis*, a plan of study for Princess Mary, recommends Seneca's tragedies but is silent about Terence or Plautus; and in a parallel programme for Charles Mountjoy, son of William Blount, lord Mountjoy, Vives approves of Terence for 'daily conversation' and recommends Seneca's tragedies, Aristophanes, Euripides, and Sophocles (*Vives and the Renascence Education of Women*, ed Foster Watson [1912], pp 147, 245-6, 249).

ca 1525 r
271 An honest widow avoids 'the tauerne, daunces, and common playes, / And wanton maygames' (John C. Meagher, ed, 'Robert Copland's *The Seven Sorrows*,' *ELR*, 7 [1977], 39, lines 440-1; STC 5734).

1526 r
272 A story about a John Adroyns (Androyns) who played the Devil in a stage play in a Suffolk market town (*Mery Tales*, pp 7-11; STC 23663-4; identified with Woodbridge, Suffolk (for which see below), by V.B. Redstone, 'The Sandling,' *PSuffIANH*, 10 [1898-1900], 65).

1527-8 r
273 Thomas Arthur and three of the king's interluders made £30 travelling through England playing interludes and plays (according to a bill in Chancery by George Maller, another King's interluder whom they deserted and against whom Arthur, who paid Maller £26 to apprentice for a year to be taught playing with the goal of becoming a king's player, entered an action of trespass; G.H. Overend, 'On the Dispute between George Maller, Glazier, and Trainer of Players to Henry VIII., and Thomas Arthur, Tailor, his Pupil,' *The New Shakspere Society's Trans*, 1st ser, 7 [1877-9], 425-9; Bernard Miles, 'Elizabethan Acting,' *TLS*, 2 April 1954, p 217; PRO, C.1.546/77).

1530 r
274 Many entries about plays, players, and playing places in John Palsgrave's English-French dictionary: 'Boke bearer in a playe' (translating 'prothocolle'); 'Bourde or game' (for 'ieu'); 'Commedy of a christmas playe' (for 'commedie'); 'Interlude' (for 'moralité'); 'Mommery' (for 'mommerie'); 'Mummar' (for 'mommevr'); 'Pagiant in a playe' (for 'mistere'); 'Playe an enterlude' (for 'farce'); 'Playe maker' (for 'factevr' and 'factiste'); 'Player in a playe' (for 'parsonnage'); 'Playe of sadde matters' (for 'moralité'); 'Spectacle a thyng to beholde' (for 'spectacle'); 'Stage playe' (for 'matire'); 'Stage a scaffolde' (for 'estage' and 'beffroy'); 'Vysar for a mummar' (for 'faulx uisaige'); 'Make romme maysters here cometh a player' (for 'Faictez place mes sieurs voicy venir ung ioueur'); and 'I Mumme in a mummynge' and 'Lette vs go mumme to nyght in womens apparayle' (for 'Ie mumme' and 'Allons mummer a nuyct en acoustremens de femmes'; John Palsgrave, *Lesclarcissement de la Langue Francoyse 1530* [Scolar Press, 1969], III, fols 20v, 21r, 25v, 42r, 49, 52r, 54v-55r, 66, 72v, 295r, 305r; STC 19166).

1530 r
275 Petition to the king for support from a former King's scholar at Cambridge who, having become master at St Paul's school and having

played, by command of the king and council, comedies before ambassadors and other foreign visitors, now is sick and has received some help for himself, his wife, and his children from the school's overseers (probably John Ritwise; *L. & P. Hen. VIII*, Addenda, I.i, no 717, p 242).

1530 r
276 Some sacrifices and ceremonies express Christ, and the circumstances and virtues of his death, 'so plainly, as if we should play his passion on a scaffold, or in a stage-play, openly before the eyes of the people' (from the prologue to Leviticus; William Tyndale, *Doctrinal Treatises*, PS 47 [1848], p 422).

1531 16 January r
277 Statute requires that vagabonds caught practising 'dyvers & subtyle craftye & unlawfull games & playes' be whipped (*Statutes*, III, 328-32, 22 Hen. VIII c 12).

1531 r
278 Sir Thomas Elyot commends classical comedies, and interludes in English, as moral accounts warning youth against vices, but he describes May games as vain, scornful things (and refers to kings in them and in interludes; *The Boke Named The Gouernour*, ed Henry H.S. Croft [1883], I, 123-8, 266; II, 270).

1532 r
279 William Umpton, formerly a royal servant, lies imprisoned in the Tower for saying that the fifty-two points for which St Thomas Becket died were just 'a dance called Robin Hood' and for questioning why St Thomas was a saint rather than Robin Hood (*L. & P. Hen. VIII*, V, no 1271, p 551).

1533 4 February r
280 Players in interludes, sights, revels, jousts, tourneys, barriers, solemn watches, or other martial feats or disguisings are excepted from restrictions in the statute concerning apparel (*Statutes*, III, 430-2, 24 Hen. VIII c 13).

1533 26 October r
281 Sir Christopher Garneys writes to Cromwell from Calais that 'the lord steward and head officers at banquets and disguisings lay their

staves on the heads of unruly persons, and thrust torches in their faces' (*L. & P. Hen. VIII*, VI, no 1350, p 540).

ca 1534-40 r

282 John Bale wrote the following lost plays in English, termed by him comedies or tragedies, according to his own bibliographical works, 'Anglorum Heliades' (1533-6, with additions to 1539; plays 1-6, which Bale describes as being written for John de Vere, earl of Oxford and Great Chamberlain), 'Fasciculus Carmelitarum' (ca 1527-33, with additions to ca 1540; plays 1-2, 10-12), the *Index* (1548; plays 1-4, 7-19), and *Scriptorum* (1557; plays 1-4, 7-19; in this [I, 702], Bale also says that Cromwell released him from ecclesiastical examinations at York [in 1534] and London [in 1536] on account of the comedies he had produced), on the basis of which lists plays 1-6 may be dated ca 1534-6, plays 7-11 ca 1537, play 12 ca 1538, plays 13-18 ?ca 1538-40, and play 19 after 1541 (Davies, pp 209-13, 231-6, 241; Thora B. Blatt, *The Plays of John Bale* [1968], pp 20-34; Stratman 5323-46):

1 / 'Vitam Diui Ioannis Baptiste,' in fourteen 'libri' (the life of John the Baptist);

2 / 'De Christo Duodenni,' a comedy (on Christ at twelve years old);

3 / 'De Christi Passione,' in two 'libri,' a comedy;

4 / 'De Christi Resurrectione,' in two 'libri,' a comedy (also called 'De sepultura & resurrectione,' possibly Bale's play on the harrowing of hell, for which see under THORNDON);

5 / 'Super Oratione Dominica' (on the Lord's Prayer);

6 / 'De Septem Peccatis' (on the seven sins);

7 / 'Super Vtroque Regis Coniugo,' in two 'libri' (on the two marriages of the king);

8 / 'De Sectis Papisticis,' in two 'libri' (on Popish sects);

9 / 'Erga Zoilos quosdam,' in two 'libri' (also called 'Contra Momos & Zoilos');

10 / 'De Traditionibus Papistarum,' in two 'libri' (also called 'Proditiones Papistarum'; on the treacheries of the papists);

11 / 'Contra Corruptores Verbi dei' (also called 'In uerbi peruersores' and 'Contra adulterantes Dei uerbum'; against the corrupters of God's word);

12 / 'De Traditione Thome Becketi' (also called 'De Thomae Becketi imposturis'; on the treason of Thomas Becket);

13 / 'De baptismo & tentatione,' in two 'libri,' a comedy (on the baptism and temptation; evidently played together at Kilkenny in

1553, the first is lost and the second is probably Bale's *Temptation of Our Lord*);

14 / 'De Lazaro suscitato,' a comedy (on the raising of Lazarus);

15 / 'De pontificum consilio,' a comedy (on the council of the high priests);

16 / 'Festum Simonis Leprosi,' a comedy (also called 'De Simone leproso'; on the feast of Simon the leper);

17 / 'De coena & pedrum lotione,' a comedy (on the lord's supper and the washing of the feet);

18 / 'Imaginem amoris' (the image of love); and

19 / 'Pammachii tragoediam transtuli,' in four 'libri' (Thomas Kirchmeyer's *Pammachius* [1541], translated).

1535-6 r

283 Richard Morison proposes (a) a yearly feast or triumph to celebrate England's delivery from the Pope, and (b) the prohibition of 'playes of Robyn hoode, mayde Marian, freer Tuck ... [and] the shiref of Notyngham' in favour of others about 'the abhomynation and wickednes of the bisshop of Rome, monkes, ffreers, nonnes, and suche like, and ... thobedience' due to the King (Sydney Anglo, 'An Early Tudor Programme for Plays and Other Demonstrations against the Pope,' *JWCI*, 20 [1957], 176-9; *L. & P. Hen. VIII*, XVII, App, no 2, p 707 [dated 1542]; redated by G.R. Elton, *Policy and Police* [1972], p 185; Collier, I, 128, n, quotes from a draft address by the House of Commons to the king [nd; unlocated] proposing that there should be fewer holy days, especially at harvest time, because of the 'many grete abhomynable & execrable vices, ydle and wanton sportes, and plaies of the staige' then).

1537 1 May p

284 A May game play 'of a king how he should rule his realm,' with a character named Husbandry who 'said many things against gentlemen more than was in the book of the play' (acted in Suffolk; and the shire justices are ordered to look to 'games and plays'; *L. & P. Hen. VIII*, XII.i, nos 1212, 1284, pp 557, 585).

1537 r

285 John Young, one of Queen Jane's players with John Slye, David Sotherne, and John Mounffeld, complains in Chancery about an action of debt by one who hired out to them ca 1536 a defective horse for carrying their playing garments in a tour of the north parts 'in exercising theire usuall feates of playinge in interludes' (C.C. Stopes, *Shakespeare's Environment*, 2nd edn [1918], pp 235-7; PRO, C.1.931/39).

1538 r
286 The publisher's stock of John Rastell includes 'the second part of the play of Epicure' and other (extant) play-texts (Roberts, pp 36, 38).

1539 13 July r
287 French diplomatic correspondence notes that there is not a village feast or pastime anywhere in the country lacking 'sports and follies' deriding the Pope (*L. & P. Hen. VIII*, XIV, no 1261, p 558).

1540 6 July r
288 Henry VIII calls the Pope '"abomination," "son of perdition," "idol," and "Antichrist," as commonly they do in the feasts and pastimes which are daily made' (letter of Charles de Marillac, French ambassador; *L. & P. Hen. VIII*, XV, no 848, p 418).

1541 22 July r
289 Prohibition of the practice of dressing children 'to counterfeit priests, bishops, and women' on the feasts of St Nicholas, St Catherine, St Clement, the Holy Innocents, etc (*Proclamations*, I, 301-2; *L. & P. Hen. VIII*, XVI, no 1022, p 487).

ca 1541-62
290 Nicholas Grimald's lost plays include 'Fama,' a comedy or tragicomedy, and 'Athanasius siue Infamia,' a comedy (both before 1547, according to Boas); 'Christus Nascens,' a comedy (probably ca 1541, the date of 'Christus Redivivus'); 'Protomartyr,' a tragedy probably about St Stephen (although St Alban is possible); and two comedies in English, 'De puerorum in musicis institutione' (only in *Index*), and 'Troilus,' out of Chaucer (*Index*, pp 302, 304; *Scriptorum*, I, 701-2; Boas, pp 32-3).

1542 ?March r
291 Draft proclamation against heretical books like those of Bale; and orders that no printer print any play without his and the author's names, and date of printing, or without giving his first copy to the town mayor two days before publication (*L. & P. Hen. VIII*, XVII, no 177, pp 79-80).

1542 r
292 Nicholas Udall's commentary and annotations on Erasmus' *Apoph-thegmes* (1542; STC 10443) sometimes appear to draw on contemporary experience of drama: 'comedies' are defined as 'merie entreludes,' and 'tragedies' as 'sadde entreludes whiche wee call staige plaies' (sig **6r); Socrates said many times that cloth of gold and purple, precious stones, jewellery, arras, and 'the other delices of ryche menne' are more fit for disguisings in stage plays than for the life of man (sig b5r); in old times the 'places' where May games, open sights, and shows of games were exhibited 'wer made circlewise round about with settles or benches of marble, staier wise one aboue an other,' on which the people sat and beheld the games and sights (sig g2v); and the course of one's life is compared to 'plaiyng a parte in an entrelude' (sig K6v; cf also the many references to plays by Terence, Sophocles, Euripides, etc, at sigs **5r, c6r, c7, e2, e3v, i1r, s9r, F9v-G1r, K5v-6r, V4v, and V5r; cf Udall's translation of *The First Tome or Volume of the Paraphrase of Erasmus vpon the Newe Testamente* [1548], 'Matt,' fol 26; 'Mark,' fol 50r, 78r; 'Acts,' fol 60r [STC 2854]).

1543 22 January-12 May r
293 Statute prohibits the printing or performance of all plays contrary to religious doctrine as prescribed in 1540, although plays and inter-ludes 'for the rebuking and reproching of vices, and the setting foorthe of vertue' that do not meddle with scriptural interpretation contrary to the king's doctrine remain lawful (*Statutes*, III, 894-7, 34-5 Hen. VIII c 1).

ca 1543-8
294 Nicholas Udall's 'Comoedias plures' and translation of 'Trogoe-diam de Papatu' for Queen Catherine Parr (two books; *Illvstrivm*, fol 233v, and *Scriptorum*, I, 717; Udall's play of Ezechias [see under ETON COLLEGE 1537-9]? or the dialogue by Bernardino Ochino, an undra-matic translation of which by John Ponet was printed in 1549? for which see *Index*, p 239, and STC 18770-1).

1544 r
295 The bishops of England are said to persecute players of interludes who, having left off lies and corruption, now persuade the people to worship God according to his laws rather than theirs, and tell the truth (that the Pope is Antichrist; Henry Stalbrydge, pseud [John

Bale], *The Epistle Exhortatorye of an Englyshe Christiane vnto his Derelye Beloued Contreye of Englande* [1544], fols 16, 19r; rpt with intro by Peter Davison [1972]; STC 1291).

1545 26 May r
296 Vagabonds, including 'common players' (gamblers?), to be ordered to the king's galleys (*Proclamations*, I, 352).

1545 r
297 Roger Ascham, in *Toxophilus*, compares an archer who swings his bow about himself to 'a man with a shaft [turning] to make room in a game place' (*Ascham*, II, 143).

1545-6 r
298 Draper's bill for red material of five coats for the players of Queen Catherine Parr (*L. & P. Hen. VIII*, XXI.i, no 645, p 321).

1546 8 July r
299 All books by selected authors including [John] Bale are to be burned, and each printer of plays is to submit the first copy to the mayor of his city for approval before publication (*Proclamations*, I, 373-6; cf APC, I, 509).

1546 r
300 All 'oure shewes or daunces called maskes in Englande & bone-fyres,' as used in some parts, are like Roman bacchanalia and should be banished among Christians; and the 'disguisyng and mummyng' at Christmas 'in the Northe partes came out of the feastes of Pallas' (done with visors and painted visages; *An Abridgement of the Notable Worke of Polidore Virgile*, comp Thomas Langley [1546], sigs liv, N7r, and cf C1v, G5r, k5v; STC 24654).

1547 May-June r
301 Letters between Stephen Gardiner, bishop of Winchester, and Edward Seymour, duke of Somerset, Lord Protector, mention players who meddle in matters of justification and the sacraments (some who wrote plays formerly against Henry VIII's proceedings being yet unpunished); and Foxe's defence of players, 'set up of God' to bring down the Pope, as having 'done meetly well already' (Foxe, VI, 31, 34-5, 57).

1547-51 r

302 Five plays, including 'a tragidie in anglishe of the vniust suprimacie of the bisshope of rome' and 'a play called old custome' (the first probably John Ponet's translation of the dialogue by Bernardino Ochino, published 1549 [STC 18770-1]), are noted in an inventory of the effects of John Dudley, Lord Lisle, son of the earl of Warwick (Greg, IV, 1651; and cf under TEXTS ca 1519-28, ca 1520-2, and 1528-33, and under LONDON ca 1545-7r).

1548 r

303 Sir Thomas Elyot's Latin-English dictionary, as augmented by Thomas Cooper (*Bibliotheca Eliotae (1548)*, facs edn, intro Lillian Gottesman [1975]; STC 7661), has many references to plays and playing: 'player of enterludes' ('Actor,' 'Ludio,' 'Ludius,' 'Scaenicus'; sigs B1r, Qq7r, Ooo4v); 'an enterlude, wherin the common vices of men and women are apparantly declared in personages, a comedie' ('Comoedia'; sig Q2r); 'a plaier of comedies, or enterludes' ('Comoedus,' 'Scaenaticus, vel scaenatilis'; sigs Q2r, Ooo4v); 'a maker of enterludes' ('Comicus'; sig Q2r); 'a masker, or he that weareth a vysour. also the visour it selfe' ('Larua,' and cf 'Laruatus'; sig Pp4v); 'any playe or pastyme, or an interlude' ('Ludicrum'; sig Qq7r); 'a player in enterludes or stage plaies' ('Ludio,' 'Ludius'; sig Qq7r); 'plaie in actes, mirthes in woordes, a sporte, a game, a pastyme' ('Ludus'; sig Qq7r); 'sightes: as the pageantes at London on Midsomer nyght. sometyme ... suche triumphes as be made by kynges, with iustyng and turneiyng' ('Ludi'; sig Qq7v); 'a plaiyng' ('Lusio'; sig Qq8r); 'a player' ('Lusor'; sig Qq8r); 'a plaie' ('Lusus'; sig Qq8r); 'a dissarde that canne feigne and counterfaite euery mans gestures' ('Pantomimus'; sig Aaa4r); 'a stage, wheron pageauntes bee sette' ('Pegma, or Pecma'; sig Bbb4r); 'a place whiche serueth onely for enterludes or comedies to be plaied in, which was in the forme of a halfe circle' ('Scaena'; sig Ooo4v); 'a thyng to be seene or looked on, a sight, a pageant, a plaie, sometyme the self beholding, also the place from whense men dooe beholde thynges, a scafolde' ('Spectaculum'; sig Rrr1v); 'Spectacula theatrica, plaies exercised in the Theatre' (sig Xxx2v); 'a little Theatre' ('Theatridium'; sig Xxx3r); 'a Theatre, a place made halfe rounde, wherin the people assembled to beholde plaies and sundrie exercises. sometyme it signifieth the multitude, that beholdeth: sometime the sight or plaie sette foorth in that place' ('Theatrum'; sig Xxx3r); 'a writer of tragedies' ('Tragicus'; sig

Xxx8v); 'a tragedie, whiche is an enterlude, wherin the personages dooe represent some historie or fable lamentable for the crueltee and miserie therin expressed' ('Tragoedia'; sigs Xxx8v-Yyy1r); and 'a plaier in a tragedie' ('Tragoedus'; sig Yyy1r).

1549 March r
304 A Latin version of Sophocles' tragedies by Vitus Winshemius, who made it for use by young people and dedicated it to Edward VI, was published at Frankfort (Baldwin 1, I, 245).

1549 12 April r
305 Hugh Latimer, bishop of Worcester, complains that once on his way home from London he was prevented from preaching at a town, as he had arranged, because its parish church had been locked up and the parishioners had gone out to gather for Robin Hood ('Seven Sermons before Edward VI, On each Friday in Lent, 1549,' in *English Reprints*, ed Edward Arber, VI [1869], pp 173-4).

1549 9 June r
306 The first Act of Uniformity of the Anglican service prescribed penalties for speaking against it in any interludes or plays (*Statutes*, IV.i, 38, 2-3 Edw. VI c 1).

1549 June-July r
307 Articles of complaint by men of Cornwall and Devon include a rejection of the new English service, which is compared to a Christmas game (Frances Rose-Troup, *The Western Rebellion of 1549* [1913], pp 127, 221, 472, 474-6, 493).

1549 6 August r
308 Performance of all plays, interludes, and dialogues in English is prohibited from 9 August to 1 November throughout the realm (*Proclamations*, I, 478-9).

1549 r
309 Sir Thomas Chaloner, in the preface to his translation of Erasmus' *Moriae Encomivm*, says that to touch men by name in books or plays is unfitting; Folly enters asking for the attention one gives 'plaiers,' jesters, and fools ('Fori circulatoribus' or mountebanks); 'ludibriis' is Englished 'maygames'; in rendering Erasmus' passage on a stage play

interrupted by someone plucking off a player's garments (as players acting a woman, a youth, a king, and God), and on life as a stage play where men play various parts, Chaloner writes 'the maker of the plaie, or bokebearer causeth theim to auoyde the skaffolde' for 'choragus educat e proscenio'; and Erasmus' mention of a theatre is glossed, 'a place where the commen plaies were plaied' (*Folie*, pp 3, 8, 20-1, 37-8, 52, and cf pp 14, 29, 106, 133, 159; STC 10500; D. Erasmus, *Moriae Encomivm Id Est Stvltitiae Lavs*, ed Clarence H. Miller, *Opera*, IV, 3 [1979], pp 72-3, 86-7, 104-5; Erasmus wrote *Moriae* in Thomas More's London house in 1509 [p 14]).

1550 22 June r
310 Edward VI's own journal records that a privy search was made through Sussex for 'il plaiers' (*Literary Remains*, p 280).

1550 5 August-11 November r
311 Sir Thomas Hoby, visiting Augsburg, translates into English 'the Tragedie of Free Will,' probably *Libero Arbitrio* by Francesco Negri de Bassano, and later dedicates it to William Parr, marquess of Northampton ('The Travels and Life of Sir Thomas Hoby, Kt. of Bisham Abbey, Written by Himself. 1547-1564,' ed Edgar Powell, in *The Camden Miscellany*, X, CS 3rd ser, 4 [1902], p 63; cf STC 18419 and Greg 63).

1550 r
312 God is pleased by the representation of his passion in the sacrifices described in Leviticus, and in the sacraments, but not 'by stageplays; which are at this day greatly set by, although scarce godly, by no small number of trifling and fantastical heads' (in a work dedicated and presented to Edward VI; *The Decades of Henry Bullinger, Minister of the Church of Zurich. Translated by H.I.*, ed Thomas Harding, PS 10 [1850], II, 194).

1550 r
313 Youths should stage comedies such as the quarrel of the shepherds of Abraham and Lot, Isaac's seeking and marrying his bride, Rebekah, and Jacob's fortunate service with his uncle Laban, and tragedies about 'the holy patriarchs, kings, prophets, and apostles, from the time of Adam' (not classical Greek and Latin plays), for moral instruction or from piety (Martin Bucer's *De Regno Christi*, written for and in 1551

presented to Edward VI by Bucer, then at Cambridge: *Melanchthon and Bucer*, ed W. Pauck, the Library of Christian Classics, XIX [1969], pp 349-52 [in English translation]; also in *EES*, II.i, 329-31).

1551 28 April r
314 All players of interludes, plays, or other matter in English must show a special licence under the king's sign, or one signed by six of the Privy Council (*Proclamations*, I, 514-18).

1551 May r
315 A Venetian diplomat reports that comedies are part of English demonstrations of contempt for the Pope (*Venice*, V, p 347).

before 1552 r
316 Formerly one of the duke of Somerset's players, one Miles can testify how the waters at Bath heal gout (William Turner, *A Booke of the Natures and Properties as Well of the Bathes in England as of Other Bathes in Germany and Italy* [1562], sig B1r; STC 24351).

ca 1552 March r
317 A proposed act for restraint of apparel, in Edward VI's hand, excepting players (not made law; *Literary Remains*, pp 494, 497).

1552 27 October r
318 Richard Ogle sends to the Council a forged licence taken from 'the players' (*CSP*, p 46).

1552 r
319 Many entries about players, plays, and playing places in Richard Huloet's English-Latin dictionary, some of which may illustrate English practice: 'Commune playes and gaye syghtes, as be at London on mydsomer nyght' (translating 'Munera,' 'Pegmata,' and 'Ludi'); 'Disard in an enterlude' (for 'Pantomimus' and 'Samnio'); 'Enterlude players' and 'Game players' (for 'Ludij, Ludiones'); 'Masker or maske player' (for 'Larua,' 'Laruatus,' 'Personatus'); 'Maskynge vysoure' (for 'Larua'); 'Place of beholdynge or lokynge about' (for 'Spectaculum'); 'Player' (for 'Lusor'); 'Player in enterludes' (for 'Comoedus,' 'Histrio,' 'Plaupes'); 'Playes celebrated or done once in fiue yeres' (for 'Actia'); 'Playes exercised vpon scaffoldes' (for 'Amphiteatrales ludi'); and 'Sightes as pageauntes and suche lyke' (for 'Ludiorum'; *Abecedarium*

Anglico-Latinum 1552, Scolar Press facs [1970], sigs F3r [and Z3r], I2r, K5v, N3v, Z2v, Z3r, Ff4r; STC 13940; see also A6v-B1, B5v, F1r, F2r, H6v, Q5r, R2r, T6, V6r, Y2v, Y4v, Z5v, Aa3r, Aa5v, Dd1v, Ff4v, Gg1v, Gg6r, Ii5v, and Ll4v).

1553 18 August r
320 No play or interlude to be printed or played without a special royal licence (*Proclamations*, II, 5-8; cf APC, IV, 426).

1554 after 25 July r
321 Some papists made interludes and pageants following the wedding of Philip and Mary (Holinshed, IV, 61).

1554 r
322 *Temp.* Edward VI, players of interludes, inspired by the Devil to heresy, 'set forth openly before mens eyes the wicked blasphemye, that they had contriued for the defacing of all rites, ceremonies, and all the whole order, vsed in the administration of the ... Sacramentes' (John Christopherson, *An Exhortation to All Menne to Take Hede and Beware of Rebellion* [1554], sig T3; STC 5207).

1555 13 June r
323 Heretical books including all works by [John] Bale to be surrendered to ecclesiastical authorities for burning or other disposal (*Proclamations*, II, 57-60).

1555 24 June r
324 Order that Sir Thomas Cheney, Lord Warden of the Cinque Ports, the mayors of Canterbury and Rochester, and the sheriff of Kent allow no May games in that county (APC, V, 151).

1556 30 April r
325 The Council asks Francis Talbot, earl of Shrewsbury, (a) to instruct the justices of the peace in the north to prohibit all plays and interludes, and (b) to order Sir Francis Leek to send to him the company of six or seven persons, supposedly Leek's own liveried servants, playing throughout the north certain plays and interludes with 'very naughty and seditious matter' about Philip and Mary, the state, and the Catholic faith (E. Lodge, *Illustrations of British History, Biography, and Manners*, 2nd edn [1838], I, 260-2; Leek has not been identified).

1556 7 May r
326 The Select Council makes orders against players 'strolling through
the Kingdom, disseminating seditions and heresies' (*CSP*, p 82).

1557 11 July r
327 Order to Justices of the Peace of Essex to permit no interludes
(*APC*, VI, 118-9).

1557 r
328 Generally persons choose fair, well-favoured young men 'to play a
virgins part or a woers part, or suche like,' in an interlude (contemporary reference within a borrowing from Cicero by Roger Edgeworth,
chancellor of Wells Cathedral, in his *Sermons* [*STC* 7482], fol 213v, cited
by J.W. Blench, *Preaching in England in the Late Fifteenth and Sixteenth
Centuries* [1964], pp 215-16).

ca 1558? r
329 *Temp.* Henry VIII-Edward VI, all interludes and plays were made
of 'gods word' (E.P., in the preface to his translation of Thomas Cranmer's *A Confutation of Vnwritten Verities* [?1558], sig A4r; *STC* 5996).

1559 7 April r
330 The Queen's proclamation in writing banns all plays and interludes until All Hallows tide (Machyn, p 193; Holinshed, IV, 184; a
London civic order of 18 April, suggesting that this proclamation may
have applied only to the City, directs it to be sent back to Sir William
Cecil at his request [Mill-Chambers, pp 298-9]).

1559 11 April r
331 Crown order forbids future performances 'of certain plays and
games on holidays ... in abuse and derision of the Catholic religion, of
the mass, of the Saints, and finally of God' (*Venice*, VII, no 58, p 65;
and also 'of the clergy,' no 62, p 71).

1559 16 May r
332 Prohibition of the playing of any interlude openly or privately
unless licensed by a mayor, or two justices of the peace, or a lieutenant for a shire; and of any play 'wherein either matters of religion or
of the governance of the estate of the commonweal' are treated (*Proclamations*, II, 115-16).

1559 19 July r
333 Injunctions for religion require that no play be printed unless it is licensed by the queen's Court of High Commission in London (*Proclamations*, II, 128-9).

1562 7 May r
334 Players of interludes are excepted from existing statutes of apparel (*Proclamations*, II, 203).

1572 r
335 Among popish abuses yet remaining in the English church is the minister's habit of rushing through services to make way for an interlude to be played, in the church itself if no where else can be got ('An Admonition to the Parliament,' in *Puritan Manifestoes: A Study of the Origin of the Puritan Revolt*, ed W.H. Frere and C.E. Douglas [1954], p 29, and cf p 22; STC 25427).

1579 r
336 An attack on the Whitsunday descent of an artificial dove with fireworks from the church roof, on the Ascensiontide pulling up of a Christ figure by ropes and a vice in it, and on processional playing of the Passion, as papist interludes; and a recommendation of a Robin Hood play or morris dance over a priest's 'apishe toies' ([Philips van Marnix van Sant Algegonde], *The Bee Hiue of the Romishe Church*, trans George Gylpen the elder [1579], fol 201, and cf fols 62r, 212r; STC 17445).

1589 r
337 Anderson, parson of Stepney, once had the Potter's part in the (Robin Hood) morris dance in a market-town on the 'edge' of Bucks. or Beds. (Martin Marprelate's 'The Just Censure and Reproofe,' in *Marprelate*, pp 369-70).

1595 July r
338 Justices of the Peace for Devon abolish all ales, revels, May games, and plays on Sundays and holy days, and at night (sessions held at Exeter; A.H.A. Hamilton, *Quarter Sessions from Queen Elizabeth to Queen Anne* [1878], pp 28-9; orders of suppression followed in 1599, 1607, 1622, and 1631 [pp 29, 73, 116]).

1602 r
339 The 'Guary miracle,' a Cornish interlude of scriptural history played on a 'stage' in an earthen amphitheatre, 40-50 feet in diameter, with devils, and with a prompter 'Ordinary' following the actors with his book; and one actor's practical joke on him (Richard Carew, *The Svrvey of Cornwall* [1602], fols 71r-2r; *STC* 4615).

1604 r
340 Churchwardens are forbidden to permit any 'ludos scenicos' in their churches, chapels, or cemeteries ('Constitutiones sive canones ecclaesiastici' [no 88], *Concilia*, IV, 395).

1605-6 r
341 Any player in a stage play, interlude, show, May game, or pageant 'jestingly or prophanely' speaking or using the name of God, Christ Jesus, the Holy Ghost, or the Trinity is to be fined (*Statutes*, IV, 1097).

ABINGDON (Oxfordshire or Berkshire)

1437 r
342 Robert Nevill, bishop of Salisbury, forbids that there be 'homines laruati' or 'effigies dyabolica comitantes' in the town procession of St Helen's church on the Sunday after 3 May, the feast of the Fraternity of the Holy Cross (Arthur E. Preston, *Christ's Hospital Abingdon: the Almshouses, the Hall and the Portraits* [1929], p 24 ['Masked men or figures implying devilry']; transcription courtesy of Abigail Young).

1445 3 May r
343 Pageants, plays, and May games by the Fraternity of the Holy Cross on its feast day (in notes from a register copied in 1638; *Liber Niger Scaccarii*, ed T. Hearne [1728], p 599).

1559-87
344 Visiting players (H.T. Riley, 'The Manuscripts of the Corporation of Abingdon. – Additional Report,' *2nd Report*, HMC [1871], pp 149-50; Frederick S. Boas, 'Visits of Professional Players to Abingdon, 1558-87,' *TLS*, 4 July 1929, p 535; these and other town dramatic records are being re-edited by A.F. Johnston as part of REED Berkshire collections).

1566 r
345 Setting up of Robin Hood's bower (J. Ward, 'Extracts from the Church-wardens Accompts of the Parish of St. Helen's, in Abington, Berkshire,' *Arch*, 1 [1770], 16).

ADDLETHORPE INGOLDMELLS (Lincolnshire)

ca 1543-50 p
346 Several payments to players appear in churchwardens' accounts (Kahrl, p 1).

ALDEBURGH (Suffolk)

1573-4 p
347 The earl of Leicester's men played in the church (J.C. Coldewey, ed, 'Playing Companies at Aldeburgh 1556-1635,' *Collections Volume IX*, MalS [1971 (1977)], p 19).

1582-3 r
348 Play? with devil (his coat; Coldewey, p 20).

AMERSHAM (Buckinghamshire)

1529-30 r, 1539-40 r
349 The lord for Robin Hood; and a receipt of 'the lades for Robyn Hode' (F.G. Lee, 'Amersham Churchwardens' Accounts,' *Records of Buckinghamshire*, 7 [1897], 44; *The Edwardian Inventories for Buckinghamshire*, transcr J.E. Brown, ed F.C. Eeles, Alcuin Club Collections, 9 [1908], p 126).

ANDOVER (Hampshire)

1473 p
350 Players for the parish church (*The Early Churchwardens' Accounts of Hampshire*, ed John F. Foster [1913], p 9).

ARNESBY (Leicestershire)

1510 April r
351 Parishioners 'ludant in cimiterio ad inhonesta ro ...' (A.W. Gibbons, 'Documents Relating to Leicestershire, Preserved in the Episcopal Registers at Lincoln,' *AASRP*, 21 [1891-2], 317).

ASHBURTON (Devon)

1492-1564
352 Corpus Christi play(s) with King Herod 1537-8r, God (or Christ) 1555-6r, 1557-9, and St Rosmonus 1555-6 (*Churchwardens' Accounts of Ashburton, 1479-1580*, ed Alison Hanham, Devon & Cornwall Rec. Society, NS 15 [1970], pp 19-152).

1526 r, 1542 r
353 Robin Hood and his fellows, all with tunics (Hanham, pp 78, 109; cf Wasson, p 68).

1531-44
354 Play or game at Christmas, in the church 1533-6 (by visiting Exeter players 1534-5), possibly with devils (Hanham, pp 89-113).

AVELEY (Essex)

1564 r
355 St James' day, July 25, is the 'play-day' (Frederick Emmison, 'Tithes, Perambulations and Sabbath-breach in Elizabethan Essex,' in *Antiquary*, p 205).

AXBRIDGE (Somerset)

ca 1570-1603
356 Plays in the church (H. St George Gray [reported lecture], *PSomANHS*, 91 [1946], 27).

1582-3 p
357 Play by the children of Wells grammar school and Wells cathedral choristers in the parish church (*MSS Wells*, II, 304).

BALDOCK (Hertfordshire)

1st-4th centuries? r
358 A fine fragmentary life-size tragic mask, made of pottery, and 'boldly modelled' with mouth opening and holes for nostrils and eyes, was found here (I.M. Stead, 'A Roman Pottery Theatrical Face-mask

and a Bronze Brooch-blank from Baldock, Herts.,' *Antiq*, 55 [1975], 397-8, with fig 1; Wacher, *Towns*, p 68, pl 5).

BANBURY (Oxfordshire)

1555-6 p
359 Accounts have payments for 'Dycher and Bramley' plays and towards a city pageant celebrating the charter of incorporation granted in 1554 (twelve crafts subsidized the pageant and players' gear was brought from Coventry; *Banbury Corporation Records: Tudor and Stuart*, ed J.S.W. Gibson and E.R.C. Brinkworth, Banbury Hist. Society, 15 [1977], pp 16-17).

BARDNEY (Lincolnshire)

1246 r
360 The abbey is granted control over shows and other entertainments (A.H. Thompson, 'Notes on the History of the Abbey of St. Peter, St. Paul, and St. Oswald, Bardney,' *AASRP*, 32 [1913-14], 53).

BARKING ABBEY (Essex, now Greater London)

1279 r
361 Celebrations on Innocents' day, formerly performed by children, are to be undertaken by nuns lest they become 'ludibrium' (*Registrum Epistolarum Fratris Johannis Peckham, Archiepiscopi Cantuariensis*, ed C.T. Martin, RS 77, I [1882], pp 82-3; termed '"mystery" play' in *VCHEssex*, p 117).

1363-76 r
362 Liturgical representation of the harrowing of hell, and a 'Visitatio Sepulchri,' for both of which Abbess Katherine of Sutton was responsible (text ed J.B.L. Tolhurst, *The Ordinale and Customary of the Benedictine Nuns of Barking Abbey*, I, HBS 65 [1927], pp 106-10; Young, I, 164, 381-4, and facs, pl X; Lipphardt, V, 1458-61, no 770; and Nancy Cotton, 'Katherine of Sutton: The First English Woman Playwright,' *ETJ*, 30 [1978], 475-81).

BARNSTAPLE (Devon)

1474-82
363 'ludatores,' 'ludariis,' and 'lusores,' often at Christmas (courtesy of John Wasson; see also his 'Folk Drama in Devon,' ISSMT conference [1980], p 2).

1532-1637
364 Visiting players and interluders, including players in the church 1548-9p (*Reprint of the Barnstaple Records*, ed J.R. Chanter and T. Wainwright [1900], II, 98, 105, 117-18, 143, 155-7; Murray, II, 197-200; *Halliwell-Phillipps*, p 142; and courtesy of John Wasson).

BASSINGBOURN (Cambridgeshire)

1511 20 July p
365 On St Margaret's day, the play 'off the holy martir seynt georg,' with garments, properties, playbooks (one of which a priest bore), three 'Fawchones' and four 'tormentoures axes,' a dragon, and a croft to play in (Cox, pp 270-4).

BATH (Somerset, now Avon)

1481-2 p
366 'le playeres,' with 'ludi,' evidently in the churchyard (cf references to a John Somerkyng 1435-41, and to the 'Regi attumnali' 1484-95; Charles B. Pearson, 'Some Account of Ancient Churchwarden Accounts of St. Michael's, Bath,' *TRHS*, 7 [1878], 314-15; 'The Churchwardens Accounts of the Church & Parish of S. Michael without the North Gate, Bath, 1349-1575,' ed C.B. Pearson, *PSomANHS*, NS 3-6 [1877-80], viii, xv, 46, 51, 83-4, 87-8, 90-2 [consecutively paginated]).

BATH AND WELLS, diocese of

1258? r
367 Statutes of Bishop William of Bitton I require that priests denounce in their churches any who make 'inhonestos ludos' in churchyards (*Councils & Synods*, p 601).

BATTENHALL (Worcester, now Hereford and Worcester)

1525-35
368 Visiting players; players of St Peter's (1535); and the Robin Hood and Little John of Ombersley (performing for Prior William More of Worcester ?at his manor here; *More*, pp 221-405).

BATTLE ABBEY (Sussex, now East Sussex)

1478-1522
369 Visiting actors and players (as with puppets), sometimes for Christmas and Epiphany (Allan Evans, 'Actors in the Account Rolls of Battle Abbey,' HLQ, 6 [1942], 103-5; *Halliwell-Phillipps*, p 101).

BEAMINSTER (Dorset)

1630 r
370 Blasphemous puppet 'shows and sights' (Murray, II, 206).

BELVOIR CASTLE (Leicestershire)

1530-1618
371 Visiting and household players and mummers; a play by fellows of an unidentified college for the earl in 1542, away from home; and masques (the household accounts of the earls of Rutland, at this his seat and elsewhere; *The Manuscripts of his Grace the Duke of Rutland, K.G. Preserved at Belvoir Castle*, IV [ed H.M. Lyte and W.H. Stevenson], HMC [1905], pp 270-514; Price, pp 136-7).

BERKELEY CASTLE (Gloucestershire)

1420-1
372 Disguisings and visiting 'ludentes' at Christmas (courtesy of Peter H. Greenfield; cf C.D. Ross, 'The Household Accounts of Elizabeth Berkeley, Countess of Warwick, 1420-1,' TBGAS, 70 [1951], 81-105).

BERMONDSEY (Surrey, now Greater London)

1444 August p
373 'a play ... of a knight cleped fflorence,' possibly 'Florice et Blanch-fleur' (probably with auspices at the abbey here; 'Bale's Chronicle,' p 117).

BETHERSDEN (Kent)

1519-21 p
374 The play of St Christina, on three playing days, with play-
wardens, rehearsal, riding with the banns, deviser (and his gear),
dressing chamber, and a timbered stage (*Churchwardens' Accounts at
Betrysden 1515-1573*, transcr Francis R. Mercer, Kent Recs., 5 [1928], pp
3-5, 9-12, 78-80).

BEVERLEY (Yorkshire, E.R., now Humberside)

ca 1220 p
375 'repraesentatio Dominicae resurrectionis' in St John's churchyard,
with both 'verbis et actu' by masked persons, 'larvatorum,' in summer,
at which one boy climbed into the triforium of the church (*The Historians of the Church of York and its Archbishops*, ed J. Raine, RS 71, I
[1879], pp 328-30; Axton, 'Modes,' pp 27-8, links this play with folk
'ludi'; possibly one form of the Anglo-Norman *La Seinte Resureccion*,
according to a correspondent, 'A Canterbury Manuscript,' *The Times*,
28 December 1937, pp 13-14; and Legge, p 322).

1377-1539
376 Corpus Christi pageants and play were presented by the crafts at
stations as directed by the town governors, and in 1423 Master Thomas Bynham, a Friar Preacher, composed banns to be proclaimed
throughout the town; there was also a Corpus Christi procession, and
the crafts erected and ornamented wooden viewing stands called
'castles' (*Beverley Town Documents*, ed Arthur F. Leach, Selden Society
14 [1900], pp 33-101; A.F. Leach, *Report on the Manuscripts of the Corporation of Beverley*, HMC [1900], pp 46-173; Nelson, pp 91-9; and
'Some English Plays and Players, 1220-1548,' *An English Miscellany
Presented to Dr. Furnivall*, ed W.P. Ker, A.S. Napier and W.W. Skeat
[1901], pp 218-19, gives a list ca 1520):
   1 / the falling of Lucifer (Tilers);
   2 / the making of the world (the creation; Saddlers);
   3 / the making of Adam and Eve (Paradise; in 1391, by the Hairers
[in particular, by one John of Arras], with one car, two visors, two
angels' wings, a worm, shirts, sword, linen boots, and other materials
[p 66]; Walkers);

4 / the breaking of God's commandments (Ropers);

5 / graving and spinning (Creelers);

6 / Cain (Glovers);

7 / Adam and Seth (Shearmen);

8 / Noah's ship (Watermen);

9 / Abraham and Isaac (Bowyers and Fletchers);

10 / the salutation of Our Lady (Mustardmakers and Chandlers);

11 / Bethlehem (Husbandmen);

12 / the shepherds (Vintners);

13 / the three kings of Cologne (Goldsmiths; in 1455, also by the Painters, Masons, and Glaziers);

14 / Simeon (Fishers);

15 / the fleeing to Egypt (Coopers);

16 / the children of Israel (Shoemakers);

17 / the disputation in the temple (Scriveners);

18 / St John Baptist (Barbers);

19 / the pinnacle (Laborers);

20 / the raising of Lazarus (Milners);

21 / Jerusalem (Skinners);

22 / the maundy (Bakers);

23 / the praying at the mount (Litsters);

24 / sleeping Pilate (Tailors);

25 / black Herod (Merchants);

26 / deeming Pilate (in 1520 the pageant was not covered with 'vestibus honestis' [p 172]; Drapers);

27 / the scourging (Butchers);

28 / the 'Stedynynge' or crucifixion (Cutlers and Potters);

29 / the stanging (Weavers);

30 / the taking off the cross (Barkers);

31 / the harrowing of Hell (the redemption of Adam and Eve; Cooks);

32 / the resurrection (Wrights);

33 / the castle of Emmaus (Gentlemen);

34 / the ascension (Smiths);

35 / the coronation of Our Lady (Priests); and

36 / doomsday (Merchants).

1389 r
377 Procession of the Guild of St Elene on her feast day with a fair youth dressed as St Elene and two old men representing the finding of

the cross; and the Guild of St Mary has a 'pageant Virgin with her son, and Joseph and Simeon' and two angels, all costumed guild members, going in procession on 2 February to the church where the Virgin offers her son to Simeon at the high altar (Westlake, p 233; Smith, pp 148-9).

1441 r, 1467 r
378 Pater Noster 'ludus' or play, with pageants of eight 'lusores,' 'Viciouse' (by the gentry), Envy, Pride, Sloth, Gluttony, Anger, Avarice, Lechery, performed at eight stations (each by a large group of crafts; Leach, *Report*, pp 128-9, 142-3; Nelson, pp 97-8).

1445-1573
379 Men of Long Riston and Cottingham with proclamations of their 'ludi' in the market place in 1445-6; and visiting players in 1541-73 (Nelson, pp 98, 233-4; Leach, *Report*, pp 175-82).

1537 25 January r
379.5 John Fraunces, a town baker, deposes that about a week ago two townsmen tried to persuade him to accompany them and 'other good fellows "as it were a mumming"' (ie in masks?) to the house of one Catherall so as to 'beat and coil' a group of 'ancient men of the town' who were gathered there and with whom they had a quarrel over town privilege (*L. & P. Hen. VIII*, XII.i, no 201.viii, p 97; noted by Thomas Pettitt, 'Early English Traditional Drama: Approaches and Perspectives,' *RORD*, 25 [1982], 9, 24).

BEWDLEY (Worcestershire, now Hereford and Worcester)

1572 p
380 Queen's players in the church (J.R. Burton, *A History of Bewdley* [1883], pp xii-xxxv).

BICESTER PRIORY (Oxfordshire)

ca 1377-99
381 A 'magnus ludus' at a feast on a Sunday within the octave of Peter and Paul in early July (priory accounts; *The History of Bicester, Its Town and Priory*, comp J.C. Blomfield [1884; pt 2 of *Deanery of Bicester*,

8 pts (1882-94)], p 161; cf p 166 for a payment to a player in 1408-9; courtesy of T. De Welles).

1432-51
382 Payments to players for an interlude on Christmas night 1432, in St Eadburga's feast 15? June 1433, at Christmas 1439, on St John Evangelist's feast 27 December 1446, and at Christmas 1451 (priory accounts; *History of Bicester*, pp 178, 181, 183, 186-7; these accounts are misdated here by one year; courtesy of T. De Welles).

BILLERICAY (Essex)

1579 p
383 Play in the chapel (churchwardens from Great Burstead were involved; Coldewey, 'Demise,' p 248; *Antiquary*, p 205).

BISHOP'S STORTFORD (Hertfordshire)

1490?-1541
384 Parish plays (irregularly, in ?1490, 1491, 1504 [of Braughing, Herts.], 1510, 1523, and 1541 [of Stanstead, Herts.]: *The Records of St. Michael's Parish Church, Bishop's Stortford*, ed J.L. Glasscock [1882], pp 21-43).

BISHOPSTOKE (Hampshire)

1551 ca 18 December r
385 Henry Brabon, in the house of a relation the week before Christmas, dressed down one of the servants as a heretic and knave for beginning to study a part in the 'Comedie' *Three Laws*, and required the servant to tell its 'compiler,' John Bale, the rector, that he was one too (John Bale, *An Expostulation or Complaynte agaynste the Blasphemyes of a Franticke Papyst of Hamshyre* [1552?], sigs C2v-C3r; STC 1294; Davies, p 221; text of *The Three Laws*, written 1538, in *The Dramatic Writings of John Bale*, ed John S. Farmer, EED [1907], pp 1-82; TFT 23; Greg 24; STC 1287-8 [publ 1548?]; Stratman 5398-406; Houle 49).

BODMIN (Cornwall)

1469-72 p
386 Receipt from the player in the church hay William Mason and his fellows ('Receipts and Expenses in the Building of Bodmin Church,

A.D. 1469 to 1472,' ed John J. Wilkinson, *The Camden Miscellany, Volume the Seventh*, CS NS 14 [1875], p 11).

1539 r, 1566 r
387 Church inventories listing coats for Jesus (two in 1539, three in 1566), tormentors (four in 1539, three in 1566), and devils (two in 1566; H.M. Whitley, 'The Church Goods of Cornwall at the Time of the Reformation,' *JRIC*, 7 [1881-3], 121-2).

BOSTON (Lincolnshire)

1288 July p
388 Tournament at St Botulph's market with participants who disguised either as monks or as regular canons (*The Chronicle of Walter of Guisborough*, ed Harry Rothwell, CS 3rd ser, 89 [1957], pp 224-5, and cf pp 217-18; Knighton, I, 280-1).

1518-46
389 Bailiffs' accounts of the Guild of the Blessed Virgin Mary record the carriage of Noah's ship by eight men at Pentecost and at Corpus Christi in 1518-19, and mention pageant materials in 1538-9; and a Common Council order of 11 June 1546 requires the pageants not to process that year (Kahrl, pp 3-4; A.F. Leach, 'Schools,' *The Victoria History of the County of Lincoln*, II, ed William Page [1906], p 454).

1525-6 r
390 The Guild of the Blessed Virgin Mary rewards visiting 'lusores' and pays for crowns for the town waits when Nicholas Feild's daughter is 'queen' (Kahrl, p 4; and 'A Boston Guild Account,' Lincolnshire Archives Office, *Archivist's Report*, 16 [1964-5], 42).

1579 17 February r
391 The 'play of the passion' of Christ is licensed to be played at the hall garth at Easter or Pentecost (Borough of Boston, Council Minutes, I, fol 185r; cf R.B. Walker, 'Reformation and Reaction in the County of Lincoln, 1547-1558,' *AASRP*, NS 9, pt 1 [1961], 52; also performed in 1587 according to Pishey Thompson, *The History and Antiquities of Boston* [1856], p 211, but the History of Boston project transcript of the minutes for 1587 does not refer to any play).

BOUGHTON STREET (Kent)

1535 p
392 Corpus Christi play on Whitsunday and at least one other play-
day (notes in churchwardens' accounts; John S. Burn, *Registrum Ecclesiae Parochialis* [1829], pp 8, 236).

BOXFORD (Suffolk)

1529-35
393 Stoke play 1529-34; and a local play in 1535 by a 'propyrte pleyer'
and players 'which cam owt of strange placys' (to raise money for
rebuilding the church steeple; Galloway-Wasson, pp 135-8; see also
G.E. Corrie, 'On the Parish Accounts of Boxford in Suffolk from A.D.
1529 to 1596,' *Antiquarian Communications*, CAS 1 [1859], 266, for the
1535 entry).

BRAINTREE (Essex)

1523 p
394 Play of St Swithin in the church (W.A. Mepham, 'Mediaeval Plays
in the 16th Century at Heybridge and Braintree,' *EssR*, 55 [1946],
14-16; Coldewey, p 226).

1525 2 July p
395 Play of St Andrew in the church (Mepham; Coldewey)

1534 p
396 Play of 'Placy Dacy als St Ewe Stacy,' ie Placidus or St Eustace, to
raise funds for church building (Mepham; Coldewey).

1567-79
397 Plays; playbook; and leasing of players' apparel (Mepham;
Coldewey, pp 226-7).

BRANDSBY (Yorkshire, N.R., now North Yorkshire)

1615 p
398 The play of Robin Hood and the sheriff, acted by local recusants
(Aveling, p 289).

BRAUNTON (Devon)

1561-4
399 Robin Hood and Little John, and their coats (Wasson, p 67; date courtesy of John Wasson).

BRAY (Berkshire)

1623 r
400 Garments for Maid Marian, morris dancers, and a fool in the church (Charles Kerry, *The History and Antiquities of the Hundred of Bray* [1861], p 30; courtesy of A.F. Johnston).

BRIDGNORTH (Shropshire)

ca 1300 r
400.5 Men 'de terra domini R. de Mortuo Mari' came to the town 'ad quandam carolam causa ludendi' (PRO Miscellaneous Inquisitions C. 145/67/20, as cited by R.E. Latham, *Dictionary of Medieval Latin from British Sources*, fascicle II C [1981], p 285, sv 'carola, -us,' 3, where it is glossed 'playground, (?) dancing ring').

1550-1604
401 Visiting players (H.C.M. Lyte, 'The Manuscripts of the Corporation of Bridgnorth,' *10th Report*, HMC, App, pt 4 [1885], pp 431-2).

1588 p
402 Persons playing Robin Hood (Lyte, p 431).

BRISTOL (Gloucestershire, now Avon)

1256 16 July r
403 One John Knoyl was drowned by misadventure 'in playing' in the Avon River with others before the king, who was in the town at the time of 'the said play' (*Calendar of the Patent Rolls* [Henry III], IV, for 1257-8 [1908], p 488; courtesy of T. De Welles).

1348 r
404 Chaplain in a chantry in St Augustine's Abbey is not to 'frequent plays or unlawful games' (*Descriptive Catalogue of the Charters and Muniments ... at Berkeley Castle*, comp I.H. Jeayes [1892], pp 163-4).

1461 p
405 Pageants for the entry of Edward IV (text in 'The Receyvyng of Kyng Edward the iiijth at Brystowe,' *Political, Religious, and Love Poems*, ed F.J. Furnivall, EETS OS 15, 2nd edn [1903], p 5; Withington, I, 151-2; *IMEV* 3880):
　1 / William the Conqueror and four lords (with a four-line text), and a giant; and
　2 / St George on horseback, a king and a queen and his daughter, a dragon that is slain, and angels.

ca 1479-1508 r
406 St Catherine's players, rewarded for their 'playes' at the doors of the mayor and sheriff, and others every 24 November, St Katherine's eve; and a prohibition of disguised Christmas mummers (Robert Ricart, *The Maire of Bristowe is Kalendar*, ed Lucy T. Smith, CS NS 5 [1872], pp 80, 85).

1486 23-4 May p
407 Pageants at the entry of Henry VII (text in Leland, IV, 198-202; *IMEV* 2200.5, 2212.5, 3884.5):
　1 / King Bremmius (Brennius);
　2 / Prudentia;
　3 / Justicia;
　4 / 'The Shipwrights Pageannt,' without speeches; and
　5 / an elephant with a castle, in which was the Lord's resurrection.

1499-1558, 1644 r
408 Baker's Guild Corpus Christi pageant in procession (Alderman Fox, 'The History of the Guilds of Bristol,' *TBGAS*, 3 [1878-9], 91, 95-7; Robert E. Finnegan, 'Research in Progress: Gloucestershire and Bristol,' *REEDN*, 1977.1, pp 9-10).

1526 r
409 Hose for Robin Hood and Little John paid for by St Nicholas Church (John Taylor, 'St. Nicholas Crypt, Bristol,' *JBAA*, 31 [1875], 374).

1532-1635
410 Visiting players, at the guildhall ca 1535-57 and at 'St. Ausende' (?) in 1537 (*City Chamberlains' Accounts in the Sixteenth and Seventeenth*

Centuries, ed D.M. Livock, Bristol Record Society 24 [1966], pp 38-9;
Murray, II, 207-19; *Halliwell-Phillipps*, pp 107, 131, 142, 148).

1577-8 p
411 Lord Berkeley's players, whose 'matter was what mischief worketh
in the mynd of man'; and Lord Sheffield's players with 'the Court of
Comfort' (Murray, II, 214-15).

BROME (Suffolk)

ca 1454-99
412 'The Brome Play of *Abraham and Isaac*' (text ed Davis 1, pp 43-57;
facs edn, Davis 2, pp 47-65; auspices at Brome Hall, the manor of the
Cornwallis family, seem likely; Stratman 3328-78; *Manual* 16; Harvey-
Dietrich, p 409).

BROUGH-ON-HUMBER (Yorkshire, E.R., now Humberside)

ca 140-4 r
413 Marcus Ulpius Januarius, aedile of the village of Roman Petuaria,
presented a '[new] stage' for the theatre, at his own expense (R.G.
Collingwood and R.P. Wright, *The Roman Inscriptions of Britain*, I
[1965], no 707, p 237; and Wacher, *Towns*, pl 77, p 394; the town was
probably abandoned ca 370, according to J.S. Wacher, *Excavations at
Brough-on-Humber 1958-1961*, RRCSAL, 25 [1969], p 24).

BUNGAY (Suffolk)

1407-8 p
414 Town 'ludentes' (Bungay priory accounts; Galloway-Wasson,
p 140).

1444-5 p
415 The town wait, a minstrel, 'ad vnum interludum' at Christmas
(priory accounts; Galloway-Wasson, p 140).

1514 16 June r
416 A town bailiff and two others broke and threw down five
pageants that were carried about the town on Corpus Christi day:
'hevyn pagent, the pagent of all the world, Paradys pagent, Bethelem

pagent, & helle pagent' (Galloway-Wasson, pp 140-1; cf John R. Daniel-Tyssen, 'Corpus Christi Pageants at Bungay, 1514,' *The Eastern Counties Collectanea* [1872-3], p 272).

1526 r, 1543 p
417 Game book; and game on Corpus Christi day (Galloway-Wasson, pp 141-2; Gray. B. Baker, 'Extracts from Churchwardens' Books ... *Bungay St. Mary*,' *The East Anglian*, 1 [1864], 375; 2 [1866], 149).

1558-91
418 Interlude or game with game books, players' parts, game gear such as visors, 'heares,' and apparel (borrowed from Thomas Howard, earl of Surrey, and at Norwich in 1566, from Wymondham in 1568; made out of old copes by 1577); performed in Holy Trinity churchyard in 1566(-7?) with a scaffold and Kelsaye the vice's pastime before and after the play on both days, and in the Castle yard 'in the Boothes & elleswher' with a stage in 1568 (Galloway-Wasson, pp 143-6; cf Gray. B. Baker, 'Church Ale-games, and Interludes. *Bungay Holy Trinity*,' *The East Anglian*, 1 [1864], 291-2, 304, 334-6).

1570 r
419 Gloves for 'the wyttche' (a Plough Monday festivity? Galloway-Wasson, p 146).

BURNLEY (Lancashire)

1580 12 May r
420 Proposal to suppress the 'lewed pastymes' and 'dancinge' of 'Robyn hoode and the May games,' which caused 'the last yere sturres' here (*The Farington Papers*, ed Susan M. ffarington, cs 39 [1856], pp 128-30; courtesy of David George).

BURY ST EDMUNDS (Suffolk)

12th-13th centuries r
421 The abbey had a Plautus and Terence (Montague R. James, *On the Abbey of S. Edmund at Bury*, CAS Octavo Publs 28 [1895], pp 27, 103).

1197 r
422 Abbot Sampson prohibits 'spectacula' in the churchyard of St
Edmund's, after a disturbance at one during Christmas (*Chronica Joce-
lini de Brakelonda, de Rebus Gestis Samsonis Abbatis Monasterii Sancti
Edmundi*, ed Johanne G. Rokewode, CS 13 [1840], pp 68-9).

1389 r
423 The Guild of Corpus Christi in St Edmund's church, according to
the guild certificate, sponsored 'quoddam interludium de Corpore
Christi' (Karl Young, 'An *Interludium* for a Gild of Corpus Christi,'
MLN, 48 [1933], 84-6).

1477 r
424 Weavers' pageant of the Ascension of God, and of the gifts of the
Holy Ghost, among other pageants in the Corpus Christi procession
(William D. Macray, 'The Manuscripts of the Corporation of Bury St.
Edmunds,' *14th Report*, HMC, App 8 [1895], pp 133-8; cited as [West]
Suffolk R.O. B9/1/2 by Galloway-Wasson, p 147, n 2).

1506-31
425 'ludentes' in the prior's hall and chamber 1506-7, 1520-1; and
visiting 'lusores' 1530-1 (Galloway-Wasson, p 148; Macray, p 157).

1550 r
426 Statutes for the Free Grammar School of Edward VI state that the
'chaster plays of Plautus and Terence' will be taught in the third form
(*VCHSuffolk*, II, 314).

1558 r
427 Corpus Christi pageants are mentioned in a note of rents at this
time (Margaret Statham, 'The Guildhall, Bury St. Edmunds,'
PSufflANH, 31 [1970 for 1968-9], 145).

CAISTER, by Great Yarmouth (Norfolk)

1456-9 r
428 William Worcester, who has entered the service of Sir John Fastolf
as his secretary in 1436, seems to have acquired from Fastolf by 1456
from John Free, fellow of Balliol College, Oxford, Bodl. ms Auct. F.3.25
(summary catalogue no 2929), which includes Sophocles' *Ajax* and

Electra and Euripides' *Hecuba Orestes* and *Phoenissae* all in Greek (this ms belonged, at any rate, to Free [d 1465], Worcester [d ca 1480-3], and Fastolf [d 1459 at his castle here]; *Greek Manuscripts in the Bodleian Library,* intro R.W. Hunt [1966], p 34; Emden 1, II, 724-5, and III, 2086-7; *DNB,* VI, 1099-104).

CALNE (Wiltshire)

1551 r
429 Vice's coat ('Ancient Inventory of Calne Church Goods' [ed John N. Ladd], *WiltANHM,* 4 [1858], 208).

CAMBORNE (Cornwall)

ca 1495-1501
430 *The Life of Saint Meriasek* (that is, *Beunans Meriasek*), copied by one Rad[olphus]? Ton in 1504 (text: *The Life of Saint Meriasek, Bishop and Confessor,* ed W. Stokes [1872]; and *The Life of Meriasek: A Medieval Cornish Miracle Play,* trans Markham Harris [1977]; sometimes associated with Glasney; Stratman 3716-20).

1540 p, 1547 p
431 Plays noted in churchwardens' accounts (*The Medieval Cornish Drama,* ed Charles Thomas, Cornwall Archaeological Society, Special Bibliography no 3 [1969], p 6).

before 1700 r
432 'Plain an Gwarry' or playing place, at Race (Charles Thomas, 'Parochial Check-Lists of Antiquities. Hundred of Penwith, Eastern Division. 5: Parish of Camborne,' *CA,* 9 [1970], 141).

CAMBRIDGE (Cambridgeshire)

1344 r
433 Peterhouse College statutes require fellows to avoid theatrical spectacles and games in churches, ?market-places, and rings (*Early Cambridge University and College Statutes,* ed James Heywood [1855], p 34 [2nd pagination]; 'ludis theatralibus ludibriorum spectaculis publicis in Ecclesiis, theatro, vel Stadiis,' Boas, p 25; probably copied from Merton College statutes [James B. Mullinger, *The University of Cam-*

bridge, I (1873), pp 230-1; see also *Documents Relating to the University and Colleges of Cambridge* [1852], II, 31, 73).

1353 r
434 'ludo filiorum Israel,' of the Corpus Christi guild (*Cambridge Gild Records,* ed M. Bateson, CAS Publs, Octavo Ser, 39 [1903], p 51).

1386 r
435 Comedy with a pall or cloak, six visors, and six beards at the College of Michael-House (*HEP,* III, 302; untraced record, as noted in MS, II, 344; another Warton fabrication? see Boas, p 2, n 1).

1452 r
436 A library catalogue for King's College lists two volumes of Seneca's tragedies (Montague R. James, *A Descriptive Catalogue of the Manuscripts Other than Oriental in the Library of King's College, Cambridge* [1895], p 82).

1457-1504
437 'ludentes,' 'lusores,' and 'ludo' at King's Hall ('The Academic Drama at Cambridge: Extracts from College Records,' ed G.C.M. Smith, in *Collections Vol. II. Part II,* MalS [1923], p 151; for 'ludi' of 1507-9, see Alan B. Cobban, *The King's Hall within the University of Cambridge in the Later Middle Ages* [1969], pp 227-8).

1482-1564
438 Visiting 'lusores,' including some from local parishes; and plays and disguisings at King's College, often at Christmas, with a 'theatrum' made in 1552-3 and 1555-6 ('Academic Drama ... Extracts,' pp 151, 214-17; *Medwall,* pp 6, 8).

ca 1494-1502 r
439 Terence replaces Priscian on the university arts curriculum and has equal weight with Aristotle (M.B. Hackett, *The Original Statutes of Cambridge University* [1970], pp 68, 300-2; for records of the Terence lecturer, Gilbert Gefferay in 1505-7, and John Philip in 1508, see *Grace Book B,* ed Mary Bateson, I [1903], pp xix, 232; Bateson also says that Caius Auberinus, who lectured ca 1492-1503, had read Terence previously [pp xix, 44, 175, 185]; *Grace Book* γ, ed William G. Searle [1908], p 49).

1501-1615
440 Visiting players (at the guildhall in 1531 and 1548), paid largely from the town accounts (Charles H. Cooper, *Annals of Cambridge*, I-II [1842-3], I, 255-II, 145; and H.T. Riley, 'Downing College, Cambridge: The Bowtell Collection,' *3rd Report*, HMC [1872], pp 322-3).

1510-11 p, 1516-17 p
441 Comedies by Terence in King's Hall ('Academic Drama ... Extracts,' p 228).

1520-32 r
442 Thomas Arthur's (Artour) tragedies of *Microcosmus* and *Mundus Plumbeus* (G.C.M. Smith, *College Plays Performed in the University of Cambridge* [1923], p 50; *Index*, p 429; *Scriptorum*, I, 709-10).

1521 r
443 A private copy of Terence (F.J. Norton, 'The Library of Bryan Rowe, Vice-Provost of King's College (†1521),' *TCBS*, 2 [1954-8], 345, no 39).

1522-3 p
444 Comedy by Plautus at Queens' College, probably where Stephen Gardiner played Periplectomenus, Thomas Wriothesley Palaestrio, and William Paget Miliphippa ('Academic Drama ... Extracts,' pp 183, 229; John Leland's 'Encomia Illustrium Virorum,' in Leland, V, 117-18; *L. & P. Hen. VIII*, XX.ii, no 788, pp 376-7; Leicester Bradner, 'The First Cambridge Production of *Miles Gloriosus*,' *MLN*, 70 [1955], 400-3).

1531-68
445 Plays at Christ's College (with a fool in 1551-2, and a Latin play in 1553-4; 'Academic Drama ... Extracts,' pp 204-9).

1536 Christmas p
446 Aristophanes' *Plutus*, performed in Greek, at St John's College (Mullinger, *The University of Cambridge*, II [1884], p 73; Smith, p 51; John Strype, *The Life of the Learned Sir Thomas Smith*, new edn [1820], pp 10-14, says that this performance was used to exhibit the new pronunciation developed by Smith as reader in Greek [notably Euripides] from 1533).

ca 1536-9? r
447 Three dialogues by Robert Radcliffe, of Jesus College (ie earl of
Sussex? or his cousin Ralph, of that same college, the dramatist
schoolmaster at Hitchin?), for presentation to Henry VIII: 'A Governance of the Church,' 'Between the Poor Man and Fortune,' and 'Between Death and the Goer by the Way' (texts: *Ecclesia: A Dialogue by
Ravisius Textor Translated from the* Dialogi Aliquot *by His Contemporary
Radcliffe,* ed Hertha Schulze [1980]; the other two dialogues, also in
National Library of Wales Brogyntyn ms 24, are so far unpublished,
but see, for a brief notice, Alfred J. Horwood, 'The Manuscripts of J.R.
Ormsby-Gore, Esq., M.P., of Brogyntyn, Co. Salop.,' *2nd Report,* HMC
[1874], p 85, and Reginald L. Hine, *Hitchin Worthies* [1932], pp 37-42).

1536-44
448 *Absalom,* by Thomas Watson, probably written at St John's College
(text ed and trans J.H. Smith, *A Humanist's 'Trew Imitation': Thomas
Watson's 'Absalom,'* Illinois Studies in Lang. and Lit., 52 [1964]; and
Roger Ascham, *The Scholemaster 1570* [1967], fol 57; for the Elizabethan
poet, a different Thomas Watson who translated Sophocles' *Antigone,*
see *ES,* III, 506-7).

1536-1642
449 Plays and comedies at Queens' College, with a 'theatru*m*' made in
the hall at various times 1546-54 ('Academic Drama ... Extracts,' pp
183-94, 229).

1542-3 r
450 Roger Ascham writes Richard Brandesby that since John Cheke
became Regius Professor of Greek in 1540 and publicly read through
twice, without fee, authors like Sophocles and Euripides, those two
playwrights are now more familiar to the university than Plautus was
when Brandesby was here, and there are more copies of Isocrates than
of Terence (*Ascham,* I.i, xxxvii, 26; in *Toxophilus* [1545] Ascham again
mentions Creke's complete reading of Sophocles and Euripides, but
'privately in his chamber,' and in a letter to Cranmer in January 1545
Ascham regrets the loss of Cheke [to be tutor to Prince Edward in July
1544], and of his influence [as above], although Nicholas Carr succeeded Cheke and carried on such lectures [*Ascham,* II, 67-9; III,
315]).

1543 January-February p
451 Dialogue by Ravisius Textor, probably the comedy with 'miles gloriosus' (which may well be 'Thersites'); and acting of 'the Dialogue of the Weaver'; for both of which Master Perne was responsible at Queens' College ('Academic Drama ... Extracts,' p 184; Smith, p 51; *Annals*, V [1908], p 278; Boas, pp 20-1).

ca 1544
452 *Jephthah*, a play in Greek by John Christopherson (text ed and trans F.H. Fobes [1928]; and a Latin version, for which see Bodl. ms Tanner 466, fols 126-53, Bernard M. Wagner, 'The Tragedy of Iephte,' *TLS*, 26 December 1929, p 1097, and F.S. Boas, 'The Tragedy of Iephte,' *TLS*, 30 January 1930, p 78).

1545 March p
453 Thomas Kirchmayer's anti-catholic *Pammachius* at Christ's College (*Correspondence of Matthew Parker, D.D. Archbishop of Canterbury: 1535-75*, ed J. Bruce and T.T. Perowne, PS 49 [1853], pp 20-30; *APC*, I, 162).

1545 r
454 Henry VIII's statutes for St John's College require (1) the annual appointment of a Christmas lord, paid to prepare six dialogues 'aut festiva aut litteraria spectacula'; (2) comedies and tragedies to be acted between Epiphany and Lent; and (3) students to occupy their four short vacations with literary pursuits or the acting of dialogues, comedies, or tragedies (not in the statutes of 1530, or earlier; *Early Statutes of the College of St. John the Evangelist in the University of Cambridge*, ed J.E.B. Mayor [1859], pp 139, 249).

1545 r
455 The inventory of printer and bookseller Nicholas Pilgrim's books at his death includes printed books of Plautus, Terence, Aristophanes in Latin and in Greek, and Sophocles' tragedies (George J. Gray and William M. Palmer, *Abstracts from the Wills and Testamentary Documents of Printers, Binders, and Stationers of Cambridge, from 1504 to 1699* [1915], pp 14-16, 22, 24, 26).

ca 1546 p
456 Aristophanes' comedy *Pax*, in Greek, performed at Trinity College and set forth for the university by John Dee, 'with the performance of

the *Scarabaeus* [the beetle] his flying up to Jupiter's palace, with a man and his basket of victuals on her back: whereat was great wondring' (John, monk of Glastonbury, *Chronica sive Historia de Rebus Glastoniensibus*, ed Thomas Hearne [1726], II, 501-2 [John Dee's 'compendious rehearsal,' App 4]).

1546 r
457 Comedy of 'Laelia Modenas,' that is, a version of the Italian *Gl'Ingannati*, at Queens' College ('Academic Drama ... Extracts,' p 196; Wilson-Hunter, pp 113-14); a Queens' College statute of this year specifies penalties for students, fellows, and scholars who ignore college comedies or tragedies, expenses for which are defrayed from the common chest (Mullinger, *Cambridge*, II, 73, n 1; for the statutes of 1559, see *Documents Relating to the University and Colleges of Cambridge* [1852], III, 54).

ca 1546-62
458 Costumes for the following characters: Decons, Leno, knight, shipman, fool, Aulos, the Devil, Rusticus, Paupertatis, Jupiter or Jove, Death, devils, Egyptian, Jews, Mardochiens, Gnato, young men, Enolios, Dives, Harcutes, Phredia, two soldiers, parasite, Thraso's servant, the king, and a woman (Sandra Billington, 'Sixteenth-century Drama in St. John's College, Cambridge,' *RES*, NS 29 [1978], 1-10).

1546-1642
459 Plays and shows at Trinity College, often at Christmas; with a 'theatru*m*' in 1547-8 ('Academic Drama ... Extracts,' pp 153-74).

1547 2 February r
460 Coats and faces for devil and death at Queens' College ('Academic Drama ... Extracts,' p 195).

1548 January-February p
461 Plays of *Persa* by Plautus, *Adelphi* by Terence, and *Heli* (perhaps by Hieronymus Ziegler) at Queens' College ('Academic Drama ... Extracts,' p 186).

1549 February-March p
462 Plays of *Poenulus* by Plautus and *Hypocrisis* by W. Gnaphaeus at Queens' College ('Academic Drama ... Extracts,' pp 187, 196; *College Plays*, p 104).

1549 8 April r
463 Edward VI's statutes for the university, read out in the senate on 6
May, require the professor of Greek to teach authors including Euripides (*A Collection of Letters, Statutes, and Other Documents ... Illustrative
of the History of the University of Cambridge*, ed John Lamb [1838], p
125).

1549 2 July r
464 Royal injunctions for the university change the lecture on Terence
to one on rhetoric and rule out the 'dominus ludorum' at Christmas
(*Collection*, ed Lamb, pp 140, 143, and cf p 230 [a reference to 'the
terence schole dores,' 12 May 1557]; also *Visitations*, II, 208; Baldwin 1,
I, 217-18, indicates that young Prince Edward seems not to have been
taught Terence or Plautus).

1550 1 October r
465 Roger Ascham writes of the hall of St John's College, 'theatrali
more ornata' after Christmas (*Ascham*, I, 212).

1550-1 p
466 Play at Corpus Christi College ('Academic Drama ... Extracts,'
p 210).

ca 1550-65 r
467 Thomas Browne's tragedy 'Thebais' (Cooper, p 510).

1551-2
468 Play with 'caelum,' and a 'lusus' by John Mey, performed at
Queens' College; Mr Malham's play *Troas* (*Troades*, by Seneca?), and
Mr Rudde's play *Menechmus* (by Plautus?), recorded at Trinity College
('Academic Drama ... Extracts,' pp 155, 188, 197; Edwin W. Robbins,
'The Play of Theano,' MLN, 58 [1943], 417-22, suggests that Mey's play
dealt with Theano, queen of Icaria; cf below under ca 1553 and
1553-4).

ca 1551-4
469 *Gammer Gurton's Needle*, by Mr S., Mr of Art, probably William
Stevenson, and acted at Christ's College at one time; plays by Sir
Stephenson 1550-3 and Mr Stephenson 1553-60 were performed at
Christ's College (text ed H.F.B. Brett-Smith [1920]; TFT 48; Arber, I,
206 ['Dyccon of Bedlam']; Greg 67; STC 10137.2 seq, 23263; Dust-Wolf,

pp 113-16; 'Academic Drama ... Extracts,' pp 206-9; the attribution to Stevenson is made first by Henry Bradley, 'The Authorship of "Gammer Gurton's Needle,"' *The Athenaeum*, no 3693, 6 August 1898, p 204, and *Representative English Comedies*, ed Charles M. Gayley, I [1903], pp 197-204; for other attributions, see David E. Baker, *Biographia Dramatica*, ed Isaac Reed [1782], I, 434-5, and II, 132 [John Still, bishop of Bath and Wells]; Charles H. Ross, 'The Authorship of "Gammer Gurton's Needle,"' *Anglia*, 19 [1897], 297-318, *Marprelate*, pp 33, 140, 167, and Boas, pp 83-7 [John Bridges, dean of Salisbury]; and Charles W. Roberts, 'The Authorship of *Gammer Gurton's Needle*,' *PQ*, 19 [1940], 97-113 [Sebastian Westcott]).

1552 r
470 Every year at Trinity College comedies or tragedies, one Greek and the other Latin, are to be performed after Epiphany before the start of term (college statutes; Mullinger, *The University of Cambridge*, II, 620).

1552-3 r
471 A play or character, Seneca's? 'Hyppolitus,' is mentioned in King's College accounts (courtesy of Alan H. Nelson).

ca 1553 r
472 Costumes for the prologue, Apollo, Thraso, Hanno Poenus, angel, Venus, Theano, Mercury, poet, and fool, borrowed by John Mey, at Queens' College ('Academic Drama ... Extracts,' pp 195-8).

1553 p
473 Nicholas Robinson's comedy 'Strylius,' acted at Queens' College (Cooper, p 505; source untraced by Boas, p 22, n 1).

1553 p
474 Show played at Trinity College at Christmas called 'Anglia deformata and Anglia Restituta' ('Academic Drama ... Extracts,' pp 156-7).

1553-4 r
475 Plautus' comedy of 'Stichus,' and a tragedy by John Mey, at Queens' College ('Academic Drama ... Extracts,' pp 188-9).

1554-5 p
476 Play 'de crumena perdita,' exhibited by Matthew Hutton at Trinity College ('Academic Drama ... Extracts,' p 158).

1555-1605
477 Plays at St John's College ('Academic Drama ... Extracts,' pp 219-26).

1556-7 r
478 A Terence, a Plautus, and a (Greek) Aristophanes in the university library (J.C.T. Oakes and H.L. Pink, 'Three Sixteenth-Century Catalogues of the University Library,' TCBS, 1, iv [1952], 315, 323, 326, nos 11 [now CUL ms Ff.4.39], 105, 155).

1557 1 January p
479 A show at Trinity College court 'of the wynninge of an holde and takinge of prisoners,' with minstrelsy, guns, and squibs (John Mere's journal, in *Collection*, ed Lamb, p 196; also *Annals*, II, 111-12).

1557 6 January p
480 Plays at the Falcon and at the Saracen's Head (Mere's journal, in *Collection*, p 197; also *Annals*, II, 112; see PLATE 22).

1557 7 January p
481 Comedy of Plautus in Trinity College (Mere's journal, in *Collection*, p 198; also *Annals*, II, 112; Alan H. Nelson informs me that Mere names *Rudens* as the play).

1557 23 May p
482 The duke of Norfolk's players played 'in the [guild] hall' and at the Falcon (Mere's journal, in *Collection*, p 233).

ca 1557-69 r
483 A printed Terence in Corpus Christi College (John M. Fletcher and James K. McConica, 'A Sixteenth-Century Inventory of the Library of Corpus Christi College, Cambridge,' TCBS, 3 [1959-63], 198, no 115).

1559-60 p
484 Mr Penny's *Sapientia Solomonis* at Trinity College ('Academic Drama ... Extracts,' p 160).

1562-3 p
485 *John Baptist* and John Foxe's *Christus Triumphans* at Trinity College (Smith, pp 57-8; *Two Latin Comedies*, pp 34, 376; I.D. McFarlane, *Buchanan* [1981], thinks the former is not likely to be George

Buchanan's *Baptistes* [p 385]; the prompt book for this may be the copy of the 1556 edition at Harvard, for which see under OXFORD 1562).

1564 8 August p
486 Nicholas Udall's 'Ezechias' by King's College (Smith, p 59; cf under ETON COLLEGE 1537-9).

1566-7 p
487 *Jephthes* at Trinity College (Smith, p 60).

1570-5?
488 *Herodes* at Trinity Hall (Smith, p 61).

ca 1571 p?
489 *Misogonus* (text ed Lester E. Barber [1979], who attributes the original play to Anthony Rudd here, and a revision represented by the ms state [of 1577] to Laurentius Bariona, ie Laurence Johnson, schoolmaster at Kettering, Northants.; Stratman 6104-13; Houle 36; G.C. Moore Smith, '"Misogonus,"' *TLS*, 10 July 1930, p 576, suggests that Rudd did this play at his own college, Trinity).

CANTERBURY (Kent)

ca 80-ca 400 r
490 Roman theatre at Durovernum Cantiacorum, a gravel earthwork structure at first, rebuilt ca 210-20 into a formal vaulted masonry structure seating about 7000 persons and demolished by about ca 1100 (Sheppard Frere, 'The Roman Theatre at Canterbury,' *Britannia*, 1 [1970], 83-113 and figs 1-13; and his *Roman Canterbury: The City of Durovernum*, 3rd edn [1962], pp 11-12 and figs 10, 17; Wacher, *Towns*, pp 181-5, 192-3).

ca 1170-1331
491 Copies of Terence at Christ Church Priory (and several listed ca 1284-1331; James, pp 9, 55).

1348-9 p
492 Royal 'hastiludia' or jousts for Edward III with visored men and ladies (the latter masked, at least, on entering the city; Nicolas, pp 29-30, 42, 116, 118, 122).

1444 p
493 Treasurers' accounts reward the town players on Good Friday
(C.E. Woodruff and W. Danks, *Memorials of the Cathedral & Priory of Christ in Canterbury* [1912], p 262).

1445-9 p
494 Obedientiaries' accounts have payments for a Christmas interlude; and visiting 'lusores' and 'ludentes,' before the prior (C.E. Woodruff, 'Notes on the Inner Life and Domestic Economy of the Priory of Christ Church, Canterbury, in the Fifteenth Century,' *Arch. Cant.*, 53 [1941], 7).

1451 p
495 Players of Canterbury, and visiting players, at the priory (R.A.L. Smith, *Canterbury Cathedral Priory: A Study in Monastic Administration* [1943], p 199; cf pp 32, 50).

ca 1472-94 r
496 William Tilley of Selling, prior of Christ Church, probably owned Corpus Christi College Cambridge ms 403, a 15th-century Euripides, and obtained it from the Continent (Montague R. James, *The Sources of Archbishop Parker's Collections of Manuscripts*, CAS 32 [1899], p 9).

ca 1490-1520 r
497 A book of Abraham and Isaac, belonging to the 'Schaft,' the religious guild, in the choir chest (J.M. Cowper, 'Accounts of the Church-wardens of St. Dunstan's, Canterbury, A.D. 1484-1580,' *Arch. Cant.*, 17 [1887], 80, 146-8; other books or legends, as of Corpus Christi, St Anne, Halloween, etc, for which see V.S.D. [John B. Bunce], 'Church Goods of St. Dunstan's, Canterbury, 1500,' *Gentleman's Magazine*, 162 [1837], 569-71, have been accepted as playbooks by Cowper, p 147, and 16 [1886], 298, and *MS*, II, 344).

ca 1491-7 r
498 Seneca's tragedies, and all six extant plays by Terence, are books in St Augustine's Priory (James, pp 305, 345, 367).

1494 r
499 Crafts are to support, as of old time, the then neglected Corpus Christi play (date possibly as late as 1504; J.B. Sheppard, 'The Records of the City of Canterbury,' *9th Report*, I, HMC [1883], p 174).

1501-2 p
500 A play of the three kings of Cologne and of their henchmen, with three beasts, a 'castle,' scaffolds, and a star (for a banquet in the guild-hall? Dawson, pp 189-90).

1504-55
501 The pageant of St Thomas Martyr, with children playing knights in harness, a painted head and gloves for St Thomas, an angel moved by a vice, a leather bag for blood, and a cart borne by two or three men (which was renewed with wheels in 1520-1), was repressed after 1538, made a play with a stage and four tormentors in 1542-3, and briefly revived in 1554-5 (J.B. Sheppard, 'The Canterbury Marching Watch with its Pageant of St. Thomas,' *Arch. Cant.*, 12 [1878], 27-46; Dawson, pp 191-8; Murray, II, 222, n 7; for the 1532 watch, see Peter Clark, *English Provincial Society from the Reformation to the Revolution* [1977], pp 416-17, n 16; for the old pageant wagon in 1563-4, see Sheppard, 'Records,' p 156).

1519-20 r
502 The wardens of the Grocers' pageant paid for torches burned about it (*Churchwardens' Accounts of the Parish of St. Andrew*, ed Charles Cotton [1916], p 41).

1520-1641
503 Visiting players, in the court hall ca 1542-9 and the 'Cheker' in 1546-7 (Dawson, pp 8-21; *Halliwell-Phillipps*, p 134).

1526 r
504 Civic orders concerning the waits, notably their playing at May games (Civis, 'Minutes, Collected from the Ancient Records and Accounts ... of Canterbury,' *Kentish Gazette* [ca 1800-2], no XXI).

1538 September p
505 John Bale's company acted before Thomas Cromwell at St Stephen's (*L. & P. Hen. VIII*, XIV.ii [1895], no 782, p 337).

1539 2 January p
506 An interlude about King John and putting down the Pope and St Thomas martyr acted by John Bale's company (John Bale's *King Johan*, the A-text, ca 1538, ed Barry B. Adams [1969] with B-text alterations ca 1547-60; facs ed W. Bang, *Bales Kynge Johan nach der Handschrift in der*

Chatsworth Collection, MKAED 25 [1909]; *L. & P. Hen. VIII*, XIV.ii, no 782, p 339; *Miscellaneous Writings and Letters of Thomas Cranmer*, ed J.E. Cox, PS 24 [1846], pp 387-8; Stratman 5364-89; Houle 22; see PLATE 21).

1541 r
507 Statutes for Canterbury Cathedral grammar school specify the teaching of Terence's comedies in the third form (Leach, p 467).

1557 June-August r
508 Arrest of players at the order of the mayor, the sending of 'their lewde playe booke' and examinations to the Privy Council, which then instructs the city to proceed against them (*APC*, VI, 110, 148-9).

1560 May r
509 A man preferring to 'go to Romney where there is a good play' quarrels about a play (with a friar or priest) by John Bale in the house of alderman George May; and about this time Bale accuses conservative citizens of mocking Protestant preachers with May games (Leslie P. Fairfield, *John Bale: Mythmaker for the English Reformation* [1976], pp 145-7; and Peter Clark, 'Josias Nicholls and Religious Radicalism, 1553-1639,' *The Journal of Ecclesiastical History*, 28 [1977], 134-5).

1563 p
510 The town and cathedral organized anti-catholic plays (Clark, 'Josias Nicholls,' p 135).

1576-7 r
511 One who was dressed in 'the devylls clothes' whipped a man and a woman (are these old play garments? Sheppard, 'Records,' p 157).

1639 p
512 One person that had 'a shew of the Creation' (Murray, II, 234).

CANTERBURY, diocese of

1213-14 r
513 Archbishop Stephen Langton's statutes prohibit 'inhonesti ludi qui ad lasciviam invitent' in churchyards and churches, and forbid clergy visiting 'spectaculis' (*Councils & Synods*, pp 26, 35).

1295-1313
514 The so-called statutes of Archbishop Robert Winchelsey forbid priests frequenting 'spectacula' and 'ludos noxios vel prohibitos,' and prohibit 'ludi' in the church or churchyard (*Councils & Synods*, pp 1384, 1388).

CARLISLE (Cumberland, now Cumbria)

1345 31 July p
515 An affray between Edmund Walays, servant of John Kirkby, bishop of Carlisle, and Walter Cole, a servant of lord Petre, when the clerks made a 'ludum' or 'miraculum' on a sunday, the eve of St Peter ad vincula, in the market place (PRO C49/46/16 [8, 10], two depositions; courtesy of Audrey Douglas and A.F. Johnston).

CASTILLY (Cornwall)

ca 1275-1325 r
516 Henge remodelled as a 'Plain an Gwarry' or playing place for an audience of up to 2000 people (Charles Thomas, 'The Society's 1962 Excavations: The Henge at Castilly, Lanivet,' *CA*, 3 [1964], 3-14; Bakere, pp 26-7, doubts that this may not be instead a 'place of judicial assembly').

CASTLE HEDINGHAM (Essex)

1490-1 p
517 Visiting players, and a disguising and pageant, at Christmas at the seat of John de Vere, earl of Oxford, for which linen, canvas, and other disguising stuff were purchased at Bury and London (*Household Books*, pp 515-19; de Vere's accounts are here attributed mistakenly to Thomas, earl of Surrey: see M.J. Tucker, 'Household Accounts 1490-1491 of John de Vere, Earl of Oxford,' *EHR*, 75 [1960], 468-74).

CATTERICK (Yorkshire, N.R., now North Yorkshire)

1st-4th centuries? r
518 A Celtic type of face mask, probably made 'in the Nene Valley potteries, around modern Peterborough ... one of the largest centres of pot manufacture in Roman Britain, particularly in the fourth century,'

was found here at Roman Cataractonium, where there was also a small theatre (letter of 25 June 1982 from John Wacher; cf his *Towns,* pl 6, p 69; his *Roman Britain* [1978], pp 254-5; and *Britannia,* 3 [1972], 279-80; see PLATE 1).

CHAGFORD (Devon)

1513-39 r
519 Church 'pageants,' probably not dramatic, 1513-39; playing in 1544 (G. Wareing Ormerod, 'Historical Sketch of the Parish of Chagford,' *RTDevA,* 8 [1876], 74; see also *The Church Wardens' Accounts of St. Michael's Church, Chagford, 1480-1600,* transcr Francis M. Osborne [1979]).

1555-88
520 Robin Hood and his company; or hoodsmen (John Wasson, pp 67-8, and his 'Folk Drama in Devon,' ISSMT conference [1980], p 2).

CHELMSFORD (Essex)

1562-76
521 Four plays in 1562, probably from Midsummer day into August, using scaffolds and stages, a painted pageant carried by ten men, and bushes for the 'enclosinge of the pighetell,' having vices, prophets, devils (with flaps), and Aaron, and employing one Burles (the property player?) and his boy (possibly the first play had a vice [with coat, scalp, and dagger], hell, and the temple, and the last two plays had heaven, the temple, Christ [in a leather coat], and a giant); afterwards, costumes were used for other plays and rented out to neighbouring towns and itinerant troupes (W.A. Mepham, 'The Chelmsford Plays of the Sixteenth Century,' *EssR,* 56 [1947], 148-52, 171-8; Coldewey, pp 294-322; his 'The Digby Plays and the Chelmsford Records,' *RORD,* 18 [1975], 103-21, argues that the four plays of 1562 were, in order, 'The Conversion of St. Paul,' 'Herod's Killing of the Children,' and, in two parts, 'Mary Magdalene').

CHESHUNT (Hertfordshire)

ca 1548-50 r
522 Roger Ascham, schoolmaster to Princess Elizabeth chiefly here, writes Sturm, the Strassburg schoolmaster, that she used to read

Sophocles' tragedies with him (in the afternoons; *Ascham*, I.i, lxiii, 192).

CHESTER (Cheshire)

ca 70-350 r
523 Roman amphitheatre at Deva, for about 8000 persons (of timber until ca 100; F.H. Thompson, 'The Excavation of the Roman Amphitheatre at Chester,' *Arch*, 105 [1976], 127-239, with appendices by Nigel J. Sunter and O.J. Weaver).

1422-74 (-1521?)
524 Corpus Christi play, with perhaps eleven mainly New Testament pageants, including the flagellation of Christ and the crucifixion (1422r; *Chester*, ed Lawrence M. Clopper, REED 3 [1979], pp 6-25; generally his 'The History and Development of the Chester Cycle,' MP, 75 [1978], 219-46; and Nelson, pp 154-8).

1431 p
525 St George's 'playes' (*Chester*, p 8).

1489-1515
526 Play of the Assumption of Our Lady (before Prince Arthur 3 or 4 August 1499, at the abbey gate; performed three times in all; *Chester*, pp 20-1, 23-4, where one list attributes the subject to the town wives).

1498-1602
527 Midsummer show with pageants, players, and characters from guild cycle plays (eg, 'little' God, God, Simeon, Mary Magdalene, Judas, doctors, devils, Balaam and his ass), and later with giants, unicorn, dromedary, lynx, camel, ass, dragon, hobbyhorses, and naked boys (*Chester*, pp 21-206; Nelson, pp 165-8).

1515 p, 1577-8 p
528 Shepherds' play in St John's churchyard (see below under 1521-75; *Chester*, pp 23-4, 124).

before 1521-75
529 Whitsun plays were performed on wheeled carriages, following rehearsals (including a general one) by the crafts, and ridings of the

banns and the 'regenal' (final performance at Midsummer 1575; possibly the old Corpus Christi play? with many additional Old Testament pageants, as follows; *Chester*, pp 24-117, from the list of 1539-40, as played over three days, with the names of extant texts in parentheses from *The Chester Mystery Cycle*, ed R.M. Lumiansky and David Mills, EETS SS 3 [1974], for Huntington ms 2; *The Chester Mystery Cycle: A Facsimile of MS Bodley 175*, intro R.M. Lumiansky and David Mills, LeedsTMMDF I [1973]; *The Chester Plays*, ed Hermann Deimling and Dr Matthews, 2 vols, EETS ES, 62, 115 [1892, 1916 for 1914], for BL Harl. ms 2124; *The Chester Plays*, ed Thomas Wright, Shakespeare Society [1843, 1847], for BL Add. ms 10305; Stratman 3412-682; *Manual* 9; Harvey-Dietrich, pp 400-1; cf F.M. Salter, *Mediaeval Drama in Chester* [1955], and Nelson, pp 158-65):

1 / the falling of Lucifer (the fall of Lucifer; Barkers or Tanners);

2 / the creation of the world (Adam and Eve; Cain and Abel; Drapers and Hosiers);

3 / Noah and his ship (Noah's flood; Waterleaders and Drawers of Dee);

4 / Abraham and Isaac (Abraham, Lot, and Melchysedeck; Abraham and Isaac; Barbers, Wax Chandlers, and Surgeons);

5 / King Balaack and Balaam with Moses (Moses and the Law; Balaack and Balaam; Cappers, Wiredrawers, and Pinners);

6 / the nativity of Our Lord (the annunciation and the nativity; Wrights, Slaters, Tilers, Daubers, and Thatchers);

7 / the shepherds' offering (the shepherds; with records mentioning the angel's hymn, Joseph, the four shepherds' boys [Trowe, Hankyn, Harvey, and Tud], many foodstuffs, and a painted ox, ass, and magpie; Painters, Embroiderers, and Glaziers);

8 / King Herod and the mount victorial (the three kings; Vintners and Merchants);

9 / the three kings of Cologne (the offerings of the three kings; Mercers and Spicers);

10 / the slaying of the children of Israel by Herod (the slaughter of the innocents; Goldsmiths and Masons);

11 / the purification of Our Lady (the purification; Christ and the doctors; with records mentioning curtains, Joseph, crowned Mary, Dame Anne, angels, doctors, and Simeon, and the gilding of the faces of 'little' God and God; Blacksmiths, Furbishers, and Pewterers);

12 / the pinnacle with the woman of Canaan (the temptation; the woman taken in adultery; Butchers);

13 / the raising of Lazarus from death to life (the blind Chelidonian; the raising of Lazarus; Glovers and Parchment Makers);

14 / the coming of Christ to Jerusalem (?Christ at the house of Simon the leper; Christ and the money-lenders; Judas's plot; with records mentioning Mary Magdalene, Martha, Judas, six children of Israel, Caiaphas, Annas, two knights, the gilding of God's face, the painting of the jailors' faces [the torturers' 'heads'?], and playing gear such as coats and gloves; Corvisers);

15 / Christ's maundy where he sat with his apostles (the last supper; the betrayal of Christ; Bakers and Milners);

16 / the scourging of Christ (the trial and flagellation; with records mentioning Annas, the tormentors, Herod's visor, and clothes for him and Pilate; Fletchers, Bowyers, Coopers, Stringers, and Turners; for another text, see 'The "Trial and Flagellation": A New Manuscript,' ed F.M. Salter, in *The Trial & Flagellation with Other Studies in the Chester Cycle*, ed W.W. Greg, MalS [1935], pp 1-73);

17 / the crucifying of Christ (the passion; Ironmongers and Ropers);

18 / the harrowing of hell (the harrowing of hell; Cooks, Tapsters, Hostilers, and Innkeepers);

19 / the resurrection (the resurrection; Skinners, Cardmakers, Hatters, Pointers, and Girdlers; for another, fragmentary text, see 'The Manchester Fragment of the "Resurrection,"' ed W.W. Greg, in *Trial*, pp 85-100);

20 / the castle of Emmaus and the apostles (Christ on the road to Emmaus; doubting Thomas; Saddlers and Fusters);

21 / the ascension of Christ (the ascension; Tailors);

22 / Whitsunday, the making of the creed (Pentecost; Fishmongers or ?Fleshmongers);

23 / prophets before the day of doom (the prophets of Antichrist; Clothworkers or Shearmen);

24 / Antichrist (Antichrist; Dyers and Bellfounders); and

25 / doomsday (the last judgment; Websters and Walkers).

1529 p, 1531 r
530 Play of Robert of Sicily, performed at the High Cross in 1529 (*Chester*, pp 26, 484).

1539-40 r
531 The colleges and priests are to bring forth a play on Corpus Christi with the mayor's assent (*Chester*, p 33).

1543-59
532 A prophet with gloves on Palm Sunday at Chester Cathedral (*Chester*, pp 45-62).

1552-1614
533 Trinity parish churchwardens' accounts record a Christmas ceremony with a star, a pully, and a cord (*Chester*, pp 52-284).

1555 r
534 Prohibition of disguised mummings at Christmas (*Chester*, p 56).

1588 p
535 A play called 'the storey of Kinge Ebrauk with all his sonne' (*Chester*, p 156).

1610 23 April p
536 Entry of Prince Henry with procession of St George, Peace, Plenty, Envy and Love (*Chester*, pp 258-60).

CHEVET (Yorkshire, W.R., now West Yorkshire)

1526 14 January p
537 A play, a masque, and a banquet at night for the marriage of Roger Rockley, and Elizabeth Nevill, daughter of Sir John Nevill (later sheriff of Yorkshire; J. Croft, *Excerpta Antiqua* [1797], pp 78-83).

CHICHESTER (Sussex)

ca 70-ca 195 r
538 Roman amphitheatre at Noviomagus Reg(i)norum (G.M. White, 'The Chichester Amphitheatre: Preliminary Excavations,' *AntiqJ*, 16 [1936], 149-59; Wacher, *Towns*, pp 247-8).

CHICHESTER, diocese of

1245-52 r
539 Statutes of Bishop Robert (Richard?) Wich prohibit 'inhonesti ludi qui ad lasciviam invitant' from churchyards (*Councils & Synods*, p 461).

1289 r
540 Statutes of Bishop Gilbert of St Leofard require clergy to stay away from 'illicitis spectaculis' (*Councils & Synods*, p 1083).

CHUDLEIGH (Devon)

1561 r
541 Coats for Robin Hood, Little John, the vice, and others (Wasson, p 67, his 'Folk Drama in Devon,' ISSMT conference [1980], p 2, and his 'Guide,' pp 64–5).

CIRENCESTER (Gloucestershire)

1st-5th centuries r
542 Roman amphitheatre, at first of timber, then of masonry, and finally reduced to a fort, at Corinium Dobunnorum (John S. Wacher, 'Cirencester 1962,' *Antiq J*, 43 [1963], 23-6, and 'Cirencester 1963,' *ibid*, 44 [1964], 17-18 and pl 20; P.D.C. Brown and Alan D. McWhirr, 'Cirencester, 1966,' *ibid*, 47 [1967], 185-8; and Wacher, *Towns*, pp 290-1, 299, 314-15).

2nd-4th centuries? r
542.5 Remains of foundation walls within the town are of a Roman theatre, with a probable diameter of 192 ft (P.D.C. Brown and Alan D. McWhirr, 'Cirencester, 1966,' *Antiq J*, 47 [1967], 194-5, fig 5, and pls XXXIII.a, XXXIV.b; their 'Cirencester, 1967-8. Eighth Interim Report. I. The Excavations,' *Antiq J*, 49 [1969], 235; and Alan McWhirr, 'The Roman Town Plan,' in *Studies in the Archaeology and History of Cirencester*, ed Alan McWhirr, BAR 30 [1976], p 11 and fig 1.1).

CLERKENWELL (Middlesex, now Greater London)

ca 1300-1 r
543 The constable of the vill, as a result of the petition of the prioress of Clerkenwell to the king, is instructed to prevent Londoners damaging priory property while attending their 'miracles et lutes' (ca 1300); a royal writ instructs the mayor and sheriffs of London (8 April 1301) to proclaim against 'luctas [wrestling] et alios ludos' at Clerkenwell because of the audience's trampling of the priory crops, hedges, and ditches (W.O. Hassall, 'Plays at Clerkenwell,' MLR, 33 [1938], 564-7;

the writ appears also in his *Cartulary of St. Mary Clerkenwell*, CS 3rd ser, 71 [1949], p 260).

1384 29 August p
544 A five-day 'ludum valde sumptuosum' by the clerks of London at Skinners Well (Malverne, p 47).

1385 12 August r
545 Proclamation by the mayor and aldermen prohibiting 'the performance of the play that customarily took place at Skynnereswelle or any other such play' ('ne nul jew entreludie nautre jewee') until news of the king's venture against Scotland (*Letter-Books*, H, p 272).

1390 after 24 August p
546 The London clerks' 'play of the Passion of our Lord and the Creation of the World' at Skinners Well after St Bartholomew's day (royal payment 11 July 1391; *Issues*, pp 244-5; performance dated 18 July for three days in all, before the king, queen, and nobles according to Stow, *Survey*, I, 15).

1391 18 July p
547 The London clerks' 'ludum satis curiosum' of the Old and New Testaments, performed over four days at Skinners Well (Malverne, p 259; over three days before the king, queen, and nobles according to Stow, *Survey*, I, 93).

1409 24-28 July p
548 A 'great play showing how God created Heaven and Earth out of nothing and how he created Adam and on to the Day of Judgment' before the king, prince, and nobility, who sat on a timber scaffold (J.H. Wylie, *History of England under Henry the Fourth*, IV [1898], p 213, from the royal wardrobe accounts; cf III [1896], p 246, and for the date, IV, 298; on four days, one Wednesday to Friday and the following Sunday, at Skinners Well or Clerkenwell, according to *Chronicle*, p 91; over eight days according to *Great Chronicle*, p 87, and Stow, *Survey*, I, 93, and II, 31, 171, which also attributes the play to the parish clerks; see also 'Gregory's Chronicle,' p 105).

1410-11 p
549 A 'gret pley from the begynnyng of the worlde' at Skinners Well, performed over seven days before the nobility (*Friars' Chronicle*, p 12).

COLCHESTER (Essex)

61 r
550 Tacitus refers to a city theatre here within the walls of Roman Camulodunum (*The Annals of Tacitus*, ed Henry Furneaux, 2nd edn, rev H.F. Pelham and C.D. Fisher, II [1907], XIV.32, p 274), and remains of mortar foundations of a later, post-Boudican theatre with a diameter of 71 metres exist (Philip Crummy, 'The Roman Theatre at Colchester,' *Britannia*, 13 [1982], 299–302 and figs 1–3; see also M.R. Hull, *Roman Colchester*, RRCSAL, 20 [1958], p 80; and Wacher, *Towns*, pp 106-9).

ca 100-ca 210 r
551 The largest known Roman theatre in Britain, at first of timber with raised rectangular wooden stage, was rebuilt with masonry, staircases, and a roofed stage ca 150 near a large temple and was demolished early in the third century, at what is now Gosbecks Farm outside the old city walls (Rosalind Dunnett, 'The Excavation of the Roman Theatre at Gosbecks,' *Britannia*, 2 [1971], 27-47, figs 1-5, describes this as being 'clearly a religious building'; Hull, *Colchester*, pp 267-9; D.R. Wilson, 'Roman Britain in 1967. I. Sites Explored,' *Journal of Roman Studies*, 48 [1968], 196-7; and Wacher, *Towns*, pp 112-13).

1490 2 May p
552 Parish display of 'monstraciones' and 'recordaciones' in aid of the church (musters and memorials? *The Red Paper Book of Colchester*, ed W.G. Benham [1902], p 109).

1527 r
553 Two persons fined for gathering corn 'for Seynt Martyns pley' (W.G. B[enham]., '"Seynt Martyns Pley" at Colchester,' *EssR*, 48 [1939], 83).

COVENTRY (Warwickshire, now West Midlands)

1392-1580
554 The Corpus Christi play, often after several rehearsals (occasionally with a clerk bearing the playbook or 'originall'), was played by the city guilds in ten pageants, some of them new in 1519, on movable pageant wagons (roofed, in some accounts), each pageant being performed several times, all under the supervision of the city council

(*Coventry*, ed R.W. Ingram, REED 4 [1981], pp 3-294, 334-5, 455-85; see also Ingram's '"To find the players and all that longeth therto": Notes on the Production of Medieval Drama in Coventry,' in *The Elizabethan Theatre* V, ed G.R. Hibbard [1975], pp 17-44; '"Pleyng geire accustumed belongyng & necessarie": Guild Records and Pageant Production at Coventry,' REED *Proc.*, pp 60-92; and 'The Coventry Pageant Waggon,' MET, 2 [1980], 3-14; Nelson, pp 142-53; Stratman 3739-811):

1 / the annunciation to the massacre of the innocents, by the Shearmen and Tailors (recorded from 1434; text in 'The Shearmen and Taylors' Pageant,' in *Two Coventry Corpus Christi Plays*, ed Hardin Craig, 2nd edn, EETS ES 87 [1957], pp 1-32; *Manual* 13; Harvey-Dietrich, pp 408-9);

2 / the presentation in the temple, and the dispute with the elders, by the Weavers (recorded from 1424; late guild accounts deal with Mary, Joseph, Simeon, his mitre, his clerk, Jesus' sleeves, hose, and head, the little child, Anne, angels, gloves, beards, and playbook; text, revised by Robert Crowe in 1535 from a partly-existing earlier version, in 'The Weavers' Pageant,' in *Two Coventry Corpus Christi Plays*, pp 33-71; *Manual* 13; Harvey-Dietrich, pp 408-9);

3 / the betrayal, trial, and crucifixion, by the Smiths (recorded from 1428; with God or Jesus [having leather coat, gilded wig, girdle, sudary, and gloves], Herod [on horse or brought in by four men, with gown, scepter, crest, and painted head], Malchus, Judas, Dycar the beadle, Pilate [with hat], Pilate's wife Dame Procula [or Percula], Pilate's son [with battle-axe and scepter], Caiphas, Annas, Peter [with gilded wig], four tormentors, two princes, two knights, the Demon, the cross, four scourges, a pillar, a falchion, and the 'originall'; with the Porter, by 1560; and with two damsels, the cock-crowing, and the hanging of Judas [by noose and hook], by 1573, and the gibbet of 'Jeȝie' in 1576; and various payments for hats, caps, wigs, hoods, mitres, coats, gloves, and beard);

4 / the descent from the cross, the resurrection, the harrowing of hell, and the meeting with the Maries, by the Cappers (recorded from 1534 [but they assumed the Cardmakers' and Saddlers' pageant, itself recorded from 1435]; with Pilate [having mall, club, head, gown, gloves, doublet, and balls], God and the Spirit of God [both having head and coat], the Mother of Death, four knights, Our Lady [crowned], two bishops [having mitres], two angels [wearing albs], Mary Magdalene [having coat and kirtle], two other Maries [having heads and coifs], the Demon [having head, mall, club, and coat], two stars, and painted hell mouth; with the Castle of Emmaus, by 1552; a Prologue or Preface,

three fools' heads, crosses for God and the Spirit of God, and Adam's spade and Eve's distaff, from 1567; and 'god and dede man,' by 1576);

5 / doomsday, by the Drapers (recorded from 1392; with two demons [with faces and hose], three white souls, three black souls, four angels [with wings], three patriarchs, God [with gloves], and hell-head, ca 1537-9; rewritten 1556-7? by Robert Crowe? with three worlds to be set on fire, a barrel for the earthquake, prologue, a pillar for the worlds, pulpits for angels, two worms of conscience, two spirits, hell mouth and a fire at it, diadems, 'playing of the protestac-yon,' and the pharisee [with hat]);

6 / the Whittawers' and Butchers' pageant (recorded from 1403; see also *Cal. Inq. Misc.*, VII [1968], no 245, pp 123-7 [courtesy of R.W. Ingram]; and *Calendar of the Close Rolls* [Henry IV], II, for 1402-5 [1929], p 290);

7 / the pageant of the Pinners, Tilers, and Wrights (recorded from 1435; about the taking down of Christ from the cross? see *Coventry*, p 543), taken over afterwards by the Coopers (recorded from 1547);

8 / the Girdlers' pageant (recorded from 1445? or 1495?);

9 / the Mercers' pageant (recorded from 1445? or 1526);

10 / the Tanners' pageant (recorded from 1506? or 1518); and

11 / the Painters' pageant (ca 1526-32? probably one of the above; see *Coventry*, pp xvii, 563-4).

1398 17 September r
555 Richard II had 'a sumpteous theatre and listes royall' prepared for the judicial combat of the dukes of Norfolk and Hereford then (Halle, 'Henry the fourthe,' fol 2v; see also Holinshed's account in *Coventry*, pp 3-5).

1416-1561, 1576-80
556 Hock Tuesday, a show of the defeat of the Danes by the citizens of Coventry (followed by the binding of the menfolk by the parish wives; also 1566r, 1591r; *Coventry*, pp 7, 215, 233, 271-6, ?332-5; Charles Phythian-Adams, 'Ceremony and the Citizen: The Communal Year at Coventry 1450-1550,' *Crisis and Order in English Towns 1500-1700*, ed Peter Clark and Paul Slack [1972], pp 66-7, 69; and see under KENIL-WORTH).

1456 14 September p
557 Pageants by John Wedurby of Leicester with speeches for the entry of Queen Margaret (text in *Coventry*, pp 29-35, 548-9; *IMEV* 2781):

1 / a tree of Jesse, with Isaiah and Jeremiah;
2 / St Edward and St John the Evangelist;
3 / the four cardinal virtues;
4 / angels;
5 / the nine conquerors or worthies in nine pageants (including Arthur, by the Smiths); and
6 / virgins, with St Margaret slaying the dragon.

1457 16 June p
558 Corpus Christi play performed before Queen Margaret at Little Park Street End, except for doomsday, which could not be played for lack of daylight (*Coventry*, p 37; Nelson, p 148).

1461 p
559 The entry of Edward IV, with the Smiths' pageant of Samson and his three knights (*Coventry*, p 40).

1474 28 April p
560 Pageants for the entry of Prince Edward, with speeches (text in *Coventry*, pp 53-5; Queen Elizabeth evidently accompanied him [p 56]; *IMEV* 3881):
1 / King Richard (II) and thirteen nobles;
2 / three patriarchs, with the twelve sons of Jacobus;
3 / St Edward, with ten estates;
4 / three prophets and the children of Israel;
5 / the three kings of Cologne with two armed knights; and
6 / a king and queen in a tower, and their daughter with a lamb who kneels before St George as he saves her from the dragon.

1485 2 June p
561 Richard III came to see the Corpus Christi plays (*Coventry*, p 66).

1487 29 June p
562 Henry VII came to see the plays on St Peter's day (*Coventry*, pp 67-8; McGee-Meagher, p 36).

1490-1 p
563 A play about St Catherine performed in the Little Park (*Coventry*, p 74).

1493 6 June p
564 Henry VII came to see the plays at Corpus Christi tide 'by the Grey Friers' and greatly commended them (*Coventry*, p 77).

1498 17 October p
565 Pageants for the entry of Prince Arthur, with speeches (text in
Coventry, pp 89-91; *IMEV* 1075, 2834):
   1 / the nine worthies, and King Arthur's speech;
   2 / the Queen of (or Dame) Fortune, and virgins, in the Barkers'
pageant;
   3 / angels; and
   4 / St George killing the dragon.

1505-6 p
566 Mumming or 'interludo' at [St Mary's] Priory (Mary D. Harris,
'The Manuscripts of Coventry,' *TBGAS*, 37 [1914], 187; *The Coventry Leet
Book*, ed M.D. Harris, EETS OS 134-5, 138, 146 [1907-13], pp li-lii, n 12;
Coventry, p xx).

1505 p
567 A play of St Christian in the Little Park (*Coventry*, p 100).

1511 p
568 Three pageants at the entry of Henry VIII and Catherine: the nine
orders of angels; 'beautifull Damsells'; and a 'goodly Stage Play'
(*Coventry*, p 107; McGee-Meagher, p 64).

1519 p
569 The king's players (paid by the Holy Trinity Guild; *Coventry*,
p 115).

ca 1520-2 r
570 The Pardoner in John Heywood's *The Four P.P.* describes his visit
to hell, where he met an old acquaintance, a devil who often played
the Devil in the Coventry Corpus Christi play (*Heywood*, p 53).

1525 2 February p
571 Players, and Robert Crowe's pageant or subtlety 'the Golden flecc,'
for the Cappers (*Coventry*, p 123).

1526 r
572 Story of a Warws. curate who, preaching on the twelve articles of
the creed, told his listeners, 'go your way to couentre / and there ye
shall se them all playd in corpus cristi playe' (*Mery Tales*, pp 96-100;
STC 23663-4).

1526 p
573 The Mercers' pageant was shown at the entry of 'the Lady Mary' (ie Princess Mary; *Coventry*, p 125).

1533-63
574 A giant and his wife, and pageants including a hart, in the Midsummer Watch (and on St Peter's eve until 1549; *Coventry*, pp 136-225, 474-81, 504; these two events are recorded as early as 1421 [pp 7-8]).

1539 17 January r
575 Mayor William Coton writes to Thomas Cromwell requesting him to direct letters to the Coventry council for reformation of the over-heavy public expenses of the city on such occasions as the commoners' plays and pageants at Corpus Christi (which contribute to the city's decay; *Coventry*, pp 148-9).

1539-46
576 Corpus Christi Guild procession with Mary (having gloves), SS Catherine and Margaret, Gabriel (bearing the lily and wearing coat and hose), ten apostles, James, Thomas, four burgesses, and eight virgins (*Coventry*, pp 152-74; the procession goes back at least to 1445 [pp 16-17]).

1553 20 November r
577 Players imprisoned in Coventry (for sedition? *APC*, IV, 368; C.R. Manning, 'State Papers, Relating to the Custody of the Princess Elizabeth at Woodstock, in 1554: Being Letters between Queen Mary and her Privy Council, and Sir Henry Bedingfield ...,' *NA*, 4 [1855], 201-2, 205-6; one of these players must have been John Careless, a weaver, who, although jailed in Coventry ca 1554-6, was released briefly to play in the pageant about the city [Foxe, VIII, 170]; cf *Coventry*, pp 207-8, 569-70, 592).

1566 17 August p
578 Pageants of the Tanners, Drapers, Smiths, and Weavers at the entry of Elizabeth I (*Coventry*, p 234).

1584 p
579 The 'new play of the Destruction of Ierusalem,' a tragedy by Mr Smythe of Oxford (John Smith of St John's College); with Simon, Phy-

nea, Justus, Ananus, Eliazar, the captain, Johannes, Merstyars, Jacobus, Hippenus, Jesus, Zacharias, Pristus, Zilla, Mathias, Esron, Niger, Solome, the children to Solome, the Chorus, and the Temple (*Coventry*, pp 303-9, 587; Thomas Fuller, *The Worthies of England*, ed John Freeman [1952], p 421, relates that Thomas Legge [see below, App ii, under 'Legg'] 'composed a tragedy of the destruction of Jerusalem' that 'some plagiary filched ... from him, just as it was to be acted').

1591 p
580 A civic play of the Destruction of Jerusalem, or the Conquest of the Danes, or the History of Edward IV (*Coventry*, pp 332-5).

1638-9? p
581 Players showing the creation of the world (*Coventry*, pp 442-3).

COVENTRY AND LICHFIELD, diocese of

1252 r
582 Articles of inquiry for the diocese ask about 'ludi' done on consecrated ground (*Annales Monastici*, I, 298).

COWICK (Yorkshire, W.R., now Humberside)

1323 7 January p
583 Payment of 40s. to four 'clers de Sneyth [Snaith, Yorks., W.R.] iuantz entreludies en la sale de Couwyk deuant le Roi et monsire Hugh de doun le Roi [Hugh le Despenser]' (J.C. Davies, 'The First Journal of Edward II's Chamber,' *EHR*, 30 [1915], 668-9, 678).

CRANOE (Leicestershire)

1576 July-August r
584 The rector, who suffered puppet plays in the church, agrees not to allow any further ones, 'by morrys daunce or otherwise' (*Lincoln Episcopal Registers in the Time of Thomas Cooper, S.T.P. Bishop of Lincoln A.D. 1571 to A.D. 1584*, ed C.W. Foster, LRS 2 [1912], pp 137-8).

CRONDALL (Hampshire)

1555-6 p
585 Morris players before the lady Marquess of Exeter (*The Early Churchwardens' Accounts of Hampshire*, ed John F. Williams [1913], p 119).

CROSCOMBE (Somerset)

1475-1526
586 Robin (or Robert) Hood and Little John, a 'king's' revel or sport (Hobhouse, pp 4-31, 38).

CROWLE (Worcestershire, now Hereford and Worcester)

1527-34
587 Visiting players; and the tenants of Cleeve Prior, playing with Robin Hood, Maid Marian, and others (with a reference to five pageants in 1533; at the manor of Prior William More of Worcester; *More*, pp 252-386).

CROXTON (near Thetford, Norfolk?)

ca 1461-1511 r
588 *The Play of the Sacrament* (text only; see Davis 1, pp lxx-lxxxv, 58-89; Bevington, pp 754-88; facs edn, Davis 2, pp 91-131; Stratman 3812-26; *Manual* 18; for the identification of the town, see Galloway-Wasson, pp 106, 111, under Thetford, 1506-7 and 1524-5 [payments to the Croxton guild], and John Wasson, 'Visiting Entertainers at the Cluniac Priory, Thetford 1497-1540,' *Albion*, 9 [1977], 132-3; Cecilia Cutts, 'The Croxton Play: An Anti-Lollard Piece,' MLQ, 5 [1944], 45-60, would date the play not long after 1461).

CUCKFIELD (Sussex)

1528 r
589 The free grammar school teaches the Eton curriculum, with Terence in the third form (*The Victoria History of the County of Sussex*, II, ed William Page [1907], pp 418-19).

CULWORTH (Northamptonshire)

ca 1531-47 r
590 The Torchmen's accounts in the churchwardens' book record income from hobby-horse 'pleyers' who in most years danced with painted clothes on the evening of New Year's day (Cawte, pp 18-21).

CUMBERWORTH (Lincolnshire)

1566 r
591 Players' coats, made from church vestments, have been cut in pieces (Edward Peacock, 'English Church Furniture, A.D. 1566,' *LN&Q*, 14 [1916-17], 112).

DARTMOUTH (Devon)

1494 p
592 Play in St Saviour's church on Easter Day (churchwardens' accounts; courtesy of John Wasson; cf Hugh R. Watkin, *Dartmouth*, I [1935], p 327).

1526-8 p
593 Payment to the king's players (Watkin, p 264).

1552-3 p
594 Players at church (courtesy of John Wasson).

DEPTFORD (Kent, now Greater London)

1550 19 June p
595 Edward VI watches the admiral of the navy, with various pinnances, attack with fireworks, and take, a castle with soldiers and its attendant galley on the Thames (*Literary Remains*, p 279).

DERBY (Derbyshire)

1572 p
596 Play of Holofernes by townsmen (recorded in BL Add ms 6705, fol 94r; also quoted by Collier, I, xxi).

DEREHAM (Norfolk)

ca 1519? r
597 May games (report of a lecture by Walter Rye; 'Life in "Merry England,"' *Norfolk and Norwich Notes and Queries*, 3rd ser [1904-5], 23).

DEVIZES (Wiltshire)

1556 r
598 Worm Cliff, the town's 'common playing place' (B.H. Cunnington, *Some Annals of the Borough of Devizes*, I [1925], pp 10, 15).

DITTON PARK, near Windsor (Buckinghamshire)

1520-1 p
599 Visiting players at this the household of Princess Mary (the royal household moved among a number of seats, of which this appears to be its winter base at this time; *L. & P. Hen. VIII*, III.ii, no 2585, p 1099).

1521-2 p
600 A Christmas lord of misrule, with interludes; and men playing the friar and the shipman, and a disguising of twelve men covered in straw (probably at Ditton; *L. & P. Hen. VIII*, III.ii, no 2585, pp 1099-100).

DONCASTER (Yorkshire, W.R., now South Yorkshire)

1540 p
601 The 'Fyssher Play' at Corpus Christi (Borough of Doncaster, *A Calendar to the Records of the Borough of Doncaster*, II [1900], p 73).

1575 p
602 Visiting players in the church (*Calendar*, IV, 54).

1582 r
603 Corpus Christi pageants of the Weavers, Walkers and Shearmen, and the Cordwainers or Shoemakers (*Calendar*, IV [1902], pp 36-7, 86).

1655 r
604 Corpus Christi pageant of Glovers and Skinners (*Calendar*, IV, 24).

DONINGTON ON BAIN (Lincolnshire)

1563-5 r?
605 A parish agreement to fine players not keeping to their times includes a revised cast-list for 16-17 parts in a play of a king, steward,

soldan, Holofernes, Duke, messengers, knights, herald, and young men, evidently undertaken to fund a dyke (Kahrl, pp 6-7).

DORCHESTER (Dorset)

1st-4th centuries r
606 Roman amphitheatre at Durnovaria, adapted from the site of a Neolithic henge at Maumbury Rings (*An Inventory of Historical Monuments in the County of Dorset*, II [1970], pt 3, pp 589-92; Wacher, *Towns*, pp 318-19; see PLATE 8).

DOVER (Kent)

1389 r
607 A Terence in Dover Priory (now BL Royal ms 15.A.12; James, pp 489, 523).

1443-4 p
608 Town accounts reward visiting men who came 'cum diuersis ludis' (William Boys, *Collections for an History of Sandwich in Kent* [1792], p 795).

1452-1641
609 Visiting 'ludentes' and players (as with puppets, of interludes, or with banns), in St Martin's church in 1477-8 and at the market place in 1551; also, plays at Christmas from 1452 to 1510 (Dawson, pp 23-53).

DOWNHAM (Cambridgeshire)

1410 1 January p
610 'Lusores' of Isleham playing before the prior of Ely at his palace here (Beadle, I, 142, cited from CUL Add ms 2953; see also below under ELY).

ca 1486-1500 r
611 Moral verse written in the side window of the palace, as 'pronounced' by John Alcock, bishop of Ely, during rebuilding here: 'To give to Players, and to sacrifice to Deviles, is all one' (Bentham [1817], pp 84-5; cf [1812], p 183).

DUNHEVED otherwise LAUNCESTON (Cornwall)

1521-2 p, 1531 p
612 Visiting players (Richard and Otho B. Peter, *The Histories of Launceston and Dunheved, in the County of Cornwall* [1885], p 177).

DUNMOW (Essex)

1527-42
613 Corpus Christi pageants and plays to 1542 (with playbook), made by one Parnell in 1527-8, and contributions towards which came from various towns, and playing garments from Chelmsford; and unspecified games, Mays, and plays (as of a Christmas lord, and by children at Christmas), with a fool, to 1551 (Andrew Clark, 'Great Dunmow Revels, 1526-1543,' *EssR*, 19 [1910], 194-8; W.A. Mepham, 'Mediaeval Drama in Essex: Dunmow,' *EssR*, 55 [1946], 57-65, 129-36; Coldewey, pp 235-60; and J.W. Robinson, 'Three Notes on the Medieval Theatre,' *TN*, 16 [1961], 61-2).

1532-6
614 Visiting players rewarded by the prior of (Little) Dunmow Priory (*L. & P. Hen. VIII*, VIII [1885], no 865, pp 338-40).

1545-6 p
615 Receipts of 'the [athletic?] games of the Bysshope of Seynte Andrewe'; and of the 'Eston' and Margaret Roding plays (Coldewey, pp 258-9; dated 1547 on p 44).

DUNSTABLE (Bedfordshire)

ca 1100-19
616 'ludum de Sancta Katerina [St Catherine], – quem "Miracula" vulgariter appellamus' by Geoffrey, later abbot of St Albans, probably intended for Henry I at his nearby palace at Kingsbury Regis (Geoffrey borrowed choir copes from St Albans' sacrist for the play, and they were accidentally destroyed when his house caught fire the night [after the play?]; *Gesta Abbatum*, I, 73; C.B.C. Thomas, 'The Miracle Play at Dunstable,' *MLN*, 32 [1917], 337-44).

1530 r
617 Puppet play (?) at Christmas (*Visitations in the Diocese of Lincoln 1517-1531*, II, ed A.H. Thompson, LRS 35 [1944], pp 7-8).

DUNS TEW (Oxfordshire)

1584 September-October p
618 An interlude played in the church on a Saturday evening after service (*The Archdeacon's Court: Liber Actorum, 1584*, vol I, ed E.R. Brinkworth, Oxfordshire Rec. Society, 23 [1942 for 1941], pp 124-5).

DURHAM (Durham)

12th century r
619 Two manuscripts of Terence, one with glosses, in Durham Cathedral; one survives in catalogues of 1391 and 1416 (*Catalogi Veteres Librorum Ecclesiae Cathedralis Dunelm*, ed B.B., SS 7 [1839], pp 4, 9, 32, 109).

ca 1149-54
620 'Rithmus Laurentii de Christo et eius Discipulis,' a Latin 'peregrinus' ?dramatic dialogue by Laurentius, prior of Durham (text: Udo Kindermann, 'Das Emmausgedicht des Laurentius von Durham,' *Mittellateinisches Jahrbuch*, 5 [1968], 79-100; Lipphardt, V, 1615-33, nos 809-10; for other works by Laurentius, who was chanter here before he became prior, see *Dialogi Laurentii Dunelmensis Monachi ac Prioris*, ed James Raine, SS 70 [1880]; and A. Hoste, 'A Survey of the Unedited Work of Laurence of Durham with an Edition of his Letter to Aelred of Rievaulx,' *Sacris Erudiri*, 11 [1960], 249-65).

1403-1532
621 Corpus Christi procession and play, 'of old time,' with individual plays by at least the following guilds, probably performed on Palace Green (M.H. Dodds, 'The Northern Stage,' *AA*, 3rd ser, 11 [1914], 37; C.E. Whiting, 'The Durham Trade Gilds,' *TAASDurN*, 9 [1939-43], 143-416; J.J. Anderson, 'The Durham Corpus Christi Play,' *REEDN*, 1981:2, pp 1-3; and for a late Tudor description of the procession by itself, see *Rites of Durham*, ed J.T. Fowler, SS 107 [1903], pp 107-8):

1 / Butchers and Fleshers (1403r; F.J.W. Harding, 'The Company of Butchers and Fleshers of Durham,' *TAASDurN*, 11 [1970 for 1958-65], 93-100; only a procession in 1520, according to Whiting, p 175);

2 / Weavers and Websters (1450r; Anderson, and cf Whiting, p 147);

3 / Cordwainers (1464r; Anderson; cf Dodds; not in Whiting);

4 / Barber-surgeons and Waxmakers (1468r; Whiting, pp 158, 408);

5 / Goldsmiths, Plumbers, Pewterers, Potters, Glaziers, and Painters (1532r; Whiting, pp 204, 397-8); and

6 / Smiths (18th-century references to 'pageant money,' probably surviving from a much earlier period; Whiting, pp 293, 415).

1417-18 p
622 'pueris ludentibus' before the prior on St Stephen's day (*Extracts from the Account Rolls of the Abbey of Durham*, III, ed Canon Fowler, SS 103 [1901], p 614).

1433-4 p
623 Visiting 'players' (probably minstrels; R.B. Dobson, *Durham Priory 1400-1450* [1973], p 105).

1484-94
624 John Shirwood, bishop of Durham (died 1494), owned printed copies of Terence, Seneca's tragedies, and Plautus (bought in Italy and later acquired at Shirwood's death by his successor Richard Fox; P.S. Allen, 'Bishop Shirwood of Durham and his Library,' *EHR*, 25 [1910], 455-6).

1532-3 p, 1539-40 p
625 Visiting players (*The Durham Household Book; or, The Accounts of the Bursar of the Monastery of Durham. From Pentecost 1530 to Pentecost 1534*, ed James Raine, SS 18 [1844], pp 143, 340 [with a payment of 1496 to Robert Walssch for 'two days playing']).

DURHAM, diocese of

ca 1241-9?
626 Among statutes for peculiars of the church of Durham is a prohibition of 'inhonesti ludi' in churchyards (as in the Salisbury diocesan statutes of 1217-19); and the statutes of Bishop Nicholas Farnham prohibit for Durham diocese any 'ludos' in consecrated places (*Councils & Synods*, pp 440, 432).

EASTHAMPSTEAD (Berkshire)

1502 16 October r
627 Payment was made here on this day for 'a disare that played the Sheppert' before Queen Elizabeth during her progress from Wales (she arrived from Ewelme, Oxon., after 13 October and left before 25 October; *The Privy Purse Expenses of Elizabeth of York ...*, ed Nicholas H. Nicolas [1830], p 53).

EAST HARLING (Norfolk)

1452 r
628 The 'original' of an interlude played at the church gate (Extraneus, 'Church Ales and Interludes,' *The East Anglian*, 1 [1864], 383; Galloway-Wasson, p 5).

1457-67 p, 1494 p
629 Visiting (game) players (Extraneus, 'Church Ales,' p 383; Galloway-Wasson, p 5 [except 1494]).

EASTON (Wiltshire)

1368 r
630 Canons of the Trinitarian priory, according to Robert Wyvil, bishop of Salisbury, rode out to games and plays (Edward Kite, 'Wiltshire Topography [1659-1843], with some Notes on the Late Sir Thomas Phillipps, and his Historical Collections for the County,' *Wiltshire Notes and Queries*, 6 [1908-10], 158-9).

EAST RETFORD (Nottinghamshire)

1499 18 August r
631 Bequest to a guild of a gilded and jewelled circlet for the image of the Virgin, for a 'ludo de Mankynd, et aliis ludis' (*Test. Ebor.*, IV, 164; Wenzel, pp 393-4).

ELTHAM (Kent, now Greater London)

1384-5 r
632 Gilbert Prince, painter of London, was paid for works undertaken for 'ludis regis' here and at Windsor on these two Christmases (7-8

Richard II; T.F. Tout, *Chapters in the Administrative History of Mediaeval England*, IV [1928], p 391, n 8).

1393 6 January p
633 London presented a mumming to Richard II (the Mercers supplying five mummers; Caroline M. Barron, 'The Quarrel of Richard II with London 1392-7,' *The Reign of Richard II*, ed F.R.H. Du Boulay and C.M. Barron [1971], p 195; with 'glorioso apparatu,' according to Malverne, p 278).

1400-1 p
634 A great mumming of twelve aldermen and their sons by men of London for Manuel II, emperor of Constantinople, at court during Christmas (*Chronicle*, p 87; D.M. Nicol, 'A Byzantine Emperor in England: Manuel II's Visit to London in 1400-1401,' *University of Birmingham Historical Journal*, 12 [1969], 215, n 32).

1415' 6 January r
635 Arrest of lollards planning to kill the king in a mumming at court here ('Gregory's Chronicle,' p 108).

1424 r
636 Lydgate's 'A Mumming at Eltham,' with Bacchus, Juno, and Ceres, a ballad by Lydgate before Henry VI and Queen Catherine his mother at Christmas (text in *Minor Poems*, II, 672-4; *IMEV* 458).

1426 p
637 The London players of Jack Travaill, and four boys of Thomas Beaufort, duke of Exeter, performing interludes, were at court here before Henry VI at Christmas (Wolffe, p 37).

1427 p
638 Payments to '*Jakke Travaill & ses Compaignons*, feisans diverses Jeuues & Entreludes,' and '*autres Jeweis de Abyndon*, feisantz autres Entreludes,' before the king at Christmas (ca 25 December-4 Februaryp; date from Wolffe, p 37; Thomas Rymer, *Foedera* [1727], X, 387).

1516 6 January p
639 Richard Gibson prepared a revels at court, including a comedy by William Cornyshe and the chapel children with Calcas (played by Cornyshe), Troilus, Pandar, 'Kryssyd' like a widow of honour, Dio-

mede, Ulysses, and the Greeks; and a herald (also played by Cornyshe) who announced an assault by knights on a timber castle holding a queen and six ladies (one called Faith) who made speeches written by Cornyshe (*L. & P. Hen. VIII*, II.ii, pp 1470, 1505-6; a fuller transcription appears by Hillebrand, pp 324-5; Halle, fols 57v-8r; Holinshed, III, 613).

1526 January r
640 Schedule of wages for Richard Hole and other of the king's players in his Eltham household book (*L. & P. Hen. VIII*, IV.i, no 1939.9, p 869; Collier, I, 97, n, notes a payment in Michaelmas this year to the king's 'lusores,' including Richard Hole and George Mayler).

ELY, diocese of

ca 1550-6? r
641 Memorandum about the (?Cambridge) chancellor's view of the order to be taken about plays, etc, done for profit in churches and churchyards (*Ely Episcopal Records*, comp A. Gibbons [1891], p 36).

ELY PRIORY (Cambridgeshire)

1479 29 August p
642 Subtlety with dialogue of 'Pastor Bonus,' the Bishop, and St Andrew (and a presenter?) at the 'Convivium' celebrating the installation of John Morton as Bishop of Ely (*The Customs of London, otherwise Called Arnold's Chronicle*, ed Francis Douce [1811], pp 238-41; Bentham [1812], App, nos XXIX-XXX, pp 34*-6*; and pp 179-80, n 11; *IMEV* 3563.5; ref courtesy of A.F. Johnston).

1518 23 June p
643 The king's players (possibly this entry and the one below belong under DOWNHAM at the prior's manor there; C.T. Flower, 'Obedientiars' Accounts of Glastonbury and Other Religious Houses,' *TSPES*, 7 [1911-15], 53).

1526-32 p
644 Visiting 'ludentes' before the prior (at Christmas in 1532; Bentham [1817], p 52; Beadle, I, 142-3, from CUL Add ms 2957).

ETON COLLEGE (Berkshire)

1444 r
645 College statutes require scholars and fellows not to frequent
'tabernas, spectacula, aut alia loca inhonesta' (*The Ancient Laws of the
Fifteenth Century, for King's College, Cambridge, and for the Public School
of Eton College*, ed James Heywood and Thomas Wright [1850], p 537).

1447-8 p
646 Players (courtesy of A.F. Johnston).

1485 25 December p
647 Play (courtesy of A.F. Johnston).

1519 r
648 The *Vulgaria* of William Horman, schoolmaster here 1486-94,
schoolmaster at Winchester 1494-1502, and fellow here 1502-35 (*Vulgaria: London, 1519*, The English Experience, 745 [1975]; STC 13811),
has many references to plays and playing that may reflect his experiences as well as his teaching here: the loaning of a Terence (fol 86v);
'we haue played a comedi of greke,' '... a comedy of latten' ('Representauimus fabulam palliatam,' '... fabulam togatam'; fol 87r); 'There were
.v. coursis in the feest: and as many paiantis in the pley' ('in ludis'; fol
189r); 'In solemne shewynges ['festinis spectaculis']: that be done a
nyghtis tyme men hange vp masis / full of burnynge lampis' (fols
191v-2r); 'play' ('ludicrum'; fols 279v, 281r, 282v); 'The mayre made
shewyngis and pleyes ['ludos'] throught al the wardis of the cyte' (fol
279v); 'a may kynge,' as an annual custom ('rex vernalis'; fol 279v);
'He can pley the desard with a contrefet face ['Morionem'] proprely'
(fol 280r); 'I wyll haue made .v. stagis / or bouthis in this pleye' ('scenas in hos ludos'; fol 280r); 'pleyers garmentis both for sad partis and
mad' ('scenicae vestes / tam as graues quam ridiculas personas'; fol
280r); 'I wolde haue a place in the middyl of the pley: that I myght se
euery paiaunt' ('Cupio hic fieri orchestra'; fol 280r); 'The apperel of
this pley ['Choragium'] coste me moche money' (fol 280v); 'who dyd
the coste of this pley ['choragus'] for the plesure of the people?' (fol
280v); 'This felowe ['gesticulator'] pleyeth well with poppettis' ('ocilla
... sigilla ... puppas'; fol 281r); 'a parte in a playe' ('operam in ludicro';
fol 281r); 'pryncipall player' ('princeps personatorum'; fol 281v); 'who

shalbe players?' ('Qui ludicras partes sustinebunt'; fol 281v); 'I haue
played my parte without any fayle' ('Aedidi opera*m* ...'; fol 281v); 'I
delyte to se enterludis' ('ludicra'; fol 281v); 'The stag*is* of the play
['Theatru*m*'] fel al downe; and no man hurt that sate in the setis' ('in
foris'; fol 281v); 'Orde*n* me a lokyng place i*n* the play' ('podiu*m* siue
stibadiu*m*'; fol 281v); and 'The trogettars ['Praestigiatores'] behynd a
clothe shew forth popett*is* that chatre / chyde / iuste / and fyghte to
gether' (fol 282v; cf fols 278v, 282r).

1525-73
649 Plays by the schoolmaster and children in the hall, sometimes
with a stage, often at Christmas: interludes and comedies 1550-1 and
1553-4, with fool and visors 1550-6, and beards 1548-9 and 1552-3
(Motter, pp 261-4; different accounts, noting that the Dean of Windsor supplied playing clothes in ?1533-4, are cited in *VCHBucks*, II,
183-4).

ca 1529-31 r
650 The school timetable scheduled the teaching of Terence each Monday in both third and fourth forms (from a timetable sent to Saffron
Walden as a model; Leach, p 451; and for the 1528 Eton curriculum,
see under CUCKFIELD above).

1537-9 p?
651 Nicholas Udall, schoolmaster, possibly wrote his play of Ezechias
(=Henry VIII?) for performance by the boys here (A.R. Moon, 'Nicholas Udall's Lost Tragedy "Ezechias,"' *TLS*, 19 April 1928, p 289;
Scheurweghs, pp xxxv-xxxviii; Eton records 1534-45 exist but do not
have evidence of any plays, according to Motter, p 55, and a new
search by A.F. Johnston; Edgerton, pp 12, 82, 122-3, suggests 1545 or
1546, after Udall had left Eton; cf under CAMBRIDGE 1564 8 August and
under LONDON 1537-42).

EVERSHOLT (Bedfordshire)

1552 2 September r
652 Four playing coats, made out of six church curtains (*The Edwardian Inventories for Bedfordshire*, ed F.C. Eeles and transcr J.E. Brown,
Alcuin Club Collections, 6 [1905], p 2).

EVERTON (Bedfordshire)

1418 5 June p
653 A complaint against John Potter of Everton by Richard Naseby of Girtford (?), who claims Potter owes him 5s. for playing costumes ('vestiment*es* licalib*us*') taken from him and his fellows for playing on this day (Blunham manor court plea cf 23 November; Beds. County Record Office, L 26/51, m 12d [i], courtesy of the owner the Rt Hon Lady Lucas, Winchester, Hants.).

EVESHAM (Worcestershire, now Hereford and Worcester)

1530 r
654 Joseph Hunt's introductory lecture on Terence's *Eunuchus* to the novices (text in *The Letter Book of Robert Joseph, Monk-scholar of Evesham and Gloucester College, Oxford 1530-3*, ed Hugh Aveling and W.A. Pantin, OHS NS 19 [1967 (1964)], pp 56-9).

EXETER (Devon)

1333 r
655 Bishop John Grandisson requires the Exeter Cathedral vicars choral not to perform scandalous plays on Holy Innocents day as accustomed (Wasson, 'Folk Drama in Devon,' p 1).

1348 11 July r
656 'Order of Brothelyngham' has set up a lunatic abbot in the city 'Theatro' as a 'ludus' (*The Register of John de Grandisson, Bishop of Exeter, (A.D. 1327-1369)*, ed F.C. Hingeston-Randolph, II [1897], pp 1055-6; Cecily Radford, 'Early Drama in Exeter,' *RTDevA*, 67 [1935], 365, suggests that this may have been rebuilt in 1387 as 'the Pale' next Westgate, for wrestling, and in her 'Had Roman Exeter an Amphitheatre?', *Devon and Cornwall Notes & Queries*, 18 [1934-5], 375-7, she mentions as a possibility the supposed Roman site Danes Castle, which had been proposed as the amphitheatre of Isca Dumnoniorum [cf *ibid*, pp 30-1, 85, 133, 184-5; and Wacher, *Towns*, p 331]; Marshall cites contemporary English works using 'theatrum' strictly as 'public square' or 'marketplace'; that this and the next entries allude to a formal playing structure seems unlikely [p 381]).

1352 12 August p?
657 Attempt to halt play or buffoonery insulting the leather-dressers
to be enacted that day in the city 'Theatro' (*Register*, II, 1120; Radford,
'Early Drama in Exeter,' p 363).

1408-32 p
658 Plays (at the Black Friars in 1409; A.G. Little and R.C. Easterling,
The Franciscans and Dominicans of Exeter, History of Exeter Research
Group Monograph 3 [1927], p 39; Radford, pp 367-8).

before 1413-1525
659 Corpus Christi play or 'lusione' performed annually 'of old
custom ... until a little while ago,' and newly ordered in 1413 to be
played Tuesday in Whitsun week by civic guilds, notably the Skinners,
in pageants with speeches from the play's 'ordinale'; later maintained
by the fraternity of Corpus Christi (long gaps in the records; Cecily
Radford, 'Three Centuries of Playgoing in Exeter,' *RTDevA*, 82 [1950],
241-2, 267; and John Wasson, 'Records of Early English Drama: Where
they Are and What they Tell us,' *REED Proc.*, p 138).

1418-19 p
660 'lusores' (courtesy of John Wasson).

1419 r, 1441-56
661 May play; procession of the May, with an elephant (Wasson, 'Folk
Drama in Devon,' pp 1, 3; Radford, p 367).

1426-7 p
662 'lusoribus ludentis lusionem Robyn hood' (Wasson, 'Guide,' pp
74–5; Radford, p 367; Wasson, p 67).

1430 p
663 'lusoribus ludentibus Natale Christi' in the guildhall; and a 'histri-
one' of the duke of Gloucester (courtesy of John Wasson; Radford, p
367, sees this as the nativity of Christ played by the duke of Gloucester's company).

1432 p?
664 Players who played 'de la Tornament de Totyngham' in the Castle
(Radford, p 368; cf *IMEV* 2615).

1457-8 p
665 'ludo' mentioned in St John's Bow churchwardens' accounts
(courtesy of John Wasson).

ca 1470-80
666 Mimes on St George day (a play?) at Holy Trinity (Wasson, p 66,
and his 'Folk Drama in Devon,' pp 1-2).

1487-8 p
667 'lusione' at Frerenhay, the Franciscans' house, and a 'lusione
voc*ata* Robyn Hode' (Exeter St John's Bow churchwardens' accounts,
courtesy of John Wasson).

1508-54
668 Robin Hood and Little John at St John at Bow; in 1510 the city
council forbids Robin Hood plays and restricts parishes to presenting
them on dedication days (records with long gaps; Radford, 'Three
Centuries of Playgoing,' pp 243-4; Wasson, p 67, and his 'Folk Drama
in Devon,' pp 1-2).

1528-1635
669 Visiting players; including an interlude on Corpus Christi by
Queen Mary's players in the guildhall (Murray, II, 270-3; and courtesy
of John Wasson).

EXETER, diocese of

1287 r
670 The statutes of Bishop Peter Quinel (or Quivel) require parish
priests to denounce publicly in their churches 'ludos inhonestos'
played in churchyards as well as 'ludos teatrales et ludibriorum spectacula,' and forbid clergy to attend 'spectacula' (*Councils & Synods*, pp
1009, 1013).

1360 r
671 Prohibition of 'ludos ineptos et noxios' made by clerics and boys
25-28 December at Exeter Cathedral and the collegiate churches of
Ottery St Mary, Crediton, and Glasney (*The Register of John de Grandisson, Bishop of Exeter, (A.D. 1327-1369)*, ed F.C. Hingeston-Randolph, III
[1899], pp 1213-15; cf Bakere, pp 30-31).

EYE (Suffolk)

1536 p, 1540 p
672 Players on Corpus Christi; and players (Galloway-Wasson, p 159; cf his 'Records of Early English Drama: Where they Are and What they Tell us,' REED *Proc.*, p 139).

EYNSHAM (Oxfordshire)

1196 r
673 Customary Easter resurrection play including the angel's appearance to the women at the tomb, the conversation of Peter and John, and the appearance of Christ to Mary Magdalene in the garden ('Visio Monachi de Eynsham,' ed P.M. Huber, *Romanische Forschungen*, 16 [1904], 653; trans Valerian Paget, *The Revelation to the Monk of Evesham Abbey* [1909], pp 61-2; Woolf, p 18).

FARWAY (Devon)

1567 p
674 Robin Hood (courtesy of John Wasson).

FAVERSHAM (Kent)

1530-1625
675 Visiting players (Dawson, pp 57-66).

FINCHINGFIELD (Essex)

1524-5 p
676 'ludum,' probably here (mentioned in Thetford accounts; Galloway-Wasson).

FINSBURY (Middlesex, now Greater London)

ca 1524-6 r
677 Players' costumes, as for a gallant, a priest, and a woman, used for court plays and disguisings at John Rastell's stage in Finsbury Fields along Old Street (leased from his death in 1536), and hired out for summer stage plays and winter interludes (H.R. Plomer, 'New Documents on English Printers and Booksellers of the Sixteenth Century,'

Trans. of the Bibliographical Society, 4 [1896-8], 153-83; and his 'Notices of English Stationers in the Archives of the City of London,' *ibid*, 6 [1900-2], 24; Reed, pp 230-3).

FOLKESTONE (Kent)

1514-1621
678 Visiting players (Dawson, pp 68-73).

FORDWICH (Kent)

1568-1633
679 Visiting players (Dawson, pp 75-9).

FOUNTAINS ABBEY (Yorkshire, W.R., now North Yorkshire)

1456-9 p
680 The monastery's own 'lusores,' and visiting 'lusores'; and 'ludo-rum corporis xpi,' for the conduct of which Thomas Barber of York was paid (*Memorials of the Abbey of St. Mary of Fountains*, III, ed J.T. Fowler, SS 130 [1918], pp 17-18, 59-61; 20, 65, 90-1).

FRILFORD (Oxfordshire)

ca 1st-4th centuries r
680.5 A circular amphitheatre was made in a valley descending to the River Ock, just east of a Romano-British temple, by building a bank 11 to 14 meters wide from materials probably available as a result of the lowering of the enclosed arena, about 45 meters in diameter, into the ground; the bank has east and west entrances and a rectangular chamber to the south, 'probably the remains of a shrine of Nemesis, or possibly a beast-pen' (Richard Hingley, 'Recent Discoveries of the Roman Period at the Noah's Ark Inn, Frilford, South Oxfordshire,' *Britannia*, 13 [1982], 306-8 and figs 5-6).

GATESHEAD (Durham, now Tyne and Wear)

1490 r
681 Painted star for church (-play? *Memoirs of the Life of Mr. Ambrose Barnes*, ed W.H.D. Longstaffe, SS 50 [1867 for 1866], p 262; M.H. Dodds, 'The Northern Stage,' AA, 3rd ser, 11 [1914], 33).

GLASTONBURY (Somerset)

1428 p
682 'ludentes' at Christmas and Midsummer (W.E. Daniel, 'Church-wardens' Accounts, St. John's Glastonbury,' *Notes & Queries for Somerset and Dorset*, 4 [1895], 141).

1500 p
683 'les pagetts cum j play in la belhay' on Corpus Christi; also a record of Robin (or Robert) Hood (Daniel, pp 334-6).

GLOUCESTER (Gloucestershire)

1283 ?6 December p
684 The clerks' St Nicholas miracle play ('ludentibus miracula sancti Nicholai') and their boy bishop (Arnold Taylor, 'Royal Alms and Oblations in the Later 13th Century: An Analysis of the Alms Roll of 12 Edward I (1283-4),' in *Antiquary*, p 123).

1550-1641
685 Visiting players and Abbot of Misrule; and players of the city 1553-4p (W.H. Stevenson, 'The Records of the Corporation of Gloucester,' *12th Report*, HMC, App 9 [1891], pp 465-71; Murray, II, 276-85).

ca 1565-75 p
686 'the Cradle of security,' a moral stage play with a prince ('the wicked of the world'), courtiers, three ladies called Pride, Covetousness, and Luxury, an old man in blue with a serjeant at arms ('the end of the world'), another old man in red bearing a sword ('the last judgement'), and wicked spirits (a plot summary by R. W[illis]., who saw the performance standing between his father's legs as he sat on a bench; *Mount Tabor* [1639], pp 110-14; STC 25752).

GLOUCESTER, diocese of

1551-2 r
687 The interrogatories of John Hooper, bishop of Gloucester, ask parishioners if they annoy their minister with 'plays' during divine service (*Visitations*, II, 291).

GREAT TEY (Essex)

ca 1496-1593
688 The town's common playing place, where local archers and 'lusores
... habere uti et gaudere Joca sua' ('Mr. [Thomas] Astle on the Tenures,
Customs, &c. of his Manor of Great Tey,' *Arch*, 12 [1796], 38-9).

GREAT YARMOUTH (Norfolk)

1462-1512
689 Liturgical play? with a star, at St Nicholas church (churchwardens' accounts; Charles J. Palmer, *The History of Great Yarmouth,
Designed as a Continuation of Manship's History of that Town* [1856],
p 117; Galloway-Wasson, p 16).

1473-1508
690 Plays at Corpus Christi (1473p, 1486p) and Bartholomewtide (24
August 1489p); a game played on Corpus Christi ('Christmas' day in
Palmer; 1493p); and game players then (1508p; Palmer, p 118; Galloway-Wasson, pp 15-16).

1492-1596
691 Game players and game place at which interludes or plays were
played (a game place house or 'domus' was used by both players and
audience from at least 1538; David Galloway, 'The "Game Place" and
"House" at Great Yarmouth, 1493-1595,' *TN*, 31 [1977], 6-9; Galloway-
Wasson, pp 11-15).

1531-57
692 Visiting players (Galloway-Wasson, pp 12-14; cf Murray, II, 286).

GREENWICH (Kent, now Greater London)

1452-3 Christmas p
693 Richard Bulstrode was paid £25. 9s. for stuff and wages for a 'dis-
gisynge' made before Henry VI and Queen Margaret at their manor of
Pleasaunce in 'festo Natalis Domini' (A.R. Myers, 'The Household of
Queen Margaret of Anjou, 1452-3,' *BJRL*, 40 [1957-8], 88, 422).

1486 6 January p, Christmas r
694 Disguisings at court, made by Richard Pudsey or Puddesay (*Materials Hen. VII*, I [1873], p 337, and II, 60, 83).

1487-8 Christmas p
695 Many plays; and a disguising on 1 January (Leland, IV, 235).

1489-90 p
696 No disguisings at court, 'and but right few Pleys' (Leland, IV, 255-6).

1499 p
697 May game ('Court Festivals,' p 35).

1506 14 May-ca 14 June p
698 A challenge to feats of arms and wrestling at this time by Lady May from a 'ship,' on behalf of her servants (Francis H. Cripps-Day, *The History of the Tournament in England and France* [1918], App VI, pp xlv-xlvii; *Memorials Hen. VII*, p 302; dated by Kipling, pp 132-3).

1507 May-June p
698.5 Feats at arms by the servants of the Lady of May, probably represented by the Princess Mary, who is set on a stage under a hawthorn made by Flora to oversee the jousts (location uncertain; 'The Justes of the Moneths of May and June,' in *Remains of the Early Popular Poetry of England*, ed W.C. Hazlitt, II [1866], pp 109-30; STC 3543 [publ 1507?]; sometimes confused with the jousts at Kennington in 1441; cf Kipling, pp 133-6).

1511 1 May p
699 A moving pageant ship called Fame, leading Henry VIII and the court from the woods to a jousting (Halle, fols 11v-12r; *Great Chronicle*, p 375; Holinshed, III, 561-2).

1512 1 and 6 January p
700 Richard Gibson, under Sir Harry Guildford, arranged a pageant castle and dungeon, 'Le Fortress dangerous' (with six ladies, William Cornyshe, and the chapel gentlemen), assaulted by Henry VIII and five other lords and knights and left as 'broken store' (1 January); and a disguising after the manner of a 'meskelyng' in Italy in which a rope was used for the hall traverse (6 January; *L. & P. Hen. VIII*, II.ii, pp

1497-8; Halle, fols 15v-16r; Holinshed, III, 567; cf below under 7 March 1519).

1512 1 June p
701 Royal joust having three pageants with knights: a satin fountain; a horse litter; and 'The dolorous Castle' (*L. & P. Hen. VIII*, II.ii, 1498-9; Halle, fol 21r; Holinshed, III, 572).

1513 6 January p
702 Richard Gibson prepared a royal pageant called the 'riche Mount,' on which were set precious stones, herbs, roses, and a burning beacon with six lords and six ladies (the latter within), and drawn by wildmen (*L. & P. Hen. VIII*, II.ii, pp 1499-1500; Halle, fol 22; Holinshed, III, 574).

1514 31 December p
703 Richard Gibson prepared a royal disguising or mummery in the queen's chamber (*L. & P. Hen. VIII*, II.ii, pp 1500-1, and cf Addenda, I.i, no 121, p 35; Halle, fol 55v).

1515 6 January p
704 On Sir Harry Guildford's instructions, Richard Gibson prepared a royal pageant called 'the Pavilion on the Place Perilous,' a stage, with a battle of wildmen and knights, and speeches by William Cornyshe and the chapel gentlemen explaining the 'intent' (with the children; the pageant was spoiled later 'with press'; *L. & P. Hen. VIII*, II.ii, pp 1466, 1501-2; and cf Addenda, I.i, no 121, p 35; Halle, fol 55v; Holinshed, III, 609).

1516 20 May p
705 A play was provided by William Cornyshe for the king's post-jousts banquet for Margaret, Queen of Scots (noted in an account by Richard Gibson; courtesy of W.R. Streitberger).

1517 6 January p
706 Royal pageant called the Garden of Esperance with many flowers, with six knights and ladies, William Cornyshe as the explicator on horseback, and the chapel children (*L. & P. Hen. VIII*, II.ii, p 1509; Halle, fol 59; Holinshed, III, 617).

1518 7 October p
707 Royal pageant with Turks, Report riding Pegasus, a castle with knights who fought the Turks, a rock and a cave of peace with dis-

guisers and an infant queen (*L. & P. Hen. VIII*, II.ii, pp 1514-17, and no 4491, p 1380; III, p 1557; Halle, fol 66 [dating the event 8 October]; Holinshed, III, 633-4; *Venice*, II, nos 1088-9, pp 465-7).

1519 January-March r
708 Masquing expenses of Henry Courtenay, earl of Devon (once in the presence of Henry VIII; *L. & P. Hen. VIII*, III.i, no 152, pp 49-51; cf Alfred J. Horwood, 'The Manuscripts of the Right Honourable the Earl of Devon, at Powderham Castle, Co. Devon,' *3rd Report*, HMC, App [1872], p 216).

1519 7 March p
709 A comedy by Plautus on a stage and a royal disguising, a 'maska-lyne' after the manner of Italy, with ladies dressed like 'Egipcians' (*L. & P. Hen. VIII*, III.i, no 113, p 35, and p 1535; Halle, fols 67v-68r).

1519 31 December p
710 Court mummery arranged by Richard Gibson (*L. & P. Hen. VIII*, III.iii, pp 1551-2).

1520 1 February p
711 Challengers for a tilt enter the queen's chamber in a disguising with a 'tryke' or 'spell' wagon holding a lady (Halle, fol 70r; *L. & P. Hen. VIII*, III, 1552-3; Holinshed, III, 641).

1520 3 November p
712 Royal masque with nobles dressed as friars (*L. & P. Hen. VIII*, III.iii, p 1556).

1520 9 December ?p
713 Revels with disguisers dressed as mariners and friars (*L. & P. Hen. VIII*, III.iii, p 1556).

1521 4 January p
714 Revels at court with a disguising of eight reisters (German cavalry soldiers; *L. & P. Hen. VIII*, III.iii, p 1556).

1521 11-12 February p
715 Masques, including one of friars (*L. & P. Hen. VIII*, III.iii, p 1557).

1521-2 p
716 Richard Gibson arranged Christmas revels for 29 December-1 January that include masquing (*L. & P. Hen. VIII*, III.iii, p 1557).

1522 4-5 June p
717 Masques, with three foresters, four hunters, a keeper, woodwoses, a 'stuffed body,' and a pageant on 5 June, devised by William Cornyshe with the king for the Emperor Charles (Halle, fols 95r-96r; *L. & P. Hen. VIII*, III.ii, no 2305, pp 976-7; *Venice*, III, no 466, p 236; and see under WINDSOR [15 June]).

1524-5 December-February p
718 Royal jousts (begun when two ladies led two old knights – the king and Charles Brandon – by reins) and a great timber pageant, the Castle of Loyalty (arranged by Richard Gibson), equipped with drawbridges, ditches, and bulwark, for assaults in the tiltyard; followed by a masque 29 December, in which the chapel gentlemen were bridled and led by ladies (*L. & P. Hen. VIII*, IV.i, no 965, pp 418-19; Halle, fols 133v-4r; McGee-Meagher, pp 82-3).

1526 p
719 Pageant? and masques at court (14 January, 17 February; *L. & P. Hen. VIII*, IV.i, no 1888, pp 837-8).

1526-7 p
720 Revels, masques, and disguisings at court this Christmas (Halle, fol 154v).

1527 6 May p
721 Richard Gibson arranged revels in the disguising hall (or 'Revels House') at the Long House in the tiltyard: a play (rhymed dialogue in both English and Latin) by the chapel children about the disputes between Love or Cupid, and Riches or Plutus, introduced by Mercury, and Justice, and to be judged by the king, appointed to do so by Jupiter; and a pageant disguising with a towered mount and cave; and John Rastell's 'pageant of the Father of Hevin' (a ceiling design? the roof 'bare the weather'; *L. & P. Hen. VIII*, IV.ii, nos 3097-8, 3107, pp 1390-3, 1415; for accounts for building the Long House, see IV.ii, no 3104, pp 1394-7; Halle, fols 156v-8r; *Venice*, IV, no 105, pp 57-61; McGee-Meagher, p 85; and Sydney Anglo, 'La Salle de Banquet et le Théâtre Construits à Greenwich pour les Fetes franco-anglaises de 1527,' in *Le Lieu Théâtral à la Renaissance*, ed Jean Jacquot, Élie Konigson, and Marcel Oddon [1964], pp 273-88).

1527 after 10 May p
722 Combats and comedies in the disguising house for the French ambassadors (*Calendar of State Papers and Manuscripts ... Milan*, I, ed Allen B. Hinds [1912], no 804, pp 512-13).

1527 10 November p
723 Pageant disguisings in the disguising hall with an arbour and fountain, a 'place of plesyer'; and a Latin tragedy or 'farsa' by Paul's boys, led by John Ritwise, Master of St Paul's School, about the captive pope as freed by Wolsey (Clement VII), with characters Religion, Ecclesia, Veritas (like three novices), Heresy, False Interpretation, Corruptio Scriptoris (like ladies of 'Beeme' [Bohemia]), Luther (a 'party' friar), his wife (a 'frowe of Spyers' [Spires] in Almain), SS Peter, Paul, and James (three abbots), a cardinal, two serjeants, the dauphin and his brother, the Emperor's chancellor, his messenger, three Almains, commoners, Ladies Peace, Quietness, and Tranquillity, and others (*L. & P. Hen. VIII*, IV.ii, nos 3563-4, pp 1603-6; see also no 3518, pp 1586-7, an apparent reference to this farce [representing 'Defiance'] in a letter dated 26 ?October 1527, from the emperor's court at Burgos; Halle, fols 165-6r; *Spain*, III.ii [1877], no 240, p 458; McGee-Meagher, p 86; see PLATE 19).

1527-8 Christmas p
724 Masques and disguisings at court (Halle, fol 181).

1528 25-31 December p
725 At this time Wolsey caused farces to be played in French, 'with great display,' during the visit of Cardinal Lorenzo Campeggio (*L. & P. Hen. VIII*, IV.iii, no 5133, pp 2255-7; cf Sidney Thomas, 'Wolsey and French Farces,' *TLS*, 7 December 1935, p 838).

1535 16 June r
726 Queen Anne gave several 'braues mommeries' for the king at one of her residences (location uncertain; *Spain*, V.i, no 174, p 493; *L. & P. Hen. VIII*, VIII, no 876, p 346).

1538 20-3 March p
727 The king 'cannot be one single moment without masks, which is a sign that he purposes to marry again' (location uncertain; *Spain*, V.ii,

no 220, p 520; *L. & P. Hen. VIII*, XIII.i, no 583, p 215, and no 784, p 294, for an April rumour of a marriage).

1540 1 January p
728 Play by the chapel children for the king (Kempe, pp 69-70; *L. & P. Hen. VIII*, XIV.ii, no 757, p 284).

1540 6 January p
728.5 Masques and other disports for the king and Anne of Cleves on their wedding night (Halle, fol 240v).

1540 2 February p
729 The king's works' accounts (18 January-15 February) deal with setting up a scaffold or 'stadge for the players' for a play on Candlemas night in the king's chamber (location uncertain; *L. & P. Hen. VIII*, XVI, no 398.ii[3], p 203).

1548 11-13 February p
730 Jousts or triumph before a fortress with thirty men against about one hundred attackers; four Shrovetide masques, of which one was of Moors (having long gloves, black-leather nether stocks, headpieces, bells, darts, swords, and visors); and the king's players, for which a canvas-covered oven was provided (Shrove Tuesday was 13 February; *Literary Remains*, p 221; APC, II, 163; Feuillerat 1, pp 26, 29-33; De Selve, nos 302-4, pp 283-7).

1551-2 p
731 Christmas revels at court, including:
1 / masques of Argus, Moors, and Amazons women of war, at court (Feuillerat 1, p 85); and
2 / the entry of the Lord of Misrule George Ferrers, by a device as if he was coming out of the moon, in a chariot with retinue (eight counsellors, cofferer, master of ordnance, gentlemen ushers, pages, herald, trumpeter, ambassador, interpreter, vice or dizzard [with dagger and ladle with pendant bauble], juggler, marshal, minstrel, and dancers), including the king's fool William Somer, who made a play combat that perhaps relates to a pair of stocks, with manacles, a pillery, a gibbet, weapons, prisons, and a heading axe and block that appear in the revels' properties made for this occasion (Ferrers also carried a club and had a seat with canopy; Feuillerat 1, pp 56-81).

1552 6 January p
732 Play or dialogue of Riches and Youth, 'wither of them was bettir,'
with fighting at barriers by men including some dressed as Almains
and as friars (*Literary Remains*, pp 387-8; probably 'the playe of
yeowthe at crystmas' and possibly by Sir Thomas Chaloner, for which
see Feuillerat 1, pp 60, 63, 268-9, 278, 299, and *Folie*, p xlix; neither of
these is the extant *Interlude of Youth*, ca 1513; cf Wallace, p 71).

1552-3 p
733 Christmas revels at court, including:
   1 / the entry of the Lord of Misrule George Ferrers, 26 December,
in a device to come out of a waste outside the world, the 'vastum
vacuum,' with herald, interpreter, ambassador, six counsellors, a
divine (an almoner?), a philosopher, an astronomer, a poet, pages,
marshals, physician, an apothecary, a master of requests (an advo-
cate?), a civilian (?), two dizzards, two gentlemen ushers, four friars,
sergeants at arms, footmen, messenger, trumpeter, juggler, tumbler,
and Irish man and woman; a combat of the Lord of Misrule, apparently with a serpent or dragon equipped with head and mouth of
plate with stops to burn like fire; and possibly some business with
stocks, pillery, and heading axe (Feuillerat 1, pp 89-125; Holden, pp 27,
92; Machyn, p 28; Ferrers was appointed Lord of the Pastimes, November 1552 [*APC*, IV, 181]; see also LONDON, 1552 4 January and 1552-3);
   2 / masques: eight satyrs – ?the covetous men with long noses; babi-
ons; graziers – ?the 'Pollenders,' with torchbearers as soldiers (in all,
twelve 'savage men'); and Diana and women hunters, with torchbearers as matrons (Feuillerat 1, pp 106, 109, 116, 190-4, 286; *Loseley mss*);
and
   3 / Sir George Howard's device for a Twelfth Night play or triumph
or pageants of Cupid, an image of a little winged and blindfolded boy
with bow and arrows, Venus in a triumphal chair attended by two
fools, her three ladies, Mars in a chair, his three gentlemen, ladies
Idleness and Daliance, the Marshal and his band (from whom Cupid is
rescued by Venus), the herald 'Coeur Ardant,' and the Lord of Misrule's counsellors (Howard was the Lord's 'master of the horse'; Feuillerat 1, pp 89, 93-125).

1557 31 January p
734 Lord of misrule of the Lord Treasurer came to the Mayor of London with a retinue including a devil and Death with a dart in hand
(Machyn, p 125).

GRIMLEY (Worcestershire, now Hereford and Worcester)

1524-31
735 Visiting players, and a play at a church ale (1530), at the manor of Prior William More of Worcester (*More*, pp 198-325).

GRIMSBY (Lincolnshire, now Humberside)

1431 r
736 A complaint in the town court rolls concerns 'Ioly Walte and Malkyng,' certain 'instrument*a* joci' (Ian Lancashire, '"Ioly Walte and Malkyng": a Grimsby Puppet Play in 1431,' REEDN, 1979.2, pp 6-8).

1499-1585
737 Town chamberlains' accounts reward visiting players, 'lusores,' 'luditores,' and 'ludi' or plays of nearby towns (Kahrl, pp 11-17).

1527 18 June r
738 Borough court books order 'the play of holy John of bowre' prepared (Kahrl, p 12).

1602 p
739 Play on Whitsunday (M.J. Thorpe, *Calendar of State Papers, Relating to Scotland*, II [1858], p 815).

GUILDFORD (Surrey)

1347 22-8 December p
740 'ludos d*o*m*i*ni R*e*gis,' a tournament-disguising at Christmas for Edward III (with visors of women, bearded men, and angels, and with heads of dragons, peacocks, and swans; Nicolas, pp 37-8, 116, 120; cf Arthur Beatty, 'Notes on the Supposed Dramatic Character of the "Ludi" in the Great Wardrobe Accounts of Edward III,' MLR, 4 [1908-9], 474-7).

HADLEIGH (Suffolk)

1547-8 r
741 Church accounts note the making of a stage in the church (dramatic? Galloway-Wasson, p 162).

1597 r
742 Prohibition of forthcoming Whitsuntide stage plays (Galloway-Wasson, pp 162-3; *APC*, XXVII, 97).

HAGWORTHINGHAM (Lincolnshire)

1537-8 p
743 Churchwardens' accounts have payments to players (Editors, 'Hagworthingham Church Book,' *LN&Q*, 1 [1888-9], 8).

HAILES ABBEY (Gloucestershire)

15th century r
744 A copy of Terence's 'Andria,' now in BL Royal ms 8.D.XVII, item i (Williams, p 137).

HALSTEAD (Essex)

1529 p
745 Play in the church (W.A. Mepham, 'Mediaeval Plays in the 16th Century at Heybridge and Braintree,' *EssR*, 55 [1946], 15-16; Coldewey, p 226).

1589 r
746 Glibbery of Halstead, a priest, once having been a vice on a stage in a play, left his pulpit to join either the Summer Lord with his May game, or Robin Hood with his morris dance, just then going by the church (Martin Marprelate's 'Hay Any Worke for Cooper,' in *Marprelate*, pp 226-7).

HAMPTON COURT (Middlesex, now Greater London)

1544 January r
747 Household accounts of Henry VIII pay Mr Crane (of the chapel) for playing before him this Christmas here, as well as his own players (BL Add ms 59900, fols 67v-8r).

1544 21 April r
748 Masques and revels, using Turks' heads, took place in the previous (regnal) year (*L. & P. Hen. VIII*, XIX.i, no 369, pp 244-5; Jeaffreson, pp 602, 604 [date uncertain]).

1546 24-8 August p
749 There were 'rich maskes' nightly with the Queen and ladies at
court for the visit of Claude d'Annebaut, admiral of France (Wriothesley, I, 173; a warrant for materials for these (?), November 1546, is
noted in *L. & P. Hen. VIII*, XXI.ii, no 475.15, p 224, and cf no 775, pp
448-9; McGee-Meagher, p 96).

1547-8 Christmas p
750 Revels included masquing and a tower like that of Babylon for a
play, evidently the king's own 'Comediam de meretrice Babylonica,'
written at this time (Feuillerat 1, pp 26, 269-70; *Index*, p 67; according
to *King's Works*, III [1975], p 44, a 'Tower of Babylon' was done by
architectural artist Robert Trunckey, under the direction of Nicholas of
Modena, evidently for Henry VIII; French correspondence refers to 'des
beaulx mistères et farses' on Epiphany at court [De Selve, no 284, p
266]).

1574 2 February r
751 Masque of six virtues, not performed at Hampton Court (Feuillerat 2, p 206).

HARLOW (Essex)

2nd century r
751.5 Three fragments of 'an imported pipe-clay theatre-mask' are
finds from a well at Holbrooks (River Way) not far from a Roman
temple (Boris Rankov, 'Roman Britain in 1981. I. Sites Explored,'
Britannia, 13 [1982], 371-2).

HARWICH (Essex)

1553 p, 1557 p
752 Visiting players twice in the church (Coldewey, pp 336-7).

HASCOMBE (Surrey)

1579 ?5 January p
753 'a kynge playe' at the church (of the three kings of Cologne?
despite the date, probably a folk play: J.G.N., 'A King Play,' *N&Q*, 2nd
ser, 12 [July-December 1861], 210).

HATFIELD (Hertfordshire)

1552 February r
754 Payment to one Heywood (John?) and to Sebastian (Westcott, master of Paul's song school by 1557) for 'the charge of the children' with carriage of players' garments ('Household Expenses of the Princess Elizabeth during her Residence at Hatfield October 1, 1551, to September 30, 1552,' ed Viscount Strangford, *The Camden Miscellany*, II, CS 55 [1853], p 37; probably Paul's boys, according to ES, II, 12).

HATFIELD BROAD OAK (Essex)

1556 r
755 The stage play that was to be presented at Shrovetide is halted (*APC*, V, 234, 237-8; cf VI, 118-19).

HAUGHLEY (Suffolk)

1538 r
756 Sir Robert Cooke, vicar of the town, leaves all his 'play boks' to his brother Robert (*Wills and Inventories from the Registers of the Commissary of Bury St. Edmund's and the Archdeacon of Sudbury*, ed Samuel Tymms, CS 49 [1850], p 129).

HAVERING (Essex, now Greater London)

1523 6 January p
757 Visiting players before Princess Mary and her household, briefly at this place (*L. & P. Hen. VIII*, III.ii, no 3375.1, p 1409).

HEALAUGH (Yorkshire, N.R., now North Yorkshire)

1568 r
758 Inventory of Thomas, Lord Wharton of Healaugh, includes revels apparel for three fools (with two daggers), two bishops, and two peers, and for masking (*Yorkshire Probate Inventories 1542-1689*, ed P.C.D. Brears, YorkASRS, 134 [1972], p 33).

HEDON (Yorkshire, E.R., now Humberside)

1390 6 January p
759 'ludentes' in the morning in the chapel of St Augustine (J.R. Boyle, *The Early History of the Town and Port of Hedon* [1895], pp 140, li; with undated records of visiting players, *temp* Henry V-Edward VI, pp lv-lxiv).

HEIGHLEY CASTLE (near Audley, Staffordshire)

ca 1500-20
760 A window of painted glass, once at Betley (three miles away) and formerly owned by John Touchet, lord Audley, whose seat was here until 1536, depicts eleven figures and a May pole: a fool with ass's ears, bauble, and bells; six dancers; minstrel; hobby horse, with a ladle in his mouth; a crowned lady, probably a May queen; and a Franciscan friar (Friar Tuck? E.J. Nicol, 'Some Notes on the History of the Betley Window,' *JEFDSS*, 7:2 (December 1953), 59-67 and colour front; and Charles G.O. Bridgeman, 'Note on the Betley Morris Dance Window,' *Collections for a History of Staffordshire*, William Salt Archaeol. Society NS [1924 for 1923], pp 3-19 and front; the window is now at Leigh Manor, near Minsterley, Shrop.).

HENLEY-ON-THAMES (Oxfordshire)

1455 r, 1499-1542
761 King play or game at Whitsun; in 1531 termed the May game, with one playing the dizzard; with a 'ludi de Robyn Hode' 1499r, and 'Robyne Hoodys money' 1520p (*Henley Borough Records. Assembly Books I-IV, 1395-1543*, ed P.M. Briers, Oxford Rec. Society [1960], pp 58, 125-229).

1511 r
762 'lusum resurrectionis et processionem in die Dominica in octaua Pasche' (*Henley Borough Records*, p 168).

1531-41/2 r
763 Corpus Christi procession (with 'pagent gere,' 1535; Briers, pp 200-30).

HENWICK (Worcestershire, now Hereford and Worcester)

1533 6-7 July p
764 Play at Henwick Hall for the profit of All Hallows' Church (supported by Prior William More of Worcester; *More*, p 370).

HEREFORD (Herefordshire, now Hereford and Worcester)

1286 r
765 Bishop Richard Swinfield excommunicated citizens for attending a Jewish wedding where a ?play was performed (Dew, pp 26-7; Klausner, p 21).

1440 30 April r
766 One 'libri de lusionibus' (plays? W.D. Macray, 'The Manuscripts of the Corporation of Hereford,' *13th Report*, HMC, App 4 [1892], p 300; record now lost? see Klausner, p 23).

1486 p
767 Pageants for the entry of Henry VII on Whitmonday: St George and the dragon; St Ethelbert and two bishops; and Our Lady and virgins (texts: Leland, IV, 197-8; *IMEV* 2199.5).

1503 r, 1548 r
768 Pageants 'of ancient history' for the Corpus Christi procession, ceased by 1548 (Macray, 'Manuscripts,' pp 288-9, and cf p 305; Richard Johnson, *The Ancient Customs of the City of Hereford*, 2nd edn [1882], pp 116-20).
  1 / Adam and Eve (Glovers);
  2 / Cain, Abel, and Moses, Aaron ('Eldest seriant'; ie the town serjeant);
  3 / Noah's ship (Carpenters);
  4 / Abraham, Isaac, Moses with four boys (Chandlers);
  5 / Jesse (Skinners);
  6 / the salutation of Our Lady (Fletchers);
  7 / the nativity of Our Lord (Vintners);
  8 / the three kings of Cologne (Tailors);
  9 / the purification of Our Lady, with Simeon (the 'belman');
  10 / the '... deitours,' going with the Good Lord (Drapers);
  11 / 'Fleme Jordan' (Saddlers);
  12 / the Castle of Israel ('Cardeners'; Carders?);

13 / the Good Lord riding on an ass, with the twelve apostles (Walkers);

14 / the story of Sheer Thursday (Tanners);

15 / the taking of Our Lord (Butchers);

16 / the tormenting of Our Lord, with four tormentors, and the lamentation of Our Lady; and St John the Evangelist ('The eldest seriant');

17 / 'Portacio crucis usque montem Oilverii' (Cappers);

18 / Jesus hanging on the cross (Dyers);

19 / Longinus with his knights (Smiths);

20 / Mary and John the Evangelist ('The eldest sariant');

21 / Joseph of Arimathea (Barbers);

22 / 'Sepultura Christi' (Dyers);

23 / the three Maries ('The eldest seriant');

24 / 'Milites armati custodes sepulcri' (Porters);

25 / Pilate, Caiaphas, Annas and Mahownde (Mercers);

26 / knights in harness (Bakers); and

27 / Saint 'Keterina' with three tormentors (journeymen Cappers).

ca 1509-47 r
769 Letter to the mayor asking leave 'to make a game or give-ale' (William D. Macray, *Catalogue of and Index to MS. Papers, Proclamations, and Other Documents, Selected from the Municipal Archives of the City of Hereford* [1894], p 10).

HEREFORD, diocese of

1348 6 October r
770 Bishop John Trilleck prohibits 'lud*um* theatralis fieri in ecclesiis' (Klausner, p 21).

HERTFORD (Hertfordshire)

1427-8 r
771 Christmas revels at the court of Henry VI: 'A Mumming at Hertford,' with the mutual complaints of six rustic husbands and their wives, and the king's judgment; a 'disguysing' devised by Lydgate for Christmas (text in *Minor Poems*, II, 675-82; IMEV 2213; dated by Richard F. Green, 'Three Fifteenth-Century Notes,' ELN, 14 [1976], 14-17).

HEYBRIDGE (Essex)

1516-32
772 Plays, to which Damyon the property player contributed in
1516-17 and 23 towns in 1526-7; and pageant players with tabernacle,
fool, and one to bear the book, on 12 May 1532p (*The First Book of the
Churchwardens' Accounts of Heybridge, Essex*, transcr John Pridden, ed
W.J. Pressey [nd], pp 8, 10, 41-4; *The Second Book*, transcr and ed W.J.
Pressey [nd], pp 3, 43 [a receipt from sale of 'ye Deuylls head,' 1559];
W.A. Mepham, 'Mediaeval Plays in the 16th Century at Heybridge and
Braintree,' *EssR*, 55 [1946], 8-14).

HICKLING PRIORY (Norfolk)

1512-20
773 Visiting *ludi* and interludes (Galloway-Wasson, pp 17-18; Richard
Beadle, 'Entertainments at Hickling Priory, Norfolk, 1510-1520,' REEDN,
1980:2, pp 17-19).

HINCHINGBROOKE (Huntingdonshire, now Cambridgeshire)

1564 10 August p
774 Actors followed Elizabeth I to Sir Henry Cromwell's seat from
Cambridge to perform their representation of the imprisoned bishops,
including the bishop of London carrying a lamb that he ate, and a dog
entering with a sacramental wafer in his mouth; and the queen de-
parted angrily midway with her torches (*Simancas*, I [1892], no 263,
p 375; Boas, pp 382-5).

HITCHIN (Hertfordshire)

ca 1550-7 r
775 At his school's theatre in the refectory of the dissolved Carmelite
friary, Ralph Radcliffe had his pupils perform his plays, which included the following works (*Index*, p 333; *Scriptorum*, I, 700; cf *The
Victoria History of the County of Hertford*, ed William Page, III [1912],
p 12; and 'Appendix,' *Arch*, 18 [1817], 448; according to Hampson,
p 302, Radcliffe destroyed the mss of his plays at his death):

1 / 'De Grisilidis Chauceriane rara patientia' (comedy; Chaucer's Clerk's tale of Griselda);

2 / 'De Melibeo Chauceriano' (comedy; Chaucer's tale of Melibeus);

3 / 'De Titi et Gisippi firmissima amicitia' (comedy; Titus and Gisippus);

4 / 'De Sodome et Gomorre incendio' (tragedy; the burning of Sodom and Gomorrah);

5 / 'De Ioannis Huss Bohemie nati condemnatione' (tragedy; the condemnation of John Huss);

6 / 'De Iona a deo ad Niniuitas ablegati defectione' (comedy; Jonah's revolt);

7 / 'De Lazaro a diuitis edibus abacto' (comedy; Dives and Lazarus);

8 / 'De Iudith Bethuliensis incredibili fortitudine' (comedy; the courage of Judith);

9 / 'De Iobi iusti afflictionibus' (comedy; the afflictions of Job); and

10 / 'De Susanne per iudices iniquos ob lese pudicitie notam diuina liberatione' (tragedy; the deliverance of Susannah from the sinful judges).

HOLBEACH (Lincolnshire)

1539 p
776 Churchwardens' accounts concern the four men who bore the 'Marye Cartt' or pageant, at Corpus Christi, and its ?'cloud' (Kahrl, p 18).

1547 r
777 Coats for Herod, the apostles, and the three kings of Cologne, and the 'Dracon' are sold by the churchwardens (William Stukeley, *Itinerarium Curiosum* [1724], I, 18-20).

1560 p
778 Churchwardens' accounts reward players (Kahrl, p 19).

HONITON (Devon)

1571-2 p
779 Visit of Robin Hood of Colyton (and a Robert Hood in 1576-7; Wasson, p 67).

HORBLING (Lincolnshire)

1558-9 r
780 Players' coats, made out of a Romanist vestment and three banner clothes, the first for Richard Colsonne, a scholar, and the rest for children (Peacock, pp 107-8).

HORNCHURCH (Essex, now Greater London)

1566 r
781 Players in the church 'the which did playe and declare certayn things against the ministers' (original now lost; see Coldewey, 'Demise,' p 246).

HOXTON (Middlesex, now Greater London)

ca 1551-6 p
782 King's players' 'play of Self-love' for Sir Thomas Chaloner (MS, II, 201; for his seat here, see *Folie*, pp xxxiii-xxxiv). See also below under LONDON 1553-4r.

HULL, or KINGSTON UPON HULL (Yorkshire, E.R., now Humberside)

1439-95
783 Visiting 'ludentes' from Cottingham and Hessle; and the players of Barton (Anna J. Mill, 'The Hull Noah Play,' MLR, 33 [1938], 490, 496).

1463 r
784 The Guild of the Blessed Virgin Mary pays for an angel and garlands (Hugh Calvert, *A History of Kingston upon Hull* [1978], p 96).

1469-1536 p
785 Noah play (with speeches, written by Nicholas Helperby in 1487-8) on Plough Day, with Noah (who has a pilch, coat, and mittens), Noah's wife and children, and God 'in the ship,' which had wheels (also mentioned 1551r; Mill, 'The Hull Noah Play,' pp 489-505).

1531 23 September r
786 Order that mayors are to reward minstrels, players, etc only at their own expense (Mill, 'The Hull Noah Play,' p 490).

HUNSTANTON HALL (Norfolk)

1523-1632
787 Visiting players (accounts of Sir Thomas Le Strange to 1539, of Sir Nicholas Le Strange to 1543; Galloway-Wasson, pp. 19-28; cf Daniel Gurney, 'Extracts from the Household and Privy Purse Accounts of the Lestranges of Hunstanton, from A.D. 1519 to A.D. 1578,' *Arch*, 25 [1834], 458, 498).

HYTHE (Kent)

1486-1616
788 Visiting players, bann-criers, and 'lusores' (at the Swan in 1499-1500; Dawson, pp 82-8).

INGATESTONE HALL (Essex)

1553-5 p
789 The children of Paul's at a marriage in September 1553; mummers on 6 January 1555, Mr Bower with the children of the Chapel that month, and one called Killcalf that year; and visiting players 1559-61, all for the household of Sir William Petre, either here or at his London house in Aldersgate Street (Price, pp 83-6; F.G. Emmison, *Tudor Food and Pastimes* [1964], pp 75-9).

IPSWICH (Suffolk)

ca 1400-1542
790 Pageants on Corpus Christi, evidently tabernacles, by at least 1443 the responsibility of the Corpus Christi Guild, include the following (Galloway-Wasson, pp 170-83; John Wasson, 'Corpus Christi Play and Pageants at Ipswich,' RORD, 19 [1976], 99-108; also records for 1443-1542 in Nathaniell Bacon's *Annalls of Ipswiche*, ed W.H. Richardson [1884], pp 102-220):
    1 / St George (Gentlemen, Pewterers, Plumbers [dealers in lead], Saddlers, Masons, Tilers, and Armourers);

2 / St John (the Tailors);

3 / St Eligius (Goldsmiths, Blacksmiths, Locksmiths, and Blade-smiths);

4 / St Thomas Martyr (the Barbers and Waxchandlers);

5 / St Luke (the [Wrights and] Carpenters, Carvers, Bowyers, Fletchers, Wheelwrights, Coopers, Pattenmakers, and Turners; with the Glaziers, Painters, and Scriveners *temp* Henry VII);

6 / pageant of the Weavers or Websters, Fullers (in 1437 separate pageants), Hatmakers, and Cappers;

7 / pageant of the Shoemakers (or Cordwainers) and Tanners;

8 / a dolphin (the Fishmongers);

9 / the bull (the Butchers and Tallowchandlers);

10 / pageant of the Skinners, Glovers, Cardmakers, and Pursers;

11 / the Assumption of the Blessed Mary (Drapers, Clothmakers, Dyers, and Shearmen);

12 / pageant of the Mercers, Haberdashers, and Pointers;

13 / a ship (Merchants, Mariners [or Shipmen], and Brewers);

14 / pageant of the Bakers and Waferers; and

15 / 'Tabernaculum dominicum' (the receptable for the Host? the Carmelite Friars, Friars Preachers, and Friars Minor; later with clergy and religious).

1407 r
791 Plea of John Seteler for the arrest of Thomas Fanmaker for refusing to give up the original of diverse plays (V.B. Redstone, 'Ipswich Borough Records. Sixth Article. (No 5.-Henry IV.),' *East Anglian Daily Times*, 2 March 1928; see BL copy of the reprinted series, shelfmark 010358.ppp.11, pp 4-5).

1445p, 1492-1531
792 Out-of-town and town 'lusores' on Corpus Christi, with stages (1445); and a civic Corpus Christi play (a 'librum Corporis Xpi' of 1492, and an annual 'ludus siue le pagent' before 1502, a 'Corpus Cristi pley' by 1515 [for which in 1505 John Stangilts provided the staging and John Parnell the ornaments], which was laid down in 1531; Galloway-Wasson, pp 172-3, 175-82; Wasson, 'Pageants at Ipswich,' pp 102-4, and his 'Guide,' pp 80-1).

1511 r
793 The 'pageant of George' (Bacon, *Annalls*, p 183).

1528 r
794 Statutes for Cardinal Wolsey's College Grammar School here require scholars to read Terence in the third form (Baldwin 1, I, 124-5;
not the eighth form as well, as stated in *VCHSuffolk*, II, 330).

1530-1625
795 Visiting players (Galloway-Wasson, pp 182-4; John Webb, *Great
Tooley of Ipswich* [1962], p 133, for 1530-1; 'Players at Ipswich,' ed E.K.
Chambers, *Collections Vol. II. Part III* [MalS, 1931], pp 258-84, from
1555 onwards).

ISLINGTON (Middlesex, now Greater London)

1557 12 December p
796 Play scheduled for dissenters at the Saracen's Head, Islington; the
'communyon' should have been played (Foxe, VIII, 444-6; Machyn, p
160; O.L. Brownstein, 'The Saracen's Head, Islington: A Pre-Elizabethan Inn Playhouse,' *TN*, 25 [1971], 68-72).

KENDAL (Westmorland, now Cumbria)

1575-1612 r
797 Corpus Christi play, with pageants; or 'other stage playes' (*A Boke
off Recorde or Register*, ed R.S. Ferguson, Cumberland and Westmorland
Antiquarian and Archaeological Society, ES 7 [1892], pp 91, 136-7;
A.W. Douglas, 'Research in Progress,' *REEDN*, 1979.1, pp 13-16; MS, II,
373).

1612 r
798 The town holds the privilege of its fair or charter by a yearly stage
play (Heywood, *Apology*, sig G3r).

1621 July r
798.5 A Star Chamber deposition of this date shows that the town
vicar, supporting tenants against many local 'Lordes of the Mannors'
in a disagreement over customary tenure, caused 'Players and Actors
in a stage playe [performed at Kendal Castle] publicklie to personate
and represent the persons' of these lords in 'a representacon of hell' (a
play written ca 1615, condoned by the town corporation, and costumed with apparel lent from private wardrobes; information of John

Walter, ed Nicholas Davis, 'Allusions to Medieval Drama in Britain: A Findings List [1],' MET, 4:2 [1982], 76).

before 1631 p
799 Corpus Christi play, acted shortly after James' accession in 1603 (Weeuer, p 405).

1644 r
800 An old man about sixty years old from Cartmel parish told preacher John Shaw that he had heard of Christ (and salvation by his blood) '"once in a play at Kendall, called Corpus Christi play, where there was a man on a tree, and blood ran down," &c.' ('The Life of Master John Shaw,' *Yorkshire Diaries and Autobiographies in the Seventeenth and Eighteenth Centuries*, ed Charles Jackson, SS 65 [1877], pp 138-9).

KENILWORTH (Warwickshire)

1575 17 July p
801 Entertainments for Elizabeth I at the earl of Leicester's seat (*Laneham*, pp 26-40, 45) included:
1 / a bride ale with a morris dance having Maid Marian and the fool; and
2 / the Hock Tuesday show of the defeat of the Danes by the English, done by men of Coventry (repeated 19 July).

KENNINGTON (Surrey, now Greater London)

1377 25 January p
802 A mumming in a procession from Newgate to Kennington to meet Richard II, with masked squires, knights, emperor, pope, twenty-four cardinals, and foreign legates (*Anonimalle Chron.*, pp 102-3; Stow, *Survey*, I, 96-7; Withington, I, 104).

1441 May p
803 Feats at arms by the servants of the Queen of May (with her officer at arms April; Richard F. Green, 'A Joust in Honour of the Queen of May, 1441,' N&Q, 225 [1980], 386-9; H. Cripps-Day, *History of the Tournament* [1918], App VI, pp xlv-xlvii).

804 *cancelled*

KING'S LYNN (Norfolk)

1370-1 p
805 'ludentes' (Galloway-Wasson, p 36; cf H. Harrod, *Report on the Deeds & Records of the Borough of King's Lynn* [1874], p 80; the same as the one 'ludenti' noted by J.C. Jeaffreson, 'The Manuscripts Belonging to the Corporation of the Borough of King's Lynn Co. Norfolk,' *11th Report*, HMC, App 3 [1887], p 221).

1384-5 p
806 'ludent*ibus* int*e*rlud' die Corp*o*ris Xpi'; and 'ludent*ibus* int*e*rlud' S*a*nc*t*i Thome Martiris' (Galloway-Wasson, p 38; Jeaffreson, 'King's Lynn,' p 223).

1399 p, 1430-8
807 One 'ludus,' the Guild of St Giles and St Julian (1399); and players, for the guild (Galloway-Wasson, pp 39, 45-7).

1410 p
808 Play on Corpus Christi? (Harrod, *Report*, p 87, but not in Galloway-Wasson).

1415-16 p
809 Visiting 'Iogulatori Ludenti' from Cambridge (Galloway-Wasson, p 43).

ca 1440 r
810 The first English-Latin dictionary, by Galfridus Grammaticus, a Dominican friar at the Black Friars, includes terms on plays and players: 'Bane of A play' (for 'Banna'), 'Borde, or Game' (for 'ludus'), 'Bord*e*r, or playere' (for 'lusor'; see also under 'Pleyar*e*'), 'Boordone, or to play' (for 'ludo'), 'Game, pley' (for 'ludus'), 'Int*e*rlege of a play' (for 'p*re*ludiu*m*,' 'Int*e*rludiu*m*'), 'Ioy, or play that be-gynnyþ w*it*h sorow and endyth w*it*h gladnesse' (for 'Co*m*media'; see also under 'Play'), 'Ioy, or pley þ*a*t bege*n*nyþ w*it*h sadnesse *and* endyth w*it*h sorow *and* grevowsnesse' (for 'Tragedia'; see also under 'Pley'), 'Mu*m*mar' and 'Mu*m*myng' (for 'Mussator,' 'Mussac*i*o'), 'Pagente' (for 'pagina'), 'Pley' (for 'ludus'), 'Pley, of su*m*e [or 'somyr'] game' (for 'Sp*e*ctaculum'), 'Pleyng*e* garme*n*t' (for 'ludix'), 'Playynge place' (for 'Diludiu*m*'), 'Pleyy*n*' (for 'ludo'), 'Scaffold, stage' (for 'fala,' 'Machinis'),

'Spectacle' (for 'Spectaculum'; *The Promptorium Parvulorum. The First English-Latin Dictionary*, ed A.L. Mayhew, EETS ES 102 [1908], cols 32, 44, 63, 186, 239-40, 296, 325, 351-2, 427, 675; cf *Promptorium Parvulorum 1499*, Scolar Press facs [1968]).

1445-6 r
811 'ludus' by 'lusores' and with persons singing 'le Mary & Gabriel,' performed several days at Christmas, before the mayor and council, at the hall of St George's and St Trinity's (on the eve of 6 January and on a Saturday or Sunday night; this play was apparently the one taken by 'ludentes' to lord de Scales' seat, for which see below under MIDDLE-TON [1445-6]; Galloway-Wasson, pp 47-8; Harrod, *Report*, p 88).

1447-84
812 Corpus Christi 'ludi' and 'lusores,' generally in the market place; a Corpus Christi procession 1461-98 (Galloway-Wasson, pp 49-54; cf S.J. Kahrl, 'Learning about Local Control,' REED *Proc.*, p 116).

1509 9 December r
813 Town constables are to watch, especially in Christmas, for vaga-bonds and 'ryottours players' (Galloway-Wasson, p 56).

1520-1 p, 1528-9 p
814 Visiting 'joculatores' and 'ludatores' (Galloway-Wasson, pp 58-9).

KINGSTHORPE (Northamptonshire)

1547-8 r
815 King and queen for the May games are to be chosen on Easter after evensong (with a fine for anyone refusing the office; *Kingsthorpi-ana*, ed J.H. Glover [1883], p 94).

KINGSTON UPON THAMES (Surrey, now Greater London)

1505-65
816 Plays: on the resurrection? 1513-14r; on a stage at Easter 1520p, 1565p (D. Lysons, *The Environs of London*, I [1792], pp 229-30).

1506-39
817 May game, or Robin Hood game or gathering, or Kingham game, with Little John, Maid Marian, and the friar (all with coats); linked

with the Lord of Misrule, morris dance, fool, and dizzard (Henry T. Riley, 'The Corporation of Kingston-on-Thames,' *3rd Report*, HMC [1872], p 331; W.E. St Lawrence Finny, 'Mediaeval Games and Gaderyngs at Kingston-upon-Thames,' *Surrey Archaeological Collections*, 44 [1936], 102-36).

KIRK DEIGHTON (Yorkshire, W.R., now North Yorkshire)

1464 January r
818 Bequest to the 'Somer-game light' (*Test. Ebor.*, V, 103 n).

KIRKHAM (Cheshire)

1496 r
819 Parishioners 'servabant lez Somergame' in the chapel here (in Chester according to J.S. Purvis, *Tudor Parish Documents of the Diocese of York* [1948], p 161, n).

LANCASTER (Lancashire)

16th century? r
820 An oak panel formerly at Lancaster Castle depicts seven figures: a lady with a ladle (labelled 'Maid Marian'?), a minstrel, a nude girl dancer (or boy made to look like a girl), three morris men, and a fool with cap, bells, and bauble (Anne G. Gilchrist, 'A Carved Morris-Dance Panel from Lancaster Castle,' *JEFDSS*, 1:2 [December 1933], 86-8 and pl).

before 1631 p
821 Corpus Christi play (seen by Weeuer, p 405).

LANCHESTER (Durham)

1293 r
822 Vicars of the collegiate church, according to its statutes, are not to frequent 'such spectacles or syghtes, which ar comonly called *Myracles*' (Robert Surtees, *History and Antiquities of the County Palatine of Durham*, II [1820], p 309).

LANERCOST PRIORY (Cumberland, now Cumbria)

1307 r
823 Miracle plays organized by James de Cowpen, harper and King of Heralds, for Queen Margaret (of France) here or at Carlisle (Bullock-Davies, pp 79, 101, 122, 182; Axton, 'Modes,' p 27; entry transcribed by Richard Rastall, 'Minstrels and Minstrelsy in Household Account Books,' REED Proc., p 7).

LANHERNE (Cornwall)

1466-7 r
824 Christmas disguising and moresque in the household of Sir John Arundell, in Mawgan-in-Pydar, for which a variety of materials such as paper and bells were bought (H.L. Douch, 'Household Accounts at Lanherne,' JRIC, NS 2 [1953-4], 27-9; cf J.J. Alexander, 'The Early Arundells,' Devon and Cornwall Notes & Queries, 20 [1939], 155-7).

LANTHONY ABBEY (Gloucestershire)

14th century r
825 The library included Plautus' 'Aulularia' and a Terence (H. Omont, 'Anciens Catalogues de Bibliothéques anglaises,' Centralblatt für Bibliothekswesen, 9 [1892], 218, 220, nos 314, 403; Williams, pp 154, 157, 161).

LEICESTER (Leicestershire)

1st-4th centuries? r
826 A sherd of pottery found here at Roman Ratae Coritanorum has two names scratched on it, Verecunda the 'LVDIA' (?'ludia,' that is, 'player,' or perhaps a dancer) and Lucius the gladiator, perhaps itinerant entertainers (Inscriptiones Britanniae Latinae, ed Aemilius Hübner, Corpus Inscriptionum Latinarum, VII [1873], no 1335.4, p 249; Wacher, Towns, p 357).

1467 r, 1523-43
827 Riding of the George between St George's day and Whitsunday, with a dragon (Records of the Borough of Leicester ... 1327-1509, ed M. Bateson, rev W.H. Stevenson and J.E. Stocks, II [1901], p 293, a can-

celled, late addition to a 1467 record; *Records of the Borough of Leicester ... 1509-1603*, ed M. Bateson, rev W.H. Stevenson and J.E. Stocks, III [1905], pp 24-50).

1476 p
828 Passion play (by players, not the crafts; on 26 March 1477, there was debate whether to hand over play profits and stuff to the craft pageants, but the city council chose its own wardens; *Records of the Borough of Leicester*, II, 297; Kelly, pp 27-8, 187-8).

1491-1507
829 Plays in St Mary de Castro church (1491p, 1499p); and a ?representation requiring 'the garment of Jesus,' angel heads, and wings (1504-7r; cf 'the king's game,' 1520; Kelly, p 14; Nichols, *History and Antiquities*, I, ii, 309-11).

ca 1492-6 r
830 A Terence in Leicester Abbey library (John Nichols, *The History and Antiquities of the County of Leicester*, I, ii [1815], p 104; cf M.V. Clarke, 'Henry Knighton and the Library Catalogue of Leicester Abbey,' *EHR*, 45 [1930], 103-7).

1494-1556
831 Whitsuntide procession from St Martin's church to St Margaret's, at times with the twelve apostles, virgins, the figure of St Martin, and the Mary tabernacle; with Herod in 1546-7 and three shepherds in 1555-6; and from St Mary de Castro, with twelve apostles and others, 1493-1516 (Thomas North, *A Chronicle of the Church of S. Martin in Leicester* [1866], pp 70-3, 114, 140; Kelly, pp 7-10; Nichols, *History and Antiquities*, I, ii, 309-11).

1525-6 r, 1534 p
832 Robin Hood (1525r, 1534p); and May games and pageants or ridings of St George and the twelve months brought into Newarke College (1525r); 'ludum vocat Robynhud Play' for St Leonard's church (1526r; *Visitations in the Diocese of Lincoln, 1517-1531*, III, ed A.H. Thompson, LRS 37 [1947 for 1940], pp 144-5, 152, 172-3, 181-2; A.P. Moore, 'Proceedings of the Ecclesiastical Courts in the Archdeaconry of Leicester, 1516-1535,' *AASRP*, 28, pt i [1905], 202, 208; Kelly, pp 60-1, 191).

1530-1642
833 Visiting players (*Records of the Borough of Leicester*, III, 30-450; Kelly, 190-266).

1544-7
834 Palm Sunday prophet reading the passion at St Martin's church (North, *Chronicle*, pp 54, 84).

1550-1 p
835 A play in the church (*Records of the Borough of Leicester*, III, 70).

1559-61
836 Payment of, and loan to, players by St Martin's church (North, *Chronicle*, p 151).

LENTON (Nottinghamshire)

1580 19 November r
837 Lord Henry Berkeley's players fighting in the church (R.F.B. Hodgkinson, 'Extracts from the Act Books of the Archdeacons of Nottingham,' *Trans. of the Thoroton Society*, 30 [1926], 50).

LEOMINSTER (Herefordshire, now Hereford and Worcester)

1348 r
838 Bishop John Trilleck prohibits exhibitions or plays in 'L. church' that have ribaldry or obscenity (probably Leominster, according to Dew, p 66; Ludlow or Ledbury is more likely, according to EES, II.i, 55).

ca 1535-43 r
839 Townsfolk go 'ons a yere ... to sport and play' to a ditched area on a hillside just east of the town, a place 'now caullyd Comfort-castle' (Leland, *Itin.*, II, 74-5).

LEVERINGTON (Cambridgeshire)

1518-66
840 Visiting players and bann-criers, often at Christmas ('Leverington Parish Accounts,' *Fenland Notes and Queries*, 7 [1909], 188, 298-300, 332-3).

LEVERTON (Lincolnshire)

1526 p, 1575-95
841 Churchwardens' accounts reward visiting players, riding and crying their bann in 1526, and playing in the church in 1595 (Kahrl, p 20; Pishey Thompson, *The History and Antiquities of Boston* [1856], pp 569, 572).

LEWES (Sussex)

1558 r
842 Visiting players (*The Town Book of Lewes 1542-1701*, ed L.F. Salzman, Sussex Rec. Society, 48 [1945-6], p 10).

LICHFIELD (Staffordshire)

ca 1188-98 r
843 'representacio pastorum' (Christmas night), and two miracles, 'representacio Resurreccionis dominice' on Easter morning and 'representacio peregrinorum' on Easter Monday (as revised in the 13th-14th centuries; *Statutes of Lincoln Cathedral*, arranged by Henry Bradshaw, ed Christopher Wordsworth, II [1897], pp 15, 23; text in 'The Shrewsbury Fragments'? [Davis 1, pp xiv-xxii, 1-7; also reconstructed by Young, II, 514-23, with facs, pl XIII; Smoldon, pp 394-9; Stratman 4385-409; *Manual* 2]).

1348 9 April p
844 Royal 'hastiludia' or jousts, at which there were many visored ladies (for Edward III; Nicolas, pp 26-9, 40, 114-15, 117-18, 121).

LIMEBROOK (Herefordshire, now Hereford and Worcester)

1422 16 June r
845 Ordinances for the priory here state that the prioress is not to licence the sisters any more to attend 'comyn wakes or fetes, spectacles, and other worldly vanytees, and specially on holy dayes,' and that 'all maner of mynstrelseys, enterludes, dawnsyng, or revelyng' within the priory is forbidden (*Registrum Thome Spofford, Episcopi Herefordensis. A.D. MCCCCXXII-MCCCCXLVIII*, ed Arthur T. Bannister, CYS 23 [1919], pp 81-2).

ca 1570-80
846 Actor's part for God the Father ('Processus Satanae,' ed W.W. Greg, *Collections Vol. II. Part III* [MalS, 1931], pp 239-50; Stratman 4366-7, 6219; *Manual* 33).

LINCOLN (Lincolnshire)

ca 100-200 r?
847 There was possibly a Roman theatre or wooden amphitheatre here at Lindum (J.B. Whitwell, *Roman Lincolnshire*, History of Lincolnshire 2 [1970], p 22; Christina Colyer, *Lincoln: the Archaeology of an Historic City* [1975], p 12; Wacher, *Towns*, p 134).

1236-1390
848 In a letter of 1236? to the Dean and Chapter of Lincoln Cathedral, Robert Grosseteste, bishop of Lincoln, prohibits the customary 'festum stultorum' on the Circumcision and in 1390 William Courtenay, archbishop of Canterbury, still draws attention to the clerics' 'strepitus truffas garulaciones et ludos' then (Kahrl, pp 98-100).

ca 1272-1307
849 'La Batailplace,' a public area of two acres outside Lincoln, is where its citizens customarily come to play ('ludere') at all times, its friars to preach, and all to have their easements (*Rotuli Hundredorum Temp. Hen. III & Edw. I* [ed W. Illingworth and J. Caley], I, Record Commission [1812], pp 312, 320, 323, 398).

1317-87
850 Cathedral accounts record a 'ludus' of the three kings at Epiphany, with a star, 1318-22 and 1384-7 (Kahrl, pp 24, 26).

1321-69
851 Cathedral accounts pay for a 'ludus' of St Thomas the apostle, often at Easter in the nave (Kahrl, pp 24-5).

1321-1509
852 Cathedral records note a ceremony involving a dove drawn by a cleric, and once an angel, at Pentecost (*Statutes of Lincoln Cathedral*, ed Henry Bradshaw and Christopher Wordsworth [1892-7], I, 336; II, cxviii, 165; Kahrl, pp 26-7, 32, 41).

1384-91
853 Cathedral accounts pay for a 'ludus resurreccionis,' once at Easter (Kahrl, p 26).

1389 r
854 The Cordwainers process to the monastery, St Catherine's priory, with Mary, Joseph, St Blaise and two angels, and there are games there (H.F. Westlake, *The Parish Gilds of Mediaeval England* [1919], pp 172-3).

1389 r, 1521 r
855 The Guild of 'Minstrels and Actors' processes to the cathedral about Pentecost ('histriones' or 'mimi'? Westlake, p 173; *Lincoln Wills*, I, ed C.W. Foster, LRS 5 [1914], pp 101-2, has a reference to this guild in 1521).

1393-1561
856 Cathedral accounts pay for a representation with Mary, the Angel, and sometimes Elizabeth and prophets on Christmas morning to about 1543, and afterwards for a ceremony with a star then (Kahrl, pp 26-67).

1397-1521
857 The Pater Noster 'ludus,' 'lusus,' or play, a civic production by 1521 (Kahrl, pp 27-50). A late text is probably *The Castle of Perseverance*, in *Macro Plays*, pp 1-111; Bevington, pp 796-900; facs ed David Bevington, Folger Facsimiles 1 (1972); the early text, as described in the banns, was written in a Lincolnshire dialect, with auspices near Lincoln (perhaps at the battle place), for which see Walter K. Smart, 'The "Castle of Perseverance": Place, Date, and a Source,' *The Manly Anniversary Studies in Language and Literature* (1923), pp 42-53, and Jacob Bennett, 'The *Castle of Perseverance*: Redactions, Place, and Date,' MS, 24 (1962), 141-52. There is no room here to argue for an identification of this play with the Pater Noster play, but see lines 1917 and 2398 for the virtues' use of the Paternoster (later the rosary) to ward off the vices (and cf lines 1649, 2213, 2358, 2362); and the present ms, ca 1440, has a new ending with the Four Daughters of God and is written by a Norfolk scribe. For discussions of the 'staging diagram,' see Richard Southern, *The Medieval Theatre in the Round* (1957), Schmitt, and PLATE 11; Stratman 5421-49, 6014-18; *Manual* 27; Houle 5.

1420 r
858 A 'visus' called 'Rubum quem viderat' is arranged by Thomas Chamberleyn at Christmas (Christopher Wordsworth, *Notes on Mediaeval Services in England* [1898], p 127; perhaps with Moses, according to Chambers, ELCMA, p 8; document unlocated by Kahrl, p 29, n 1).

1441-2 p
859 'Ludus' of St Laurence (Kahrl, p 30).

1447-8 p
860 'Ludus' of St Susanna (Kahrl, p 31).

1452-3 p
861 A 'ludus' of King Robert of Sicily (Kahrl, p 31).

1454-5 p
862 'Ludus' of St James (Kahrl, p 32).

1455-6 p
863 'Ludus' of St Clara (Kahrl, p 32).

1457-1538
864 Representation or 'visus' of the Ascension or the Assumption of the Blessed Virgin on St Anne's feast takes place in the cathedral nave up to 1469; and from 1483 this 'Ludum siue serimonium,' generally known as the Coronation, is played and shown in the civic St Anne's day procession (Kahrl, pp 32-62).

1472-1554
865 A Corpus Christi 'ludus,' 'lusus,' or play is done by 1477-81 in the chamber of John Sharpe in the cathedral close, but on 6 July 1554 the city orders that the play be brought forth (Kahrl, pp 35-65).

1514-55
866 St Anne's Guild and the city crafts, with garments on loan from knights and gentry, bring forth the sight or pageants of St Anne's guild on St Anne's day, with kings, prophets and two Maries; and probably the Cordwainers' pageant of Bethlehem (which included a great gilded head with eight beams, three stars, two angels, and doves

and was carried by six bearers accompanied by three shepherds), and a Noah's ship (Kahrl, pp 42-69; and Nelson, pp 104-13).

1529-32 p
867 The Cordwainers' Guild has players on several occasions, in 1529-30 in the guildhall (Kahrl, pp 56-7).

1564-7 r
868 The standing or stage play of 'olde thobye' or Tobit, or of his son Tobias, is performed over two days in July 1564 in Broadgate, with a hell mouth and nether 'chap' or jaws, a prison, the chamber of Sarah (Tobias's wife), a great idol with a club, a tomb, the cities of Nineveh, Jerusalem, and Rages in Media, the king's palace at Lachish, and a firmament with a fiery cloud; and civic minutes propose additional performances at Pentecost 1566 and 1567 (Kahrl, pp 67-8; and Nelson, pp 117-18).

1564-5 r
869 'Crying Christmas,' a dialogue of three senators played by the city waits at the crying of Christmas (text ed Kahrl, pp 101-3).

LINCOLN, diocese of

1230 r
870 Interrogatories ordered by Hugh of Wells include a question about 'ludi' in consecrated places (*Concilia*, pp 627-8).

ca 1235-6 r
871 Bishop Robert Grosseteste's statutes prohibit all 'ludi' from consecrated ground (*Councils & Synods*, p 274).

ca 1235-53 r
872 Instructions to the archdeacons of the diocese to refrain from 'ludos' called 'miracula' made by clerks and other 'ludos' called 'inductionem Maii sive Autumpni' (*Councils & Synods*, pp 479-80).

ca 1236 r
873 A letter by Bishop Grosseteste to his archdeacons forbids 'ludos' in churches and churchyards (*Councils & Synods*, p 204).

LINSTEAD (Kent)

1482 r
874 Parishioners are allowed to use a field described as 'a Playing-place' (Arthur Hussey, *Testamenta Cantiana* [1907], p 195).

LITTLE BARFORD (Bedfordshire)

1528 13 December r
875 Bequest by John Slade of Blunham, Beds., of 'all my play book*es* and garment*es* with all the pr*o*perties and o<ther> thyng*es* belongyng to the saim' to the church here (Beds. County Record Office, ABP/R 2, fol 192d; cf Joyce Godber, *History of Bedfordshire 1066-1888* [1969], p 105).

LODDON (Norfolk)

1554-6 p
876 'the gaudayes' 1554-5 and a game week 1556 (Galloway-Wasson, p 78; cf J. Copeman, 'Autographs of Sir Miles Hobart and Anthony Hobart,' NA, 2 [1849], 65-6).

LONDON AND WESTMINSTER

For dramatic activities in the environs of London, in what is now Greater London, see BERMONDSEY, CLERKENWELL, DEPTFORD, ELTHAM, FINSBURY, GREENWICH, HAMPTON COURT, HAVERING, HORNCHURCH, HOXTON, ISLINGTON, KENNINGTON, KINGSTON UPON THAMES, MERTON, PUTNEY, RICHMOND, SHOOTERS HILL, SHOREDITCH, SOUTHWARK, STEPNEY, SYON ABBEY, and WEST HAM.

ca 1st-4th centuries
877 Fragments of three masks, two from excavations for rebuilding of the Bank of England (a ritual deposit from the Walbrook river?), and one from the Roman waterfront site at St Magnus, are possibly imports depicting 'grotesque old men,' likely 'worn in semi-religious performances and processions' (G.D. Marsh, 'Three "theatre" Masks from London,' *Britannia*, 10 [1979], 263-5 and fig 4).

ca 1170-82 r
878 'London in place of shows in the theatre and stage-plays [as at Rome] has holier plays, wherein are shown forth the miracles wrought by Holy Confessors or the sufferings which glorified the constancy of Martyrs' (William Fitz Stephen's 'Descriptio Londoniae,' trans H.E. Butler, in F.M. Stenton, *Norman London: An Essay*, new edn, Hist. Assoc. Leaflets, 93-4 [1934], p 30).

ca 1193 r
879 Literary allusion to a 'theatrum' in a work condemning entertainers (*The Chronicle of Richard of Devizes*, ed J.T. Appleby [1963], p 65).

1207 r
880 At Emperor Otto's entry, London dressed itself in 'solempnitatem pallis et aliis ornamentis circumornata' (pageants? 'Annales Londonienses,' *Chronicles*, I, 13-14).

1236 January p
881 At the procession of Eleanor of Provence to Westminster for coronation, 'quibusdam prodigiosis ingeniis et portentis' (Matthew Paris, *Chronica Majora*, ed Henry R. Luard, RS 57, III [1876], pp 336-7; 'many Pageants, and strange deuises,' according to Stow's *Survey*, I, 95).

1295 8 October p
882 Thomas Turbeville was led on a hackney from the Tower to Westminster with his tormentors riding about him dressed like devils ('turmenturs ... del deble atireez'; Bartholomew Cotton, *Historia Anglicana*, ed Henry R. Luard, RS 16 [1859], pp 306, 439; courtesy of T. De Welles).

1298 19 August p
883 St Magnus, by the Guild of Fishmongers, and pageants in a civic procession for Edward I's victory (Stow, *Survey*, I, 96; Withington, I, 124-5).

1299 p
884 A play ('spel') or game of King Arthur, his knights, and the round table, in a tournament for Edward I's (second) marriage to Margaret of France in London, and a set of challenges at a banquet with disguised

figures including two squires and the Loathly Damsel (Roger S. Loomis, 'Edward I, Arthurian Enthusiast,' *Speculum*, 28 [1953], 118-21).

1312 13 November p
885 Londoners celebrate the birth of Prince Edward with 'carols of people in costume' for a fortnight from this day (*Chronicles of the Mayors and Sheriffs of London, A.D. 1188 to A.D. 1274. The French Chronicle of London, A.D. 1259 to A.D. 1343*, trans H.T. Riley [1863], p 214).

1313 4 February p
886 Fishmongers' procession, from Westminster to Eltham, with Queen Isabella and a pageant ship, to celebrate the birth of the future king ('Annales Londonienses,' *Chronicles*, p 221; Withington, I, 126).

1331 22 September p
887 One day before a Cheapside tournament, a procession of Edward III, William de Montacute, earl of Salisbury, and other knights dressed like Tartars, 'ad similitudinem Tartarorum,' and led on golden chains by their ladies ('Annales Paulini,' *Chronicles*, I, 354-5; cf the June 1331 procession through London where knights wore masks [p 353]).

1334 14 December r
888 Civic prohibition, at time of war, of persons going about disguised with 'false faces' at Christmas to houses in the City in order to play at dice (*Memorials*, p 193).

1343 p
889 A Smithfield tournament waged on three days after Midsummer with knights dressed as the Pope and twelve cardinals (Murimuth, pp 146, 230).

1352 ca 30 November r
890 Civic proclamation forbidding persons to go about at night with a mask (a 'fause visage'; *Letter-Books*, G, p 3).

1357 May p
891 King John of France, led captive to London by Edward the Black Prince, encountered near a woods a (ceremonial) ambush by five hundred men in green, foresters who appeared like robbers; and during

the king's royal entry on 24 May there was a Cheapside pageant of two beautiful maidens suspended 'in quadam catasta' (a cage?) with cords (*Anonimalle Chron.*, pp 40-1; *Chronica Johannis de Reading et Anonymi Cantuariensis 1346-1367*, ed James Tait, Univ. of Manchester Historical Ser., 20 [1914], pp 204-5).

1359 27-9 May p
892 Tournament in which Edward III, his sons, and certain noblemen performed as the mayor of London and twenty-four aldermen against all comers (*Chronica Johannis de Reading*, pp 131-2, 275).

1362 p
893 Cheapside tournament with 'the Seven Deadly Sins' as challengers (*Chronica Johannis de Reading*, pp 150-1, 294).

1372 25 December r
894 Civic proclamation that none should go about the City with visors to play at dice (*Letter-Books*, G, p 303).

1374-5 p
895 The 'actors' of London played before the abbot and convent on the feasts of St Peter and St Edward ('histriones'? Herbert F. Westlake, *Westminster Abbey: The Church, Convent, Cathedral and College of St. Peter, Westminster* [1923], II, 315).

1375 p
896 Dame Alice Perrers rode as lady of the sun in a procession from the Tower through Cheapside before the Smithfield jousts (*Chronicle*, p 70).

1376 December r
897 Civic proclamation against wearing masks and playing dice (*Letter-Books*, H, p 54).

1377 15 July p
898 Richard II was received by London at Cheapside with a castle pageant having four virgins and a mechanical angel that came down to offer him a golden crown (Walsingham, I, 331-2; trans in EES, I, 54-5; *Anonimalle Chron.*, pp 107-8).

1378 r
899 The scholars of Paul's school petition Richard II 'to prohibit some unexpert People from presenting the History of the Old Testament, to the great Prejudice of the said Clergy, who have been at great Expence in order to represent it publickly at *Christmas*' ([Robert Dodsley, ed] *A Select Collection of Old Plays*, I [1744], p xii; unknown source, as noted in MS, II, 380-1).

1380 December r
900 Civic proclamation against wearing visors or masks and playing at dice (*Letter-Books*, H, p 157).

1383 7 January p
901 Goldsmiths' guild pays for a pageant castle with three female characters at the entry of Anne of Bohemia (Herbert, II, 217-18).

1385-6 p
902 Two boys, 'ludentes' at Westminster Abbey (E.H. Pearce, *The Monks of Westminster* [1916], p 99).

1387 ?7 January r
903 Civic proclamation against wearing masks and playing with dice (*Letter-Books*, H, p 293).

1387 December r
904 Civic proclamation forbidding anyone going as a '"mummer" or playing any game with a mask or other strange guise' (*Letter-Books*, H, p 322).

1388-9 r
905 'ludo regis,' with twenty-one linen coifs for counterfeiting men of law at court in Christmas (*HEP*, II, 220).

1390 ca May-July r
906 Civic order to keep night watch during 'revels and jousts' (at Smithfield beginning 10 October; *Letter-Books*, H, pp 353-4).

1392 21 August p
907 Procession by Richard II and Queen Anne through London, welcoming them by pageants including the following (Richard de Maid-

stone, 'The Reconciliation of Richard II. with the City of London,' *Political Poems and Songs Relating to English History*, ed Thomas Wright, RS 14, I [1859], pp 282-300, partly trans in EES, I, 64-71; Malverne, p 275; Withington, I, 129-31 [which excerpts from Bodl. ms Ashmole 793, a 15th-century chronicle]; Walsingham, II, 210-11; Knighton, II, 320; Helen Suggett, 'A Letter Describing Richard II's Reconciliation with the City of London, 1392,' EHR, 62 [1947], 209-13):

1 / a castle in Cheapside near the Great Conduit with two youths as angels who descend with crowns for the king and queen;

2 / God and angels, represented at St Paul's; and

3 / a forest wilderness on Temple Bar gate with John Baptist, wild beasts, and an angel who descends with tablets.

1393 p
908 Play of St Catherine (*Chronicle*, pp 80, 154).

1393 r
909 Civic prohibition against persons going about the City or the suburbs 'with visor or false face' at Christmas (*Memorials*, p 534).

1393-4 p
910 Londoners came to Westminster at Christmas with 'diverso apparatu,' dancing, and music for the king (Malverne, p 281).

1396 r
911 St Paul's canons are prohibited frequenting 'ludos vel spectacula inhonesta' (translated early in the 16th century as 'vnhonest playes and spectacles'; W.S. Simpson, 'The Charter and Statutes of the College of the Minor Canons in S. Paul's Cathedral, London,' *Arch*, 43, pt 1 [1871], 176, 192-3).

1400 r
912 The Merchant Tailors' guild contributes to the Lord Mayor for the 'Mommyng' at Christmas at the Guildhall (C.M. Clode, *Memorials of the Guild of Merchant Taylors of the Fraternity of St. John the Baptist, in the City of London* [1875], p 62).

1404 November r
913 Civic proclamation forbidding wearing of mask or visor at Christmas (*Letter-Books*, I, p 38).

1404-42
914 The Drapers' guild allows 20s. for rushes, minstrels, players, etc
(1404-5r), and has players at its annual feast (1429-42; Herbert, I, 467;
A.H. Johnson, *The History of the Worshipful Company of Drapers of London*, I [1914], pp 321, 326, 330, 338, 343, and cf p 267).

1405 13 December r
915 Civic prohibition against persons going about the City or the
suburbs 'with visors or false faces' at Christmas (*Memorials*, p 561).

1412-18 p
916 Interlude, *ludus*, revels (*Early Records of Furnival's Inn*, ed D.S.
Bland [1957], pp 24-5, and his 'Interludes in Fifteenth-Century Revels
at Furnivall's Inn,' RES, 3 [1952], 263-8).

ca 1412-34? r
917 Lydgate's poem, 'an ordenaunce of a precessyoun of þe feste of
corpus cristi made in london': a description of the 'figures,' 'many
vnkouþe signe,' and 'diuers liknesses' (of pageants? *Minor Poems*, I,
35-43, and lines 6-8, 217-18; IMEV 3606; for the Skinners' procession
on Corpus Christi, ca 1327-1548, see Nelson, pp 173-5).

1413 15 April p
918 Pageantry (?) for the coronation procession of Henry V (a giant
was erected at London Bridge; Charles Welch, *History of The Tower
Bridge* [1894], p 120).

1413-14 p
919 Boys of Westminster School 'ludentibus coram Domino' at Westminster (E.J.L. Scott, 'The Westminster Play,' *The Athenaeum*, 17
November 1900, p 655; E.K. Chambers suggests, instead, a boy-bishop
revel [24 November 1900, p 692]; cf Tanner, p 56).

1415 23 November p
920 Pageants for Henry V's entry into London after Agincourt (*Gesta
Henrici Quinti. The Deeds of Henry the Fifth*, ed and trans F. Taylor and
J.S. Roskell [1975], pp 100-13, 191-2; Giles, pp 53-60; J.H. Wylie, *The
Reign of Henry the Fifth*, II [1919], pp 257-68; and other chronicles, for
which see Withington, I, 132-7):
   1 / a giant and giantess;

2 / antelope, lion, St George, and the hierarchy of angels;
3 / the prophets;
4 / the twelve apostles and twelve 'kings of the English succession,
martyrs and confessors';
5 / a castle with virgins and angels; and
6 / the sun enthroned, with archangels.

1417 23 December r
921 Proclamation against the wearing of visors or false faces at night,
and against mumming at Christmas (*Memorials*, p 658; Mill-Chambers,
p 286).

1418 r
922 Mayor's proclamation that during Christmas no one walk at night
'in eny man*e*re mo*m*myng, pleyes, ent*e*rludes, or eny þ *er* disgisynges'
with pretended beards, painted visors, or 'disfourmyd or colourid visages' (*A Book of London English 1384-1425*, ed R.W. Chambers and M.
Daunt [1931], pp 96-7; *Letter-Books*, I, p 209; *Memorials*, p 669; see
PLATE 9).

1421 14, 24 February p
923 Various pageants, which included giants, lions, castles, angels,
apostles, martyrs, confessors, and virgins, made by the City when
Queen Catherine of Valois entered London from Eltham, and when
she rode from the Tower to Westminster (attributed to Thomas de
Elmham, *Vita & Gesta Henrici Quinti*, ed Thomas Hearne [1727], pp
297-8; *Great Chronicle*, p 115; 'ludicis et vario apparatu,' according to
Walsingham, II, 336; Welch, *Tower Bridge*, p 120).

ca 1424-30 r
924 Lydgate's 'Bycorne and Chychevache,' a 'deuise of a peynted or
desteyned clothe,' also termed a 'fourome of desguysinges,' with nar-
rator and speaking pictures, for a London citizen (*Minor Poems*, II,
433-8; IMEV 2541; Schirmer, p 100, considers this a mumming).

1425 p, 1435 p
925 Players at the Brewers' Guild election feast; 'four Clerkis of London for a Play' in 1435 (Mia Ball, *The Worshipful Company of Brewers: A
Short History* [1977], p 50; Chambers, MS, II, 382, also mentions players
in 1433).

ca 1425-35? r
926 A Londoner, probably an Oxford graduate, denies himself for-
ever all 'spectacula,' that is, 'dances (*choreas*), buckler-play, dicing,
wrestling, and the like' (W.A. Pantin, 'Instructions for a Devout and
Literate Layman,' *Medieval Learning and Literature: Essays Presented to
Richard William Hunt*, ed J.J.G. Alexander and M.T. Gibson [1976], pp
400, 421).

1426 r, 1496-1555
927 Play to be done annually by visiting players for the Blacksmiths'
guild on their quarter day, shortly after Twelfth Day, at the cony feast
(Anne Lancashire, 'Plays for the London Blacksmiths' Company,'
REEDN, 1981.1, pp 12-14; and Arthur Adams, *The History of the Worshipful Company of Blacksmiths* [1951], p 25, for 1497-9).

ca 1427
928 'A Mumming at London,' Lydgate's 'deuyse of a desguysing'
before the great estates of England, with Dames Fortune, Prudence,
Rightwisness, Fortitude or Magnificence, and Fair and Wise Attemper-
ance (text in *Minor Poems*, II, 682-91; IMEV 1928).

1427 p
929 Pageantry in the spring for the return of John of Lancaster, duke
of Bedford, from France (with effigies of a princess, Abraham, Isaac,
Jacob, Joseph, Moses, Joshua, the duke of Bedford, Judas Maccabaeus,
the centurion of the Roman senate, St Alban the prince, Henry, first
duke of Lancaster, Hector, and Hercules standing on London Bridge;
Welch, *Tower Bridge*, pp 120-1).

1429 6 January r
930 'A Mumming for the Mercers of London,' Lydgate's 'lettre made
in wyse of balade' for Jupiter's pursuivant sent with mummers before
William Estfeld, mayor of London (*Minor Poems*, II, 695-8; IMEV 2210).

1429 2 February r
931 'A Mumming for the Goldsmiths of London,' Lydgate's 'lettre
made in wyse of balade' for a herald, Fortune, presenting David, the
twelve tribes of Israel, and his ark in a disguising before William Estfeld, mayor of London (*Minor Poems*, II, 698-701; IMEV 3301).

1429 November p
932 Coronation procession of Henry VI, with pageantry (a 'mimic queen,' with maidens and pages, appeared at London Bridge; Welch, *Tower Bridge*, p 121).

1432 21 February p
933 Pageants for the entry of Henry VI into London (text: Lydgate's 'King Henry VI's Triumphal Entry into London, 21 Feb. 1432,' *Minor Poems*, II, 630-48; 'Letter of John Carpenter, Common Clerk of the City of London ...,' *Munimenta Gildhallae Londoniensis*, RS 12, ed Henry T. Riley, III [1862], App III, pp 457-64; *Great Chronicle*, pp 156-70; *IMEV* 227.5, 578.5, 728.5, 1240.5, 1924.4, 1929.3, 3785.8, 3799, 3866.3; Withington, I, 141-7):

1 / a giant on a tower;

2 / empresses Nature, Grace, and Fortune in a tower, with seven maidens (presenting the seven gifts of the Holy Ghost), and seven other virgins (presenting glory, clemency and pity, might and victory, prudence and faith, health, and love and peace);

3 / Dame Sapience and the seven liberal sciences: Grammar, Logic, Rhetoric, Music, Arithmetic, Geometry, and Astronomy, each with a famous practitioner (respectively, Priscian, Aristotle, Cicero, Boethius, Pythagorus, Euclid, and Albumazar);

4 / a king with Mercy, Truth, Clemency, two judges, and eight sergeants;

5 / Mercy, Grace, and Pity, with a paradise, beside which appear Enoch and Elijah;

6 / a castle and a tree of Jesse; and

7 / the Trinity with angels.

1432 p
934 Payment to 'lez playersz de Glowceter' (*Facsimile of First Volume of MS. Archives of the Worshipful Company of Grocers of the City of London, A.D. 1345-1463*, ed John A. Kingdon [1886], II, 213).

1437 10 December r
935 Civic order that no one go visored at night during Christmas (*Letter-Books*, K, p 215).

1442-98 p
936 Players and play (1497-8) at the Cutlers' guild cony feast at Christmas (payments to players – four of them from 1486 on – between

these limits on this occasion are regular; Anne Lancashire, 'Players for the London Cutlers' Company,' REEDN, 1981:2, pp 10-11; Charles Welch, *History of the Cutlers' Company of London*, I [1916], pp 177, 304, 311).

1445 28 May p
937 Pageants for the entry of Queen Margaret of Anjou: Peace and Plenty; Noah's ship; Madame Grace, chancellor of God; St Margaret; the five wise and five foolish virgins; the Heavenly Jerusalem; resurrection and doomsday (text, written to comment on and ?accompany the pageants: Carleton Brown, 'Lydgate's Verses on Queen Margaret's Entry into London,' MLR, 7 [1912], 225-34; Robert Withington, 'Queen Margaret's Entry into London, 1445,' MP, 13 [1915-16], 53-7; Gordon Kipling, 'The London Pageants for Margaret of Anjou: A Medieval Script Restored,' MET, 4:1 [1982], 5-27; IMEV 2200).

1449 25 December p
938 Plays and recreations for Henry VI (*Issues*, p 473).

1451 17 December r
939 Civic prohibition of going with mummings, disguisings, and visors and painted faces at Christmas (Mill-Chambers, p 286).

1451 p
940 Playing the prophet on Palm Sunday at St Mary at Hill church (Henry J. Feasey, *Ancient English Holy Week Ceremonial* [1897], pp 75-6; not in Littlehales' edn, for which see below at 1485).

1454-1512
941 Plays or players, occasionally at Candlemas (*Records of the Worshipful Company of Carpenters*, II, ed Bower Marsh [1914], pp 17-217).

1464 p
942 A pageant on London Bridge for the coronation of Elizabeth Woodville: having angels (with hair and wings), the holy spirit (a figure), St Paul (acted by Robert Clerk), St Elizabeth (acted by Salamon Batell), and Mary Cleophas (acted by Edmund Herte), among which were eight artificial figures (six of them women); and including six ballads written and limned by John Genycote and put on tablets affixed to the pageant, as well as singing by the boys of St Magnus and by the master of the clerks' guild and 25 persons (EES, I, 324-31).

1476-1540
943 The Drapers' guild wardens ask for money to cover entertainment including players, sometimes visiting, generally at their mayor's feast (1481, 1485-1540 [including one playing the friar in 1518]; and in 1539 the parish clerk and his company of players, possibly from St Swithin's; Johnson, *History of the Worshipful Company of the Drapers of London*, I, 157, 278, 356; Herbert, I, 469, n, and cf I, 462; Robertson-Gordon, pp 132-8, 183-4).

1477 28 June p
944 The Drapers' guild contributes a pageant borne by some men, and the nine worthies, to the Midsummer Watch on St Peter's night (ie eve; Johnson, *History of the Worshipful Company of the Drapers of London*, I, 158, n 1; II [1915], pp 273-4).

1478 22 January p
945 Anthony Woodville, earl Rivers, in the dress of a white hermit, St Anthony, at a Westminster jousting entered 'in the house of an Hermite' (William H. Black, 'Narrative of the Marriage of Richard Duke of York with Ann [countess] of Norfolk, the 'Matrimonial Feast,' and the Grand Justing A.D. 1477,' *Illustrations of Ancient State and Chivalry from Manuscripts Preserved in the Ashmolean Museum*, Roxburghe Club [1840], pp 32-40; Kipling, pp 123-5).

1481 23 October r
946 Civic order that there be no disguising or pageant, 'as it hath been used nowe of late afore this tyme,' when the Mayor goes from his house to the water on the way to Westminster for the oath-taking, or from the water to his house on the way back (*Letter-Books*, L, p 187).

1485 ?September p
947 Plays and pastimes, after Henry VII's entry into London (Halle, fol 1v).

1485 r, 1500 r
948 Garments for pageants hired out; and angel wings and three diadems sold (St Mary at Hill churchwardens' accounts, in *Illustrations*, p 100 [1485-7 records are lost, according to *The Medieval Records of a London City Church (St. Mary at Hill) A.D. 1420-1559*, ed Henry Littlehales, EETS OS 125 (1904), p 127]; and Littlehales, p 241).

ca 1485-1509 r
949 A ceremonial account of how a foreign queen ought be received into England for marriage to the king requires that during the coronation procession from the Tower to Westminster there be at the conduit in Cornhill 'a sight w*ith* angelles singinge, and freche balettes y*e* ron in latene, engliche, and ffrenche, mad by the wyseste docturs of this realme' (*AR*, I, 302-3).

1487 3 November p
949.5 An 'angel descending from the roof of St. Paul's to cense' Henry VII during his entry into the City after the battle of Stoke (McGee-Meagher, pp 36-7).

1487 23 November p
950 'gentilmanly Pajants' for Queen Elizabeth's procession by water from Greenwich to the Tower, including 'The Bachelers Barge' with a red dragon spouting flames (later, in her procession to Westminster for coronation, there were children dressed as virgins and angels, with songs, in various parts of the city; Leland, IV, 218, 220).

1487 p
951 Players were paid for a play at the general feast of the guild of the Assumption of Our Blessed Lady at the house of the archbishop of York, Thomas Rotherham (H.F. Westlake, *St Margaret's Westminster* [1914], p 55).

1489-90 p
952 Christmas at court had 'right few Pleys' (Leland, IV, 256)

1490 3, 10, 30 January p
953 Disguising (?play) of the Inner Temple at Gray's Inn (3rd); disguising of Gray's Inn at the Inner Temple (10th); and the Inner Temple disguising at home (A.C. Baugh, 'A Fifteenth-Century Dramatic Performance at the Inns of Court,' *Tennessee Studies in Literature*, 11 [1966], 71-4).

1490 2 February p
954 A play at Whitehall before the king and court (Leland, IV, 256).

1491 25 December p
955 Players (*Early Records of Furnival's Inn*, ed D.S. Bland [1957], p 34).

1491-2 r
956 Inventory of players' garments for the prophet on Palm Sunday, the Virgin, a child, three old women and others (Collier, I, 82-3).

1491-1509
957 Royal and visiting players, puppet players, Abbots of Misrule, May (games), disguisings (with moresques), and pageants by William Cornyshe and others, at the court of Henry VII (also at Greenwich, Sheen or Richmond, and other palaces outside London; 'Court Festivals'; supplemented by BL Add. ms 59899 [Henry VII's personal accounts, 1502-5]).

1493 r
958 Preparations for disguisings as such are not the business of the king's chamberlain, of the ushers of the chamber, either in the hall or the great chamber (AR, I, 313).

1494 6 January p
959 Pageant of St George with a castle, the king's daughter (a virgin), and a dragon at Westminster Hall (*Great Chronicle*, pp 251-2; Anglo, 'Cornish,' pp 348-50; McGee-Meagher, pp 39-40; Richard Daland provided 'certain spectacles, or theatres, commonly called scaffolds ... for performance of "the disguisyngs"' [*Issues*, p 516]; the hall was 'staged Round abowte with Tymber, that the people myght easely behold' [*Chronicles of London*, ed Charles L. Kingsford (1905), p 200]; cf PRO, S.P. 46/123, fol 56).

1494 Michaelmas r
960 Royal fees for the 'lusoribus Regis,' or the players of the king's interludes, John English, Edward Maye, Richard Gibson, and John Hamond (*Issues*, p 516; for a receipt dated 17 May with the players' signatures, see Collier, I, 36-8 [with a facs of the signatures]).

1494-1580
961 Visiting 'lusores' or players, with play, interlude, disguising, or 'commedia,' often on the Purification (*The Records of the Honorable Society of Lincoln's Inn. The Black Books*, I, ed W.P. Baildon [1897], pp 104-418).

1499 November p
962 Pageants at six stations, evidently for the visit of certain Spaniards (Withington, I, 165).

ca 1500 r
962.5 An undated ordinance of 'lez rulez an auncient temps' used in the twelve days of Christmas at Gray's Inn describes the election of a king of Christmas who sat only on festival days, with revels especially (1) after the mid-day banquet and after the post-church supper on Christmas day, and (2) in the hall after supper on Epiphany, the conclusion of which was celebrated by a semi-dramatic carol, 'fare well et have good daye' (*The Reports of Sir John Spelman*, I, ed J.H. Baker, Selden Society 93 [1977], pp 233-4; the editor identifies this carol with 'Now haue gud day' [sung by Christmas; Greene, no 141, p 85], but the latter is clearly meant for Candlemas, not Epiphany).

1501 12 November p
963 Pageants for the entry of Catherine of Aragon (text in 'The Voyage, &c. of the Princess Catharine of Arragon to England, on her Marriage with Prince Arthur ... with a Particular Account of her Progress to London,' *AR*, II, 259-81; *Great Chronicle*, pp 297-310, 447-8; Halle, fols 52v-53r; *Chronicles of London*, pp 229 [on 6 May 1500 the city was authorized to collect a tax to prepare these pageants], 234-48; *Friars' Chronicle*, p 27; Kipling's 'The Dating of the Privy Council Plans for the Reception of Katharine of Aragon' [three versions, late 1499-1501], pp 173-4; *Letters and Papers Illustrative of the Reigns of Richard III. and Henry VII.*, ed James Gairdner, RS 24, I [1861], p 411; Anglo, pp 56-97; McGee-Meagher, pp 44-8; *IMEV* 671.5, 1270.4, 1273.8, etc; cf *The Traduction & Mariage of the Princesse* [1501?], sig [A3v]; *L. & P. Hen. VIII*, IV.iii, no 5791, p 2587; *STC* 4814):

1 / St Catherine, St Ursula, and virgins;

2 / a castle with two knights, Policy and Noblesse, and a bishop Virtue;

3 / the sphere of the moon, with Raphael, Alphonso the Wise of Castile, Job, and Boethius;

4 / the sphere of the sun, with Prince Arthur, angels (and Fronesis, 'Understanding');

5 / the throne of the Godhead, four figures like prophets, angels, and the Prelate of the Church; and

6 / the throne of Honour, the seven virtues Faith, Hope, Charity, Justice, Temperance, Prudence, and Fortitude, and virgins.

1501 14 November p
964 Pageant at St Paul's after the wedding of Arthur and Catherine: a mount with the kings of France, a ship with the king of England, and

a castle with the king of Spain (AR, II, *289-90; *Great Chronicle*, p 310; with disguisings that night at court, according to Halle, fol 53v).

1501 18-28 November p
965 Jousts at Westminster and disguisings, plays, and pageants, probably created by John Atkinson, William Cornyshe, and John English, in Westminster Hall to celebrate the wedding (AR, II, *298-*318; Anglo, 'Cornish,' pp 350-3; *Great Chronicle*, pp 313-15; *Chronicles of London*, pp 248-53; Kipling's 'William Cornish, John English, and the Disguisings of 1501,' pp 175-7; according to 'Certain Notes Taken out of the Entertainment of Katherine, Wife of Arthur, Prince of Wales, Oct. 1501,' *Miscellaneous State Papers* [ed Philip Hardwicke] [1778], I, 19, Jacques Hault and William Pawne were appointed to prepare disguisings and moresques; Anglo, pp 99-103):

1 / a procession into the lists with pageants: chapels, a turreted pavilion, a hermit, a ship, a dragon led by a giant, and a mount with a maiden led by a wildman (18 November);

2 / a disguising of three pageants, a castle with ladies and children, drawn by beasts; a ship with one like Princess Catherine, with Hope and Desire, and with mariners; and a mount of Love with knights who, having seen their ambassadors Hope and Desire rejected by the ladies and having been refused entry themselves, assault the castle until the ladies yield and emerge to dance (19 November; for the text of a song by William Cornyshe possibly intended for this disguising, see Greene, no 463, pp 282, 497-8; but see below under 4 March 1522 for a more likely occasion);

3 / an interlude, and a disguising with two pageants, probably by John English (Kipling, pp 176-7): an arbour with lords, and a windowed, lighted lantern with ladies (21 November);

4 / a procession into the tiltyard by a pageant ship with mariners and shooting serpentines (24 November);

5 / a procession into the tiltyard by a pageant chariot holding a lady and drawn by beasts (as on 19 November); and a disguising with two linked mounts, one like a green garden, with lords, and the other full of sunburnt minerals and precious stones, with ladies of Spain (25 November; for the Scot Walter Ogilvie's account of this revel, see Kipling, p 110, n 35); and

6 / see under RICHMOND (1501 28 November p).

1502 June? p
966 A disguising (between 11 June and 9 December; *Privy Purse Expenses of Elizabeth of York* ..., ed Nicholas H. Nicolas [1830], pp 21, 78; she was on progress from mid-July to late October).

1503-7
967 Yearly plays by the churchwardens and parish of St Andrew's, Holborn, for church works (cited from John Bentley's 'Monuments,' ca 1584, by J.P. Malcolm, *Londinium Redivivum*, II [1803], p 188; Cox, p 279).

1503-9 r
968 Royal fees for the king's interluders, John English, William Rutter, John Scott, Richard Gibson, and John Hamond (*Issues*, p 516, for 1503-4; Collier, I, 38, and ES, II, 78, n 2 [Gibson and 'others'], for 1505-6; and Robert Henry, *The History of Great Britain*, 5th edn [1814], XII, 456, for an annuity for Gibson and 'alijs lusoribus domini regis' in 1508-9).

1504-68
969 Midsummer watch or show on the eves of 23 and 28 June (to 1541) and Lord Mayor's show on 29 October (from 1540; Robertson-Gordon, pp 1-50; 'A Calendar of Dramatic Records in the Books of the London Clothmakers' Company (Addenda to *Collections III*),' *Collections Volume V*, MalS [1959 (1960)], pp 1-16; Machyn, pp 155-6; Wriothesley, I, 100; a vivid description of the 1521 show, lasting from 11 pm to 2 am, appears in *Venice*, III, no 244, pp 136-7; and cf IV, no 482, p 220 [1529]; and the city agreed on 5 May 1521 that the pageant 'devised by [John?] Rastell' standing at the Little Conduit by the stocks should go forth [Reed, p 45]; for the pageants of this year, see below under 3-4, 9-11). The Midsummer Show was cancelled, evidently by the king's command, in 1539 (*L. & P. Hen. VIII*, XIV.i, no 1144, p 515; *Lisle Letters*, V, 542). The pageants up to 1558, with a few after that year, excluding the giants and wife-giants – sometimes hired from Barking or St Giles – are as follows:
   1 / St Blythe (1512);
   2 / Achilles (1512; see also Withington, I, 177);
   3 / the Assumption of the Virgin Mary (1512-41);
   4 / the castle of war (1512-36, with four armed children, a drawbridge, and a Turkish horseman attacking in 1521; and termed

the Castle of Denham (with fireworks) in 1535 and the Castle of Monmouth in 1536 [after civic officials]?);

5 / the martyrdom of St Thomas Becket (played by Thomas Bakehowse?), with Tracy the knight (William de Tracy, played by Robert Johnson), the Crosier (played by Richard Stabyll), the Jewess (played by Robert Hynstok), the Gaoler, and Gilbert Becket (played by Richard Mathewe), with a pageant prison (1519; hired from St Giles');

6 / Our Lady and Elizabeth (1519, hired from Barking; 1535);

7 / the soldan, played by John Mayne in 1519 and by Richard Matthew in 1541 (1519-24, 1541);

8 / the maundy, with God and the twelve apostles played by children with beards (1519);

9 / the tree of Jesse (1521, with all the prophets, turning about by a vice or mechanism; 1529; twelve prophets in 1530);

10 / St John Evangelist (1521, with the Isle of Patmos, some towers, and two boys; 1529; 1535, with dragon and child playing the executioner);

11 / a king of Moors with long sword, wild-fire, and sixty moors who stripped off their breeches and were naked (1521, described as Pluto in the Venetian account, with naked boys dyed black like devils, and a fire-spitting serpent; 1536);

12 / St George, choking the dragon, and delivering St Margaret (1521);

13 / Herod at table on a stage, with Herodias' daughter, the tumbler, the executioner, and St John the Baptist in prison (1521); with goodly speeches (1553), as well as with a lion (1554; Machyn, pp 48, 73); and with a text having speeches for John and four boys (1568);

14 / St Ursula (1523, 1529);

15 / a mount (1532);

16 / St Christopher, with a hermit (1534);

17 / a lady with a gilded Roman 'M' as a device, and three ladies in waiting (the Virgin Mary? 1534);

18 / King Solomon, with children playing two women (1535);

19 / the King, with five children (? Henry VIII; 1535; see below under 1535 23p/?28r June);

20 / Corpus Christi, with six children (1535);

21 / King William the Conqueror and the French king (1535);

22 / Christ disputing with the doctors in the temple; with Joseph and Mary (1541);

23 / a Rock of Rock Alum, with two children (1541);

24 / St Margaret, four child angels, and ?dragon (with speeches; 1541);

25 / wildmen, and a great boat with ordnance (1551);

26 / devil and wildmen (1553-5; Machyn, pp 47, 73, 96);

27 / pageant (a foist?) with children, a gentlewoman, a camel, and speeches written by ?Nicholas Grimald (1556; cf Machyn, pp 117-18); and

28 / pageant with speeches for David, Orpheus, Amphion, Arion, and Topas (1561; text).

1506 24 January r

970 Erasmus visits Lambeth to present his Latin translation of Euripides' *Hecuba* to William Warham, archbishop of Canterbury, which was published later that year in Paris, together with the *Iphigenia* (itself translated in England and dedicated also to Warham, in the second edition; *The Correspondence of Erasmus*, II, trans R.A.B. Mynors and D.F.S. Thomson, annot Wallace K. Ferguson [1975], pp 107-10, 133-5; Erasmus had previously given these translations, for approval, to Thomas Linacre, William Grocyn, William Latimer, and Cuthbert Tunstall [p 99, n 15]; for a London edition of 1519, see Ferdinand Vander Haeghen, *Bibliotheca Erasmiana* [1972], II, 25).

1508 February r

971 Two children (musicians?) of Sir Thomas Brandon come to play before Edward Stafford, third duke of Buckingham, evidently at his London house, the Red Rose (*L. & P. Hen. VIII*, III.i, no 1285, p 496).

1508 23 June p

972 'Spectacula' on St John's eve (Bernard André, 'Annales Henrici Septimi,' *Memorials Hen. VII*, p 121).

1509 11 May r

973 Livery for the funeral of Henry VII was given to 'the king's players,' John English, Thomas Scotte, Bartholomew Hamond, Thomas Sudborough (Sydburgh), and Richard Gibson (*L. & P. Hen. VIII*, I [1920], no 20, p 16).

1509 25-6 June p

974 Pageants of Lady Pallas, a castle, and of Diana, a park with deer, at Henry VIII's coronation tournament at Westminster (Halle, fols 4v-6r; *Great Chronicle*, pp 341-2; Holinshed, III, 550-2).

1509-10 p
975 Reward for 'ludatores' at Christmas (*Minutes of Parliament of the Middle Temple*, ed and trans Charles T. Martin [1904], I, 30).

1509-22
976 Players, disguisings, Lords of Misrule, revels, pageants, and mummings at court (in the king's household and Richard Gibson's revels accounts – the latter with very detailed itemization of costume materials – for Eltham, Greenwich, New Hall, Richmond, and other seats as well as Westminster and York House; *L. & P. Hen. VIII*, II.ii, pp 1441-80, 1490-1517; III.iii, pp 1533-45, 1548-59; Addenda, I.i, no 121, p 35 [1514], and no 273, p 75 [1519]; for two annuities of 1516 to John English and the other king's players, see II.i, no 2736, pp 874-5; see PLATE 16).

1510 18 January p
977 Disguising of Robin Hood, his men (in green coats and hose), and Maid Marian by Henry VIII in the queen's chamber (*L. & P. Hen. VIII*, II.ii, p 1490; Halle, fol 6v; Holinshed, III, 554).

1510 28 February p
978 Disguising or mummery at Westminster by the king and others dressed as Turks, Russians, Prussians, and Moors (*L. & P. Hen. VIII*, II.ii, pp 1445, 1490-2; Halle, fols 6v-7r [dating the event 10 February]; Holinshed, III, 554-5).

1510 23, 28 June p
979 Henry VIII sees the Midsummer Watch in disguise at the King's Head in Cheap (the 23rd) and with his queen publicly (the 28th; *Songs, Carols, and Other Miscellaneous Poems*, ed Roman Dyboski, EETS ES 101 [1908 for 1907], p 156).

1511 12-13 February p
980 Royal jousts by the four knights of Queen Noble Renown of the land called *Coeur Noble*, with knights *Coeur Loyal* (Henry VIII), *Bon Voloir*, *Bon Espoir*, and *Valiant Desire*; and in the Great Hall of Westminster, a pageant of a castle in a forest, having foresters and a maiden, and being drawn by a lion and an antelope or 'olyvant' (on which were two maidens) that wildmen led (on 12 February), and with lesser pageants of a castle and of *La maison du refuge* (and knights

dressed as a recluse and pilgrims; on 13 February); and an interlude including shipmen by William Cornyshe and the chapel children and gentlemen, and in Whitehall a wheeled pageant called the Golden Arbour in the Orchyard of Pleasure with a disguising of the above four 'Chivaliers,' and with John Kite disguised in a gown with eighty faces and a rolled cap like one of a Baron of the Exchequer; after which disguising both the wagon and the revellers' costumes were ransacked by spectators (*The Great Tournament Roll of Westminster*, intro by Sydney Anglo [1968]; Halle, fols 9r-11r; *Great Chronicle*, pp 368-74, 456; *L. & P. Hen. VIII*, II.ii, pp 1450, 1494-7; Holinshed, III, 560-1).

1511 p
981 Interlude at Christmas for the Skinners' company (Robertson-Gordon, p 136).

1514 May p
982 In jousts Henry VIII and Charles Brandon, duke of Suffolk, entered as white and black hermits (Halle, fols 46v-7r).

1515 April-May r
983 Unfinished pageant to be called the Palace 'Marchallyn' (?Marshalling), with ten towers and an armed king and nobles, the 'house framed passant to be borne by men' (*L. & P. Hen. VIII*, II.ii, pp 1503-4).

1515 p
984 Resurrection pageant, hired by the monastery of the Holy Trinity (or Christchurch, Aldgate) from the keepers of Barking procession, for Easter (*L. & P. Hen. VIII*, II.i [1864], no 115, p 38).

1518 18 June r
985 John Colet's statutes for St Paul's School imply that Terence is to be taught (Lupton, App A, p 279; the 'Carmen de Moribus,' written by William Lily, master of the school 1510-22, to his students, requires the reading of Terence [William Lily and John Colet, *A Short Introduction of Grammar: 1549*, Scolar Press facs (1970), sig D7v; STC 15611; by 1528 Wolsey intended this grammar to be used throughout England (Baldwin 1, I, 122)]; and Robert Laneham, who was admitted to the Mercers' company in 1557, recalls that he read Terence at school, and he attended both St Paul's and St Anthony's [*Laneham*, pp 85-6; R.J.P.

Kuin, 'Robert Langham and his "Letter,"' *N&Q*, 223 (1978), 426-7]; cf David Scott, 'William Patten and the Authorship of 'Robert Laneham's *Letter*,"' *ELR*, 7 [1977], 297-306).

1518 October p
986 A mummery of twenty-four men and women dancers at the palace of the bishop of London, Richard FitzJames (3 October); and comedies and pageants (5-10 October; *Four Years at the Court of Henry VIII. Selection of Despatches Written by the Venetian Ambassador, Sebastian Giustinian, and Addressed to the Signory of Venice, January 12th 1515, to July 26th 1519*, trans Rawdon Brown [1854], II, 224-35; *Venice*, II, no 1088, pp 464-5; Halle, fols 65v-66r; Holinshed, III, 633; *L. & P. Hen. VIII*, II.ii, nos 4481, 4491, pp 1377, 1380; French diplomatic reports said that the king went mumming at the lodging of the Admiral, Thomas Howard, earl of Surrey [*L. & P. Hen. VIII*, II.ii, no 4544, p 1391]; and see under GREENWICH).

1518 r
987 Children of the May game (from the churchwardens' accounts of St Margaret, Westminster; John E. Smith, *A Catalogue of Westminster Records* [1900], p 43).

1519-28
988 Prophets on Palm Sunday, one with a beard, at St Stephen, Walbrook (Cox, p 255; Thomas Milbourn, 'Church of St Stephen Walbrook,' *Trans. of the London and Middlesex Archaeological Society*, 5 [1877-81], 361).

1519-34
989 Prophets with wigs (?reading the Passion) on a scaffold on stages on Palm Sunday at St Peter Cheap church (possibly from 1447; W.S. Simpson, 'On the Parish of St Peter Cheap, in the City of London, from 1392 to 1633,' *JBAA*, 1st ser, 24 [1868], 263).

1520 r
990 Printed copies of Plautus' comedies, and of the works of Seneca, in the library of the Oxford scholar, William Grocyn, who lived mainly in London ('Linacre's Catalogue of Books Belonging to William Grocyn in 1520 Together with his Accounts as Executor Followed by a Memoir of William Grocyn,' *Collectana*, 2nd ser, OHS 16 [1890], pp 320-1, 324).

1520 5-7 January p
991 Henry VIII visits Wolsey's place in masquing apparel (5 January); a pageant (6 January); and a masque (7 January; *L. & P. Hen. VIII*, III.iii, p 1552).

1521 3 January p
992 Royal disguising at York Place, Wolsey's palace (*L. & P. Hen. VIII*, III.iii, p 1556; see PLATE 20).

1521 31 December p
993 Wolsey entertained the Emperor's ambassadors at court with many disguisings and interludes (Halle, fol 90r).

1521-2 p
994 There were many mummeries at court this regnal year (Halle, fol 90r).

1521-4 r
995 Payments for the writing of plays (5s.; 1521) and for writing a play for the grammar and singing boys at Westminster Abbey (16d.; 1524; noted in the sub-almoner's notebook; Tanner, pp 56-7; the second item is dated ca 1526 by H.F. Westlake, *Westminster Abbey: The Last Days of the Monastery* [1921], p 35).

1522 3 March p
996 Wolsey entertained the king and the Emperor's ambassadors with a play and a masque (Halle, fol 92r).

1522 4 March p
997 A pageant castle called 'Chateau Vert' at Wolsey's York House with ladies Beauty, Honour, Perseverance, Kindness, Constance, Bounty, Mercy and Pity; ladies of India (guarding them), named Danger, Disdain, Jealousy, Unkindness, Scorn, Malebouche, and Strangeness; and lords (assaulting and winning the castle) Amorous, Nobleness, Youth, Attendance, Loyalty, Pleasure, Gentleness, and Liberty, all led by Ardent Desire (of which the chapel children played ones in the castle); sixteen mantles and cloaks for whom were garnished with 'reasons' or 'rolls written with divers words and poyems' (*L. & P. Hen. VIII*, III.iii, pp 1558-9; Halle, fol 92); the text possibly in-

cluded William Cornyshe's carol 'Yow and I and Amyas,' of a knight Desire, a lady in a castle, a portress Strangeness, Kindness, and Pity (*Music & Poetry*, pp 402-3; but see Greene, no 463, pp 282, 497-8).

1522 6 June p
998 Pageants at the entry of Charles V include the following (eight triumphal arches, according to *Venice*, III, no 466, p 236; text of Latin verses by William Lily is translated and paraphrased in English in *Of the tryumphe and the verses* [Richard Pynson, 1522], STC 5017, for which see C.R. Baskervill, 'William Lily's Verse for the Entry of Charles V into London,' *Huntington Library Bulletin*, 9 [1936], 1-14 (also giving civic payments to Lily for these speeches); STC 15606.7; Withington, I, 174-9; Anglo, pp 186-202; Halle, fols 96-8v; *L. & P. Hen. VIII*, III.ii, no 2306, p 977; McGee-Meagher, pp 79-80; a schedule of pageants, changed by the time of the entry, appears in *A Collection of Scarce and Valuable Tracts* [of Lord Somers], 2nd edn, ed Walter Scott, I [1809], 32-3, the document for which is not now known):
  1 / two giants, Hercules and Samson;
  2 / Jason and the Golden Fleece, a dragon, two bulls, and Medea;
  3 / Charlemagne, with Roland, Oliver, the Pope, the King of Constantinople, the Patriarch of Jerusalem, Charles, the emperor, and Henry VIII;
  4 / genealogical tree from John of Gaunt;
  5 / King Arthur and ten subject princes;
  6 / England an island with the emperor in a castle, the king in an arbour, the elements, planets, stars, and the 'father off hevyn' (also the pageant of roses and a maiden mentioned in the early schedule?);
  7 / the 'Castellum pudiciae' with the four cardinal virtues;
  8 / genealogical tree from Alphonso of Castile (not in the early schedule, which lists the story and progeny of King Solomon); and
  9 / the Assumption of Our Lady, with Michael, Gabriel, the heavens, the apostles, St George, St John Baptist, St Edmund, St Edward the Confessor, Henry VI, St Dunstan, St Thomas a Becket, and St Erkenwaldus.

ca 1522-30 p
999 John Ritwise acted with Paul's boys his tragedy of 'Dido' out of Vergil before Cardinal Wolsey (location uncertain; Wood, I, col 35; cf Cooper, p 529).

1523 27 December r
1000 William Babyngton of London, '"master de miserule," at the
Christmas games,' kills Robert Wolfe or Ulpe in 'le Flete' messuage in
St Bride's parish (pardoned 30 May 1524; *L. & P. Hen. VIII*, IV.i, no 390,
p 170).

1523-40
1001 Prophets on Palm Sunday (also 1493-4, 1518-20? payments
1523-5 to Mr Northfolk, his company, and the children in the playing
week [after Christmas] to make merry, probably relate to his job in
keeping the choir and organs; *The Medieval Records of a London City
Church (St. Mary at Hill)*, pp 321-82; Hugh Baillie, 'Some Biographical
Notes on English Church Musicians, Chiefly Working in London
(1485-1560),' *R.M.A. Research Chronicle*, 2 [1962], p 47).

1525 18 June p
1002 Disguisings in celebrations at Bridewell Palace for the creation
of Henry's illegitimate son Henry Fitzroy as duke of Richmond and
Somerset (Halle, fol 143v; termed 'a magnificent pageant' in *Spain*, III.i
[1873], no 120, p 211).

1526-7 p
1003 Disguising or play by John Roo (written ca 1506-7) performed at
Christmas at Gray's Inn: Dissipation and Negligence, ruling Lord
Governance, put Lady Public Weal(th) from him; and Rumor Populi,
Inward Grudge, and Disdain of Wanton Sovereignty expelled them
from him and restored her; the 'tragedy' was 'partly ... matter against
the cardinal Wolsey,' and Simon Fish, of Gray's Inn, acted the part
touching him and had to flee overseas to escape Wolsey's anger (Halle,
fols 154v-5r; Foxe, IV, 657; Marie Axton, *The Queen's Two Bodies:
Drama and the Elizabethan Succession* [1977], p 2, mentions a letter of 6
February 1527 by Archbishop Warham about this play in PRO, SP 1/40,
fol 25).

1526-40
1004 An angel on Palm Sunday 1526-7r (?hired), 1539-40r; a priest,
and a child who played 'messynger' 1535-7p; and players in the
church 1539-40p, at St Andrew Hubbard church (J.C. Crosthwaite,
'Ancient Churchwardens' Accounts of a City Parish,' *BrMag*, 34
[1848], 183, 396, 401-2).

1527 3 January p
1005 At Wolsey's palace, an unexpected royal disguising of shepherds;
Plautus's comedy *Menaechmei* in Latin by Wolsey's gentlemen on a
stage; and a pageant of Venus, Cupid, six nymphs, and six old men as
shepherds (*Venice*, IV, nos 3-4, pp 2-3; G. Cavendish, *The Life and
Death of Cardinal Wolsey*, ed R.S. Sylvester, EETS ES 243 [1959], pp 25-8;
Halle, fol 154v).

1528 7 January p
1006 At Wolsey's palace hall, Terence's *Phormio* played by Paul's boys;
and a complaint by Religion, Peace, and Justice for Wolsey's help
(*Venice*, IV, no 225, pp 115-16).

1528 r
1007 Civic licence that only the parish of All Hallows in the Wall
could make a stage play from Easter (12 April) to Michaelmas (29
September; Mill-Chambers, p 287); such a play, evidently staged on
scaffolds, grossed over five pounds in the 1528[-9] accounts (*The
Churchwardens' Accounts of the Parish of Allhallows, London Wall, in the
City of London*, ed Charles Welch [1912], pp 57-8).

1528-9 r
1008 John Scott, one of the king's players, was imprisoned in Newgate
for rebuking the sheriffs, and died at his house from exposure during
the time that he was led between two officers from Newgate through
the City and back again just before his release (*Friars' Chronicle*, p 34).

1529 r
1009 Civic licence that only the parish of Christ Church, St Katharine's, could set up a stage play from 20 April to 29 September (Mill-
Chambers, pp 287-8).

1529-30 r
1010 A play on St Margaret's day noted in the churchwardens'
accounts (H.F. Westlake, *St. Margaret's Westminster* [1914], p 175).

1529-30 p
1011 Players (*Wardens' Accounts of the Worshipful Company of Founders
of the City of London 1497-1681*, ed Guy Parsloe [1964], p 80).

1529-31

1012 Chapel children, playing; royal and visiting players at Christmas (household accounts of Henry VIII; *Trevelyan*, pp 146-77; *L. & P. Hen. VIII*, V, 307-17; Collier [1879], I, 115, n 1, refers to a payment of 1530 to John Roll, Richard Hole, and Thomas Sudbury, king's players).

1530 p

1013 A play by the children of John Wilmot, Clerk of the Market (Sylvia Thrupp, *A Short History of the Worshipful Company of Bakers of London* [1933], p 161).

1531 January p

1014 Thomas Boleyn, earl of Ormond and Wiltshire, entertained for supper – evidently at his London house – Claude de la Guiche, the new French ambassador, with a farce acted of Cardinal Wolsey going down to hell; and the 'Duke' (probably Thomas Howard, 3rd duke of Norfolk) ordered the farce to be printed (*Spain*, IV.ii [1882], no 615, pp 40-1).

1531-57

1015 Palm Sunday pageants (1531-3p); players in the church (1539-40p); and players on Easter morning (1557; *St. Martin-in-the-Fields: The Accounts of the Churchwardens 1526-1603*), ed John V. Kitto [1901], pp 28, 60, 165).

1533 29 May p

1016 The mayor's water pageants for Anne Boleyn include two foists, one with a great red dragon casting wild fire, and around about monsters and wildmen; and the other with a mount, a white falcon, and virgins (*L. & P. Hen. VIII*, VI, no 601, p 276; Holinshed, III, 779-80).

1533 31 May p

1017 Pageants for the coronation procession of Anne Boleyn (text in '[John] Leland's and [Nicholas] Udall's Verses before the Coronation of Anne Boleyn,' *Ballads from Manuscripts*, ed Frederick J. Furnivall, I, pt 1, Ballad Society [1868], pp 364-401; *L. & P. Hen. VIII*, VI, no 564, p 251, and no 601, p 277; *Venice*, IV, no 912, p 418; *Spain*, IV.ii, nos 1073, 1077, 1081, 1107, pp 682, 700, 704, 755 ('le triomphe'); Wriothesley, I, 19; 'Copy of a Letter from Archbishop Cranmer to Mastyr Hawkyns, Relating to the Queens Catharine of Arragon and Anne Boleyn,' ed

Henry Ellis, *Arch*, 18 [1817], 79-80; Halle, fols 212v-15r; Holinshed, III, 782-3; Withington, I, 180-4; McGee-Meagher, pp 89-90; and cf 'The Noble Triumphant Coronation of Queen Anne, Wife unto the Most Noble King Henry the VIIIth,' *An English Garner*, ed Edward Arber, II [1879], pp 41-60; ie STC 656 [1533]; for facs see Alfred Fairbank and Berthold Wolpe, *Renaissance Handwriting* [1960], pl 23, and Beal, I, ii, fasc XXXII [from (4) below]):

1 / children dressed as merchants;

2 / Apollo, and the nine Muses on Parnassus (Udall);

3 / a castle with a falcon, an angel, St Anne, and the three Maries with their issue (Udall);

4 / the three Graces (Udall);

5 / Juno, Pallas, Mercury, Venus, and Paris (Udall);

6 / virgins;

7 / children of St Paul's School, on a scaffold, with verses; and

8 / a tower with the four cardinal virtues (possibly an error for [4] above).

1533 November p

1018 Jean du Bellay notes that, to the Pope's great displeasure, Henry VIII 'feist jouer on [ou] permist estre jouées des farces dedans Londre fort ignominieuses' in which people went through the streets masked and dressed as cardinals, 'qui portoyent en crouppe des p......... et des bardaches' (P.A. Hamy, *Entrevue de François Premier avec Henry VIII, à Boulogne-sur-Mer, en 1532* [1898], doc 114, p ccclxxviii; cf the note by Edward Lord Herbert of Cherbury that a comedy was represented at court, 'to the no little defamation of certain Cardinalls,' according to news at Rome; *The Life and Raigne of King Henry the Eighth* [1649], p 368).

1534 7 January r

1019 John Husee writes Lord Lisle that the Inns of Court kept Christmas revels 'with such pastimes as hath not been seen, and the Pope is not set by' (*L. & P. Hen. VIII*, VII, no 24, p 13).

1534-9 r

1020 John Farlion (Farlian), the first yeoman or keeper of the king's vestures or apparel of masks, revels, and disguisings (stored at Warwick Inn), from 20 November 1534, just after Richard Gibson's death, to Farlion's own death 25 July 1539 (*L. & P. Hen. VIII*, VII, no 1498.41, p 560; XIV.i, no 1318, p 574; for men who carried out earlier revels, from other posts, see E.K. Chambers, *Notes on the History of the Revels Office under the Tudors* [1906], pp 3-7, and generally above).

1535 23 p/?28 r June
1021 The king saw from a house an outdoor pageant ('triomphe') on a chapter of the Apocalypse where the heads of ecclesiasts were cut off (?by Henry VIII; *Spain*, V.i [1886], no 179; *L. & P. Hen. VIII*, VIII [1885], no 949).

ca 1535 r
1022 A play book priced 2d, in the shop of Wynkyn de Worde or his successors (William A. Jackson, 'A London Bookseller's Ledger of 1535,' *The Colophon*, NS 1, no 4 [Spring 1936], 502).

1536 May r
1023 Masquing hose belonging to Lady Jane Rochford appears in a court inventory (*L. & P. Hen. VIII*, X, no 1011, p 416).

1536 r
1024 Allhallows Staining churchwardens hire a pair of wings, a wig, and a crest for an angel on Palm Sunday (A. Povah, *The Annals of the Parishes of St. Olave Hart Street and Allhallows Staining* [1894], p 365; date from Guildhall Library ms 4956/1, fols 141r, 144v).

1536-47
1025 Plays and masques at court, often over Christmas (revels' accounts 1536-7, 1539-40, 1543-7; Kempe, pp 69-73; Jeaffreson, pp 602-4; and *Folger*, II, 67-83), including:
    1 / see under GREENWICH (1540 1 January);
    2 / masques of mariners and of Almains, with 'monstrous' torch-bearers, on Shrove Sunday and Tuesday (dated 1543 in *Catalog*, p 68, and 1547-8 by Kempe, pp 69-70);
    3 / see under HAMPTON COURT (1544 21 April); and
    4 / masque of wildmen, 1546-7 (Kempe, p 73).

1537 12 June r
1026 Henry VIII urges Stephen Gardiner, bishop of Winchester, to demand that the French king suppress a newly-printed book of which

Henry has a copy, originally 'written in form of a tragedy' by one Carle, servant to the French ambassador in England, in his house here as an attack on Henry himself (*L. & P. Hen. VIII*, XII.ii, no 78, pp 27-8; cf XII.i, no 1315, p 597).

1537-42
1027 Masques, and visiting and royal players at court, including Udall, schoolmaster of Eton, for playing (February 1538; as 'Woodall'), and Bale and his fellows (January 1539), and the chapel children (personal accounts of Thomas Cromwell, *L. & P. Hen. VIII*, XIV.ii, no 782, pp . 329-40; of Sir Thomas Henneage for the king, *L. & P. Hen. VIII*, Addenda, I.i, no 1284, p 438; and of the king, *L. & P. Hen. VIII*, XIII.ii, no 1280, pp 528-9, 538-9; XIV.ii, no 781, p 308; XVI, nos 380, 1489, pp 178-9, 185, 699-705; the king's masquing in March 1538 appears in XIII.i, no 583, p 215; Christmas 'mummeries' of 1540-1 are noted in no 373, p 170).

1538 3-5 October r
1028 Interlude called *Rex Diabole*, with 'these new scripture [or ecclesiastical] matters,' for over 40s, and 'a suit' of players' garments (of silk?), hired by John Husee, the London agent of Lady Honor Lisle, evidently for use at her Calais seat, the Staple Inn: these garments suffered water damage when the ship returning with them in a chest from Calais in late March or early April 1539 was lost at Margate, so that when he returned them to the hire-merchant in London Husee had to pay amends (*L. & P. Hen. VIII*, Addenda, I.ii, nos 1360, 1362, pp 462-3; XIV.i, nos 690, 713, 791, pp 341, 350, 377; *Lisle Letters*, V, 237-8, 437-8).

1539 February p
1029 John Heywood's masque of King Arthur's knights, with hobbyhorses, at Cromwell's house before 11 February and at court 22 February; in this there may have been a female Divine Providence who played before the king at this time (*L. & P. Hen. VIII*, XIV.ii, no 782, pp 339-40; Reed, pp 61-2).

1539 29 April r
1030 John Young's grant to be one of the king's interluders, '*vice* John Roo, deceased' (*L. & P. Hen. VIII*, XIV.i, no 906.14, p 423).

1539 17 June p
1031 A triumph on the Thames before Westminster Palace: a battle
where the bishop of Rome and his cardinals, in one barge, were defeated and cast into the river by those in the king's barge (Wriothesley,
I, 99-100; *Correspondance Politique de MM. de Castillon et de Marillac
Ambassadeurs de France en Angleterre (1537-1542)*, ed Jean Kaulek,
Inventaire Analytique des Archives des Affaires Étrangères [1885],
no 123, p 105).

1539-47
1032 John Bridges, the second yeoman or keeper of the king's vestures
or apparel for the king's masks, revels, and disguisings, from 21 October 1539 to ca 1547 (*L. & P. Hen. VIII*, XIV.ii, no 435.48, p 159; XVIII.i,
no 436, p 264; XVIII.ii, no 231, p 126; XIX.i, no 275.6, p 165; Feuillerat
1, esp p 265, where an inventory of the [then late] king's household
goods on 14 September 1547 lists a box with six visors; for an inventory of revels' stuff housed in Warwick Inn then, including stuff for a
palmers' masque, see *L. & P. Hen. VIII*, II.ii, p 1517 [misdated 1518; see
Chambers, *Notes*, p 8, n 1]; and for a manuscript on offices at court
late in the reign of Henry VIII, with mention of the Revels, and eight
players of interludes, see Alfred J. Horwood, 'The Manuscripts of Matthew Ridgway, Esq., of Dewsbury,' *4th Report*, HMC, App [1874], p
404).

1540 p
1033 Children played the prophets on Palm Sunday at St Alphage's
church (*Records of St. Alphage, London Wall*, comp G.B. Hall [1882],
p 17).

1540-4 p
1034 Visiting players, including the prince's and the king's players, before the Princess Mary (at court, possibly at Richmond, Westminster,
and Hampton Court; *Privy Purse Expenses*, ed Frederick Madden
[1831], pp 83, 104, 140).

1541 p
1035 Shermons, keeper of the Carpenters' Hall in Christ's parish, pro-
cured an interlude to be played openly that railed against priests and
called them knaves (at Shoreditch? Foxe, V, 446).

1542 March r
1036 The Convocation of Canterbury petitions the king 'to correct the public plays and comedies which are acted in London, to the contempt of God's Word' (*L. & P. Hen. VIII*, XVII, no 176, p 79).

1542 11 April r
1037 The mayor instructs that no common plays or interludes be permitted in any craft hall or public place until further notice (Mill-Chambers, pp 288-9).

1542 1 July r
1038 Song after the play of 'the battle betwixt the Spirit [the Devil?], the Soul and the Flesh,' played by Suffolk men (*L. & P. Hen. VIII*, Addenda, I.ii, no 1547; this may be the book called the 'batell of the spryte and ye flesshe,' of which six copies are listed in [?] Edward Whitchurch's inventory, for which see Leslie M. Oliver, 'A Bookseller's Account Book, 1545,' *Harvard Library Bulletin*, 16 [1968], 154; cf Arber, I, 412, for a 'ballett' – a term commonly used for an interlude – of 1569-70 called 'the sprete the flysshe ye Worlde and ye Devell').

1542-6 r
1039 Quarterly wages to Henry VIII's players, Robert Hinstock (Hynstock), George Birch, and Richard Parowe (Parrowe; the treasurer of the chamber's payments; *L. & P. Hen. VIII*, XVII, no 880, p 478 [1542]; and the king's payments, XX.ii, no 1035, p 515 [1545]; and cf Collier, 2nd edn, I, 133, for a payment of March 1546 to eight players).

1543 2 April r
1040 The City orders the arrest of anyone setting up bills for plays and interludes, especially of persons responsible for the bill concerning Dr [Hugh?] Weston [rector of St Nicholas Olave?] and Dr [Nicholas?] Wilson [prebendary of Hoxton?]; and recognizances not to allow interludes or common plays at their dwellings are signed by William Blytheman, of the earl of Northumberland's Place, George Gadlowe, and Thomas Hancokkes (Mill-Chambers, pp 289-90; on 31 March the mayor showed the Privy Council evidence of the 'licentiows manner' of players (*APC*, I, 103-4]).

1543 10 April r
1041 Twenty joiners, including Hawtrell, Lucke, and Lucas, briefly jailed for making a disguising on a Sunday; and four players of the

Lord Warden were jailed for playing contrary to the mayor's order
(*ACP*, I, 109-10, 122).

1544 October r
1042 Interludes or common plays to be played, not in 'suspicious,
dark, and inconvenient places' within the City, or during hours of
divine service, but only in houses of the nobility, gentry, and City
officials and solid citizens, in open streets, and in guild common halls
(*Proclamations*, I, 341-2).

1544-6 r
1043 The Founders' and Weavers' guilds rent out their halls to players
for playing (*Wardens' Accounts*, ed Parsloe, pp 99-100, 102 [for playing
from St Nicholas day until after Christmas], 106; Frances Consitt, *The
London Weavers' Company*, I [1933], pp 159, 255, 259).

1544-7
1044 Alexander Nowell, schoolmaster of Westminster School, institutes
Christmas plays by the boys; his prologues to Terence's *Adelphi*
(Christmas 1544 and ?1545), Seneca's *Hippolytus* (Christmas 1546?),
and Terence's *Eunuchus* are in Nowell's notebook, Brasenose College
ms 31, fols 10-13r ff (unedited? not seen; Baldwin 1, I, 172-3, 177-8;
Tanner, p 57).

1544-59
1045 Sir Thomas Cawarden, the first master of the revels and masks,
by patent 16 March 1544, overseeing a lieutenant, a clerk comptroller,
a clerk, and a yeoman (*L. & P. Hen. VIII*, XIX.i, no 275.6, p 165; XX.i, no
465.28-9, p 213; XXI.i, no 970.15, p 482; also *APC*, IV, 195, 205-6; for the
new revels buildings at Blackfriars, 1547-8, see Feuillerat 1, pp 3-8; for
the changing personnel under Cawarden, see Chambers' *Notes*, pp
1-18, Feuillerat 1, *passim*, and generally the 'Constitucions' ca 1544-53
[in Chambers, supplemented by John Doebler, 'A Lost Paragraph in
the Revels Constitution,' *SQ*, 25 [1974], 286-7, correcting *SQ*, 24 [1973],
333-4] and the anonymous report ca 1573; and for revels' inventories
of apparel for falconers, priests, cardinals, Turks, friars, pilgrims, a boy
to play the prophet, Almains, Astronomers, 'frows,' and Egyptians ca
1547-8, and for mariners, Venetian senators patrons of galleys, galley
slaves, Turkish magistrates, Greek worthies – Hercules, Jason, Perseus,

Pyrothus, Achilles, and Theseus – Albany's warriors, Turkish archers, Irish kerns, falconers, palmers, Turkish commoners, huntresses, Venuses or amorous ladies, nymphs, Turkish women, St Nicholas, Egyptians, cardinal, vices, a masque of 'frowees,' and priest ca 1555 [Feuillerat 1, pp 11-23, 180-96, 251]).

1545 12 January r
1046 The City orders the earl of Hertford's players from henceforth only to play in the houses of the mayor, sheriffs, aldermen, or substantial citizens (Mill-Chambers, p 291).

1545 6 February r
1047 Repetition of the proclamation of October 1544 (Mill-Chambers, pp 291-2; *EES*, II.i, 327-8; Peter Goodstein, 'New Light on an Old Proclamation,' *N&Q*, 215 [1970], 212).

1545 r
1048 Bishop Stephen Gardiner 'forbad the players of london ... to play any mo playes of Christe / but of robin hode and litle Johan / and of the Parlament of byrdes and suche other trifles' (W. Wraghton, pseud [William Turner], *The Rescvynge of the Romishe Fox Other Wyse Called the Examination of the Hunter Deuised by Steuen Gardiner. The Seconde Covrse of the Hvnter at the Romishe Fox & hys Aduocate ... Steuen Gardiner* [1545], sig G2r; cf sig H4v; *STC* 24355; noted by J.A.W. Bennett, *The Parlement of Foules* [1957], pp 1-2, n 3).

1545 r
1049 Prophets (probably from 1539 at least, reading the Passion; *The Transcript of the Registers of ... S. Mary Woolnoth ... with ... Extracts from the Churchwardens' Accounts*, ed J.M.S. Brooke and A.W.C. Hallen [1886], pp xvii-xix).

ca 1545-7 r
1050 Court play with Virtue, Zeal (both scholars?); Insolence and Diligence (both gentlemen?); Old Blind Custom (a priest); Hunger of Knowledge (a London apprentice); and Thomas of Croydon, a collier (Albert Feuillerat, 'An Unknown Protestant Morality Play,' *MLR*, 9 [1914], 94-6; C.R. Baskervill, 'On Two Old Plays,' *MP*, 14 [1914-17], 16; and cf above under GENERAL 1547-51r).

1546 26 February r
1051 Repetition of the proclamation of October 1544 (Mill-Chambers, p 293).

1546 2 May r
1052 Arrest of five of the earl of Bath's players for performing 'lewde playes' in the suburbs (*ACP*, I, 407; released 6 May on bond).

1546 29 September r
1053 Annuity of John Young, one of the king's players of interludes, and actors of comedies, payable from the death of Thomas Sudborough (*L. & P. Hen. VIII*, XXI.ii, nos 199.116, 332.12, pp 88, 156; cf Collier, 2nd edn, I, 133-4, n 3).

1547 19 February p
1054 Civic pageants, with texts, for Edward VI's procession to Westminster for coronation (*Literary Remains*, pp cclxxviii-ccxci; Withington, I, 185-7; McGee-Meagher, pp 97-8):

1 / a conduit with speeches by two children;

2 / Valentine and Orson;

3 / a flower-covered rock with a fountain and Grace, Nature, Fortune, and Charity;

4 / Sapience and the seven liberal sciences (Grammar, Logic, Rhetoric, Arithmetic, Geometry, Music, Astronomy; for a 'spyre' for Astronomy [Archimedes' spiral?], and other pageant costumes, as for women, lent to London men by the Office of the Revels, see Feuillerat 1, p 249).

5 / the heavens, a phoenix, and two lions, with children representing Edward himself, Regality, Justice, Mercy, and Truth; and the golden fleece with two bulls and a serpent;

6 / England;

7 / King Edward the Confessor, his page, and a maiden holding a lamb by a string; and St George; and

8 / Truth, Faith, and Justice.

1547 20-27 February p
1055 Revels for the coronation of Edward VI at Westminster include a pageant mount, with gilded sun beams, and a play on 22 February, Shrove Tuesday, with friars, cardinals, the pope, and priests (one of them possibly acted by the king himself); and an interlude of the story

of Orpheus in Westminster Hall then as well (Feuillerat 1, pp 3-8, 22, 256, 260; *Literary Remains*, p cccii; McGee-Meagher, pp 97-8; French correspondence refers to 'farses' with popes and cardinals on this date [De Selve, nos 122, 124, pp 106, 108]).

1547 17 March r
1056 All players' bills are to be pulled down Sunday mornings and brought to the mayor (Mill-Chambers, p 293).

1547-9
1057 Royal players; chapel children, playing (household accounts of Edward VI; *Trevelyan*, pp 195, 201-5; pt II, CS 84 [1863], pp 17-37; among players named in 1547 to be retained in the king's service [others are to be discharged] are Richard Cok, John Birch, Henry Heryet, and John Smyth [Collier, I, 138-9; ES, II, 82, n 1]; by Midsummer 1547 Robert Hinscoke and George Birch are singled out for wages as players of interludes [Feuillerat 1, p 280, n 86.3]).

1547-53
1058 Plays, pageants, the king's players, mummeries, a vice, and masques in the court revels of Edward VI (Feuillerat 1, pp 1-145, 190-4, 251-2, having very detailed accounts of costume materials; *Literary Remains*, p 388; additional documents are noted in *Loseley mss* and McGee-Meagher, pp 98-104; see also under GREENWICH). Masques on the following themes appear:
   1 / pilgrims (1547? p 6);
   2 / Prester John (1548? pp 190-1);
   3 / friars (1549-50; p 42);
   4 / Almains (1548-50; pp 34-5, 43);
   5 / hermits (1549-50; pp 41-3);
   6 / lance-knights (1549-50; p 42);
   7 / palmers (1549-50; pp 42-3);
   8 / Irish men and women (1550-1; possibly at Greenwich; pp 47-9, and cf pp 53-5);
   9 / a 'dronken Maske' (1552; p 52);
   10 / Greek worthies, including Hercules (1553; intended for Shrovetide but, along with the following four masques, postponed until Easter and Mayday; pp 129-45);
   11 / Medioxes, half-death, half-man (1553);
   12 / bagpipes (1553);

13 / cats (1553); and

14 / tumblers going on their heads (1553).

ca 1547-58 r
1059 Interlude with Honour, a king; Wisdom, a woman with two faces; Knighthood, a knight; Loyalty, a woman; Justice, a judge; Mercy; Religion, a preacher; God's Word or Scripture, a woman; Science, a scholar; Reason; Service, a serving man; Affection; Labour, a woman with many hands; Diligence; Pride, a pope; Wrath, a bishop; Envy, a friar; Covetous, a parson; Gluttony, a 'Sole preste'; Lechery, a monk; and Sloth, a hermit (Feuillerat 1, p 245).

1548-9 p
1060 Playings in the Founders' guild hall (*Wardens' Accounts*, ed Parsloe, p 111).

1549 27 May r
1061 Citizens are ordered to keep their youths and servants from May games and interludes on holy days; and John Wylkynson, a currier, who allows interludes and plays to be made in his dwelling house, is ordered to cease doing so (Mill-Chambers, p 293; [William] *Harrison's Description of England in Shakspere's Youth*, part IV, ed Frederick J. Furnivall and C.C. Stopes [1908], p 313 [not in Mill-Chambers]).

1549 4 July r
1062 The Mayor is to appeal to the Lord Chancellor, Richard lord Rich, for help in staying 'all comen interludes & pleyes' in the City and suburbs (*Harrison's Description of England*, IV, 313-14; not in Mill-Chambers).

1549 7 November r
1063 The City council orders that the two secondaries of the Compters, Mr Atkyns and Mr Burnell, are to peruse all interludes to be played by any common player in the City or suburbs and to report to the Mayor, who will rule whether they may be performed (*Harrison's Description of England*, IV, 314; not in Mill-Chambers).

1549 p
1064 A Shrovetide play by the king's players with a king, a dragon with seven heads, six priests, and seven hermits (Feuillerat 1, pp 39-40).

1549-55 p
1065 The children of Paul's play (once upon viols) and sing on the Merchant Tailors' guild feast day (Clode, *Memorials of the Guild of Merchant Taylors*, pp 526, 528-9).

1550 2 February r
1066 Combat at barriers at court with a 'devise' where the defenders protect lady Love from ascending a gallows ladder to hang (*The Manuscripts of his Grace the Duke of Rutland, K.G. Preserved at Belvoir Castle*, I [ed H.M. Lyte and W.H. Stevenson], HMC [1888], p 55).

1550 29 May p
1067 Masquing at court for the French ambassador (at Whitehall? Wriothesley, II, 40).

1550 8 June p
1068 François de Vendôme, vidame de Chartres, entertains the duke of Somerset and the marquess of Northampton with masques and 'other conceites' (*Literary Remains*, p 276).

1550 17 November r
1069 Order against any 'Comedies, called *Interludes*' at Gray's Inn out of term times, except at Christmas; the costs for apparel for such comedies are to be shared by all the society then in commons (Sir William Dugdale, *Origines Juridiciales*, 3rd edn [1680], p 285; a lost manuscript now, according to Reginald J. Fletcher, ed, *The Pension Book of Gray's Inn* [1901], p 496).

1550 23 December r
1070 The following common players of interludes within the City were bound by recognizance not to play any interlude or common play without a special licence by the king or his council: John Nethe, Robert Southyn, Robert Drake, Robert Peacocke, John Nethersall, Robert Sutton, Richard Jugler, John Ronner, William Readyng, Edmund Stokedale, John Rawlyns, John Crane, Richard Gyrke, John Radstone, Oliver Page, Richard Pokeley, Richard Parseley, and William Clement (*Harrison's Description of England*, IV, 314-15; not in Mill-Chambers).

1551 r
1071 Lord marquess of Dorset's players are licensed to play only in his presence (*APC*, III, 307).

1552 4 January p
1072 Entry of the royal court's Lord of Misrule George Ferrers into the City with his retinue, which included harquebusiers, in a mock Midsummer watch that included a beheading of ?a hogshead of wine (Feuillerat 1, pp 59, 89; Machyn, pp 13-14; and see also under GREENWICH).

1552 26 May p
1073 A May pole with a giant came to Fenchurch Street parish and was destroyed by the mayor's order (Machyn, p 20).

1552 9 June r
1074 Wages and livery to John Browne, one of the king's players of interludes (*CSP*, p 40).

1552 10 June r
1075 The 'cowper' who was jailed in the Tower 'for making of playes' is released (*APC*, IV, 73).

1552 10 December r
1076 A report on royal revenues 1550-1 includes customary payments for the Master and Yeoman of the Revels; the Master of the Chapel Children; John Young, player in interludes; and players of interludes Robert Hinstock, George Birch, Richard Coke, Richard Skinner, Henry Harriot, John Birch, and Thomas Southey (*The Report of the Royal Commission of 1552*, ed W.C. Richardson [1974], pp 17, 19-20, 117; cf Collier, 2nd edn, I, 136, n 1 for payments of 30 September).

1552 r
1077 Among goods in church inventories are fifteen 'Robyne Hoodes Cottes' at Holy Trinity the Less, an embroidered vestment called 'the players' coat' at St Dionis Backchurch, eleven stained linen players' coats at St Lawrence Jewry, and five garments, collars, 'crownetes,' and wigs for prophets at St Magnus (H.B. Walters, *London Churches at the Reformation with an Account of their Contents* [1939], pp 48, 129, 239, 327, 348).

1552-3 r
1078 Christmas revels at court, including:

1 / the entry into London of the king's Lord of Misrule with his retinue, including harquebusiers, in a mock Midsummer watch on 6 January, and his meeting with the Sheriff's Lord of Misrule, with jailors
and prisoners (Machyn, pp 28-9, 157; Wriothesley, II, 80; Feuillerat 1,
pp 89-92, 119, 281; *Loseley mss*; and see under GREENWICH 1552-3);
and

2 / 'a play of Esops Crowe' by the King's players, probably about the
mass (the actors, most of whom played birds, were in learning on 28
December; Holden, pp 27, 92; STC 1244; Feuillerat 1, p 282; L.B.
Campbell, 'The Lost Play of *AEsop's Crow,*' MLN, 49 [1934], 454-7).

1553 8 March r
1079 Civic council orders (2 March), as follows, are proclaimed (Mill-
Chambers, pp 294-5):

1 / that no three-men's songs are allowed outside common plays or
interludes; and

2 / that no such plays are lawful in any house or house's yard,
garden, or backside on holy days before 3 pm.

1553 17 March p
1080 Procession of the Sheriff of London as Lord of Misrule with the
Devil, a soldan, giants, Jake-of-lent, a ?priest shriving him, a doctor
his physician, and Jake's wife bringing physicians to save his life
(Machyn, p 33).

1553 April-May p
1081 At court, planned for Shrovetide or Candlemas and deferred until
Easter and May day, William Baldwin's play on the state of Ireland,
with Irishmen and devils; and a play by [John] Heywood for twelve
boys, possibly with Fame (having a coat and cap with eyes, tongues,
and ears), if he is not in Baldwin's play instead (Holden, pp 6 [n 3],
27, 92; Feuillerat 1, pp 134-43; APC, IV, 210).

1553 20 May r
1082 The earl of Northumberland asks Sir Thomas Cawarden to
appoint two fair masques, one of men and another of women, for the
celebration of three noble marriages at Durham House on 25 May
(including that of Lady Jane Grey and Guildford Dudley; Jeaffreson,
p 608; Feuillerat 1, p 306).

1553 30 September p
1083 Civic and other pageants for the coronation procession of Mary I
through London, including the following (*The Chronicle of Queen Jane,
and of Two Years of Queen Mary*, ed John G. Nichols, CS 48 [1850], pp
27-30; Wriothesley, II, 103; Machyn, pp 43, 45; *Friars' Chronicle*, p 84;
'London Chronicle,' pp 29-30; Stow, *Chronicles*, pp 1072-4; Clode,
Memorials of the Guild of Merchant Taylors, p 528; Holinshed, IV, 6-7;
and Withington, I, 188-9):
   1 / a pageant with a child in girl's apparel borne up in a chair
by two men (by the Genoese; with four great giants and speeches,
according to Machyn, p 45);
   2 / a mount with four children (the Easterlings);
   3 / a royal ship;
   4 / six gowned persons, and an angel with trumpet (the Florentines);
   5 / Grace, Virtue, and Nature;
   6 / a pageant with children in women's apparel;
   7 / in Paul's churchyard, two pageants, one by the school, with Mr
[John] Heywood sitting in the pageant under a vine and addressing
the queen in Latin and English; and
   8 / a castle.

1553 p
1084 Players at Christmas for the Weavers' guild (Consitt, *London
Weavers' Company*, I, 283).

1553 r
1085 *Respublica*, to be performed by [?the Chapel] boys (text: *Respublica: An Interlude for Christmas 1553, Attributed to Nicholas Udall*, ed
W.W. Greg, EETS OS 226 [1952]; TFT 25; Stratman 6270-86; Houle 44).

1553-4 r
1086 Christmas play by the chapel gentlemen for the coronation of
Mary I with characters Genus humanum, five virgins, Reason, Verity,
Plenty, Self-love, Care, Scarsity, Disceit, Sickness, Feebleness, Deformity, Epilogue, Good Angel, and Bad Angel (delayed until Christmas?
Feuillerat 1, pp 149-51, 289-90).

1553-8
1087 Plays, pageants, and masques in the court revels of Mary and
Philip (Feuillerat 1, pp 147-242, having very detailed accounts of cos-

tume materials; McGee-Meagher, pp 108-14; for Mary's players of interludes, see Edmond Malone, *The Plays and Poems of William Shakespeare* [1821], III, 45, and Collier, I, 164, and II, 83). Masques on the following themes appear:

1 / Greek worthies or six Hercules, with six mariners as torchbearers (1 November 1554; pp 161-5, 292; Francis Yaxley writes Sir William Cecil that on Sunday night [7 October 1554] at court there was 'a brave maskery of cloth of gold and sylver, apparailed in maryners garments' [*Original Letters, Illustrative of English History*, ed Henry Ellis, 3rd ser, III (1846), p 313]);

2 / eight patrons of galleys like Venetian senators, and six galley slaves for torchbearers (Christmas 1554-5; pp 166-71);

3 / six Venuses or amorous ladies with six cupids as torchbearers (Christmas 1554-5; pp 166-71);

4 / six Turkish magistrates and six Turkish archers as torchbearers (Shrovetide 1555; Shrove Tuesday was 26 February; pp 172-7);

5 / eight goddess huntresses with eight Turkish women as torchbearers (Shrovetide 1555; pp 172-7); and

6 / Almains, pilgrims, and Irishmen (25 April 1557; pp 225-8, 302-3).

1554 19? April r
1088 Civic prohibition, on behalf of the queen, of May games and (associated?) interludes or stage plays (Mill-Chambers, pp 295-6).

1554 18 August p
1089 Civic triumphs and pageants at the entry of Philip of Spain ([John Elder] *The Copie of a Letter Sent in to Scotlande, of the Ariuall and Landynge, and Moste Noble Marryage of the Moste Illustre Prynce Philippe ... and of his Triumphyng Entries in the Noble Citie of London* [1555], sigs B5v-C4v; STC 7552; Foxe, VI, 557-9; Withington, I, 189-94; Tucker Orbison, 'Research Opportunities at the Inns of Court,' RORD, 20 [1977], 30; *Friars' Chronicle*, p 91; 'London Chronicle,' pp 37-8; Wriothesley, II, 122; *The Chronicle of Queen Jane*, pp 78-81, 145-51 [the latter a reprint of Elder's account]; McGee-Meagher, pp 106-7; cf Anglo, pp 327-39):

1 / the giants Corineus Britannus and Gogmagog Albionus;

2 / the nine worthies, with Henry VIII and Edward VI;

3 / Prince Philip on horseback;

4 / the four noble Philips: king of Macedonia, the Roman emperor, and dukes of Burgundy *Bonus* and *Audax*;

5 / Orpheus on a mount, the nine Muses, and wild beasts;

6 / a genealogical tree from Edward III; and

7 / a castle; and Mary and Philip, crowned by Sapientia, with Justicia, Equitas, Veritas, and Misericordia.

1554 11 November r

1090 Lord Henry Maltravers at Arundel Place requests to borrow 'one maske, yf it be possible of allmay*n*s,' from Sir Thomas Cawarden, Master of the Revels (Feuillerat 1, p 249).

1554-5 Christmas p

1091 Plays by Nicholas Udall at court (Feuillerat 1, pp 159-60, 166).

1555 7 March r

1092 Civic prohibition, on behalf of the queen, of minstrelsy and any kind of 'interlude or playe' in alehouses, taverns, or victualling houses (Mill-Chambers, pp 296-7).

1555 26 May p

1093 May game with giants at St Martin's in the Field (Machyn, p 89).

1555 3 June p

1094 May game at Westminster with giants and devils (Machyn, p 89).

1555 7 August r

1095 Among books received here for Cardinal (Reginald) Pole were Seneca's works and Aristophanes in Greek (Emden 2, p 733, nos xxix, lxviii).

1555 24 December r

1096 William Baldwin's three-hour comedy 'Love and Life' concerning 'the way to lyfe,' 'comprehending a discourse of the hole worlde,' a play then 'in learnyng,' to be ready within ten days, offered to the court and desired by the Inns of Court; with sixty-two characters, natural and allegorical, all of whose names begin with 'L,' where a husbandman Lamech and his servant Lob meet the three Ladies Lust, who offers them a sumptuous whore (Lady Lechery), Luck, who offers

Lordship, and Love, who offers Life; after being lost from following
the first, the two recover through Luck and Lordship, from whom,
however, they come to Lack by means of Largess and 'Larracine'
(?Larceny), and only by Love are they able to go to Light and attain
Life (from the letter's endorsement, dated Tuesday Christmas eve 1556
[in which, however, 24 December was a Thursday]; there were Christmas plays at court in 1555-6; Feuillerat 1, pp 215-17, and cf p 199;
'Love and Live' was Baldwin's motto, according to Holden, p 9; Bale
mentions Baldwin's 'Comoedias' [*Scriptorum*, II, 108]; for the remaining
characters, see under 'L' in the General Index).

1555 r
1097 Edmund Bonner, bishop of London, prohibits the clergy of St
Paul's from frequenting 'ludis illicitis et inhonestis' (*Visitations*, II,
376-7).

1555? p
1098 London clerks play some holy play at a guild dinner (G.N. Pitt,
Notes on the History of the Armourers' & Brasiers' Company [1914], p 23;
courtesy of Anne Lancashire).

1556 11 February r
1099 Sir William Paget asks Sir Thomas Cawarden, Master of the
Revels, for masquing apparel for the ambassador of Venice, Giovanni
Michiel (Feuillerat 1, p 250).

1557 9 March r
1100 Civic prohibition of all stage plays or interludes on holy days
(Mill-Chambers, pp 297-8).

1557 29 April p
1101 A (musical?) interlude of the children of Paul's at the Drapers'
Hall for the ambassador of Muscovia and Russia (Robertson-Gordon,
pp 138-9).

1557 30 May p
1102 May game in Fenchurch Street with a riding of the nine
worthies, with speeches, the soldan, an elephant and castle, and others
(Machyn, p 137).

1557 7 June p
1103 Stage play of the Passion of Christ began at the Grey Friars (Machyn, p 138).

1557 13 June p
1104 'certaine naughtie plaies' acted; the players are to be apprehended and sent to the Commissioners for Religion (APC, VI, 102).

1557 29 July p
1105 Stage play 'of a goodly matter' at St Olave's church (in Silver Street) at night, 8 pm to midnight, which ended with a good song (Machyn, p 145).

1557 5 September p
1106 Halting of a 'lewde' play called 'Sacke full of Newes' to be played at the Boar's Head without Aldgate, and a brief arrest of the players (APC, VI, 168-9).

1557 6 September p
1107 The Lord Mayor is authorized to free the players jailed yesterday, and is instructed to allow plays only between All Saints and Shrovetide, and only after approval by the ordinary (APC, VI, 169).

1557 31 December p
1108 On New Year's eve a Lord of Misrule entered London from Westminster with many disguised in white (Machyn, p 162).

1557-68
1109 Rental of Trinity Hall from St Botolph without Aldersgate by players (Charles T. Prouty, 'An Early Elizabethan Playhouse,' ShS, 6 [1953], 64-74; see PLATE 23).

before 1558 r
1110 Whitsuntide ceremony of the descent of a dove, and dumb shows or 'Spectacles' of the Nativity, Passion and Ascension of Christ, in St Paul's (William Lambarde, *Dictionarium Angliae Topographicum & Historicum* [1730], pp 459-60; put down in 1547-8, according to *Friars' Chronicle*, p 56).

1558 4 September p
1111 Masque at the marriage of ?alderman John White (Machyn, p 172).

1558 28 November p
1112 Queen Elizabeth processes through London to the Tower and in some places there are children with speeches (Machyn, p 172).

1558 7 December r
1113 A recognizance not to allow any interlude or stage play, unless licenced, in his mansion house, yard, garden, or other property is signed by William Aston (Mill-Chambers, p 298).

1558-9 p
1114 All men of the Pewterers guild pay towards the play at the Yeomanry feast 'as they haue done in tymes past' (Charles Welch, *The History of the Worshipful Company of Pewterers of London* [1902], I, 201, 205).

1559 6 January p
1115 A *farsa* before Elizabeth in the day, and a mummery after supper, of crows dressed as cardinals (with hats), asses as bishops, wolves as abbots; and in London about this time there was a masquing of friars (*Venice*, VII, no 10, p 11; *Folger*, II, 80).

1559 14 January p
1116 Civic pageants for Elizabeth's coronation (*The Quenes Maiesties Passage through the Citie of London to Westminster the Day before her Coronacion* [by Richard Mulcaster], facs, ed James M. Osborn, intro Sir John Neale [1960]; STC 7591 [cf 7590]; Machyn, pp 185-6; Wriothesley, II, 143; Norman Davis, 'Two Early Sixteenth-Century Accounts of Royal Occasions,' *N&Q*, 218 [1973], 122-3; for the provision, by the Revels' office, of garments to be used here, see David M. Bergeron, 'Elizabeth's Coronation Entry (1559): New Manuscript Evidence,' *ELR*, 8 [1978], 3-8; McGee-Meagher, pp 58-62; Arber, I, 96; Withington, I, 199-202):

1 / 'The vniting of the two houses of Lancastre and Yorke,' with Henry VII, his Queen Elizabeth, Henry VIII, Anne Boleyn, and Elizabeth I;

2 / 'The seate of worthie gouernance,' with Elizabeth I, Pure Religion, Love of Subjects, Wisdom, and Justice, with their opposites Superstition and Ignorance; Rebellion and Insolency; Folly and Vain Glory; and Adulation and Bribery;

3 / 'The eight beatitudes' (from Matt. v);

4 / two mounts, one 'A decayed common weale,' the other 'A florishyng commonweale' (or 'a qwyke tre and a ded'; Machyn, p 186), with winged Time, an old man with a scythe; the daughter of Time, Truth, who presented a Bible to the queen;

5 / 'Debora with her estates, consulting for the good gouernment of Israel,' with a palm tree, Queen Deborah the judge, and her nobility, clergy, and commonalty; and

6 / a child dressed as a poet.

1559 6 February r

1117 Placards posted at street corners invite Londoners to taverns to pay to see newly invented 'plays in derision of the Catholic faith, of the Church, of the clergy, and of the religion'; one play represented Philip, Mary I, and Cardinal Pole and reasoned 'about such things as ... might have been said by them in the matter of religion'; and 'the arguments to construct these comedies' were given out by Sir William Cecil, secretary to the Council (*Venice*, VII, nos 18, 69, pp 27, 80-1; *Simancas*, I [1892], p 62, and cf p 247).

1559 24 June p

1118 May game around the City (and ?at Greenwich 25 June p) with St John Zachary; a giant; the nine worthies with speeches; a pageant with a queen with speeches; St George and the dragon; Robin Hood, Little John, Maid Marian, and Friar Tuck, with speeches (Machyn, p 201).

1562 21 July p

1119 At the Bridgehouse, three masques, including one of friars and one of nuns (who danced together), at a wedding feast for the daughter of John Nicolls, comptroller of works at London Bridge (Machyn, pp 288, 391).

1563 22 February r

1120 Edmund Grindal, bishop of London, writes Sir William Cecil to recommend that all plays be inhibited by proclamation within the

City, or three miles about it, for one year, with penalties for offending players and for the owners of the houses where the 'lewd interludes' occur; the offenders Grindal calls 'histriones, common players' who daily set up their bills (*The Remains of Edmund Grindal*, ed William Nicholson, PS 23 [1843], pp 268-9).

1565 p
1121 Players performing interludes in the churchyard of Christ Church, St Katharine's, Aldgate, during Easter and Whitsun weeks, and on Sundays and holy days between them, and up to Michaelmas; with scaffolds there (for the audience; J.P. Malcolm, *Londinium Redivivum*, III [1803], pp 309-10; Cox, p 279).

1566 17 January p
1122 *Sapientia Solomonis* (text in *Sapientia Solomonis, Acted before the Queen By the Boys of Westminster School*, ed Elizabeth R. Payne, Yale Studies in English, 89 [1938]; original version by Sixt Birck, printed in 1547).

1567-8 p
1123 Plays called 'witte and will' and 'prodigallitie' performed before Elizabeth at Whitehall (Feuillerat 2, p 119). These have been tentatively identified as:
  1 / *The Marriage of Wit and Science* (text ed Arthur Brown, MalS [1960 (1961)], and Trevor Lennam, *Sebastian Westcott, the Children of Paul's, and 'The Marriage of Wit and Science'* [1975], pp 61, 81-197; TFT 43; Arber, I, 399; Greg 55; STC 17466 [publ 1570]; Stratman 6041-56; Houle 33); and
  2 / *The Contention between Liberality and Prodigality* (text ed W.W. Greg, MalS [1913]; TFT 98; Greg 190; STC 5593 [publ 1602]; Stratman 5459-64; Houle 23; cf Lennam, *Sebastian Westcott*, p 61).

1574 1 January p
1124 'Truth, Faythfullnesse, & Mercye' played by the Children of Westminster at Whitehall (Feuillerat 2, p 193).

1582 r
1125 Description of the lost *Play of Plays and Pastimes*, with Life, Delight, Recreation, Glut, Tediousness, and Zeal, acted at the Theatre; ?also played at court as *Delight* by Leicester's men twice in 1580-1 (ES, IV, 217-18; II, 89).

1583 22 February p
1126 A 'play set out al by one virgin' at the Theatre (ES, I, 371, n 4).

1588-91 p
1127 *The Seven Deadly Sins*, originally by Richard Tarlton (theatrical plot; W.W. Greg, *Dramatic Documents from the Elizabethan Playhouses* [1931], pp 105-22).

1591 22 March p
1128 Play of Jerusalem by Strange's men (also performed 25 April; *Henslowe's Diary*, ed R.A. Foakes and R.T. Rickert [1961], p 17).

1591 29 October p
1129 George Peele's *Descensus Astraeae*, a pageant with such characters as Superstition, Ignorance, Charity, Hope, and Faith (Withington, II, 25-6).

1594 3/17/31 January p
1130 Play of Abraham and Lot by Sussex's Men (*Diary*, pp 20-1).

1594 3/10 June p
1131 Play of Hester and Ahasuerus (*Diary*, p 21).

1596-7 p
1132 Play of Nebuchadnezzar by the Admiral's Men (acted 8 times 19 December-21 March; *Diary*, pp 55-7).

1600-2 r
1133 Play of Judas by William Haughton, William Bird and Samuel Rowley for the Admiral's Men (*Diary*, pp 135, 185-6).

1602 12 January p
1134 Play of Pontius Pilate (*Diary*, p 187).

1602 r
1135 Plays with the hanging of Absalom, for Worcester's Men; of Jephthah by Anthony Munday and Thomas Dekker for the Admiral's Men; of Joshua by Samuel Rowley for the Admiral's Men; of Tobias by Henry Chettle for the Admiral's Men; and of Samson by Rowley and Edward Juby for the Admiral's Men (*Diary*, pp 200-5, 217, 296).

1604 15 March p
1136 Pageants for the entry of James I include the riding of St George and St Andrew; Astraea, Virtue, the four cardinal virtues, Envy and Zeal (Withington, I, 222-6).

1606 July-August p
1137 Solomon's temple and the coming of the queen of Sheba, for James and the king of Denmark at Theobalds; and a fireworks pageant of the seven deadly sins at sea off Gravesend (*ES*, I, 172; Withington, I, 229).

1609 29 October p
1138 Lord Mayor's pageant with St Andrew and St George (Withington, II, 30).

1611 p
1139 Lord Mayor's show, Anthony Munday's *Chryso-Thriambos*, with St Dunstan (Withington, II, 31).

1612 p
1140 Lord Mayor's show, Thomas Dekker's *Troia Nova Triumphans*, with the battle between the Throne of Virtue and Castle of Envy (holding Ignorance, Sloth, etc; Withington, II, 31-2).

1613 p
1141 Lord Mayor's pageant, Thomas Middleton's *Triumphs of Truth*, with an Angel and moral figures like Zeal, Error, Envy, Truth with Graces and Virtues, Religion, Perfect Love, Chastity and Meekness (Withington, II, 33-5).

ca 1613-22 p
1142 A performance of Christ's Passion on Good Friday night at Ely House, Holborn (William Prynne, *Histriomastix* [1633], p 117; STC 20464a; *MS*, II, 382).

1620, 1631, 1637 p
1143 Lord Mayor's show with St Catherine (Withington, II, 83).

1620-4 p
1144 *The Virgin Martyr*, on St Dorothea, by Thomas Dekker and Philip Massinger (G.E. Bentley, *The Jacobean and Caroline Stage*, III [1956], pp 263-4).

1621 May r
1145 James I to see the 'History of Abraham' at the Banqueting House (*Collections Volume VI. Dramatic Records in the Declared Accounts of the Treasurer of the Chamber 1558-1642*, ed D. Cook and F.P. Wilson, MalS [1961], p 119).

1622 r
1146 *Herod and Antipater*, by Gervase Markham and William Sampson (text; *Annals*, p 114).

1623 p
1147 Lord Mayor's show with the eight beatitudes (Withington, II, 82-3).

LONDON, diocese of

ca 1215-22 r
1148 Prohibition of 'ludi' from consecrated places, including churchyards and church porches (R.M. Woolley, 'Constitutions of the Diocese of London, c. 1215-22,' *EHR*, 30 [1915], 297-8).

1245-59 r
1149 The statutes of Bishop Fulk Basset prohibit all 'ludi' from consecrated places, especially churchyards and church porches (*Councils & Synods*, pp 647, 649).

1542 r
1150 Edmund Bonner, bishop of London, prohibits clergy allowing 'common plays, games, or interludes' in churches or chapels (*Visitations*, II, 88; *L. & P. Hen. VIII*, XVII, no 282, pp 156-7).

1550 r
1151 Interrogatories of Bishop Nicholas Ridley ask his clergy whether any persons speak against the Book of Common Prayer in interludes or plays (*Visitations*, II, 234).

1554-5 r
1152 Edmund Bonner, bishop of London, in a general visitation asks if his clergy use 'common games or plays,' if any parishioners of four-

teen years or more go to 'games and other plays, disport and pastimes' during divine service, and if any plays slandering religion have been printed or sold; and Bonner prohibits the first two points (*Visitations*, II, 333, 348, 354, 364, 366-7).

LONGLEAT (Wiltshire)

ca 1562? p
1153 Robin Hood play in the house of John Thynne (David Burnett, *Longleat* [1978], p 30).

LONG MELFORD (Suffolk)

ca 1554-9 r
1154 Palm Sunday procession with a boy prophet, pointing to the sacrament and singing (transcript of 1692 of the written memories of the Marian churchwarden Roger Martyn; William Parker, *The History of Long Melford* [1873], p 72).

1555 p
1155 Games; and proclaiming them at Braintree and Ipswich (Galloway-Wasson, p 185; Parker, *History*, p 106).

LONG SUTTON (Lincolnshire)

1542-74
1156 Visiting players, bann-criers, and 'bayne,' in the church in 1547-8 (Kahrl, pp 70-4).

LOUTH (Lincolnshire)

1516-57
1157 St James' churchwardens' accounts list a book including the whole 'Regenall' of Corpus Christi play (1516) and pay towards the pageants in procession on Corpus Christi and for four men bearing pageants; and Grammar School accounts reward the schoolmaster Mr John Goddall for play costs in 1555-6 and at Corpus Christi 1556-7 in the market place (Kahrl, pp 78-84).

1527-1625
1158 The same church accounts reward visiting players, some with banns, others in the church (1556-7), and a nearby town 'bayne' and play (Kahrl, pp 80-4).

1567-8 r
1159 Grammar School accounts reward Mr Pelsonne for setting out an interlude (Kahrl, p 84).

LUDLOW (Shropshire)

1554-1627
1160 Visiting players; including interluders in 1554 and children players in 1562, both in the castle (J.O. Halliwell, *Notices of Players Acting at Ludlow* [1867]).

LYDD (Kent)

1428-1636
1161 Visiting 'lusores,' bann-criers, puppet player, and 'foote' and other players (*Records of Lydd*, trans and transcr Arthur Hussey and M.M. Hardy, ed Arthur Finn [1911]; Dawson, pp 91-112).

1456 4 July p
1162 Play of St George (Dawson, p 93).

1489-90 r
1163 New Romney men see the 'originalem lud'' of Lydd here (Dawson, p 124).

1526-34
1164 Play of St George, with a new play-book, performed in 1532-3 on four play days, once before Richard? Gibson of London, who had been helping the town with its play since 1526 (in rewriting it? Dawson, pp 189, 199-200; churchwardens' accounts note that two wardens of this play visited Gibson in 1527 about play apparel [*Records of Lydd*]).

LYME REGIS (Dorset)

1549-1634
1165 Visiting players, several times *temp.* Mary in the church (Cyril Wanklyn, *Lyme Leaflets* [1944], pp 12-13, 20-1, 39-40; Murray, II, 327; *Halliwell-Phillipps*, pp 113, 115).

MAIDSTONE (Kent)

1589 p
1166 Coronation day pageant with children (Dawson, p 201).

MALDON (Essex)

1447-1635
1167 Visiting 'lusores,' players, and town plays and 'lusi,' as in the market place (1469), the corn market (1469), and the Carmelite friars (in 1537, evidently with stage timber there by 1541; A. Clark, 'Maldon Records and the Drama,' *N&Q*, 10th ser, 7 [1907], 181-3, 422-3; 8 [1907], 43-4; Coldewey, pp 262-84).

1540-62
1168 Town play (using scaffolds and having John Baptist in calves' skins and Christ in a coat, 11 July 1540; Burles the property player in 1562; and the sale of costumes in 1563-4; Clark, 'Records,' pp 182-3, 342-3, 422; W.A. Mepham, 'Municipal Drama at Maldon in the Sixteenth Century,' *EssR*, 55 [1946], 169-75, 56 [1947], 34-41; Coldewey, pp 261-78).

MANCHESTER (Lancashire, now Greater Manchester)

1552 r
1169 John Bradford, one of Edward VI's six itinerant chaplains, preached here, according to a popular tradition, that because the people were ungodly the mass should again be said in the church and 'the play of Robin Hood acted there; which accordingly came to pass in queen Mary's reign' (Richard Hollingworth's mid-17th-century ms history of the town, cited in *The Writings of John Bradford, M.A.*, ed Aubrey Townsend, II, PS 7 [1853], p xxviii, n 1; and cf pp xxv-xxvii).

MANNINGTREE (Essex)

ca 1588-99 r
1170 'a playe of strange moralitie / Shewen by Bachelrie of Maningtree' ('The Choise of Valentines,' attributed to Thomas Nashe, *Works*, ed Ronald B. McKerrow, 2nd edn with corrections by F.P. Wilson [1958], III, 404).

1603 February r
1171 'The towne of Manitre in Essex holdes by stage playes' (*The Diary of John Manningham of the Middle Temple 1602-1603*, ed Robert P. Sorlien [1976], p 187).

1606 r
1172 Cruelty is acted '(like the old Morralls at *Maningtree*) by Tradesmen' ('The Seuen Deadly Sinnes of London,' *The Non-Dramatic Works of Thomas Dekker*, ed Alexander B. Grosart, II [1885], p 73).

1612 r
1173 The town holds the privilege of its fair, or charter, by a yearly stage-play (Heywood, *Apology*, sig G3r).

MASHAM (Yorkshire, N.R., now North Yorkshire)

1609-10 p
1174 Winter performance of *St. Christopher* at the home of Sir Thomas Danby (G.W. Boddy, 'Players of Interludes in North Yorkshire in the Early Seventeenth Century,' *NYorkCROJ*, 3 [1976], 107-8).

MAXSTOKE PRIORY (Warwickshire)

1430 2 February p
1175 'ludum' by boy choristers of this monastery in the castle of William de Clinton, lord Clinton, here (MS, II, 384; record not extant, according to J.R. Holliday, 'Maxstoke Priory,' *Trans. Birmingham and Warwickshire Arch. Soc.* for 1874 [1878], p 93; CP, III, 315).

1431-58
1176 Visiting players (Holliday, pp 91-3).

MELTON MOWBRAY (Leicestershire)

1556 r
1177 Robin Hood's play (for two years; Kelly, p 64).

MERE (Wiltshire)

1561-3 p
1178 Vice or fool at church ale ('The Churchwardens' Accounts of Mere,' transcr Thomas H. Baker, *WiltANHM*, 35 [1907-8], 34; *ECA*, p 48).

MERTON (Surrey, now Greater London)

1349 6 January p
1179 'ludos R*eg*is,' a tournament-disguising, having visors with heads of dragons and of men (for Edward III at his manor of Banstead; Nicolas, pp 43, 122-3).

METFIELD (Suffolk)

1509 r
1180 Bungay game (Galloway-Wasson, p 186).

METTINGHAM COLLEGE (Suffolk)

1403-1527
1181 Visiting players, and puppet players or 'lusores,' often over Christmas (Richard Beadle, 'Dramatic Records of Mettingham College, Suffolk, 1403-1527,' *TN*, 33 [1979], 125-31 [BL Add mss 33985-90]; and Galloway-Wasson, pp 188-9 [BL Add mss 40069-70]).

MIDDLETON (Norfolk)

1445-6 p
1182 Play before Thomas de Scales, lord Scales, at Christmas by King's Lynn townsmen (Galloway-Wasson; dated 1444-5 by H. Harrod, *Report on the Deeds & Records of the Borough of King's Lynn* [1874], p 87; *CP*, XI, 504-7; see also under KING'S LYNN).

MILDENHALL (Suffolk)

1505 p
1183 A play of St Thomas [a Becket?] on St Thomas day (probably 29
December) for the guild of St Thomas a Becket in the hall yard (Galloway-Wasson, p 190; cf his 'The Morality Play: Ancestor of Elizabethan
Drama?' *CompD*, 13 [1979], 218).

1510 p, 1529 p
1184 Players at the May ale; 'ludo vocat*us* Maygame' (with a May ale
recorded by 1508; Galloway-Wasson, pp 191-2; Wasson, 'Guide,' pp
78-9).

1540-1 p
1185 Play or church ale (Galloway-Wasson, p 192).

MISSENDEN ABBEY (Buckinghamshire)

1528-30 r
1186 Payments to players at Christmas (*The Cartulary of Missenden
Abbey*, III, ed J.G. Jenkins, HMC JP1 [1962], pp xxii-xxiii; courtesy of T.
De Welles).

MOATENDEN, near Headcorn (Kent)

1576 r
1187 Friars' annual Trinity Sunday procession where the Devil is put
to flight (William Lambarde, *A Perambulation of Kent* [1826], p 300).

MOREBATH (Devon)

1533 Easter r
1188 Receipt from players (*The Accounts of the Wardens of the Parish of
Morebath, Devon. 1520-1573*, transcr J.E. Binney [1904], p 49).

1540-7?
1189 St George pageant or play (a horse and a dragon; and a 'city' was
constructed in a churchyard, 1540, according to Wasson, p 66; Binney's *Accounts* records the wardens of St George 1522-73, and there
are references to the tabernacle of St George, his horse, and the dragon
[eg, pp 32, 61, 72]; and Wasson, 'Guide,' pp 70-1).

MORPETH (Northumberland)

1666 r
1190 A town custom before the civil war was to select one young man
to be St George (and the other young men his attendants), who on St
George's day would come to church and, at the creed, 'stand up and
draw his sword' (Walter C. Trevelyan, 'Observations in a Northern
Journey, Taken Vaccon. 1666, by John Stainsby, of Clement's Inn,
Gent.,' AA, 3 [1844], 121).

MOUNT EDGCUMBE (now Cremyll, Cornwall)

ca 1556? p
1191 Armed men, led by one Trevanian (?), an enemy of Sir Richard
Edgecombe (fl 1556), came here to his seat at Christmas, but their
armour and weapons were only painted paper, and their intention was
only to join ladies of the house in dancing, after which 'Pastimes'
there was a banquet at which Trevanian took off his vizard and proposed a marriage between a nephew who entered dressed in a
nymph's attire, and one of Edgecombe's daughters (John Prince,
Danmonii Orientales Illustres: or, the Worthies of Devon [1701], p 285;
courtesy of T. De Welles).

MUCHELNEY (Somerset)

1437 r
1192 Order that the gate through which monks go for 'shows' be shut
up (*The Register of John Stafford, Bishop of Bath and Wells, 1425-1443*, ed
Thomas S. Holmes, SomRS 31-2 [1915-16], pp 209-10).

NETHERBURY, Slape Manor in (Dorset)

ca 1566 r
1193 Robin Hood and Little John, at church ales (Hutchins, II, 108).

NEWCASTLE UPON TYNE (Northumberland, now Tyne and Wear)

1427-1581 (1589?)
1194 Corpus Christi plays (*Newcastle upon Tyne*, ed J.J. Anderson, REED
[1982], pp 3-132, 163; Henry Bourne, *The History of Newcastle upon*

Tyne [1736]; John Brand, *The History and Antiquities of the Town and County of the Town of Newcastle upon Tyne*, 2 vols [1789]; James Walker and M.A. Richardson, *The Armorial Bearings of the Several Incorporated Companies of Newcastle upon Tyne* [1824]; *History of Newcastle and Gateshead*, ed Richard Welford, vols I-II [1884-5]; and *Extracts from the Records of the Merchant Adventurers of Newcastle-upon-Tyne*, ed F.W. Dendy, II, SS 101 [1899]. The plays were evidently performed on Corpus Christi day (although some historians – Anderson excepted – believe that they followed Corpus Christi day in 1568, according to testimony about Sir Robert Brandling's will in *Depositions and Other Ecclesiastical Proceedings from the Courts of Durham* [ed James Raine], SS 21 [1845], p 123; *Newcastle*, REED, pp 57-8, 174; Dendy, pp 161, 171; Welford, II, 416); the performance (with banns), Anderson argues, being accomplished separately from the Corpus Christi procession at several locations on one day and done on 'cars' carried by porters (cf his 'The Newcastle Pageant "Care,"' MET, 1 [1979], 60-1). The following pageants have been recorded:

1 / the creation of Adam, by the Bricklayers and Plasterers (1454r; Walker, p 49; Welford, I, 334);

2 / Noah's ark, by the Shipwrights (text: Bourne, pp 139-41; facs by John Anderson and A.C. Cawley, 'The Newcastle play of *Noah's Ark*,' REEDN, 1977.1, pp 11-17; ed Davis, pp xl-xlvii, 19-31; Stratman 4303-30; *Manual* 14);

3 / the offering of Isaac by Abraham, by the Slaters and Bricklayers (1452r and 1568p [unnamed], 1579r; Brand, II, 350-1, 370, n b; Walker, p 39; Welford, II, 133, 424);

4 / the deliverance of the children of Israel out of thralldom, bondage, and servitude of King Pharaoh, by the Millers (1578r; Brand, II, 348, 372; Walker, p 36; Welford, II, 508);

5 / the kings of Cologne, with messenger, star, and playbook, by the Goldsmiths, Plumbers, Glaziers, Pewterers, and Painters (1536r; Bourne, p 14; Brand, II, 352, 371, n d; Walker, pp 41, 59; Welford, II, 151);

6 / the flying of Our Lady into Egypt, also by the Bricklayers and Plasterers (1454r; as above for [1]);

7 / the purification? erroneously identified play by the Smiths (1437r; *Newcastle*, REED, p xxxvii, n10; Brand, II, 318-19, 370; Walker, pp 15, 58 [where so named]; Welford, I, 298);

8 / the baptizing of Christ, by the Barber-Surgeons and the Wax and Tallowchandlers (1442r; Brand, II, 341, 370; Walker, p 26; Welford, I, 308);

9 / the last supper? play supported by the Fullers and Dyers 1477r, with God's coat and maundy loaves 1561p (Brand, II, 320, 370-1, n c; Walker, pp 18, 58-9; Welford, I, 375; II, 370);

10 / the bearing of the cross, by the Weavers (1525r; Brand, II, 339; Walker, p 24; Welford, II, 97);

11 / 'our Saviour's Sufferings,' by the Saddlers (1460; Bourne, p 21; Brand, II, 316, 370; Walker, p 14; Welford, I, 339; J.C. Hodgson, 'The Company of Saddlers of Newcastle,' AA, 3rd ser, 19 [1922], 1-3);

12 / the burial of Christ, by the Housecarpenters and Joiners (1579r; Brand, II, 345, 372; Walker, p 31; Welford, II, 513);

13 / the descent into hell? erroneously identified play by the Tailors (1537r, 1560r; Newcastle, REED, p xxxvii, n10; Bourne, pp 86-8; Brand, II, 315-16; Walker, pp 9, 59, n [where so named]; Welford, II, 154-6, 364);

14 / the burial of Our Lady St Mary the Virgin, by the Masons (1581r; Brand, II, 346, 372; Walker, p 32); and

15-22 / plays, or contributions to them, by the Coopers (1427r, 1575r), Glovers (1437r), Skinners (1438r), Tanners (1532r), Curriers, Feltmakers, and Armourers (1545r), Vintners (1552-3r?), Cooks (1575r), and Joiners (contributing to 'any general play ...'; 1589r; Brand, II, 317, 344, 347-9, 359, 370-2; Walker, pp 8, 29, 33, 37, 59-60; Welford, I, 274-5, 297; II, 238, 467, 470); and see below under 1552.

1503 25 July p
1195 The fifth earl of Northumberland, Henry Algernon Percy, received Margaret Tudor here on her progress to Edinburgh with a banquet having 'games/dauncers sportes. & songes' (Newcastle, REED, p 10; Leland, IV, 277-8).

1510-11 r
1196 A canvas-and-timber dragon appears in a civic procession (for St George's day? Newcastle, REED, pp 13-14; John Anderson, 'The Newcastle Dragon,' MET, 3.2 [December 1981], 67-8).

1552 p
1197 Five plays put on by the Merchant Adventurers, of which one, the Hostmen's play, was paid for by the city (Newcastle, REED, pp xii-xiii, 24, 55; Brand, II, 371; Extracts, ed Dendy, II, 164; John Anderson suggests that the Hostmen's play, also performed in 1568, was a Harrowing of Hell or Doomsday play).

1554 r
1198 Civic act forbidding apprentices to mum or to wear beards (*Newcastle*, REED, pp 24-6; Brand, II, 227-8n).

1554-96 p
1199 Hogmagog (a giant; *Newcastle*, REED, pp 26-113; *Extracts*, ed Dendy, II, 165, 168, and cf p xxi for a suggestion that this was one of the plays of 1552; 'Extracts from the Municipal Accounts of Newcastle-upon-Tyne,' ed M.A. Richardson in his *Reprints of Rare Tracts & Imprints of Rare Manuscripts*, III [1849], p 22).

1568 May r
1200 Town play with bann and Beelzebub (possibly a giant; *Newcastle*, REED, p 56; 'Extracts,' ed Richardson, p 17).

NEW HALL, or Beaulieu, at Boreham (Essex)

1519 3 September p
1201 Richard Gibson prepares two masques (of old men and of ?youths) and a pastime for Henry VIII and the court; and William Cornyshe's play by the chapel children portraying Lust, Summer, the Moon, the Sun, Winter, the Wind, and Rain (*L. & P. Hen. VIII*, III.ii, pp 1538, 1550-1; and cf Addenda, I.i, no 273, p 75; Halle, fols 68v-9r).

NEW ROMNEY (Kent)

1387-1625
1202 Visiting 'lusores,' bann-criers, and players, at the Crockhill (Crockley Green) in 1441-2 (Henry T. Riley, 'The Manuscripts of the Corporation of New Romney,' *5th Report*, HMC, I [1876], pp 533-54; Dawson, pp 120-43).

1432-3 p
1203 Town players (*5th Report*, p 541).

1456 10 May r
1204 John Craye and Thomas a Nasshe, wardens of the play of the resurrection, recover a sum from John Lylye in court (Henry T. Riley, 'Court Books of the Corporation of New Romney,' *6th Report*, HMC, I, App [1877], p 541).

1463-4 p
1205 A payment for 'ludo interludii Passionis Domini' (Dawson, p 120).

1497-8 r
1206 Town bann-criers are ordered to carry in their banns or bills of it before St George's day (*5th Report*, p 551).

1513-45
1207 In 1516 the town chooses wardens for the play of Christ's Passion, to be done 'as from olden time' (probably the 'lusus' paid for in 1513-14 and 1517-18, and 'Le Playboke' noted about 1516-17) but the Lord Warden of the Cinque Ports in May 1517 requires them to get the king's permission before playing it, a fact that may explain the visits that townsmen made to Richard? Gibson in London in 1525-6 about the 'arrayment' for a play and in 1532-3 to 'know his mynde of our play,' although a probable performance in 1539-40 (when there are payments for playing gear and play-rehearsal in Lent) seems to lack any indication of a prior visit to London (Dawson, pp 130-5; Riley, *5th Report*, pp 552-3).

1555 27 December r
1208 A stage play was planned for the following Pentecost with the following groups of parts, and town accounts pay for their writing out, the making of a falchion to rehearse the play, and a visit to the Lord Warden for his good will, but it was apparently not performed after all (players' recognizances; Dawson, pp 136-7, 202-4):

1 / Herod, his two knights, his messenger, six tormentors (Mischance, False at Need, Untrust, Faintheart, Unhappe, Evil Grace), Pilate, his messenger, Caiphas, his messenger, Annas, his handmaid, and the second devil;

2 / the blind man, his boy, father, and mother, SS Peter, Simon, Matthew, Andrew, John, James, James the less, Thomas, Philip, Bartholomew, and Jude, Judas, two pharisees, Lazarus, Martha, Magdalene, Martha's servant, a neighbour, and a Jew; and

3 / the doctor, the Virgin Mary, three (?) princes, Malcus, Mary Salome, the third devil, and Simon of Cyrene.

1560 p
1209 Whitsuntide play on four days with stages for Pilate and princes, Annas and the tormentors, the pharisees, and Herod; with Heaven,

'the longe A Galye,' the Cave, Hell, the three crosses, and the city of 'samary' (Samaria?); with the godhead, the centurion, Judas, John Baptist, and the pascal lamb; and with bann-criers and a fool (and with players mentioned in 1566-8; Dawson, pp 137-8, 204-11, the latter a list of gifts towards the plays, as well as accounts).

NIDDERDALE, Gowthwaite Hall at
(Yorkshire W.R., now North Yorkshire)

1609 2 February p
1210 *St. Christopher*, with Reprobus, the Emperor, the Devil, and a hermit, played at the home of Sir John Yorke; with an interlude, 'a disputation between a Catholic priest and an English minister,' with a fool, an ?angel, and one or two devils, one of whom carries off the minister (G.W. Boddy, 'Players of Interludes in North Yorkshire in the Early Seventeenth Century,' *NYorkCROJ*, 3 [1976], 95-130; Christopher Howard, *Sir John Yorke of Nidderdale 1565-1634* [1939], pp 20-6; Aveling, p 289).

ca 1628 r
1211 Anti-protestant play, with the Devil and King James (J.S. Burn, *The Star Chamber* [1870], p 119).

NONSUCH (near Ewell, Surrey)

1558 24 July r
1212 Thomas Coppley asks to borrow a court masque for his marriage revels from Sir Thomas Cawarden (Feuillerat 1, p 251).

NORTHAMPTON (Northamptonshire)

1461 r
1213 Abraham and Isaac play (text only; see Davis 1, pp xlvii-lviii, 32-42; facs edn, Davis 2, pp 31-45; Stratman 3883-99; *Manual* 17).

1581 r
1214 Pageants were stored in St George's Hall within the previous fifty years (J.C. Cox, *The Records of the Borough of Northampton* [1898], II, 181-4).

NORTH CURRY (Somerset)

1314 r
1215 Wastel bread cut in three for old Christmas game by tenants in villeinage (*MSS Wells*, I, 335).

NORTHILL (Bedfordshire)

ca 1561-4
1216 Two vices (at a church ?ale; J.E. Farmiloe and Rosita Nixseaman, 'Elizabethan Churchwardens' Accounts,' *Publications of the Bedfordshire Historical Record Society*, 33 [1953], 7).

NORWELL (Nottinghamshire)

ca 1399-1413 r
1217 The manor customs *temp.* Henry IV note that the lord's tenants at mowing time are to be feasted and 'to divert themselves with plays the remainder of the day' in Northyng meadow (William Dickinson, *Antiquities, Historical, Architectural, Chorographical, and Itinerary, in Nottinghamshire*, pt 2, vol I [1803], p 151).

NORWICH (Norfolk)

ca 1260
1218 The three Maries at matins on Easter (*The Customary of the Cathedral Priory Church of Norwich*, ed J.B.L. Tolhurst, HBS 82 [1948], p 94; Lipphardt, II, 564, no 411).

1301-80
1219 Visiting minstrels or players at the monastery, often on Trinity Sunday (H.W. Saunders, *An Introduction to the Obedientiary & Manor Rolls of Norwich Cathedral Priory* [1930], pp 182-3).

1389-1558
1220 Corpus Christi procession, with ?pageants such as the Griffin and a tree of paradise, and an angel, 1545-58 (JoAnna Dutka, 'Mystery Plays at Norwich: Their Formation and Development,' *LeedsSE*, NS 10 [1978], 111, 115-16; and Nelson, pp 128-31).

15th century-1527
1221 St Luke's Guild, on Monday and Tuesday in Whitsun week, presented the 'sight' of 'many and diuers disgisinges and pageauntes as well of the liff and marterdams of diuers and many hooly sayntes as also many other lyght and feyned figures and pictures of other persones and bestes' (Davis, pp xxvii-xxviii; generally Dutka, pp 107-20; and Nelson, pp 119-21).

ca 1400-1500
1222 Descent of an angel from the cathedral roof on the feasts of Trinity and Corpus Christi (Saunders, *Introduction*, p 103).

1408-?1553
1223 Pageant and riding of St George, Margaret, angels, and the dragon, with which the George makes 'a conflict' ('Account of the Company of St. George in Norwich. From Mackerell's History of Norwich, MS. 1737,' NA, 3 [1852], 315-74 [and p 335]; *Records of the Gild of St. George in Norwich, 1389-1547*, trans Mary Grace, Norfolk Rec. Society, 9 [1937], pp 6-149; and Nelson, pp 121-2).

1443 5 March p
1224 Shrove Tuesday riding of the king of Christmas (played by John Gladman of the 'Bachery' Guild on a horse trapped with tinfoil, and with three men carrying before him a crown, a scepter, and a sword), preceded by persons disguised as the twelve months and Lenten (clad in herrings' skins, and followed by his horse, trapped with oyster shell), and by other disguisers 'making merthe and disporte and pleyes,' to the priory (this ended in a riot; *The Records of the City of Norwich*, ed W. Hudson and J.C. Tingey, I [1910], pp 345-6).

1469 p
1225 Two pageants: one, with a speech, written out by Geoffrey Spirleng, of the salutation of Mary and Elizabeth, with angels, two giants, two patriarchs, twelve apostles, sixteen virgins, three empresses, and Gabriel; another performed by 'Fakke' and his boys (Henry Harrod, 'Queen Elizabeth Woodville's Visit to Norwich in 1469,' NA, 5 [1859], 35-6; in general, organized by Pernell of Ipswich, 'qui frequentat prouidere subtilia ludorum et Stacionum,' for which see Mark Eccles, '*Ludus Coventriae* Lincoln or Norfolk?' *Medium AEvum*, 40 [1971], 138-9; and Galloway-Wasson, under Ipswich, 1491).

1473 r

1226 W. Woode, horse-keeper to John Paston II, was kept for the past
three years (at Norwich? or about Caistor?) 'to pleye' St George,
Robin Hood, and the Sheriff of Nottingham (probably a bitter jesting
allusion; *Paston*, I, 461; for the supposed text, see 'Robin Hood and the
Sheriff of Nottingham: A Dramatic Fragment, c. 1475,' ed W.W. Greg,
Collections Part II [MalS, 1908], pp 117-24; facs edn, Davis 2, pp 73-7;
Robyn Hood, pp 203-7; Stratman 6545, 6550, 6566-661; *Manual* 34).

ca 1530-65

1227 Pageants and plays in Pentecost week, including the following
pageants (from a list ca 1530; Davis 1, pp xxix-xxx; Hudson and
Tingey, II, 126, 135, 171, 230; and Nelson, pp 124-37):

    1 / the creation of the world (Mercers, Drapers, Haberdashers);

    2 / Hell cart (Glaziers, Stainers, Scriveners, Parchment Makers, Car-
penters, Gravers, Carriers, Collarmakers, Wheelwrights);

    3 / Paradise (Grocers, Raff-men; also in a procession for the birth of
Prince Edward in 1537; text: 'The Story of the Creation of Eve, with
the Expelling of Adam and Eve out of Paradise' [from 1533], in Davis
1, pp xxii-xxxvi, 8-18; Stratman 4335-49; *Manual* 15; a new manu-
script, reported by F.I. Dunn, 'The Norwich Grocers' Play and the
Kirkpatrick Papers at Norwich,' *N&Q*, 217 [1972], 202-3, is edited by
JoAnna Dutka, 'The Lost Dramatic Cycle of Norwich and the Grocers'
Play of the Fall of Man,' *RES*, forthcoming; a facsimile, 'The 18th-
Century Transcript of the Norwich Grocers' Play,' is forthcoming in
REEDN). Accounts in 1534 pay for fruits (for the tree; also in 1557), a
new hair with a crown for the serpent, gloves for Adam, Eve, the
Father, and the Angel, players for those parts, and Sir Stephen Prewett
for making 'a newe ballet'; in 1556, a hair and crown for the angel; in
1557, a crown and hair for the bearer of the Griffin; and in 1558, hire
of an angel's coat, two crowns, and a hair. An inventory of pageant
properties in 1563 lists a pageant, that is, a painted wainscot house on
a four-wheeled cart; a square top for the house, and a gilded Griffin;
various flags; a red rib; stained coat, hose, bag, and cap for Dolor; two
stained coats and hose for Eve; stained coat and hose for Adam;
stained coat, hose, and tail for the serpent, with a white hair; an
angel's coat and over-hoses of 'apis skynns'; three painted cloths to
hang about the pageant; a face and hair for the Father; two hairs for
Adam and Eve; and other goods, such as for horses.

    4 / Abel and Cain (Shearmen, Fullers, Thickwoollenweavers, Cover-
lightmakers, Masons, Limeburners);

5 / Noah's ship (Bakers, Brewers, Innkeepers, Cooks, Millers, Vintners, Coopers);

6 / Abraham and Isaac (Tailors, 'Broderers,' Reders, Tilers; by 1537; Dutka, p 109);

7 / Moses and Aaron with the children of Israel and Pharaoh with his knights (Tanners, Curriers, Cordwainers; pageants of God in the burning bush, Moses, and Aaron, and the cart, 1534r; *Notices and Illustrations of the Costume, Processions, Pageantry, &c. Formerly Displayed by the Corporation of Norwich* [1850], p 7);

8 / the conflict of David and Golias (Smiths);

9 / the birth of Christ with the shepherds, and the three kings of Cologne (Dyers, Calenderers, Goldsmiths, Goldbeaters, Saddlers, Pewterers, Braziers);

10 / the baptism of Christ (Barbers, Waxchandlers, Surgeons, Physicians, Hardwaremen, Hatters, Cappers, Skinners, Glovers, Pinners, Pointmakers, Girdlers, Pursers, Bagmakers, Skeppers, Wiredrawers, Cardmakers);

11 / the resurrection (Butchers, Fishmongers, Watermen); and

12 / the Holy Ghost (Worstedweavers; by 1529; Dutka, p 113; Hudson and Tingey, II, 175).

ca 1534-42 r

1228 John Leland sees a copy of Terence at the Carmelite convent here (Leland, III, 28).

1534-1638

1229 Visiting players; games and interludes, in particular, by players and gameplayers in the assembly chamber of the common hall at the Blackfriars or the game place or Master 'Castylden's' place ca 1539-45, regularly with a stage, or a booth, or a scaffold of barrells and timber for the players (*EES*, II.i, 332-4; David Galloway, *Norwich*, II, REED [forthcoming]; Murray, II, 361-72).

1546 9 November p

1230 Queen's players' interlude in the common hall, with a scaffold, the matter being the market of mischief (*EES*, II.i, 333; Galloway; *Notices*, p 14; Murray, II, 362).

1547 9 January p

1231 Students of the grammar school under schoolmaster Byrde played an interlude in the common hall chapel (Blackfriars; *EES*, II.i,

333; Galloway; L.G. Bolingbroke, 'Pre-Elizabethan Plays and Players in Norfolk,' NA, 11 [1892], 351; *Notices*, p 14).

1547 ?February p
1232 Triumph for the Coronation of Edward VI, including a pageant of King Solomon, and the mermaid (Galloway; *Notices*, p 13, dated 1546; Thomas Nicholas gave his pageant called the 'Moremayd' to the city in 1540; Hudson and Tingey, II, 168; and Nelson, p 125).

1551-2 p
1233 Lord marquess' (of Dorset?) gameplayers are rewarded for a play 'at the gyldhall of zacheus' (Galloway).

1556 June p
1234 Pageants for the mayor's installation include one of Time performed by civic waits at St Peter Hungate, with a speech written by schoolmaster John Buck; a castle with an orator, having a speech written by Buck, at St John's; and the four cardinal virtues with an orator, all having speeches, at St Andrew's (*Notices*, pp 14-15, dated 1550; the text for Time alone is printed by George A. Stephen, 'The Waits of the City of Norwich through Four Centuries to 1790,' NA, 25 [1933-5], 56-8; Withington, II, 16-17; and C.A. Janssen, 'The Waytes of Norwich and an Early Lord Mayor's Show,' RORD, 22 [1979], 57-64; Galloway).

1558-9 p
1235 An interlude made and played by schoolmaster John Buck for the mayor (Janssen, 'The Waytes of Norwich,' p 58).

1578 16 August p
1236 Civic pageant of Deborah, Judith, Esther and Queen Martia for the entry of Elizabeth I (Bernard Garter, *The Ioyfvll Receyuing of the Queenes Most Excellent Maiestie into hir Highnesse Citie of Norvvich* [London: Henry Bynneman (1578)], sigs C2r-C3r; STC 11627-8; McGee-Meagher, pp 100-2).

NORWICH, diocese of

1240-3 r
1237 Bishop William Raleigh's statutes prohibit 'ludi' on consecrated grounds, and particularly in churchyards and church porches (*Councils & Synods*, pp 351, 353).

NOTTINGHAM (Nottinghamshire)

1562 May r
1238 Plots for three masques before Elizabeth I in Nottingham Castle (cancelled before performance; 'Dramatic Records from the Lansdowne Manuscripts,' ed E.K. Chambers, *Collections Part II* [MalS, 1908], pp 144-8; McGee-Meagher, pp 71-2):

1 / Argus or Circumspection, keeper of the prison Extreme Oblivion; Pallas and ladies Prudentia and Temperantia, with captives Discord and False Report;

2 / Peace and Friendship at the Court of Plenty, a castle with two porters, Ardent Desire and Perpetuity;

3 / Discretion at the castle, with Valiant Courage (Hercules), who wins over Disdain and Prepensed Malice.

NUN COTON (Lincolnshire)

1531 30 April r
1239 The prioress is forbidden to allow any lord of misrule or disguising in nuns' or other apparel as had occurred in the past (Edward Peacock, 'Injunctions of John Longland, Bishop of Lincoln, to Certain Monasteries in his Diocese,' *Arch*, 47.i [1882], 56).

OTFORD (Kent)

1348-9 p
1240 'ludos R*egis,*' a tournament-disguising, at Christmas, with visors with heads of men, lions, elephants, wildmen, and virgins (for Edward III; Nicolas, pp 43, 122).

OXFORD (Oxfordshire)

ca 1225 p
1241 Public letters or proclamations by 'Genius of Christmas'? Discretion, and 'Transaetherius' before or addressed to Robert Grosseteste as newly-elected King of Christmas at the university (text in 'The "Rex Natalicius,"' *Collectanea*, 1st ser, ed C.R.L. Fletcher, OHS 5 [1885], pp 39-49; 'elaborate fooling,' amusing types of the model rhetorical letter, according to E.F. Jacob, '*Florida Verborum Venustas*: Some Early Examples of Euphuism in England,' *BJRL*, 17 [1933], 285; Chambers, *MS*, I,

411-12, and Boas, p 4, n 1, would date these in the 14th-16th centuries).

before 1350 r
1242 No member of the university is to celebrate the feast of North or South 'nations' by dancing visored or crowned with leaves (*Statvta Antiqva Vniversitatis Oxoniensis*, ed Strickland Gibson [1931], p 83; courtesy of John Elliott).

1360 29 August p
1243 Play by the parishioners of West (now Long, or Earl's) Wittenham on the day of the decollation of St John Baptist ?at Exeter College (H.T. Riley, 'Exeter College, Oxford,' *2nd Report*, HMC [1871], p 128).

ca 1387-1400 r?
1244 Chaucer's 'Miller's Tale,' set in Oxford, includes a clerk Absolon who plays 'Herodes upon a scaffold hye' (*Chaucer*, line A3384; the Miller, who cries out 'in Pilates voys' (A3123), alludes bawdily in this tale to the stories of the miracle plays of Noah and his wife, of St Joseph's 'trouble,' and of Gabriel's annunciation to Mary; see Kelsie B. Harder, 'Chaucer's Use of the Mystery Plays in the *Miller's Tale*,' MLQ, 17 [1956], 193-8; Beryl B. Rowland, 'The Play of the *Miller's Tale*: A Game within a Game,' *ChauR*, 5 [1970], 140-6; and her 'Chaucer's Blasphemous Churl: A New Interpretation of the *Miller's Tale*,' in *Chaucer and Middle English Studies in Honour of Rossell Hope Robbins*, ed Beryl Rowland [1974], 43-55).

1400 r
1245 Statutes of New College, or St Mary's College of Winchester in Oxford, prohibit scholars and fellows frequenting 'tabernas, spectacula, vel alia loca inhonesta' (*Statutes of the Colleges of Oxford* [1853], I, 47 [separate pagination for each set of statutes]).

ca 1410 r
1246 A Terence at Merton College (F.M. Powicke, *The Medieval Books of Merton College* [1931], no 711, p 193).

1437-8 r
1247 Statutes of All Souls College prohibit scholars and fellows from frequenting 'tabernas, spectacula vel alia loca inhonesta' (*Statutes of the Colleges*, I, 43).

1439 r, 1444 r
1248 Humphrey of Lancaster, duke of Gloucester, gave to the university in 1439 Seneca's tragedies and in 1444 a Terence (*Epistolae Academicae Oxon.*, ed Henry Anstey, OHS 35-6 [1898], I, 182, 237; H.H.E. C[raster]., 'Index to Duke Humphrey's Gifts to the Old Library of the University in 1439, 1441, and 1444,' *The Bodleian Quarterly Record*, 1 [1914-16], 134).

1442 r
1249 A copy of Terence's comedies (beginning part way through 'Andria') was written here for William Grey, university chancellor (who gave it back in 1478, being now ms 276 in *Catalogue of the Manuscripts of Balliol College Oxford*, comp R.A.B. Mynors [1963], pp xxvii, 292; for the six comedies of Terence owned by Alexander Bell [d 1474], see p xxiii).

ca 1444-16th century
1250 Christmas plays at St Peter's in the East (Hobhouse, p xiv).

ca 1457-61
1251 Thomas Chaundler's moral play *Liber Apologeticus* (text: *Liber Apologeticus de Omni Statu Humanae Naturae. A Defence of Human Nature in Every State* (c. 1460). *A Moral Play by Thomas Chaundler*, ed Doris E. Shoukri, Modern Humanities Research Association Publs., 5 [1974]; Leland, IV, 156 [ms at Wells Cathedral Library]).

1461-80
1252 Visiting 'players' at New College; those of Edward IV and of Prince Edward, probably their minstrels (unpublished thesis by Shirley Bridges, 'The Life of Chaundler,' cited by Shoukri, ed, *Liber Apologeticus* [1974], pp 16, 38)

1474-6 r
1253 Lincoln College Library catalogue of 1474 includes Terence's comedies, Seneca's tragedies, and Plautus' comedies, given to it in 1465 by Robert Flemyng, former chaplain to Henry VI (Emden 1, I, 700, items xxii, xxiii, xxvi, xxviii; for these and a Terence in a list of 1476, see R. Weiss, 'The Earliest Catalogues of the Library of Lincoln College,' *The Bodleian Quarterly Record*, 8 [1935-7], 350 [items 74, 78, 80], 352 [item 18]).

1479 r
1254 Magdalen College statutes prohibit scholars and fellows from frequenting 'tabernas, spectacula, vel alia loca inhonesta' (*Statutes of the Colleges*, II, 41).

1483 r
1255 Among books valued by Thomas Hunt, a stationer, were several Terences ('Day-Book of John Dorne, Bookseller in Oxford, A.D. 1520,' ed Falconer Madan, *Collectanea*, 1st ser, ed C.R.L. Fletcher, OHS 5 [1885], pp 141-3).

1485-1635
1256 'lusores' and 'lusiones' at Christmas, plays, interludes, comedies (from 1537), and tragedies (from 1539) at Magdalen College; with mention of a 'theatrum' in 1553-4 and 1557-8 (Alton, pp 43-62).

1486-7 r
1257 'ornamento lusorum vocato le capp mayntenaunce' at Magdalen College (Alton, p 44).

1494 r
1258 An ms of Seneca's tragedies was deposited in Merton College (Powicke, *Medieval Books*, no 1114, pp 221-2).

ca 1495-9 r
1259 Sports and 'plays' in the Oxford vacation are mentioned in a Magdalen College *vulgaria*, which also refers to the 'doer' (author) and men players (with their parts) of a delightful play ('ludicrum') of King Solomon, performed 'yesterday' (*School Book*, pp 26-7; the editor identifies this with Thomas More's play on the same subject, for More studied at Oxford ca 1492-4 and his letter mentioning that play also appears in this manuscript [pp xxvi-xxix]; see under GENERAL RECORDS ca 1501 November).

ca 1495-1513 r
1260 All Souls College library had an ms of Seneca's tragedies ca 1495-1556, a Plautus ca 1505 and another, given by Richard Topclyffe, ca ?1512-13 (N.R. Ker, *Records of All Souls College Library 1437-1600*, OBS NS 16 [1971], nos *1025, *1067, 1360, pp 40, 48, 60, 87-8, 109, 123, 127; cf Sir Edmund Craster, *The History of All Souls College Library*, ed E.F. Jacob [1971], p 33).

1495-1521
1261 Easter play at Magdalen College (?also termed a play of Mary Magdalene 1506-7, and with Christ and women 1518-9; Alton, pp 45-8).

ca 1505-15 r
1262 The university's first register records a comedy of Terence on the grammar curriculum (James K. McConica, *English Humanists and Reformation Politics under Henry VIII and Edward VI* [1965], p 87).

1507 20-30 January r
1263 In a visitation of Magdalen College at this time John Burgess, senior, said that the fellows use copes (from the sacrist) in the Christmas 'interludiis'; and John Burgess, junior, said that Francis Pollard, a demy, was in town at Christmas dressed with open sleeves like an actor (*A Register of the Members of St. Mary Magdalen College, Oxford*, NS 1, ed William D. Macray [1894], pp 55-6; Pollard failed to get his degree [p 147]; courtesy of John Elliott).

1507 r
1264 Statutes of Balliol College prohibit college members being at 'ludis inhonestis aut prohibitis aut vitium incitantibus, aut doctrinam impedientibus et contentionem provocantibus,' and mingling with 'histriones' and 'ioculatores' (*Statutes of the Colleges*, I, 18-19).

ca 1508 r
1265 A Terence ms in Canterbury College (W.A. Pantin, *Canterbury College Oxford*, OHS NS 6, I [1947], p 87).

1512 11 March r
1266 Edward Watson is awarded a degree in grammar on condition that he compose one hundred poems in praise of the university, and one comedy, within the next year (*Register of the University of Oxford*, I, ed C.W. Boase [1885], p 298).

ca 1512-27 r
1267 A schoolboy at Magdalen College School writes in his English exercise book, 'Me semeth it is tyme to leue owre plays, sportes and mery conseittes ... [after] this cristinmes holidays' (Nicholas Orme, 'An Early-Tudor Oxford Schoolbook,' *RenQ*, 34 [1981], 22 [item 2]; cf pp

30 [item 51], 32 [item 63, where he lists dicing, cards, tables, chests, singing, dancing, drinking, and reveling among these kinds of play).

1513 20 January p
1268 A 'ludus optimus' in Merton College hall (Boas, p 12, n 1; courtesy of John Elliott).

1513 p
1269 A play in Shrovetide at Lincoln College (Vivian Green, *The Commonwealth of Lincoln College 1427-1977* [1979], p 107).

1513-79 r
1270 Students and fellows at the university (by ca 1501-40) with playtexts in their possession included the following:
   1 / John Valyn, a Terence (inventoried 1513[ii]; Emden 2, p 742);
   2 / Lionel Jackson, fellow of Balliol College, a Terence (inventoried October 1514[xi]; p 722);
   3 / John Haywood, a Terence (inventoried December 1514[xii]; p 722);
   4 / William Wodrofe, a Terence (inventoried ca 1530[ix]; p 742);
   5 / Morgan Griffith, two copies of Terence (inventoried 1539[xiii, xv]; p 722);
   6 / Bysley, a Terence and a Plautus (inventoried 1543[vi, xlvi]; p 716);
   7 / Thomas Symons, fellow of Merton College, 'Commedia sacra' (inventoried 1553[cxx]; p 739);
   8 / David Tolley, Christ Church student: two copies of Plautus, a Terence, two copies of Aristophanes (one in Latin), Seneca's tragedies and his 'Hercules Furens,' Euripides' tragedies and 'Rhesus' (attributed), and Sophocles' tragedies and his 'Ajax' (inventoried November 1558[viii, xxxiv, lxviii, lxxi, lxxii, lxxxiii, lxxxix, cxxii, cxxxvi, cciv, ccxxi]; pp 740-1);
   9 / Gabriel Dunne, bequest to St John's College of printed books of Aristophanes and Euripides (1558[xxxv, xliii]; pp 720-1);
   10 / Thomas Paynell, bequest to St John's College of a printed Plautus (1564[xxxvi]; p 729);
   11 / Thomas Daye, canon of Christ Church, two copies of Terence (inventoried 1568[cxxv]; p 719); and
   12 / John Lewes, manciple of University College, Seneca's tragedies and Terence (inventoried 1579[xxxiv, xlvi]; pp 725-6).

1517 r
1271 Statutes of Corpus Christi College state that the Professor of
Humanity is to lecture on authors such as Plautus and Terence, and
the Greek Lecturer on authors such as Aristophanes, Euripides, and
Sophocles, each Tuesday, Thursday, and Saturday (*Statutes of the
Colleges*, II, 48-9).

1520 r
1272 Sale of printed editions of 'roben hod,' Terence (many), Aristophanes' *Plutus* in Greek (many), Plautus' 'commedia' (two), 'mundus a
play,' and 'saint jon euuangeliste en trelute' ('Day-Book of John
Dorne,' ed Madan, pp 71-177, and see 'Index I' for individual book
nos; a Terence and Seneca's tragedies appear in Madan's 'Supplementary Notes,' *Collectanea*, 2nd ser, OHS 16 [1890], pp 460-1).

1525 3 July r
1273 Cardinal Wolsey's statutes for Cardinal's College state that a
Reader of Humanity is to lecture privately on authors such as Plautus
and Terence, and that a Professor of Humanity in Greek is to lecture
publicly on authors such as Aristophanes, Euripides, and Sophocles
(*Statutes of the Colleges*, II, 71-2, 127, 178).

ca 1525-72
1274 A translation of Euripides' tragedies from Greek into Latin by
Thomas Kay or Caius, university registrar 1534-52 and master of University College 1561-74 (lost; *Index*, p 441; Emden 2, pp 325-6).

1529-30 r
1275 Visiting stage players in 1530, and a comedy prepared for acting
by the canons in 1529, at Cardinal's College (*L. & P. Hen. VIII*, IV.iii, no
6788, pp 3065-6).

ca 1530-41 r
1276 John Sheprey translated Euripides' 'Hecuba' and 'Hercules
Furens' from Greek into Latin (*Scriptorum*, I, 713; according to Emden
2, p 514, he translated Seneca's 'Hercules Furens').

1533-7
1277 Visiting players at New College (and 'ludos' in 1552-3; Alton, pp
40-2).

ca 1533-44
1278 John Hoker, fellow of Magdalen College, wrote a comedy called 'Piscator, siue Fraus Illusa' (*Index*, p 217; *Scriptorum*, I, 712).

1534 26 January r
1279 Richard Croke writes Cromwell from Oxford about a 'device intended to have been played' at Gloucester College (now Worcester College), 'a place of monks,' if Mr Robert Carter had not stopped it; the text is now held by the Commissary, Dr William Tresham (*L. & P. Hen. VIII*, VII, no 101, pp 38-9).

1534-42 r
1280 John Leland saw two books of Seneca's tragedies here, one at Balliol College (Leland, III, 58, 66).

1539 June r
1281 Thomas Bedell left with Alexander Nowell books including Terence and Seneca's tragedies (Baldwin 1, I, 174).

1541 r
1282 Nicholas Grimald's *Christus Redivivus*, written at Brasenose College (text ed and trans L.R. Merrill, *The Life and Poems of Nicholas Grimald*, Yale Studies in English, 69 [1925]; *Index*, p 302; *Scriptorum*, I, 701).

ca 1541-6
1283 Nicholas Grimald's *Archipropheta*, written at Christ Church (text ed and trans Merrill, *Life and Poems*; and performed there at Christmas 1548? see W.G. Hiscock, *A Christ Church Miscellany* [1946], pp 165-6; *Index*, pp 301-2; *Scriptorum*, I, 701).

1544-5 r
1284 John Foxe's *Titus et Gesippus*, written and revised (text in *Two Latin Comedies*, pp 51-197).

1545 r
1285 John Foxe says that he has extracted the argument of a comedy from 'Solomon's Ecclesiastes' (John H. Smith, ed, *Two Latin Comedies*, pp 11-12).

1548-51 p
1286 Comedies at Exeter College (Charles W. Boase, *Register of the Rectors and Fellows, Scholars, Exhibitioners and Bible Clerks of Exeter College Oxford*, I [1879], pp xxix, 38; misdated 1458 by Boas, p 25, n 1).

ca 1553-6
1287 Tragedy at New College at Christmas with three kings, a queen (?), two dukes, six counsellors, three gentlewomen, a young prince; and a masque (Feuillerat 1, p 250; Albert Feuillerat, 'Performance of a Tragedy at New College, Oxford, in the Time of Queen Mary,' MLR, 9 [1914], 96-7).

1554 12 December r
1288 Dean and Chapter of Christ Church allows funds for only two comedies and two tragedies in Latin and in Greek at Christmas (Boas, pp 7, 17).

1555 r
1289 Statutes of the College of St John the Baptist state that the Professor of Greek was to lecture on Aristophanes, Euripides, and others (*Statutes of the Colleges*, III, 50).

1555 r
1290 Statutes of Trinity College require the teacher of Latin to interpret authors such as Terence and Plautus on Tuesdays, Thursdays, and Saturdays (Baldwin 1, I, 105).

1556-80
1291 Visiting players, in 1556-7 at the guildhall (*Selections from the Records of the City of Oxford*, ed William H. Turner [1880], pp 267-411).

1558 r
1292 Jasper Heywood's English translation of Seneca's *Troas*, undertaken as a Fellow of All Souls College ?late in this year, a New Year's gift for Queen Elizabeth (text in *Jasper Heywood and his Translations of Seneca's 'Troas,' 'Thyestes' and 'Hercules Furens,'* ed H. de Vocht, MKAED 41 [1913], pp 1-86; Greg 28; STC 22227-27a [publ 1559]).

1562 r
1293 Laurence Humphrey, President of Magdalen College, asks John Foxe for permission to produce his *Christus Triumphans* there (*Two*

Latin Comedies, pp 34, 376; the prompt book for this may be the copy of the 1556 edition at Harvard).

ca 1564-74 p
1294 'A certaine company of country plaiers' performing the story of Isaac (played by a boy with a beard), among other things (John P. Driscoll, SJ, 'A Miracle Play at Oxford,' *N&Q,* 205 [1960], 6, citing Edmund Bunny's *A Briefe Answer* [1589], pp 152-3; *STC* 4088).

PENRYN (Cornwall)

ca 1375
1295 The Cornish *Origo Mundi, Passio Domini Nostri,* and *Resurrexio Domini Nostri* (text ed Edwin Norris, 2 vols [1859]; newly trans by Markham Harris, *The Cornish Ordinalia* [1969]; probably written at the Collegiate Church of Glasney, with auspices in the town itself; Stratman 3688-715; Robert Longsworth, *The Cornish Ordinalia: Religion and Dramaturgy* [1967]; however, Bakere, pp 31-48, distinguishes sharply between the Glasney-based 'Origo Mundi' and the 'Passio,' associated with West Penwith [Marazion and the river Hayle are named], and supports Phyllis Pier Harris' unpublished suggestion that authorship by one Sir Reginald de Sancto Austolo, a rector of St Just-in-Penwith who occupied a prebend at Glasney in 1358, would account for the odd distribution of place-names in these plays; Southern 1, pp 237-60, discusses staging).

PENSHURST (Kent)

1574 p
1296 Robin Hood players, in accounts for Robert Sydney and his sisters (C.L. Kingsford, *Report on the Manuscripts of Lord De L'Isle & Dudley Preserved at Penshurst Place,* II, HMC [1934], p 268).

PETERBOROUGH (Northamptonshire, now Cambridgeshire)

ca 1194 r
1297 Abbot Benedict bequeathed a book with Terence to the abbey; and by the late 14th century it had Seneca's tragedies too (M.R. James, *Lists of Manuscripts Formerly in Peterborough Abbey Library,* Supplement to the Bibliographical Society Trans., 5 [1926], pp 21, 47).

1468-74
1298 Hiring out of players' garments by the church of St John Baptist (*Peterborough Local Administration. Parochial Government before the Reformation: Churchwardens' Accounts 1467-1573 with Supplementary Documents 1107-1488*, ed W.T. Mellows, Northants. Rec. Society, 9 [1939], pp 1-15).

1479 p
1299 Players playing in the church of St John Baptist at Christmas (*Parochial Government*, p 33).

1548 p
1300 Payment to visiting players on Christmas eve by Peterborough Cathedral Dean and Chapter (*Peterborough Local Administration. The Last Days of Peterborough Monastery*, ed W.T. Mellows, Northants. Rec. Society, 12 [1947], p 96).

PLYMOUTH (Devon)

1479-96 r, 1515-16 p
1301 Corpus Christi pageant and players (the Tailors' pageant, 1479-96r: R.N. Worth, 'The Early Commerce of Plymouth,' *PlyIDCNHS*, 6 [1876-8], pp 299-300, and his *Calendar of the Plymouth Municipal Records* [1893], pp 34-5; the record of 1515-16 players courtesy of John Wasson).

1515-1635
1302 Visiting players and interluders, regularly in the guildhall 1537-42 (with town players 1544-5, players at Christmas 1546-7, and players in the church 1549-50, 1559-60, 1565-6, and the boys of Totnes playing there 1573-4; Murray, II, 380-5; Worth, *Calendar*, pp 111-51; W.H. Cornish, 'Presidential Address. Strolling-Players in the West when Shakespeare Trod the Boards,' *PlyIDCNHS*, 22 [1949-56], 147-60; and courtesy of John Wasson).

PLYMSTOCK (Devon)

1568-70 p
1303 Players in the church and at Christmas according to churchwardens' accounts (courtesy of John Wasson).

PONTEFRACT (Yorkshire, W.R., West Yorkshire)

1664 18 April r
1304 'Pagent in Corpus X'ti playe called Noe' to be brought forth, according to the ordinances of the Wrights, Bowyers, Coopers, Patteners, Turners, Sawers, and Sewers (a late surviving reference; the regulation may be as early as ca 1484; *The Booke of Entries of the Pontefract Corporation. 1653-1726*, ed Richard Holmes [1882], pp 371-4).

POOLE (Dorset)

1508-9
1305 Robin Hood collections (courtesy of A.F. Johnston).

1512-51
1306 Visiting players, at the church in 1551; in 1512 the mayor agreed to call a special meeting to authorize payment to the king's players, should they visit the town (Victor J. Adams, 'When the Players Came to Poole,' *Dorset Year Book* [1978], p 129; and courtesy of A.F. Johnston).

PRESTON (Lancashire)

before 1631 p
1307 Corpus Christi play (seen by Weeuer, p 405).

1638 r
1308 William Sandes' show called 'the Chaos' (David George, 'Records of Interest at the Lancashire Record Office,' REEDN, 1979:2, pp 2-6).

PULLOXHILL (Bedfordshire)

ca 1486-93 r
1309 A play made, on one occasion, for St James' church (E.W. Ives, 'In Aid of the Restoration Fund – A Medieval Example,' *N&Q*, 207 [1962], 162-3).

PUTNEY (Surrey, now Greater London)

1567 p
1310 *Sapientia Solomonis*, by the Westminster School boys before Bishop Grindal (*ES*, II, 73).

RAMSEY ABBEY (Huntingdonshire, now Cambridgeshire)

14th century r
1311 A Terence ms in the library catalogue (*Chronicon Abbatiae Rame-seiensis*, ed W.D. Macray, RS 83 [1886], p 361; cf James W. Thompson, *The Medieval Library* [1967], p 122, n 87).

RAYLEIGH (Essex)

1550 1 June p
1312 Stage players performed for the parish on Trinity Sunday (H.W. King, 'Inventories of Church Goods 6th Edw. VI.,' *Trans. of the Essex Archaeological Society*, 5 [1873], 119-20).

1574 r, 1580 p
1313 Painted stuff (for plays) in the church; and players in a certain man's yard (Coldewey, 'Demise,' p 246; Frederick Emmison, 'Tithes, Perambulations and Sabbath-breach in Elizabethan Essex,' in *Anti-quary*, pp 205-6).

READING (Berkshire)

1347-8 p
1314 Royal 'hastiludia' or jousts, with some persons wearing vizards of red sheep skin (for Edward III; Nicolas, pp 38-9, 120-1).

1382-1631
1315 Visiting players; and the local 'lusores' in St Laurence's church 1433-4p (William D. Macray, 'The Manuscripts of the Corporation of Reading,' *11th Report*, pt VI, HMC [1888], pp 172-210; Alexandra F. Johnston, 'Folk Drama in Berkshire,' ISSMT conference paper [Dublin, July 1980], p 4).

1498 r, 1538-9?
1316 Kings of Cologne, with horses, on May Day (Charles Kerry, *A History of the Municipal Church of St. Lawrence, Reading* [1883], pp 228, 235).

1498-1508, 1530 r
1317 Robin Hood play or May play, with Robin Hood's men, coat, and hose (in 1505 from Finchampstead; Kerry, pp 227-37; with a Maid

Marian coat in 1530, according to Alexandra F. Johnston, 'Folk Drama in Berkshire,' ISSMT conference [1980], p 3).

1502-57
1318 King play or game at Whitsuntide (Kerry, pp 235-6; *The Church-wardens' Account Book for the Parish of St. Giles, Reading*, pt I, 1518-46, trans W.L. Nash [1881], pp 9-75; and courtesy of A.F. Johnston).

1506 p
1319 A play with Adam and Eve, evidently on Corpus Christi in the Forbury with a scaffold (Kerry, pp 233-4; date courtesy of A.F. Johnston).

1506 p, 1534-6 r
1320 Resurrection play, for the 'reformyng' and book of which a Mr Laborne was paid in 1534-6 (Kerry, pp 237-8; dates courtesy of A.F. Johnston).

1507-8 p
1321 Pageant of the passion on Easter Monday at the church (employing boards; Kerry, pp 237-8; dates courtesy of A.F. Johnston).

1511 p, 1515 r
1322 Cain's pageant, in 1515 in the market place (Kerry, p 237; dates courtesy of A.F. Johnston).

1540-1 p
1323 Loreman was paid for playing the prophet on Palm Sunday (Kerry, p 238).

1542 p
1324 Play in the abbey (St Lawrence churchwardens' accounts; courtesy of A.F. Johnston).

RICHBOROUGH (Kent)

ca 285-350 r
1325 Roman amphitheatre or arena at Rutupiae (Charles R. Smith, *The Antiquities of Richborough, Reculver, and Lymne, in Kent* [1850], pp 52, 161-72; B.W. Cunliffe, 'The Development of Richborough,' *Fifth Report*

on the Excavations of the Roman Fort at Richborough, Kent, ed B.W. Cunliffe, RRCSAL, 23 [1968], pp 248-9).

RICHMOND or SHEEN (Surrey, now Greater London)

1501 28 November p
1326 Final revels celebrating the wedding of Prince Arthur and Catherine of Aragon: a disguising with a two-storey tabernacle or chapel, lords with conies below, ladies with white doves above, and with sea-horses and children of the chapel within mermaids (AR, II, p *318; Anglo, pp 101-2; Wallace, p 13, from his *The Children of the Chapel at Blackfriars 1597-1603* [1908], p 69, misdates as 1485 the reference to this event in BL Harl. ms 69, fol 34v).

1502 26 January p
1327 Celebrations for the marriage of Margaret Tudor and James IV of Scotland: a hall pageant with many lighted windows, like a lantern, from which emerged moresques; and a disguising (Leland, IV, 263; McGee-Meagher, pp 48-9).

1508 December p
1328 Disguisings, moresques, interludes (also termed comedies and tragedies), and three pageants of a castle, a tree, and a mount at court (A.R. Myers, 'The Book of the Disguisings for the Coming of the Ambassadors of Flanders, December 1508,' BIHR, 54 [1981], 120-9; 'Court Festivals,' pp 24-5; '"The Spousells" of the Princess Mary, Daughter of Henry VII., to Charles Prince of Castile. A.D. 1508,' ed James Gairdner, in *Camden Miscellany,* IX, CS NS 53 [1895], p 30; a Spanish version, 'Las Solemnidades y Triunfos,' is in *Relaciones Históricas de los Siglos XVI y XVII,* foreword by Francisco R. de Uhagón, La Sociedad de Bibliófilos Españoles, 260 [1896], pp 14-27; cf *L. & P. Hen. VIII,* II.ii, p 1443).

1510 14 November p
1329 Richard Gibson arranged a mummery and disguising in the queen's chamber (*L. & P. Hen. VIII,* II.ii, pp 1492-3; Halle, fols 8v-9r; McGee-Meagher, p 62).

1511 6 January p
1330 A pageant of a rich mount with a golden tree with roses and pomegranates; a disguising with green, red, white, and black knights;

and a moresque coming out of the hill with a lady and a fool, all in a
revel devised by Mr Harry Guildford (L. & P. Hen. VIII, II.ii, pp 1493-4;
Halle, fol 9r; Holinshed, III, 558).

1514 6 January p
1331 Interlude with a moresque, devised by Sir Harry Guildford, of six
persons including Ladies Venus and Beauty, and a fool (L. & P. Hen.
VIII, I [1920], no 2562, pp 1122-3; Collier fabricates a record that this
interlude was called Cornish's 'tryumpe of Love and Bewte,' showed
Venus and Beauty taming a savage man and a lion, and included a
quatrain from a song by Venus and Beauty [I, 64-5]; Dr D. Cooper's
song 'I have bene a foster,' from a manuscript that John Stevens dates
ca 1515 [Music & Poetry, pp 386, 409 (text)], seems likely to have been
part of the entertainment from the forester's references in the song to
Lady Venus and Beauty, although William H.G. Flood, Early Tudor
Composers [1925], p 65, argues for the pageant-disguising 15 June
1522, for which see under WINDSOR).

1525-6 p
1332 Wolsey celebrated Christmas here with plays and disguisings
(Halle, fol 146r).

1535 r
1333 A book of Terence in the king's library here (Henri Omont, 'Les
Manuscrits français der Rois d'Angleterre au Chateau de Richmond,'
Études Romanes dédiées à Gaston Paris [1891], p 11).

1538 March r
1334 Heywood and his children playing an interlude (Privy Purse
Expenses of the Princess Mary, ed Frederick Madden [1831], p 62).

1547?
1335 A Newe Dialog betwene Thangell of God, & the Shepherdes in the
Felde by Thomas Becon, a chaplain to the household of Edward Seymour at Sheen (STC 1735.5; not seen; a dialogue? described as 'a
Protestant nativity play' and 'a patchwork of gospel verses' by John N.
King, 'Protector Somerset, Patron of the English Renaissance,' PBSA, 70
[1976], 310, 326).

1550 3 June p
1336 Masquing at the marriage of John Dudley, lord Lisle, the earl of Warwick's son, at Sheen (Wriothesley, II, 41; *Literary Remains*, pp 273-5).

1552-3 r
1337 Visit of ?the earl of Oxford's players to Sheen, home of Henry Grey, duke of Suffolk, in the winter (Davey, p 229).

1579 5 January p
1338 Children of Paul's act 'A Morrall of the marryage of Mynde and Measure' at Richmond (Feuillerat 2, p 286).

RIPON (Yorkshire, W.R., now North Yorkshire)

1312 r
1339 Prohibition of clergy at 'spectaculis publicis, ludibriis, et ... teatricalibus ludis' (*Memorials of the Church of SS. Peter and Wilfrid, Ripon*, II, ed J.T. Fowler, SS 78 [1886], p 68).

1439-40 p, 1447-8 p
1340 'ludentes' at Christmas, Epiphany, and Easter (*Memorials*, III, ed J.T. Fowler, SS 81 [1888], pp 235, 240).

ROCHESTER (Kent)

1202 r
1341 An ms Terence here (W.B. Rye, 'Catalogue of the Library of the Priory of St. Andrew, Rochester, A.D. 1202,' *Arch. Cant.*, 3 [1860], 59).

ROSSINGTON (Yorkshire, W.R., now South Yorkshire)

1299-1300 p
1342 A boy playing ('ludenti') before Prince Edward (*Liber Quotidianus Contrarotulatoris Garderobae. Anno Regni Regis Edwardi Primi Vicesimo Octavo. A.D. MCCXCIX & MCCC* [1787], p 163).

ROTHERHAM (Yorkshire, W.R., now South Yorkshire)

ca 1484-99 r
1343 The college founded here by Thomas Rotherham, archbishop of York, has a copy of Terence's comedies in its library (Montague R.

James, *A Descriptive Catalogue of the Manuscripts in the Library of Sidney Sussex College, Cambridge* [1895], p 5).

RYE (Sussex, now East Sussex)

1455-77
1344 Visiting players (in the church 1474-5, and the churchyard, 1477; H.T. Riley, 'The Manuscripts of the Corporation of Rye,' *5th Report*, pt 1, HMC [1876], pp 491-5).

1506 p
1345 Visiting players of Towne Mallyng, that is, South Malling, playing at the (former mayor's) house owned by Lawrence Stephens (Leopold A. Vidler, *A New History of Rye* [1934], p 49).

1522 p
1346 Play of the Resurrection at Easter on a stage, with 'the part of Almighty God' (William Holloway, *The History and Antiquities of the Ancient Town and Port of Rye* [1847], p 491).

SAFFRON WALDEN (Essex)

1466-75
1347 Visiting and town 'ludi' (courtesy of John C. Coldewey; for a record of 1474, see W.A. Mepham, 'A General Survey of Mediaeval Drama in Essex: The Fifteenth Century,' *EssR*, 56 [1945], 57).

1547-1631
1348 Visiting players (Andrew Clark, 'Players' Companies on Tour,' *N&Q*, 10th ser, 12 [1909], 41-2).

ST ALBANS (Hertfordshire)

ca 155-ca 395 r
1349 Roman theatre at Verulamium, with stage having a wooden floor, and after ca 200 with curtain-slot (from which the curtain was raised to cover the stage), proscenium, and stage buildings (structurally altered several times, converting a theatre where performances occurred in the central arena, ca 155-60, into an ordinary Roman theatre with enlarged stage, and returning to the central arena structure

ca 300, when a triumphal arch was added; Kathleen K. Kenyon and Sheppard S. Frere, *The Roman Theatre of Verulamium* [ca 1963]; and Kathleen M. Kenyon, 'The Roman Theatre at Verulamium, St. Albans,' *Arch*, 84 [1935], 213-61; Wacher, *Towns*, pp 210-11; see PLATES 2-3).

ca 300 (22 June) r
1349.5 St Alban was to be beheaded before a multitude at an open place ('harena,' ie 'arena' and possibly 'amphitheatre') outside the city walls and across the river Coln, but he actually suffered martyrdom about a half mile away on a hill, more worthy for a holy death (*Bede's Ecclesiastical History of the English People*, ed Bertram Colgrave and R.A.B. Mynors [1969], pp 30-3 [i.7]).

12th century r
1350 The library of the Benedictine abbey owned a 12th-century Terence written and illustrated there with ink-drawings of masked actors (now Bodl. ms Auct. F.2.13 [summary cat no 27603]; for an account of the two artists, the so-called Apocrypha Master and the Master of the Leaping Figures, see Larry M. Ayres, 'The Role of an Angevin Style in English Romanesque Painting,' *Zeitschrift für Kunstgeschichte*, 37 [1974], 220-1 and figs 41-2; cf Leslie W. Jones and C.R. Morey, *The Miniatures of the Manuscripts of Terence Prior to the Thirteenth Century: The Text* [1931], pp 68-93; Ker, p 94; see PLATES 5-6).

ca 1328-49 r
1351 The constitutions of Abbots Richard de Wallingford and Michael de Mentmore prohibit their clergy from attending 'illicita spectacula' or being 'aliis ludentibus' (*Gesta Abbatum*, II, 469).

ca 1329-34 r
1352 Abbot Richard de Wallingford gave four books from the monastery library including a Terence to Richard Bury, Keeper of the Privy Seal, later bishop of Durham (*Gesta Abbatum*, II, 200).

1444 30 June p
1353 'a play of Eglemour and Degrebelle,' ie Sir Eglamour of Artois and his son Degrabell ('Bale's Chronicle,' p 117).

ST BENET OF HULME (near Ludham, Norfolk)

1372-3 r
1354 Payment of two trumpeters 'in ludo de hornyg*es*' (Horning; John Wasson, 'Records from the Abbey of St Benet of Hulme, Norfolk,' REEDN, 1980.2, pp 19-21).

ST BREOCK (Cornwall)

ca 1588? r
1355 A play of Suzanna (undated) and the visiting Robin Hood of St Columb Major (churchwardens' accounts; Bakere, pp 18-19).

ST COLUMB MAJOR (Cornwall)

14th-16th century r
1356 'Plain an Gwarry' or playing-place (Nance, p 194, but modern according to Cornish, p 473).

1586-97 r
1357 Coats for morris dancers and a friar among 'Robbyn hoodes clothes' (R.M. Serjeantson, 'The Church and Parish Goods of St. Columb Major, Cornwall,' *The Antiquary*, 33 [1897], 345; Bakere, pp 18-19).

ST IVES (Cornwall)

14th-16th century r
1358 'Plain an Gwarry' or playing-place, at Stennack (Vivien Russell, 'Parochial Check-Lists of Antiquities. Hundred of Penwith, Western Division. 12: Parish of St. Ives,' CA, 8 [1969], 116).

1573 r
1359 Interlude in the playing place (John H. Matthews, *A History of the Parishes of Saint Ives, Lelant, Towednack and Zennor* [1892], p 144).

1575 p
1360 A six-day play with a structure for Heaven (Matthews, p 148).

1577-84
1361 Visiting players (Matthews, pp 151-6).

1584 p, 1588 p
1362 The Robin Hood (Matthews, pp 155, 157).

ST MARY DE PRÉ, near St Albans (Hertfordshire)

ca 1486-93
1363 Payments for wassails at New Year's and Epiphany, for harpers and players at Christmas, and for May games (Dugdale, III, 359-60; *The Victoria History of the County of Hertford*, IV, ed William Page [1914], p 431, n 39).

SALISBURY (Wiltshire)

1222 r
1364 Two 'coronae ... de latone ad representationes faciendas,' in a cathedral inventory (*Vetus Registrum Sarisberiense Alias Dictum Registrum S. Osmundi Episcopi*, ed W.H. Rich Jones, RS 78, II [1884], p 129).

1319 r
1365 Roger Martival, bishop of Salisbury, orders that no money or valuable commodity be given out of the cathedral alms-fund to those called 'menestralli' or sometimes 'ludorum homines' (*Statutes and Customs of the Cathedral Church of the Blessed Virgin Mary of Salisbury*, ed C. Wordsworth and D. Macleane [1915], pp 266-9).

1461-90
1366 'de diuersis jocalibus regibus & reginis' in 1461; 'le Kyngplay' in 1469; 'Alys [or King] Plaies' in the summer of 1490; 'lusores' with costumes at Corpus Christi in 1469; and pageants at Corpus Christi in 1490, evidently for a procession on both latter occasions (for or at St Edmund's church; *Churchwardens' Accounts of S. Edmund & S. Thomas, Sarum 1443-1702*, ed Henry J.F. Swayne, Wilts. Rec. Society [1896], pp xvi-xvii, 8-9, 13, 36-7; *Calendar of State Papers, Domestic Series ... Addenda, 1580-1625*, ed M.A.E. Green [1872], p 101).

1478-1524
1367 Riding of 'the George' between St George's Day and Whitsunday (Charles Haskins, *The Ancient Trade Guilds and Companies of Salisbury* [1912], p 40).

1496 p
1368 St Christopher, a giant, with his sword bearer, mace bearer, and Hob Nob, for the entry of Henry VII (on his way to Clarendon; Frank Stevens, 'The Giant and Hob Nob and their Story,' *The Festival Book of Salisbury*, ed F. Stevens, Salisbury, South Wilts & Blackmore Museum [1915], pp 63-4).

1541 r
1369 Richard Spencer, a priest turned player in interludes, was burned here for 'matter concerning the sacrament of the altar' (Foxe, V, 443).

1564 p, 1570 p
1370 The Tailors' Midsummer pageant with a giant, three black boys, the Devil, and Maid Marian (Haskins, pp 171-3; Marian K. Dale, 'The City of New Salisbury,' *A History of Wiltshire*, VI, ed Elizabeth Crittall, V.C.H. [1962], pp 135-6).

SALISBURY, diocese of

1217-19 r
1371 The statutes of Bishop Richard Poore prohibit 'inhonesti ludi qui ad lasciviam invitent' in churchyards (*Councils & Synods*, p 93).

SANCREED (Cornwall)

ca 1500
1372 'a Mirable Play' in 'the place' of an amphitheatre in this parish, now a field called 'Plain Gwarry,' after which two men fought, one of whom died (P.A.S. Pool, ed, 'The Penheleg Manuscript,' *JRIC*, NS 3 [1959], 200-1; for the 'Plain-an-Gwarry,' see Vivien Russell, 'Parochial Check-Lists of Antiquities. Hundred of Penwith, Western Division. 5. Parish of Sancreed,' *CA*, 1 [1962], 111).

SANDON (Essex)

1562 r
1373 Play, proceeds of which went for a bridge (Coldewey, p 59).

SANDWICH (Kent)

1458-1577
1374 Visiting 'ludentes,' 'ludatores,' 'lusores,' disguisers, and players, including ones showing a May, at the friars' in 1502-3, the fish market in 1508-9, and the Bull 1518-22 (Dawson, pp 146-54).

SEALE (Surrey)

1611 p
1375 Vice or fool at church ale (W.H. Hart, 'On the Churchwardens' Accounts, and Other Records Relating to the Parishes of Seal and Elstead, in the County of Surrey,' *Surrey Archaeological Collections*, 2 [1864], 35).

SELBY ABBEY (Yorkshire, W.R., now North Yorkshire)

1398 24 June p
1376 Clerks of Selby, 'ludentibus coram domino abbate' ('Account Roll of Selby Abbey, 1397-8,' *YorkAJ*, 15 [1899], 410, 413).

1431-1532
1377 Players, sometimes boys, as above; and visiting companies (*EES*, I, 332-9).

SHERBORNE (Dorset)

1543-72
1378 Corpus Christi play acted on boards or scaffolds in the church before the two low altars, with playbooks, painted garments, and visages for players; the standing of people on the church at the play in 1548; and rental of properties and garments by nearby towns from 1550, and of the church house for interludes in 1567 (A.D. Mills, 'A Corpus Christi Play and Other Dramatic Activities in Sixteenth-Century Sherborne, Dorset,' *Collections Volume IX*, MalS [1971 (1977)], pp 1-15; and for a recollection in 1603, see Joseph Fowler, *Mediaeval Sherborne* [1951], p 323).

1573-4 p
1379 Corpus Christi play in the churchyard with Sodom clothes, a gilded 'face,' and Lot's wife (made of a peck of wheaten meal), where

the audience sat on 'standinges' or stood on the church leads, and the players arrayed themselves in 'backer' tents that served as tiring-houses (possibly the play performed as well in 1576; Mills, pp 12-13).

1575 r
1380 Making of a vice coat (Mills, p 13).

SHERBURN IN ELMET (Yorkshire, W.R., now North Yorkshire)

1312 17 August r
1381 Vicar reproved for attending 'ludis teatralibus' (*The Register of William Greenfield Lord Archbishop of York 1306-1315*, pt I, ed William Brown, SS 145 [1931], pp 68-9).

SHERE (Surrey)

1526-7 p, 1534 p
1382 King game (on Whitsunday, 24 May 1534; Owen Manning, *The History and Antiquities of the County of Surrey*, cont William Bray, I [1804], pp 530-1).

SHERIFF HUTTON (Yorkshire, N.R., now North Yorkshire)

1525-6 p
1383 Rewards to players by Henry Fitzroy, duke of Richmond and Somerset and earl of Nottingham (Henry VIII's natural son; *L. & P. Hen. VIII*, IV.i, no 2063.2, p 928; dated 1526-7 by Collier, I, 97-8).

SHIPDHAM (Norfolk)

1536 p
1384 Game players at Christmas (from churchwardens' accounts; Galloway-Wasson, p 82).

SHOOTERS HILL (Kent, now Greater London)

1515 1 May p
1385 Meeting of Henry VIII and the queen with Robin Hood, Little John, Friar Tuck, and Maid Marian (played respectively by Yay or Ghay, Thomas Wawen, Wynsberry, and Thomas Villiers) at Shooters Hill, and later with ladies May, Flora, Humidity, Vert, Vegetave, Pleas-

ance, and Sweet Odour in a horse-drawn pageant and as played by ?the children of the chapel (*L. & P. Hen. VIII*, II.i, no 410, p 120 [with 'certain pasteboard giants carried upon cars' in procession], and II.ii, pp 1504-5; Halle, fols 56v-7r; there were also 'tall pasteboard giants' on cars in the procession back to Greenwich, according to *Venice*, II, no 624, p 248; Holinshed, III, 611-12).

SHOREDITCH (Middlesex, now Greater London)

1536 3 July p
1386 Henry VIII and others rode from York Place to the earl of Rutland's seat at Holywell nunnery in a masque of Turkish garments to celebrate the marriages of the children of three earls (Wriothesley, I, 50-1).

SHREWSBURY (Shropshire)

1494-1617
1387 Plays and interludes, sometimes by townsmen and in the quarry (1494, 1532; still customary by 1570), and at Pentecost, once with a dizzard; town interluders William Taylor and others (May 1549); and visiting players, 'interlusores,' and 'lusores' (H. Owen and J.B. Blakeway, *A History of Shrewsbury* [1825], I, 262, 267, 327-31, 394; W.D. Macray, 'The Municipal Records of Shrewsbury,' *15th Report*, pt X, HMC [1899], pp 13-36; Murray, II, 389-93; *Halliwell-Phillipps*, pp 101, 114).

1515-16 p
1388 Play and show, 'ludum & demonstracionem,' of the martyrdom of Feliciana and Sabina in Whitsun week in the quarry (Owen and Blakeway, I, 328; Macray, p 32).

1517-18 p
1389 Interlude of the three kings of Cologne at Pentecost (Macray, p 32).

1521-52
1390 Abbot of Marsham (Marham, Mardall, Marrall), played in May (Owen and Blakeway, I, 332-3; Macray, p 33).

1526-7 p
1391 'Saynt Kateryne is play' (expenditures for this are listed in the town bailiffs' accounts; courtesy of J.A.B. Somerset).

1542 p
1392 'interlusores,' with 'interlusus,' in the churchyard of St Chad (Owen and Blakeway, I, 330).

1552-3 p
1393 Robin Hood 'interlusoribus' (Macray, p 36).

1561 p
1394 Thomas Ashton's 'first playe upon the Passion of Christ' (George W. Fisher, *Annals of Shrewsbury School*, rev J.S. Hill [1899], p 5).

1566 p
1395 Ashton's play at Whitsuntide in the quarry for which Elizabeth I, on progress, was too late to see; possibly his play of Julian the Apostate (misdated, respectively, 1565 and 1556 [?also 1565] by William Phillips, 'William Cartwright, Nonjuror, and his Chronological History of Shrewsbury,' *TShropANHS*, 37 [1914], 54, and T. Phillips, *The History and Antiquities of Shrewsbury* [1779], p 201; redated in *ES*, III, 210-11, and IV, 83, and by Fisher, *Annals*, p 18).

1569 p
1396 Ashton's second, 'greate playe,' of the Passion of Christ at Whitsuntide in the quarry (dated variously 1567-9 in records: Phillips, *History*, pp 136, 201; 'Early Chronicles of Shrewsbury, 1372-1603,' ed W.A. Leighton, *TShropANHS*, 3 [1880], 268; and Fisher, *Annals*, pp 18-19 [whose date is used here]).

1587 r
1397 Bounded by the Severn and the city wall is 'a ground, newe made Theator wise, / Both deepe and hye, in goodly auncient guise,' seating above 10,000 for plays, baitings, and wrestling, with a cockpit; 20,000 saw 'Astons Play' here (Thomas Churchyard, *The Worthines of Wales* [1587], sig L1r; *STC* 5261; cf Arthur Freeman, 'A "Round" Outside Cornwall,' *TN*, 16 [1961], 10-11).

SILCHESTER (Hampshire)

1st-4th centuries? r
1398 Roman amphitheatre at Calleva Atrebatum, for perhaps 2700 persons (George C. Boon, *Roman Silchester: The Archaeology of a Romano-British Town*, rev edn [1974], pp 148-51, pl 2, and final Plan; Sheppard Frere, *Britannia* [1967], p 261; Wacher, *Towns*, p 264).

SLEAFORD (Lincolnshire)

1480 r
1399 Accounts of the Holy Trinity Guild note a 'Ryginall' of the play for the Ascension, with the writing of speeches, and a painted garment for God (MS, II, 395, from BL Add ms 28,533).

1533-4 r
1400 Personal accounts for Sir John Hussey, lord Hussey, of Sleaford, at this time chamberlain for Princess Mary, have a payment to four players (*The Victoria History of the County of Lincoln*, II, ed William Page [1906], p 329, n 13).

SNETTISHAM (Norfolk)

1469-1536
1401 Games, dances, Mays, processions, and gatherings, generally from other towns (churchwardens' accounts; Galloway-Wasson, pp 86-93; and cf David Galloway, 'Comment: The East Anglian "game-place": Some Facts and Fictions,' REEDN, 1979.1, p 25).

1485 p
1402 Plays (date uncertain; Galloway-Wasson, p 87).

SOUTHAMPTON (Hampshire)

1485-1635
1403 Visiting players, as at the Dolphin in 1539-40 and at the town hall in 1555-6 (C.E.C. Burch, *Minstrels and Players in Southampton 1428-1635* [1969], pp 12-45; *Lisle Letters*, I, 163-4; *Halliwell-Phillipps*, p 121).

SOUTH KYME (Lincolnshire)

1601 31 August p
1404 Stage play or interlude called 'the Death of the Lord of Kyme' near Sir Edward Dymocke's house: a libel against the earl of Lincoln, with the characters of Lord Pleasure, the Lord of South Kyme, the Devil, the Vice or Fool, and a minister (Norreys J. O'Conor, *Godes Peace and the Quenes* [1934], pp 108-26, 144-5).

SOUTHWARK (Surrey, now Greater London)

1444-59
1405 Plays, sometimes by clerks, on St Lucy's day (13 December) and on St Margaret's day (20 July; J.P. Collier, 'St. Margaret's, Southwark,' *BrMag*, 32 [1847], 484-96, 638-9; 33 [1848], 2-3).

1547 5 February r
1406 Stephen Gardiner, bishop of Winchester, protests that 'certain players of my Lord of Oxford's' in Southwark intend to have 'a solemn play' at the time of his services for the late king (Patrick F. Tytler, *England under the Reigns of Edward VI. and Mary* [1839], I, 21-2; *CSP*, p 1).

1555 7 April p
1407 Children with hired playing garments and six pair of gloves played the prophets on Palm Sunday (Newington District Library, Southwark, St Olave's churchwardens' accounts, p 41).

SOUTHWELL (Nottinghamshire)

1248 r
1408 Statutes forbid canons going to 'spectaculorum' (*Visitations and Memorials of Southwell Minster*, ed Arthur F. Leach, CS NS 48 [1891], p 208).

1496 r
1409 A vicar choral promises not to frequent 'publica spectacula' any more (*Visitations and Memorials*, pp 58-9).

SPALDING (Lincolnshire)

1391 r
1410 A place in the township is called 'Pleyingplace' (*Select Cases in the Court of King's Bench under Richard II, Henry IV and Henry V*, VII, ed G.O. Sayles, Selden Society, 89 [1971], p 91; courtesy of T. De Welles).

STALLINGBOROUGH (Lincolnshire, now Humberside)

before 1567 r
1411 Cloth for a cross is sold by the church to players who then deface it (Peacock, p 144).

STAMFORD (Lincolnshire)

1465-83
1412 Town hall books indicate that the 'ludus Corporis Christi' will be played in 1480 as in 1479, the first six pageants in 1482, and the remaining five in 1483 (in 1465-6 the 43 crafts are organized into eleven 'pageants'; Kahrl, pp 87-9).

STEPNEY (Middlesex, now Greater London)

1309 28 May p
1413 Tournament in which Giles Argentine entered as King of the Greenwood ('Annales Paulini,' *Chronicles*, I, 157, 267).

ca 1424-30
1414 Lydgate's 'The Mumming at Bishopswood,' with Vere and May; a ballad by Lydgate at a May day dinner for the sheriffs of London and their brethren, at Bishop's Wood, a place belonging to the bishop of London (text in *Minor Poems*, II, 668-71; IMEV 2170).

1567 r
1415 Play called 'the storye of Sampson' with scaffolds at the Red Lion Inn in Stepney (*Records of the Worshipful Company of Carpenters*, III, ed Bower Marsh [1915], pp xx, 95-6).

STETCHWORTH (Cambridgeshire)

15th century? r
1416 A graffito, in the church of St Peter, of a ?stage hell-mouth (a
cat-like head within a rectangular frame, possibly a scaffold; John
Marshall, 'The Medieval English Stage: A Graffito of a Hell-mouth
Scaffold?' TN, 34 [1980], 99-103 and pl 8).

STEYNING (Sussex, now West Sussex)

early 16th century r
1417 A king's play was performed to raise funds for the church (A
History of the County of Sussex, VI, pt I, ed T.P. Hudson, VCH [1980],
p 238).

STOGURSEY (Somerset)

1210 September p
1418 King John paid his chamberlain Warin fitz Gerold 20s. 'ad ludum
suum' (Henry C.M. Lyte, 'Curci,' PSomANHS, 66 [1921], 114).

STOKE-BY-NAYLAND, Tendring Hall at (Suffolk)

1465-6 p
1419 Players twice rewarded by Sir John Howard (to the players of
Stoke, the place of his seat, in January 1466; Beriah Botfield, Manners
and Household Expenses of England in the Thirteenth and Fifteenth Centuries [ed Thomas H. Turner] [1841], pp 325, 511).

1481-3 p
1420 Visiting players rewarded by John, Lord Howard, at this his seat
and perhaps at Colchester and London; a play at 'the church' on
Whitsun Monday 1482; and a Christmas disguising in 1482-3, with
payments for materials including paper, glue, and foil (Household
Books, pp 104-339; Collier, History, 2nd edn [1879], I, 30, n, says that
Howard's own players were John Hobbis, Thomas Pout, Burges, and
Richard Newman, but in Collier's discussion of plays and players in
Household Books, pp xxii-xxv, he does not mention these names or this
troupe, and although they appear to occur irregularly in the house-

hold book [eg, pp 8 (Hobbes) and 82 (Richard Borgeis)], no entry identifying them as players has been found).

1526-7 p
1421 Visiting players rewarded by Thomas Howard, duke of Norfolk (Galloway-Wasson, p 194).

1528 3, 5 January r
1422 Three messes of players were fed by the duke of Norfolk with his household (J.D. Alsop, 'Players at Stoke Mansion, 1528,' *TN*, 35 [1981], 87).

STONOR (Oxfordshire)

1481-2? p
1423 Visiting players in Christmas at the seat of Sir William Stonor (*The Stonor Letters and Papers 1290-1483*, ed Charles L. Kingsford, CS 3rd ser, 30 [1919], II, 139-40).

STRATFORD-UPON-AVON (Warwickshire)

1541-57
1424 Riding of St George and the dragon (with a vice, 1543r; *Minutes and Accounts of the Corporation of Stratford-upon-Avon and Other Records 1553-1620*, I, trans Richard Savage, ed Edgar I. Fripp, Dugdale Society Publs, 1 [1921], pp xix-xx).

STRATTON (Cornwall)

1536-9 p, 1543 r
1425 Players, at the church house; and Robin Hood players (Edward Peacock, 'On the Churchwardens' Accounts of the Parish of Stratton, in the County of Cornwall,' *Arch*, 46, pt 1 [1880], 214-15, 233-4).

SUTTERTON (Lincolnshire)

1510-24
1426 St Mary's churchwardens' accounts include payment to the 'play light' in 1510-11 (Bodl. ms Rawl. D 786), for players' candles in 1520-3, and for a play on the Assumption of the Virgin in 1523-4 (Kahrl, pp 91-3).

1518-31
1427 Churchwardens' accounts pay visiting town players, once riding their play, and for gatherings for nearby town plays (Kahrl, pp 91-3).

1532 January p
1428 These same records have a receipt of the plough players' account (Kahrl, p 92).

SWAFFAM (Norfolk)

1508-19
1429 Stages made on Childermass day and on Palm Sunday (with sepulchre); whipcord for angels on Corpus Christi 1515-16, with a procession 1536-7 (churchwardens' accounts; Galloway-Wasson, pp 99-100).

1511-12 p, 1541-2 r
1430 Game players and game gear (Galloway-Wasson, pp 99, 101).

1545-6 r
1431 Pageants, with gunpowder (Galloway-Wasson, p 101).

SYON ABBEY (Middlesex, now Greater London)

1535 r
1432 Richard Reynolds, fellow of Corpus Christi College, Cambridge, and a monk here, bequeathed copies of Seneca's tragedies and of Euripides' 'Hecuba' and 'Iphigenia at Aulis' to the abbey (*Catalogue of the Library of Syon Monastery Isleworth*, ed Mary Bateson [1898], pp 8, 60).

TAMWORTH (Staffordshire)

1536 p, 1539 r
1433 Corpus Christi play, possibly a Doomsday play: on 15 June 1536, Corpus Christi day, an actor playing the Devil in this play came with his chain by one of the spectators, Sir Humfrey Ferrers, the lord of Tamworth Castle, and unwittingly broke his shins with it; three years later a velvet jacket and some money were bequeathed to the wardens of the Corpus Christi play (Ian Lancashire, 'The Corpus Christi Play of Tamworth,' N&Q, 224 [1979], 508-12).

TATTERSHALL (Lincolnshire)

1498-9 r
1434 A 'versus prophete' was copied out at the collegiate church for the Palm Sunday procession (precentor's accounts; David S. Josephson, *John Taverner: Tudor Composer* [1975, 1979], pp 17, 219).

TAUNTON (Somerset)

1504 r
1435 Bequest of red damask and silk mantles to the 'Mary Magdaleyn play' at the sepulchre service in the church of St Mary Magdalene (*Somerset Medieval Wills. (Second Series.) 1501-1530*, ed F.W. Weaver, SomRS 19 [1903], p 53; see PLATE 15).

TAVISTOCK (Devon)

1561-2 p
1436 Town play in the church; and visiting players (W.H. Cornish, 'Presidential Address. Strolling-Players in the West when Shakespeare Trod the Boards,' *PlylDCNHS*, 7 [1949-56], 154).

TEWKESBURY (Gloucestershire)

ca 1525 27 November r
1437 The Council for the Princess Mary writes Cardinal Wolsey to ask whether or not to appoint a Lord of Misrule to provide for interludes, disguisings, or plays on Christmas or Twelfth Night (letter dated at Tewkesbury; *Original Letters Illustrative of English History*, ed H. Ellis, 2nd edn [1825], I, 270-1; *L. & P. Hen. VIII*, IV.i, no 1785, p 792).

1567-85
1438 Stock of players' costumes and gear belonging to the abbey was loaned out to players, some from nearby towns: armour, weapons, eight gowns and cloaks, seven jerkins, four caps, six sheepskins for Christ's garments (added 1577-8), eight heads of hair for the apostles (1585), ten beards, a face or visor for the Devil (1585), 'thunderheades' (drums? F.S. Boas, 'Play in Ancient Abbey. Tuesday's Production at Tewkesbury. An Old Practice,' *The Observer*, 15 January 1933, p 8, and his 'Tewkesbury Abbey's Theatrical Gear,' *TLS*, 16 March 1933, p 184).

1575-6 p
1439 Play in the abbey church (Boas, 'Theatrical Gear,' p 184).

1600 p
1440 Three stage plays in the abbey on the first three days of Whitsun week to help finance a new stone battlement on the top of the abbey tower (Boas, 'Play in Ancient Abbey,' p 8; ΓCA, pp 34-5).

THAME (Oxfordshire)

1456-65
1441 Plays (the organs are borne home from 'owr pley' in 1465; 'The Churchwardens' Accounts of the Parish of St Mary, Thame,' trans W.P. Ellis, *Berks., Bucks., and Oxon. Archaeol. Journal*, 9 [1903-4], 119; NS 10 [1904-5], 57; NS 16 [1910], 89; Frederick G. Lee, *History, Description, and Antiquities of the Prebendal Church of the Blessed Virgin Mary of Thame* [1883], col 47).

1474-1501
1442 Robin Hood ale at Whitsuntide (Ellis, NS 19 [1913-14], 22; Lee, cols 26, 49).

1482-3 p
1443 Play called St George (Ellis, NS 20 [1914-15], 119).

1488-9 r
1444 Play of 'Fabine & Sabine' (?Fabianus and Sebastianus; Ellis, 9 [1903-4], 53-4).

1516 p, 1523 p
1445 Resurrection play (in 1523, with parts of the three kings of Cologne and Herod, for Corpus Christi; Lee, cols 50, 53; J. Howard Brown and William Guest, *A History of Thame* [1935], p 71).

1535 p
1446 Resurrection play 'de Clay' (a proper name? Lee, col 58).

THATCHAM (Berkshire)

1568 r
1447 Vice's coat (S. Barfield, *Thatcham, Berks, and Its Manors* [1901], II, 95; date courtesy of A.F. Johnston).

THETFORD PRIORY (Norfolk)

1497-1540
1448 Visiting 'lusores' (eg, with 'popynys'), 'ludentes,' 'iocatori,' or players, often at Christmas and Epiphany; and a payment to 'M[r William] Cornessh,' the king's servant, in 1511-12 (Galloway-Wasson, pp 104-15; cf Richard Beadle, 'Plays and Playing at Thetford and Nearby 1498-1540,' *TN*, 32 [1978], 4-11).

1510-31
1449 Local 'ludi,' Mays, and plays: the May of St Peter's (1510-11, 1518-19); the play in St Cuthbert's parish (1510-11); 'ludum St. Trinity' (the parish? 1520-1); and a Christmas 'ludo' (1530-1; Galloway-Wasson, pp 107-13).

THORNBURY (Gloucestershire, now Avon)

1507-8 r
1450 Visiting players this Christmas day and Epiphany (John Gage, '... Extracts from the Household Book of Edward Stafford, Duke of Buckingham,' *Arch*, 25 [1834], 318-19, 324-5).

1521 1 January r
1451 French men and two French women playing the 'Passion of our Lord' by a 'vise' for the duke of Buckingham (*L. & P. Hen. VIII*, III.i [1867], no 1285, p 500; date from PRO, E.36.220, p 12).

THORNDON (Suffolk)

1536 19 November r
1452 John Bale admitted preaching that people should not believe the creed's article, 'descendit ad inferna,' as it is set forth in painted cloths or glass windows, 'or lyke as my self had befor tyme sett yt forth in the cuntre ther in a serten playe' (that is, at Thorndon, his parish), where Christ fights violently with devils to possess the faithful souls (*L. & P. Hen. VIII*, XI, no 1111, p 446; Thora B. Blatt, *The Plays of John Bale* [1968], p 27, quotes from the original).

THORNTON ABBEY (Lincolnshire, now Humberside)

1440 r
1453 The sacrist is forbidden to lend vestments to 'ludentes' (as he has done already) playing 'ludos noxios,' 'ludibria vel spectacula,' abroad among lay folk (*Visitations of Religious Houses*, III, ed A.H. Thompson, LRS 21 [1929], pp 372, 381-2).

1529 p
1454 Players are paid (C.T. Flower, 'Obedientiars' Accounts of Glastonbury and Other Religious Houses,' *TSPES*, 7 [1911-15], 55).

THORPE ST PETER (Lincolnshire)

1547 p
1455 Churchwardens' accounts pay players, once on Candlemas (Kahrl, p 94).

TILNEY (Norfolk)

1499 6 January r
1456 Payment to 'luditores,' possibly for the church dedication day (*The Transcript of the Churchwardens' Accounts of the Parish of Tilney All Saints, Norfolk. 1443 to 1589*, transcr A.D. Stallard [1922], p 83; not in Galloway-Wasson).

1547-63 p
1457 Players at Christmas 1547 and 1563 and Easter 1549 (*Transcript*, pp 170, 174, 201; cf Galloway-Wasson, p 118, for the first item).

TILTY ABBEY (Essex)

1549-50 p
1458 Visiting players at Christmas 27 December-9 January at the home of George Medley (W.H. Stevenson, *Report on the Manuscripts of Lord Middleton, Preserved at Wollaton Hall, Nottinghamshire*, HMC [1911], pp 520-1; Davey, pp 183-4, refers to [the same?] visits of players here ['Tylsey'] ca 16 December 1551-20 January 1552).

TINTINHULL (Somerset)

1447-8 p
1459 Visiting king ('Regis') from Montacute, paid 3d (Hobhouse, p 183; Robert W. Dunning, 'The Middle Ages,' in *Christianity in Somerset*, ed R.W. Dunning [1976], p 13).

1451-2 p
1460 'unius ludi vocati Christmasse play' by five persons in the church house to raise money for a new stone screen with wooden loft (Hobhouse, p 184; Dunning, 'Middle Ages,' p 18).

1512-13 p
1461 Robin Hood's ale, 'only this once' (Hobhouse, p 200).

TITCHFIELD (Hampshire)

1538 1 February r
1462 Anthony Gedge and other servants of Thomas Wriothesley make merry nightly 'with Christmas plays and masks' at his house, the former abbey, run by his wife Jane while Wriothesley, later earl of Southampton, is at court (*L. & P. Hen. VIII*, Addenda, I.ii, no 1304, pp 445-6; cf *CP*, XII.i, 122-6; Nicholas Udall had lived here by 1541 as Wriothesley's servant – are these Udall's plays [cf Edgerton, pp 40-6]?).

TIVERTON (Devon)

1523-4 p
1463 Visiting players at the seat of Catherine (Courtenay), countess of Devon (*L. & P. Hen. VIII*, IV.i, no 771, pp 339-40).

TOPCLIFFE (Yorkshire, N.R., now West Yorkshire)

1534 r
1464 Two men were occupied for two weeks in carrying disguising stuff here, the usual home of Henry Percy, 6th earl of Northumberland, from Warkworth, another of his castles (John C. Hodgson, *A History of Northumberland*, V, Northumberland County History Committee [1899], pp 55-6).

TRURO (Cornwall)

ca 1535-43 r
1465 The site of a ruined castle a quarter of a mile west of the town and formerly belonging to the earl of Cornwall 'is now usid for a shoting and playing place' (Leland, *Itin.*, I, 198).

WADDINGHAM (Lincolnshire)

before 1567 r
1466 Parson of St Peter's church made children's playing coats (Peacock, p 157).

WAKEFIELD (Yorkshire, W.R., now West Yorkshire)

ca 1556-76
1467 Every craft is to bring forth its pageant of Corpus Christi day and to give forth speeches of the same in Easter holidays (1556); one Gyles Dolleffe is to bring in the 'regenall' of this play, and the play masters are accountable to the town gentlemen and burgesses (1559-60); and in 1576 the Ecclesiastical Commissioners instruct the Wakefield burgesses not to show anything of the Trinity, the sacraments of baptism or communion, or of idolatry in pageants in their Whitsuntide Corpus Christi play ('The Burges Court, Wakefield. 1533, 1554, 1556, and 1579,' ed J.W. Walker, in *Miscellanea Vol. II*, YorkASRS 74 [1929], pp 20-2; see Jean Forrester and A.C. Cawley, 'The Corpus Christi Play of Wakefield: A New Look at the Wakefield Burgess Court Records,' *LeedsSE*, 7 [1974], 108-15, for evidence that additional records of 1556 may be an invention; Gardiner, p 78; Nelson, pp 82-7; for a text possibly representing this 'regenall,' or part of it, see *The Wakefield Pageants in the Towneley Cycle*, ed A.C. Cawley [1958], and above under TEXTS, ca 1450-?1576).

WALBERSWICK (Suffolk)

1479-99
1468 Visiting Mays and games from neighbouring towns (Galloway-Wasson, pp 201-3; *Walberswick Churchwardens' Accounts A.D. 1450-1499*, transcr R.W.M. Lewis [ca 1948], pp 71, 245, 253).

WALSALL (Staffordshire, now West Midlands)

1493-4 r
1469 Ordinance by the mayor and his brethren that repair and main-
tenance of 'the play Garmentes' be charged, in three parts, to the following crafts ('Church-wardens' Accounts All Saints' Church Walsall
1462-1531,' ed and trans Gerald P. Mander, *Collections for a History of
Staffordshire* for 1928, William Salt Archaeological Society [1930], pp
224-5):
   1 / Smiths, Braziers, Millers, Bakers, and Curriers (or Carriers?) and
Limeburners;
   2 / Shearmen, Tailors, Mercers, Drapers, Glovers, Seamsters, and
Barbers; and
   3 / Corvisers, Bakers, Butchers, Carpenters, and 'Flescharrus'
(Fleshers? Fletchers? and one unknown craft, name deleted).

WALSHAM-LE-WILLOWS (Suffolk)

1533-81 r
1470 Game place with a raised, round, stone-walled bank in the
middle for the use of stage plays (Kenneth M. Dodd, 'Another Elizabethan Theatre in the Round,' *SQ*, 21 [1970], 125-56).

WANTAGE (Berkshire)

1590-1 p
1471 Vice at the revel (Alexandra F. Johnston, 'Folk Drama in Berkshire,' ISSMT conference paper [Dublin, July 1980], p 3).

WARWICK (Warwickshire)

1553-4 p
1472 Visiting players (*Halliwell-Phillipps*, p 127).

WELLS (Somerset)

ca 1270 r
1473 Impersonation of Caiphas in Palm Sunday procession (*Dean
Cosyn and Wells Cathedral Miscellanea*, ed and trans A. Watkin, SomRS
56 [1941], p 131; text: Carleton Brown, 'Caiphas as a Palm-Sunday

Prophet,' *Anniversary Papers by Colleagues and Pupils of George Lyman Kittredge* [1913], pp 105-17; and Brown's 'A Textual Correction,' MLN, 29 [1914], 60-1; *Manual* 1).

1331 r, 1338 r
1474 The Dean and Chapter prohibit 'ludos theatrales' with 'monstra larvarum' by the clergy of Wells in the church between Christmas and the octave of Holy Innocents, at Pentecost, and at other feasts (*Dean Cosyn and Wells Cathedral Miscellanea*, pp 20-3; Herbert E. Reynolds, *Wells Cathedral: Its Foundation, Constitutional History, and Statutes* [nd], pp 75, 79, 87-8, uses a copy written in 1634).

1331-2 p
1475 Edward III kept Christmas here 'ubi fiebant multa mirabilia sumptuosa' (Murimuth, p 65).

ca 1331-8 r
1476 Prohibition of 'Ludi vel Spectacula' in the cathedral cloister or churchyard (Reynolds, *Wells Cathedral*, p 86).

1407-19
1477 Easter play with St Saviour or Holy Saviour (with a tunic, gown, or robe), palmers (with two beards), and the Maries (with three mantles; *MSS Wells*, II, 42-60).

1470-1 p
1478 Play with three Maries, with hempen wigs, on Passover night (*MSS Wells*, II, 94).

1478-1506
1479 Visiting players (*MSS Wells*, II, 97, 132, 164, 196).

1491 r
1480 A man charged with heresy before the Consistory Court at Wells denied having 'libris anglicanis de interludis, anglice: Ordinals for pleyes' (*Dean Cosyn and Wells Cathedral Miscellanea*, p 155).

1497-98 r
1481 Money derived from a 'tempus de Robynhode' (Henry T. Riley, 'The Corporation of Wells, Somerset,' *1st Report*, HMC [1874], p 107).

1540 r
1482 John Leland saw in the cathedral library a 'Terentius pulcherrimus' (Leland, IV, 155; cf C.M. Church, 'Notes on the Buildings, Books, and Benefactors of the Library of the Dean and Chapter of the Cathedral Church of Wells,' *Arch*, 57 [1901], 210-11).

1607 p
1483 Summer May game pageants in procession (C.J. Sisson, *Lost Plays of Shakespeare's Age* [1936], pp 157-85) include the following:
  1 / the Lord of the May;
  2 / the Pinner of Wakefield;
  3 / Robin Hood and his men;
  4 / the 'Sparked Calf';
  5 / St George, his knights, and the dragon;
  6 / Mother Bunch;
  7 / Diana and Acteon;
  8 / Noah and his ark;
  9 / the giant and giantess; and
  10 / the Soldan of Egypt and his queen.

1613 20 August p
1484 Shows for the Queen by six companies, including the following ([J.O. Halliwell?] 'Proceedings of the Association,' *JBAA*, 16 [1860], 319-20):
  1 / Noah building the ark; Vulcan; Venus and Cupid; and the dragon who devoured the virgins (Hammermen);
  2 / 'a carte of old virgines ... their attires made of cowtayles,' with their St Clement and his friar riding (Tanners, Chandlers, and Butchers);
  3 / ss Crispian [and Crispianus] (Cordwainers);
  4 / Herod and Herodias, her daughter, and St John Baptist beheaded (Tailors);
  5 / the giant and giantess; King Ptolomeus, his queen, and his daughters, to be devoured by the dragon; St George and his knights, who slew the dragon and rescued the virgin; Diana, her nymphs, and Acteon (Mercers).

WELTON IUXTA LOUTH, or LITTLE WELTON (Lincolnshire)

before 1567 r
1485 An alb in the church is sold to four players (Peacock, p 160).

WEST HAM (Essex, now Greater London)

1576 p
1486 Two plays in the church by common players in Lent, with people standing on the communion table (Coldewey, pp 330-3, and his 'Demise,' pp 246-7).

WHITBY ABBEY (Yorkshire, N.R., now North Yorkshire)

1394-6
1487 'Ludentes' in the hall at Christmas and New Year's, and a man 'qui ludebat cum Jak,' 1394-5; 'ludentes' on Corpus Christi as well as 'tripidiantes' (dancers?) then, two 'ludatores' (?), and a 'mimo ludenti in sacco' (a bag?), ca 1394-6 (*Cartularium Abbathiae de Whiteby*, ed J.C. Atkinson, II, SS 72 [1881], pp 608, 621-4; reconstructed from unreliably edited texts of George Young, *A History of Whitby, and Streoneshalh Abbey* [1817], p 923 [1394-5; not seen], and Lionel Charlton, *The History of Whitby, and of Whitby Abbey* [1779], pp 260-2 [ca 1394-6]; and courtesy of Christopher Dean).

WIGTOFT (Lincolnshire)

1525 p, 1532 p
1488 Churchwardens' accounts reward the bann-criers of Swineshead and Spalding (M.F., 'Extracts from the Churchwardens Accompts of Wigtoft, a Village near Boston, in Lincolnshire,' *Illustrations*, pp 195-249).

WILDERSPOOL (Cheshire)

ca 80-ca 300
1489 A life-size pottery 'actor's' mask in orange-pink ware from the Stockton Heath kilns is abandoned here (F.H. Thompson, *Roman Cheshire* [1965], pp 84-5, fig 21, no 1; a colour postcard photograph is available at the Museum and Art Gallery, Warrington [courtesy of John Astington]).

WILLENHALL (Staffordshire, now West Midlands)

1498 10 June p
1490 Captains called Abbot of Marham or Robin Hoods from neighbouring towns are at Willenhall fair on Trinity Sunday to gather

money for the churches and are charged with riot (W.K. Boyd, 'Staffordshire Suits in the Court of Star Chamber, *temp.* Henry VII. and Henry VIII.,' *Collections for a History of Staffordshire*, NS 10, pt 1 [1907], pp 80-1).

WILTON ABBEY (Wiltshire)

1379 r
1491 Ralph Erghum, bishop of Salisbury, forbids the nuns to 'entertain themselves with superstitious plays or games' (*A History of Wiltshire*, III, ed R.B. Pugh and Elizabeth Crittall, VCH [1956], p 238).

WIMBORNE MINSTER (Dorset)

1573 p, 1589 p
1492 Plays in the church house of Wimborne Minster (Hutchins, III, 262).

WINCHESTER (Hampshire)

965-75 r
1493 'Visitatio Sepulchri,' also called 'Quem Quaeritis,' at Easter (text: *Regularis Concordia: The Monastic Agreement*, ed and trans Dom T. Symons [1953], pp 49-50; there is an Old English interlinear translation in BL ms Cotton Tiberius A.III; Young, I, 249-50, and facs, pl VII; ed and trans, Bevington, pp 27-8; Smoldon, pp 90-2; Lipphardt, II, 539-41, nos 394-5, locates the two texts at Canterbury; see PLATE 4).

978-80 r
1494 'Quem Quaeritis' trope (text ed W.H. Frere, *The Winchester Troper from MSS. of the Xth and XIth Centuries*, HBS 8 [1894], p 17; ed and trans, Bevington, p 29; Smoldon, pp 93-100, and pl IIIa; Stratman 710-16; Lipphardt, II, 576-8, nos 423-4).

1384 14 April r
1495 Prohibition of participation by the clergy and laity of Winchester Cathedral in 'ludibriorum spectacula' and 'ludos inhonestos' in general (*Wykeham's Register*, ed T.F. Kirby, II, Hampshire Rec. Society [1899], p 410).

1400 11 September r
1496 School statutes forbid scholars and fellows frequenting 'tabernas, spectacula, vel alia loca inhonesta' (T.F. Kirby, *Annals of Winchester College* [1892], pp 82, 491).

1400 p
1497 'lusores' of the city come with their 'tripudio' (dance) to Winchester College (Mackenzie E.C. Walcott, *William of Wykeham and his Colleges* [1852], p 206).

1415 24 June p
1498 Players at the feast of the Tailors' Fraternity of St John the Baptist (Henry T. Riley, 'The Corporation of Winchester,' *6th Report*, App 1, HMC [1877], p 601).

ca 1440-50 r
1499 (1) *Occupation and Idleness* and (2) *Lucidus and Dubius*, two interludes in Winchester College ms 33A (fasc and transcripts, Davis 2, pp 133-208; IMEV 3352.5; the first is undoubtedly a school play, and the appearance of Doctrine, a doctor of divinity of a university, to schoolboy Idleness suggests auspices at Winchester College, founded in conjunction with New College, Oxford, from which every year the warden and two fellows came to the school in visitation [A.F. Leach, 'Schools,' *A History of Hampshire and the Isle of Wight*, VCH, II [1903], p 269]; the second seems to be a dialogue, like its source, for which see B.S. Lee, 'Lucidus and Dubius: A Fifteenth-Century Theological Debate and its Sources,' *Medium Aevum*, 45 [1976], 79-96).

1441 28 December p
1500 Boys of the monastery, and of St Elizabeth's chapel, disguised as girls, 'saltantibus, cantantibus, et ludentibus,' at St Mary's Abbey (HEP, II, 231).

1466-79
1501 'interludentes,' civic 'lusores,' and 'ludentes' in the hall recorded at Winchester College (HEP, II, 98, n 2; for a modern view of this hall, see PLATE 13).

1486 p
1502 'Christi Descensus ad Inferos, or Christ's descent into hell,' performed by boys of St Swithun's Priory and Hyde Abbey before

Henry VII (*HEP*, III, 163; redated in MS, II, 396, n 4; not found in Warton's *Description of the City, College, and Cathedral of Winchester* [1750] or in his *Notes, & Corrections* to that volume, ed Thomas Phillipps [1857]; another Warton fabrication?).

1490 r
1503 The boys of Hyde Abbey appear at Wolvesey, the bishop's palace, in masks and other garments (*HEP*, II, 231-2).

ca 1529-31 r
1504 Winchester College taught boys in its fourth form Terence some six days a week (Leach, pp 448-9; timetable sent to Saffron Walden as a model).

1556-1625
1505 Visiting 'ludentes' and players, as in the common hall in 1556-7 (Murray, II, 404-6).

WINCHESTER, diocese of

1224? r
1506 Statutes of Bishop Peter des Roches prohibit 'inhonesti ludi' in churchyards (*Councils & Synods*, p 135).

1247 r?
1507 Statutes of Bishop William Raleigh prohibit 'ludi' from church porches or churchyards (*Councils & Synods*, p 412).

1262-5
1508 Statutes of Bishop John Gervais prohibit having 'ludi spectabiles' on saints' feasts, and forbid clergy from frequenting 'spectaculis' (*Councils & Synods*, pp 709-10).

WINDSOR (Berkshire)

1361 r
1509 Visors, tunics, and various other things were supplied for 'the king's play' during the visit of Peter, king of Cyprus (Stella M. Newton, *Fashion in the Age of the Black Prince: A Study of the Years 1340-1365* [1980], pp 77, 122 n 18).

1400 6 January r
1510 A plan by members of the nobility to kill Henry IV during a mumming by certain 'lusores' of London before him at Windsor Castle (*Great Chronicle*, p 83; *Chronicle*, pp 85-6; Giles, p 7; 'ludorum natalitiorum' according to Walsingham, II, 243).

1428 23 April p
1511 'lusores' and 'tripudiatores' of France at St George's feast (Harris Nicolas, *Proceedings and Ordinances of the Privy Council of England*, III, Record Commission Publication, 16 [1834], p 294; located at Hertford in Easter by Wolffe, p 45).

ca 1430
1512 'A Mumming at Windsor,' Lydgate's 'devyse' for which was how St Clotilda converted Clovis, king of France, and how by miracles at Joye-en-Vale and Rheims the fleurs-de-lys and the golden ampulla came to the kings of France; a story 'shewed' before Henry VI at Christmas shortly before his coronation (*Minor Poems*, II, 691-4; IMEV 2212).

1449-50 p
1513 Easter (?) 'ludo' in St George's Chapel Royal (courtesy of A.F. Johnston; cf under LONDON 25 December 1449 for royal payments probably relating to this).

1522 15 June p
1514 Play or farce devised by William Cornyshe at Windsor with Amity (or Friendship), Prudence and Policy, and Might, taming and bridling a horse (representing Francis I); and a pageant-disguising with three foresters, four hunters, a keeper, and wildmen (*L. & P. Hen. VIII*, III.ii, no 2305, pp 976-77; Halle, fols 98v-9r; *Spain*, II [1866], no 437, pp 443-5; Anglo, 'Cornish,' pp 357-60; and see under GREENWICH [4-5 June]).

1538-9 p
1515 Visiting players (R.R. Tighe and J.E. Davies, *Annals of Windsor* [1858], I, 511).

1553 p
1516 Players of William Parr, marquess of Northampton, at his own house (J.D. Alsop, 'Entertainments of the Marquess of Northampton in

1553,' *N&Q*, 222 [1977], 500-1; the location of his household at this time is unclear, but Parr was constable of Windsor Castle 1550-3, according to *CP*, IX, 670).

WINSLOW (Buckinghamshire)

1580 r
1517 'a godly interlude' in the church (W.H. Hale, *Precedents in Causes of Office Against Churchwardens and Others* [1841], p 85).

WISTOW (Yorkshire, W.R., now North Yorkshire)

1469 p
1518 'unum ludum estivalem vulgariter vocatum Somergame' in a 'Somerhouse' with king, queen, knights, seneschal, and harpist (Parker, pp 20-3).

WITHAM ON THE HILL (Lincolnshire)

1554 p
1519 Churchwardens' accounts reward players in the church (Kahrl, p 95).

WITNEY (Oxfordshire)

before 1558 r
1520 Show or interlude of the Resurrection with puppets for Christ, Mary, the watchman ('Jack Snacker') and others (William Lambarde, *Dictionarium Angliae Topographicum & Historicum* [1730], pp 459-60; Young, II, 542-3).

WITTON, near Northwich (Cheshire)

1558 r
1521 Statutes of the Free Grammar School here mention Terence among Latin authors to be taught (Nicholas Carlisle, *A Concise Description of the Endowed Grammar Schools in England and Wales* [1818], I, 131).

WIX PRIORY (Essex)

1509 8 September r
1522 Nuns forbidden 'to permit any public spectacles of seculars'
(*VCHEssex*, p 124; courtesy of J.C. Coldewey).

WOLLATON HALL (Nottinghamshire)

1521-75
1523 Visiting players at the seat of the Willoughby family, notably Sir
Henry; the 'players of paules' appeared at Christmas 1521 (the family
was also located at Middleton, Warw., to which some of these visits
were probably made; W.H. Stevenson, *Report on the Manuscripts of Lord
Middleton, Preserved at Wollaton Hall, Nottinghamshire*, HMC [1911], pp
334-521; Price, p 143).

WOODBRIDGE (Suffolk)

ca 1475-1500 p?
1524 St George and the dragon, and religious plays, by the canons
of the Augustinian priory (Vincent B. Redstone, 'The Sandling,'
PSufflANH, 10 [1898-1900], 65; and his 'Social Condition of England
during the Wars of the Roses,' *TRHS*, NS 16 [1902], 184).

WOODBURY (Devon)

1574-7
1525 Robin (Robert) Hood and his house (and a fool 1554-74; T.N.
Brushfield, 'The Church of All Saints, East Budleigh. Part II.,' *RTDevA*,
24 [1892], 341; Wasson, 'Guide,' pp 58-9).

WORCESTER (Worcestershire, now Hereford and Worcester)

11th century r
1526 An ms of Terence, noted in a list from Keynsham Abbey, Som.,
but perhaps originally from Worcester Priory (H.M. Bannister, 'Bishop
Roger of Worcester and the Church of Keynsham, with a List of Vestments and Books Possibly Belonging to Worcester,' *EHR*, 32 [1917],
388-91).

1424 p
1527 'ludentes' paid on Corpus Christi (*Compotus Rolls of the Priory of Worcester of the XIVth and XVth Centuries*, ed Sidney G. Hamilton, WorcsHS [1910], p 68).

1450 April r
1528 Episcopal order against 'ludis inhonestis' in Worcester Cathedral (Klausner, p 21).

1467-1584
1529 At least five pageants by crafts in 1467 civic ordinances, to go or not annually as decided at Hocktide (last performance in 1566; in 1584 a lease was made for the vacant place where the pageants 'do stand'; Smith, pp 385, 407-8; Klausner, p 21).

1486 r
1530 Pageants for Henry VII, at Whitsunday, with speeches by Henry VI and a doorkeeper (unperformed text: Leland, IV, 192-7; IMEV 3885.5).

1489-90 p
1531 Visiting 'lusores' at the cathedral almonry school (*Documents Illustrating Early Education in Worcester. 685 to 1700*, ed Arthur F. Leach, WorcsHS [1913], p 1).

1519-35
1532 Children and visiting players; players of St Michael's (1519), St Peter's (1520), and St Kenelmus (1521); Robin Hood and his men (1519, 1530; by men of St Helen's [1529] here or at Battenhall); and players at 'ye more' in 1530 (all performing for Prior William More; *More*, pp 77-403; and see also under BATTENHALL, CROWLE, and GRIMLEY).

1556 r
1533 Players' garments in the probate inventory of draper William Specheley (Klausner, p 21).

1576 r
1534 A cathedral inventory notes players' 'gere' or apparel for a friar, a woman, a ?knight, and a devil (R.L. Poole, 'Muniments in the Pos-

session of the Dean and Chapter of Worcester,' *14th Report*, HMC, App 8 [1895], p 187).

WORCESTER, diocese of

1240 r
1535 Statutes of Bishop Walter Cantilupe prohibit 'ludis,' particularly 'ludi ... inhonesti,' in consecrated places such as churchyards, and forbid clergy to avoid 'ludis inhonestis' and 'ludos fieri de rege et regina' (*Councils & Synods*, pp 297, 313, 321).

1551-2 r
1536 The interrogatories of John Hooper, bishop of Gloucester, for this diocese ask parishioners if they annoy their minister with 'plays' during divine service (*Visitations*, II, 291).

WORFIELD (Shropshire)

1502-3 p, 1520-1 p
1537 Plays (also possibly a King play at Whitsuntide 1503; 'The Churchwardens' Accounts of the Parish of Worfield,' ed H.B. Walters, *TShropANHS*, 3rd ser, 3 [1903], 110, 115; 4 [1904], 107).

WOTTON UNDER EDGE, Wortley in (Gloucestershire)

1344 r
1538 Endowment of chapel chantry specifies that its priest is not to frequent plays or unlawful games (E.S. Lindley, 'A History of Wortley in the Parish of Wotton under Edge, I,' *TBGAS*, 68 [1949], 51).

WRESSLE (Yorkshire, E.R., now Humberside)

ca 1511-15 r
1539 Ceremonial ordinances for the household of Henry Algernon Percy, the fifth earl of Northumberland, refer to disguisings, interludes, or plays in the great chamber at the wedding supper of an earl's daughter; and to a Twelfth Night revels in the great hall that allowed for a three-part spectacle (Ian Lancashire, 'Orders for Twelfth Day and Night circa 1515 in the Second Northumberland Household Book,' *ELR*, 10 [1980], 6-45; for evidence that Wressle, rather than Leconfield,

was the earl's main seat at this time, see p 14, n 27; see also PLATES 17-18):

1 / an interlude, a comedy, or a tragedy;

2 / a disguising of ladies and gentlemen; and

3 / morris dancers entering from a pageant-like 'towr or thing devisid for theim,' all organized by a master of the revels.

ca 1511-20 r

1540 The fifth earl's almoner, if he makes interludes, is to have a servant to write the parts; and he has a servant ca May 1511 ('The Earl of Northumberland's Houshold-Book. The Regulations and Establishment of the Household of Henry Algernon Percy, The Fifth Earl of Northumberland, At his Castles of Wresill and Lekinfield in Yorkshire. Begun Anno Domini M.D.XII.,' *AR*, IV, 61, 92, 97, 199).

ca 1511-27

1541 The fifth earl's budget schedules allow for visiting players (of earls and of lords) between Christmas and Candlemas (*AR*, IV, 45, 138, 254).

1514-16 r

1542 Disguising stuff is purchased for use at Christmas in the earl's household (*L. & P. Hen. VIII*, IV.ii, no 3380.ii, p 1530; and PRO, E.36.226, pp 16, 38, 54).

ca 1524-7 r

1543 The fifth earl's budget schedules allow for his chapel to play 'the Play of the Nativite' on Christmas morning in the chapel; for the chapel and 'other his Lordshipis Servaunts' to play 'the Play of Resurrection' on Easter morning in the chapel, and 'the Play' on Shrove Tuesday night; the Master of the Revels to oversee and order the earl's 'Playes Interludes and Dresinge' in the twelve days of Christmas; and the earl's four players to come to the earl yearly at Christmas and other times when he commands from them plays and interludes in his house (*AR*, IV, 256, 258-9, 262).

WRITTLE (Essex)

1442-3 r

1544 Accounts of Humphrey Stafford, duke of Buckingham, have a payment for carriage of timber and brick 'to the house outside outer gates called disguising chamber' (P.A. Rahtz, *Excavations at King John's Hunting Lodge, Writtle, Essex, 1955-57*, Society for Medieval Archaeology Monograph Ser 3 [1969], pp 10, 13).

1443-4 p
1545 'lez disgisyng*es*' at Christmas for the household of Humphrey Stafford, duke of Buckingham, probably at his manor here (*Compota Domestica Familiarum de Bukingham et d'Angouleme*, ed William B.D.D. Turnbull, Abbotsford Club, 3 [1836], p 23; for another possible location, at Maxstoke, and for Thomas Berston [who is named in this accounting], see Rawcliffe, pp 66-7, 235).

WROXETER (Shropshire)

1st-2nd centuries r?
1546 A Roman enclosure behind the temple at Viroconium Cornoviorum, used for ?amphitheatrical shows or religious plays (Wacher, *Towns*, p 373).

WULFHALL (Wiltshire)

ca 1536-44? p
1547 Visiting players here at the house of Edward Seymour, earl of Hertford, or at Beauchamp House in London, including Paul's choristers (J.E. Jackson, 'Wulfhall and the Seymours,' *WiltANHM*, 15 [1875], 174; Price, pp 121-3).

WYE (Kent)

1447 r
1548 Wye College statutes prohibit members attending summer games (W.S. Morris, *The History and Topography of Wye* [1842], p 128).

WYMONDHAM (Norfolk)

1519 r
1549 Stuff belonging to a play at the 'howse for saint Thomas' ?church is noted in a will (Galloway-Wasson, p 124).

1538-52
1550 Watch and play, apparently rehearsed ('recordyng the play'),
with a wood and canvas giant, properties, and game players' apparel
including two vice coats (one of diverse colours), a coat armour (of Sir
William Knevett), devil's shoes, moss for a woodwose, four doctors'
hoods, two women's kirtles, two children's gowns, five knights' coats,
and a vice cap (Galloway-Wasson, pp 128-32; cf G.A. Carthew, 'Extracts from Papers in the Church Chest of Wymondham,' NA, 9 [1884],
145-7; H. Harrod, 'Some Particulars Relating to the History of the
Abbey Church of Wymondham in Norfolk,' Arch, 43, pt 2 [1872],
272).

1545-6 p
1551 Churchwardens' accounts note the setting forth of a pageant in
procession, and the 'husbondes of the play' (Galloway-Wasson, p 130).

1549 6-8 July p
1552 A play called 'Wyndhamgame' on Saturday night, Sunday, and
Monday was the occasion of Robert Kett's rebellion (Galloway-
Wasson, p 131; and Barrett L. Beer, '"The Commoyson in Norfolk,
1549": A Narrative of Popular Rebellion in Sixteenth-century Eng-
land,' The Journal of Medieval and Renaissance Studies, 6 [1976], 73-99;
town 'ludi ac spectacula' of old custom, according to Alexander
Neville, De Furoribus Norfolciensium Ketto Duce [1575], sig C1v; trans R.
W[oods]., Norfolkes Fvries [1615], sigs B2v-B3r; STC 18478, 18480;
Holinshed, III, 963-4, calls it 'a publike plaie').

1583-1621
1553 Game place with 'stages,' later called Bridewell (Galloway-
Wasson, p 132).

YEAVERING (Northumberland)

ca 605-40 r
1554 A *villa regia* of the Northumbrian kings, also known as Ad Gef-
rin, this site has archaeological remains of a bank of nine (earlier only
three) tiered seats, a concentric timber 'theatre' or assembly place that
was modelled on a Roman theatre, had screens like sounding boards,
and faced a small platform or dais (demolished ca 640; Brian Hope-
Taylor, *Yeavering: An Anglo-British Centre of Early Northumbria*, Dept. of

the Environment Archaeological Reports, 7 [1977], pp 119-22, 154, 158-9, 168-9, 241-4, 279-80, 316-19, and figs 12, 55-7, 63, 75-8, 109; pls 90-104, 108).

YEOVIL (Somerset)

1516-87
1555 Robin (Robert) Hood and Little John plays; and hire of players' garments by Sherborne (1566) and Leigh (1569), Dorset (L. Brooke, *The Book of Yeovil* [1978], p 133; John Goodchild, 'Elizabethan Yeovil: as Recorded in Churchwardens' Accounts,' *PSomANHS*, 88 [1943], 60-71).

YORK (now North Yorkshire)

1220-5 r
1556 Presentations of the shepherds on Christmas night and of the three kings on Epiphany, with stars (*York*, ed Alexandra F. Johnston and Margaret Rogerson, REED 1-2 [1979], p 1).

1366 p
1557 Christmas interlude at St Leonard's hospital (*York*, p 2).

ca 1370 r
1558 Mss of six comedies of Terence, 'comedia vitalis de amphitrione' (ie *Geta*), and Seneca's tragedies at the Augustinian friary (M.R. James, 'The Catalogue of the Library of the Augustinian Friars at York,' *Fasciculus Ioanni Willis Clark Dicatus* [1909], items 453, 489, 510, pp 64, 70, 72).

1376 r
1559 Bequest by clerk William de Thorp of 'libros meos de ludis' to Sir Richard de Yhedyngham (*York*, p 3).

1376-1580
1560 The Corpus Christi play was performed from about 4:30 a.m. on a single day at Corpus Christi (on its eve in 1426, the feast itself being reserved for the procession) by players acting on pageant wagons drawn to various stations or sites through the city (the last generally being the Pavement) before audiences who watched and heard the

speeches from windows, scaffolds, or the street. The play was funded
by pageant silver collected by pageant masters of each craft guild responsible, in part or in full, for a pageant and for storing its wagon in
a pageant house (these were mainly in Toft Green, otherwise called
Pageant Green) and was subject to civic control up until 1580, when
the city council reserved performance until an approval (of the text)
by Edwin Sandes, archbishop of York, and Matthew Hutton, dean of
York Minster, that was apparently never forthcoming. The text is in
York Plays, ed L.T. Smith [1885]; present evidence dates the ms with
limits 1463-77, for which see Richard Beadle and Peter Meredith, 'Further External Evidence for Dating the York Register (BL Additional MS
35290),' *LeedsSE*, NS 11 [1980], 51-8; cf Nelson, pp 38-81; Richard J.
Collier, *Poetry and Drama in the York Corpus Christi Play* [1978], the
only book wholly devoted to this cycle; Clifford Davidson and David
E. O'Connor, *York Art: A Subject List of Extant and Lost Art Including
Items Relevant to Early Drama*, EDAM Reference Ser, 1 [1978]; Stratman
4857-5184; Harvey-Dietrich, pp 407-8; and *Manual* 10. The following
pageant list is based on the second list in the 1415 'Ordo' in *York* (for
the records and their relation to the texts, see *York, passim* and pp
657-85; Meg Twycross, '"Places to Hear the Play": Pageant Stations at
York, 1398-1572,' *REEDN*, 1978:2, pp 10-33; and A.F. Johnston, '*Errata*
in *York*,' *REEDN*, 1980:1, pp 35-8):

1 / the creation of heaven and earth (Tanners; Barkers in text);
2 / the work of the five days (Plasterers);
3 / the formation of Adam and Eve (Cardmakers);
4 / the prohibition of the tree of knowledge (Fullers);
5 / the deceit of the Devil in a serpent (the fall of man; Coopers);
6 / the assigning of work to Adam (expulsion from the garden;
Armourers);
7 / Cain killing Abel (Glovers);
8 / the building of Noah's ark (Shipwrights);
9 / Noah's ark during the flood (Fishmongers and Mariners);
10 / the sacrifice of Isaac by Abraham (Parchment Makers; and
Bookbinders in text);
11 / Pharaoh with Moses and the children of Israel (Hosiers);
12 / the annunciation to Mary by Gabriel (Spicers);
13 / Joseph wishing to send her away secretly (Founders; and
Pewterers in text);
14 / Bethlehem with the new-born boy (Tile-thatchers);
15 / the offering of the shepherds (Chandlers);

16 / Herod questioning the three kings (Goldsmiths; then Masons [in text]; then Minstrels);

17 / the offering of the three kings (Goldsmiths);

18 / the presentation of Christ in the temple (St Leonard's Hospital; then Masons, who with the Hatmakers and Laborers had the present text, Mary's purification and the prophecies of Simeon and Anna [no XLI]);

19 / how Christ fled into Egypt (Marshals);

20 / slaughter of the innocents in place of Christ (Girdlers; and Nailers in text);

21 / the discovery of Christ in the temple among the learned men (Spurriers and Lorimers);

22 / the baptism of Christ by John (Barbers);

23 / the marriage in Cana of Galilee (no text; Taverners);

24 / the temptation of Christ in the desert (Smiths);

25 / the transfiguration of Christ (Curriers);

26 / the feast in Simon's house (no text; Ironmongers);

27 / the woman taken in adultery (Plumbers; now joined with the next pageant under the Capmakers);

28 / the raising of Lazarus (Capmakers);

29 / Jerusalem, with citizens and children (Skinners);

30 / the selling of Christ by Judas (the conspiracy; Cutlers);

31 / the supper of Christ with the disciples (the last supper; Bakers, whose accounts mention painted diadems; by Baxters in text);

32 / washing of the apostles' feet (no text; subsumed in previous pageant? Waterleaders);

33 / the capture of Christ praying on the mount (the agony and betrayal; Cordwainers);

34 / the mocking of Christ before Caiphas (trial before Caiaphas; Bowyers and Fletchers);

35 / the accusation of Christ before Pilate (first trial before Pilate; Tapissers; and Couchers in text, with the episode of the dream of Pilate's wife);

36 / the presentation of Christ before Herod (Dyers; by Litsters in text);

37 / the second accusation before Pilate, the remorse of Judas, and the purchase of the Field of Blood (only in text; Cooks and Waterleaders);

38 / the contrition of Judas before the Jews (no text; subsumed in preceding pageant? Cooks);

39 / the hanging of Judas (where he hung himself and 'crepuit medius' [pp 31, 716]; no text; Saucemakers);

40 / the condemnation of Christ by Pilate (Tilemakers);

41 / the scourging and crowning with thorns (no text; Turners and Bowlmakers);

42 / the leading of Christ and the manifestation to Veronica (the road to Calvary; Shearers);

43 / the division of the vestments of Christ (no text; subsumed in next pageant? Millers);

44 / the stretching out and nailing of Christ (Painters; and now Pinners);

45 / the raising of Christ on the mount (no text; subsumed in preceding pageant? Latteners);

46 / the death of Christ on Calvary (Butchers);

47 / the harrowing of hell (Saddlers);

48 / the resurrection of Christ (Carpenters);

49 / the appearance of Christ to Mary Magdalene (Winedrawers);

50 / the appearance of Christ to the pilgrims (travellers to Emmaus; Wool-packers; Sledmen in text);

51 / the appearance of Christ to the apostle Thomas and to others (Scriveners);

52 / the ascension of Christ to heaven (Tailors);

53 / the descent of the Holy Spirit (Pentecost; Potters);

54 / the death of the Blessed Virgin (Drapers);

55 / the appearance of Our Lady to Thomas (only in text; Weavers);

56 / the carrying of the body of Mary (Fergus; no text; Masons; then Linenweavers);

57 / the Assumption of the Blessed Mary (no text; now subsumed in next pageant; Woollenweavers);

58 / her crowning (the Mayor, etc; then Innholders, as in text); and

59 / the last judgment (Mercers). An indenture of 11 June 1433 between the Mercers and their pageant masters lists the following parcels in the pageant gear: a pageant with four wheels; hellmouth; three garments and three visors (with six faces) for devils; shirts, hose, visors, and wigs for two evil and two good souls; two pair of angel wings with iron in the ends; two trumps and two reeds; four albs, three diadems with three visors, and four diadems with four yellow wigs for apostles; a cloud and two pieces of a wood rainbow; a 'Wounded' shirt and a diadem with gilded visor for God; a large red damask hanging for the back of the pageant, six smaller hangings for the sides,

and one to hang up back of God; four irons to bear up heaven; four 'finale coterelles' and an iron pin; an iron 'brandreth' with ropes at the four corners for God to sit on in going up to heaven; an iron heaven with a wood 'naffe'; seven pieces for clouds, red with gold stars (for heaven), blue, and red with gold sunbeams and stars for the highest of heaven; seven large and four smaller gilded angels holding up God's Passion; nine smaller red angels made by a cord to run about in heaven; two short wood 'rolls' to put forth the pageant; and five banners and one streamer (pp 55-6; with major repairs to these in 1451-2, 1461-2 [including a new pageant made for souls to rise out of], and 1526 [including a Trinity 'hus']; see also Peter Meredith, 'The Development of the York Mercers' Pageant Waggon,' MET, 1 [1979], 5-18; Philip Butterworth, 'The York Mercers' Pageant Vehicle, 1433-1467: Wheels, Steering, and Control,' MET, ibid, pp 72-81; and PLATE 10).

ca 1385-95
1561 Friars have taught the paternoster in English, 'as men seyen in þe pley of ȝork' ('De Officio Pastorali,' *Wyclif*, p 429, in the English version only, by John Purvey or an assistant, for which see Workman, II, 329-30, 156, 165).

1388 14 May r
1562 At a royal inquiry here a jury learns that men of diverse crafts hold (ie store) diverse play-pageants ('paginas diversas ludor*um* suorum') in the hall of the archbishop's palace; and at Corpus Christi next the jury will know what these men pay for this space (Alexandra F. Johnston, 'York pageant house: new evidence,' REEDN, 1982:2, pp 24-5; *Cal. Inq. Misc.*, V, for 1387-93 [1962], no 99, p 74).

1388-1575
1563 Members of the Pater Noster Guild are to ride with the players of their 'ludus de vtilitate or*a*cionis d*o*minice,' or the Pater Noster play, where vices or sins are reproved and virtues are commended (with 'ludum Accidie' 1400r; owned by chaplain William Downham before 1465 in many 'libri'; undertaken by the Guild of St Anthony by 1446 and the city by the dissolution; and probably in the three playbooks taken but not returned (corrected) by Edmund Grindal, archbishop of York, in 1575; *York*, pp 6-378, 645-8; see also Alexandra F. Johnston, 'The Plays of the Religious Guilds of York: The Creed Play and the Pater Noster Play,' *Speculum*, 50 [1975], 55-90).

1396 1 June p
1564 Corpus Christi play before Richard II (a single pageant wagon appears to be used; *York*, p 9).

1442 p
1565 'ludo de vyne yerde' (*York*, p 60).

1446 r
1566 Play about St James the apostle in six pageants (*York*, p 68).

1446-9
1567 Local and visiting 'lusores,' 'ludentes,' or players (*York*, pp 66-77).

1446-1568
1568 Sir William Revetour, chaplain of St William's Chapel on Ouse Bridge, leaves in 1446 to the Corpus Christi Guild, on condition that it be performed every twelve years if possible, the English 'Orygenal' or playbook of the Creed play (the 'Registre' in 1565?), and play stuff, which came to include 25-34 banners, 13 diadems with wigs and one gilded mask for Christ and the apostles, a royal crown with scepter and a glove, a papal mitre, two episcopal mitres, twelve rolls written with articles of the faith, and a key for Peter; by 1495 the play is performed on St Bartholomew's eve after banns on Whitmonday; after the dissolution the play came under civic control, and the city decided against playing it on the advice of Matthew Hutton, dean of York Minster (*York*, pp 68-353, 633, 639; see also Johnston's 'Plays of the Religious Guilds of York').

1447-8 r
1569 'Ludentes' with 'Ioly Wat & Malkyn' (*York*, pp 70, 72).

1455 r
1570 The 'ludum oreginale' of St Dennis (cf two 'ludentes' from the parish of St Denys in 1449; *York*, pp 77, 88).

1483 29 August p
1571 Entry of Richard III, welcomed 'per diversas visiones & ornamenta Ciuitatis'; the Creed play was also put on for him on Sunday 7 September (*York*, pp 130-3; for a now-missing letter of 23 August by John

Kendale, the king's secretary, calling on the city to receive Richard with pageants and 'soch good speches as can goodly ... be devised,' see Robert Davies' *Extracts from the Municipal Records of ... York* [1843], pp 163-4, and found earlier in Francis Drake's *Eboracum* [1736], p 116).

1486 June p
1572 A play arranged and played by Sir Henry Hudson, a chaplain, and three other clerks for Henry VII; and eight pageants at his entry (*York*, p 145; and for the pageants, pp 139-43, 146-52; *IMEV* 1186, 2214-16) include the following:
  1 / a heaven; a world with trees and flowers that bowed to a red rose into which, by a vice, a white rose was conveyed and on which a crown descended from a cloud; and Ebrauk (Ebraucus) with his city;
  2 / the six Henries and Solomon, with ships betokening Henry VII's landing at Milford Haven;
  3 / a show, and hailstones (comfits) coming from it by a vice;
  4 / a castle and David; and
  5 / Our Lady coming from, and her Assumption to, heaven.

1487 1 August p
1573 Henry VII, two days after his second entry into the city, sees the Corpus Christi play (*York*, pp 154-5).

ca 1509-47 p
1574 Religious interlude of St Thomas the Apostle once on 23 August during this period (alleged record, now lost; *York*, pp 649-50).

ca 1510 r
1575 William Melton, chancellor of York (1496-1528), urges those in holy orders against 'ludis theatralibus' and 'turpi lucri ludis' (*Sermo Exhortatorius Cancellarij Eboracum hijs Qui ad Sacros Ordines Petunt Promoueri* [1510?], sig A7r; STC 17806; his will, dated 1528, lists books including a Terence [*Test. Ebor.*, V, 258]).

1519 15 October r
1576 Bequest to the 'Somer-game lyght' in the parish church of St Michael's (*York*, p 219).

1527 p, 1540-2 p
1577 'luditores' at the common hall; and visiting players (*York*, pp 243, 269-81).

1538 April-May r
1578 Neville Mores, a stationer, had a Terence in his inventory (D.M. Palliser and D.G. Selwyn, 'The Stock of a York Stationer, 1538,' *The Library*, 5th ser, 27 [1972], 216).

1541 15 September p
1579 Shows (unfinished) and the merchants' pageant, for the entry of Henry VIII and Queen Catherine Howard (*York*, pp 271-7).

1546-58
1580 The Guild of St Christopher and St George sponsors the riding and play of St George (played by John Stamper in 1554) with pageant of St Christopher (his head), the king and the queen, the maiden, and the dragon (*York*, pp 289-327; Eileen White, '"Bryngyng Forth of Saynt George": The St. George Celebrations in York,' MET, 3.2 [December 1981], 114-21).

1555 26 February p
1581 Shrove Tuesday pastime in which certain young men defended a fort and others assaulted it (*York Civic Records*, V, ed Angelo Raine, YorkASRS 110 [1946 for 1944], p 117).

1556 11 May r
1582 Royal commission to the city that no players of interludes be allowed to play or go about (*York Civic Records*, V, 144-6; cf *York*, p 322).

ca 1570-2
1583 Riding of Yule, Yule's wife, and children on 21 December, terminated on the request of Edmund Grindal, archbishop of York (for a possible text, see *York*, pp 359-62, 368-9; STC 26098.5 [Addenda]).

YORK, diocese of

1241-55? r
1584 Statutes forbid clergy from frequenting 'illicitis spectaculis' (*Councils & Synods*, p 486).

1343 r
1585 Constitution of Archbishop William Zouche requiring abstinence from 'ludis' and 'spectaculis' on Good Fridays (*York*, pp 1-2).

1367 r
1586 John Thoresby, archbishop of York, prohibits 'spectacula' or 'ludi' in consecrated places (*Concilia*, III, 68).

ca 1538
1587 Edward Lee, archbishop of York, instructs his clergy to abstain from 'houses of games and plays' on holy days (*Visitations*, II, 51).

ca 1570-6
1588 The register of Edmund Grindal, archbishop of York, shows that lords of misrule, summer lords and ladies, and disguised persons in Christmas or at May games are prohibited from coming into any church, chapel, or churchyard at any time, namely during divine service or a sermon, to play any 'vnseemelye partes with scoffes ieastes wanton gestures or rybaulde talke' (*York*, pp 358-9).

YOXFORD (Suffolk)

1537 r?
1589 Vicar Thomas Wylley's plays as he offered them for Thomas Cromwell's patronage (*L. & P. Hen. VIII*, XII.i [1890], no 529):

1 / a reverent receiving of the sacrament as a Lenten matter declared by six children representing Christ, the Word of God, Paul, Austin, a child, a nun called Innocency;

2 / a play against the Pope's counsellors, Error, Colle Clogger of Conscience, and Incredulity;

3 / a play called a Rude Commonalty;

4 / and one in the making called the Woman on the Rock, in the fire of faith affining and purging in the true purgatory.

Wales

1135 r
1590 Gruffydd ap Rhys had guests entertained at his court in South
Wales with 'pob chwareuon hud a lledrith a phob arddangos' ('games
of illusion and phantasm, and all kinds of spectacles'; Jones, p 2, citing
O. Jones, E. Williams, and W. Pughe, *The Myvyrian Archaiology of
Wales*, 2nd edn [1870], p 558).

ca 1582 r
1591 One person playing the Devil (*MSS Welsh*, II, i [1902], p 367;
Jones, pp 6-7).

ABERGAVENNY (Monmouthshire, now Gwent)

1537 6 November r
1592 Parishioners including John ap Poll ap John, Jenkyn da Blether,
John Bengreth, Thomas Coke, Jenkyn ap Gwilliam, Lloyd? Vynneth,
and William ap Poll ap Jenkyn, gathered money to pay for church
bells by going about 'into the countrie with games and playse' (PRO
E.315.117, fol 18; general reference from Glanmor Williams, *The Welsh
Church from Conquest to Reformation* [1962], p 457).

CAERLEON (Monmouthshire, now Gwent)

ca 80-ca 300 r
1593 Roman amphitheatre at Isca, mainly for military games, built to
hold about 6000 persons (destroyed only from about the beginning of

the reign of Edward I; R.E.M. Wheeler and T.V. Wheeler, 'The Roman Amphitheatre at Caerleon, Monmouthshire,' *Arch*, 78 [1928], 111-218; and Mortimer Wheeler and V.E.N. Williams, *Caerleon Roman Amphitheatre and Prysg Field Barrack Buildings, Monmouthshire* [1970], especially the authors' reconstruction, pp 10-11).

ca 2nd-3rd centuries r
1594 A tragic mask in ivory, 'very finely executed' and probably imported, was found here (J.M.C. Toynbee, *Art in Britain under the Romans* [1964], p 359, pl LXXXIIa).

ca 1191 r
1595 Gerald of Wales in his *Itinerarium Kambriae* refers to seeing here the remains of 'loca theatralia' (*Giraldi Cambrensis Opera*, RS 21, VI, ed James F. Dimock [1868], p 55).

CAERWENT (Monmouthshire, now Gwent)

1st-5th centuries? r
1596 Roman amphitheatre at Venta Silurum (T. Ashby, A.E. Hudd, and A.T. Martin, 'Excavations at Caerwent, Monmouthshire, on the Site of the Romano-British City of Venta Silurum, in the Years 1901-1903,' *Arch*, 59 [1904], 104-13; Wacher, *Towns*, p 386, questions that this is an amphitheatre).

CARMARTHEN (Carmarthenshire, now Dyfed)

1st-4th centuries? r
1597 Roman amphitheatre at Moridunum (Wacher, *Towns*, p 392).

RHUDDLAN (Flintshire, now Clwyd)

1281-2 p
1598 Gift of a shilling to 'a certain player' (a minstrel? George Davies, 'Queen Eleanor at Rhuddlan,' *The Cheshire Sheaf*, 1st ser, 3 [1883], 94).

ST. ASAPH, diocese of

1556 r
1599 Bishop Thomas Goldwell prohibits priests from using 'common or unlawful games or plays' (*Visitations*, II, 410).

TOMEN-Y-MUR (Merionethshire, now Gwyned)

1st-2nd centuries? r
1600 Roman fort with a possible amphitheatre (V.E. Nash-Williams, *The Roman Frontier in Wales* [1954], pp 36-7).

Scotland

13th century r
1601 Scottish synodal statute forbids 'ludi' in sacred places (*Concilia Scotiae*, II, 52; *Statutes of the Scottish Church*, p 56).

ca 1214-15 r
1602 Soon after his coronation (4 December 1214) Alexander II, as a sign of mourning for his father, William I, ordered that there be 'na playis nor bankettis' for the next year (Bellenden, p 218).

1225 r
1603 The Provincial Council of Scotland forbids 'ludi' in churches and churchyards (*Concilia*, I, 611).

ca 1265 r
1604 The common people celebrate 'in comoediis et in tragoediis' the story of Robert Hode, Little John, and their fellows (who are mentioned at this date here; Joannis de Fordun, *Scotichronicon* [1759], II, 104).

ca 1342-76? r
1605 Women shame themselves who 'prese vnto playes pepull to beholde'; and summer queens and games in May were invented in Troy (*The 'Gest Hystoriale' of the Destruction of Troy: An Alliterative Romance Translated from Guido de Colonna's 'Hystoria Troiana,'* ed G.A. Panton and D. Donaldson, EETS OS 39, 56 [1869, 1874], p 96, line 2923, and p 54, lines 1625-8).

ca 1430 r
1606 Poor 'Shavelings,' hired by priests for singing at services, 'by
muttering and mumbling out a certain Task and Jargon of *Psalms*,
which was appointed every day ... made a collusive kind of a Tragedy,
sometimes contending in alternate Verses and Responses; otherwhiles
making a *Chorus* between the Acts, which at last closed with the
Image, or Representation, of *Christs* Death' (Buchanan, fol 111;
'... nunc choros inter actus adhibentes tragoediae speciem exhibebant,
quae Christi morte imaginaria claudebatur,' as trans in *The History of
Scotland* [1690], p 346).

before 1487 r
1607 In 'How the Good Wife Taught her Daughter' young women are
prohibited from attending 'clerk-playis' and pilgrimages unless accompanied by 'viss folk of age' (John Barbour, *The Bruce*, ed Walter W.
Skeat, STS 32, II [1894], p 206, lines 83-4).

ca 1490-1520 r
1608 William Dunbar's allusions to plays and pageants (*Dunbar*)
include the following:
    1 / 'Than cryd Mahoun for a heleand [highland] padʒane: / Syne ran
a feynd to feche Makfadʒane / Far northwart in a nuke' ('[Fasternis
Evin in Hell],' p 153, lines 109-11, ca 1507 [cf pp 335-6]);
    2 / a wife claims that she should be 'at fairis be found, new faceis to
se, / At playis and at preichingis and pilgrimages greit' ('The Tretis of
the Tua Mariit Wemen and the Wedo,' p 44, lines 70-1); and
    3 / Dunbar's loss of heart for songs, ballads, and 'playis' in winter
('[In Winter],' p 191, lines 4-5).

ca 1500? r
1609 In the story of Clariodus and Meliades, mainly set in England,
court revels in the hall include pageants played between courses of a
feast by persons arrayed in 'play coats' by 'great inchanters and subtill
magicianis,' dancing by virgins with Homeric stories and merry 'fabil-
lis' of Guido de Colonna, 'syns of padʒeanis playit dumbe,' 'intermei-
sis,' and interludes (*Clariodus; A Metrical Romance: Printed from a
Manuscript of the Sixteenth Century*, ed Edward Piper, MaC 9 [1830], II,
lines 1661-70; III, 2396-7; IV, 1285-6; V, 783-8, 961-3, 1620-2, 1806,
1862-4, 2732; IMEV 548.5).

ca 1501 r
1610 At a banquet of the Muses in Gavin Douglas's 'The Palice of Honour' they 'eit with interludis betwene' and see Vergil play 'the sportis of Daphnis and Corydone,' and Terence play 'the comedy / Of Parmeno, Thrason, and wise Gnatone' ('Eunuchus'; *Poetical Works*, ed John Small [1874], I, 45, lines 17-18, and 47, lines 6-9; *IMEV* 4002.5).

1503 p
1611 Margaret Tudor, at her entries into Edinburgh, Stirling, St Andrews, Dundee, St John's Town of Dalry, Aberdeen, Glasgow, and Linlithgow, received such banquets, farces, and plays as were never before seen at a queen's entry in Scotland (Pitscottie, I, 240).

ca 1511-26 r
1612 'Quho ca*n* say more tha*n* schir Iames Inglis [abbot of Culross, d 1531] says, / In ballatts, farses, and in plesand playis? / Bot Culrose hes his pen maid Impotent' ('The Testament, and Complaynt, of our Souerane Lordis Papyngo,' in Lindsay, *Works*, I, 57, lines 40-2 [in the context of court literature]; cf Mill, pp 58-9, 329-30).

1528 r
1613 Sir David Lindsay relates how he has, to amuse the young James V, played 'fairsis on the flure' and disguised himself, one time like a fiend, another like 'the greislie gaist of gye' ('The Dreme of Schir Dauid Lyndesay,' in Lindsay, *Works*, I, 4, lines 13, 15-18).

1531 r
1614 The ordinances of the Visitor General of the Cistercian order in Scotland (as sent to the convent of Deer, Aberdeen) require monks not to attend 'spectacula' (*Illustrations of the Topography and Antiquities of the Shires of Aberdeen and Banff*, ed Joseph Robertson, IV, SpaldC 32 [1862], p 9).

1537 r
1615 Triumphs, farces, and plays to be made for the entry of the new Scottish queen, Madeleine of France, as at Edinburgh, Leith, Dundee, Brechin and Montrose, Aberdeen, St John's Town of Dalry, Stirling, Glasgow and Ayr, Linlithgow, St Andrews, and Cowper of Fife, were cancelled because of her sudden death (Pitscottie, I, 369).

ca 1545-68 r
1616 May was formerly celebrated with the 'game' where 'men ȝeid everich one, / With Robene Hoid and Littill Johne / To bring in bowis and birkin bobbynis' (*The Poems of Alexander Scott*, ed James Cranstoun, STS 36 [1896], pp xii, 23, 132-3).

ca 1550 r
1617 In old time the two wardens of the borders of England and Scotland determined that there should be no contact between their people, such as 'conuentions on holy dais at gammis and plays' (Robert Wedderburn, *The Complaynt of Scotland (c. 1550)*, ed A.M. Stewart, STS 4th ser, 11 [1979], p 84).

1555 r
1618 Parliament prohibits the choosing of Robert Hoods, Little Johns, Abbots of Unreason, and Queens of May on pain of imprisonment, or banishment, or fine (*The Acts of the Parliament of Scotland*, ed Thomas Thomson, II, Rec. Com. Publs, 36 [1814], p 500).

1558 ca 24 April r
1619 Sir Richard Maitland, in his poem on Queen Mary's marriage on this date to the dauphin of France, says: 'All burrowis townis euerilk man ȝow prayis / To mak bainfyris fairseis and clerk playis' (*The Maitland Folio Manuscript*, ed W.A. Craigie, STS NS 7, I [1919], p 28, lines 19-20; cf *The Maitland Quarto Manuscript*, ed W.A. Craigie, STS NS 9 [1920], p 20, lines 19-20).

1558 May-June r
1620 A Scot in Paris on the wedding day of Mary, Queen of Scots, to the Dauphin reports such sport in the miseries of spectators trying to get coins thrown as largesse that he wished Plautus was present 'to mak a merie clerk play of ther [un]happy spedingis' (Douglas Hamer, 'The Marriage of Mary Queen of Scots to the Dauphin: A Scottish Printed Fragment,' *The Library*, 4th ser, 12 [1931-2], 422-3, 425, and fig).

1574 7 March r
1621 The General Assembly of the Church forbids all clerk plays, comedies, and tragedies on the 'Canonicall Scripture, alsweill new as old,' and allows only those profane plays not made on 'authentick

partes of the Scripture,' and then only if reviewed before public showing and if not intended for the Sabbath (*Kirk of Scotland*, I, 322-3).

1577 1 April r
1622 The General Assembly of the Church asks the Lord Regent to do
away with plays of Robin Hood, King of May, and such others on the
Sabbath (repeated 24 April 1578, as 'played either be bairnes at the
schools or others,' and 2 July 1591; *Kirk of Scotland*, I, 388; II, 405-7,
410, 784; and cf II, 440).

1580 10 April r
1623 The Council orders that, in accordance with a special public fast
ordained that month for Lothian and the Merse, there be no 'using of
Robene Hude and uther vane and unlesum gammis' then (*The Register
of the Privy Council of Scotland*, III, ed David Masson [1880], p 277).

ABERDEEN (Aberdeen, now Grampian)

1440-79
1624 'ludo de ly haliblude' at the Windmill-hill (1440r, 1445r) or Corpus Christi play (1449r, 1479r; Mill, pp 115-16; cf *Extracts from the
Council Register of the Burgh of Aberdeen. 1398-1570*, ed John Stuart,
SpaldC 12 [1844], pp 395, 410).

1440-1555, 1565-71
1625 Abbot of Bonaccord, also called Robin Hood and Little John
(from 1508); generally on St Nicholas' day and in May; in 1553 the
town ordered that banqueting be reduced in favour of one or two
'generall plais' or farces (Mill, pp 131-55; cf *Extracts*, pp 14-459).

1442-1526
1626 Procession, play, or 'offerand' on Candlemas (2 February) with
pageants on the following subjects (lists of 1442, 1506; Mill, pp
116-23; cf *Extracts*, pp 9-445):
    1 / the emperor and two doctors (Litsters);
    2 / the three kings of Cologne (Smiths and Hammermen or Gold-
smiths);
    3 / Our Lady, St Bride, St Helen, and Joseph (Tailors);
    4 / two bishops and four angels (Skinners);
    5 / Simeon and his disciples (Websters and Walkers);

6 / the messenger and Moses (Cordwainers);

7 / 'wodmen' ('Fleshowarez'; Fleshers?); and

8 / three knights in harness (Masons).

1471 p
1627 'ludum de bellyale' (Mill, p 117; Chambers, ELCMA, p 64).

1511 May p
1628 'pleasant padgeanes playit prattelie' by the city (?guilds) for the entry of Queen Margaret ('[To Aberdein],' *Dunbar*, pp 135-7; Mill, pp 158-9):

1 / the salutation of the Virgin;

2 / the offering of the three kings;

3 / the angel with the sword expelling Adam and Eve from Paradise;

4 / the Bruce (Robert I, king of Scots), riding;

5 / the royal Stewarts (a genealogical tree?); and

6 / twenty-four maidens in green, singing.

1526 r
1629 Pageants and pastimes to be prepared for James V (Mill, p 159).

1530-56
1630 Pageants in the Corpus Christi procession include the following (list of 1531; Mill, pp 124-31; cf *Extracts*, pp 449-59):

1 / St Bestien and his tormentors (Fleshers);

2 / St Laurence and his tormentors (Barbers);

3 / St Stephen (Stewin) and tormentors (Skinners);

4 / St Martin (Cordwainers);

5 / the Coronation of Our Lady (Tailors);

6 / St Nicholas (Litsters);

7 / St Ion (Websters, Walkers, and Bonnetmakers);

8 / St George (Baxsters);

9 / the Resurrection ('writtis,' Masons, Slaters, Coopers); and

10 / the 'barmen' of the cross (Smiths, Hammermen).

ca 1540 r
1631 A printed book of Terence (Paris, ca 1505), owned by the first Professor of Humanity here, John Vaus (d ca 1540; J. Durkan and R.V. Pringle, 'St Andrews Additions to Durkan & Ross: Some Unrecorded

Scottish Pre-Reformation Ownership Inscriptions in St Andrews University Library,' *The Bibliotheck*, 9 [1978-9], 20).

1541 p
1632 Triumphs and plays prepared by the town, university, and schools for James V and his queen (Lesley, p 159; cf his *De Origine*, p 430, and Dalrymple's trans, II, 247 [comedies]; Mill, p 159).

1553 r
1633 Terence is prescribed at Aberdeen Grammar School ('Statuta et Leges Ludi Literarii Grammaticorum Aberdonensium. 1553,' *The Miscellany of the Spalding Club*, V, ed John Stuart [1852], p 400; also in *Bon Record*, ed H.F. Morland Simpson [1906], pp 98, 106; the statutes are printed at the end of a late edition of John Vaus' *Rudimenta Artis Grammaticae* [Paris, 1553]; STC 24623.7).

1574 18 August r
1634 The Privy Council orders the civic bailiffs to prohibit and punish the superstitious keeping of papist feast days 'and all playis' at those times (*The Register of the Privy Council of Scotland*, II, ed John H. Burton [1878], p 390).

ABERDEEN, diocese of

13th century r
1635 Prohibition of 'turpes et inhonesti ludi' in churches and churchyards (*Concilia Scotiae*, II, 38, 40; *Statutes of the Scottish Church*, nos 68, 76, pp 40, 42).

ARBROATH (Angus, now Tayside)

1503 1 January p
1636 Guisers for the court here (*ALHTS*, II, 353; Mill, p 319).

1528 r
1637 Play (Mill, p 164)

1565 r
1638 Lord of Reason (Mill, p 164).

ARBUTHNOTT (Kincardine, now Grampian)

1570 r
1639 Seventeen men indicted for treasonable choosing of Robert Hood and Abbot of Unreason in this parish and in the bounds of 'Meirnis' (Pitcairn, I, 15-16).

AYR (Ayr, now Strathclyde)

1496 r
1640 Abbot of Unreason (Mill, p 165).

1506 August r
1640.5 The Queen of May (paid by the Court; ALHTS, III, 332; Mill, p 323).

1534-41 r
1641 Clerk play (Mill, pp 165-6; *Ayr Burgh Accounts 1534-1624*, ed George S. Pryde, SHS 3rd ser, 28 [1937], p 72).

1539-54
1642 Robin Hood and Little John; sometimes termed plays (Mill, pp 165-7; *Accounts*, pp 84-120, and cf 'Jacques playis' in 1543-4 [p 95]).

BORTHWICK (Midlothian, now Lothian)

1547 16 May r
1643 The town's Abbot of Unreason (Sir Walter Scott, *Provincial Antiquities and Picturesque Scenery of Scotland* [1826], I, 37-40, 48; Mill, pp 28-9).

CRAIGIE (?Tayside)

1508 before 15 February r
1644 Two men are convicted of robbery near the church under the guise of 'mummyn(g)' (Pitcairn, I, *50-1).

CRANSTON, parish of (Lothian)

1590 r
1645 May and Pasche plays; Robin Hood, and Abbot of Unreason (Mill, p 170).

CUPAR (Fife)

1552? 7 June p
1646 Performance of Lindsay's *Satyre of the Thrie Estaitis* on Castle Hill
on Whitsun Tuesday (for text, see Lindsay, *Works*, II, 8-404 [left-hand
pages]; Mill [*PMLA*], pp 637-45; Kantrowitz, pp 11-27; Stratman
5966-99; Houle 45).

DALKEITH (Midlothian, now Lothian)

1582-90
1647 Plays of the Abbot of Unreason, or Robin Hood and Little John;
or May or Pasche plays (Mill, pp 168-70).

DIRLETON (East Lothian, now Lothian)

1585 May p
1648 The play of Robin Hood, for James VI (Calderwood, IV, 366).

DUMBARTON (Dunbarton, now Strathclyde)

nd
1649 Robin Hood (Mill, p 24; no stated source).

DUNFERMLINE (Fife)

1576 r
1650 The General Assembly permits the town to play a play not on the
canonical parts of scripture (*Kirk of Scotland*, I, 375; cf Mill, pp 175-6).

DUMFRIES (Dumfries, now Dumfries and Galloway)

1532 r
1651 The play of Good Friday and Whitsunday (Mill, p 171).

1534-70
1652 Robin Hood and Little John, or Pasche plays (Mill, pp 171-2).

DUNDEE (Angus, Tayside)

ca 1450 r?
1653 Corpus Christi procession including the following properties: six
pair of angel's wings, three miters, Christ's garments and head, thirty-

one swords, St Thomas' spear, St Blasius' body, St John's coat, a cradle and three 'barnis maid of cloth,' twenty wigs, the four evangelists (?), St Catherine's wheel, St Andrew's cross, a wooden 'worm,' a wooden 'haly lam,' St Barbara's castle, Abraham's hat, and other goods (Mill, pp 172-3).

1490 23 July ?p
1654 French men played for the court here (*ALHTS*, I, 170; Mill, p 314).

1521 r
1655 Robin Hood (Mill, p 173).

ca 1540-5 p
1656 James Wedderburne's anti-papist comedies and tragedies in Scots, including a tragedy on the beheading of John the Baptist (acted at the West Port); a comedy on the history of 'Dyonisius the Tyranne' (acted on the town playing field); and a counterfeit conjuring of a ghost as practised by Friar Laing, formerly the king's confessor (Calderwood, I, 142).

1553 p
1657 Play at the West Field (Mill, p 173).

EDINBURGH (Midlothian, now Lothian)

1446-78
1658 'lusores,' 'ludi,' 'le mumre,' 'jociis,' and interludes at court, generally at Christmas (once at Shrovetide; *The Exchequer Rolls of Scotland*, ed George Burnett, V [1882], 266, 318, 396, 607; VII [1884], 423, 501; VIII [1885], 333, 404, 512; Mill, pp 310-12).

1480-1510?
1659 'The Maner of the Crying of ane Playe,' formerly attributed to William Dunbar, banns (for a Robin Hood play?) spoken by Wealth, or Blind Harry (text: *The Asloan Manuscript*, ed W.A. Craigie, STS NS 16, II [1925], pp 149-54; *IMEV* 1119.3; for another text, titled 'Ane Littill Interlud of the Droichis Part of the Play,' see *The Poems of William Dunbar*, ed John Small, STS 24, II [1893], pp 314-20; the attribution to Dunbar is rejected by J.W. Baxter, *William Dunbar: A Biographical Study* [1952], p 226, although see Beal, I, ii, 57).

1492-1579
1660 Robert/Robin Hood and Little John, or Abbot of Narent or Unreason, or Lord of Disobedience; sometimes plays (Mill, pp 219-24; ERBE [1869], pp 66, 176).

1494-1516
1661 Procession with Hammermen's Herod, his (four-six) knights, the four wives, and two doctors, playing (a Slaughter of the Innocents' play? Mill, pp 225-32; and her 'The Edinburgh Hammerman's Corpus Christi Herod Pageant,' *Innes Review*, 21 [1970], 77-80).

1497-1550
1662 Court revels including town guisers and Robin Hood, Abbot of Unreason, Corpus Christi play (by Edinburgh guisers? 1503-4), the Queen of May (at the abbey gate, 1506), mummings, 'Wantones and hir tua marowis' who sang (1507), plays by David Lindsay (1511), Sir James Inglis (1511, 1526), and William Lauder (1549), farce, guise, the king's Robin Hood (1531), masquing, and a bard called Hercules (1545; locations for some of these revels may be outside Edinburgh; ALHTS, I, 309-27; II, 112-476; III, 127-372; IV, 125-330; V, 254-432; VI, 186-255; VII, 276-7; VIII, 282-386; IX, 73-393; Mill, pp 316-32).

1503 7 August p
1663 At Margaret Tudor's approach to Edinburgh, a knight came with his Lady Paramour from a pavilion, another knight took her from him, and they tournied; and at Margaret's entry into the city the following pageants appeared (Leland, IV, 288-90; McGee-Meagher, pp 49-50):
    1 / angels in towers;
    2 / Paris and the three goddesses, with Mercury, whose golden apple Paris gives to Venus;
    3 / the salutation of Gabriel to the Virgin, and the solemnization of the marriage of the Virgin and Joseph; and
    4 / the four virtues Justice (with Nero), Force (with Holofernes), Temperance (with Epicurus), and Prudence (with Sardanapalus).

1503 13 August p
1664 'a Moralite' by John English and his interluders, that is, Henry VII's players, for James IV and Margaret Tudor ('Johannes and his

Company' also performed 8, 11 August; the three 'gysaris' who played a play? *ALHTS*, II, 387, and Mill, p 320; Leland, IV, 296-300; Buchanan, fol 148r, says that there were nothing but 'spectacula, pompae, & conuiuia, & saltationes' after the marriage).

1507 r
1665 Goldsmiths' pageant of the passion (Agnes Mackenzie, *Scottish Pageant*, 2nd edn, I [1952], p 44; courtesy of Anna J. Mill).

1507 June p
1666 Tournament of the Wild Knight and Black Lady (a moor), with wildmen (*ALHTS*, III, 258-410; Mill, pp 325-6; McGee-Meagher, p 55).

1508 May-June r
1667 Jousting by James IV as the Wild Knight, 'with counterfutting of the round tabill of King Arthour' (with the Black Lady and her two maidens; Lesley, p 78; cf his *De Origine*, p 334, and Dalrymple's trans, II, 128; *ALHTS*, IV, 63-129; Mill, p 327); at the end of this tournament of the 'Black' Knight (the king; term used only by Pitscottie) and the Black Lady there was a three-day triumph and banquet at Holyrood House, between each service of which was a farce or a play, 'sum be speikin sum be craft of Igramancie quhilk causit men to sie thingis aper quhilk was nocht'; and on the third day, in the last farce and play, the necromancer Andrew Forman, bishop of Moray, made a cloud come out of the hall roof, open, and enclose the Black Lady so that she was seen no more (Pitscottie, I, 242-44; misdated 1505; McGee-Meagher, p 56).

1515 26 May p
1668 John Stewart, duke of Albany, governor of Scotland, was received with 'sindre ferses and gude playis' by the town (Lesley, p 102; cf his *De Origine*, p 359, and Dalrymple's trans, II, 157 [comedies]).

1537 r
1669 The death of the Scottish queen, Madeleine of France, shortly after her arrival in Scotland from France forced the city to cancel preparations for a triumphant entry, to include 'Disagysid folkis, lyke Creaturis deuyne, / On ilk scaffold, to play ane syndrie storie' (Lindsay, *Works*, I, 109, lines 110-11; Pitscottie, I, 369, 373).

1538 after June p
1670 Triumph, farces, and plays for the entry of Mary of Guise (Pit-scottie, I, 381; Mill, pp 179-80; ERBE [1871], pp 89-91).

1552 7 October r
1671 James Henderson's offer to the city council to build a new civic play grounds, for lawful martial pastimes and for playing 'interludis in to draw pepill till the toune,' on the land between 'the Gray Freyr porte and the Kirk of Field' (Mill, p 351; ERBE [1871], p 172).

1553 p, 1555 r
1672 Clerk play, ca June in the first year and 6 January in the second, both on scaffolds, the latter in the Tolbooth (Mill, pp 180, 182-3; ERBE [1871], pp 276, 295; Edinburgh Records, pp 76, 133).

1554 10 June p
1673 Play, probably one with a moresque before the queen, 'at the trone' (Mill, pp 180-1; ERBE [1871], pp 193-4, 283; Edinburgh Records, p 109).

1554 ?before August r
1674 The city constructs a play field on the Greenside (records covering 1554-6; Mill, pp 351-2; ERBE [1871], pp 195-7, 282, 320 [a Council order of 18 August 1554 (p 197), seems not to be in Mill]; Edinburgh Records, pp 106, 178).

1554 ?18 August p
1675 A play before the queen on the playing field, with gibbets, scaffold, and probably a king, a bishop, a fool, and an angel; possibly Lindsay's Satyre of the Thrie Estaitis (Mill, pp 181-2; ERBE [1871], pp 198-9, 283-4; Edinburgh Records, p 110; for the text, see Lindsay, Works, II, 9-405 [right-hand pages only]; facs edn, The English Experience, 137 [1969]; STC 15681-2 [publ 1602]; Mill [PMLA], p 645; Stratman 5966-99; Houle 45).

1554 r
1676 Farce and play by William Lauder before the queen (Mill, p 182; ERBE [1871], p 206).

1555 p?
1677 Two days 'that the tovn maid ther mestris' (from a payment to a musician in the Hammermen's accounts; glossed as '?mystery-play' in

A Dictionary of the Older Scottish Tongue, IV, ed A.J. Aitken [1967], p 325; *The Hammermen of Edinburgh*, ed John Smith [1906], p 159, reads 'ministers').

1556 r
1678 Edward Henryson, public lecturer in Greek here, owned a printed Aristophanes (Durkan-Ross, p 116).

1558 July p
1679 Triumph for the queen's marriage, with a play of the seven planets by William Lauder (with a part written by William Adamsoun), a grey and a black friar, Cupid, and a fool (Mill, pp 183-8; *Edinburgh Records*, pp 241, 269-73).

1561 12 May p
1680 George Durye, chosen to be 'Lord of (In)obedience' among craftsmen and servants of the city, entered it 'in Robert Hude' despite the opposition of civic officials on route (Durye was chosen in April, and his rebellion continued into July and August; Pitcairn, I, *409-10).

1561 21 July r
1681 Craftsman James Killone (Kellone, Gilloun), condemned to be hanged for entering the city 'and playing with Robene Hud' (with 'Robene Huides playes'), was freed when the citizens rioted (*A Diurnal of Remarkable Occurrents that Have Passed within the Country of Scotland since the Death of King James the Fourth till the Year M.D.LXXV.*, BanC 43 [1833], pp 65-6, 283-5; Calderwood, II, 123-5; Pitcairn, I, *410).

1561 3 September p
1682 Pageants for the entry of Mary, Queen of Scots (Mill, pp 190-1; *A Diurnal*, pp 67-9; McGee-Meagher, pp 65-8):
    1 / an angel descending out of a cloud with the keys of the city and with books;
    2 / Fortune, Love, Justice, and Policy;
    3 / a sacrifice: a wooden priest at mass, put to the flames? or Korah, Dathan, and Abiram, burnt while they sacrificed in idolatry; and
    4 / a dragon, burnt.

1562 30 April r
1683 The queen's letter to the city council forbidding the election of Robin (Robert) Hood, Little John, or the Abbot of Unreason there in

May or at any other time is proclaimed (Mill, p 223; *Edinburgh Records*, p 367).

1572 May r
1684 Despite poverty and a scarcity of victuals, the citizens had their May-time pleasures of 'ald tymes, viz. Robin Hude and Litill Johne' (*A Diurnal*, p 263).

1579 September p
1685 Pageants at the entry of James VI (Mill, pp 193-4; *The Historie and Life of King James the Sext*, ed Thomas Thomson, BanC 13 [1825], pp 178-9; Calderwood, III, 458-9, with a date of 17 October; McGee-Meagher, p 103):
1 / the wisdom of Solomon, with two women contending for the young child;
2 / a boy, coming out of a globe with keys to the city;
3 / Peace, Justice, Plenty, and Policy (or the four cardinal virtues);
4 / Dame Religion;
5 / the story of Bacchus;
6 / the signification of the seven planets, with Ptolemy; and
7 / 'ane breiff fabill' for the abolition of the Pope and the mass (only in Mill, p 194).

1590 1 May p
1686 Pageants for the entry of James and his queen, including nos (2)-(4) presented in 1579 (Mill, pp 201-4).

1598 p
1687 A comedy, played by school children at the Tolbooth, with five friars, a pope, and two cardinals (Mill, pp 205-6).

1617 19 June p
1688 Play with fireworks before the king, with the palace of St Androis, the Castle of Envy (with St George for its badge, and the captain of the castle, Envy), and St Andrew fighting a dragon (W.J. Hardy, *The Manuscripts of Lord Kenyon*, HMC, 14th Report, App, IV [1894], pp 22-3; cf Mill, pp 206-7, 344-5).

1633 15 June p
1689 Pageant of the Genius of Edinburgh, Religion, Superstition, Justice and Oppression, the first of seven for the entry of Charles I (Mill, p 215).

FINTRY (?Stirling, now Central)

1578 June p
1690 Six townsmen indicted of making an Abbot of Unreason
(Pitcairn, I, 81).

GLASGOW (Lanark, now Strathclyde)

1462 r
1691 Provision for an interlude by masters and students at the University on the feast of the translation of St Nicholas (*Munimenta Alme Universitatis Glasguensis*, ed Mr Innes, MaC 72 [1854], II, 39-40; Mill, pp 75, 246-7).

1558 r
1692 The Old Green is the 'palestram de Glasgw lusoriam' (probably athletic games; Robert Renwick, *Glasgow Memorials* [1908], pp 73-4).

1599 r
1693 Play and pastime on Corpus Christi night (Mill, p 244).

HADDINGTON (East Lothian, now Lothian)

1530-52
1694 Abbot of Unreason; with play garments (Mill, pp 249-53).

1534-41 r
1695 Pageants played on Corpus Christi or Midsummer day (Mill, p 249).

1545-6 Christmas r
1696 Preaching, Master George Wishart complained that, although two or three thousand townsfolk would attend 'ane vane Clerk play' here, scarcely one hundred would come for a sermon (Knox, I, 138).

1565 p
1697 Play by schoolmaster for his scholars to perform 'against the ministers, and [they?] baptised a cat in the name of the Father, the Son, &c.' (before 20 March; Robert Keith, *History of the Affairs of Church and State in Scotland*, ed John P. Lawson, 3 vols, Spottiswoode Soc 1, II [1845], p 269; Mill, p 90).

1589 r
1698 Civic repression of Pasche plays, including Robin Hood, Abbot of Unreason, and the play or 'trik' of Samuelston (Mill, pp 254-5).

INVERNESS (Inverness, now Highland)

1574-5 r
1699 Abbot of Unreason on Whitsunday (Mill, p 257; *Records of Inverness*, ed William Mackay and Herbert C. Boyd, I [1911], pp cvi, 238, 243).

JEDBURGH ABBEY (Roxburgh, now Borders)

1285 p
1700 A musical 'ludi' with a 'phantasma,' 'ane ymage of ane dede man, nakitt of flesche & lyre, *with* bair banys,' interrupting a ring dance at the wedding feast of Alexander III (Joannis de Fordun, *Scotichronicon* [1759], II, 128; Bellenden, p 244; Mill, p 48).

LANARK (Lanark, now Strathclyde)

1488 ?p
1701 Guisers for the court are here (*ALHTS*, I, 93; Mill, p 313).

1488-1507
1702 Corpus Christi processional pageants (termed ?a play) with St George, the dragon, the chapel, Christ, ladies, the kings of Cologne, and 'the actouris hattis' (*Extracts from the Records of the Royal Burgh of Lanark with Charters and Documents Relating to the Burgh* A.D. *1150-1722* [1893], pp 2-3, 7, 12-18; Mill, pp 261-2).

LASSWADE (Midlothian, now Lothian)

1583 r
1703 Robin Hood, Little John, and May plays (Mill, pp 169-70).

LEITH (Midlothian, now Lothian)

1581 January p
1704 The Pope's castle or palace on boats in the river were assaulted and set on fire (Mill, p 55, n 3).

LINLITHGOW (West Lothian, now Lothian)

1488-1501
1705 Patrick Johnson and the town players; guisers; and the town Abbot of Unreason in revels for the court here (*ALHTS*, I, 91, 118, 184; II, 111; Mill, pp 313-14, 317).

1540 6 January p
1706 Interlude of 'the noughtines in Religion, the presumpcon of Busshops, the collucon of the spirituall Courtes, called the Concistory Courts in Scotland, and mysusing of preists,' at Epiphany, performed in the palace hall before James V and Mary of Lorraine (Lindsay's *Satyre of the Thrie Estaitis*; for a summary of text, see Lindsay, *Works*, II, 1-6; *L. & P. Hen. VIII*, XV, no 114, p 36; Kantrowitz, pp 11-27, argues that this interlude is perhaps an earlier draft of our [quite different] extant text; Stratman 5966-99; Houle 45; Mill [*PMLA*], pp 636-7).

LINTON (Peebles, now Borders)

1610-12 r
1707 May or Pasche plays called Lord or Abbot of Unreason, Robin Hood, and Little John (Mill, pp 257-60).

MELROSE (Roxburgh, now Borders)

1496 27 December ?p
1708 Guisers for the court are here (*ALHTS*, I, 308; Mill, p 315).

MUTHILL (Perth, now Tayside)

1583 p
1709 Clerk play put on by schoolmaster John Wod on the Sabbath (*Stirling Presbytery Records 1581-1587*, ed James Kirk, SHS, 4th ser, 17 [1981], pp 118-19; Mill, p 289).

PEEBLES (Peebles, now Borders)

1472 r
1710 Abbot of Unrest (Mill, p 263).

1555 r
1711 Robin Hood (Mill, p 263).

PERTH (Perth, now Tayside)

1485-1553, 1577 p
1712 Corpus Christi play, with Adam, Eve, St Eloy, the mermaid, the Devil, his man, his 'chepman,' the serpent, angel and two little angels, clerk, St Erasmus, the cord-drawer, king, three tormentors; termed clerk play in 1546? in 1553 the Trinity is added, and the devil's man, one of the little angels, clerk, St Erasmus, the cord-drawer, king, and three tormentors do not appear (Mill, pp 264-77; and her 'The Perth Hammermen's Play: A Scottish Garden of Eden,' *Scottish Historical Review*, 49 [1970], 146-53).

1503 26 June ?p
1713 The town Robin Hood for the court here (*ALHTS*, II, 377; Mill, p 319).

before 1542?
1714 Lyndsay's *Satyre of the Thrie Estaitis*, in the 'Amphitheatre' (John Row, *The History of the Kirk of Scotland, from the Year 1558 to August 1637*, ed David Laing, Wodrow Society [1842], p 7; Mill [*PMLA*], pp 645-6; Stratman 5966-99; Houle 45).

1545 r
1715 Robin Hood (Mill, p 265).

1577-88
1716 St Tobert's play, with devil (St Cuthbert? Mill, pp 276-81).

ST ANDREWS (Fife)

1460 8 April r
1717 '... otio ludis et spectaculis vacantes' are frequented by the university's scholars, to its displeasure (*Acta Facultatis Artium Universitatis Sanctiandree 1413-1588*, ed Annie I. Dunlop, St Andrews Univ. Publ., 56 [1964], p 134; Mill, p 284).

1508 5 December r
1718 The university prepares 'ludis' for the visit of the king and queen at Christmas (*Acta*, p 290).

1514 8 May r
1719 To prevent defamatory statements against persons 'in ludis et proclamacionibus,' the regents of the place at which they are made are to examine them (*Acta*, pp 308-9; Mill, pp 284-5).

ca 1523-59
1720 John Grierson, Provincial of the Dominicans in Scotland, had a Terence that was printed in 1504 for Wynkyn de Worde (in the Black-friars' library; John Durkan and Julian Russell, 'John Grierson's Book-List,' *The Innes Review*, 28 [1977], 40, 45).

1530-4 r
1721 Friar William Arth's sermon comparing the Abbot of Unreason to lawless present-day prelates; and Sandie Furrour, accused by priests of heresy, at the court 'lapp up mearely upoun the scaffold, and, casting a gawmound, said, "Whair ar the rest of the playaris?"' (Knox, I, 40, 43).

1538 June p
1722 Farces and plays were made for the entry of Mary of Guise: at the New Abbey gate Sir David Lindsay's 'trieumphant frais' (or farce) showed a great cloud come out of the heavens and divide in half to reveal a fair lady like an angel delivering the keys of Scotland to her (Lindsay thus exhorting the queen 'to serue her god, obey hir hus-band, and keep hir body clene'); and after dinner at the palace (Pit-scottie, I, 378-9).

ca 1538 r
1723 James Stewart, prior of St Andrews and half-brother of Queen Mary, owned a printed works of Seneca (Durkan-Ross, p 147).

1574 1 August p
1724 'the comede mentionat in Sanct Lucas Euuangel of the forlorn sone' licenced for performance at this time (on a Sunday, out of preaching hours), on the application of elder Patrick Auchinleck, on condition that it be first revised by the rector and others (*Register of the Minister, Elders, and Deacons of the Christian Congregation of St. Andrews*,

Part First: 1559-82, ed David H. Fleming, SHS, 4 [1889], p 396; possibly the clerk play played by the grammar school scholars outside of preaching time, as defended by the town minister Robert Hamilton on 24 February 1575, for which see 'Extracts from the Buik of the General Kirk of Edinburgh,' *Miscellany of the Maitland Club*, pt I, MaC 25 [1833], pp 114-15; Mill, pp 285-6, n 2).

1574 11 August r
1725 The General Assembly of the Church inquires into the violation of the Sabbath by profane plays by the town ministers, elders, and deacons (*Kirk of Scotland*, I, 312).

1575 February-March r
1726 Robin Hood plays, as performed by servants and young children before 24 February, were investigated; and on 2 March these plays were again prohibited (*Miscellany of the Maitland Club*, pt I, pp 114-15; and Mill, p 286).

ST ANDREWS, diocese of

14th century r
1727 Prohibition of '[ludos] inhonestos' in churches and churchyards (*Concilia Scotiae*, II, no 164, p 73; *Statutes of the Scottish Church*, p 77).

ST JOHN'S TOWN OF DALRY
(Kirkcudbright, now Dumfries and Galloway)

1541 p
1728 Triumph made by the town for the queen (Lesley, p 159).

SAMUELSTON (East Lothian, now Lothian)

1589-1603
1729 Play or 'trik,' evidently a Pasche play or May play associated with the Abbot of Unreason (Mill, pp 254-5).

STIRLING (Stirling, now Central)

1496-1500
1730 Abbot of Unreason or Abbot of Narent for the court here (*ALHTS*, I, 270; *The Exchequer Rolls of Scotland*, VIII, ed George Burnett [1888], p 260; Mill, pp 315, 312).

ca 1535-6 p
1731 Friar Kyllour's play, 'the Historye of Christis Passioun,' on Good Friday morning for the king, in which the people were persuaded that present-day bishops and religious were like the priests and pharisees who persecuted Christ (Knox, I, 62).

1543 20 August p
1732 Crowning of Queen Mary with triumph, 'playis, phrassis and bankating and great danceing' (Pitscottie, II, 15).

STRAGEATH, near Muthill (Perthshire, now Tayside)

1583 p
1733 Clerk play with 'mekill baning and swering, sum badrie and filthie baning,' performed by schoolmaster John Brown's 'bairnis' on the Sabbath (*Stirling Presbytery Records 1581-1587*, ed James Kirk, SHS, 4th ser, 17 [1981], pp 118-19, 122, 129-30, 141; Mill, pp 289-91).

Ireland

ca 1400?
1734 'Visitatio Sepulchri' in the church of St John the Evangelist (text; see Young, I, 347-50; Stratman 419-21; Lipphardt, V, 1467-72, nos 772-72a).

ca 1490?-1570
1735 Pageants of St George's day (J.T. Gilbert, *Calendar of Ancient Records of Dublin*, I [1889], pp 242, 476):
  1 / the Emperor, two doctors, the Empress, two knights, and two maidens;
  2 / St George on horseback, four trumpeters, and four horsemen;
  3 / a maiden leading the dragon; and
  4 / the king and queen of 'Dele' or Grief with two knights and two maidens.

1498-1569
1736 Sixteen Corpus Christi pageants, 'made by an olde law,' in procession, which were as follows in 1498 (Gilbert, *Calendar*, I, 239-41, 392, 440; II, 3-4, 54):
  1 / Adam and Eve, with an angel following who bears a sword (the expulsion);
  2 / Cain and Abel with altar and offerings;
  3 / Noah and his ship;
  4 / Abraham and Isaac with their altar, a lamb, and an offering;
  5 / Pharaoh and his host;

6 / the body of the camel led by Joseph, and carried by porters; Our Lady and her child (?going from Egypt), and Moses and the Israelites;

7 / the three kings of Cologne riding with offerings, following the star;

8 / the shepherds and an angel singing *Gloria in Excelsis*;

9 / Christ in his passion with three Maries and angels;

10 / Pilate, his lady, his fellowship, and his knights (the Tailors, also known as the Guild of St John the Baptist, paid those playing Pilate – in 1554-5 – and the Emperor and Empress in their pageant then and in 1567 [John J. Webb, *The Guilds of Dublin* (1929), pp 90-2]);

11 / Annas and Caiaphas;

12 / Arthur, with his knights;

13 / the twelve apostles;

14 / the prophets;

15 / the tormentors with painted garments;

16 / the nine worthies riding with their followers (1554r; also performed in 1557 for the Chief Governor, Thomas Radcliffe, earl of Sussex, and in 1561 for his heir the third earl, according to Walter Harris, *The History and Antiquities of the City of Dublin* [1766], pp 145-6, 312-13); and

17 / the dragon.

1509 r
1737 One 'ludenti' with lights at Christmas and Candlemas, and Whitsun players with angels and dragon, in St Patrick's Cathedral accounts (1509-10p? J.T. Gilbert, *A History of the City of Dublin* [1861], I, 37).

1528 p
1738 Stage plays every day in Christmas on Hoggen Green for the Lord Deputy, Piers Butler, earl of Ossory (Gilbert, *History*, III, 3-4):

1 / Adam and Eve (the Tailors);

2 / Crispin and Crispianus (the Shoemakers);

3 / Bacchus (the Vintners);

4 / Joseph and Mary (the Carpenters);

5 / Vulcan (the Smiths);

6 / Ceres (the Bakers);

7 / the Passion of Our Saviour (the Priors of St John of Jerusalem, the Blessed Trinity, and All Hallows); and

8 / the deaths of the Apostles (the same).

1541 13 June p
1739 'Epulas, Comoedias, & certamina ludicra' given on the day Henry VIII was made King of Ireland by the Irish Parliament; according to Harris, the nine worthies were played at this time on Corpus Christi (16 June; James Ware, *Rerum Hibernicarum Annales, Regnantibus Henrico VII. Henrico VIII. Edwardo VI. & Maria* [1664], pp 160-1; Harris, *History*, pp 144-5).

DUBLIN, diocese of

1367 Lent r
1740 Archbishop Thomas Minot at his provincial council in Kilkenny prohibits, for all Dublin province, 'ludi teatrales et ludibriorum spectacula' in cemeteries (Aubrey Gwynn, 'Anglo-Irish Church Life: Fourteenth and Fifteenth Centuries,' *A History of Irish Catholicism*, ed Patrick J. Corish, II [1968], no 4, p 50; cf Clark, p 10).

KILKENNY (Kerry)

1553 20 August p
1741 At the market cross, young men played John Bale's [1] 'a Tragedye of Gods promises in olde lawe' in the morning, and in the afternoon [2] 'a Commedie of sanct Johan Baptistes preachinges / [3] of Christes baptisynge and [4] of his temtacion in the wildernesse' (John Bale, *The Vocacyon of Johan Bale to the Bishoprick of Ossorie in Irelande* [December 1553], fol 24; STC 1307; 'Christes baptisynge' [3] is lost, but for the other texts see *The Dramatic Writings of John Bale, Bishop of Ossory*, ed John S. Farmer, EED [1907], pp 83-125 [1], 127-50 [2], and 151-70 [4]; and facs edns, TFT 21 [1], TFT 22 [4], and 'A Brefe Comedy or Enterlude of Iohan Baptystes Preachynge in the Wyldernesse' [4], *The Harleian Miscellany*, ed William Oldys, annot Thomas Park, I [1808], pp 101-14 [the earliest extant text, an antiquarian edition of 1744]; Greg 22-3; STC 1279 [1547-8?], 1305 [1547?]; Stratman 5347-63, 5390-7).

1580-ca 1650
1742 Corpus Christi and Midsummer plays, often done at stations (though the resurrection play was once done in St Mary's church 25 June 1588), with a book of Corpus Christi plays 1637, and with the

following groups of characters (Patrick Watters, 'Notes of Particulars Extracted from the Kilkenny Corporation Records Relating to the Miracle Plays as Performed There from the Year 1580 to the Year 1639,' *The Journal of the Royal Historical and Archaeological Association of Ireland*, 4th ser, 6 [1883-5], 238-42; John G.A. Prim, 'Olden Popular Pastimes in Kilkenny,' *Trans. of the Kilkenny Archaeological Society for 1852-53*, 2 [1853-5], 327-8; Clark, pp 22-5):

1 / a trumpeter;

2 / Christ, John the Evangelist, the Virgin Mary, and the other three Maries, with the sepulchre (a resurrection play);

3 / St Michael, Satan, and another devil (Belphegor), playing the resurrection (?the harrowing of hell); and

4 / the conqueror, Charlemagne, Julius Caesar, Joshua, Godfrey, and Hector (the nine worthies).

Other

ARDRES (France)

1520 17, 24 June p
1743 Disguisings by Henry VIII and his retinue at the French king's palace while Francis masqued at Henry's new palace at Guines (Halle, fols 80, 83; *L. & P. Hen. VIII*, III.iii, nos 704.1, 870, pp 239-40, 312, 1554; *Venice*, III, nos 50, 90, pp 26, 30, 71-2; Joycelyne G. Russell, *The Field of Cloth of Gold* [1969], pp 164-70, 177-81, with use of additional French materials; for plans for two mummeries, one at Guines Castle, another at Ardres, for which both participants and apparel were to be decided by Henry, see John Caley, 'Two Papers Relating to the Interview between Henry the Eighth of England, and Francis the First of France,' *Arch*, 21 [1827], 182-3, 189):

1 / a mummery of Eastlanders, old men, and ?Greeks or Albanians (17 June); and

2 / Henry VIII as Hercules, leading the nine worthies; gold-bearded men; and two groups of women, in Genoese and Milan dress (24 June).

CALAIS (France)

1513 June-September r
1744 Ten members of 'the King's minstrels and players' accompanied Henry VIII to Calais in the middle ward of his force invading France (*L. & P. Hen. VIII*, I [1920], no 2053.2, p 925).

1514 May r
1745 'great pageants' were to have been performed for the (unrealized) marriage of Henry VIII's sister Mary to Charles, prince of Castile (*Venice*, II, no 505, p 199).

1520 11, 12 July p
1746 A masque (11 July); eight companies of maskers in mummeries devised by Henry VIII himself, with William Cornyshe's pageants, at a banquet at the Exchequer for the king and Charles V to have taken place originally in the great banqueting house (12 July; Halle, fol 84v; 'Meeting of King Henry VIII. and the Emperor Charles V. at Gravelines,' *Rutland Papers*, ed William Jerdan, CS 21 [1842], pp 54, 56-7; *L. & P. Hen. VIII*, III.i, no 804, pp 281-2; *Venice*, III, nos 50, 104, pp 31, 80).

1520 July r
1747 Henry VIII's banqueting house, an amphitheatre structure with a canvas roof that blew off in a great wind before it could be used for pageants and masques before the king and Charles V (Richard Turpin, *The Chronicle of Calais*, ed John G. Nichols, CS 35 [1846], pp 29-30; described as a 'theatre' in *Venice*, III, no 50, pp 32-4; cf Anglo, pp 159-68 [drawing on *Le Triomphe festif ... fait ... en la ville de Calais* (1520)], and Richard Hosley, 'The Theatre and the Tradition of Playhouse Design,' in *The First Public Playhouse: The Theatre in Shoreditch 1576-1598*, ed Herbert Berry [1979], pp 60-74).

ca 1520-6, 1531-3
1748 'Comoediam, Ite in uineam' by John Bourchier, Lord Berners, acted customarily 'in the great church at Calais after vespers' (lost; *Scriptorum*, I, 706; *Illvstrivm*, fol 216v, refers just to 'comoedias'; Wood, I, 73; cf N.F. Blake, 'Lord Berners: A Survey,' *Medievalia et Humanistica*, NS 2 [1971], 119-32; Bourchier's translation [1532], *The Golden Boke of Marcvs Avrelivs* [1535], refers to 'counterfaitynge players of farces and mummeries' and to interludes [fols 25r, 27r; cf fols 40r, 140-1; STC 12436).

1521 August-November p
1749 An attack on Wolsey ca 1529 refers to 'mummeries' in his wasteful triumph at 'our [en]countering at Calais,' evidently his mediation between warring France and the Empire at this time (*L. & P. Hen. VIII*, IV.iii, no 5750, p 2560).

1532 25-8 October p
1750 Masquings, pageants, and pastimes at the meeting of Henry VIII
and the king of France here (*Venice*, IV, nos 822, 824, pp 363, 368; *The
Privy Purse Expences of King Henry the Eighth, from November* MDXXIX, *to
December* MDXXII, ed Nicholas H. Nicolas [1827], p 270; Halle, fol
209r; *L. & P. Hen.* VIII, V, no 1484, pp 623-4; on Sunday night, 28
October, at Staple Hall, Anne Boleyn led a masque before the two
kings, according to *The Maner of the Tryumphe at Caleys & Bulleyn. The
Second Pryntyng / with Mo Addicions as It Was Done in Dede* [London:
Wynkyn de Worde, 1532], sig A4r; STC 4351).

1540 June r
1751 An inventory of the goods of Arthur, Viscount Lisle, and his
wife Honor, in the Staple Inn, his residence when he was Deputy of
Calais (compiled as he lay in the Tower under arrest), lists twelve
'maskyn gownes' with buckram hoods and caps (*Lisle Letters*, VI,
157-8, 201; cf *L. & P. Hen.* VIII, XV, no 853, pp 425-7 [not listed]).

1547 19-22 February p
1752 Tournament and triumphs in honour of the coronation of
Edward VI: six participants dressed as Turks entered the field (20 February); and on the last night (22 February, Shrove Tuesday) the Lord
Deputy, George Lord Cobham, gave a banquet at his house with interludes and masques, including one by the challengers dressed as pilgrims ('Calais Papers,' *Calendar of State Papers, Foreign Series, of the
Reign of Edward VI., 1547-1553*, ed William B. Turnbull [1861], nos 43,
47, pp 306-10).

GUINES (France)

1520 11-22 June r
1753 'Robert the Devil,' an attendant to noble jousters at the Field of
Cloth of Gold (*L. & P. Hen.* VIII, III.iii, p 1555).

Doubtful Texts and Records

ca 55-4 BC
1754 King Cassivelaunus celebrated his second victory over Julius
Caesar by inviting his chief subjects to a feast at Trinovantum (later
London) where there were 'diuersos ludos' (*The Historia Regum Britanniae of Geoffrey of Monmouth*, ed Acton Griscom [1929], pp 313-14;
probably athletic games, not the 'many disguisinges, playis, minstrelsy,
and sportes,' as stated in *The Household of Edward IV: The Black Book and
the Ordinance of 1478*, ed A.R. Myers [1959], p 83).

1st-4th centuries? r
1754.5 A large semicircular Roman structure at Wycomb, near Ando-
versford, Gloucs, not far from a temple, may be a theatre (W.L. Lawrence [communication], *Proceedings of the Society of Antiquaries of
London*, 2nd ser, 2 [1861-4], 304, 425; *The Roman West Country: Classical Culture and Celtic Society*, ed Keith Branigan and P.J. Fowler [1976],
p 112).

1st-4th centuries?
1755 Elliptical earthwork 'amphitheatre' of Roman construction at
Charterhouse, 'in all probability used ... for sports and pastimes,' but
both smaller and differently oriented than the usual Roman amphitheatre (H. St George, Gray, 'Excavations at the "Amphitheatre," Charter-
house-on-Mendip, 1909,' *Proceedings of the Somersetshire Archaeological &
Natural History Society*, 55 [1910 for 1909], 118-37 and pls I-IV).

721/4-40?
1756 A fragmentary Harrowing of Hell dialogue with narrative links,
supposed to be a liturgical play, in an ms copy ?written for Aethel-

weald, bishop of Lichfield ca 818-30 and ?derived from an exemplar associated with Aethelweald, bishop of Lindisfarne ca 721/4-40 (David N. Dumville [ed], 'Liturgical Drama and Panegyric Responsory from the Eighth Century? A Re-examination of the Origin and Contents of the Ninth-Century Section of the Book of Cerne,' *JTS*, NS 23 [1972], 374-406).

9th century
1757 A dialogue of Joseph and Mary in the seventh Advent lyric of the Exeter book (Jackson J. Campbell, *The Advent Lyrics of the Exeter Book* [1959], pp 58-61; Nicoll [1931], pp 212-13, following others, regards it as possibly dramatic, but Campbell, p 22, and Albert S. Cook, 'A Remote Analogue to the Miracle Play,' *JEGP*, 4 [1902], 421-51, and 'A Dramatic Tendency in the Fathers,' *JEGP*, 5 [1903-5], 62-4, points out detailed parallels in 4th-century dialogues by Greek and Latin church fathers; cf Neil D. Isaacs, 'Who Says What in "Advent Lyric VII"? (*Christ*, lines 164-213),' *PLL*, 2 [1966], 162-6).

ca 868-80 p
1758 King Alfred, disguised as a minstrel with his instrument, entered the tents of the Danes to show 'his enterludes & songes' and so learn of his enemy's strategy (Robert Fabyan, *The New Chronicles of England and France*, ed Henry Ellis [1811], p 167; the source, William of Malmesbury's *De Gestis Regum Anglorum*, ed William Stubbs, RS 90, I [1887], p 126, describes Alfred as 'sub specie mimi ... joculatoriae professor artis').

ca 1125 r
1759 A 'peregrinus' play at Malmesbury, Wilts, in Easter (Walther Lipphardt, 'Liturgische Dramen,' *Die Musik in Geschichte und Gegenwort*, VIII, ed F. Blume [1960], col 1020, from a clause relating the monks' attention to pilgrims having come to St Aldhelm's shrine, in *Willelmi Malmesbiriensis Monachi de Gestis Pontificum Anglorum Libri Quinque*, ed N.E.S.A. Hamilton, RS 52 [1870], p 440).

ca 1130
1760 Three Latin plays, with some French refrains, by Hilarius: 'Suscitacio Lazari,' 'Ludus super Iconia Sancti Nicolai,' and 'Historia de Daniel Representanda' (*Hilarii Versus et Ludi*, ed John B. Fuller [1929]; Young, II, 212-18, 337-41, 276-86; 'Suscitacio' is ed and trans by Bevington, pp 155-63; Stratman 1373-7, 1405-11, 1458-64; Hilarius' allu-

sions to English persons in his writing has led some to conclude that he was English, but his home appears to have been in Angers; Frank, p 52, n 1; Legge, p 312).

1171 p
1761 Miracle plays, masques, and mummeries witnessed by Henry II at Christmas at 'Hogges' near Dublin (record unlocated: Chambers, MS, II, 365, found an undocumented reference to these performances by W.F. Dawson, *Christmas* [1902], p 52; Dawson's source is probably William Sandys, *Christmastide* [1852?], p 26, for whom see also below at 1587p).

ca 1200-30
1762 Two supposed Anglo-Norman dramatic versions of the four daughters of God by Guillaume Herman and Stephen Langton (Adolphus W. Ward, *A History of English Dramatic Literature*, rev edn [1899], I, 105-6; in fact a single poem by Guillaume le Clerc of Normandy; see Hope Traver, *The Four Daughters of God*, Bryn Mawr College Monographs, 6 [1907], pp 31-3).

1224 4 May
1763 Five Franciscan friars, the first in England, were mistaken for 'mummers' by certain monks belonging to Abingdon and were driven away (in a miracle story by Bartholomew of Pisa in his 'Liber Conformitatum,' trans J.S. Brewer, *Monumenta Franciscana*, RS 4, I [1858], pp 632-3).

ca 1250
1764 'The Harrowing of Hell,' a poem with dialogue and, in one text, speech prefixes (termed 'dramatic' by William H. Hulme, ed, *The Middle-English Harrowing of Hell and Gospel of Nicodemus*, EETS ES 100 [1907], pp 2-23; Stratman 3944-68).

1296 r, 1332 r
1765 Two names in the Lay Subsidy Rolls, John le Pleyer (Herts) and William (Galfr.) le Pleyer (Surrey; Bertil Thuresson, *Middle English Occupational Terms*, Lund Studies in English 19 [1950], p 190).

ca 1314
1766 Robert Baston's 'Tragoedias uulgares' (one book; *Illvstrivm*, fol 127r, and *Scriptorum*, I, 370; probably poems, the very existence of

which is questionable, according to A.G. Rigg, 'Antiquaries and Authors: the Supposed Works of Robert Baston, O. Carm.,' in *Medieval Scribes, Manuscripts & Libraries: Essays Presented to N.R. Ker*, ed M.B. Parkes and Andrew G. Watson [1978], pp 322, 326, 330).

1316 r
1767 William Wheatley made two hymns addressed to St Hugh, bishop of Lincoln, not for a Christmas day play at Lincoln but for a 'poetic exercise' (Roger S. Loomis, 'Was There a Play on the Martyrdom of Hugh of Lincoln?' *MLN*, 69 [1954], 31-4, and Leo Spitzer, 'Istos Ympnos Ludendo Composuit,' *ibid*, pp 383-4).

ca 1317-60 r
1768 The bishop of Ossory, Richard Ledred, wrote songs for his clergy so that they would refrain from songs 'teat*ra*libus' (trans 'associated with revelry' by Richard L. Greene, ed, *The Lyrics of the Red Book of Ossory*, Medium AEvum Monographs, NS 5 [1974], pp iii-iv).

1324 r
1769 Robert Busse, abbot-elect of Tavistock, gave gifts at Exeter to 'ystrionibus maribus ac feminis' (Cecily Radford, 'Medieval Actresses,' *TN*, 7 [1952-3], 48; for contemporary female minstrels such as Matilda Makejoy, see Bullock-Davies, pp 137-8).

ca 1326-1538 p
1770 The prior's 'ludi' of Durham, Jarrow, Wearmouth, Finchale, Holy Island, and Farne, (quarterly) periods of feasting and perhaps 'relaxation' for 'ludentes' at his various manor houses at Beaurepaire (Bear Park), Pittington, Witton, etc; these 'ludi,' formerly thought to involve dramatic plays, sometimes linked with singers and the boy bishop, and at Finchale enjoyed a 'camera ludencium' or 'le Playerchambre' ca 1411-65 (*Extracts from the Account Rolls of the Abbey of Durham*, ed Canon Fowler, 3 vols, SS 99-100, 103 [1898-1901], pp 15-698; *The Durham Household Book*, ed James Raine, SS 18 [1844], pp 9-339; *The Inventories and Account Rolls of the Benedictine Houses or Cells of Jarrow and Monk-Wearmouth*, ed James Raine, SS 29 [1854], pp 56, 119-35, 215-32; *The Priory of Finchale*, ed James Raine, SS 6 [1837], pp lviii-ccccxli; James Raine, *The History and Antiquities of North Durham* [1852], pp 124, 130 [Holy Island, 1501-2, 1536-7], 358 [Farne, 1536-7]; *Wills and Inventories Illustrative of the History, Manners, Language, Statistics, &c. of the Northern Counties of England*, ed James Raine, I, SS 2

[1835], p 95; *The Wars of Alexander*, ed Walter W. Skeat, EETS ES 47 [1886], p xix; and R.B. Dobson, *Durham Priory 1400-1450* [1973], pp 97-8, says that the production of miracle plays and mysteries at these periods 'seems hardly likely').

1344 r
1771 Illuminations of two pageants or puppet shows, and of masked dancers, from a romance of Alexander written in 1338 in French at Bruges probably at the request of David II of Scotland (then in France; see Nicoll, figs 121 and 115; Falconer Madan and H.H.E. Craster, *A Summary Catalogue of Western Manuscripts in the Bodleian Library at Oxford*, II, i [1922], no 2464, pp 381-2, for Bodl ms 264).

1348 r
1772 Forty or fifty wealthy women dressed as men 'quasi comes interludii' attended tournaments at this time (Knighton, II, 57-8; translated as 'player of interludes' by Baskervill, p 81 and n 1, but as 'as if they were taking part in the sport' by Richard Barber, *Edward, Prince of Wales and Aquitaine* [1978], p 94).

1357 r
1773 By means of John Gaytryge's English translation of the 'Lay Folks' Catechism' by John Thoresby, archbishop of York, accounts of the deadly sins, the works of mercy, and the ten commandments were sent 'in smale pagynes' to the common people (units of paper, not 'pageants'; David A. Lawton, 'Gaytryge's Sermon, *Dictamen*, and Middle English Alliterative Verse,' *MP*, 76 [1978-9], 331; cf EETS OS 118 [1901], pp xvii-xix).

1360 r
1774 Bishop Beaupré of Exeter prohibited plays in his diocese noting 'in one of these plays Adam and Eve appear naked, the Devil displayed his horns and tail, and Noah's wife boxed the Patriarch's ears before entering the Ark' (no such bishop has been found; P. Berresford Ellis, *The Cornish Language and its Literature* [1974], p 37).

1382 r
1775 A poem attacking the Franciscans, supposedly for their Passion plays (*Reliquiae*, I, 322-3; Lawrence G. Craddock, 'Franciscan Influences on Early English Drama,' *Franciscan Studies*, 10 [1950],

383-417; probably referring to wall-paintings, according to R.H. Robbins, ed, *Historical Poems of the XIVth and XVth Centuries* [1959], pp 163-4, 335-7; IMEV 2663).

ca 1387-1400 r
1776 Chaucer's doubtful allusions to plays include the following:
  1 / a knight entering on a mechanical brass horse after the third course of a birthday feast for King Cambiuskan, 'An apparence ... As jogelours pleyen' ('The Squire's Tale,' *Chaucer*, lines F76-171, F218-19; a 'one-man masque' with pageant car according to Fifield, 'Chaucer'); and
  2 / Sir Thopas as a puppet hero ('Sir Thopas,' *Chaucer*, pp 164-6; Ann S. Haskell, 'Sir Thopas: the Puppet's Puppet,' *ChauR*, 9 [1975], 253-61).

ca 1388? r
1777 'Goddis halydays *non observantur honeste*, / For unthryfty pleyis *in eis regnant manifeste*,' probably referring to games of chance, not religious plays (*Satirical Songs and Poems on Costume*, ed Frederick W. Fairholt, Percy Society, 27 [1849], p 45; variant 'onthryfty pley' in *Political Poems and Songs*, ed and trans Thomas Wright, RS 14, I [1859], p 272; IMEV 3113).

15th century
1778 Fragment of a supposed Passion play in English, speeches by John, Mary, and Jesus, in a Latin sermon (*Catalogue of Manuscripts Preserved in the Chapter Library of Worcester Cathedral*, comp John K. Floyer, ed Sidney G. Hamilton, WorcsHS [1906], p 6; IMEV 14, 427.5).

15th century r
1779 Mystery plays at Leeds (Collier, I, 11, followed by other writers; Chambers, MS, II, 375-6, suggests that the error results from the presence of the York plays ms in Ralph Thoresby's library, as listed in a separately paginated catalogue [no 17, p 73] bound up with Thoresby's *Ducatus Leodiensis: or, the Topography of ... Leedes*, 2nd edn, ed T.D. Whitaker [1816]).

1401 Christmas
1780 Letters to Princess Blanche by Phoebus, Jenneste (queen of joy), Dalida (sultan of Babylon), Nature, Virtue, Venus, Penelope, Cleo-

patra, and others present knights to take part in a tournament at Eltham, to be attended by Manuel Palaeologus, emperor of Constantinople (whether the tournament itself had participants who assumed allegorical names is unclear; Dietrich Sandberger, *Studien über das Rittertum in England* [1937], pp 70-4).

1416 May p
1781 A dialogue or dumbshow representation of incidents in the life of St George for Henry V and the Emperor Sigismund at Windsor (Collier, I, 20; Chambers, MS, I, 224, and II, 132, 396-7, cites *Chronicle*, p 159, to 'resolve' this play into a cake, a subtlety; for other subtleties, see *Great Chronicle*, pp 117-19, 152, 414, 418-19).

1442 22 January r
1782 'divers works of charity and piety by them [the London parish clerks] yearly performed and found within the City aforesaid for forty years past and more' (from Henry VI's charter to the parish clerks; Reginald H. Adams, *The Parish Clerks of London* [1971], p 118; translated as '... year by year by themselves, exhibited and invented,' and considered a reference to their [Clerkenwell, not City] plays, by James Christie, *Some Account of Parish Clerks* [1893], p 61; and after him by Chambers, MS, II, 381).

ca 1450-99
1783 An Irish prose version of the harrowing of hell, 'almost exclusively ... dialogue,' with Satan, the seven deadly sins, and Christ (BL Add ms 30512, fols 80v-7r, copied at the time; and two later mss: texts ed J.E. Caerwyn Williams, 'An Irish Harrowing of Hell,' *Études Celtiques*, 9 [1960-1], 44-78).

1452-3 r
1784 A Scottish play of St Andrew: the record concerns the town itself (Craig, p 333; corrected by A.J. Mill, 'The Records of Scots Medieval Plays: Interpretations and Misinterpretations,' *Bards and Makars*, ed A.J. Aitken, M.P. McDiarmid, and D.S. Thomson [1977], p 139).

ca 1460-83 r
1785 Edward IV was accustomed to see 'the Citty Actors' at his palace at St John's (error for Edward VI? Heywood, *Apology*, sig E1v, citing Stow generally; source unlocated, but possibly a confusion of the Pri-

ory of St John, Clerkenwell [near which the London parish clerks had their scriptural plays, and which Stow describes as a store-house for the king's toils and tents ca 1540-50], with the palace or royal manor of St James, Westminster, erected ca 1531-2 on the grounds of St James' hospital and often used by the Tudors [Stow, *Survey*, II, 84, 101; cf Feuillerat 1, p 149]; there are no records, apparently, of London actors *temp.* Edward IV).

ca 1480 r
1786 John Scogan, jester to Edward IV, authored one book of 'Comoedias quasdam' at court (*Scriptorum*, II, 68; is this not what Andrew Borde later published as *The Iestes of Skogyn* [ca 1570; a late reprint], STC 21850.3-51? but cf below under 1613, and Welsford, pp 41-2).

1485 Christmas p
1787 A play by the king's chapel at court (Wallace, p 12, followed by *ES*, II, 28, draws this record, he says, from Collier, I, 46, although Collier has nothing about such a performance in either his 1831 or 1879 editions [but cf (1831), I, 64]).

1485 p
1788 William Ireland's forged play-text, 'The Divill and Rychard,' supposedly performed at Henry VII's coronation at Westminster by Paul's clerks and boys (J.W. Robinson, 'An Interlude or Mystery Play by William Ireland, 1795,' *CompD*, 13 [1979], 235-51; this also notes some play-titles, modelled on texts by Medwall, Heywood, Bale, and Wever, in a forged catalogue of Shakespeare's books).

1494 r
1789 A play of St Catherine at Edinburgh: the record concerns a place-name (Craig, p 332; corrected by Mill, 'Records,' p 139).

1498
1790 John Skelton's 'The Bowge of Courte,' verse dialogue and narrative performed with a ship pageant at court? (Leigh Winser, '*The Bowge of Courte:* Drama Doubling as Dream,' *ELR*, 6 [1976], 3-39; text ed Robert S. Kinsman, *John Skelton: Poems* [1969], pp 11-28).

ca 1500?
1791 Craft pageants in Nottingham including 'the raising of Lazarus, or St. George and the Dragon' (Duncan Gray, *Nottingham through*

500 Years, 2nd edn [1960], p 44; see REEDN, 1977.2, p 25, notes 19-20).

1503 r
1792 An ordinance 'in restraint of plays,' passed at Edinburgh (Davidson, p 99; record not located according to Mill, p 97, n 1).

1503-4 p
1793 A play of St Mary Magdalen at Thetford Priory, Norfolk: this is actually a 'play of Mydenale,' Mildenhall, Suffolk (Coffman, p 62; *Annals,* p 14; see under THETFORD PRIORY).

1504? 31 March p
1794 John Skelton's moral interlude *The Nigramansir,* with the Necromancer, Beelzebub the Devil, a notary public, Simony, and Philargyria or Avarice; about the trial of these latter two by the devil (supposedly played at court at Woodstock, Oxon., and printed by Wynkyn de Worde in 1504; HEP, III, 287-9, with a long plot summary from a copy belonging to William Collins; also called 'The Trial of Simonie' [III, 310]; now thought a fabrication, for which see MS, II, 440-1, and Greg, II, 960-1; Rodney M. Baine, 'Warton, Collins, and Skelton's *Necromancer,'* PQ, 49 [1970], 245-8, uses a letter by Warton [to David Garrick, dated just before HEP was published] that mentions this play to argue for its authenticity).

1515 p
1795 Fabricated record that the king's players acted an interlude by 'Mayster Midwell' (Henry Medwall) 'of the fyndyng of Troth, who was caryed away by ygnoraunce & ypocresy,' the fool's part being the best, but that the play was not liked, 'yt was so long,' and the king left for his chamber before the end (Collier, I, 65; Reed, pp 95-6; see also under LONDON [1514 6 January p]).

ca 1518-19 p
1796 John Winchcombe, clothier, is supposed to have entertained Henry VIII, Queen Catherine, and Cardinal Wolsey at the merchant's own house in Newbury, Berks., with a pageant of poor children disguised as Diana, goddess of Chastity, nymphs, four prisoners (Bellona, and her three daughters Famine, Sword, and Fire), Fame, and Victory (fiction possibly based on Elizabeth I's entry into Norwich in 1578;

'The pleasant Historie of Iohn Winchcomb, In his yonguer yeares called Iack of Newbery,' *The Works of Thomas Deloney*, ed Francis O. Mann [1912], pp 36-7, 514).

1520 r
1797 A breaking up of Christmas revels at Lincoln's Inn (without reference to plays as such; R.J. Schoeck, 'Christmas Revels at the Inns of Court: "A Sudden Order against Plays" in 1520,' *N&Q*, 197 [1952], 226-9; correcting his own 'Satire of Wolsey in Heywood's "Play of Love,"' *N&Q*, 196 [1951], 113, following D.S. Bland, 'Wolsey and Drama at the Inns of Court,' ibid, pp 512-13).

1521-2 r
1798 Payment 'for saynt' george levereys' is queried as for play-costumes (*Lambeth Churchwardens' Accounts 1504-1645 and Vestry Book 1610*, ed Charles Drew, II, Surrey Rec. Society, 20 [1950], p 420).

1525-6 p
1799 Fabricated entries supposed in the cofferer's accounts of the fifth earl of Northumberland in London: a royal masque, visiting players, and Percy's chaplain William Peres, making a Christmas interlude (see PRO, E.36.226, pp 241-51; Collier, I, 86-8; and Ian Lancashire, 'Orders for Twelfth Day and Night circa 1515,' *ELR*, 10 [1980], 13, n 24).

1527 p
1800 A 'solempne (sic) play' presented by the players of Henry Courtenay, earl of Devon, at his mother the countess' funeral at Tiverton (unlocated record; Cecily Radford, 'Three Centuries of Playgoing in Exeter,' *RTDevA*, 82 [1950], 243, dates this 1525, but see *CP*, IV, 330; is this entry not a garbled allusion to the 'solemn play' of 1547 in Southwark at the time of services for Henry VIII?).

1532 12 May p
1801 Play with pageant players and fool at 'Weybridge, Essex' (see under HEYBRIDGE; Cox, pp 274-5).

1533 r
1802 A proclamation forbidding playing of interludes about controversial doctrines (the date is an error for [18 August] 1553; Warton's misreading of Foxe's *Actes & Monumentes* [1576], pp 1338-9 [*STC* 11224], in *HEP*, IV, 115, followed by Collier, I, 119, and Chambers, *MS*, II, 220).

1536 r
1803 The Heavenly Jerusalem and other religious 'subtilties,' evidently elaborate pastries ('Plan of a Pageant,' *L. & P. Hen. VIII*, X, no 1016, p 421; revels possibly for Jane Seymour, according to Robert W. Bolwell, *The Life and Writings of John Heywood* [1921], p 173).

1539 r
1804 Sir Richard Charnell is paid 'for correkyn ye seruyce of thomas beckytt' (at Bungay; described as a play in Galloway-Wasson, but Charnell was probably striking Becket's name out of the liturgy; see Denis Stevens, 'Music in Honor of St. Thomas of Canterbury,' *Musical Quarterly*, 56 [1970], 327).

1554-8
1805 Pageant disguising and 'the Play of Holophernes' for Princess Elizabeth at Hatfield House in Shrovetide 1556; a play by Paul's boys there when Queen Mary visited Elizabeth, in either April 1558 or 1554; and revels, masquing, and disguisings when Elizabeth visited Mary and Philip at Hampton Court one Christmas (1557? Thomas Warton, *The Life of Sir Thomas Pope* [1780], pp 86-91; HEP, III, 312-13; all fabrications, according to H.E.D. Blakiston, 'Thomas Warton and Machyn's Diary,' *EHR*, 11 [1896], 282-300).

1555 7 February p
1806 '*Jube the cane*, a play ... and a maske [afterwards],' after supper at the marriage of Henry Stanley, lord Strange, and the earl of Cumberland's daughter: *Juego de cannas* was a Spanish sport at casting canes (Machyn, pp 82, 342-3, 401; 'the play ... of the cane' was also done at Westminster 25 November 1554, according to *Friars' Chronicle*, pp 92-3, and 'London Chronicle,' pp 39-40; cf Collier, I, 146, n; and 'Jube the Sane,' ca 1547-53, in *Annals*, p 30).

before 1558? r
1807 Elizabeth I is supposed to have translated a play by Euripides into Latin (Horatio Walpole, *A Catalogue of the Royal and Noble Authors of England, Scotland, and Ireland*, ed Thomas Park [1806], I, 85; cf H.H.E. Craster, 'An Unknown Translation by Queen Elizabeth,' *EHR*, 29 [1914], 721-3).

1587 p
1808 A play of Samson at a barn in Penryn, Cornwall, in which the noise of drums and trumpets, and the shouts of the audience – 'just at the time Sampson was let loose on the Philistines' – frightened off a landing party of Spaniards intent on plundering the town (William Sandys, 'On the Cornish Drama,' *JRIC*, 1, iii [1865], 18; Heywood's *Apology*, sig G2r [not Stephen Gosson's *School of Abuse*, an attribution that results from a misreading of the Shakespeare Society edition (1841) of it and Heywood's *Apology*], tells the story, without mentioning a dramatic subject, about an acting troupe visiting Penryn ca 1600).

1613 r
1809 In a French village's 'stage' play of 'the resurrection of the Lord' at Easter for which the Parson played Christ with a banner in his hand, his one-eyed 'lemman' the Angel in his grave, and two of the simplest townsmen the three Maries, these two, at Scoggin's instigation, answered the Angel's question, 'whom you seeke?' with 'the Parsons lemman with one eye'; at which she scratched one of them in the face, he buffeted her in return, the Parson and his clerk came to her defence, and the whole town joined in the brawl (*Scoggins Iestes* [1613], sigs A8v-A9r; *STC* 21851; Willard Farnham, 'Scogan's *Quem Quaeritis*,' *MLN*, 37 [1922], 289-92, argues that this jest reflects English practice and that Scoggin is not Edward IV's jester but Chaucer's friend Henry Scogan, but Neil C. Brooks, 'Scogan's *Quem Quaeritis* and Till Eulenspiegel,' *MLN*, 38 [1923], 57, traces the jest to a German edition of Till Eulenspiegel in 1515; cf Farnham's 'John (Henry) Scogan,' *MLR*, 16 [1921], 120-8).

ca 1620-50?
1810 An ms play in Latin, 'Sanctus Tewdricus sive Pastor bonus, Rex et Martyr,' with St Tewdricus, Maurice, king of the Silures, his brother Arthur, Malcolm, and Ulfadus; in nine scenes by nine authors, Richard Simons, William Parry, Richard Smith, Frances Simons, Daniel Gifford, Henry Chamberling, Charles Peeters, Thomas Beveridge (who also wrote the song at the end), and Nicholas Tempest (not seen; *Annals*, p 16, following Coffman, p 60, and Craig, p 333, suggests 'ment. 1701, Carnarvon, Bangor,' but Alfred J. Horwood, 'The Manuscripts of Reginald Cholmondeley, Esq., of Condover Hall, Shropshire,' *5th Report*, pt 1, HMC [1876], p 340, appears not to date the ms, which

is listed following a copy of a work by John Selden; the ?only source for the story of Teudiric, who lived ca 620-88, and for his defeat of the Saxons and death, is in Nat. Lib. of Wales ms 17110E, ed A. Gwenoguryn Evans and John Rhys in *The Text of the Book of Llan Dav* [1893; facs, 1979], pp 141-3, which states that this book, at Llandaff at least until 1619, was lent to Selden ca 1619-27 [pp x-xi]; cf Wendy Davies, *The Llandaff Charters* [1979], pp 97, 186; probably a Jesuit play from St Omer, for which see William H. McCabe, 'The Play-List of the English College of St. Omers 1592-1762,' *Revue de Littérature Comparée*, 17 [1937], 355-75, and 'Notes on the St. Omers College Theatre,' PQ, 17 [1938], 225-39).

APPENDIXES AND GENERAL INDEX

All reference numbers here are those of this guide. The following abbreviations are used:

attri attributed to
b banns
bc banncriers
c(cs) comedy(ies)
CC Corpus Christi
ch(s) character(s)
d(ds) disguising(s)
di(dis) dialogue(s)
ds disguisers
e(s) entry(ies)
f(fs) farce(s)
g(gs) game(s)
gpl(s) gameplayer(s)
gs gisers
i(is) interlude(s)
in interluders
interls interlusores
io iocatores
jo joculatores
l(li) ludus(-i)
ld ludatores
ls lusores
lt ludentes

ltd liturgical drama
m(ms) masque(s)
mi(mis) miracle(s)
mm(mms) mummer(s)
mo(mos) moresque(s) or
  morris(es)
mu(mus) mummery(ies)
mum(s) mumming(s)
nd no date
p(ps) play(s)
pa Passion
pg(pgs) pageant(s)
pl players
pp puppets
pr(s) property(ies)
pw playwright
r revels
s(ss) show(s)
so(sos) song(s)
t(ts) tragedy(ies)
tc(s) tragi-comedy(ies)
tr(trs) triumph(s)

I

An Index of Playing Companies to 1558

A COMPANIES IDENTIFIED BY PLACE-NAMES

References to each civic, town or parish playing company are listed chronologically under the name of the troupe's home site. A typical entry consists of the date of the record, the site visited by the troupe, the abbreviated name for that troupe in the record, and a bibliographical reference. Almost all this evidence appears in records from sites other than that of the troupe in question. Where the home site itself has records of dramatic activity (and thus appears in the main body of this guide), I have briefly summarized whatever from that evidence may bear on its travelling company.

1 Abergavenny, Gwent
A parish troupe that toured the countryside with games and plays.
1537 Abergavenny (pl? **1592**).

2 Abingdon, Oxfordshire
There were town players of the Fraternity of the Holy Cross in 1445 (**343**).
1427-8 Hertford? ('jouers' making interludes; **771**).

3 Aldermaston, Berkshire
1382-3 Reading (lt; **1315**, p 172)
1388-9 Reading (lt; **1315**, p 172).

4 Appledore, Kent
1467-8 Lydd (showers of the play; **1161**, p 95).
1488-9 New Romney (bc; **1202**, p 124).

1516-17 Lydd (bc; **1161**, p 99).
1517-18 New Romney (ls/bc; **1202**, p 131).

5 Ash (near Sandwich), Kent
1462-3 Sandwich (ld; **1374**, p 146).

6 Atherstone upon Stour, Warwickshire
1457-8 Maxstoke Priory (ls of 'Adryston'; **1176**, p 93).

7 Bardwell, Suffolk
1505-6 Thetford (g; **1448**; Galloway-Wasson).

8 Barton-upon-Humber, Lincolnshire (now Humberside)
1493-5 Hull (pl; **783**).

9 Beccles, Suffolk
1466-7 Mettingham College (three ls and 'trepidatoribus'; **1181**,
  p 127).
1472-3 Mettingham College (four with l; two men, one with pp; ibid).
1512-13 Hickling Priory (l; l of Beccles and ?North Walsham; **773**;
  Galloway-Wasson).

10 Benenden, Kent
1527-8 Lydd (pl; **1161**, p 103).

11 Bethersden, Kent
The town play of St Christina was put on over three days in 1519-21
(**374**).
1508-9 New Romney (bc; **1202**, p 129).
1517-18 Lydd (pl; **1161**, p 100).
1520-1 Lydd (pl; **1161**, p 101).

12 Billericay, Essex
1521-2 Lydd (pl; **1161**, p 101).
1526-7 Stoke-by-Nayland (four pl; **1421**).

13 Bishop Auckland, Durham
1539-40 Durham (ls; **625**, p 340).

14 Bishop's Caundle, Dorset
1558 Sherborne (town rents pl garments; **1378**, p 9).

15 Blythburgh, Suffolk
1479 Walberswick (May; **1468**).
1491 Walberswick (May; **1468**).
1492 Walberswick (May; **1468**).
1495 Walberswick (May; **1468**).
1498 Walberswick (May; **1468**).
1499 Walberswick (May; **1468**).

16 Boughton Street, Kent
This town had a Corpus Christi play in 1535.
1484-5 Dover (pl of 'Boghton'; other towns with this name exist, but
    Boughton Street is on the main road to Dover near Canterbury; **609**,
    pp 29, 182).

17 Bramfield, Suffolk
1494 Walberswick ('brownfeld' g? Galloway-Wasson say Brownfield,
    Suffolk, which I have not found; **1468**).

18 Braughing, Hertfordshire
1504 Bishop's Stortford (p; **384**, p 29).

19 Brookland, Kent
1494-5 Hythe (bc; **788**, p 84). New Romney (bc/l; **1202**, p 125).
1499-1500 Hythe (ls; **788**, p 85).
1505-6 Hythe (ls; **788**, p 86).
1506-7 New Romney (bc/l; **1202**, p 129).
1510-11 Dover (pl; **609**, p 33).
1517-18 Lydd (pl; **1161**, p 99).
1518-19 Lydd (bc; **1161**, p 100).
1519-20 Lydd (pl; **1161**, p 101). New Romney (common criers; **1202**,
    p 131).
1520-1 Lydd (bc; **1161**, p 101).
1521-2 New Romney (pl; **1202**, p 132).
1533-4 Lydd (bc; **1161**, p 104).
1534-5 New Romney (pl proclaiming p; **1202**, p 134).

20 Bungay, Suffolk
There were town 'ludentes' in 1407-8, and Corpus Christi pageants or
game in 1514 and ca 1526-43 (**414, 416, 417**).
1509 Metfield (g; **1180**).

21 Burstwick, Yorkshire, E.R. (now Humberside)
nd Hedon (ls *temp.* Hen. V-Edw. VI; **759**, p lx).

22 Burton Pidsea, Yorkshire, E.R. (now Humberside)
nd Hedon (ls *temp.* Hen. V-Edw. VI; **759**, pp lv, lviii).

23 Calais, France
1486-7 Dover (pl; **609**, p 29).

24 Cambridge, Cambridgeshire
1415-16 King's Lynn ('Iogulatori' lt; **809**).

25 Cannock, Staffordshire
1522 Wollaton Hall (pl of 'Canke'; **1523**, p 350).

26 Canterbury, Kent
The town had players 1444-51, a Corpus Christi play by 1494, a play
on the three kings of Cologne in 1501-2, and the pageant watch and
later play of St Thomas Becket 1504-55 (**493-5, 499-501**).
1462-3 Sandwich (ls; **1374**, p 146).
1486-7 Dover (pl; **609**, p 29).
1489-90 Dover (pl; **609**, p 30). Sandwich (ds; **1374**, p 148).
1497-8 Sandwich (pl; **1374**, p 149).
1526-7 Lydd (pl; **1161**, p 102).
1535-6 Lydd (pl; **1161**, p 104).

27 Castle Cary, Somerset
1558 Sherborne (town rents pl garments; **1378**, p 9).

28 Chelmsford, Essex
1490 Castle Hedingham (pl; **517**, p 517).
1537-8 Dunmow (town rents pl garments; **613**, p 247).

29 Cheshire
1526 Wollaton Hall (p; **1523**, p 386).

30 Cinque Ports
1540 Bristol (pl; **410**, p 105).

31 Cleeve Prior, Worcestershire (now Hereford and Worcester)
1531 Crowle (pl; **587**, p 332).

32 Coggeshall, Essex
1481 Stoke-by-Nayland (pl; **1420**, p 145).
1482-3 Stoke-by-Nayland (four pl of 'Cokale'; **1420**, p 336).

33 Coleshill, Warwickshire
1441-2 Maxstoke Priory (ls of 'Colsell'; **1176**, p 92).

34 Colyton, Devon
1571-2 Honiton (Robin Hood; **779**).

35 Cornwall
1534-5 Barnstaple (pl; **364**; Wasson; cf II, 117).

36 Cottingham, Yorkshire, E.R. (now Humberside)
1439-40 Hull (lt; **783**).
1442-3 Hull (lt; **783**).
1444-5 Hull (lt; **783**).
1445-6 Beverley (proclamation of *li* of 'Cocyngham'; **379**, pp 98, 234).
1475-6 Hull (lt; **783**).

37 Coventry, Warwickshire (now West Midlands)
The town Corpus Christi play ca 1392-1580 drew many noble and
royal visitors, and there were a Hock Tuesday play 1416-1561 and
several saints' plays in the Tudor period, but these are not likely to
have been done by travelling companies (**554, 556**).
1432-3 Maxstoke Priory (ls; **1176**, p 92).
1433-4 Maxstoke Priory (ls; *ibid*).
1435-6 Maxstoke Priory (ls; *ibid*).
1441-2 Maxstoke Priory (ls; *ibid*).
1442-3 Maxstoke Priory (ls; *ibid*).
1457-8 Maxstoke Priory (ls; *ibid*).
1529 Battenhall (four pl; **368**, p 286).
1530 Court (pl; **1012**; V, 317; and p 162).

38 Cranbrook, Kent
1520-1 Battle Abbey (men playing; **369**, p 105).

39 Crowland, Lincolnshire
1470 Peterborough (town hires pl? garments; **1298**, p 6).

40 Datchet, Berkshire
1521-2 Ditton Park (man playing a friar; **600**).

41 Daventry, Northamptonshire
1433-4 Maxstoke Priory (ls; **1176**, p 92).

42 Deal, Kent
1462-3 Sandwich (ld; **1374**, p 146).

43 Deeping, Lincolnshire
1474 Peterborough (town hires pl? garments; **1298**, p 15).

44 Derbyshire
1542 Belvoir Castle (six pl, not playing; **371**, p 322).

45 Dersingham, Norfolk
1526 Snettisham (May; **1401**).
1536 Snettisham (May; **1401**).

46 Docking, Norfolk
1488 Snettisham (g; **1401**).

47 Donington, Lincolnshire
A play of Holofernes is recorded here ca 1563-5.
1524-5 Sutterton (pl; **1426**, p 92).

48 Dover, Kent
There were plays at Christmas ca 1452-1510 that were possibly the work of townsmen (**609**, pp 23-33).
1527-8 Lydd (pl; **1161**, p 103).

49 Dunnington, Yorkshire, E.R. (now North Yorkshire).
1446 York (three lt; **1567**, p 67).

50 Dunwich, Suffolk
1481-2 Mettingham College (ls; **1181**, p 127).

51 Dymchurch, Kent
1516-17 Lydd (pl; **1161**, p 99).

52 Easton, Great and Little, Essex
ca 1547 Dunmow (Eston and Margaret Roding p; **615**).

53 Edinburgh, Lothian
The town gisers who played at court in 1503-4 may have been Corpus
Christi players; in 1507 the Goldsmiths' pageant of the passion is
mentioned. There were clerk plays ca 1553-5; one John Arthur played
Robin Hood in 1549.
1503 Court (gs; **1662**; II, 356).
1504 Court (gs; **1662**; II, 414, 418).
1544 Court (Robert Hood; **1662**; VIII, 282).
1547 Court (Robert Hood; **1662**; IX, 73-4).
1549 Court (Robin Hood; **1662**; IX, 316).
1550 Court (Robert Hood; **1662**; IX, 393).

54 Elham, Kent
1497-8 Sandwich (pl; **1374**, p 149).
1505-6 Dover (pl; **609**, p 32).
1508-9 Dover (pl; **609**, p 33). Hythe (bc; **788**, p 86).
1533-4 Dover (showers of b of stage p; **609**, p 38).

55 Essex
Possibly the items for 1494-1503 belong under Henry Bourchier, earl
of Essex (for whose players see below).
1494 Court (four pl; **957**, p 28).
1496 Court (pl; **957**, p 30).
1497 Court (pl; **957**, p 32).
1498 Court (pl; **957**, pp 32, 34).
1503 Court (pl; **957**, fol 10r).
1525-6 Lydd (foot pl; **1161**, p 102).
1526-7 Lydd (pl; *ibid*).
1529-30 New Romney (pl; **1202**, p 133).
1531-2 Lydd (pl; **1161**, p 103).
1540-1 Folkestone (pl; **678**, p 69). Lydd (pl; **1161**, p 105).

56 Eton College, Berkshire
Christmas plays by the schoolboys appear 1525-73 **(649)** and probably
continued after Nicholas Udall became schoolmaster in 1534.
1538 Court (schoolmaster Woodall playing; **1027**; no 782, p 334).

57 Evesham, Worcestershire (now Hereford and Worcester)
1520 Worcester (four pl; **1532**, p 101).

58 Exeter, Devon
The only known dramatic activity here in the sixteenth century was
evidently the Robin Hood play (1508-54; **668**).
1534-5 Ashburton (pl/g; **354**).

59 Faversham, Kent
Published town records give no evidence of a local troupe (**675**).
1445-9 Canterbury (ls/lt; **503**, p 7).
1516-17 Lydd (**1161**, p 99).
1519-20 Lydd (pl; **1161**, p 100).
1525-6 Lydd (pl; **1161**, p 102).
1526-7 Lydd (pl; *ibid*).

60 Finchampstead, Berkshire
1505 Reading (Robin Hood; **1315**, p 4).

61 Folkestone, Kent
Published town records give no evidence of a local troupe (**678**).
1473-4 Lydd (bc; **1161**, p 97).
1474-5 New Romney (bc; **1202**, p 121).
1477-8 Dover (pl; **609**, p 26). Lydd (bc; **1161**, p 97).
1478-9 New Romney (bc/ls; **1202**, p 122).
1531-2 New Romney (pl; **1202**, p 133).
1532-3 Lydd (bc; **1161**, p 104).
1533-4 New Romney (pl with b; **1202**, p 134).

62 Frampton, Lincolnshire
1525-6 Sutterton (ps of Frampton and Kirton; **1426**, p 92).
1542 Leverington (p; **840**, p 298).

63 France
1428 Windsor (ls; **1511**).
1490 Dundee (pl; **1654**, p 314).
1494 Court (French pl; **957**, p 28).
1495 Court (French pl; **957**, p 29).
1521 Thornbury (pl; **1451**, p 500).

64 Frieston, Lincolnshire
1542-3 Long Sutton (pl/bc; **1156**, p 70).

65 Fring, Norfolk
1475 Snettisham (May; **1401**).
1491 Snettisham (g; **1401**).

66 Garboldisham, Norfolk
1457 Harling (g; **629**).

67 Gislingham, Suffolk
1505-6 Thetford (Walsham and Gislingham g; **1448**; Galloway-
  Wasson).

68 Gloucester, Gloucestershire
There were a clerks' play in 1283 and town players in 1553-4 (**684,
685**).
1432 London (pl; **934**).
1481-2? Stonor (pl; **1423**).
1520 Worcester (four pl; **1532**, p 123).

69 Great Bircham, Norfolk
1469 Snettisham (g; **1401**).
1521˙ Snettisham (May; **1401**).
1533 Snettisham (May; **1401**).
1535 Snettisham (May; **1401**).
1536 Snettisham (May; **1401**).

70 Great Chart, Kent
1489-90 New Romney (bc/l; **1202**, p 124).
1516-17 Lydd (pl; **1161**, p 99).

71 Great Yarmouth, Norfolk
Game players and Corpus Christi plays appear here 1473-1508, and
the game place lasts to the end of the sixteenth century (**690, 691**).
1510-11 Mettingham College (three lts; **1181**; Galloway-Wasson).

72 Grimoldby, Lincolnshire
1514-15 Grimsby (p; **737**, p 12).

73 Grimsby, Lincolnshire (now Humberside)
The town prepared 'the play of holy John of bowre' in 1527 (**738**).
1527-8 Louth (pl/bc of p; **1157**, p 80).

74 Hadleigh, Suffolk
There was a stage in the church in 1547-8.
1481-2 Stoke-by-Nayland (pl; **1420**, p 146).
1526-7 Stoke-by-Nayland (four pl; **1421**).

75 Hadley, Kent?
1537-8 Canterbury (pl; location unidentified; **503**, p 10).

76 Ham Street, Kent
1454 Lydd (ls showing l; **1161**, p 92).

77 Hastings, Sussex (now East Sussex)
1532-3 New Romney ('playes'; **1202**, p 133).

78 Heacham, Norfolk
1475 Snettisham (May; **1401**).
1487 Snettisham (May; **1401**).
1489 Snettisham (May; **1401**).
1501 Snettisham (May; **1401**).
1508 Snettisham (May; **1401**).

79 Henley-on-Thames, Oxfordshire
The town had a king play or game in 1455, a Robin Hood play
1499-1520, and a Resurrection play in 1511 (**761, 762**).
1382-3 Reading (lt; **1315**, p 172).
1504 Reading (Robin Hood; **1315**, p 4).

80 Herne, Kent
1429-30 New Romney (p; **1202**, p 541).
1440-1 Lydd (pl showing p; **1161**; Finn, p 80).
1444? Lydd (pl; **1161**; Finn, p 97).
1452-3 Dover (lt; **609**, p 23).
1462-3 Sandwich (ld; **1374**, p 146).
1476-7 Dover (pl; **609**, p 26).
1483-4 Dover (pl; **609**, p 28).

81 Hessle, Yorkshire, E.R. (now Humberside)
1444-5 Hull (lt; **783**).

82 High Halden, Kent
1500-1 New Romney (bc/l; **1202**, p 127).
1511-12 New Romney (bc/l; **1202**, p 130).

83 High Wycombe, Buckinghamshire
1494 Court (three pl; **957**, p 29).
1498 Court (pl; **957**, pp 32, 34).

84 Holland, parts of, Lincolnshire
1541 Belvoir Castle (four pl; **371**, p 321).

85 Horning, Norfolk
1372-3 St Benet of Hulme (l; **1354**).

86 Howden, Yorkshire, E.R. (now Humberside)
1531-2 Selby (five ls/lt; **1377**; I, 338-9).

87 Hythe, Kent
The published town records give no evidence of this troupe (**788**).
1399-1400 New Romney (pl; **1202**, p 535).
1465 Lydd (pl; **1161**, p 95).
1465-6 Sandwich (ls; **1374**, p 147).
1465-7 New Romney (ls; **1202**, p 120).
1473-4 Lydd (bc; **1161**, p 97).
1481-2 Dover (bc; **609**, p 28).
1482-3 Dover (pl; *ibid*). New Romney (bc; **1202**, p 123).
1494-5 New Romney (bc/l; **1202**, p 125).
1503-4 New Romney (bc/l; **1202**, p 128).
1504-5 New Romney (bc/l; **1202**, p 128).
1518-19 Lydd (pl; **1161**, p 100).
1520-1 Lydd (pl; **1161**, p 101).
1532-3 New Romney (Robin Hood 'playes'; **1202**, p 133).

88 Isleham, Cambridgeshire
1410 Downham (ls lt; **610**).

89 Ivychurch, Kent
1521-2 Lydd (bc; **1161**, p 101).
1530-1 Lydd (bc; **1161**, p 103).

90 Ixworth, Suffolk
1508-9 Thetford (p; **1448**; Galloway-Wasson).

91 Kelvedon, Essex
1482 Stoke-by-Nayland (pl of 'Esterforde,' ie Easterford Kelvedon; **1420**, p 148).

92 Kenninghall, Norfolk
1463 Harling (g; **629**).
1467 Harling (pl; **629**).
1494 Harling ('Keninghale'; **629**).
1511-12 Thetford (p; **1448**; Galloway-Wasson).

93 King's Lynn, Norfolk
The town Guild of St Giles and St Julian had players in 1399 and 1430-8 (**807**), and plays on Corpus Christi in 1410 and 1447-84 (**808**, **812**); this troupe may also have performed this play of Mary and Gabriel at home in 1445-6 (**811**).
1445-6 Middleton (p; **1182**).

94 Kingston upon Thames, Surrey (now Greater London)
The town had a Resurrection or Easter play ca 1505-20 and a May, Robin Hood, or Kingham game ca 1506-39 (**816**, **817**).
1505 Court (pl; **957**, p 39).

95 Kirton, Lincolnshire
1525-6 Sutterton (pl of Frampton and Kirton; **1426**, p 92).

96 Lancashire
Possibly the players of Wigan (see below under which name).
1524 Wollaton Hall (pl; **1523**, p 364).
1542 Belvoir Castle (four pl, not playing; **371**, p 322).

97 Latchingdon, Essex
1453 Maldon (pl; **1167**, p 181).
1469 Maldon (ls showing 'lusum'; *ibid*).

98 Launceston, Cornwall
1521-2 Dunheved (pl of Plymouth and Launceston; **612**).

99 Lavenham, Suffolk
1491 Castle Hedingham (Tydeman suggests, instead of Lavenham, Langham, several miles from Stoke [p 216]; pl; **517**, p 519).
1526-7 Stoke-by-Nayland (four pl; **1421**).

100 Leeds, Yorkshire, W.R. (now West Yorkshire)
1531-2 Selby (five ls/lt; **1377**; I, 338-9).

101 Leighton Buzzard, Bedfordshire
1481-2 Stonor (pl; **1423**).

102 Lewes, Sussex (now East Sussex)
1526-7 Lydd (pl; **1161**, p 102).

103 Lichfield, Staffordshire
1524 Wollaton Hall (pl; **1523**, p 379).

104 Lincoln, Lincolnshire
At this time the city still had its Christmas morning representation with Mary and the Angel, and the cathedral representation of the Ascension, Assumption, or Coronation of the Virgin (**864**).
1540 Belvoir Castle (pl; **371**, p 312).
1542 Belvoir Castle (five pl, not playing; **371**, p 322).

105 Linlithgow, Lothian
See below under Patrick Johnson for what appears to be this town's troupe (App 1.B).
1504 Court (the Pinners' Abbot of Unreason; **1662**; II, 430).

106 Liskeard, Cornwall
1538-9 Barnstaple (pl; **364**; II, 105).

107 London
By 1430 the Brewers, Blacksmiths, and Drapers were paying players and playing companies to perform at their annual feasts: one such troupe was probably Jack Travaill's, patronized by the king; another, a group of clerks in 1435 (**925**, and cf **1098**), was possibly a shrunken, late survival of the large numbers that contributed to the great Clerkenwell scriptural cycles in the reigns of Richard II and Henry IV. Both the Inns of Court and some local parishes were providing auspices for

players by the reign of Henry VII, and the Reformation saw many professional troupes center themselves in London (although the noble patrons of such troupes no doubt had provincial seats as well as houses in the city). In 1545 'the players of London' had come to mean, not a city-sponsored troupe (there was none), but rather any and all troupes acting from time to time in the city and its suburbs (**1048**).

1374-5 London (actors? **895**).
1426 Eltham (pl; **637**).
1447 York (four lt; **1567**, p 69).
ca 1460-83 Doubtful Records (actors? **1785**).
1484-5 Dover (four pl; **609**, p 29).
1497 Court (pl; **957**, p 32).
1498 Court (pl; **957**, p 34).
1499 Court (pl; **957**, p 35).
1503 Court (pl; **957**, fol 10r).
1505 Court (pl; **957**, fol 74r).
1533-4 Bristol (pl; **410**; II, 207).
ca 1536-44? Wulfhall (Paul's choristers/pl; **1547**, p 174).

London and Westminster also had two companies of choirboys who were known to have played, those from St Paul's Cathedral and those from Westminster School.

1 / Paul's boys. See Trevor Lennam, 'The Children of Paul's, 1551-1582,' *The Elizabethan Theatre II*, ed David Galloway (1970), pp 20-36.
1378 London (pl; **899**).
1485 Doubtful Records (pl; **1788**).
1521 Wollaton Hall (pls; **1523**).
ca 1522-30 London (p; **999**).
1527 Greenwich (pl? **723**).
1528 London (pl? **1006**).
ca 1536-44 Wulfhall (pl? **1547**).
1549-55 London (pl; **1065**).
1553 Ingatestone Hall (or London; children; **789**, p 86).
1552 Hatfield (pl? **754**).
1554 or 1558 Doubtful Records (pl; **1805**).
1557 London (i; **1101**).

2 / Westminster School.
1413-14 London (lt; **919**).

108 Long Itchington, Warwickshire
1457-8 Maxstoke Priory (ls; **1176**, p 93).

109 Long Melford, Suffolk
1555 Braintree; Ipswich (b? **1155**).

110 Lopham, Norfolk
1457 Harling (g; **629**).
1494 Harling ('Lopham' g? **629**).
1504-5 Thetford (g; **1448**; Galloway-Wasson).

111 Lydd, Kent
There was a town St George's play in 1456 and 1526-34 (**1162**, **1164**).
1408-9 New Romney (pl; **1202**, p 537).
1422-4 New Romney (May; **1202**, p 540).
1432-3 New Romney (pl; **1202**, p 541).
1455 Rye (showing p; **1344**, p 491).
1456-7 New Romney (ls; **1202**, p 120).
1467-8 New Romney (ls; *ibid*).
1476-7 New Romney (bc of 'lusi'; **1202**, p 121). Rye (pl; **1344**, p 495).
1478-9 New Romney (bc, 'lusi'; **1202**, p 122).
1486-7 Hythe (ls; **788**, p 83). New Romney (bc; **1202**, p 124).
1489-90 Dover (pl; **609**, p 30).
1493-4 New Romney (bc; **1202**, p 125).
1494-5 New Romney (l; **1202**, p 126).
1503-4 Hythe (bc; **788**, p 85). New Romney (bc/l; **1202**, p 127).
1508-9 Hythe (bc; **788**, p 86).
1509-10 New Romney (bc/l; **1202**, p 129).
1518-19 New Romney (bc; **1202**, p 131).

112 Lympne, Kent
1518-19 Lydd (pl; **1161**, p 100).

113 Madingley, Cambridgeshire
1489-90 Cambridge (ls; **438**, p 151).

114 Maidstone, Kent
1492-3 Dover (pl; **609**, p 30).
1520-1 Battle Abbey (pl; **369**, p 105).
1527-8 Lydd (pl; **1161**, p 103).

115 Margaret Roding, Essex
ca 1547 Dunmow (Elsenham and Margaret Roding g; **615**).

116 Marsh Chapel, Lincolnshire
1515-16 Grimsby (pl; **737**, p 12).

117 Martley, Worcestershire (now Hereford and Worcester)
1519 Worcester (pl; **1532**, p 91).

118 Maxstoke Priory, Warwickshire
1430 Lord Clinton's castle (boys/l; **1175**).

119 Middleton, Warwickshire
1521 Wollaton Hall (pl; **1523**, p 337).
1523 Wollaton Hall (pl; **1523**, p 351).

120 Mildenhall, Suffolk
The town's play of St Thomas (a Becket?) appears in 1505 and a May
game in 1510, 1529, and probably 1540-1 (**1183-5**).
1505-6 Thetford (p; **1448**; Galloway-Wasson).

121 Mile End, Middlesex (now Greater London)
1501 Court (pl; or Mile End, Essex? **957**, p 37).

122 Montacute, Somerset
1447-8 Tintinhull ('king'; **1459**).

123 New Romney, Kent
Town players are recorded in 1432-3 and a local Resurrection or
Passion play 1456-1518; by 1555 the Passion play has returned at
Whitsuntide (**1203-5**, **1207-9**).
1428 Lydd (pl; **1161**; Finn, p 15).
1430 Lydd (pl; **1161**; Finn, p 26).
1432 Lydd (pl; **1161**; Finn, p 43).
1437 Lydd (showing 'sport'; **1161**; Finn, p 69).
1439-40 Lydd (showing May; **1161**; Finn, p 75).
1440-1 Lydd (pl; **1161**; Finn, p 79).
1450-2 Lydd (ls; **1161**, p 91).
1454 Lydd (ls showing l; **1161**, p 92).
1462-3 Lydd (pl; **1161**, p 94).
1466 Lydd (pl showing p; **1161**, p 95).

1474-5 Rye (pl; **1344**, p 494).
1476-7 Lydd (pl; **1161**, p 97).
1479-80 Lydd (bc; **1161**, p 98).
1503-4 Hythe (bc; **788**, p 85).
1516-17 Lydd (bc; **1161**, p 99).
1525-6 Lydd (bc; **1161**, p 102).
1532-3 Lydd (bc; **1161**, p 104).
1547-8 Dover (b/pl; **609**, p 40).

124 Newark-on-Trent, Nottinghamshire
1541 Belvoir Castle (children pl; **371**, p 313).

125 Northrepps, Norfolk
1515-16 Hickling Priory (l; **773**, p 18).

126 North Walsham, Norfolk
1512-13 Hickling Priory (l of Beccles and 'Walss''; **773**; Galloway-
Wasson; Beadle, p 18, expands to 'Walss*ingham*').

127 Norwich, Norfolk
Liturgical drama at the cathedral begins ca 1260 (**1218, 1222**), and in
1469 a special pageant is performed for Queen Elizabeth by 'Fakke'
and his boys (**1225**). Whitsun pageants and plays dominate civic drama
here through the 15th and 16th centuries (**1221, 1227**).
1406 Mettingham College (lt; **1181**, p 126).
1472-3 Mettingham College (three lt with two l; **1181**, p 127).
1515-16 Hickling Priory (l; **773**, p 18).

128 Nottingham, Nottinghamshire
1541 Belvoir Castle (pl; **371**, p 313).

129 Ombersley, Worcestershire (now Hereford and Worcester)
1535 Battenhall (Robin Hood; **368**, p 405).

130 Oxfordshire
Perhaps these are the players of John de Vere, earl of Oxford (for
whom see below).
1496 Court (pl; **957**, p 30).

131 Perth, Tayside
1503 Court (Robin Hood; **1713**).

132 Picardy, Flanders
1475-6 Dover (one pl; **609**, p 26).

133 Plymouth, Devon
There are Corpus Christi players here as late as 1516, and other town players in 1544-5 (**1301, 1302**).
1521-2 Dunheved (pl of Plymouth and Launceston; **612**).

134 Reading, Berkshire
Local players, from 1433-4 to 1557, performed not only plays on many scriptural subjects including Adam and Eve, Cain, the kings of Cologne, and the Passion, but Robin Hood and King plays (**1315-24**).
1489-90 Sandwich (pl; **1374**, p 148).

135 Riccall, Yorkshire, E.R. (now North Yorkshire)
1527-8 Selby (four ld; **1377**; I, 336-7).

136 Ringstead, Norfolk
1475 Snettisham (g; **1401**).

137 Ripon, Yorkshire, W.R. (now North Yorkshire)
Local 'ludentes' appear on religious feasts 1439-48 (**1340**).
1457-8 Fountains Abbey (ls; **680**, p 61).

138 Riston, Long (Yorkshire, E.R., now Humberside)
1445-6 Beverley (proclamation of *li*; **379**, pp 98, 233-4).

139 Rochester, Kent
1521-2 Lydd (pl; **1161**, p 101).
1539-40 New Romney (pl; **1202**, p 135).

140 Roding, Essex
1533 Dunmow (p; **614**; no 865, p 339).

141 Ruckinge, Kent
1430 Lydd (pl showing p; **1161**; Finn, p 27).
1430-1 New Romney (p; **1202**, p 541).

142 Rye, Sussex (now East Sussex)
The town Resurrection play was performed in 1522 (**1346**).
1478-9 Lydd (ls; **1161**, p 97).
1493-4 New Romney (bc/l; **1202**, p 125).
1495-6 New Romney (bc/l; **1202**, p 126).
1518-19 New Romney (ls of Winchelsea and Rye; **1202**, p 131).
1520-1 Lydd (pl; **1161**, p 101).

143 St Albans, Hertfordshire
In 1444 the town had a play of Sir Eglamour and his son Degrabell
(**1353**).
1502 Court (pl; **957**, fol 8v).

144 St Mary in the Marsh, Kent
1512-13 New Romney ('lusorum beate marie,' two miles north of
    New Romney; **1202**, p 130).

145 Sandon, Essex
1453 Maldon (pl; **1167**, p 181).

146 Sandwich, Kent
The town records give no evidence of a local troupe (**1374**).
1483-4 Dover (pl; **609**, p 28).
1484-5 Dover (pl; **609**, p 29).

147 Sedgeford, Norfolk
1506 Snettisham (May; **1401**).
1507 Snettisham (May; **1401**).
1508 Snettisham (May; **1401**).
1509? Snettisham (May; **1401**).
1535 Snettisham (May; **1401**).

148 Shelfanger, Norfolk
1508-9 Thetford (p; **1448**; Galloway-Wasson).

149 Sherborne, Dorset
There was a Corpus Christi play here 1543-73 (**1378-9**).
ca 1553-8 Lyme Regis (pl; **1165**, p 39).

150 Shernborne, Norfolk
1506 Snettisham (May; **1401**).
1507 Snettisham (May; **1401**).

151 Sindlesham, Berkshire
1421-2 Reading (pl of Sindlesham and Sonning; **1315**, p 173).

152 Sittingbourne, Kent
1516-17 Lydd (pl; **1161**, p 99).
1517-18 Lydd (pl; **1161**, p 100).
1521-2 Lydd (pl; **1161**, pp 101-2).

153 Sleaford, Lincolnshire
There was an Ascension play here in 1480 (**1399**).
1541 Belvoir Castle (four pl, not playing; **371**, p 321).

154 Slimbridge, Gloucestershire
1420-1 Berkeley Castle (lt; **372**).

155 Snaith, Yorkshire, W.R. (now Humberside)
1323 Cowick (four pl/is; **583**).

156 Solihull, Warwickshire (now West Midlands)
1522 Wollaton Hall (pl; **1523**, p 338).
1523 Wollaton Hall (pl; **1523**, p 364).

157 Sonning, Berkshire
1421-2 Reading (pl of Sindlesham and Sonning; **1315**, p 173).

158 South Elmham, Suffolk
1473-4 Mettingham College (two lt; **1181**, p 127).

159 South Malling, Sussex
1506 Rye (pl of Towne Mallyng; **1345**).
1520-1 Battle Abbey (pl; or Malling, near Maidstone, Kent? **369**,
  p 105).

160 Spalding, Lincolnshire
The town had a playing place as early as 1391 (**1410**).
1532 Wigtoft (bc; **1488**).
1533-4 Thetford (io; **1448**; Galloway-Wasson).

161 Stallingborough, Lincolnshire
1514-15 Grimsby (p; **737**, p 12).

162 Stamford, Lincolnshire
Perhaps these garments were hired for the town's Corpus Christi play
1465-83 (**1412**).
1472   Peterborough (hire of pl? garments by John Glaseer; **1298**, p 9).

163 Stanstead Abbots and St Margaret, Hertfordshire
1541 Bishop's Stortford (p; **384**, p 43).

164 Stoke-by-Nayland, Suffolk
1466 Tendring Hall, Stoke-by-Nayland (pl; **1419**, p 325).
1529 Boxford (p; **393**).
1530 Boxford (p; **393**).
1532 Boxford (p; **393**).
1534 Boxford (p; **393**).

165 Stoke Rochford, or North and South Stoke, Lincolnshire
1541 Belvoir Castle (four pl; **371**, p 321).

166 Stone, near Appledore, Kent
1468-9 Lydd (pl/bc; **1161**, p 95).

167 Stow Maries, Essex
1469 Maldon (ls showing p; **1167**, p 181).

168 Suffolk
1512 Court (four pl; **976**, p 1454).
1542 London (p; **1038**).

169 Surrey
1500-1 Dover (pl; **609**, p 32).

170 Swineshead, Lincolnshire
1524-5 Sutterton (pl; **1426**, p 92).
1525 Wigtoft (bc; **1488**).
1525-6 Boston ('Baynerdes'/p; **389**, p 4).
1526 Leverton (pl/bc; **841**, p 20).

171 Tamworth, Staffordshire
A Corpus Christi play is recorded here 1536-9 (**1433**).
1521 Wollaton Hall (pl; **1523**, p 337).

172 Taunton, Somerset
A Mary Magdalene play was done in the town by 1504.
1535-6 Exeter (four playing lads; **669**; Wasson).

173 Tenterden, Kent
1489-90 Dover (pl; **609**, p 30).
1518-19 Lydd (pl; **1161**, p 100).
1519-20 Lydd (pl; *ibid*).
1520-1 Battle Abbey (pl; **369**, p 105).

174 Thanet, Isle of, Kent
1467-8 Dover (pl; **609**, p 24).

175 Thirsk, Yorkshire, N.R. (now North Yorkshire)
1457-8 Fountains Abbey (ls; **680**, p 59).

176 Thorington, Suffolk
1481 Stoke-by-Nayland (pl of 'Turton Strete'; **1420**, p 104).

177 Topcliffe, Yorkshire, N.R. (now North Yorkshire)
1457-8 Fountains Abbey (ls; **680**, p 59).

178 Torrington, Devon
1478-9 Barnstaple (ld; **363**).

179 Ulting, Essex
1459 Maldon (p; **1167**, p 181).

180 Upper Broughton, Nottinghamshire
1524 Wollaton Hall (pl of 'Browton'; location uncertain; **1523**, p 379).

181 Wakefield, Yorkshire, W.R. (now West Yorkshire)
Corpus Christi pageants appear here ca 1556-76 (**1467**).
1446 York (one lt; **1567**, p 67).

182 Walsham le Willows, Suffolk
A game place is recorded here 1533-81 (**1470**).
1505-6 Thetford (Walsham and Gislingham g; **1448**, p 5).

183 Walsoken, Norfolk
1555-6 Long Sutton (pl; **1156**, p 71).

184 Welby, Lincolnshire
1499-1500 Grimsby (townsmen riding their l; **737**, p 11).

185 Wenhaston, Suffolk
1493 Walberswick (g showed; **1468**).

186 West Wittenham, Berkshire (now Oxfordshire)
1360 Oxford (p; **1243**).

187 Whaplode, Lincolnshire
1518-19 Sutterton (pl; **1426**, p 91).
1530-1 Sutterton (pl riding p; **1426**, p 92).

188 Wigan, Lancashire (now Greater Manchester)
1541 Belvoir Castle (pl; **371**, p 312).

189 Wimborne Minster, Dorset
The church house here has plays as late as 1589 (**1492**).
1494 Court (pl; **957**, p 28).

190 Wincanton, Somerset
1557 Sherborne (town rents pl garments; **1378**, p 9).
1558 Sherborne (town rents pl garments; *ibid*).

191 Winchelsea, Sussex (now East Sussex)
1476-7 Rye (pl; **1344**, p 495).
1516-17 Lydd (pl; **1161**, p 99).
1518-19 New Romney (ls of Winchelsea and Rye; **1202**, p 131).

192 Withern, Lincolnshire
1547-8 Louth (bc/p; **1158**, p 83).

193 Wittersham, Kent
1426-7 New Romney (showing interlude; **1202**, p 540).
1440 Lydd (pl showing p; **1161**; Finn, p 79).
1441-2 New Romney (showing p; **1202**, p 542).

194 Wokingham, Berkshire
1385-6 Reading (lt; **1315**, p 172).
1423-4 Reading (lt; **1315**, p 173).
1427-8 Reading (lt; *ibid*).

195 Woodham Ferrers, Essex
1453 Maldon (pl; **1167**, p 181).

196 Worcester, Worcestershire (now Hereford and Worcester)
Corpus Christi pageants were played here 1424-1566, and Robin Hood
plays 1519-30, but players' apparel is mentioned in 1556 as part of the
goods of a draper, William Specheley, and in 1576 as cathedral property (**1527**, **1529**, **1532-4**).
1530 Battenhall (four pl; **368**, p 303).
1555-6 Dover (pl with the children of Worcester; **609**, p 42).

197 Wotton, Gloucestershire
1420-1 Berkeley Castle (lt; **372**).

198 Wrexham, Clwyd
1540 Shrewsbury (interls/lt; **1387**; Owen, p 330).

199 Writtle, Essex
The first duke of Buckingham had disguisings here in 1442-4, and
even by 1521 it was a family manor (Rawcliffe, p 67). This troupe may
belong to the third duke's retinue.
1507 Thornbury (four ls; **1450**, pp 324-5).

200 Wye, Kent
1491-2 New Romney (bc; **1202**, p 125).

201 Wymondham, Norfolk
The town play is recorded 1538-52, but a will of 1519 listing play stuff
suggests an earlier history of town drama (**1549-52**).
1515-16 Hickling Priory (l; **773**, p 18).
1533-4 Thetford (io; **1448**; Galloway-Wasson).
1537 Hunstanton (pl; **787**; Galloway-Wasson).
1537-8 Thetford (io; *ibid*).

202 Yateley, Hampshire
1419-20 Reading (ls; **1315**, p 173).

203 Yetminster, Dorset
1555-6 Sherborne (townsmen rent pl garments; **1378**, p 8).

204 York (now North Yorkshire)
At present the only evidence that the home of the best-known civic
Corpus Christi cycle (**1560**) had ecclesiastical players of this sort is a
clerk's possession of play-books in 1376, and a play by four clerks
before Henry VII in 1486 (**1559, 1572**).
nd Hedon (pl; *temp.* Hen. V-Edw. VI; **759**, p lxii).
ca 1496 Selby (ld of the abbey of Mary; **1377**; I, 334-5).
1527-8 Selby (five ld/five boys of the abbey of Mary lt; **1377**; I, 336-7).

205 Unidentified places
1489 Snettisham ('Walsyrton' g; identified by Galloway-Wasson as
being in Norfolk but otherwise unlocated; Walsoken, Norfolk?
1401).
1555-6 Banbury ('Dycher and Bramley plays'; **359**, p 16).

B COMPANIES IDENTIFIED BY PATRON OR PLAYER TO 1558

References to each playing company are listed chronologically under
the surname of the troupe's patron or principal player. A typical entry
consists of the date of the record, the site visited by the troupe, the
abbreviated name for that troupe in the record, and a bibliographical
reference. I have briefly summarized such evidence that exists about a
troupe's actors and movements and activities and is found in the main
body of this guide.

206 Anne Boleyn (ca 1507-36)
2nd queen of Henry VIII (28 May 1533-17 May 1536). The queen's
players (in 1534 John Slye led a company of four and in 1535 William
Slye was the chief player):
1534 Worcester (four pl; **1532**, p 388).
1535 Battenhall (pl; **368**, p 405).

207 Anne of Cleves (1515-57)
4th queen of Henry VIII (6 January-9 July 1540). The queen's players:
1540 Court (pl; **1027**; no 380, p 179).

208 Arthur (1486-1502)
Prince of Wales, first son of Henry VII. The prince's players:
1494-5 New Romney (ls; **1202**, p 126).
1495-6 Shrewsbury (pl; **1387**; Owen, I, 267).
1498-9 London (ls; **961**, p 119).
1499 Court (pl; **957**, p 34).
1500-1 Wells (pl; **1479**, p 164).
1501 Court (pl; **957**, p 36).

   Arundel, earls of. See under: Fitz Alan otherwise Mautravers, William (1438-87); Fitz Alan, Thomas (1487-1524); Fitz Alan, William (1524-44).

209 Audley, Lady Elizabeth
2nd wife of Thomas, Baron Audley of Walden, and daughter of Thomas (Grey), marquess of Dorset; seats at Walden monastery from 1538 and at Christchurch, or Cree Church, Aldgate, London, by 1531 (*CP*, I, 348-50). Lady Audley's players:
1547-8 Saffron Walden (pl; **1348**, p 41).

210 Audley, Thomas (ca 1488-1544)
Baron Audley of Walden, and Lord Chancellor 1533-44; for his seats, see above under Lady Elizabeth Audley (*CP*, I, 348-50). The Lord Chancellor's players:
1537 Court (pl; **1027**; no 782, p 333).
1537-8 Canterbury (pl; **503**, p 10).
1538 Court (pl; **1027**; no 782, p 334).
1538-9 Thetford (io 'domini schaunler'; **1448**; Galloway-Wasson).
1539 Cambridge (pl; **440**; I, 394).
1539-40 Thetford (io; **1448**; Galloway-Wasson).

211 Bale, John (1495-1563)
Antiquarian; playwright; Reformation preacher; probably in the employment of Thomas Cromwell, Lord Privy Seal (Davies, pp 203-30). Bale and his fellows, perhaps to be identified with Cromwell's troupe (for which see below):
1538 Canterbury (pl; **505**; no 782, p 337).
1539 Canterbury (pl; **506**).

212 Ballys, Thomas
Leader? of a two-man company, the other being William Freman.
1521-2 Thetford (io; **1448**; Galloway-Wasson).

213 Barbor, Richard
With his fellows, performing a 'ludo.'
1476-7 Barnstaple (l; **363**).

Bath, earl of. See under: Bourchier, John (1539-61).

214 Beaufort, Thomas (before 1397-1426)
Duke of Exeter (1416-26); seat at Greenwich (CP, V, 200-4). Boys of?
1426 Eltham (four boys playing is; **637**).

Bedford, earl of. See under: Russell, Francis (1555-85).

215 Belknap, Sir Edward (ca 1472-1521)
Royal councillor; one responsible in part for the hall at Guines for the
Field of the Cloth of Gold in 1521 (W.C. Richardson, *Tudor Chamber
Administration 1485-1547* [1952], pp 198-214); seat at Weston, Warwickshire. Mister Belknap's players:
1519 Worcester (four pl; **1532**, p 77).
1520 Worcester (four pl; **1532**, p 99).
1521 Wollaton Hall (pl; **1523**, p 334).
1524 Wollaton Hall (pl servants of Mr Beltnoppe and Mr Lewsys
     [perhaps Lewys appe John, a Welshman]; **1523**, pp 378-9).

Bergavenny, Baron. See under: Nevill, George (1492-1535).

216 Berkeley, Henry (1534-1613)
Lord Berkeley (1553-1613); seat at Berkeley Castle, Gloucs. (CP, II, 138).
Lord Berkeley's players:
1556-7 Bristol (pl; **410**; II, 209).

Berners, Baron. See under: Bourchier, John (1474-1533).

217 Boleyn, George (ca 1505?-36)
Viscount Rochford (1529-30), Baron Rochford (before 13 July 1530-6),
Lord Warden of the Cinque Ports (1534-6; CP, X, 140-2; XI, 51). The
Lord Warden's players:
1535-6 Lydd (pl; **1161**, p 104).

218 Bourchier, Henry (ca 1404-83)
Earl of Essex (1461-83), Lord Treasurer (1455-6, 1460-2, 1471-83), and
Steward of the Household (1463-71; CP, V, 137-8). The earl of Essex's
players:
1469 Maldon (ls/lt; **1167**, p 181).
1482 Stoke-by-Nayland (pl; **1420**, p 149).

219 Bourchier, Henry (ca 1473-1540)
Earl of Essex (1483-1540); seat at Gaynes Park, Essex (CP, V, 138-9).
The earl of Essex's players:
1482 Stoke-by-Nayland (pl; **1420**, p 149).
1499 Court (pl; **957**, p 34).
1514-15 Dover (pl; **609**, p 34).
1526-7 Stoke-by-Nayland (four pl; **1421**).

220 Bourchier, John (ca 1468-1533)
Lord Berners (ca 1467-1533), Chancellor of the Exchequer (1516-27),
and Deputy of Calais (1520-6, 1531-3; CP, II, 153-4). Lord Berners'
players:
1529-30 Dover (pl; **609**, p 38). Thetford (io; **1448**; Galloway-Wasson).

221 Bourchier, John (ca 1500-61)
Earl of Bath (1539-61); seats at Tawstock, Devon, and in Milk Street,
London (CP, II, 16-17). The earl of Bath's players:
1540-1 Barnstaple (pl; **364**; Wasson).
1542-3 Barnstaple (pl; **364**; Wasson). Bristol (pl showing pastime; **410**;
    II, 208).
1546 London (pl; **1052**).

222 Brandon, Charles (ca 1484-1545)
Duke of Suffolk (1514-45), who married Mary, the French queen and
sister of Henry VIII; seats at Suffolk Place, Southwark, Tattershall,
Lincs., and Westhorpe Hall (CP, XII.i, 454-61). *Hick Scorner* (ca 1514)
has been suggested as written for an early troupe sponsored by Brandon. The duke of Suffolk's players:
1520-1 King's Lynn (jo and bearward; **814**).
1525 Shrewsbury (four interls; **1387**; Owen, I, 328).
1529-30 Southampton (pl; **1403**, p 41).
1530 London (pl; **943**, p 137).
1530-1 Southampton (pl; **1403**, p 42).

1531 London (pl/two p; **943**, p 184).

1531-2 Great Yarmouth (ld; **692**; Galloway-Wasson).

1532-3 Thetford (io; **1448**; Galloway-Wasson).

1538 Court (pl; **1027**; no 782, p 334).

1538 Cambridge (pl; **440**; I, 392).

1538-9 Thetford (io; **1448**; Galloway-Wasson).

1539 Cambridge (pl; **440**; I, 394).

1539-40 Louth ('servants videlicet fabule actoribus'; **1158**, p 82). Lydd (pl; **1161**, p 105).

1540 York (earl of Suffolk's pl; **1577**, p 269).

1540-1 Bristol (pl, not playing; **410**, II, 208). Lydd (pl; **1161**, p 105).

1541 Court (pl; **1027**; no 1489, p 700).

1541-2 Dover (pl; **609**, p 39). Folkestone (pl; **678**, p 69). Lydd (pl; **1161**, p 105).

223 Brandon, Sir Thomas (?-1510)

See *DNB*, II, 1132. His children:

1508 London (children pl; **971**).

224 Braye, Sir Edward

His interluders:

1549 Shrewsbury (in of Sir John Brydges and Sir Edward Braye; **1387**; Owen, I, 330).

1550-1 Norwich (pl; **1229**; Galloway).

225 Brewderer, Walter

Leader? of a troupe of fellow 'ludentes':

1428 Glastonbury (lt; **682**, p 141).

226 Brews, Sir Thomas

Seat at Topcroft, Norfolk. His 'lusores':

1454-5 Mettingham College (ls/lt with pp; **1181**, p 127).

1473-4 Mettingham College (lt; *ibid*).

Bridgwater, earl of. See under: Daubeney, Henry (1538-48).

227 Brooke, George (ca 1497-1558)

Lord Cobham (1529-58), of Cobham, Kent; seat at Cowling Castle, Kent (*CP*, III, 347-8). Lord Cobham's players:

1538 Court (pl; **1027**; no 782, p 334).

228 Brooke, John (?-1512)
Lord Cobham (1464-1512; *CP*, III, 346-7), of Cobham, Kent. Lord
Cobham's players:
1489-90 Dover (pl; **609**, p 30).

229 Browne, James
Player?
1547-8 Plymouth (set forth an i; **1302**; Wasson).

230 Brydges or Bruges, John (1492-1557)
Baron Chandos of Sudeley (1554-7); seat at Sudeley Castle, Gloucs.
(*CP*, III, 126). Lord Chandos' players:
1549 Shrewsbury (in of Sir John Brydges and Sir Edward Braye; **1387**;
    Owen, I, 330).
1558-9 Gloucester (pl; **685**; II, 277).

Buckingham, dukes of. See under: Stafford, Edward (1485-1521);
Stafford, Humphrey (1444-60).

231 Bultell
Bultell and his company, game players:
1511-12 Swaffam (g pl; **1430**).

232 Catherine of Aragon (1485-1536)
1st queen of Henry VIII (1509-33). The queen's players:
1528-9 Thetford (io; **1448**; Galloway-Wasson).
1530-1 Southampton (pl; **1403**, p 42).
1530-2 Southampton (pl [entry deleted]; *ibid*).
1531-2 Oxford (ls; **1256**, p 49).

233 Catherine Howard (ca 1522-42)
5th queen of Henry VIII (8 August 1540-13 February 1542). The
queen's players:
1541 Court (pl; **1027**; no 1489, p 700).

234 Catherine Parr (1512-48)
6th queen of Henry VIII (12 July 1543-7). The queen's players (five
persons in 1545-6):
1543-4 Canterbury (pl; **503**, p 11).
1545-6 Dover (pl; **609**, p 40). General Records (five pl; **298**).

1546 Maldon (pl; **1167**, p 422). Norwich (pl; **1230**).
1546-7 Norwich (pl; **1229**; II, 362).
1547 Maldon (pl; **1167**, p 422).
1547-8 Bristol (pl; **410**; II, 209). Dover (late queen 'Katerynge' pl; **609**, p 40).

Chandos, lord. See under: Brydges or Bruges, John (1554-7).

235 Cheney, Sir Thomas (d 1558)
Lord Warden of the Cinque Ports (1542-58); Treasurer of the Royal Household. The Lord Warden's players:
1542-3 Canterbury (pl; **503**, p 10). Dover (pl; **609**, p 39). Folkestone (pl; **678**, p 69).
1543 London (four pl; **1041**).
1543-4 Folkestone (pl; **678**, p 70).
1544-5 New Romney (pl; **1202**, p 135).

236 ·Clinton otherwise Fiennes, Edward (1512-85)
Lord Clinton (1517-85); Chief Captain of Boulogne (1548-50); Lord Admiral (1550-3, 1557-85; CP, III, 317; VII, 690-3). Players of the Lord Deputy of Boulogne or of the Lord Admiral:
1548-9 Plymouth (pl; **1302**; II, 381).
1551? Lyme Regis (pl; patron uncertain and possibly Thomas Seymour or the previous Lord Admiral, John Dudley, earl of Warwick; **1165**, p 115).

237 Clyfton, Robert
Seat at Topcroft, Norfolk. His 'lusores':
1450-1 Mettingham College (ls; **1181**, p 126).

Cobham, lord. See under: Brooke, John (1464-1512); Brooke, George (1529-58).

238 Courtenay, Henry (ca 1498-1539)
Earl of Devon (1511-39) and first marquess of Exeter (1525-39); seat at Tiverton, Devon (CP, IV, 330-1; V, 216). The marquis of Exeter's players (a list of the marquis' servants in 1538 notes singers, musicians, a fool, and one Thomas Wright, 38, a harper, singer, and juggler who can 'make pastetymes' (L. & P. Hen. VIII, XIII.ii, no 755, pp 293-4]; see also below under Grey, Thomas):

1527 Doubtful Records (pl; **1800**).
1536-7 Belvoir Castle (pl; **371**, p 280).
1537 Court (pl; **1027**; no 782, p 333).

239 Crispe (or Cripps), Nicholas
Sheriff of Kent (1558-9). His players (identification uncertain):
1558-9 Lydd (Mr 'Cripes' pl; **1161**, p 106).

240 Cromwell, Thomas (ca 1485-1540)
Chancellor of the Exchequer (1533-40); Principal Secretary to the King
(1534-40); Lord Privy Seal (1536-40); Baron Cromwell (1536-40); and
earl of Essex (17 April-29 June 1540; CP, III, 555-7). Players of the Lord
Privy Seal, of the Secretary, or of Lord Cromwell:
1536-7 Cambridge ('mimis'/lt; **438**, p 151).
1537 Shrewsbury (ls; **1387**; Owen, I, 329).
1537-8 Leicester (pl; **833**, p 41). Oxford ('histriones'; **1277**, p 41).
   Thetford (io; **1448**; Galloway-Wasson).
1538 Cambridge (pl; **440**; I, 392).
1538-9 Barnstaple (pl; **364**; II, 105).
1539-40 Thetford (io; **1448** [rough draft accounts only]; Galloway-
   Wasson).
1540 Cambridge (pl; **440**; I, 396). Maldon (pl; **1167**, p 422). York (pl;
   1577, p 269).

241 Daubeney, Henry (1493-1548)
Lord Daubeney (1508-38); earl of Bridgwater (1538-48); seat at Bridgwater, Somerset (CP, II, 311; IV, 102-5)? Lord Daubeney's or the earl of
Bridgwater's players:
1532-3 Barnstaple (pl; **364**; Wasson).
1540-1 Barnstaple (pl; **364**; Wasson).
1544-5 Plymouth (pl; **1302**; II, 381).

242 Deor, William
Leader? of a troupe of his fellow 'ludentes.'
1428 Glastonbury (lt; **682**, p 141).

   Derby, earls of. See under: Stanley, Edward (1521-72); Stanley,
   Thomas (1485-1504).

243 Devereux, Walter (ca 1490-1558)
Lord Ferrers of Chartley (1501-); Viscount Hereford (1550-); seat at
Chartley (CP, V, 326-8). His players:
1530 Grimley (pl; **735**, p 305).

Devon, earl of. See under: Courtenay, Henry.

Dorset, marquess of. See under: Grey, Henry (1530-54).

244 Dudley, John (1502-53)
Lord Admiral (1543-7, 1549-50); earl of Warwick (1547-53); duke of
Northumberland (11 October 1551-3); seat at Ely Place, London (CP, IX,
722-6). The duke of Northumberland's players:
1551-2 Barnstaple (earl of Northumberland's pl; **364**; II, 117).
1552-3 Barnstaple (pl; **364**; Wasson). Leicester (pl; **833**, p 71).
1553-4 Warwick (pl; **1472**).

245 Dudley, Robert (1532/3-88)
Lord Dudley (1558-64)? earl of Leicester (1564-88; CP, VII, 549-53).
Lord Dudley's players:
1558-9 Norwich (pl; **1229**; II, 364).

246 Edward IV (1442-83)
Reigned 4 March 1461-September/October 1470, 11 April 1471-9 April
1483. The king's players (possibly minstrels; see also Alton, pp 40, 99).
1478-9 Wells (pl; **1479**, p 97).

247 Edward VI (1537-53)
Prince of Wales (1537-47); reigned 28 January 1547-6 July 1553; prin-
cipal seats at Greenwich, Westminster, Richmond, and Hampton
Court.

1 / Players or players in interludes of the prince or the king: there are
at least four players in 1538-9, led by Thomas Yely in 1539 (**943**, p
138), who does not appear otherwise as one of Henry VIII's players,
but from 1547 to at least 1552 six men are listed in the troupe, of
whom Robert Hinstock and George Birch, who led Henry VIII's players
towards the end of his reign, seem to be the principals; and Richard

Cooke (Cok, Coke), Richard Skinner, Henry Harriot (Hariot, Heryet; he disappears after 1552 [**1087**; Collier]), John Birch, and John Smyth (only in 1547) – who is replaced by Thomas Southey in 1548 (**1057, 1076**) – are the lesser members. In 1551-2 John Browne and John Young (or Yonge, a former member of Jane Seymour's troupe) are separately mentioned as players of interludes (**1058, 1074, 1076**).

ca 1537-44 Wulfhall (pl; **1547**, p 174).

1537 Shrewsbury (ls; **1387**; Owen, I, 329).

1537-8 Canterbury (pl; **503**, p 10). Court (pl; **1027**; no 1280, p 539). Exeter (pl; **669**; Wasson). Leicester (pl; **833**, p 41). Plymouth (pl of is; **1302**; II, 380). Southampton (pl; **1403**, p 42).

1538 Cambridge (pl; **440**; I, 392).

1538-9 Canterbury (pl; **503**, p 10). Plymouth (four pl; **1302**; II, 380). Sandwich (pl; **1374**, p 154). Thetford (io; **1448**; Galloway-Wasson).

1539 Cambridge (pl; **440**; I, 394). London (pl; **943**, p 138).

1539-40 Bristol (pl; **410**; II, 208). Faversham (pl; **675**, p 57). Plymouth (pl; **1302**; II, 380). Southampton (pl; **1403**, p 42).

1540 Cambridge (pl; **440**; I, 394). Court (pl; **1027**; no 380, p 179). Court (pl; **1034**, p 83). Shrewsbury (pl; **1387**; Owen, I, 330).

1540-1 Bristol (pl; **410**; II, 208). Faversham (pl; **675**, p 57). Lydd (pl; **1161**, p 105). New Romney (pl; **1202**, p 135).

1541 Beverley (pl; **379**, p 175). Court (pl; **1027**; no 1489, p 700).

1541-2 Norwich (pl; **1229**; II, 361). Plymouth (pl/i; **1302**; Wasson).

1542 Belvoir Castle (or London? pl; **371**, p 329).

1542-3 Dover (pl; **609**, p 39). Folkestone (pl; **678**, p 69).

1543-4 Canterbury (pl; **503**, p 11). Folkestone (pl; **678**, p 70). Great Yarmouth (pl; **692**; Galloway-Wasson). Norwich (pl, not playing; **1229**; II, 362).

1544 Cambridge (pl; **440**; I, 416).

1544-5 Barnstaple (pl; **364**). Canterbury (pl; **503**, p 11). Dover (pl; **609**, p 40). New Romney (pl; **1202**, p 135). Norwich (pl; **1229**; II, 362). Plymouth (pl; **1302**; II, 381).

1546-7 Canterbury (pl; **503**, p 11). Norwich (pl; **1229**; II, 362).

1547 Court (pl; **1057**, p 195; I, 138-9; p 280). Dover (pl; **609**, p 40).

1547-8 Cambridge ('ludionibus'; **438**, p 151). Canterbury (pl; **503**, p 11). Dover (pl; **609**, p 41).

ca 1547-53 Grimsby (pl; **737**, p 13).

1548 Bristol (pl; **410**; *Halliwell-Phillipps*, p 113). Cambridge (pl; **440**; II, 22). Court (pl; **1057**; I, 201, 203, 205; II, 17-18; **730**, p 31).

1548-9 Court (pl; **1057**, p 37). Faversham (date uncertain; pl; **675**, p 58). New Romney (pl; **1202**, p 136). Norwich (pl of i; **1229**; Galloway). Southampton (pl; **1403**, p 42).

1549 Court (pl; **1064**, p 39; **1057**, pp 20, 25-6, 31).

1549-50 Norwich (pl not playing; **1229**; II, 363; Galloway).

1550 Cambridge (pl; **440**; II, 49). Maldon (pl; **1167**, p 422).

1550-1 Canterbury (pl; **503**, p 12). Dover (pl; **609**, p 41). Lydd (pl; **1161**, p 105).

1551-2 Court (pl; **1058**, pp 57, 86).

ca 1551-6 Hoxton (pl; **782**).

1552 Court (pl; **1074**; **1076**). Lyme Regis (pl; **1165**, p 113; dated ca 1547-53, p 39).

1552-3 Court (pl; **1078**). Dover (pl; **609**, p 42). Lydd (pl; **1161**, p 106).

1553-4 New Romney (pl; **1202**, p 136).

2 / The gentlemen and children of the royal chapel. De Lafontaine gives two almost identical lists of twenty gentlemen, one in 1547 and the other in 1548 (pp 5-7, 21-2); and Stopes (*Hunnis*, pp 21-2) prints a third, undated list of 32 gentlemen, apparently of Edward's reign. The chapel members are as follows (names with an asterisk continue in the chapel under Mary): John Fisher (1547-8; from 1504), *Thomas Byrd/Byrde (1547-8; nd; from 1526), Henry Stevinson/Stephinson (1547-8; from 1509?), *William Hochins/Hychyns/Hutchins (1547-8; nd; from 1520?), Thomas Bury/Burye (1547-8; from 1520), Robert Phelipps/Philipps (1547-8; nd; from 1526), *Richard Bower/Bowyer (1547-8; nd; from 1526), Richard Pigott (1547-8; from 1526), John Perrye (1547-8), *William Barbor/Barber (1547-8; nd; from 1526), *Robert Richemountt/Richemound/Richmond (1547-8; nd; from 1526), John Allen (1547-8; from 1526), Richard Stephin (1547-8), *Thomas Wayte/Whayt/Waite (1547-8; nd), Robert Okelaund/Hockland (1527-8), *Thomas Tallis/Talys/Talles (1547-8; nd), *Nicholas Mellowe (1547-8; nd), Richard Kenricke/?Barwyck (1547-8), *Thomas Wrighte/Wright (1547-8; nd), William Poope (1547-8), Emery Tuckfield (nd; from 1526), Nicholas Aurchbalde (nd; from 1526), William Walker (1547-8; from 1526), Robert Chamberleyne (nd), John Leide (nd), William Gravesend (nd), John Angell (nd), *Robert Pirrey (nd; from 1526), *Robert Stone (nd), *John Benbowe (nd), *John Sheppheard (nd), *William Mauperley (nd), *George Edwards (nd), *Robert Morcocke (nd), *William Hynnes (nd), Thomas Manne (nd), *Richard Ayles-

worth (nd), *Thomas Palfreman (nd), *Roger Kenton (nd), *Lucas
Caustell (nd), *Richard Farrant (nd), and *Edward Adams (nd). In
1548-9 Richard Bower led the chapel children in playing at court.
1548 Court (pl; **1057**, p 201).
1549 Court (pl; **1057**, p 20).

248 Elizabeth of York (1465-1503)
Queen of Henry VII (1486-1503). The queen's players (possibly
minstrels):
1492-3 Wells (pl; **1479**, p 132).
1500-1 Wells (pl; **1479**, p 164).
1501 Cambridge (pl; **440**; I, 255).

Essex, earls of. See under: Bourchier, Henry (1461-83); Bourchier,
Henry (1483-1540).

Exeter, duke of. See under: Beaufort, Thomas (1416-26).

Exeter, marquess of. See under: Courtenay, Henry (1525-39).

249 Fakke
Leader? of boys' troupe.
1469 Norwich (**1225**).

Ferrers, Lord. See under: Devereux, Walter (1501-8).

250 Fitz Alan or Mautravers or Arundell, Thomas (1450-1524)
Lord Fitz Alan (by 1461), Lord Mautravers (by 1471), or Lord Arundell de Mautravers (by 1482); earl of Arundel (1487-1524); seat at
Arundel (*CP*, I, 249-50). Lord (or earl) of Arundel's players:
1492-3 Southampton (pl; **1403**, p 40).
1499-1500 New Romney ('ludarum'; **1202**, p 127).
1502-3 Sandwich (pl; **1374**, p 149).
1508-9 Sandwich (pl showing sport; **1374**, p 150).
1509 Battle Abbey (pl; **369**; *Halliwell-Phillipps*, p 101). Shrewsbury (pl;
  1387; *ibid*).
1513-14 Dover (pl; **609**, p 34).
1514-15 Dover (pl; *ibid*).
1516-17 Lydd (pl; **1161**, p 99). Sandwich (pl; **1374**, p 151).
1517-18 Lydd (pl; **1161**, p 100).
1518-19 Dover (pl; **609**, p 35).

1519 Shrewsbury (four interls showing diverse interludes; **1387**; Owen, I, 328).
1519-20 Lydd (pl; **1161**, p 101).
1520-1 Battle Abbey (pl; **369**, p 105).
1521-2 Southampton (pl; **1403**, p 41).
1522-3 Dover (pl; date uncertain; **609**, p 36).
1523-4 Lydd (pl; **1161**, p 102). Southampton (pl; **1403**, p 41).

251 Fitz Alan otherwise Mautravers, William (1417-87)
Earl of Arundel (1438-87); Constable of Dover Castle, and Warden of the Cinque Ports (1471, 1483-7); seat at Arundel (*CP*, I, 248-9). The lord (or earl) of Arundel's players:
1477-8 Dover (pl; **609**, p 26).
1478-9 Dover (pl; **609**, p 27).
1479 Battle Abbey (pl; **369**, p 104).
1479-80 Dover (pl; **609**, p 27). Lydd (ls; **1161**, p 98).
1483-4 Dover (pl; **609**, p 28).
1486 Southampton (pl; **1403**, p 40).

252 Fitz Alan, William (ca 1476-1544)
Earl of Arundel (1524-44); seat at Arundel (*CP*, I, 250). The earl of Arundel's players:
1524-5 Southampton (pl; **1403**, p 41).
1525-6 Southampton (pl; *ibid*).
1530 Poole (pl; **1306**).
1542-3 Norwich (pl; **1229**; II, 361).

253 Fitzroy, Henry (1519-36)
Natural son of Henry VIII by Elizabeth Blount; earl of Nottingham and duke of Richmond and Somerset (1525-36); seat at Sheriff Hutton (*CP*, X, 829-30). The duke of Richmond's (Somerset's) players:
1530-1 Bury St Edmund's (ls; **425**).
1531-2 Selby (ls; **1377**; I, 336-7).
1533 Cambridge (pl of the young duke; **440**; I, 361).
1533-4 Bristol (pl; **410**; II, 207; dated 1553 in *Halliwell-Phillipps*, p 142).

Fitz Walter, Viscount. See under: Radcliffe or Ratclyffe, Henry (1542-57); Radcliffe or Ratclyffe, Robert (1529-42).

French Queen, the. See under: Mary Tudor.

254 Giles, Robert
Leader? of a troupe of players.
1477-8 Dover (pl; **609**, p 26).

Gloucester, dukes of. See under: Lancaster, Humphrey of; Richard
III.

255 Gray, John
Lord John Gray; unidentified (a brother of Henry Grey, duke of
Suffolk? see Davey, p 183).
1526 Wollaton Hall (p from him; **1523**, p 386).

256 Gresby, Thomas
Unidentified 'ludenti.'
1531-2 Selby (lt; **1377**; I, 338-9).

257 Grey, Edward (before 1504-51)
Lord Grey of Powis (1504-51; CP, VI, 142-3).
1538-9 Lydd (pl; **1161**, p 104).
1546-7 Dover (pl; **609**, p 40).

258 Grey, Henry (1517-54)
Marquess of Dorset (1530-54); duke of Suffolk (1551-4; CP, IV, 420-1);
seats at Bradgate Old Manor, Leics., and Sheen (Davey, pp 1, 223). The
marquess of Dorset's players:
1536-7 Bristol (pl; **410**; II, 207).
1539-40 Plymouth (pl/i; **1302**; II, 380; and Worth, p 151).
1540 Bristol (pl; **410**, p 107).
1540-1 Bristol (pl; *ibid*).
1542-3 Barnstaple (pl; **364**; Wasson). Exeter (pl; **669**; Wasson).
1550-1 Norwich (pl; **1229**; Galloway).
1551 London (pl; **1071**).
1551 Poole (pl; **1306**).
1551-2 Norwich (gpl; patron uncertain; **1233**).

259 Grey, Thomas (1477-1530)
Marquess of Dorset (1501-30; CP, IV, 419-20); seat at Bradgate Old
Manor, Leics. (Davey, pp 1, 223).
1529-30 Thetford ('le playarys Domini markys,' either Grey, who had
  links with East Anglia and whose son became duke of Suffolk in

1551, or Henry Courtenay, marquess of Exeter [for whom see above]; **1448**; Galloway-Wasson prefer Courtenay).

260 Guildford, Sir Edward
Lord Warden of the Cinque Ports' players:
1529-30 Southampton (pl; **1403**, p 41).
1532-3 Sandwich (pl; **1374**, p 153).

261 Halle, Antony
Leader? of a troupe of five players; he was at board at Belvoir Castle some four weeks learning to play a play at Christmas.
1541-2 Belvoir Castle (five pl; **371**, p 322).

262 Hawtrell
Leader? of a troupe of three joiners.
1543 London (three ds; **1041**).

263 Hayn, William
Leader of a group of 'ludatores'?
1478-9 Barnstaple (ld; **363**).

264 Hemings, Mr
Leader or patron of a troupe of players.
1542-3 Bristol (pl; **410**; II, 208).

265 Henry VI (1421-71)
Reigned 1 September 1422-4 March 1461, September/October 1470-11 April 1471. The king's players (probably minstrels):
1451 Canterbury (pl; **495**, p 32).

266 Henry VII (1457-1509)
Reigned 22 August 1485-21 April 1509; seats at Greenwich, Westminster, and Sheen (later Richmond).

1 / The king's players, in lists of 1494 and 1503-4, include John English, Edward Maye (1494 only), Richard Gibson, John Hamond, William Rutter (1503-4 only), and John Scott (1503-4). At Edinburgh for the wedding festivities for Margaret Tudor and James IV, this troupe is led by John English, but by 1505-9 it is identified as Richard Gibson and his fellows. After Gibson became yeoman of the revels in the first

year of Henry VIII's reign, the acting troupe evidently was headed by English.

1494 Court (pl; **957**, p 28). Court (pl; **960**).
1496 Court (pl; **957**, p 30).
1497 Court (pl; **957**, p 31).
1498 Court (pl; **957**, p 32).
1500 Court (pl; **957**, p 35).
1500-1 Wells (pl; **1479**, p 164).
1501 Court (pl; **957**, p 36).
1502 Court (pl; **957**, p 38).
1502-3 Dover (pl; **609**, p 32). Thetford (ls; **1448**; Galloway-Wasson).
1503 Court (pl; **957**, fol 10r). Edinburgh (pl; **1664**).
1503-4 Cambridge (interls/lt; **438**, p 151). Court (pl; **968**). Dover (pl; **609**, p 32).
1505 Court (pl; **957**, fol 75r).
1505-6 Court (pl; **968**). Wells (pl; **1479**, p 196).
1507 Court (four pl; **957**, p 41).
1508-9 Court (ls; **968**). Sandwich (pl showing sport; **1374**, p 150).
1509 Court (pl; **957**, p 44).

2 / The gentlemen and children of the royal chapel. De Lafontaine prints a list of 18 gentlemen in 1504 (names with asterisks recur in the chapel under Henry VIII): Edward John, William Newerk*, John Sidburgh*, Thomas Bladesmyth, John Penne*, Henry Wilkyns, John Cornysh, John Prate, Robert Fairfaux*, John Petwyn*, Thomas Sexten*, William Sturton*, Robert Penne*, John Fyssher*, John Venner, John Fowler, William Tebbe, and William Browne*. Laurence Squier was master in 1488-9 (*Materials Hen. VII*, pp 390, 436). William Cornyshe senior was master of the chapel children ca 1480-90 and his son evidently succeeded him late in the reign (see below, App II).
1485 Doubtful Records (p; **1788**).
1501 Richmond (pg; **1326**).
1505 Court (pl; **957**, fol 75r).
1506 Court (four pl; **957**, p 40).
1507 Court (four pl; **957**, p 41).
1508 Court (five pl; **957**, p 43). Richmond (pl; **957**, p 44).
1509 Court (pl; **957**, p 44).

267 Henry VIII (1491-1547)
Reigned 22 April 1509-28 January 1547; principal seats at Eltham, Greenwich, Hampton Court, Richmond, and Westminster.

1 / Players of the Lord Warden of the Cinque Ports (1494-5?), of the prince, and of the king. By 1515-21 the king's players had split into two troupes: the 'old' players, probably led by John English (who was paid up to 1531) and including (probably) John Slye, William Rutter, Thomas Sudborough, and John Scott, were active until at least 1533 (**368, 389, 587, 735, 943, 976,** and p 1493, **1012, 1403**); and the new players, evidently including George Maller (Mayler), Thomas Arthur, and Richard Hole, and perhaps John Roll (probably 'Roo') and Sudborough (the former first recorded in 1530), probably travelled in the north ca 1527-8 and had five or six members in all (**273, 640, 1012**). By 1533 the players are led by Robert Hinstock (**943, 1027**; first recorded as a player in the Lord Mayor's pageant of 1519 [**969/5**]), George Birch, and George Maller, who is replaced ca 1540 by one Richard Parrowe. Two players in the king's payroll, John Slye (the same man?), a player ca 1538-40, and John Young, who took over grants to John Roo at his death in 1539, and then to Thomas Sudborough (Sudbury) at his death in 1546 (**1027, 1030, 1053**), are possibly attached to the queen's company (for which see under Anne of Cleves, Catherine Howard, and Catherine Parr), since they belonged in 1537-8 to Jane Seymour's troupe.

1494-5 Dover (pl; **609,** pp 31, 160).
1502 Court (pl; **957,** fol 8v).
1503 Court (pl; **957,** fol 41v).
1503-4 Thetford (ls; **1448;** Galloway-Wasson).
1504 Court (pl; **957,** fols 43v, 73r).
1505 Court (pl; **957,** p 40).
1505-6 Wells (pl; **1479,** p 196).
1506-7 Thetford (ls; **1448;** Galloway-Wasson).
1510 Court (pl; **976,** p 1444).
1512 Court (pl; **976,** p 1454). Poole (pl; **1306**).
1513 Calais (pl; **1744**).
1515 Court (old pl; **976,** p 1466). Doubtful Records (pl; **1795**). London (pl/two ps; **943,** p 136).
1515-6 Plymouth (jo; **1302;** Worth, p 150).
1516 London (pl; **943,** p 136).
1516-17 New Romney (ls; **1202,** p 131).
1517 London (pl/two ps; **943,** p 136).
1517-18 Sandwich (pl; **1374,** p 152). Shrewsbury (pl; **1387;** *Halliwell-Phillipps,* p 114).
1518 Ely Priory (pl; **643**).

1518-19 Dover (pl; **609**, p 35).

1519 Court (old pl; **976**, p 1533). Coventry (pl; **569**). London (pl/two ps; **943**, p 137). Mettingham College (jo; **1181**, p 128).

1520 Court (pl; **976**, p 1539). London (pl/two ps; **943**, p 137).

1520-1 Canterbury (pl; **503**, p 8). Lydd (pl; **1161**, p 101). Plymouth (jo; **1302**; II, 380).

1521 Court (old pl and pl; **976**, p 1543).

1523-4 Plymouth (jo; **1302**; II, 380). Southampton (pl; **1403**, pp 14, 41).

1524 Grimley (pl; **735**, p 198). Mettingham College (jo; **1181**, p 128). Tiverton (pl; **1463**, p 340).

1525 London (pl; **927**, p 13).

1525-6 Boston (ls; **389**, p 4). Dover (pl; **609**, p 37). Southampton (pl; **1403**, pp 14, 41).

1526 Eltham (pl; **640**). London (pl/two ps; **943**, p 183).

1526-7 Lydd (pl; **1161**, p 102). Mettingham College (jo/ls; **1181**, p 128). New Romney (pl/bc; **1202**, p 133). Plymouth (pl; **1302**; II, 380). Thetford (io; **1448**; Galloway-Wasson).

1526-8 Dartmouth (pl; **593**).

[1527] Crowle (four pl; **587**, p 252).

1527 London (pl; **943**, p 137). Shrewsbury (in; **1387**; Owen, I, 329).

1527-8 Canterbury (pl; **503**, p 9). General Records (pl; **273**). Selby (six ld; **1377**; I, 336-7). Thetford (pl; **1448**; Galloway-Wasson).

1528 Cambridge (pl; **440**; I, 327).

[1528] Grimley (pl; **735**, p 278).

1528-9 Exeter (pl; **669**; Wasson). London (pl; **1008**). Southampton (date uncertain; pl; **1403**, pp 14, 41).

1529 Court (pl; **1012**, pp 146, 149, 157, 308-9).

[1529] Grimley (four pl; **735**, p 298).

1529-30 Canterbury (pl; **503**, p 9).

1530 Court (pl; **1012**, pp 161, 170; I, 115, n 1). Hunstanton (pl; **787**; Galloway-Wasson).

1530-1 Belvoir Castle (pl; **371**, p 270). Bury St Edmunds (ls; **425**). Canterbury (pl; **503**, p 9). Faversham (pl; **675**, p 57). Lydd (pl; **1161**, p 103). Southampton (pl; **1403**, pp 14, 41).

1530-2 Southampton (pl; **1403**, p 42).

1531 Court (pl; **1012**, pp 174, 177). Dunheved (one pl; **612**).

1531-2 Canterbury (pl; **503**, p 9). Great Yarmouth (ld; **692**; Galloway-Wasson). Oxford (ls; **1277**, p 41). Leicester (pl; **833**, p 32). Thetford (pl; **1448**; Galloway-Wasson).

1532 Shrewsbury (ls/interls; **1387**; Owen, I, 329).

1532-3 Canterbury (pl; **503**, p 9). Durham (ls; **625**, p 143). Great Yarmouth (pl; **692**; II, 286). Thetford (pl; **1448**; Galloway-Wasson).
1533 Battenhall (pl; **368**, p 363). London (pl/two ps; **943**, p 184).
1533-4 Canterbury (pl; **503**, p 9). Dover (pl; **609**, p 38). Exeter (pl; **669**;
Wasson). Great Yarmouth (pl; **692**; II, 286). Southampton (pl; **1403**,
p 42). Thetford (pl; **1448**; Galloway-Wasson).
1534 Dunmow (pl; **614**, p 339). London (pl/two ps; **943**, p 138).
1534-5 Bristol (pl; **410**; II, 207). Canterbury (pl; **503**, p 9). Norwich
(pl; **1229**, p 361). Oxford (ls; **1277**, p 41).
1535 Worcester (four pl; **1532**, p 403).
1535-6 Bristol (pl; **410**; II, 207). Dover (pl; **609**, p 38). Thetford
(io; **1448**; Galloway-Wasson).
1536-7 Bristol (pl; **410**; II, 208). Canterbury (pl; **503**, p 10). Dover (pl;
609, p 38). Lydd (pl; **1161**, p 104). Oxford (ls; **1277**, p 41). Sandwich
(pl; **1374**, p 154).
ca 1536-44 Wulfhall (pl; **1547**, p 174).
1537 Court (pl/four pl of is; **1027**; nos 782, p 333, and 1284, p 438).
Hunstanton (pl; **787**; Galloway-Wasson).
1537-8 Barnstaple (pl; **364**; Wasson). Sandwich (pl; **1374**, p 154). Thetford (io; **1448**; Galloway-Wasson).
1538 Cambridge (pl; **440**; I, 392). Court (pl; **1027**; no 1280, pp 528-9,
539).
1538-9 Canterbury (pl; **503**, p 10). Lydd (pl; **1161**, p 104). Sandwich
(pl; **1374**, p 154). Windsor (pl; **1515**).
1539 Court (pl; **1027**; no 781, p 308; **1030**).
1539-40 Canterbury (pl; **503**, p 10). Faversham (pl; **675**, p 57). Lydd
(pl; **1161**, p 105). New Romney (pl; **1202**, p 134). Norwich (pl/gpl;
1229; Galloway). Southampton (pl; **1403**, p 42). Thetford (io; **1448**;
Galloway-Wasson).
1540 Court (pl/pl of i; **1027**; no 380, pp 179, 183, 185, 189). Hunstanton (gpl; **787**; Galloway-Wasson). London (pl; **943**, p 184). Shrewsbury (pl; **1387**; Owen, I, 330). York (pl; **1577**, p 269).
1540-1 Bristol (pl; **410**; II, 208). Canterbury (pl; **503**, p 10). Faversham
(pl; **675**, p 57). Lydd (pl; **1161**, p 105). New Romney (pl; **1202**, p
135).
1541 Beverley (pl; **379**, p 175). Cambridge (pl; **440**; I, 399). Court
(pl; **1027**; no 1489, p 700).
1541-2 Dover (pl; **609**, p 39). Faversham (pl; **675**, p 57). Lydd (pl;
1161, p 105).
1542 Court (pl; **1027**; no 880, p 478; **1039**). York (pl; **1577**, p 281).

1542-3 Canterbury (pl; **503**, p 10).
1544 Court (pl; **1034**, p 140). Hampton Court (pl; **747**, fol 68r).
1545 Court (pl; **1039**).
1545-6 Folkestone (pl; **678**, p 70).
1546 Court (pl/in; **1053**).
1546-7 Canterbury (pl; **503**, p 11). Norwich (pl; **1229**; II, 363).
1547 Maldon (or 1 Edward VI? pl; **1167**, p 422).

2 / The gentlemen and children of the royal chapel. De Lafontaine
prints two lists of gentlemen, 1509 (18 names)? and 1510 (21 names;
pp 4-5); and there are two later lists, one of 1520 (33 names) and the
other of 1526 (29 names; *L. & P. Hen. VIII*, III.i, no 704.2, p 245; and
IV.i, no 1939.10, pp 870-1). The chapel members are as follows (names
with an asterisk recur under Edward VI): William Newark (1509?
from 1504), John Smythe (1509?), Dr Robert Feyrefax/Farefax
(1509?-1520; from 1504), John Sudburgh/Sidborough/Sudborow
'(1509?-20; from 1504), William Cornysshe/Cornysh (1509?-20), John
Petwyn (1509?-11; from 1504), John Weyver/Wever (1509?-20), William Sturton (1509?-11; from 1504), Robert Penne/Pende, Pend
(1509?-26; from 1504), *John Fyssher/Fissher/Fisher (1509?-26; from
1504), William Dobeney/Dawbeney/Daubney (1509?-20), William
Brown/Browne (1509?-11; from 1504), Edward Johannes/John
(1509?-11), William Crane (1509?-26), John Penne/Pende (1509?-11;
from 1504), Thomas Sexton/Sexten (1509?-11; from 1504), *Henry
Stevynson/Stevenson/Stevinson/Stephinson (1509?-26), Henry Pren-
tyce/Prentisshe (1509?-11), Davy Burten/Burton (1510-20), Mr John
Lloidd (1510-20), Thomas Farthyng (1510-20), John Gyles/Giles
(1510-20), Robert Hawkins/Hawkyns (1510-20), Sir Roger Norton
(1520), Sir William Tofte (1520), Sir John Cole (1520), Sir John Muldre
(1520), Sir Andrew Yong (1520), Sir Thomas Hal/Haule (1520-6), Sir
William Blakeden (1520), Sir Richard Elys/Elles (1520-6), *Thomas
Bury (1520-6), John Tyl (1520), William Colman (1520-6), Thomas
Cheyny (1520), *William Hogeskyn (1520), Robert Jones/Johns
(1520-6), William Rothewel (1520), John Bunting (1520), Nicholas
Horneclif (1520), William Lambe (1520), Geoffrey Write (1520), Rich-
ard Ward (1526), ...y Dogget (1526), Thomas Westcot (1526), *Emery
Tuckfyld (1526), Andrew Trace (1526), *Nicholas Archbold (1526),
*William Walker (1526), *Robert Phillipps (1526), Avery Burnett
(1526), Hugh Roodes (1526), *Thomas Byrd (1526), *Richard Bower

(1526), *Richard Pygot (1526), Edmund Bekham (1526), *Robert Pury (1526), *William Barbor (1526), John Fuller (1526), *Robert Rychmount (1526), *John Alyn (1526), and John Stephen (1526). De Lafontaine also gives two lists of the chapel children, 1509 and ?1509 (pp 3-4). James Curteys appears only in the first list, and ten names are common to the two: William Colman, William Maxe, William Alderson, Henry Meryell (Merell), John Williams, John Graunger, Arthur Lovekyn, Henry Andrewe, Nicholas Ivy (Ive), and Edward Cooke (Coke). William Cornyshe, junior (see below App II) was master of the chapel children to about 1523, when he was granted a corrody in Thetford Priory on 10 August (*L. & P. Hen. VIII*, III.ii, no 3289, p 1372; cf II.i, no 2736, p 874; III.i, nos 999, 1114, pp 365, 408). William Crane was appointed master on 12 May 1526 (IV.i, nos 1939.9 and 2218, pp 869, 991; cf IV.iii, no 5738, p 2542, and V, no 559, p 255), and Richard Bower (Bowre) succeeded him 30 June 1545 (XX.ii, no 910.11, p 447).
1511 Court (d; **976**, pp 1496-8). Court (i/pg; **980**).
1512 Court (pl; **976**, pp 1454-5). Greenwich (pg; **700**).
1515 Court (pg; **704**). Shooters Hill (pg; **1385**).
1516 Eltham (p; **639**).
1517 Court (pg; **976**, pp 1474, 1509). Greenwich (pg; **706**).
1519 Court (pl/i; **976**, pp 1533, 1536). New Hall (p; **1201**).
1520 Court (two is; **976**, p 1539).
1522 Court (pg; **997**).
1524 Greenwich (d; **718**).
1527 Greenwich (p; **721**).
1529 Court (pl; **1012**, pp 146, 307).
1530 Court (pl; **1012**, p 161).
1531 Court (pl; **1012**, p 174).
1538 Court (pl; **1027**, p 538).
1540 Court (pl; **1027**, p 178). Greenwich (p; **728**).
1541 Court (pl; **1027**, p 699).
1544 Hampton Court (Crane playing; **747**, fol 67v).

268 Herbert, Henry (ca 1538-1601)
Lord Herbert (1551-70); earl of Pembroke (1570-1601); seat at Wilton House (*CP*, X, 410-12).
1556-7 Dover (pl; **609**, p 42).

Hertford, earl of. See under: Seymour, Edward (1537-52).

269 Hopton, Mr
Edward or Walter Hopton? a servant of Cromwell? Hopton's priest
and certain children are players.
1538 Court (pl/children; **1027**; no 782, p 335).

270 Howard, John (before 1436-85)
Lord Howard (before 1470-85), duke of Norfolk (1483-5); seat at
Stoke-by-Nayland (*CP*, IX, 610-12). For a doubtful identification of his
players, ca 1481-3, see **1420**.

271 Howard, Thomas (1473-1554)
Lord Treasurer (1522-47); duke of Norfolk (1524-47; attainted
1547-53); major seats at Norwich, Kenninghall, and Framlingham,
Norfolk, although at Tendring Hall, Stoke-by-Nayland, he rewarded
visiting players in 1526-7 (**1421**; *CP*, IX, 615-20). The duke of Norfolk's
players:
1529 London (pl; **943**, p 137).
1529-30 Thetford (io; **1448**; Galloway-Wasson).
1530 Oxford (two stage-pl; **1275**).
1530-1 Bury St Edmunds (ls; **425**).
1535-6 Norwich (pl; **1229**; II, 361). Thetford (io; **1448**; Galloway-
    Wasson).
1543 Cambridge (pl; **440**; I, 407).
1543-4 Canterbury (pl of Master Treasurer; **503**, pp 11, 175).

272 Howard, Thomas (1538-72)
Duke of Norfolk (1554-72); seats at Norwich and Kenninghall (*CP*, IX,
622-4). The duke of Norfolk's players:
1556-7 Exeter (pl; **669**; II, 270). Great Yarmouth (pl; **692**; Galloway-
    Wasson). Ipswich (pl; **795**, p 261). Norwich (pl; **1229**; II, 363).
1557 Cambridge (pl; **482, 440**; II, 132). Harwich (pl; **752**, p 337).
1557-8 Ipswich (pl; **795**, p 261).
1558 Lewes (pl; **842**). Maldon (pl; **1167**, p 422).
1558-9 Norwich (pl; **1229**; II, 363).

273 Inglis, Sir James
Sir James Inglis 'and his collegis,' players at the Scottish court.
1511 Court (pl; **1662**; IV, 321).

274 James V (1512-42)
1531 Edinburgh (Robin Hood; **1662**; V, 432).

275 Jane Seymour (1509?-37)
3rd queen of Henry VIII (30 May 1536-24 October 1537). The queen's
players included John Young, John Slye, David Sotherne (Sothurne),
and John Mounffeld, and were evidently led by Sotherne.
1537 Court (pl; **1027**; no 782, p 329). General Records (pl; **285**).
1538 Court (pl; **1027**; no 1280, p 539). London (pl/two ps; **943**, p 184).

276 Johnson, Patrick
Leader? of players in Linlithgow (see above, App I[A], under this site).
1475-6 Court (li; **1658**; VIII, 333).
1477 Court (li/'joccis'; **1658**; VIII, 404).
1477-8 Court (li/is; **1658**; VIII, 512).
1488 Court (pl; **1705**, p 313).
1489 Court (pl; **1705**, p 314).

> Kings. See under: Henry VI (1422-61, 1470-1); Edward IV (1461-83);
> Richard III (1483-5); Henry VII (1485-1509); Henry VIII (1509-47);
> James V (1513-42); Edward VI (1547-53); Mary, and Philip and
> Mary (1553-8)

277 Kingston, Sir Anthony (1519-56)
His father, Sir William Kingston, of Painswick, Gloucs., was comptroller of Henry VIII's household; Anthony was a member of the Privy
Council under Edward VI (*DNB*, XI, 185). His players:
1550-1 Gloucester (pl; **685**, p 465).
1551-2 Gloucester (pl; **685**, p 466).

278 Knygh (Knyth), John
Leader? of some parish 'ludentes.'
1403 Mettingham College (lt; **1181**, p 126).
1404 Mettingham College (lt; *ibid*).

279 Lancaster, Humphrey of (ca 1390-1447)
Duke of Gloucester (1414-47); seat, a manor house called 'Bella Court,'
at East Greenwich (*CP*, V, 730-7). There were Latin comedies written
by Tito Livio Frulovisi, to whom Humphrey was patron (**50**).
1430 Exeter (a company very doubtfully attri to him; **663**).

280 Leek, Sir Francis
1556 General Records (six-seven pl; **325**).

281 Lisle, Nicholas (ca 1445-1506)
Lord Lisle (1471-1506); J.P. for Hampshire (1480-1, 1486); seat at
Thruxton, Hampshire (CP, VIII, 45)?
1503 Southampton (pl; less likely to be John Grey, Viscount Lisle
  [1480-1504], for whom see CP, VIII, 61-2; **1403**; *Halliwell-Phillipps*,
  p 121).

Lisle, Viscount. See under: Plantagenet, Arthur (1523-42).

Lord Admiral. See under: Russell, John (1540-2); Seymour, Thomas
(1547-9); Clinton, Edward (1550-4).

Lord Chamberlain. See under: Radcliffe or Ratclyffe, Robert
(1540-2); Vere, John de (1526-40).

Lord Chancellor. See under: Audley, Thomas (1533-44).

Lord Privy Seal. See under: Cromwell, Thomas (1536-40); Russell,
John (1542-55).

Lord Protector. See under: Seymour, Edward (1547-9).

Lord Treasurer. See under: Howard, Thomas (1522-47); Paulet,
William (1550-72).

Lord Warden of the Cinque Ports. See under: Henry VIII
(1494-?1504); Guildford, Edward; Boleyn, George (1534-6);
Plantagenet, Arthur (1536-42); Cheney, Thomas (1542-58).

282 Manners, Henry (1526-63).
Earl of Rutland (1543-63); seat at Belvoir Castle (CP, XI, 255-7)?
1553 Belvoir Castle (pl; **371**, p 372).

283 Manthorp, John
Leader? of a company of boy 'lusores.'
1485 Mettingham College ('pro luso'; **1181**, p 128).

284 Mary (1516-58)
Reigned 19 July 1553-24 July 1554; as Philip and Mary 25 July
1554-17 November 1558; seats at Greenwich, Hampton Court, Richmond, and Westminster.

1 / Players of the Princess (1525-33/34; 'prynces players' should perhaps sometimes be read 'prince's players'), of the queen (ca 1555?-8), and of the king and queen (1555-8). In 1531 they included William Slye and three others; and in 1553-6 John Birch, Richard Cooke, and Thomas Southey (**1087**; Collier). The first performances of Udall's *Roister Doister* (ca 1552-3), *Respublica* (1553), and *Wealth and Health* (ca 1554-5) have been linked with this troupe.

1525 Shrewsbury (in; **1387**; Owen, I, 328).
1526 Worcester (pl; **1532**, p 230).
1529 Court (pl; **1012**, p 146; and p 308). London (pl; **943**, p 137).
1530 Court (pl; **1012**, p 161).
1531 Court (pl; **1012**, p 174).
[1531] Crowle (four pl; **587**, p 331).
1531-2 Leicester (pl; **833**; III, 32).
1532 Bristol (pl; **410**, p 131).
1532-3 Dover (pl; **609**, p 38).
1533-4 Bristol (pl; **410**; II, 207).
1553-8 Court (pl; **1087**).
1555-6 Canterbury (pl; **503**, p 134). Gloucester (pl; **685**, p 468).
  Ipswich (pl; **795**, p 260). Leicester (pl; **833**; III, 85).
1556 Beverley (pl; **379**, p 178).
1556-7 Barnstaple (pl; **364**; Wasson). Bristol (pl; **410**; II, 209). Exeter
  (pl; **669**). Ipswich (pl; **795**, p 261). Louth (servants; **1157**, p 84).
  Norwich (pl; **1229**; II, 363). Oxford (pl; **1291**, p 267).
1557 Beverley (pl; **379**, p 180).
1557-8 Dover (pl; **609**, p 42). Exeter (pl; **669**; Wasson). Leicester
  (pl; **833**; III, 92).
1558 Cambridge (pl; **440**; II, 145). Lyme Regis (pl; **1165**; II, 327; dated
  ca 1553-8, p 39). Maldon (pl; **1167**, p 422).

2 / The gentlemen and children of the royal chapel. There are two lists of the chapel gentlemen, both in 1553 (see Craven Ord, 'The Accompte of Sir Edwarde Waldegrave, Knighte, Oone of the Qwenes Highness Prevy Counceile, and Mr. of her Ma*ties* Greate Warderobe,' *Arch*, 12 [1796], 372-3; Charlotte C. Stopes, 'Mary's Chapel Royal and her Coronation Play,' *The Athenaeum*, 9 September 1905, p 347; cf Stopes, *Hunnis*, pp 22-3). The same 26 gentlemen appear in both, and there are, in addition, several yeomen and a dozen (unnamed) children. The gentlemen are as follows: William Hochine (Huchons; from 1520?), Thomas Byrde (from 1526), Richard Bowre (Bowere; from 1526),

Robert Pirrey (Perye; from 1526), William Barbor (Barbour; from 1526), Robert Richmounte (Richmonte; from 1526), Thomas Wayte (from 1547), Thomas Tallis (from 1547), Nicholas Mellowe (Melawe; from 1547), Thomas Wrighte (Wright; from 1547), John Bendebowe (from *temp*. Edw. VI), Robert Stone (from *temp*. Edw. VI), John Shepherde (from *temp*. Edw. VI), William Maperley (Mauperley; from *temp*. Edw. VI), George Edwardes (Edwards; from *temp*. Edw. VI), Robert Moorecocke (Morecocke; from *temp*. Edw. VI), William Hynns (Hinnes; from *temp*. Edw. VI), Richard Ayleworthe (Aleworth; from *temp*. Edw. VI), Thomas Palfreman (Palfreyman; from *temp*. Edw. VI), Roger Cotton (Centon? from *temp*. Edw. VI, as 'Kenton'), Luke Caustell (from *temp*. Edw. VI), Richard Farraunte (Farrante; from *temp*. Edw. VI), and Edward Adame (Addams; from *temp*. Edw. VI). Richard Bower was master of the children in January 1555 (**789**).
1553 Court (pl; **1085**).
1553-4 Court (pl; **1086**).
1555 Ingatestone Hall (or London; children; **789**).

285 Mary Tudor (1495-1533)
Sister of Henry VIII; queen of Louis XII (1514-15); wife of Charles Brandon, duke of Suffolk, 1515-33; seats at Suffolk Place and Westhorpe Hall (from 1515; Walter C. Richardson, *Mary Tudor: The White Queen* [1970]). Players of the French queen (probably identical with the duke of Suffolk's players at this time):
1521-2 Thetford (io; **1448**; Galloway-Wasson).
1527-8 Thetford (io; *ibid*).
1528-9 Southampton (pl; date uncertain; **1403**, p 41).

286 Marys, John
Leader? of a Robin Hood troupe.
1536 Stratton (pl/Robin Hood; **1425**, p 233).

287 Mason, William
Leader? of a company of parish? players.
1469-72 Bodmin (one pl? **386**).

288 Naseby, Richard
Leader? of a playing troupe in ?Bedfordshire.
1418 Everton (hires out pl garments; **653**).

289 Nevill, George (ca 1470-1535)
Lord Bergavenny (1492-1535); Constable of Dover Castle; Warden of
the Cinque Ports (*CP*, I, 31-3). Players of lord Bergavenny:
1503 Court (pl; **957**, fol 10r).
1509-10 Dover (pl; **609**, p 33).
1510-11 Sandwich (pl; **1374**, p 151).
1513-14 Dover (pl; **609**, p 34).
1516-17 Sandwich (pl; **1374**, p 151).
1517-18 Lydd (pl; **1161**, p 99). Sandwich (pl; **1374**, p 152).

290 Neville, Ralph (ca 1406/07-84)
Earl of Westmorland (1425-84; *CP*, XII.ii, 549-50).
1457-8 Fountains Abbey (ls; **680**, p 60).

291 Neville, Sir Thomas
ca 1553-8 Lyme Regis (pl; **1165**, p 39).

Norfolk, dukes of. See under: Howard, Thomas (1524-47). Howard,
Thomas (1554-72).

Northampton, marquess of. See under: Parr, William (1547-53,
1559-71).

Northumberland, duke of. See under: Dudley, John (1551-3).

Northumberland, earl of. See under: Percy, Henry Algernon
(1489-1527).

Nottingham, earl of. See under: Fitzroy, Henry (1525-36).

Oxford, earls of. See under: Vere, John de (1462-75, 1485-1513);
Vere, John de (1526-40); Vere, John de (1540-62).

292 Parr, William (1513-71)
Earl of Essex (1543-53); marquess of Northampton (1547-53, 1559-71);
Constable of Windsor Castle (1550-3); seat at Windsor (*CP*, IX,
669-74)? Lord marquess of Northampton's players:
1550-1 Leicester (pl; **833**, p 68).
1551 Cambridge (pl; **440**; II, 60).
1552 Maldon (pl; **1167**, p 422).
1552-3 Dover (pl; **609**, p 42).
1553 Harwich (pl; **752**); Maldon (pl; **1167**, p 422); Windsor? (pl; **1516**).

293 Paulet, William (ca 1483-1572)
Earl of Wiltshire (1550-72); Lord Treasurer (1550-72); marquess of
Winchester (1551-72); seat at Basing, Hampshire (CP, XII.ii, pp 757-62).
The Lord Treasurer's players:
1552 Cambridge (pl; **440**; II, 65).

294 Percy, Henry Algernon (1478-1527)
5th earl of Northumberland (1489-1527); seats at Wressle and
Leconfield (CP, IX, 719-20). The lord of Northumberland's players are
recorded ca 1524-7 in his household book as a troupe of four (**1543**),
and presumably they would have been responsible for the interlude
that Percy's ceremonial order for Twelfth Night ca 1511-15 requires
for that feast (**1539**). The earl's almoner apparently supplied the troupe
with play-texts ca 1511-20 (**1540**; cf **92**). The earl also patronized a
separate body of chapel players who performed Nativity and Resurrection plays for him (**1543**).
1493 Court (pl; **957**, p 28)
1508 Thornbury (four ls; **1450**, pp 318-19).
1525-6 Doubtful Records (i; **1799**).

295 Plantagenet, Arthur (before 1484-1542)
Natural son of Edward IV; Viscount Lisle (1523-42); Governor of
Calais (1533-40); Warden of the Cinque Ports (1536-42; CP, VIII, 63-8).
Lord Lisle's or Lord Warden of the Cinque Ports' players (some of the
following entries after 1540-1 may belong to Sir Thomas Cheney's
troupe):
1526-7 Southampton (pl; **1403**, p 41).
1528-9? Southampton (pl; *ibid*).
1530 Poole (pl; **1306**).
1531-2 Lydd (pl; **1161**, p 103).
1532-3 Bristol (pl; **410**; II, 207).
1533-4 Bristol (pl; *ibid*).
1535-6 Bristol (pl; *ibid*). New Romney (pl; **1202**, p 134).
1536-7 Bristol (pl; **410**; II, 207).
1537-8 Lydd (pl; **1161**, p 104). Sandwich (pl; **1374**, p 154).
1538 Court (pl; **1027**; no 782, p 334). London (Lady Lisle hires pl
     garments; **1028**).
1538-9 Lydd (pl; **1161**, p 104). New Romney (pl; **1202**, p 134). Sand-
     wich (pl; **1374**, p 154).

1539-40 Faversham (pl; **675**, p 57). Lydd (pl; **1161**, p 105). New
    Romney (pl; **1202**, p 135).
1541-2 Dover (pl; **609**, p 39). Folkestone (pl; **678**, p 69). Lydd (pl; **1161**,
    p 105). New Romney (pl; date possibly 1542-3; **1202**, p 135).

296 Plumpton, Sir William
Patron or leader of 'lusores.'
1456-7 Fountains Abbey (ls; **680**, p 18).

297 Pontisbery, John
1479 Winchester (with his fellow lt; **1501**, p 98, n 2).

Princes. See under: Arthur (1486-1502); Henry VIII (1502-9);
    Edward VI (1537-47).

Princess. See under: Mary.

298 Pynchebek, Sir John
Leader of players?
ca 1472 Peterborough (hires pl garments; **1298**, p 10).

Queens. See under: Elizabeth of York (1486-1503); Catherine of
    Aragon (1509-33); Anne Boleyn (1533-6); Jane Seymour (1536-7);
    Anne of Cleves (1540); Catherine Howard (1540-2); Catherine Parr
    (1543-8); Mary (1553-8).

299 Radcliffe or Ratclyffe, Henry (ca 1507-57)
Viscount or lord Fitz Walter (1529-42); earl of Sussex (1542-57); seat
at Attleburgh, Norfolk (Hampson, pp 60-8; *CP*, V, 488; XII.i, 520-2).
Lord Fitz Walter's or the lord of Sussex' players:
1543 Cambridge (pl; **440**; I, 407).
1543-4 Norwich (pl with i; **1229**; II, 361; Galloway).
1544-5 Barnstaple (pl; **364**; Wasson). Norwich (pl not playing; **1229**; II,
    362; Galloway). Plymouth (pl; **1302**; II, 381).
1546-7 Dover (pl; **609**, p 40).
1547 Maldon (pl; **1167**, p 422).
1555-6 Dover (pl; **609**, p 42).

300 Radcliffe or Ratclyffe, Robert (ca 1483-1542)
Viscount Fitz Walter (1525-42); earl of Sussex (1529-42); Lord Chamberlain (1540-2); seat at Attleburgh (Hampson, pp 50-60; *CP*, XII.i,
517-20). The earl of Sussex' players:

1535-6 Dunmow (pl; **614**, p 340).

1537 Maldon (pl; **1167**, p 181).

1537-8 Thetford (io; 'domini fywatyr comitis'; **1448**; Galloway-Wasson).

1538-9 Thetford (io 'domini fyvewares'; **1448**; Galloway-Wasson).

1539 Cambridge (pl; **440**; I, 394).

1540 Maldon (pl; **1167**, p 422).

1540-1 New Romney (**1202**, p 135).

1541 Maldon (pl; **1167**, p 422).

1541-2 Bristol (pl; **410**; II, 208). Plymouth (pl/i; **1302**; II, 381). Southampton (pl; **1403**, p 42).

301 Reef, William
Leader? of a group of 'ludentes.'
1390 Hedon (lt; **759**, pp li, 140).

302 Richard II (1367-1400)
Reigned 22 June 1377 to 29 September 1399. The king's ?mummers:
ca 1377-99 General (mms; **224**).

303 Richard III
Duke of Gloucester (1461-85); reigned 26 June 1483-22 August 1485; seats at Middleham and Sheriff Hutton while duke (CP, V, 737-41).
Lord of Gloucester's players:
1482-3 Stoke-by-Nayland (four pl; **1420**, p 336).

304 Richmond, earl of (ca 1546)
Identity unknown; Henry VII was the last earl, and the title of Henry Fitzroy, duke of Richmond (1525-36), lapsed after his death until 1613 (CP, X, 828-31). His players:
1546 Cambridge (pl, paid only 20d.; **440**; I, 440).

Richmond, duke of. See under: Fitzroy, Henry (1525-36).

305 Rocheford, lord
Identity unknown: the viscountcy of Rochford became extinct at the death of Sir Thomas Boleyn, 12 March 1539 (CP, X, 140; XI, 51). Lord of 'Rochefordes' players:
1550-1 Canterbury (pl; **503**, pp 12, 177).

306 Russell, Francis (1527-85)
Lord Russell (by 1553); earl of Bedford (1555-85); seats at Chenies,
Bucks., Woburn Abbey, and Russell (or Bedford) House, on the Strand,
Middlesex (CP, II, 75-6). Lord Russell's players:
1552 Belvoir Castle (pl; **371**, p 372). Shrewsbury (in; **1387**; Owen, I,
  330).
1552-3 Barnstaple (pl; **364**; *Halliwell-Phillipps*, p 142).

307 Russell, John (ca 1485-1555)
1st lord Russell (1539-?50); Lord Admiral (1540-2); Lord Privy Seal
(1542-55); 1st earl of Bedford (1550-5); seats at Chenies, Bucks., and
Russell House, on the Strand, Middlesex (CP, II, 73-5). Lord Admiral's,
Lord Russell's, or Lord Privy Seal's players:
1540-1 Plymouth (servants/i; **1302**; II, 380; Worth, p 159).
1541 Bristol (pl; **410**, p 142).
1544 Cambridge (pl; **440**; I, 415). Great Yarmouth (gpl; **692**; Galloway-
  Wasson).
1546-7 Barnstaple (pl; **364**; Wasson). Plymouth (pl; **1302**; Wasson).
1547-8 Plymouth (pl; **1302**; II, 381; Worth, p 159).
1552-3 Barnstaple (lord Russell's pl; **364**; Wasson).

  Rutland, earl of. See under: Manners, Henry (1543-63).

308 Scrope, Henry (ca 1534-92)
Lord Scrope of Bolton (1549-92); seat at Bolton Castle (CP, XI, 548-9).
Lord Scrope's players:
1557 Beverley (pl; **379**, p 180).

  Secretary (to the king). See under: Cromwell, Thomas (1534-40).

309 Seymour, Edward (ca 1500-52)
Brother of Jane, queen of Henry VIII, and uncle of Edward VI; earl of
Hertford (1537-52); Lord Protector (1547-9); duke of Somerset
(1547-52); seats at Wulfhall and Somerset House, on the Strand,
Middlesex (CP, XII.i, 59-65). The earl of Hertford's, Lord Protector's, or
lord of Somerset's players (one of them called Miles):
ca 1536-44 Wulfhall (pl; **1547**, p 174).
1539-40 Unidentified (earl of 'Hereford's' players [the last earl of this
  title died as Henry IV]; *Halliwell-Phillipps*, p 111).

1545 London (pl; **1046**).

1547-8 Cambridge ('famulo ... exhibentis ludicra spectacula'; **438**, p 151). Canterbury (pl; **503**, p 11). Dover (pl; **609**, p 40).

1548 Cambridge (pl; **440**; II, 22).

1548-9 Canterbury (pl; **503**, p 11). Dover (pl; **609**, p 41). Leicester (pl; **833**; III, 57). Lyme Regis (pl; **1165**, p 12). New Romney (pl; **1202**, p 136). Norwich (pl; **1229**; II, 363).

1550-1 Bristol (pl; **410**; II, 209).

1551 Cambridge (pl; **440**; II, 60).

before 1552 General Records (one pl; **316**).

310 Seymour, Thomas (ca 1508-49)
Younger brother of Edward Seymour, duke of Somerset; baron Seymour of Sudeley, Gloucs. (1546-9); Lord Admiral (1546-9); seats at Sudeley Castle and beside Temple Bar, London (CP, XI, 637-9). Lord Admiral's players:

1547-8 Dover (pl; **609**, p 41).

1548 Lyme Regis (pl; **1165**, p 115).

1548-9 Dover (pl; **609**, p 41). New Romney (pl; **1202**, p 136).

1549 Cambridge (pl; **440**; II, 44).

311 Shank, John
Leader of a company of 'lusores.'

1507-8 Mettingham College ('socijs suis'; **1181**, p 128).

1509-10 Mettingham College (ls; *ibid*).

1510-11 Mettingham College ('socijs suis ludendum'; *ibid*).

Shrewsbury, earl of. See under: Talbot, George (1473-1538).

312 Slade, John
Of Blunham, Beds., an owner of playbooks, playing properties, and playing garments.

1528 Little Barford (**875**).

Somerset, dukes of. See under: Fitzroy, Henry (1525-36). Seymour, Edward (1547-52).

313 Somerset, Sir George
Unidentified patron.

1549-50 Canterbury (pl; **503**, p 12).

314 Somerset, William (ca 1527-89)
Lord Herbert (-1549); earl of Worcester (1549-89); seats at Raglan
Castle and at Hackney, by St John's, near London (*CP*, XII.ii, 852-4).
Lord of Worcester's players:
1555-6 Barnstaple (men that played; **364**; II, 155).
nd Hedon (earl of Worcester's men, *temp.* Hen. V-Edw. VI; patron
    uncertain; **759**, p lxiv).

315 Stafford, Edward (1478-1521)
Duke of Buckingham (1485-1521); seats at Thornbury – where he
rewarded visiting players in 1507-8 and 1521 (**1450, 1451**) – London
(at the Red Rose), Bletchingly, and Penshurst (*CP*, II, 390-1; Rawcliffe,
pp 67-8). Duke of Buckingham's players:
1509 Court (pl; **957**, p 44).
1521 Wollaton Hall (pl; **1523**, p 334).

316 Stafford, Henry (ca 1479-1523)
Earl of Wiltshire (1510-23; *CP*, XII.ii, 738-9). Earl of Wiltshire's players:
1515 Court (pl, not playing; **976**, p 1466).
1516 Court (pl; **976**, p 1469).

317 Stafford, Humphrey (1402?-60)
Duke of Buckingham (1444-60; *CP*, II, 388-9). He had disguisings,
probably at his manor of Writtle, in 1443-4. Duke of Buckingham's
players (?minstrels):
1451 Canterbury (pl; **495**, p 32).

318 Stanley, Edward (1509-72)
Earl of Derby (1521-72); seat at Lathom House (*CP*, IV, 209-11). Earl of
Derby's players:
1530-1 Bury St Edmunds (ls; **425**). Ipswich (pl; **795**; Galloway-
    Wasson). Thetford (io; **1448**; Galloway-Wasson).
1531-2 Selby (ls; **1377**; I, 336-7).
1532 Dunmow (one pl; **614**, p 338).
1532-3 Bristol (pl; **410**, p 105). Durham (four ls; **625**, p 143).
1533 Cambridge (pl; **440**; I, 361; Riley, p 322, reads 'pleyer').
1533-4 Bristol (pl; **410**; II, 207). Thetford (io; **1448**; Galloway-Wasson).
ca 1533-46 Wulfhall (pl; **1547**, p 174).
1536 Cambridge (pl; **440**; I, 385).
1537-8 Leicester (pl; **833**; III, 41). Thetford (io; **1448**; Galloway-
    Wasson).
1538-9 Thetford (io; **1448**; Galloway-Wasson).

319 Stanley, Thomas (ca 1435-1504)
Earl of Derby (1485-1504); seats at Knowsley and Lathom (*CP*, IV, 205-7). Earl of Derby's players:
1495-6 Shrewsbury (**1387**; Owen, I, 267).

320 Stirop, Henry
Leader? of a group of 'lusores.'
1449 York (ls; **1567**, p 77).

Suffolk, duchess of. See under: Willoughby, Catherine (1533-80).

Suffolk, duke of. See under: Brandon, Charles (1514-45); Grey, Henry (1551-4).

Sussex, earls of. See under: Radcliffe or Ratclyffe, Robert (1529-42); Radcliffe or Ratclyffe, Henry (1542-57).

321 Talbot, George (1468-1538)
Earl of Shrewsbury (1473-1538); seats at South Wingfield Manor, Derbyshire, Sheffield Lodge or Manor (by 1530), and Cold Harbour, on Upper Thames Street, London (from 1509; *CP*, XI, 706-9). Earl of Shrewsbury's players:
1495-6 Shrewsbury (pl; **1387**; Owen, I, 267).

322 Teysdaile, William
Leader of playing troupe? a single player?
1544 London (pl rents hall; **1043**; I, 255).

323 Tockes, Mr
Patron of players?
1547-8 Dover (his pl; **609**, p 40).

324 Tongyshende
Leader? of a company of 'ludentes.'
1518-19 Thetford (lt; **1448**; Galloway-Wasson; Beadle, p 6, reads 'Congyshende').

325 Travaill, Jakke
Leader of (a French?) playing troupe, evidently of London at court.
1426 Eltham (pl; **637**).
1427 Eltham (making *jeux* and is; **638**).

326 Vere, John de (1442-1513)
Earl of Oxford (1462-75, 1485-1513); seat at Castle Hedingham and
?Earls Colne (CP, X, 239-44). The earl's household at Castle Hedingham had a Christmas disguising and pageant in 1490-1 (**517**), for
which the lord of Oxford's players were possibly responsible.
1492 Court (pl; **957**, p 27).
1497-8 Sandwich (pl; **1374**, p 149).
1498 Court (pl; **957**, p 32).
1498-9 Dover (pl; **609**, p 31).

327 Vere, John de (ca 1483-1540)
Earl of Oxford (1526-40); Lord Chamberlain (1526-40); seats at Castle
Hedingham and ?Earls Colne (CP, X, 245-7). Lord Chamberlain's
players, for whom John Bale wrote plays ca 1534-6 (**282**):
1537-8 Thetford (jo; **1448**, p 7; not in Galloway-Wasson).
1541-2 Plymouth (servants; **1302**; Worth, p 159).

328 Vere, John de (ca 1516-62)
Earl of Oxford (1540-62); seats at Castle Hedingham and ?Earls Colne
(CP, X, 247-50). Earl of Oxford's players:
1547 Southwark (pl; **1406**).
1549-50 Tilty Abbey (pl; **1458**).
1551-2? Tilty Abbey (pl; **1458**).
1552-3? Sheen (pl; **1337**).
1555-6 Dover (pl; **609**, p 42).
1556-7 Bristol (pl; **410**; II, 209). Dover (pl; **609**, p 42). Norwich
    (pl; **1229**; II, 363). Oxford (pl; **1291**, p 268).
1557-8 Bristol (pl; **410**; II, 209). Canterbury (pl; **503**, p 12). Ipswich
    (pl; **795**, p 261).

Warre, lord de la. See under: West, Thomas (1476-1525).

329 Wentworth, Thomas (1501-51)
Lord Wentworth (1529-51); seats at Nettlestead, Suffolk? and Stepney
and Hackney, Middlesex (from 1550; CP, XII.ii, 497-9). Lord Wentworth's players:
1542-3 Bristol (pl showing pastime; **410**; II, 208).
1544 Bristol (pl; **410**, p 148).

330 West, Thomas (ca 1457-1525)
Lord de la Warre and lord West (1476-1525); seat at Offington, Sussex
(CP, IV, 155-6)? Lord de la Warre's players:
1492-3 Southampton (pl; **1403**, p 40).

Westmorland, earl of. See under: Neville, Ralph (1425-84).

331 Wexmake, John
Leader of a group who performed 'ludi'?
1481-2 Barnstaple (l; **363**).

332 Willoughby, Katherine (1519-80)
Baroness Willoughby de Eresby; married Charles Brandon, duke of
Suffolk (1533), was widowed in 1545, and remarried her gentleman-
usher Richard Bertie (1553); seat at Grimsthorpe, Lincs. (CP, XII.ii,
673-5). Duchess of Suffolk's or Lady Suffolk's players (at least up to
1551, when her step-daughter Frances, wife of Henry Grey, duke of
Suffolk, also held that title, to her death in 1559):
1547-8 Canterbury (pl; **503**, p 11).
1548 Peterborough (pl; **1300**).
1550-1 Long Sutton (pl; **1156**, p 71).
1552-3 Dover (pl of 'the old duchess'; **609**, pp 41-2).
1553 Belvoir Castle (pl; **371**, p 372).

333 Wilmot, John
Leader? of his children players.
1530 London (children/p; **1013**).

Wiltshire, earl of. See under: Stafford, Henry (1510-23).

Worcester, earl of. See under: Somerset, William (1549-89).

334 Wyrly, John
Leader? of a troupe of 'ludentes.'
1408 Mettingham College (lt; **1181**, p 126).

II
An Index of Playwrights

λ

1 Adam, Lewes.
   1503 Court ds (**957**, p 39).

2 Adamsoun, William.
   1558 Edinburgh p (**1679**, p 183).

3 Alwyn, Walter.
   1493-4 Court r/d (**957**, p 28).

4 Arduenne, Remaclus.
   1512-13 Texts p (**91**).

5 Arthur, Thomas (d 1532), fellow of St John's College, Cambridge
   (Venn, I, 42).
   1520-32 Cambridge ps (**442**).

6 Ascham, Roger.
   ca 1543 Texts p (**131**).

7 Ashton, Thomas (d 1578), headmaster of Shrewsbury School (*ES*, III,
   210-11).
   1561 Shrewsbury p (**1394**).
   1566 Shrewsbury p (**1395**).
   1569 Shrewsbury p (**1396**).
   1587 Shrewsbury p (**1397**).

8 Atkinson, Mr, of Trinity College, Cambridge (possibly Thomas
   Atkinson, MA [1547], BD [1554]; Venn, I, 54).
   1549-51 Cambridge p/pl (**459**, pp 154-5).

9 Atkinson, John.
   1501-2 Court ds (**957**, pp 36-8).
   1501 Court pgs (**965**).

B., R. *see* Bower, Richard

10 Balcancole, Walter, notary public.
   1449 Aberdeen scribe or author CC li (**1624**, pp 61, 117).

11 Baldwin, William (Holden, pp 6-11; Emden 2, pp 32-3).
   1553 London p (**1081**).
   1555 London c (**1096**).

12 Bale, John (1495-1563), antiquarian, Reformation preacher, bishop
of Ossory (1552-3; Davies, pp 203-30; Beal, I, ii, 53-61).
   ca 1534-40 General ps (**282**).
   1536 Thorndon p (**1452**).
   1537-42 Court pl (**1027**).
   1538 Canterbury pl (**505**).
   1539 Canterbury p (**123, 506**).
   1546 General (**299**).
   1551 Bishopstoke p (**123, 385**).
   1553 Kilkenny ps (**123, 1741**).
   1555 General (**323**).
   1560 Canterbury p (**509**).

13 Barber, Thomas, of York.
   1456-9 Fountains Abbey CC l (**680**, pp 20, 65, 90-1).

Bariona, Laurentius *see* Johnson, Laurence

14 Barley, Mr, of Trinity College, Cambridge (possibly Henry Barley,
Proctor [1553-4]; Venn, I, 89).
   1556-7 Cambridge s with Mr Gray and Mr Boyes (**459**, p 158).

15 Barnarde, Mr, of Queens' College, Cambridge (probably John
Bernard or Barnard [d 1554], Fellow [1545-54]; Venn, I, 140).
   1550-1 Cambridge l/c (**449**, p 188).

16 Baston, Robert.
   ca 1314 Doubtful Records ts (**1766**).

17 Becon, Thomas (1512-67), protestant minister and divine (*DNB*, II, 92-4).
　　1547? Richmond p (**1335**).

18 Bird, William (*alias* Borne; active ca 1597-1622), actor (*ES*, II, 303).
　　1600-2 London p (**1133**).

19 Bourchier, John, Lord Berners.
　　ca 1520-33 Calais c (**1748**).

20 Bower, Richard (d 1561), master of the chapel children at Westminster (*ES*, II, 31-3).
　　ca 1567 Texts attri p (**171**).

21 Boyes, Mr, of Trinity College, Cambridge (possibly John Boyes, matriculated in 1552; Venn, I, 195).
　　1556-7 Cambridge s with Mr Barley and Mr Gray (**459**, p 158).

22 Bridges, John, dean of Salisbury.
　　ca 1551-4 Cambridge attri p (**469**).

23 Browne, Thomas (ca 1535-85), BA (1554-5), MA (1558), Fellow (1553-64); headmaster of Westminster (1564-70; Venn, I, 238; *DNB*, III, 63-4).
　　ca 1550-65 Cambridge t (**467**).

24 Buchanan, George, Scots humanist.
　　1562-3 Cambridge p (**485**).

25 Buck, John, schoolmaster of Norwich.
　　1556 Norwich pg (**1234**).
　　1558-9 Norwich i (**1235**).

26 Burges [John], MA, Magdalen College, Oxford.
　　1506-7 Oxford 'pro scriptura lusi' (**1256**, pp 46, 97).

27 Burgh, Benedict (Emden 1, I, 309).
　　ca 1440-83? Texts g (**52**).

28 Bynham, Thomas.
　　1423 Beverley CCp b (**376**, p 160).

29 Carle, servant to the French ambassador in London.
1537 London t (**1026**).

30 Cecil, William (1520-98), chief secretary of state under Elizabeth, and later Lord Burghley (*DNB*, III, 1315-21).
1559 London 'arguments' for cs (**1117**).

31 Chaloner, Sir Thomas (1520-65), clerk of the Privy Council, king's servant, and diplomat (*Folie*, pp xxix-xlv).
1552 Greenwich attri p (**732**).

32 Chamberleyn, Thomas, of Lincoln.
1420 Lincoln *visus* (**858**).

33 Chaundler, Thomas (ca 1417-90), Chancellor of Oxford University 1457-61, 1472-9 (Emden 1, I, 398-9; **1251**, pp 1-10).
ca 1457-61 Oxford p (**61, 1251**).

34 Chettle, Henry (ca 1560-before 1608), professional playwright (*ES*, III, 263-7).
1602 London p (**1135**).

35 Christopherson, John (d 1558), Fellow of St John's College, Cambridge (1542), of Trinity College (1546), and MA (1543; Venn, I, 336; *DNB*, IV, 293-5).
ca 1544 Cambridge p (**132, 452**).

36 Clerke, George, of Thame.
ca 1516-23 Thame writer of p (not copying parts; **1445**, p 71).

37 Cockroste, Mr, of Trinity College, Cambridge (Henry Cockcroft [d ca 1567], Fellow [1547], MA [1549]; Venn, I, 362).
1549-50 Cambridge p (**459**, pp 154-5).

38 Cooper, Dr D.
1514 Richmond so (**94, 1331**).

39 Cornyshe, William (d 1502), senior, master of the chapel children at Westminster ca 1480-90, and Gentleman of the Chapel Royal 1490-1502 (see Hugh Baillie [correspondence], *Music & Letters*, 36 [1955], 310-11; a

man of this name was paid for teaching the singing boys at the Almonry School, Westminster, in 1479-80 [Leach, pp 312-13]).

1494 London pg **(959)**.
1501 Court d/three pgs/so **(957**, p 37, and **965**/2).
1503 Court 'of the chapell' **(957**, fol 41v).
1504 Court 'of the chapell' **(957**, fol 44r).

40 Cornyshe, William (d ca 1524), junior, master of the chapel children for Henry VII and Henry VIII, and Gentleman of the Chapel Royal (see above, Baillie).

1509 Court pl **(957**, p 44).
1511 Court i/pg **(980)**.
1511-12 Thetford **(1448**; Galloway-Wasson).
1512 Greenwich pg **(700)**.
1514 Richmond doubtful i **(1331)**.
1515 Greenwich pg **(704)**.
1516 Eltham c **(639)**; Greenwich p **(705)**.
1517 Greenwich pg **(706)**.
1518 Court two pgs **(976**, p 1479).
1519 Court playing **(976)**; New Hall p **(1201)**.
1520 Calais pgs **(1746)**; Court two is **(976)**.
1522 London so **(104, 997)**.
1522 Greenwich ms **(717)**; Windsor p or f **(1514)**.

41 Cowpen, James de (fl 1290-1307), or Le Roy Caupenny, king of Heralds (Bullock-Davies, pp 77-9).
Lanercost Priory mi ps **(823)**.

42 Crowe, Robert.
1392-1580 Coventry pg **(554**[2]).
1525 Coventry pg **(571)**.
1556-7? Coventry pg **(554**[5]).

43 Dee, John (1527-1608), an original Fellow of Trinity College, Cambridge; later the famous mathematician and astrologer (DNB, V, 721-9).
ca 1546 Cambridge c **(456)**.

44 Dekker, Thomas (ca 1572-1632), professional playwright (JCS, III, 241-75).
1602 London p **(1135)**.
1612 London s **(1140)**.
1620-4 London p **(1144)**.

45 Dunbar, William.
   1480-1510? Edinburgh, formerly attri b (**73, 1659**).

46 Ederrington, Sir, of Trinity College, Cambridge (unidentified).
   1552-4 Cambridge ss (**459**, pp 156-7).

47 Edward VI.
   1547-8 Hampton Court c (**750**).

48 Elizabeth I (1533-1603).
   before 1558? Doubtful Records attri p (**1807**).

49 English, John, interluder for Henry VII and VIII.
   1501 Court pg (**957**, p 37, and **965**).

50 Forman, Andrew (d 1522), bishop of Moray, later archbishop of St
Andrews (*DNB*, VII, 436-7).
   1508 Edinburgh pg? (**1667**).

51 Foxe, John (1516-87), martyrologist, and Fellow of Magdalen College, Oxford (1539-45), and MA (1543; Emden 2, pp 214-15; Beal, I, ii,
93-8).
   1544-5 Oxford p (**133, 1284**).
   1545 Oxford c argument (**1285**).
   1556 Texts p (**156**).
   1562 Oxford c (**1293**).
   1562-3 Cambridge c (**485**).

52 Frulovisi, Tito Livio, playwright to Humphrey duke of Gloucester.
   1437-8 Texts cs (**50**).

53 Fulwell, Ulpian (d 1586), rector of Naunton (from 1570; Irving
Ribner, 'Ulpian Fulwell and his Family,' *N&Q*, 195 [1950], 444-8; and
his 'Ulpian Fulwell and the Court of High Commission,' *N&Q*, 196
[1951], 268-70).
   ca 1567-8 Texts attri p (**173**).

54 Fynglwyd, Iorwerth.
   ca 1450-1520 Texts attri ps (**57**).

55 Garter, Bernard (active ca 1565-79), professional pageant-maker
and writer, possibly brother of Thomas (ES, III, 319).
   1578 Norwich pg (**1236**).

56 Garter, Thomas (active ca 1562-89?), possibly brother of Bernard.
   ca 1562 Texts attri p (**164**).

57 Geoffrey, abbot of St Albans.
   ca 1100-19 Dunstable mi l (**616**).

58 Gibson, Richard, yeoman of the revels for Henry VIII.
   1526-7/1530-2 Lydd reviser of p (**1164**, pp 189, 199).

59 Godsalfe, ?Mr, of Trinity College, Cambridge (probably John Godsalfe, Scholar [1550]; Venn, II, 228).
   1551-2 Cambridge p (**459**, p 155).

60 Gray, Mr, of Trinity College, Cambridge (unidentified).
   1556-7 Cambridge s with Mr Barley and Mr Boyes (**459**, p 158).

61 Grimald, Nicholas.
   1541 Oxford p (**127, 1282**).
   ca 1541-6 Oxford p (**129, 1283**).
   ca 1541-62 General Records ps (**290**).
   1556 London pg (**969**[27], p 39).

62 Guildford, Sir Harry, Comptroller of the Royal Household, and
occasional master of the revels for Henry VIII.
   1514 Richmond i/mo (**1331**).

63 Haughton, William (active ca 1575-1605), professional playwright
(ES, III, 334-6).
   1600-2 London p (**1133**).

64 Hault or Haute, Jacques.
   1494-1500 Court many ds (**957**, pp 29-35).
   1501 Court ds/mos (**965**).

65 Hawes, Sir, of Trinity College, Cambridge (possibly Henry Hawes, Fellow [1555]; Venn, II, 333).
    1557-8 Cambridge ss with Sir Longe (**459**, p 159).

66 Helperby, Nicholas.
    1487-8 Hull p (**785**).

67 Henry VIII.
    1520 Calais mus (**1746**).

68 Herman, Guillaume, poet.
    ca 1200-30 Doubtful Texts attri p (**1762**).

69 Heywood, Jasper (1535-98), son of John Heywood, and a jesuit (*DNB*, IX, 780-2).
    1558 Oxford t (**159, 1292**).

70 Heywood, John (ca 1497-ca 1578), virginal-player to Henry VIII (Reed, pp 35-71; Emden 2, pp 288-9; Stratman 5826-75; Robert C. Johnson, *John Heywood* [1970]; Beal, I, i, 215-17).
    ca 1513-21 General p (**93**).
    ca 1519-28 Texts attri p (**98**); Texts p (**99**).
    ca 1520-2 Texts p (**102**).
    ca 1520-33 Texts p (**103**).
    1528-33 Texts p (**107**); Texts p (**108**).
    1538 Richmond ?i (**1334**).
    1539 Court m (**1029**).
    ca 1545-9 Texts p (**136**).
    1552 Hatfield? (**754**).
    1553 London pl in pg (**1083**[7]); London p (**1081**).

71 Hilarius (active ca 1125-30), Latin poet of Angers, France (*DNB*, IX, 831).
    ca 1130 Doubtful Texts ps (**1760**).

72 Hoby, Sir Thomas (1530-66), diplomat, and translator of Castiglione's *The Courtier* (*DNB*, IX, 949-50).
    1550 General t (**311**).

73 Hoker, John (d ca 1544), Fellow of Magdalen College, Oxford (ca 1533-43), MA (1535), BTh (1540; Emden 2, pp 292-3).
ca 1533-44 Oxford c (**1278**).

74 Howard, Sir George.
1553 Greenwich p/tr (**733**[3]).

75 Hunnis, William (ca 1530-1603), Master of the Children of the Chapel Royal (from 1566; Stopes, *Hunnis*; ES, III, 349-50).
ca 1525-9 Texts attri p (**128**).
ca 1557-8 Texts attri p (**158**).

76 Hutton, Sir, of Trinity College, Cambridge (possibly Matthew Hutton [1529-1606], BA [1551-2], Fellow [1553], MA [1555], Dean of York [1567-89], etc; Venn, II, 442; DNB, X, 357-8).
1552-5 Cambridge ss/p (**459**, pp 156-7, and **476**, p 158).

77 Ingelend, Thomas (ca 1520-50), of Christ's College, Cambridge.
ca 1550? Texts p (**145**).

78 Inglis, Sir James.
1511-26 Court pl (**1662**; IV, 321; V, 316).
ca 1511-26 General fs/ps (**1612**).

79 Johnson, Laurence (active ca 1570-7), of Christ's College, Cambridge (MA [1577]), and schoolmaster of Kettering, Northants (Venn, II, 479).
ca 1571 Cambridge attri p (**489**).

80 Jordan, William.
1611 Texts p (**189**).

81 Josselyn, *dominus*, of Queens' College, Cambridge (probably John Joscelyn or Josselin [1529-1603], BA [1548-9], Fellow [1549], MA [1552]; Venn, II, 490; DNB, X, 1092-3).
1550-2 Cambridge c/lusus/t (**449**, p 188).

82 Juby, Edward (d 1618), actor (ES, II, 325).
1602 London p (**1135**).

83 Katherine of Sutton, abbess of Barking.
1363-76 Barking Abbey ltd (362).

84 Kaye, Richard.
ca 1550-70 Texts ?pg (149).

85 Kay or Caius, Thomas (d 1572), Fellow of All Souls College,
Oxford (1525-43), university registrar (1534-52), and Master of University College (1561-72; Emden 2, pp 325-6).
ca 1525-74 Oxford ts (1274).

86 Kyllour, Friar.
ca 1535-6 Stirling pa p (1731).

87 Laborne, Mr, of Reading.
1534-6 Reading p (1320).

88 Lacocke, Sir, of Trinity College, Cambridge (possibly Richard
Lacock, Fellow [1555], BA [1557-8]; Venn, III, 57).
1558-9 Cambridge pl (459, p 159).

89 Lakyn, Mr, of St John's College, Cambridge (possibly John Lakyn
[d 1595], Fellow [1553], MA [1556]; Venn, III, 35).
1556-7 Cambridge p (477, p 221).

90 Langton, Stephen, archbishop of Canterbury.
ca 1200-30 Doubtful Texts attri p (1762).

91 Lauder (Lawder), William.
1549 Court p (1662; IX, 282).
1554 Edinburgh f/p (1676, p 182).
1558 Edinburgh p (1679, p 183).

92 Laurentius, prior of Durham.
ca 1149-54 Durham l? (620).

93 Legg, Sir, of Trinity College, Cambridge (probably Thomas Legge
[1535-1607], the Elizabethan playwright [DNB, XI, 854-5; ES, III, 407-9];
possibly his play on the destruction of Jerusalem was done at Coventry in 1584 [579]).
1558-9 Cambridge Sir Legg's and Sir West's pl (459, p 159).

94 Leland, John (ca 1502-52), antiquarian (Emden 2, pp 350-1; Beal, I, ii, 299-310).
   1533 London pgs (**1017**).

95 Lily, William (ca 1468-1522), grammarian and high master of St Paul's School (Emden 1, II, 1147).
   1522 London pgs (**998**).

96 Lindsay, Sir David (d 1555; W. Murison, *Sir David Lyndsay* [1938], pp 1-19; Beal, I, ii, 311-14).
   1511 Court pl/p (**1662**; IV, 313).
   1538 St Andrews f/?pg (**1722**).
   1540-54 Cupar, Edinburgh, Linlithgow, Perth pp (**124**, **1646**, **1675**, **1706**, **1714**).

97 Longe, Sir, of Trinity College, Cambridge (possibly Robert Longe, Fellow [1555], BA [1556-7]; Venn, III, 103).
   1557-8 Cambridge ss with Sir Hawes (**459**, p 159).

98 Lumley, Lady Jane (ca 1537-77; ES, III, 411).
   ca 1550? Texts p (**144**).

99 Lupton, Thomas (active 1572-84), pageant-maker and writer (ES, III, 411).
   ca 1572-7 Texts attri p (**184**).

100 Lydgate, John (ca 1370-1451), poet (Schirmer; Emden 1, II, 1185-6).
   ca 1412-34? London CC ordinance (**917**).
   1424 Eltham mu (**37**, **636**).
   ca 1424-30 London ?d (**38**, **924**); Stepney mu (**39**, **1414**); General ts/cs (**245**).
   1426-31 Texts ?p (**42**).
   1427 Hertford mu (**44**, **771**).
   ca 1427 London mu (**43**, **928**).
   1429 London mu (**47**, **931**); London mu (**46**, **930**).
   ca 1430 Windsor mu (**48**, **1512**).
   1432 London pgs description (**933**).
   1445 London pgs description (**937**).
   ca 1450-75 Texts attri pgs (**55**).
   ca 1475 Texts attri pg (**69**).

101 Malham, Mr, of Trinity College, Cambridge (probably John Mallam or Maulham [d ca 1557], Fellow [1548], MA [1549]; Venn, III, 130).
1551-2 Cambridge p (**468**, p 155).

102 Map, Walter (ca 1140-before ca 1210), author and courtier (*DNB*, XII, 994-7).
ca 1160-85 Texts attri c (**10**).

103 Markham, Gervase (ca 1568-1637), writer (*ES*, III, 417-18).
1622 London p (**1146**).

104 Martyn, Gover.
1560 New Romney deviser of p (**1209**, pp 208, 210).

105 Massinger, Philip (1583-1640), professional playwright (*JCS*, IV, 749-830).
1620-4 London p (**1144**).

106 Maye or Mey, John (d 1598), Fellow of Queens' College, Cambridge (1550-60), MA (1553), bursar of Queens' College (1554-5; Venn, III, 166; *DNB*, XIII, 141-2).
1551-2 Cambridge lusus (**468**, p 188).
ca 1553 Cambridge (**472**).
1553-4 Cambridge di/t (**475**, p 189).

107 Medwall, Henry (ca 1462-?after 1501), chaplain to Archbishop Morton (*Medwall*, pp 3-14, 163-9; Alan H. Nelson, 'Life Records of Henry Medwall, M.A., Notary Public and Playwright; and John Medwall, Legal Administrator and Summoner,' *LeedsSE*, NS 11 [1980], 111-55).
ca 1490-1500 Texts p (**78**).
ca 1496-7 Texts p (**81**).
1515 Doubtful Records i (**1795**).

108 Merbury, Francis (1555-1611; Trevor N.S. Lennam, 'Francis Merbury, 1555-1611,' *SP*, 65 [1968], 207-22).
ca 1571-7 Texts attri p (**183**).

109 Mettam, Mr, of Trinity College, Cambridge (possibly Thomas Metham, Fellow [1555], MA [1558]; Venn, III, 180).
1558-9 Cambridge pl (**459**, p 159).

110 Middleton, Thomas (1580-1627), professional playwright (*JCS*, IV, 855-911).
  1613 London pg (**1141**).

111 More, Sir Thomas (R.W. Chambers, *Thomas More* [1938]; Beal, I, ii, 347-54).
  before 1490 General extemporaneous di (**258**).
  ca 1495-9 Oxford p (**1259**).
  ca 1501 General cs (**262**).
  ca 1514-33 General descriptions of p (**267**).
  1518 ts/cs sent to (**268**).

112 Mulcaster, Richard (ca 1530-1611), London schoolmaster (*DNB*, XIII, 1172-3).
  1559 London attri pgs (**1116**).

113 Munday, Anthony (ca 1553-1633), professional playwright (*ES*, III, 444-50).
  1602 London p (**1135**).
  1611 London s (**1139**).

114 Nevyson, Mr, of Trinity College, Cambridge (probably Stephen Nevinson [d 1580], Fellow [1547], MA [1548]; Venn, III, 245; *DNB*, XIV, 309).
  1550-1 Cambridge pl (**459**, p 155).

115 Newton, Sir, of Trinity College, Cambridge (possibly Francis Newton, BA [1551-2], MA [1555]; Venn, III, 252).
  1552-4 Cambridge ss (**459**, pp 156-7).

116 Nicholas, Thomas.
  1547 Norwich his ?pg ?tableau (**1232**).

117 Nowell, Alexander (ca 1507-1602), headmaster of Westminster School (1543-55; Emden 2, pp 419-21).
  1544-7 Texts prologues (**135, 1044**).

118 Palsgrave, John (d 1554), grammarian (Emden 2, pp 429-30).
  ca 1540 Texts p (**125**).

119 Parfre, John, of Thetford.
  1512 Texts attri p (**90**).

120 Parker, Henry (1476-1556), lord Morley (*DNB*, XV, 238-40).
ca 1500-35 General cs/ts (**261**).

121 Parnell, of Dunmow.
1527-8 Dunmow maker of CC pgs (**613**, p 236).

122 Peche, a fool.
1494 Court d (**957**, p 28).

123 Peele, George (ca 1557-96), poet and playwright (*ES*, III, 458-64).
1591 London pg (**1129**).

124 Penny, Mr, of Trinity College, Cambridge (probably Thomas
Penny [d 1589], Fellow [1553], MA [1559]; Venn, III, 342).
1559-60 Cambridge p (**484**).

125 Perne, Mr, of Queens' College, Cambridge (probably Andrew
Perne [1519?-89], Fellow [1540], Proctor [1546-7]; Venn, III, 348; *DNB*,
XV, 896-7).
1543 Cambridge di (**451**).
1545-6 Cambridge cs, one with Mr Yale (**449**, p 184).

126 Pernell, of Ipswich.
1469 Norwich pgs (**1225**).

127 Phillip, John (active 1564-94; *ES*, III, 465-6; *STC* 19863-77).
ca 1564-5 Texts attri p (**168**).

128 Pilkington, Gilbert.
ca 1450-?1576 formerly attri p; see Oscar Cargill, 'The Authorship
of the *Secunda Pastorum*,' *PMLA*, 41 (1926), 810-31; Frances A.
Foster, 'Was Gilbert Pilkington Author of the *Secunda Pastorum*?'
PMLA, 43 (1928), 124-36; M.G. Frampton, 'Gilbert Pilkington
Once More,' *PMLA*, 47 (1932), 622-35 (**58**[13]).

129 Prewett, Sir Stephen (d ca 1559), priest.
1534 Norwich 'ballet' (for p? **1227**[3]).

130 Puddesay, Richard.
1486 Greenwich ds (**694**).

131 Pyers or Peres, Sir William, poet of Henry Algernon Percy, earl of Northumberland.
    1519-20 Beverley transposer of CC p (**376**, p 171).
    1525-6 Doubtful Records i (**1799**).

132 Radcliffe, Ralph (ca 1519-59), resident of Jesus College, Cambridge (1536-8), MA (1539), schoolmaster of Hitchin (Venn, III, 414; Emden 2, p 472; Hampson, pp 301-2).
    ca 1550-7 Hitchin ps (**775**).

133 Radcliffe, Robert (the same as above?).
    ca 1536-9? Cambridge three di (**119, 447**).

134 Rastell, John (ca 1476-1536), publisher (Reed, pp 1-28; Rastell, pp 4-10).
    1517-20 Texts p (**96**).
    ca 1520 Texts attri p (**101**).
    1521 London pg ('Rastell'; **969**).
    ca 1523-5? Texts attri p (**106**).
    ca 1524-6 Finsbury stage (**677**).
    1527 Greenwich ?pg ?tableau (**721**).

135 Raynolds, Mr, of Trinity College, Cambridge (possibly Richard Reynolds [d 1606], Fellow [1551], MA [1553]; Venn, III, 445; *DNB*, XVI, 954-5).
    1552-4 Cambridge cs (**459**).

136 Redford, John (1486?-1547), master of Paul's choristers under Henry VIII (Carl F. Pfatteicher, *John Redford: Organist and Almoner of St. Paul's Cathedral in the Reign of Henry VIII* [1934], pp 10-17, and Beamer, pp 82-108, 233-4 [**134**]).
    ca 1531-47? Texts i (**113**).
    ca 1531-47 Texts i (**114**).
    ca 1544-7 Texts p (**134**).
    1547-53? Texts couplet by (**142**).

137 Redmans, Sir, of Trinity College, Cambridge (possibly Robert Redman, BA [1557-8], MA [1561]; Venn, III, 436).
    1558-9 Cambridge s with Sir Shackelocke (**459**, p 159).

138 Reynolds, Walter.
  before 1313 General ?1 (**215**).

139 Ritwise, John.
  ca 1522-30 London t (**999**).
  1527 Greenwich t/f (**723**).
  1530 General Records cs (**275**; identity uncertain).

140 Robinson, Nicholas (d 1585), Fellow of Queens' College, Cambridge (1548-63), MA (1551; Venn, III, 472; *DNB*, XVII, 34-6).
  1550-4 Cambridge l/lusum/cs (**449**, pp 188-9, and **473**).

141 Roo, John.
  1526-7 London p/d/t (**1003**).

142 Rowley, Samuel (ca 1575?-after 1624), professional playwright (*JCS*, V, 1009-14).
  1600-2 London p (**1133**).
  1602 London ps (**1135**).

143 Rudd, Anthony (d 1615), Fellow of Trinity College, Cambridge (1569), MA (1570; Venn, III, 495).
  ca 1571? Cambridge attri p (**489**).

144 Rudde, Mr, of Trinity College, Cambridge (probably Richard Rudd [d ca 1560], Fellow [1545], BD [1554]; Venn, III, 496).
  1551-2 Cambridge p (**468**, p 155).

145 S., Mr, Master of Art (possibly Sir William Stevenson, for whom see below).
  ca 1551-4 Texts p (**150**).

146 Sampson, William (ca 1600-after 1655), occasional playwright (*JCS*, V, 1042-7).
  1622 London p (**1146**).

147 Sancto Austolo, Sir Reginald de (ca 1358), rector of St Just-in-Penwith.
  ca 1375 Penryn p (**1295**).

148 Sandes, William.
   1638 Preston s (**1308**).

149 Scogan, John (fl 1480), MA at Oxford, and jester to Edward IV
(*DNB*, XVII, 940-1).
   ca 1480 Doubtful Records attri cs (**1786**).

150 Shackelocke, Sir, of Trinity College, Cambridge (probably Richard
Shacklock, BA [1555-6], MA [1559], and Fellow; Venn, IV, 47; *DNB*, XVII,
1275).
   1557-9 Cambridge pl, s with Sir Redmans (**459**, p 159).

151 Sheprey, John (d 1541), Fellow of Corpus Christi College, Oxford
(1530-41), and lector in Greek (from 1533; Emden 2, pp 513-14).
   ca 1530-41 Oxford ps (**1276**).

152 Skelton, John (d 1529), poet laureate at Oxford and Cambridge
(by 1492-3; Emden 1, III, 1705-6; Robert S. Kinsman, *John Skelton, Early
Tudor Laureate: An Annotated Bibliography c. 1488-1977* [1979]; Beal, I, ii,
489-94).
   ca 1483-1523 General ps (**256**).
   1498 Doubtful Texts p (**1790**).
   1504? Doubtful Records p (**256**[6], **1794**).
   ca 1519-20 Texts p (**97**).
   1533 Texts p (**116, 256**[5]).

153 Smythe, Mr, of Oxford (probably John Smith [d 1616], scholar of
St John's College, Oxford).
   1584 Coventry t (**579**).

154 Spirleng, Geoffrey.
   1469 Norwich pg (**1225**).

155 Stevenson, Sir William (d 1575), of Christ's College, Cambridge,
BA (1549-50), Fellow (1551-4), MA (1553; Venn, IV, 159).
   1550-4 Cambridge ps (**445**, pp 206-7).
   ca 1551-4 Cambridge attri p (**150, 469**).

156 Still, John (1543?-1608), bishop of Bath and Wells (*DNB*, XVIII,
1257-60).
   ca 1551-4 Cambridge attri p (**469**).

157 Stille, Sir, of Trinity College, Cambridge (probably Henry Style
[d 1588], BA [1550-1], Fellow [1551], MA [1554]; Venn, IV, 181).
   1549-50, 1552-4 Cambridge p/pl/ss (**459**, pp 155-7).

158 Tarlton, Richard (d 1588), actor (*ES*, II, 342-5; III, 496-7).
   1588-91 Texts plot (**187**).

159 Thorpe, Master Richard, Fellow of Queens' College (1550-8), MA
(1553; Venn, IV, 236).
   1552-3 Cambridge t (**449**, pp 189, 198).

160 Thulace, Mr, of Trinity College, Cambridge (probably William
Thewles or Theulays, Fellow [1546], MA [1547]; Venn, IV, 218).
   1549-50 Cambridge p (**459**, p 154).

161 Udall, Nicholas (ca 1504/6-56), Fellow of Corpus Christi College,
Oxford (1524-33), MA (1534), headmaster of Eton College (1534-42;
Scheurweghs, pp x-liii; Emden 2, pp 586-8; *VCHBucks*, II, 182-6;
Edgerton; Beal, I, ii, 549-51).
   1533 London pgs (**115, 1017**).
   1537-9 Eton College p (**651**).
   1538 Court pl (**1027**, p 334).
   1538 Titchfield ps? (**1462**).
   ca 1543-8 General Records p? (**294**).
   ca 1547-8 Texts p (**138**).
   1553 London attri p (**151, 1085**).
   1553-8 Texts attri p (**153**).
   1554-5 London ps (**1091**).
   1564 Cambridge p (**486**).

162 Uxenbrydge, Sir, of Trinity College, Cambridge (probably Andrew
Oxenbridge [d 1615], BA [1552-3], Fellow [1553], MA [1555]; Venn, III,
292).
   1552-5 Cambridge ss/p (**459**, pp 156-8).

163 Wager, Lewis, rector of St James' Garlickhithe, London (1560 to
his death in 1562; Wayne H. Phelps, 'The Date of Lewis Wager's
Death,' *N&Q*, 223 [1978], 420-1).
   1547-66 Texts p (**143**).
   ca 1566 Texts attri p (**170**).

164 Wager, William (ca 1537-91), rector of St Benet, Gracechurch, and of St Michael at Queenhithe (Mark Eccles, 'William Wager and his Plays,' ELN, 18 [1980-1], 258-62).
  ca 1565 Texts attri p (169).
  ca 1566 Texts attri p (170).
  ca 1568 Texts attri p (176).
  ca 1568 Texts attri p (177).

165 Wapull, George (ca 1571-85), clerk of the Stationers' Company, London (ES, III, 505).
  ca 1571-5 Texts attri p (182).

166 Watson, Edward (Emden 2, p 610).
  1512 Oxford c (1266).

167 Watson, Thomas (ca 1515/16-84), Fellow of St John's College, Cambridge (1534), MA (1536), BD (1543; Venn, IV, 350).
  1536-44 Cambridge p (120, 448).

168 Wedderburne, James.
  ca 1540-5 Dundee cs/ts (1656).

169 Wedurby, John, of Leicester.
  1456 Coventry pgs (557).

170 Wendon, Sir, of Trinity College, Cambridge (probably Nicholas Wendon, Fellow [1552], MA [1554]; Venn, IV, 365).
  1552-4 Cambridge ss (459, p 156).

171 Wentworth, Master Harry.
  1507 Court d/mo (957, p 43).

172 West, Sir, of Trinity College, Cambridge (probably Robert West [d 1610], BA [1557-8], Fellow [1560]; Venn, IV, 370).
  1558-9 Cambridge pl of Sir Legg and Sir West (459, p 159).

173 Westcott, Sebastian, master of the choristers at St Paul's.
  ca 1551-4 Cambridge attri p (469).

174 Wever, R.
  ca 1550-3 Texts p (148).

175 Wheatley, William.
   1316 Doubtful Records attri p (**1767**).

176 Woodes, Nathaniel (ca 1550-after 1594), vicar of St Mary's, South Walsham, Norf (Celesta Wine, 'Nathaniel Woodes, Author of the Morality Play *The Conflict of Conscience*,' RES, 15 [1939], 458-63).
   ca 1572-80 Texts attri p (**185**).

177 Worsley, Ralph.
   1555 Texts ps (**155**).

178 Wylley, Thomas, of Yoxford, Suffolk.
   1537? Yoxford ps (**1589**).

179 Yale, Master, of Queens' College, Cambridge (probably Thomas Yale [1526?-77], Fellow [1544-57], MA [1546]; Venn, IV, 486; DNB, XXI, 1198).
   1545-7 Cambridge cs by Masters Perne and Yale (**449**, pp 184-5).

III

An Index of Playing Places and Buildings to 1558

1st-2nd centuries
1 Tomen-y-Mur (**1600**): remains of Roman amphitheatre.

1st-4th centuries
2 Calleva Atrebatum (Silchester; **1398**): remains of Roman amphitheatre.
3 Durnovaria (Dorchester; **606**): remains of Roman amphitheatre.
See RCHM *Dorset*, II.3 (1970), pp 589-92 and pl 227.
3.5 Frilford (**680.5**): remains of Roman amphitheatre.
4 Moridunum (Carmarthen; **1597**): remains of Roman amphitheatre.
4.5 Wycomb (**1754.5**): remains of Roman theatre?
5 Catterick (**518**): remains of Roman theatre.

1st-5th centuries
6 Corinium Dobunnorum (Cirencester; **542**): remains of Roman
amphitheatre.
7 Venta Silurum (Caerwent; **1596**): remains of Roman amphitheatre.

61-ca 210
8 Colchester (**550, 551**): remains of two Roman theatres, inside and
outside the town walls.

ca 70-ca 195
9 Noviomagus Reg(i)norum (Chichester; **538**): remains of Roman
amphitheatre.

ca 70-350
10 Deva (Chester; **523**): remains of Roman amphitheatre.

ca 80-ca 400
11 Canterbury (490): remains of Roman theatre, excavated.

ca 80-ca 1191
12 Isca (Caerleon; 1593, 1595): remains of Roman amphitheatre.

2nd-4th centuries
12.5 Cirencester (542.5): excavated remains of Roman theatre.

ca 100-200
13 Lindum (Lincoln; 847): Roman theatre or amphitheatre? no known remains.

ca 140-4
14 Brough-on-Humber (413): Roman theatre, without remains.

ca 140-ca 395
15 St Albans (1349): substantial ruins of Roman theatre.

ca 285-350
16 Rutupiae (Richborough; 1325): remains of Roman amphitheatre.

ca 300
16.5 St Albans (1349.5): Roman arena or possibly amphitheatre, without physical remains.

ca 605-40
17 Yeavering (1554): excavated remains of Northumbrian theatre.

965-1384
18 Winchester Cathedral (1493, 1495): surviving, from 12th century. See Morris, p 276 (and fig 3, plans of the Minster ca 648-1093); Frederick Bussby, Winchester Cathedral 1079-1979 (1979); VCHHants, III (1908), pp 50-9 (plan opp p 50; and pls 54, 56, 58 [interior]).

ca 1100-19
19 Kingsbury Regis, palace of (616): remains? See 'Kingsbury Earthwork,' RCHM Herts, p 192; a stone barn supposed in 1816 to have been the royal hall is described and depicted in Gentleman's Magazine, 120, pt 2 (July-December 1816), 393 (letter by G.O.P.T., and engraving opp p 393); and Colvin, II, 924-5.

ca 1149-1434

20 Durham Cathedral (620, 622, 623): surviving. See Morris, p 250;
The Victoria History of the County of Durham, III, ed William Page
(1928), pp 93-123 (the cathedral), 123-36 (monastic buildings), and
plan between pp 136-7; and *Medieval Art and Architecture at Durham
Cathedral*, ed Nicola Coldstream and Peter Draper, British Archaeological Assoc. Conf. Trans. for 1977 (1980), pp 11-48, and plan opp
p 3.

ca 1188-98

21 Lichfield Cathedral (843): surviving, but considerably rebuilt in the
18th-19th centuries. See Morris, p 257; Nikolaus Pevsner,
Staffordshire (1974), pp 174-89 (plan on p 176 and pls 16-17 [inte-
rior]); and *A History of the County of Stafford*, III, ed M.W. Greenslade
(1970), p 143.

1196

22 Eynsham Abbey (673): destroyed. See Sir Edmund Chambers, *Eynsham under the Monks*, Oxfordshire Rec. Society 18 (1936), pp 40-1.

1197

23 St Edmund's churchyard, Bury St Edmund's (422): remains of the
church. See Pevsner, *Suff*, p 124.

ca 1220

24 St John's churchyard, Beverley (375): the present Minster. See
Pevsner, *YorksER*, pp 169-79.

1220-5

25 York Cathedral (1556): surviving. See Morris, pp 279-80; and G.E.
Aylmer and Reginald Cant, eds, *A History of York Minster* (1977).

1222-1499

26 Salisbury Cathedral (59, 1364): remains of Old Sarum; New Sarum
survives (completed ca 1260). See Morris, p 269.

1236-1561

27 Lincoln Cathedral, especially the nave (848, 850-3, 856, 859-65):
surviving. See Morris, p 258; Pevsner, *Lincs*, pp 81-128 (and plan on
p 87; pls 12b, 15a [interior]).

ca 1260-1380

28 Norwich Cathedral Priory Church (**1218, 1219**): surviving but extensively remodelled. See Morris, p 262; Pevsner, *Norwich*, pp 207-32 (plan on pp 208-9, and pl 20 [interior]).

ca 1270-1338

29 Wells Cathedral (**1473, 1476**): surviving. See Morris, pp 273-4; Nikolaus Pevsner, *North Somerset and Bristol* (1958), pp 278-322 (plan on p 292, and pls 9a, 14-15a, 17-20 [interior]; and for the Great Hall and lesser hall of the bishop's palace, see Wood, p 24.

ca 1272-1307

30 'La Batailplace,' Lincoln (**849**): land north of the Castle ditch, now the site of the Burton Road Hospital. See Hill, p 99, n 3, and pl 2).

ca 1275-1325

31 Castilly (**516**): remains of 'Plain an Gwarry' made on the site of a henge. See Pevsner, *Corn*, p 110, for the Castilly Henge Monument near Lower Woon Farm, Luxulyan.

1279-1376

32 Barking Abbey chapel (**361, 362**): ruins. See RCHM *Essex*, II (1921), 7-9 (and plan on p 8).

1283

33 Gloucester (**684**): possibly the Great Hall of Kingsholm, the king's residence from Saxon times to sometime before 1345 (owned at this time by Eleanor of Provence). See Colvin, I, 43, 45; II, 651-6.

1285

34 Jedburgh Abbey (**1700**): ruins of the church stand (the Abbey was ransacked in 1297 and burned twice in the reign of Henry VIII). See John G. Dunbar, *The Historic Architecture of Scotland* (1966), pp 144-5, pl 102.

14th-16th centuries

35 Constantine, Corn. (**212**): 'Plain an Gwarry,' not surviving?

36 Kea, Corn. (**212**): 'Plain an Gwarry,' not surviving?

37 Landewednack, Corn. (**212**): 'Plain an Gwarry,' not surviving?

38 Ludgvan, Corn. (212): 'Plain an Gwarry,' not surviving?
39 Newlyn East, Corn. (212): 'Plain an Gwarry,' not surviving?
40 Perranzabuloe, Corn. (212): remains of 'Plain an Gwarry.'
41 Redruth, Corn. (212): 'Plain an Gwarry,' not surviving?
42 Ruan Major and Ruan Minor, Corn. (212): 'Plain an Gwarry,' not surviving?
43 St Allen, Corn. (212): 'Plain an Gwarry,' not surviving?
44 St Buryan, Corn. (212): 'Plain an Gwarry,' not surviving?
45 St Columb Major, Corn. (1356): 'Plain an Gwarry,' not surviving?
46 St Erme, Corn. (212): 'Plain an Gwarry,' not surviving?
47 St Ewe, Corn. (212): 'Plain an Gwarry,' not surviving?
48 St Goran, Corn. (212): 'Plain an Gwarry,' not surviving?
49 St Hilary, Corn. (212): 'Plain an Gwarry,' not surviving?
50 St Ives, Corn. (1358): 'Plain an Gwarry,' not surviving?
51 St Just in Penwith, Corn. (212): remains of 'Plain an Gwarry' in Bank Square.
52 St Keverne, Corn. (212): 'Plain an Gwarry,' not surviving?
53 St Stephen-in-Brannel, Corn. (212): 'Plain an Gwarry,' not surviving?
54 Sithney, Corn. (212): 'Plain an Gwarry,' not surviving?

ca 1300
54.5 Bridgnorth (400.5): 'playground' or 'dancing ring,' not surviving?

ca 1300-1411
55 Clerkenwell or Skinners Well (543-9): not surviving. See J.W. Robinson, 'Monuments to the Medieval Theatre,' TN, 33 (1979), 86, for a plaque commemorating this site.

1307
56 Lanercost Priory (823): the church and west range of the monastery survive. See Morris, p 256; Pevsner, Cumb, pp 152-7; and William Hutchinson, The History of the County of Cumberland (1794), I, 49-57.

1323
57 Cowick (583): a manor with a hall, acquired by Edward II; replaced by a late 17th-century house? See Pevsner, YorksWR, p 171; and Colvin, II, 921-2.

1345

58 The market place, Carlisle (515): surviving. See Pevsner, *Cumb*,
pp 102-3.

1347

59 Guildford (740): a palace (with an aisled hall), in ruins by 1379.
See Colvin, II, 950-5.

1348-9

60 Otford (1240): the manor house of the archbishop, with a hall, the
walls of which were kept for the new Tudor palace built ca 1520.
See Dennis Clarke and Anthony Stoyel, *Otford in Kent: A History*
(1975), p 76 and diagram of the new palace in fig 13; and Colvin,
III.i, 3, 31, 75, 79.

1348-52

61 Exeter, 'theatro' (656, 657): probably the then market place.

1349

62 Merton (1179): a royal place at the manor of Banstead at least from
ca 1276-9, when Edward I added to it for Eleanor, to ca 1376, when
Edward III granted it to Nicholas Carew. See Colvin, II, 896-8.

1360

63 Crediton (671): Holy Cross Church, of which the extensively-
remodelled church stands, but nothing of the monastic buildings.
See Pevsner, *S-Devon*, pp 94-5.
64 Exeter Cathedral (671): surviving. See Morris, p 252; Pevsner,
S-Devon, pp 130-48 (with plan on p 131 and pls 14-15 [interior]).
65 Ottery St Mary (671): surviving but restored church, and scanty
remains of the monastic buildings. See Pevsner, *S-Devon*, pp 218-23
(and pl 16a [interior]).

1360-ca 1375

66 Glasney collegiate church (671, 1295): no remains. See Pevsner,
Corn, p 136.

1360?-1551

67 Exeter College, Oxford (1243, 1286): the old hall was replaced by a
new one in 1618. See RCHM *Oxford*, pp 56-7; and *VCHOxford*, III,
115-16, for a 1631-2 survey mentioning the old hall.

1366
68 St Leonard's Hospital, York (1557): remains only. See George Benson, *York from its Origin to the End of the Eleventh Century* (1911), II, fig 12, for a reconstruction (plan); and his 'St. Leonard's Hospital, York,' AASRP, 40 (1930-1), 111-32.

1374-1414
69 Westminster Abbey (895, 902, 919): largely surviving. See Morris, pp 274-5; Wood, pl 21b, for an engraving of the lost Abbot's hall; Colvin, I, 145; and *A to Z*, p 17.

1377
70 Kennington (802): a royal palace demolished in 1531 to provide materials for Whitehall. See Colvin, II, 967-9; and Graham J. Dawson, *The Black Prince's Palace at Kennington, Surrey*, British Archaeological Reports, 26 (1976), fig 7 (a reconstruction [plan] of palace and hall).

1377-1451
71 Bicester Priory (381, 382): a few remains only.

1384-1526
71.5 Eltham (632-40): palace whose existing Great Hall was completed in 1480. See D.E. Strong, *Eltham Palace, Kent*, with foreword by F.A. Forman (1958), pp 11-13 (and pls II-III [interior]); Colvin, II, 930-7 (and his plan of the old place on p 932, which ca 1384-8 had a dancing chamber); Pevsner, *London*, II, 458-9; and RCHM *London*, V (1930), 103-5 (and plan on p 105; pls 174-8).

1386
72 College of Michael-House, Cambridge (435): the college hall was incorporated into the structure of the Great Court of Trinity College in the mid-sixteenth century, and only fragments remain. See RCHM *Cambridge*, II, 209-44 (and final Plan).

1389
73 St Catherine's priory, Lincoln (854): not surviving. See Hill, p 346 and fig 23.

1390
74 St Augustine's Church, Hedon (759): standing, but restored 1868-76. See Pevsner, *YorksER*, pp 243-46 (and pl 25 [interior]).

1391

75 Spalding (**1410**): its 'Pleyingplace.'

76 *cancelled*

1394-6

77 Whitby Abbey (**1487**): ruins. See Sir Alfred Clapham, *Whitby Abbey, Yorkshire* (1952).

1398

78 Richard II's 'theatre' for combat, Coventry (**555**): not surviving.

1398-1532

79 Selby Abbey (**1376, 1377**): partially surviving. See Morris, p 270; Pevsner, *YorksWR*, pp 435-43 (pls 18-19 [interior]), for the wholly restored church and a few monastic remains.

ca 1400?

80 St John the Evangelist church, Dublin (**1734**): not surviving.

1400

81 The Guildhall, London (**912**): rebuilt by about 1425. See Caroline M. Barron, *The Medieval Guildhall of London* (1974), pp 15-24 and fig 1; RCHM *London*, IV (1929), pp 63-7 (plans on pp 64, 66; pl 130), for the later building (partly destroyed in 1666 and rebuilt); and *A to Z*, p 11.

1400-ca 1548

82 Windsor Castle (**138, 1510, 1511**?): surviving. See Colvin, II, 864-88 (an existing Great Hall was made over to the college of St George ca 1350-7, and a new St George's Hall was built for Edward III: both appear in Plan IV); and III.i, 302-33.

1403-1527

83 Mettingham College (**1181**): ruins. This was lodged in Mettingham Castle, of which the Gatehouse survives (Pevsner, *Suff*, p 362).

1404-1557

84 Drapers' hall, London (**914, 943, 1101**): not surviving. After 1541 the Drapers took over Thomas Cromwell's house, for which see below under 1539. See Pevsner, *London*, I, 291-2; and *A to Z*, p 11.

1407-45

85 Bungay priory (**414, 415**): partly surviving in St Mary's church. See Pevsner, *Suff*, pp 107-8.

1408-32

86 Blackfriars, Exeter (**658**): not surviving? This was a house on the north side of St Peter's churchyard outside the close.

1410

87 Downham palace (**610**): ruins of the palace as rebuilt ca 1486-1500. See *VCHCamb*, IV (1953), 92.

1412-91

88 Furnival's Inn, London (**916, 955**): demolished 1818-20. See *A to Z*, p 7; Sir Robert Megarry, *Inns Ancient and Modern* (1972), pp 54-5, pls 7-8; Pevsner, *London*, I, 363.

1420-1

89 Berkeley Castle (**372**): well-preserved, with a Great Hall from ca 1342, somewhat altered. See Colvin, III.i, 232-33; and St Clair Baddeley, 'Berkeley Castle,' *TBGAS*, 48 (1927 for 1926), 133-79, plan facing p 133, and pl V.

ca 1424-30

90 Manor of the bishop of London, Bishop's Wood (**1414**): not surviving? The large medieval church of St Dunstan (mostly 15th century, but from 13th century, and much restored) stands in Stepney today (Pevsner, *London*, II, 413-14).

1424-90

91 Worcester Cathedral, and almonry school (**1527, 1528, 1531**): cathedral surviving. See Morris, pp 277-8; *VCHWorcs*, IV (1924), pp 324-408 (plan opp p 396, and pls opp pp 401, 404-5; and plan of the surviving Deanery, formerly the Bishop's Palace, with hall, on p 407); and *Medieval Art and Architecture at Worcester Cathedral*, British Archaeological Assoc. Conf. Trans. for 1975 (1978).

1425-35

92 Brewers' Hall, London (**925**): not surviving. See *A to Z*, p 9.

1426-1555

93 Blacksmiths' Hall, London (**927**): not surviving. See *A to Z*, p 22.

1427-8

94 Hertford palace (**771**): demolished by 1609. See Colvin, II, 677-81
(early plan, with Great Hall, on p 679), and III.i, 254-7 (plan of 1564
on p 256).

1430

95 Maxstoke Castle (**1175**): surviving east range with a Great Hall of
the late 15th century, and another modernized hall. See *VCHWarw*,
IV (1947), pp 133-7 (plan on p 134).

1430-1557

96 Guildhall, Exeter (**663, 669**): surviving, but main hall and roof
rebuilt in 1466. See Peter D. Thomas, *Old Exeter* (1977), pp 96-9
(with photographs).

1431-58

97 Maxstoke Priory (**1176**): largely ruins. See *VCHWarw*, IV (1947),
136-7 (the inner gatehouse, formerly probably the Prior's house, is
now an Elizabethan farm-house).

1432?

98 Exeter Castle (**664**): surviving in part. See Pevsner, *S-Devon*, p 155
(the much-restored Norman Gate Tower, which was the keep of
Rougemont Castle, remains); Colvin, II, 647-9.

1433-1541

99 St Laurence's church, Reading (**1315, 1321, 1323**): surviving. See
Nikolaus Pevsner, *Berkshire* (1966), pp 199-200.

1437-53

100 Manor of Bella Court (later Pleasance), Greenwich (**50, 693**):
archaeological remains. See Colvin, II, 949-50; and Beryl Platts,
A History of Greenwich (1973), pp 49 (excavations of 1971), 87-101.

1439-48

101 SS Peter and Wilfrid Church, Ripon (**1340**): surviving. See Morris,
p 265; Pevsner, *YorksWR*, pp 403-11 (plan on p 405, and pl 21b
[interior]).

ca 1440-79
102 Winchester College Hall (**1499-1501**): surviving. See *VCHHants*, III
   (1908), pp 14-19 (plan of College on p 15; pls opp pp 14, 18 [interior of Hall]).

1440-5
103 The Windmill-hill, Aberdeen (**1624**): later Gallowgate-hill or the
   Porthill, an incline that has since disappeared. See Fenton Wyness,
   City by the Grey North Sea: Aberdeen (1965), pp 64, 68, and map opp
   p 8.

1441-2
104 The Crockhill, New Romney (**1202**): now Crockley Green at the
   south-west end of town. See W.A.S. Robertson, 'The Passion Play
   and Interludes at New Romney,' *Arch. Cant.*, 13 (1880), 221-2.

1442-4
105 Writtle Manor disguising chamber (**1544, 1545**): demolished before
   1566. See also Colvin, II, 1019-20; RCHM *Essex*, II (1921), p 276.

1442-98
106 Cutlers' Hall, London (**936**): not surviving. See *A to Z*, p 24; and
   Pevsner, *London*, I, 300.

ca 1444-16th century
107 St Peter's in the East, Oxford (**1250**): surviving, much restored.
   See RCHM *Oxford*, pp 143-7 (plan on p 144).

1445-6
108 Middleton manor, Norfolk (**1182**): old gatehouse alone surviving,
   as Middleton Towers. See Pevsner, *Norf*, p 258.
109 St George's Guildhall, Bishop's Lynn (**811**): surviving, much
   altered. See Vanessa Parker, *The Making of King's Lynn: Secular Buildings from the 11th to the 17th Century* (1971), pp 145-8 (outside plan
   on p 147; pls 14B [interior], 31A, 31B, 38).

1445-9
110 Christ Church, Canterbury (**494**): monastic buildings largely lost.
   See Morris, p 244; Robert Willis, 'The Architectural History of the

Conventual Buildings of the Monastery of Christ Church in Canterbury,' *Arch. Cant.*, 7 (1868), 1-206 (the archbishop's Great Hall, in ruins, was rebuilt after 1559; see pp 155-6, and pls 1-3); and William Urry, *Canterbury under the Angevin Kings* (1967), map 1(b)3.

1447-1573

111 Eton College Hall (**646-51**): surviving. See Colvin, I, 279-92 (plan on p 286; pl 19B); *VCHBucks*, II, 147-207, and III, ed William Page (1925), p 273 (plan opp p 268; for the surviving Chapel, see p 269 and pl opp p 272).

1449-50

112 St George's Chapel Royal, Windsor (**1513**). See Colvin, II, 864-88 (and Plan IV).

1451-2

113 Church house, Tintinhull (**1460**): demolished by 1497. See VCH, *A History of the County of Somerset*, III, ed R.W. Dunning (1974), p 264.

1451-1540

114 St Mary at Hill, London (**940, 1001**): partly destroyed in 1666, and later rebuilt. See Cobb, p 162; and *A to Z*, p 26.

ca 1454-99

115 Brome Hall (**412**): demolished. See David M. Wilson and D.G. Hurst, 'Medieval Britain in 1967,' *Medieval Archaeology*, 12 (1968), 193 and fig 52.

1454-1512

116 Carpenters' Hall, London (**941**): much altered, then replaced in 1880. See B.W.E. Alford and T.C. Barker, *A History of the Carpenters Company* (1968), pl 3; and *A to Z*, p 11.

1456-9

117 Fountains Abbey (**680**): ruins. See R. Gilyard-Beer, *Fountains Abbey, Yorkshire* (1970), pp 52-3 (refectory), 59 (Abbot's hall).

1457-1517

118 King's Hall, Cambridge (**437, 441**): not surviving. See RCHM *Cambridge*, II, 209-13 (King's Hall was adapted ca 1547 for the new

Trinity College, and the old hall was pulled down ca 1554-61); Alan B. Cobban, *The King's Hall within the University of Cambridge in the Late Middle Ages* (1969).

1457-1505
119 The Little Park, Coventry (**558, 563, 567**): now Little Park Street End.

ca 1460-70
120 Ely Palace, Holborn, London (**62**): not surviving. See *A to Z*, p 7.

1461-1556
121 New College, Oxford (**1252, 1277, 1287**): surviving hall. See RCHM *Oxford*, pp 86-7 (plan opp p 88; pl 153 [interior]); A.H. Smith, *New College Oxford and its Buildings* (1952), pp 34-8, 61-3 (pl opp p 34); and *New College Oxford 1379-1979*, ed John Buxton and Penry Williams (1979), pp 147-232 (articles by Gervase Jackson-Stops; plans on pp 150, 177-8; pls 36-7).

1462
122 Glasgow University (**1691**): in High Street until 1632, when buildings were begun, not now surviving. See John Durkan and James Kirk, *The University of Glasgow 1451-1577* (1977), pp 21-39 (plan of old buildings on p 32).

1462-1512
123 St Nicholas church, Great Yarmouth (**689**): destroyed by enemy bombing in 1942. See Pevsner, *Norwich*, pp 143-6 (restored in the 19th century, from ruins, and rebuilt 1957-60).

1465-1528
124 Tendring Hall, Stoke-by-Nayland (**1419-22**): a later hall of 1784 has been demolished. See Pevsner, *Suff*, pp 440-1.

1466-7
125 House of John Arundell, Lanherne (**824**): surviving, much altered? See Pevsner, *Corn*, p 116 (an Elizabethan front, and backs from later periods).

1469
126 Market place and corn market, Maldon (**1167**): not surviving?
127 Wistow 'Somerhouse' (**1518**): not surviving?

1469-72
128 St Petroc's church hay, Bodmin (**386**): the church survives.
See Pevsner, *Corn*, pp 41-3.

1474-5
129 St Mary the Virgin church, Rye (**1344**): surviving, much altered.
See Ian Nairn and Nikolaus Pevsner, *Sussex* (1965), pp 594-6.

1477-8
130 St Martin le Grand, Dover (**609**): demolished by 1539. See Charles
R. Haines, *Dover Priory* (1930), pp 16-58.

1477-81
131 Chamber of John Sharpe, in Lincoln Cathedral Close (**865**): not
surviving? See Hill, fig 9, for a map of the Close ca 1400.

1478-1522
132 Battle Abbey (**369**): remains. See Sir Harold Brakspear, 'The
Abbot's House at Battle,' *Arch*, 83 (1933), 139-66 (several halls, for
which see pp 150-3, 158-60, and plan opp p 144).

1479
133 St John Baptist church, Peterborough (**1299**): surviving. See *The
Victoria History of the County of Northampton*, II, ed R.M. Serjeantson
and W.R.D. Adkins (1906), pp 429-30 (and pl opp p 430 [interior]);
and Nikolaus Pevsner, *Bedfordshire and the County of Huntington and
Peterborough* (1968), pp 325-6.

1479-1532
134 Ely Priory (**642-4**): partly surviving. See Morris, p 251; Mac
Dowdy, *The Monastic Setting of Ely* (1974); and *VCHCamb*, IV (1953),
77-82 (plan on p 78), for various original halls, of which a Great
Hall and the Queen's Hall remain.

1481-2
135 St Michael's churchyard, Bath (**366**): not surviving.
136 Stonor Manor (**1423**): the old chapel, and probably the core of the
old house, survive in the present Stonor Park. See *A History of the
County of Oxford*, VIII, ed Mary D. Lobel, VCH (1964), pp 142-3 (and
pls).

1482

137 Playing place, Linstead (**874**).

138 St Mary's church, Stoke (**1420**): greatly altered in the 19th century. See Pevsner, *Suff*, pp 407-8.

1482-1564

139 King's College, Cambridge (**438, 471**): Great Hall demolished in 1836. See Colvin, I, 269-78 (plan of the old hall on p 270); and RCHM *Cambridge*, I, 98-136 (and final Plan).

1485-1635

140 Magdalen College, Oxford (**262, 1256, 1257, 1259, 1261, 1263, 1267**): surviving hall, much altered. See RCHM *Oxford*, pp 69-74 (college plan opp p 72); R.S. Stanier, *Magdalen School: A History of Magdalen College School Oxford* (1958), pp 15-16.

1486-1557

141 Greenwich Palace, including a disguising hall in the Long House (**694-734**): destroyed. See Beryl Platts, *A History of Greenwich* (1973), pp 118-93, and pls on pp 49, 67-8.

1487

142 Frerenhay, the Franciscans' house at Exeter (**667**).

143 London house of the Archbishop of York (**951**): on the site of Wolsey's future York Place, Westminster? not surviving.

1488-1540

144 Linlithgow palace (**1705, 1706**): partly surviving. See J.S. Richardson and James Beveridge, *Linlithgow Palace, West Lothian* (1948), pp 18-19 (and plan at the end), for the Great Hall.

ca 1490-1500

145 Archbishop's Palace, Knole (**78**): surviving, altered. See V. Sackville-West, *Knole and the Sackvilles* (1949), p 6 (and pl opp p 76 [interior]), for the Great Hall, originally built in 1460.

146 Lambeth Palace, London (**78**): Great Hall destroyed. See RCHM *London*, II (1925), p 81, for the old palace plan (hall rebuilt 1660-3; pp 79, 84); *A to Z*, p 17.

1490
147 Inner Temple, London (953): original hall not surviving. See RCHM
London, IV (1929), pp 143-5 (hall rebuilt 1868-70); *A to Z*, p 20; and
for the surviving Temple church, see Pevsner, *London*, I, 313-16.
148 St Mary's church, Gateshead (681): much remodelled and
restored. See Nikolaus Pevsner, *County Durham* (1953), p 149.
149 Whitehall, Westminster (954, ?980): not surviving. See Colvin, I,
492-3, for the 'Lesser or White Hall' (to be distinguished from
Whitehall Palace, built in the 16th century, for which see York
Place); and *A to Z*, p 17.
150 Wolvesey Palace, Winchester (1503): ruins. See *VCHHants*, V
(1912), ed William Page, pp 13-14, for a description of the old Great
Hall.

1490-1
151 Castle Hedingham, Essex (517): partly surviving. See RCHM *Essex*, I
(1916), 51-7 (the Great Hall does not survive, but the hall in the
Keep does, for which see pl opp p 55).

1490-1550
152 Gray's Inn, London (953, 962.5, 1003, 1069): hall, standing but
rebuilt 1556-60, incorporating some early work. See RCHM *London*, II
(1925), pp 53-5 (and plan on p 53; pls 84-7); *A to Z*, p 7.

1491-1507
153 St Mary de Castro church, Leicester (829): surviving, restored.
See *A History of the County of Leicester*, VCH, IV, ed R.A. McKinley
(1958), pp 375-80 (plan on p 378); and Nikolaus Pevsner, *Leicestershire and Rutland* (1960), pp 144-8.

1492-1596
154 Great Yarmouth game place and house (691): not surviving?

1494-1547
155 Westminster Hall (959, 965, 976, 978, 980, 1055): surviving. See
RCHM *London*, II (1925), pp 121-3 (plan on p 120; pls 174-80; Colvin,
I, 527-33 (and Plan III); and *A to Z*, p 17.

1494-1553
156 St Saviour's church, Dartmouth (592, 594?): surviving, much
altered in 1630s. See Pevsner, *S-Devon*, pp 113-14.

1494-1580
157 Lincoln's Inn, London **(961)**: Old Hall, built 1490-2, surviving.
See RCHM *London*, II (1925), pp 45-6, 50-1 (plan on p 46; pls 77-9);
Pevsner, *London*, I, 323; and *A to Z*, p 7.

1494-1587
158 Shrewsbury quarry **(1387-8, 1395-7)**: now the principal public
park. See Nikolaus Pevsner, *Shropshire* (1958), p 270.

ca 1496-1593
159 Common playing place, Great Tey **(688)**.

1496
160 Kirkham chapel, Cheshire **(819)**.

1497-1540
161 Thetford Priory **(1448)**: remains. See F.J.E. Raby, P.K.B. Reynolds,
and S.E. Rigold, *Thetford Priory Norfolk* (1979), p 15, for the Prior's
lodging.

1498-9
162 Tattershall Collegiate Church **(1434)**: surviving. See Pevsner,
Lincs, pp 387-90 (and pl 26b [interior]), for Holy Trinity church.

1499-1500
163 The Swan, Hythe **(788)**.

ca 1500
164 Sancreed 'Plain an Gwarry' **(1372)**: not surviving?

1500
165 St John the Baptist, 'belhay,' Glastonbury **(683)**: the church survives. See Nikolaus Pevsner, *South and West Somerset* (1958), pp 177-9.

1501-49
166 Guildhall (and court hall?), Canterbury **(500, 503)**: recently taken
down. See John Boyle, *Portrait of Canterbury*, 2nd edn (1980), p 162.

1501-79
167 Richmond or Sheen **(1326-38)**: in ruins by mid-18th century, by
now destroyed. See Philip Dixon, 'Excavations at Richmond Palace,

Surrey,' *Post-Medieval Archaeology*, 9 (1975), 103-16 and fig 1; Colvin, II, 994-1002; and *The Victoria History of the County of Sussex*, III, ed H.E. Malden (1911), pp 533-41 (pls opp pp 540 and 534 give views of 1562 and 1611).

1502-3

168 Whitefriars, the Carmelite friary, Sandwich **(1374)**: not surviving. See Edward Hasted, *The History and Topographical Survey of the County of Kent*, X (1800), pp 180-2.

1504

169 St Mary Magdalene church, Taunton **(1435)**: surviving. See Nikolaus Pevsner, *South and West Somerset* (1958), pp 310-12.

1505

170 Hall yard, Mildenhall **(1183)**.

1506

171 The Forbury, Reading **(1319)**: now Forbury Road and Forbury Gardens?

1506-31

172 Bury St Edmunds Abbey **(425)**: partly surviving. See Pevsner, *Suff*, pp 132-40 (plan on pp 134-5), for existing church, gates, cloister, and lesser remains; and A.B. Whittingham, *Bury St. Edmunds Abbey, Suffolk* (1971).

ca 1507-8

173 Ampthill Castle **(88)**: not surviving. See *The Victoria History of the County of Bedford*, III, ed William Page (1912), p 270; Leland, *Itin.*, I, 102-3.

1507-21

174 Thornbury Castle **(1450, 1451)**: not surviving? See W. Douglas Simpson, '"Bastard Feudalism" and the Later Castles,' *The Antiquaries Journal*, 26 (1946), 165-9 (plan on p 166).

1508

175 The Red Rose, London **(971)**: destroyed (later the Manor of Rose). See *A to Z*, p 24.

1508-9
176 The fish market, Sandwich (**1374**).

1509
177 St Patrick's Cathedral, Dublin (**1737**): surviving but much rebuilt and restored. See 'Proceedings at Meetings of the Royal Archaeological Institute,' *Archaeological Journal*, 88 (1931), 372-3 and pl X.

1509-10
178 Middle Temple, London (**975**): not surviving. See RCHM *London*, IV (1929), pp 147-8, for a later hall built ca 1562-73; and *A to Z*, p 20.

1509-22
179 York House or Place, London (**976, ?980, 991, 992, 997**): not surviving. See *A to Z*, p 16; and Pevsner, *London*, I, 532, 534.

1510
180 Churchyard, Arnesby (**351**): the church survives. See Pevsner, *Leics*, p 49.

1511
181 Skinners' Hall, London (**981**): destroyed in 1666. See *A to Z*, p 24; and Pevsner, *London*, I, 236-7.

ca 1511-27
182 Leconfield Castle (**92, 1539-43**): destroyed, except for moat. See Leland, *Itin.*, I, 45-6.
183 Wressle Castle (**92, 1539-43**): partly surviving. See Pevsner, *YorksER*, pp 374-5 (and pl 43 [exterior]), for a range that may have contained the hall; a series of plans and sketches ca 1600 exists in the West Sussex Record Office, Petworth House Archives 3538-47; and Leland, *Itin.*, I, 52-4.

1512-20
184 Hickling Priory (**773**): partly surviving. See Pevsner, *Norwich*, p 165.

1513
185 Lincoln College, Oxford (**1269**): hall surviving, altered. See RCHM, *Oxford*, p 66 (plan of college on p 65; pl 119).

186 Merton College, Oxford (**1268**): partly surviving. See RCHM *Oxford*, p 77, for the old Great Hall, rebuilt 1790-4 and later drastically restored (plan of college, opp p 80).

ca 1514

187 Suffolk Place, Southwark (**95**): destroyed. For the hall, and for a banqueting house in the garden, see *VCHSurrey*, IV (1912), pp 143-4; *Survey*, XXII (1950), pp 46-7, and XXV, 22-3; and C.L. Kingsford, 'London Topographical Gleanings,' *London Topographical Record*, 13 (1923), 47-8.

1515

188 The market place, Reading (**1322**): surviving.

189 St John's churchyard, Chester (**528**): the church has been much restored. See Nikolaus Pevsner and Edward Hubbard, *Cheshire* (1971), pp 148-50.

1518

190 Bishop of London's palace, London (**986**): destroyed. On the north-west side of St Paul's churchyard, with a Great Hall (Stow, II, 20).

1518-22

191 The Bull, Sandwich (**1374**).

1519

192 New Hall or Beaulieu (**1201**): partly surviving. See Colvin, III.i, 1; and, for the Great Hall in the east range pulled down ca 1738, see RCHM, *Essex*, II (1921), 24-6.

ca 1519-55

193 Merchant Tailors' Guildhall, London (**97, 1065**): enemy bombing in World War II destroyed the medieval hall, which has been since rebuilt. See RCHM, *London*, IV (1929), pp 34-6 (plan on p 35); Pevsner, *London*, I, 289-90; and *A to Z*, p 11.

1519-28

194 St Stephen Walbrook church, London (**988**): destroyed in 1666. See Cobb, pp 171-2; and *A to Z*, p 24.

1519-34
195 St Peter Cheap church, London (989): destroyed in 1666. See
Pevsner, *London*, I, 226; Cobb, pp 133, 138; and *A to Z*, p 9.

1520
196 The Exchequer, Calais (1746): not surviving? See Colvin, I, 424;
III.i, 350 (plan ca 1532).
197 Guines Palace (1743): not surviving. See Colvin, III.i, 363-70, for a
brief account of these temporary buildings.
198 Henry VIII's Banqueting House, Calais (1746, 1747): not surviving.

1520-2
199 Ditton Park (599, 600): destroyed in 1812. See Colvin, III.i, 315;
and James Hakewill, *The History of Windsor, and its Neighbourhood*
(1813), p 329.

ca 1520-33
200 Great Church, Calais (1748).

1521-75
201 Middleton Hall, Warws. (1523): partly surviving. See *VCHWarw*,
IV (1947), p 156, for the destroyed Great Hall and another, surviving hall.
202 Wollaton Hall, Notts. (1523): destroyed. The present hall was built
ca 1580-8.

1522-54
203 Queens' College, Cambridge (444, 451, 457, 460-2, 468, 473, 475):
surviving hall, altered. See RCHM *Cambridge*, II, 167-78 (plan between
pp 168-9).

1523
204 Havering palace (757): not surviving. See Colvin, II, 956-9 (plan of
1578 on p 958); RCHM *Essex*, II (1921), 126.

1523-4
205 Tiverton Castle (1463): ruins. See Pevsner, *S-Devon*, p 285, for
possible location of Great Hall.

1523-5

206 St Michael's church, Braintree (**394, 395**): surviving, with an exterior renewed in 1864-6. See Nikolaus Pevsner and Enid Radcliffe, *Essex*, 2nd edn (1965), pp 99-100.

1523-1632

207 Hunstanton Hall (**787**): partly surviving, much altered and rebuilt. See Pevsner, *Norf*, pp 213-14.

ca 1524-6

208 John Rastell's stage, Finsbury Fields (**677**): not surviving. See *A to Z*, p 10.

1524-31

209 The Prior's manor, Grimley (**735**).

1525

210 Bridewell Palace, London (**1002**): excavated ruins. See John Cherry, 'Post-Medieval Britain in 1978,' *Post-Medieval Archaeology*, 13 (1979), 277-9, fig 1, and pls XXXII-XXXIV; and *A to Z*, p 20.
211 Newarke College, Leicester (**832**): one house survives. See Pevsner, *Leics*, p 153.

1525-6

212 Sheriff Hutton Castle (**1383**): Great Hall in ruins by 1624. See Colvin, III.i, 293-5; *The Victoria History of the County of York: North Riding*, II, ed William Page (1923), pp 174-6 (plan of ruins on p 175).

1526

213 Sir John Nevill's manor, Chevet, Yorks. W.R. (**537**).

1526-40

214 St Andrew Hubbard church, London (**1004**): destroyed in 1666. See Cobb, p 137; and *A to Z, p 26*.

1527

215 The common hall, York (**1577**): destroyed by enemy action in 1942 and restored in 1960. See Pevsner, *YorksER*, p 136; and Nelson, pp 72-8.

1527-34
216 The Prior's manor, Crowle (**587**): part surviving in Crowle Court
Farm? See Nikolaus Pevsner, *Worcestershire* (1968), p 130.

1528-30
217 Missenden Abbey (**1186**). See *VCHBucks*, II, 350-1.

1529
218 The guildhall, Lincoln (**867**): 15th-century building, much
restored, with a long timber-roofed chamber on the upper floor.
See Pevsner, *Lincs*, pp 148-9.
219 Halstead church (**745**): surviving, much altered. See RCHM *Essex*, I,
149-51, for the parish church of St Andrew.
220 Thornton Abbey (**1454**): ruins of gateway and parts of Chapter
House. See Sir Alfred Clapham and P.K.B. Reynolds, *Thornton Abbey
Lincolnshire* (1956).

1529-30
221 Cardinal's College, Oxford (**1275**): hall surviving, much altered.
This later became Christ Church. See RCHM *Oxford*, pp 33-4 (plan of
the hall, p 34; pls 81, 85 [present interior]).

1529-49
222 Founders' Hall, London (**1011, 1043, 1060**): not surviving. See
*Wardens' Accounts of the Worshipful Company of Founders of the City of
London 1497-1681*, ed Guy Parsloe (1964), pp xlviii-li; Pevsner, *London*, I, 287; and *A to Z*, p 11.

1530
223 Bakers' Hall, London (**1013**): not surviving. See Pevsner, *London*, I,
249-50; and *A to Z*, p 26.

1530-1618
224 Belvoir Castle (**371**): wholly rebuilt in later periods.

1531
225 House of Thomas Boleyn, earl of Ormond and Wiltshire, London
(**1014**): not surviving.
226 Nun Coton (**1239**).

1531-57
227 The guildhall, Cambridge (**440, 482**): not surviving.
228 St Martin-in-the-Fields church, London (**1015**): not surviving,
rebuilt in 1544 and 1722-6. See Pevsner, *London*, I, 309-11; and *A to
Z*, p 3.

1531-68
229 Christ's College, Cambridge (**445, 453, 469**): hall surviving, altered.
See RCHM *Cambridge*, I, 25-37 (plan between pp 28-9).

1532-6
230 Little Dunmow Priory (**614**): partly surviving. See RCHM *Essex*, I,
175-9, for the Lady Chapel, surviving alone as the present parish
church.

1532-40
231 Staple Hall or Inn, Calais (**1750, 1751**). See Colvin, I, 424, and III.i,
339-41 (pls 30-1 are 17th-century plans of the Staple Inn).

1533
232 Henwick Hall (**764**): not surviving? See *VCHWorcs*, III, 368.

1533-6
233 St Andrew's church, Ashburton (**354**): surviving, much altered.
See Pevsner, *S-Devon*, p 39.

1533-81
234 Walsham-Le-Willows game place (**1470**): surviving as an open
green space?

1534
235 Gloucester College, Oxford (**1279**): old hall demolished in 1720.
See *VCHOxford*, III, 302-4 (old plan on p 303); and RCHM *Oxford*,
pp 123-4.
236 Warkworth Castle (**1464**): large halls survive in both the Outer
Bailey and the Keep. See Nikolaus Pevsner, *Northumberland* (1957),
pp 313-18.

ca 1535-43
237 Leominster playing place called 'Comfort-castle' (**839**): surviving.
See RCHM *An Inventory of the Historical Monuments in Herefordshire*,

III (1934), p 115, for Castle Moat, 800 yards south of the church, a four-sided enclosure about which there is a dry moat.

238 Truro playing place (**1465**): not surviving?

ca 1535-57

239 The guildhall, Bristol (**410**): not surviving. See Andor Gomme, Michael Jenner, and Bryan Little, *Bristol: An Architectural History* (1979), p 71.

ca 1536-44?

240 Beauchamp House, London (**1547**): not surviving. Formerly the house of the bishops of Coventry and Lichfield in the Strand.

241 Wulfhall manor (**1547**): partly surviving. See Nikolaus Pevsner, *Wiltshire*, rev Bridget Cherry, 2nd edn (1975), p 152 (less than a mile north-north-west of Burbage; two wings survive, one Tudor, one refronted ca 1740).

1536

242 Allhallows Staining church, London (**1024**): fell down. See Pevsner, *London*, I, 145; Cobb, pp 22-3, 176; and *A to Z*, p 26.

243 Holywell nunnery, London (**1386**): not surviving. See Stow, I, 74-5; Pevsner, *London*, II, 380; and *A to Z*, p 12.

244 St John's College, Cambridge (**446, 454, 458, 465, 477**): hall surviving, much altered. See RCHM *Cambridge*, II, 187-202 (pl 239; and final Plan); *Collegium Divi Johannis Evangelistae 1511-1911* (1911), pp 8-9 (and fig 1 on p 4 [old hall]).

1536-43

245 Stratton church house (**1425**): not surviving?

1537

246 The Carmelite friary, Maldon (**1167**).

247 St Ausende, Bristol (**410**): not identified.

1537-42

248 The guildhall, Plymouth (**1302**): not surviving.

1538

249 The palace, St Andrews (**1722**): of the priory? of which there are only a few remains. See Hubert Fenwick, *Scotland's Historic Buildings* (1974), p 188.

250 St Stephen's, Canterbury (505): surviving. See Kenneth H. Jones, 'St. Stephen's Church, Hackington, and its Possible Connection with Archbishop Baldwin,' *Arch. Cant.*, 44 (1932), 253-68 (plan opp p 268; pls III-IV [interior]).

251 Titchfield Abbey (1462): ruins. See Rose Graham and S.E. Rigold, *Titchfield Abbey, Hampshire* (1954), for an account of Wriothesley's Place House (in the middle of the abbey) and the monastic Frater that was his hall; and *VCHHants*, III (1908), pp 220-3 (with several old drawings and a plan).

1539

252 Thomas Cromwell's house, London (1029): destroyed in 1666. After 1541 the Drapers' Hall. See *A to Z*, p 11.

1539-40

253 The Dolphin, Southampton (1403): not surviving (the Dolphin Hotel stands in High Street). See Pevsner, *Hants*, p 547.

ca 1539-45

254 Norwich game place (1229): the wrestling place mentioned in 1532, repaired in 1541-3 with timberwork and banks, and evidently soon afterward taken down? See Nelson, pp 127-8.

255 Master 'Castylden's' place, Norwich (1229).

ca 1539-47

256 Assembly chamber in the Common Hall at the Blackfriars, Norwich (1229-31): surviving as St Andrew's Hall, restored in 1863. See Pevsner, *Norwich*, pp 260-1 (and pl 13a).

1540

257 Morebath churchyard (1189): St George's church survives. See Nikolaus Pevsner, *North Devon* (1952), p 126.

258 St Alphage's church, London (1033): some ruins. See Pevsner, *London*, I, 263; Cobb, pp 113, 176; and *A to Z*, p 9.

1540-53

259 West Field, Dundee, otherwise called the Playfield, outside the West Port (1656, 1657): now built over. See Frank Boyd, 'The Drama in Dundee and District,' *Handbook and Guide to Dundee and District*, ed A.W. Paton and A.H. Millar (1912), p 672.

before 1542?
260 Perth, amphitheatre at (**1714**): probably the North or South Inch.

1542
261 Reading Abbey (**1324**): remains. See *The Victoria History of the County of Berkshire*, III, ed William Page, P.H. Ditchfield, and John H. Cope (1923), pp 339-42 (and plan with frater opp p 340).
262 St Chad's churchyard, Shrewsbury (**1392**): the church was destroyed in 1788 and some ruins remain. See Nikolaus Pevsner, *Shropshire* (1958), pp 258-9.

1542-74
263 St Mary's church, Long Sutton (**1156**): surviving. See Pevsner, *Lincs*, pp 597-9.

1543
264 House of William Blytheman, the earl of Northumberland's place, London (**1040**): destroyed? See Stow, I, 149; *A to Z*, p 26.
265 House of George Gadlowe, London (**1040**): destroyed?
266 House of Thomas Hancokkes, London (**1040**): destroyed?

1543-74
267 Abbey church of St Mary, Sherborne (**1378-9**): surviving. See Morris, p 270; and RCHM *Dorset*, I (1952), p 213 (the early Guest Hall and a former Abbot's hall remain; map between pp 200-1).

1544-7
268 St Martin's church, Leicester (**834**): surviving. See Pevsner, *Leics*, pp 140-1.
269 Westminster School (**1044**): hall surviving, altered. See RCHM *London*, I, 82-3 (and pl 163); Pevsner, *London*, I, 477; and *A to Z*, p 17.

1544-8
270 Hampton Court Palace (**747-50**): surviving, including Great Hall ca 1531-6. See RCHM, *An Inventory of the Historical Monuments in Middlesex* (1937), pp 30-48 (plans between pp 48-9; pls 80, 85 [interior]); and G.H. Chettle, *Hampton Court Palace*, rev John Charlton, Ministry of Works (1971), p 32 (pl on p 16).

1544-53

271 Weavers' Hall, London (**1043, 1084**): not surviving. See *A to Z*, p 11.

1545

272 St Mary Woolnoth church, London (**1049**): pulled down in 1716. See Pevsner, *London*, I, 172-3; Cobb, p 164; and *A to Z*, p 24.

ca 1546-1642

273 Trinity College, Cambridge (**456, 459, 470, 474, 476, 479, 481**): partly surviving. See RCHM *Cambridge*, II, 209-44 (and final Plan), for a description of how Trinity College incorporated the buildings of Michael House and King's Hall and only began building its own hall in 1604.

1546-7

274 The Cheker Inn, Canterbury (**503**): some parts still standing at the south-west corner of Mercury Lane in 1911. See C.E. Woodruff, 'A Monastic Chronicle lately Discovered at Christ Church, Canterbury,' *Arch. Cant.*, 29 (1911), 65-7.

1547

275 House of the Lord Deputy, George Lord Cobham, Calais (**1752**): not surviving?

1548-9

276 SS Peter and Paul church, Barnstaple (**364**): surviving, greatly altered 1866-82. See Nikolaus Pevsner, *North Devon* (1952), pp 45-6.

1549

277 House of John Wylkynson, London (**1061**): destroyed?

1549-50

278 Tilty Abbey, the house of George Medley (**1458**): ruins, except for chapel outside the abbey gate. See RCHM *Essex*, I, 321-2.

1549-66

279 St Andrew's church, Plymouth (**1302**): destroyed by enemy bombing in 1941, since rebuilt. See Pevsner, *S-Devon*, pp 229-30.

ca 1550-7
280 Hitchin Friary refectory (**775**): ruins. See RCHM *Herts*, pp 119-20, for part of the Frater range, much altered (map on p 121); and Nikolaus Pevsner, *Hertfordshire* (1953), p 138.

ca 1550?-8
281 Nonsuch manor (**144, 1212**): destroyed, with archaeological remains of a banqueting house, which had a Great Hall on its upper floor. See *VCHSurrey*, III (1911), 268-70 (pls opp pp 268, 270); and John Dent, *The Quest for Nonsuch* (1962), pp 125-30 (plan on p 127; pl 15 [excavations]).

1550-1
282 Corpus Christi College, Cambridge (**466**): hall surviving, much altered as two-storey kitchen. See RCHM *Cambridge*, I, 48-58 (plan between pp 50-1).

ca 1551-6
283 Sir Thomas Chaloner's seat, Hoxton (**782**): not surviving.

1551
284 The market place, Dover (**609**): the present Market Square?
285 Poole church (**1306**): pulled down in 1819. See Pevsner, *Dorset*, p 318.

1551-2
286 Guildhall, Market Place, Norwich (**1233**): surviving, with 19th-century front. See Pevsner, *Norwich*, pp 48, 259; and Ian Dunn and Helen Sutermeister, *The Norwich Guildhall* (nd).

1552
287 Castle Hill, Cupar (**1646**): now the play-ground of Castlehill School. See Alexander Smith, *The County of Fife* (1952), pp 645-6.
288 Hatfield House (**754**): newly built in 1608, but old hall surviving, greatly altered? See RCHM *Herts*, pp 58-62 (plan of hall on p 61, then used as stables); and *The Victoria History of the County of Hertford*, III, ed William Page (1912), p 95 (plans opp p 92, and on p 94).

1553
289 Durham House, London (**1082**): not surviving. See Pevsner, *London*, I, 343; and *A to Z*, p 18.

290 Market (place) cross, Kilkenny (**1741**): not surviving. See *Kilkenny: Its Architecture & History*, ed Katherine M. Lanigan and Gerald Tyler (1977), pp 62-3 (with an early sketch).

1553-7
291 St Nicholas church, Harwich (**752**): totally rebuilt in 1821. See RCHM *Essex*, III (1922), 134.

ca 1553-8
292 St Michael's church, Lyme Regis (**1165**): surviving but altered in the 19th century. See Pevsner, *Dorset*, p 259.

ca 1554-9
293 Holy Trinity church, Long Melford (**1154**): surviving, altered. See Pevsner, *Suff*, pp 343-8 (pl 16b [interior]).

1554
294 Arundel Place, London (**1090**): not surviving. See Pevsner, *London*, I, 383; and *A to Z*, p 18.
295 Christ Church, Oxford (**1288**): Great Hall surviving, much altered. See RCHM *Oxford*, pp 33-4, for this, the former hall of Cardinal's College, repaired after a fire in 1720 and remodelled in the 19th century (plan of hall on p 34; pls 81, 85 [interior]).
296 Ludlow Castle (**1160**): standing ruins. See Colvin, II, 732, and III.i, 277-83 (plan on p 279); and W.H. St John Hope, 'The Castle of Ludlow,' *Arch*, 61 (1908), 257-328 (for a plan including the Great Hall, pl XLI; and for the ruins of its interior, pl XXXVII and figs 11-12, 14).
297 Play field on the Greenside, Edinburgh (**1671, 1674, 1675**): Greenside is now the north side of Calton Hill in central Edinburgh.
298 St Andrew's church, Witham on the Hill (**1519**): much restored. See Pevsner, *Lincs*, p 714.

1555
299 Ingatestone Hall (**789**): partly surviving, but Great Hall destroyed. See RCHM *Essex*, II (1921), 139-41 (plan on p 140; pl opp p 144).
300 St Olave's church, Southwark (**1407**): ruins by 1737, then rebuilt. See *VCHSurrey*, IV, 151-2; and *A to Z*, p 27.
301 Tolbooth, Edinburgh (**1672**): demolished in 1817.

1555-6

302 The town hall, Southampton (**1403**): the guildhall survives, altered, in Bargate. See Pevsner, *Hants*, pp 535-6.

ca 1556

303 Mount Edgcumbe, manor of Sir Richard Edgecombe (**1191**): destroyed in World War II. See Pevsner, *Corn*, pp 123-4.

1556

304 Worm Cliff, the playing place of Devizes (**598**).

1556-7

305 The common hall, Winchester (**1505**): the old guildhall does not survive. See *Winchester in the Early Middle Ages*, ed Martin Biddle (1976), p 336.

306 The guildhall, Oxford (**1291**): not surviving.

307 The market place, Louth (**1157**): surviving. See Pevsner, *Lincs*, pp 303-4.

308 St James' church, Louth (**1158**): well-preserved. See Pevsner, *Lincs*, pp 300-3.

1557

309 Boar's Head without Aldgate, London (**1106**): not surviving. See *A to Z*, p 13?

310 The Falcon, in Petty Curry, Cambridge (**480, 482**): the yard still exists. See RCHM *Cambridge*, II, 329; and *VCHCamb*, III (1967), p 115 (drawing of 1875 of Falcon innyard, opp p 122).

311 The Saracen's Head, Cambridge (**480**): not surviving?

312 The Saracen's Head, Islington (**796**): not surviving.

1557-68

313 Trinity Hall, London (**1109**): not surviving.

before 1558

314 St Paul's Cathedral (**1110**): rebuilt in 1634-43, destroyed in 1666, and rebuilt as at present. See *A History of St Paul's Cathedral*, ed W.R. Matthews and W.M. Atkins, 2nd edn (1964), pp 1-171, 344, and pl 14 (interior); Morris, p 260; and *A to Z*, p 22.

1558

315 House of William Aston, London (**1113**): not surviving.

316 Old Green, Glasgow (**1692**). Glasgow Green is now an open park on the Clyde in central Glasgow.

1558-9

317 Pewterers' Hall, London (**1114**): not surviving. See *A to Z*, p 26.

before 1700

318 'Plain an Gwarry,' Race, Camborne (**432**): not surviving?

IV

Chronological List of
Salient Dates and Entry Numbers

Citation numbers of entries appear under their date or under the first date of their chronological limits.

55 BC   Caesar's first invasion of Britain. **1754**
54 BC   Caesar's second invasion of Britain.
1st century AD   **358, 518, 542, 606, 680.5, 826, 877, 1398, 1546, 1596, 1597, 1600, 1754.5, 1755**
44   Claudius' triumph in Britain.
61   Boudicca's revolt; destruction of Londinium. **550**
70   **523, 538**
78   Agricola becomes governor of Britain.
80   **490, 1489, 1593**
2nd century   **542.5, 751.5, 1594**
100   **551, 847**
122   Hadrian comes to Britain.
140   **413**
155   **1349**
197   Britain is split into two provinces.
211   Severus dies at York.
285   **1325**
ca 300   **1349.5**
306   Constantius dies at York.
367   Theodosius restores order after Saxons, Picts, and Scots attack Britain.
383   Revolt of Maximus.
410   Honorius abandons Britain to its own defences.
455-88   Reign of Hengest, king of Kent. About 455 the Saxons rebel against the British.

518   British victory over the Saxons at Mons Badonicus.
ca 523   Boethius' *Consolatio Philosophiae*.
539   Death of Arthur, king of the Britains.
597   Augustine converts Aethelbert of Kent.
604   Foundation of St Paul's, London.
605   **1554**
ca 675   Caedmon.
679   **191**
721   **1, 1756**
735   Death of Bede.
ca 750?   *Beowulf*.
757-96   Reign of Offa, king of Mercia.
793   First Viking attack on Lindisfarne.
799   **192**
9th century   **2, 193, 1757**
804   Death of Alcuin.
836   Vikings sack London.
865   Vikings' great invasion.
866-71   Reign of Ethelred, king of the West Saxons.
868   **1758**
870   St Edmund, king of East Anglia, is slain by the Danes.
871-99   Reign of Alfred, king of the West Saxons.
892   Alfred begins his translations.
895   Defeat of the Danes near London by Alfred.
899   Death of Alfred.
10th century   **194, 195**
937   Battle of Brunanburh.
946   Murder of King Edmund.
ca 950   St Gall *Quem Quaeritis*
955-9   Reign of Edwy.
959-75   Reign of Edgar.
ca 960   Hroswitha of Gandersheim writes her six *comediae*.
965   **3, 1493**
973   Edgar crowned at Bath.
975-9   Reign of Edward the Martyr.
978   **4, 1494**
979-1016   Reign of Ethelred (Unraed).
980   Viking raids against England.
991   Battle of Maldon.
11th century   Liturgical plays at Limoges; *Sponsus*; Paris *Officium Stellae*. **196, 1526**

1005   **197**

1009   The Danes attack London.

1013   Wessex subdued by Svein of Denmark.

1014   *Sermo Lupi ad Anglos* by Wulfstan, archbishop of York.

1016   Reign of Edmund Ironside.

1016-35   Reign of Cnut.

1035-40   Reign of Harold Harefoot.

1040-2   Reign of Harthacnut.

1040   Macbeth murders Duncan.

1042-66   Reign of Edward the Confessor.

mid-11th century   **198**

1057   Murder of Macbeth.

1066   Reign of Harold Godwinson and his defeat by William of Normandy at Hastings.

1066-87   Reign of William I (the Conqueror).

1075   **5**

1080   **6**

1085   Order for the making of the Doomsday Book.

1087-1100   Reign of William II (Rufus).

1090   Completion of the Tower of London.

1096-9   First crusade.

ca 1097   Building of Westminster Hall.

12th century   Fleury play book; Beauvais *Peregrinus*; Montecassino *Passio*. **421, 619, 1350**

1100   **616**

1100-35   Reign of Henry I.

1109   Anglo-French war (to 1113).

1125   **1759**

1130   **7, 1760**

1135   **1590**

1135-54   Reign of Stephen.

1138   Geoffrey of Monmouth's *Historia Regum Britanniae*.

1146   **8**

1147-9   Second crusade.

1149   **9, 620**

mid 12th century   Beauvais *Ludus Danielis*.

1150   **199**

1154-89   Reign of Henry II.

ca 1155   *Ordo Virtutum* by Hildegard of Bingen; the Old Castilian *Auto de los Reyes Magos*.

1159   **200**

1160 Tegernsee *Antichrist.* **10**
1170 Murder of Archbishop Thomas Becket at Canterbury. **491, 878**
1171 **1761**
1179 **201**
1180 **11**
ca 1185 Establishment of the University of Oxford.
1188 **12, 843**
1189-92 Third crusade.
1189-99 Reign of Richard I.
1190 Richard leaves on the Third Crusade.
1191 **1595**
1193 **879**
1194 Richard I again crowned. **1297**
1196 **673**
1197 **422**
1199-1216 Reign of John.
13th century Easter play of Muri; Laon play of Joseph and his
   brothers. **1601, 1635**
1200 Jean Bodel writes *Jeu de S. Nicolas* about this time. **13, 1762**
1202 **1341**
1206 **202**
1207 **880**
1208 Publication of the interdict of Innocent III.
1209 Students at Cambridge; completion of London Bridge.
early 13th century *Courtois d'Arras*; the Passion play in the *Carmina
   Burana*.
1210 **1418**
1213 John gives in to Innocent III. **513**
1214 **1602**
1215 Magna Carta; the Fourth Lateran Council. **203, 1148**
1216-72 Reign of Henry III.
1217 Dominicans arrive in England. **1371**
1220 **204, 375, 1556**
1222 **1364**
1224 Franciscan friars first arrive in England. **1506, 1763**
1225 Gascony taken by England. **14, 205, 206, 1241, 1603**
1230 **870**
1233 Jews not of use to the crown are expelled.
1235 Naves of Lincoln and Wells cathedrals are completed. **871, 872**
1236 **848, 873, 881**

14th century   *La Passion du Palatinus; Le Jour du Jugement.* **212, 825, 1311, 1356, 1358, 1727**

1300   **18, 19, 20, 400.5, 543**

1301   Edward I makes his son prince of Wales. **1219**

1303   Robert Mannyng's *Handlyng Synne.* **213**

1307   **214, 823**

1307-27   Reign of Edward II.

1309   **1413**

1311   Introduction of the Feast of Corpus Christi.

1312   Execution of Piers Gaveston. **885, 1339, 1381**

1313   **215, 886**

1314   Defeat of the English at Bannockburn. **1215, 1766**

1316   **1767**

1317   **850, 1768**

1319   **1365**

early 14th century   Vienna and St Gall Passion plays; Mallorcan play on the conversion of Mary Magdalene.

1321   Completion of Dante's *Divina Commedia.* **851, 852**

1323   **583**

1324   **1769**

1325   **21, 216**

1326   **1770**

1327-77   Reign of Edward III.

1328   **1351**

1329   **1352**

1330   **217**

1331   **887, 1474, 1475, 1476**

1332   **1765**

1333   **655**

1334   **888**

1335   **218**

1337   Loss of Gascony; beginning of the 'Hundred Years' War.' **219**

1338   **1474**

1340   English naval victory at Sluys. **220**

1342   **1605**

1343   **889, 1585**

1344   Edward refounds the Round Table at Windsor. **433, 1538, 1771**

1345   **515**

1346   English victory at Crécy.

1347   **740, 1314**

1348   Black Death this year and the next. **404, 492, 656, 770, 838, 844, 1240, 1772**

1349   Creation of the Order of the Garter. **1179**

mid 14th century   *Les Miracles de Notre Dame*; plays from the Bibliothèque Ste Geneviève (some as late as ca 1420).

1350   **22, 1242**

1351   Statute of Labourers.

1352   **657, 890**

1353   **434**

1356   King John of France captured by the Black Prince and brought to England.

1357   **891, 1773**

1359   **892**

1360   Treaty of Calais; the release of King John. **671, 1243, 1774**

1361   Return of the Black Death. **1509**

1362   Legal pleadings to be made henceforth in English; about this time the A-text of *Piers Plowman* was written. **893**

1363   **23, 362**

1366   Parliament denies feudal tribute to the Pope. **1557**

1367   **1586, 1740**

1368   **630**

1369   Black Death; the occasion of Chaucer's 'Book of the Duchess.'

1370   **221, 805, 1558**

1372   **222, 894, 1354**

1374   **895**

1375   **24, 896, 1295**

1376   **25, 223, 897, 1559, 1560**

1377   About this time the B-text of *Piers Plowman* was written. **224, 225, 376, 381, 802, 898**

1377-99   Reign of Richard II.

1378   Beginning of the Great Schism. **899**

1379   **1491**

late 14th century   Innsbruck *Fronleichnamsspiel*; Frankfurter *Dirigier-rolle*; four Flemish *abele spelen* including *Spel van Lanseloet van Denemerken*.

1380   **26, 226, 227, 900**

1381   Peasants' Revolt.

1382   Wycliffe expelled from Oxford. **1315, 1775**

1383   **228, 901**

1384 Chaucer begins *Troilus and Criseyde* about this time. **544, 632, 806, 853, 1495**

1385 Philippe de Mézières' *Presentation of the Virgin Mary in the Temple.* **229, 545, 902, 1561**

1386 **435**

1387 Chaucer begins the 'Canterbury Tales' about this time. **230, 231, 903, 904, 1202, 1244, 1776**

1388 Harsh persecution of lollards. **905, 1562, 1563, 1777**.

1389 Pier Paolo Vergerio's *Paulus.* **377, 423, 607, 854, 855, 1220**

1390 About this time the C-text of *Piers Plowman* was written. **546, 759, 906**

1391 **547, 1410**

1392 **27, 232, 554, 907**

1393 **633, 856, 908, 909, 910**

1394 **233, 234, 1487**

1395 The lollards' twelve conclusions are posted on the doors of St Paul's and Westminster Abbey; *L'Estoire de Griseldis.*

1396 **911, 1564**

1397 **28, 857**

1398 Banishment of Hereford and Norfolk by Richard II. **555, 1376**

1399 **807, 1217**

1399-1413 Reign of Henry IV.

15th century *Fastnachtspiele* of Hans Rosenplüt and Hans Folz. **29, 30, 31, 32, 33, 235, 236, 237, 238, 744, 1221, 1416, 1778, 1779**

1400 Murder of Richard II; assassination plot against Henry IV. **34, 35, 239, 240, 634, 790, 912, 1222, 1245, 1496, 1497, 1510, 1734**

1401 Statute against lollard heresies. **1780**

1403 Battle of Shrewsbury and the death of Hotspur. **621, 1181**

1404 **913, 914**

1405 **241, 915**

1407 **242, 414, 791, 1477**

1408 **658, 1223**

1409 **548**

1410 **243, 549, 610, 808, 1246**

1412 **916, 917**

1413 **659, 918, 919**

1413-22 Reign of Henry V.

1414 Statute against lollards.

1415 English victory at Agincourt. **635, 809, 920, 1498**

1416 **556, 1781**

1417 **622, 921**
1418 **653, 660, 922**
1419 **661**
early 15th century *La Passion d'Arras* by ?Eustache Mercadé; his *Vengeance de Nostre Seigneur Jhesucrist sur les Juifs par Vespasien et Titus.*
1420 Henry V's marriage with Catherine of Valois. **372, 858**
1421 **36, 923**
1422 **244, 524, 845**
1422-61 Reign of Henry VI.
1424 **37, 38, 39, 245, 636, 924, 1414, 1527**
1425 **40, 41, 925, 926**
1426 **42, 637, 662, 927**
1427 *Moralité faict en foulois pour le chastiement du Monde.* **43, 44, 45, 638, 771, 928, 929, 1194**
1428 **682, 1161, 1511**
1429 Joan of Arc relieves Orleans from the English siege. **46, 47, 246, 930, 931, 932**
1430 **48, 663, 807, 1175, 1512, 1606**
1431 Lollard risings near London; burning of Joan of Arc; Henry VI crowned at Paris. **525, 736, 1176, 1377**
1432 **49, 382, 664, 933, 934, 1203**
1433 **623**
1435 **925**
1436 Paris is lost to the English; the personal rule of Henry VI begins.
1437 **50, 342, 935, 1192, 1247**
1439 **783, 1248, 1340**
1440 *Farce de Mestier, Marchandise, le Berger, le Temps, et les Gens.* **51, 52, 766, 810, 1453, 1499, 1624, 1625**
1441 Foundation of Eton by Henry VI. **378, 661, 803, 859, 1500**
1442 **936, 1249, 1544, 1565, 1626, 1782**
1443 **608, 1224, 1545**
1444 Enea Silvio Piccolomini's *Chrysis*, a Latin imitation of Plautus and Terence. **373, 415, 493, 645, 1248, 1250, 1353, 1405**
1445 Henry VI's marriage with Margaret of Anjou. **53, 247, 343, 379, 494, 792, 811, 937, 1182**
1446 **1566, 1567, 1568, 1658**
1447 **646, 812, 860, 1167, 1340, 1459, 1548, 1569**
1449 English surrender of Rouen. **248, 249, 938, 1513**

mid 15th century   Arnoul Greban's *Mystère de la Passion*; *Le Vieux Testament*; *Le Mystère du Siège d'Orléans*; Jacques Milet's *L'istoire de la Destruction de Troye la Grant*; *Maître Pierre Pathelin*; Italian *sacre rappresentazioni*.

1450   Jack Cade's rebellion; expulsion of the English from Normandy.
54, 55, 56, 57, 58, 250, 1528, 1653, 1783

1451   **59, 495, 939, 940, 1460**

1452   *Actes des Apôtres,* attri to Simon Greban or Jean du Prier (ca 1452-78). **436, 609, 628, 693, 861, 1784**

1453   Mental collapse of Henry VI; recovers Christmas 1454.

1454   **60, 412, 862, 941**

1455   First battle of St Albans. **761, 863, 1344, 1570**

1456   **428, 557, 680, 1162, 1204, 1441**

1457   **61, 437, 558, 629, 665, 864, 1251**

1458   **1374**

1459   **251**

1460   **62, 1717, 1785**

1461   Second battle of St Albans; Edward defeats the Lancastrians at Towton; Henry escapes to Scotland. **63, 64, 65, 405, 559, 588, 1213, 1252, 1366**

1461-83   Reign of Edward IV.

1462   **689, 1691**

1463   **252, 784, 1205**

1464   Valencian *Ordo Prophetarum*. **66, 818, 942**

1465   **1412, 1419**

1466   Imprisonment of Henry VI in the Tower. **824, 1347, 1501**

1467   English treaty with Burgundy. **378, 827, 1529**

1468   **1298**

1469   Antonio Buzario's *Cauteriaria*, about this time. **386, 785, 1225, 1401, 1518**

1470   Restoration of Henry VI; Edward IV escapes to Holland. **67, 666, 1478**

1471   Edward recovers the throne at Barnet and Tewkesbury; Henry VI murdered in the Tower. **1627**

1472   Poliziano's *La Favola d'Orfeo*. **496, 865, 1710**

1473   First printing of Terence abroad. **350, 690, 1226**

1474   **363, 560, 1253, 1442**

1475   Anglo-French treaty of Picquigny. **68, 69, 70, 586, 1524**

1476   Caxton's press at Westminster. **828, 943**

1477   **424, 944**

1478   253, 369, 945, 1367, 1479
1479   71, 406, 642, 1254, 1299, 1301, 1468
late 15th century   Redentin Easter play; the Cohen *Recueil de farces*; *Les Vigiles de Triboulet*, a sottie.
1480   72, 73, 74, 75, 1399, 1659, 1786
1481   366, 946, 1420, 1423
1482   438, 874, 1443
1483   Completion of St George's Chapel, Windsor. 254, 255, 256, 1255, 1571
1483-5   Reign of Richard III.
1484   Incorporation of the College of Heralds; first performance of Plautus' *Aulularia* in Rome. 624, 1343
1485   76, 561, 647, 947, 948, 949, 1256, 1402, 1403, 1712, 1787, 1788
1485-1509   Reign of Henry VII.
1486   Jean Michel's *Passion*. 77, 407, 611, 694, 767, 788, 1257, 1309, 1363, 1502, 1530, 1572
1487   562, 667, 695, 949.5, 950, 951, 1573, 1607
1488   *Passion de Semur*. 1444, 1701, 1702, 1705
1489   Anglo-Spanish treaty of Medina del Campo. 257, 526, 696, 952, 1163, 1531
1490   78, 258, 384, 497, 517, 552, 563, 681, 953, 954, 1503, 1608, 1654, 1735
1491   498, 829, 955, 956, 957, 1480
1492   Henry VII invades France; Peace of Étaples. 352, 691, 792, 830, 1660
1493   Juan del Encina's *Cancionero* (two Easter plays). 564, 958, 1469
1494   439, 499, 592, 629, 831, 959, 960, 961, 1258, 1387, 1661, 1789
1495   *Elckerlyc*; first edition of the Greek authors from the Aldine Press at Venice. 79, 80, 430, 1259, 1260, 1261
1496   'Magnus Intercursus' between Flanders and England. 81, 688, 819, 927, 1368, 1409, 1640, 1708, 1730
1497   Rising in Cornwall and defeat of rebels at Blackheath; capture of Perkin Warbeck; betrothal of Arthur and Catherine of Aragon; destruction of Sheen palace by fire; Johann Reuchlin's *Henno*. 1206, 1448, 1481, 1662
1498   Aristophanes is printed at Venice. 82, 527, 565, 1316, 1317, 1434, 1490, 1736, 1790
1499   Execution of Perkin Warbeck; the first Italian 'tragedy,' Antonio Caminelli's *Filostrato e Panfile*. 408, 631, 697, 737, 761, 962, 1456
16th century   83, 84, 820, 1417

1500 Dutch miracle play *Mariken van Nieumeghen*. **85, 86, 259, 260, 261, 683, 760, 948, 962.5, 1372, 1609, 1791**

1501 Marriage of Arthur and Catherine of Aragon; Fernando de Rojas' *La Celestina*. **87, 262, 440, 500, 963, 964, 965, 1326, 1610**

1502 Death of Arthur; marriage of James IV of Scotland and Margaret Tudor. **627, 966, 1318, 1327, 1537**

1503 Death of Queen Elizabeth. **768, 967, 968, 1195, 1611, 1636, 1663, 1664, 1713, 1792, 1793**

1504 **263, 501, 969, 1435, 1794**

1505 **566, 567, 816, 1183, 1262**

1506 Joanna and Philip of Castile are shipwrecked in England. **425, 698, 817, 970, 1319, 1320, 1345, 1640.5**

1507 **88, 698.5, 804, 1263, 1264, 1321, 1450, 1665, 1666**

1508 **668, 971, 972, 1265, 1305, 1328, 1429, 1644, 1667, 1718**

1509 Henry VIII marries Catherine of Aragon; Ariosto's *I Suppositi*. **769, 813, 973, 974, 975, 976, 1180, 1522, 1574, 1737**

1509-47 Reign of Henry VIII.

1510 John Colet founds St Paul's School. **89, 264, 351, 441, 977, 978, 979, 1184, 1196, 1329, 1426, 1449, 1575**

1511 **265, 365, 568, 699, 762, 793, 980, 981, 1322, 1330, 1430, 1539, 1540, 1541, 1612, 1628**

1512 England at war with France; Pierre Gringore's *Le Jeu du Prince des Sots*. **90, 91, 266, 700, 701, 773, 1266, 1267, 1306, 1461**

1513 Henry VIII wins the Battle of the Spurs; the Scots are defeated at Flodden; Machiavelli's *La Mandragola*; Juan del Encina's *Égloga de Plácida y Vitoriano*. **92, 93, 519, 702, 1207, 1268, 1269, 1270, 1744**

1514 Mary Tudor marries Louis XII of France; Lucas Fernández' *Auto de la Pasión*. **94, 95, 267, 416, 678, 703, 866, 982, 1331, 1542, 1719, 1745**

1515 Mary Tudor marries Charles Brandon; Hampton Court Palace is completed; the duke of Albany becomes Protector of Scotland; Gian Giorgio Trissino's *Sofonisba*, the first Italian tragedy; Pamphilius Gengenbach's *Die zehn Alter der Welt*. **528, 704, 983, 984, 1301, 1302, 1322, 1385, 1388, 1668, 1795**

1516 More's *Utopia*. **441, 639, 705, 772, 1157, 1445, 1555**

1517 Evil May day; Bartholomé de Torres Naharro's 'comedias'; the time of Gil Vicente's greatest moralities, *Auto da Alma* and the *Barcas* trilogy. **96, 706, 1271, 1389**

1518 Peace of London; the start of Hans Sachs' play-writing. **268, 389, 643, 707, 840, 985, 986, 987, 1427, 1796**

1519   **97, 98, 99, 374, 502, 569, 597, 648, 708, 709, 710, 988, 989, 1201, 1532, 1549, 1576**

1520   Henry VIII and Francis I at the Field of Cloth of Gold; Ariosto's *Il Negromante; Recueil Trepperel* of sotties, about this time. **100, 101, 102, 103, 269, 442, 503, 570, 599, 711, 712, 713, 814, 990, 991, 1272, 1537, 1743, 1746, 1747, 1748, 1753, 1797**

1521   Treaty of Bruges. **443, 529, 600, 612, 714, 715, 716, 855, 992, 993, 994, 995, 1390, 1451, 1523, 1655, 1749, 1798**

1522   Charles V visits England; Pope Leo X names Henry VIII 'Defender of the Faith' for attacking the Reformation. **104, 105, 444, 717, 996, 997, 998, 999, 1346, 1514**

1523   **106, 270, 394, 757, 787, 827, 1000, 1001, 1445, 1463, 1720**

1524   **676, 677, 718, 735, 1543**

1525   Wolsey gives Hampton Court to Henry VIII; Pietro Aretino's *La Cortigiano*. **271, 368, 390, 395, 571, 649, 832, 1002, 1273, 1274, 1332, 1383, 1437, 1488, 1799**

1526   Anglo-Scottish peace. **272, 353, 409, 417, 504, 537, 572, 573, 593, 640, 644, 719, 720, 841, 1003, 1004, 1164, 1382, 1391, 1421, 1629**

1527   Anglo-French alliance. **273, 553, 587, 613, 721, 722, 723, 724, 738, 1005, 1158, 1577, 1800**

1528   **107, 108, 109, 589, 669, 725, 794, 814, 875, 1006, 1007, 1008, 1186, 1422, 1613, 1637, 1738**

1529   Legatine court tries the legality of Henry's marriage; the fall of Wolsey (York Place, later Whitehall, goes to the king). **349, 393, 530, 650, 745, 867, 1009, 1010, 1011, 1012, 1184, 1275, 1454, 1504**

1530   Death of Wolsey. **110, 111, 112, 274, 275, 276, 371, 617, 654, 675, 795, 833, 1013, 1227, 1276, 1317, 1630, 1694, 1721**

1531   Henry VIII is entitled Supreme Head of the Church in England; *Gl'Ingannati*. **113, 114, 277, 278, 354, 445, 530, 590, 612, 692, 763, 786, 1014, 1015, 1239, 1614, 1748**

1532   Treaty of Boulogne; submission of the clergy to Henry VIII. **279, 364, 410, 614, 625, 1428, 1488, 1651, 1750, 1801**

1533   Marriage and coronation of Anne Boleyn; excommunication of Henry VIII; birth of Elizabeth. **115, 116, 117, 118, 280, 281, 574, 764, 1016, 1017, 1018, 1188, 1277, 1278, 1400, 1470, 1802**

1534   Acts for the submission of the clergy to the king and for the king as the supreme head of the church in England; Nicholas Udall's *Floures for Latine Spekynge Selected and Gathered oute of Terence*. **282, 396, 832, 1019, 1020, 1228, 1229, 1279, 1280, 1320, 1382, 1464, 1641, 1652, 1695**

1535 Execution of Thomas More; major suppression of religious houses begins; reform of the universities; Paul Rebhun's *Susanna*. **283, 392, 726, 839, 1021, 1022, 1333, 1432, 1446, 1465, 1731**

1536 Execution of Anne Boleyn; Henry's marriage to Jane Seymour; Ten Articles; Pilgrimage of Grace; Thomas Cromwell becomes Lord Privy Seal. **119, 120, 446, 447, 448, 449, 672, 1023, 1024, 1025, 1384, 1386, 1425, 1433, 1452, 1547, 1803**

1537 Birth of Edward; death of Jane Seymour. **121, 122, 284, 285, 379.5, 651, 743, 1026, 1027, 1589, 1592, 1615, 1669**

1538 Destruction of relics and images in southern England, including Becket's shrine at Canterbury; *Pammachius* by Naogeorg (Thomas Kirchmayer). **123, 286, 505, 727, 756, 1028, 1316, 1334, 1462, 1515, 1550, 1578, 1587, 1670, 1722, 1723**

1539 Six Articles of Religion; publication of the Great Bible (to be in all parish churches by 1540). **287, 349, 387, 506, 531, 575, 576, 625, 776, 1029, 1030, 1031, 1032, 1281, 1433, 1642, 1804**

1540 Henry VIII's marriages to Anne of Cleves (annulled in July) and Catherine Howard; Regius Professorships of Greek at Oxford and Cambridge; George Buchanan at Bordeaux writes his *Jephthes* and *Baptistes* about this time. **124, 125, 126, 288, 431, 601, 672, 728, 728.5, 729, 1033, 1034, 1168, 1185, 1189, 1323, 1482, 1577, 1631, 1656, 1706, 1751**

1541 Henry VIII's progress north to York; Giambattista Giraldi's tragedy *Orbecche*. **127, 128, 129, 130, 289, 290, 507, 1035, 1282, 1283, 1369, 1424, 1430, 1579, 1632, 1728, 1739**

1542 Execution of Catherine Howard. **291, 292, 353, 450, 1036, 1037, 1038, 1039, 1150, 1156, 1324, 1392, 1714**

1543 Henry VIII's marriage to Catherine Parr; the King's Book (of doctrine) is published; Sperone Speroni's *Canace*. **131, 293, 294, 346, 417, 451, 532, 1040, 1041, 1378, 1425, 1732**

1544 England invades Scotland and France; Henry VIII crosses the channel and captures Boulogne; the first Paris theatre, the Hôtel de Bourgogne, appears about this time. **132, 133, 134, 135, 295, 452, 747, 748, 834, 1042, 1043, 1044, 1045, 1284**

1545 *Autos* of Jorge de Montemayor. **136, 296, 297, 298, 453, 454, 455, 615, 1046, 1047, 1048, 1049, 1050, 1285, 1431, 1551, 1616, 1696, 1715**

1546 **299, 300, 456, 457, 458, 459, 749, 1051, 1052, 1053, 1230, 1580**

1547-53 Reign of Edward VI.

1547 Edward Seymour, earl of Hertford, becomes Lord Protector and duke of Somerset; repeal of Six Articles act of 1539; Valenciennes

Passion play. **137, 138, 139, 140, 141, 142, 143, 301, 302, 431, 460, 741, 750, 777, 815, 1054, 1055, 1056, 1057, 1058, 1059, 1231, 1232, 1335, 1348, 1406, 1455, 1457, 1643, 1752**

1548 First Act of Uniformity; Chantries Act. **303, 461, 522, 730, 768, 1060, 1286, 1300**

1549 New Book of Common Prayer; putting down of Robert Kett's rebellion in Norfolk and of the Prayer Book rising in the West; fall of Somerset; Juan de Pedraza, *La Aparicion que hizo Jesu Christo*. **304, 305, 306, 307, 308, 309, 462, 463, 464, 1061, 1062, 1063, 1064, 1065, 1165, 1458, 1552**

1550 Peace of Boulogne ends the war with Scotland and France; Boulogne returned to France; Olavus Petri's *Tobiae Comedia* (earliest Swedish drama); Théodore de Bèze, *Abraham Sacrifiant*; *Recueil de Londres*, French sotties, farces, moralités, appears about this time. **144, 145, 146, 147, 148, 149, 310, 311, 312, 313, 401, 426, 465, 466, 467, 595, 641, 685, 775, 835, 1066, 1067, 1068, 1069, 1070, 1151, 1312, 1336, 1617**

1551 John Dudley, earl of Warwick, becomes duke of Northumberland; first licensing of alehouses and taverns in England and Wales. **150, 314, 315, 385, 429, 468, 469, 687, 731, 782, 1071, 1233, 1536**

1552 Beheading of Edward Seymour; Forty-Two Articles; founding of many grammar schools by Edward VI; Étienne Jodelle's *Cléopâtre Captive* (first French tragedy). **316, 317, 318, 319, 470, 471, 533, 594, 652, 732, 733, 754, 1072, 1073, 1074, 1075, 1076, 1077, 1078, 1169, 1197, 1337, 1393, 1646, 1671**

1553-8 Reign of Mary (and Philip).

1553 Lady Jane Grey is proclaimed queen 10 July and is deposed 19 July; Northumberland is executed; marriage treaty between Mary and Philip of Spain; Act of Uniformity repealed and church service is restored to what it was at Henry's death; Roman Catholic bishops restored. **151, 152, 153, 320, 472, 473, 474, 475, 577, 752, 789, 1079, 1080, 1081, 1082, 1083, 1084, 1085, 1086, 1087, 1287, 1472, 1516, 1633, 1657, 1672, 1741**

1554 Wyatt's rebellion against the Spanish marriage is put down; Lady Jane Grey is executed; Mary marries Philip; Mary of Guise, the Queen Mother, becomes queen of Scotland; John Knox goes to Geneva; Durich Chiampel's *Judit e Holofernes*. **154, 321, 322, 476, 876, 1088, 1089, 1090, 1091, 1152, 1154, 1160, 1198, 1199, 1288, 1519, 1673, 1674, 1675, 1676, 1805**

1555   Return of John Knox to Scotland; Philip leaves England and his crowning as king of England is rejected by Parliament. **155, 323, 324, 359, 477, 520, 534, 585, 1092, 1093, 1094, 1095, 1096, 1097, 1098, 1155, 1208, 1289, 1290, 1407, 1581, 1618, 1672, 1677, 1711, 1806**

1556   Cardinal Pole, papal legate, becomes archbishop of Canterbury. **156, 157, 325, 326, 478, 598, 755, 1099, 1177, 1191, 1234, 1291, 1467, 1505, 1533, 1582, 1599, 1678**

1557   Philip returns to England, which declares war on France as ally of Spain; Scotland invades England; the First Covenant is signed in Scotland. **158, 327, 328, 479, 480, 481, 482, 483, 508, 734, 752, 796, 1100, 1101, 1102, 1103, 1104, 1105, 1106, 1107, 1108, 1109**

1558-1603   Reign of Elizabeth I.

1558   Calais is captured by the French; Mary Queen of Scots marries the Dauphin; accession of Elizabeth on 17 November. **159, 329, 418, 427, 780, 842, 1110, 1111, 1112, 1113, 1114, 1212, 1235, 1292, 1520, 1521, 1619, 1620, 1679, 1692, 1807**

1559   New Acts of Uniformity and Supremacy. **160, 330, 331, 332, 333, 344, 484, 836, 1115, 1116, 1117, 1118**

1560   General Assembly of Scotland approves the First Book of Discipline, mainly John Knox's work, and papal jurisdiction is ended. **161, 162, 509, 778, 1209**

1561   **163, 399, 541, 1178, 1216, 1394, 1436, 1680, 1681, 1682**

1562   Thirty-nine Articles. **164, 334, 485, 521, 1119, 1153, 1238, 1293, 1373, 1683**

1563   **165, 510, 605, 1120**

1564   **166, 167, 168, 355, 486, 774, 868, 869, 1294, 1370**

1565   **169, 686, 1121, 1625, 1638, 1697**

1566   Archbishop Matthew Parker's 'Advertisements' regularize ritual; Vestarian controversy. **170, 345, 387, 487, 578, 591, 781, 1122, 1193, 1395**

1567   **171, 172, 173, 174, 397, 674, 1123, 1159, 1310, 1411, 1415, 1438, 1466, 1485**

1568   **175, 176, 177, 679, 758, 1200, 1303, 1447**

1569   **1396**

1570   Excommunication of Elizabeth. **178, 179, 180, 356, 419, 488, 846, 1370, 1583, 1588, 1639**

1571   Enforcement of Thirty-nine Articles against clergy. **181, 182, 183, 489, 779**

1572   **184, 185, 335, 380, 596, 1684**

1573   **347, 1359, 1379, 1492**

1574 **751, 1124, 1296, 1313, 1525, 1621, 1634, 1699, 1724, 1725**
1575 Edmund Grindal becomes archbishop of Canterbury. **602, 797, 801, 841, 1360, 1380, 1439, 1726**
1576 First attempt by puritans to reform fails in Parliament; the Theatre opens in Shoreditch. **511, 584, 1187, 1486, 1534, 1650**
1577 Grindal refuses to repress puritan prophesyings; Curtain theatre opens in Finsbury. **411, 528, 1361, 1622, 1712, 1716**
1578 **1236, 1690**
1579 Stephen Gosson's *School of Abuse*. **336, 383, 391, 753, 1338, 1685**
1580 **420, 837, 1313, 1517, 1623, 1742**
1581 Legislation against Roman Catholics in England; execution of Edmund Campion. **1214, 1704**
1582 **186, 348, 357, 603, 1125, 1591, 1647**
1583 Discovery of Somerville plot to assassinate Elizabeth. **1126, 1553, 1703, 1709, 1733**
1584 The Catholic enterprise of Philip II, Parma, and the duke of Guise to depose Elizabeth and replace her by Mary Queen of Scots. **579, 618, 1362**
1585 Expulsion of Jesuits and seminarists from England. **1648**
1586 Babington plot to assassinate Elizabeth, with support of Mary Queen of Scots. **1357**
1587 Execution of Mary Queen of Scots. **1397, 1808**
1588 **187, 402, 535, 1127, 1170, 1355, 1362**
1589 **337, 746, 1166, 1492, 1698, 1729**
1590 **1471, 1645, 1686**
1591 **580, 1128, 1129**
1594 **1130, 1131**
1595 **338**
1596 **1132**
1597 **742**
1598 **1687**
1599 **1693**
1600 **1133, 1440**
1601 **1404**
1602 **339, 739, 1134, 1135**
1603 Toleration granted to Roman Catholics. **1171**
1603-25 Reign of James I.
1604 **340, 1136**
1605 **341**
1606 **1137, 1172**

1607   **1483**
1609   **1138, 1174, 1210**
1610   **188, 536, 1707**
1611   **189, 1139, 1375**
1612   **798, 1140, 1173**
1613   **1141, 1142, 1484, 1809**
1615   **398**
1617   **1688**
1618   Declaration of sports.
1620   **190, 1143, 1144, 1810**
1621   **798.5, 1145**
1622   **1146**
1623   **400, 1147**
1625-49   Reign of Charles I.
1628   **1211**
1630   **370**
1631   **799, 821, 1143, 1307**
1633   **1689**
1637   **1143**
1638   **581, 1308**
1639   **512**
1644   **800**
1655   **604**
1664   **1304**
1666   **1190**
1700   **432**
nd   **1649**

General Index

Numbers in this index do not refer to pages. Numbers in ordinary type face are paragraph numbers in the Introduction. Numbers in italic are for items in Bibliographical Abbreviations. Illustrations and maps are indexed with the prefix '*pl.*' Bold-face reference numbers (eg, **1548**) are to the citation numbers of the entries in the text. (Citation numbers with an asterisk* indicate a dramatic character who has a speaking part in a play-text.) Any other two-part number joined by a decimal point refers to items in the first three appendixes (thus 1.244 is Appendix I, item 244). Appendix IV is not indexed. The order of entries here is letter-by-letter (up to a comma or opening parenthesis). Abbreviations employed in index headings are listed at the beginning of the Appendixes.

Subject indexing is generally done by means of the actual wording or phrasing of records. Thus possibly synonymous groupings such as *lusores, ludentes,* and players, or disguisings, masques, and mummings, or hairs, heads, and wigs, are given separate headwords. Cross-references and some large, general-purpose modern subject headings (audiences; *ludi*; pageants; performance, places of; play-books; players; plays; play stuff; stages; theatre history; and theatres) will help guide the user to this distributed information. To reduce lengthy strings of numbers after a common headword, sub-headings are used freely (under general names for kinds of plays, such as comedies, farces, and interludes, for example, sub-entries include play-titles so described).

A (ch) **81***
Aaron (ch) **8***, **188(3***), **521**, **768(2)**, **1227(7)**, **1295***
Abbacuc *see* Habakkuk

abbess (ch) **42***, **1675***
abbeys
– Bardney **360**
– Barking **23**, **361**, **362**

Cobham, lord *see* Brooke, George;
   Brooke, John
Cockayne, Oswald **198**
Cock (ch) **469***
Cockcroft, Henry 2.37
cock-crowing **554(3)**
cockpit **1397**
Cockroste, Mr 2.37
Cody, E.G. *222*, **1632, 1667, 1668**
Cœur Ardant (ch) **733(3)**
– *Loyal* **980**
– *Noble* **980**
cofferer (ch) **731(2)**
Coffman, G.R. *68*, **1793, 1810**
Coggeshall, Essex **202**, 1.32
coifs **554(4), 905**
Coin, Leadall (ch) **1096**
Cok (Coke), Richard **1057, 1076**
Cokayne, G.E. *82*, 1.206-334 *passim*
Coke, Thomas **1592**
Colchester, Essex **4**, **52, 550-3, 1420**,
   3.8
Coldewey, John C. 32, 38, 64, *69-71,*
   **347, 348, 383, 394-6, 397, 521, 613,
   615, 745, 752, 781, 1167, 1168, 1313,
   1347, 1373, 1486, 1522**
Coldstream, Nicola 3.20
Cole, Sir John 1.267
– Walter **515**
Coleshill, Warw 1.33
Colet, John *230*, **265, 985**
Colgrave, Bertram **1349.5**
Coll (ch) **58(13*)**
– Hazard (ch) **152***
collarmakers, craft of **1227(2)**
collars **1077**
Colle (ch) **588***
college members
– Greek lecturer **446, 1271, 1678**
– not to attend performances **433,
   1245, 1247, 1254, 1264**
– professor of Greek **450, 463, 1273,
   1289**
– professor of humanity **1271, 1273,
   1631**
– reader of humanity **1273**
– teacher of Latin **1290**

– Terence lecturer **439, 464**
colleges and collegiate churches **66,
   155, 371**
– Crediton **671**
– Glasney **671, 1295**
– Lanchester **822**
– Mettingham **1181**
– Newarke **832**
– Ottery-St Mary **671**
– Rotherham **1343**
– St Omer **1810**
– Tattershall **1434**
– Winchester **51, 1497, 1501, 1502**
– Wye **1548**
– *see also* Cambridge; London and
   Westminster; Oxford; schools
Collett-White, J.F.J. 64
Collier, John Payne 51, *72, 176, 390,*
   **283, 517, 596, 640, 956, 960, 968,
   1012, 1039, 1053, 1057, 1076, 1087,
   1331, 1383, 1405, 1420, 1779, 1781,
   1787, 1795, 1799, 1802, 1806**
– Richard J. **1560**
collier (ch) **173***
Collingwood, R.G. 413
Collins, Fletcher, Jr 73
– Patrick J. 55
– William **1794**
Colman, William 1.267
'colmanhedge, a' (ch) **1096**
Coln, River **1349.5**
Cologne, the three kings of *see*
   Balthesar; Christ (the offering of
   the Magi); Jaspar; kings, the three;
   Melchior
Colonna, Guido de **1605, 1609**
Colsonne, Richard **780**
Colvin, H.M. *205*, **750**, 3.19, 3.33,
   3.57, 3.59, 3.60, 3.62, 3.69, 3.70,
   3.71.5, 3.82, 3.89, 3.94, 3.98, 3.100,
   3.105, 3.112, 3.139, 3.149, 3.155,
   3.167, 3.192, 3.196, 3.197, 3.199,
   3.204, 3.212, 3.231, 3.296
Colyer, Christina **847**
Colyton, Devon **779**, 1.34
combat at arms **555**
– in play **731(2)**

devices (for) **881**
- combat at barriers **1066**
- d **928**
- learned **142**
- mum **1512**
- p **1279**
- painted cloth **924**
- pg **969**
- plots of ss **731(2), 733(1, 3)**
- tower pg **1539(3)**
devices (mottos) **969(17)**
Devil, the **192, 193, 216, 322**
Devil, the (ch) **55(26*), 272, 458,
    529(2*), 554(3-4), 570, 1080, 1210,
    1211, 1370, 1404, 1433, 1438,
    1560(5), 1591, 1712, 1774, 1794**
- and Richard (forged play-text) **76,
    1788**
- chain of **1433**
- coat of **554(4)**
- ʒamena **197**
- head of **554(4), 772**
- horns of **1774**
- mall or club of **554(4)**
- pg of **229**
- processing of **1187**
- shoes of **1550**
- tail of **1774**
- visor of **1438**
- *see also* Beelzebub; Belial; Dia-
    bolus; Lucifer; *Rex Diabole*; Satan;
    spirit
devilry **342**
devils **570, 1608(1)**
devils (chs) **55(30*, 40*, 41*), 58(1*,
    30*), 75*, 85*, 143*, 189*, 339, 348,
    354, 387, 430*, 458, 460, 527, 529(1*,
    10*, 18*, 24*, 25*), 734, 969(11, 26),
    1081, 1094, 1208(1, 3), 1210, 1452,
    1534, 1550, 1560(59*), 1613, 1716,
    1742(3)**
- black **969(11)**
- clothes of **511, 1560(59)**
- faces of **554(5), 1560(59)**
- head of **554(3)**
- hose of **554(5)**
- 'stafe' of **554(3)**

- with flaps **521**
- *see also preceding entry and* Alecto;
    Belphegor; Cadodaemon; Light-
    born; Mercury; Monfras; Rybald;
    spirits; Titivillus; Torpen; Tulfric;
    Tutivillus
devisers *see under* playwrights
Devizes, Wilts **598**, 3.304
Devon
- countess of *see* Courtenay,
    Catherine
- earl of *see* Courtenay, Henry
- men of **307**
Devon, Frederick *185,* **546, 938, 959,
    960, 968**
Dew, E.N. *101,* **765, 838**
Diabolus (ch) **6*, 21*, 55(19*),
    1194(2*), 1560(24*, 35*, 47*)**
diadems **554(5), 948, 1560(31, 59),
    1568**
dialogues **44, 48,** *397,* **1, 2, 6, 9, 15?
    16, 42, 71? 85, 119, 121, 294, 302,
    447, 620, 642, 1499, 1756, 1757,
    1764? 1781**
- acted **308, 451, 454, 721, 732, 869**
- *A newe dialog* by Thomas Becon
    139, 1335
Diana (ch) **733(2), 974, 1483(7),
    1484(5), 1796**
Diccon the Bedlam (ch) **469***
dice **888, 894, 897, 900, 903**
- play at **926**
Dick (ch) **142***
Dicke Dicer (ch) **1123(2*)**
Dickinson, John **200**
- William **1217**
Dickson, Thomas *4,* **1640.5, 1654,
    1701, 1705, 1708, 1730**
dictionaries *see under* English;
    French; Latin
'Dido' (ch) **999**
Dietrich, Julia C. **55, 58, 412, 529,
    554(1-2), 1560**
Digby Plays **69,** *102,* **54, 62, 74, 75, 90,
    521**
Diligence (ch) **134*, 168*, 1050, 1059,
    1123(1*), 1646***

placards **1117**
Placebo (ch) **1646***
place of pleasure (pg) **723**
places (playing) 41, 52, 55, **292**
- *amphitheatrum* **250**
- common playing place **598, 688**
- *diludium* **259, 810**
- *loca theatralia* **1595**
- *Plain an Gwarry* pl 7, 12, *272*, **212,
  432, 516, 1356, 1358, 1372**
- 'playing place' **255, 849, 874, 1359,
  1410, 1465**
- 'theatre' **309**
- *see also under* games; performance,
  places of
Placidus (Placy Dacy) **396**
Plain an Gwarry see under places
  (playing)
planets, the seven (pg) **69, 998(6),
  1679, 1685(6)**
Plantagenet, Arthur, viscount Lisle
  225, **1751**
- his wife Lady Honor 33, **1028,
  1751**
- pl of 1.295
Plantagenet, Richard, duke of York
  945
plasterers, craft of **1194(1, 6), 1560(2)**
platea **202**
Platts, Beryl 3.100, 3.141
plaupes **319**
Plautus (Titus Maccius) 28, **200, 270,
  421, 450, 455, 464, 478, 624, 1260,
  1270(6, 8, 10), 1271, 1273, 1290**
- *Amphitruo* **153**, *243 see also under*
  Vitalis of Blois
- *Asinaria* **243**
- *Aulularia* **243, 825**
- *Captiui* **243**
- *Casina* **243**
- chaster ps 28, **426**
- *Cistellaria* **243**
- cs **267(2), 444, 481, 709, 990, 1253,
  1272**
- *Curculio* **243**
- *Epidicus* **243**
- *Menaechmi* 28, **468, 1005**

- *Miles Gloriosus* **444**
- *Persa* **461**
- *Poenulus* **462**
- *Rudens* **481**
- *Stichus* **475**
- *see also* Miliphippa; Palaestrio;
  Periplectomenus
play-books (extant texts)
- art and 19, *6, 73, 92, 114*
- atypical 30
- auspices 42, 44
- authorship 19, 44
- bibliographies 44, *153, 160, 175,
  237, 243, 263, 376, 416*
- chronological lists *11*, **1-190**
- costumes *see* play stuff
- criteria for inclusion 44
- criticism on 3, 7-9, 18-19, 25, 30,
  38, 42, 44, 50
- dates of 43-4
- dialects 25, 44, *32*
- doubtful 51, **1756, 1757, 1760, 1762,
  1764, 1778, 1780, 1783, 1790, 1810**
- editions of 39
- fraudulent 51, **1788**
- meter of 30
- music and *73, 112, 152, 177, 191,
  268, 358*
- number of 2
- printed 27-8, 30
  - repertory of patron-sponsored
    troupes? 29
- proverbs in 30
- sources for 7-9, 19, 44
- staging of *see* staging
play-books (mentioned) **284, 397,
  497, 554(2), 1022, 1164, 1194(5),
  1378**
- arrest of **508**
- bearer of **274, 309, 772**
  - termed 'Ordinary' **339**
- borne by priest **365, 554**
- burned 36, **323**
- i **628, 1480**
- *libri de lusionibus* **766**
- of the Ascension **1399**
- of CC ps **613, 659, 792, 1742**

reeds; rib; rings; robes; rolls; rosary; rushes; *sacco*; scalps; scepters; scourges; scythe; sea-horses; sepulchre; serpentines; sheepskins; shirts; skins; spade; spear; spiral; squibs; 'stafe'; stage machinery; stars; stocks; stones (precious); stool; straw; streamers; sudary; swords; tabernacles; tablets; tail; thrones; timber; tombs; torches; trumps; tunics; vestments; vices (devices); victuals; vines; weapons; wheels; whipcord; wigs; wind; windows; wings; worms

playwrights 52, 54
- almoners 995, 1540
- paid 995, 998
- terms for
  - *comicus*? 303
  - compiler 385
  - conveyor 189
  - deviser 374, 969
  - doer 1259
  - maker 274, 303? 309, 1075(?)
  - *tragicus* 303
- women 144, 362, 1807
- *see Appendix* II
Pleasance (ch) 1385
Pleasaunce, Kent, manor of 693, 3.100
Pleasure (ch) 170*, 184*, 997
- Lord 1404
- Orchyard of (pg) 980
- Prest for 184*
plega 195(2), 196(2)
pleghuses 195(2)
pleglic 196(1)
plegstowe 195(3), 196(2), 198
Plenty (ch) 536, 937, 1086, 1685(3)
- Court of (pg) 1238(2)
Pleyer, John le 1765
- William le 1765
Plomer, H.R. *304,* 78, 92, 97, 116, 677
plots, theatrical 187, 1127, 1238
Plough day
- p 785
- pl 1428

- Plough Monday pastime 86, 419
Plowman (ch) 69*, 98*
plumbers, craft of 621(5), 790(1), 1194(5), 1560(27)
Plumpton, Sir William, ls of 23, 1.296
Pluto (ch) 969(11)
Plutus (p) 446, 1272
Plutus (ch) 721
Plymouth, Devon 31, 1301, 1302, 1.133, 3.248, 3.279
Plymstock, Devon 1303
poems (as records) 49, 198, 213, 217, 219, 221, 223, 231, 234, 237, 240, 248, 256, 263, 271, 570, 907, 917, 937, 1170, 1244, 1397, 1604, 1605, 1607, 1608, 1609, 1610, 1612, 1613, 1616, 1619, 1628, 1669, 1775, 1776, 1777
Poeta (ch) 74*, 90*
poets (chs) 158*, 472, 733(1), 1085*, 1116(6)
pointers, craft of 529(19), 790(12)
pointmakers, craft of 1227(10)
Pokeley, Richard 1070
Polax (ch) 188(6*)
Pole, Cardinal Reginald 1095, 1117
- John de la, duke of Suffolk 253
Poli, bishop of 430*
Policy (ch) 963(2), 1514, 1682(2), 1685(3)
Politic Persuasion (ch) 168*
Pollard, Alfred W. 18, *234, 58 see also* STC
- Francis 1263
'Pollenders,' the (chs) 733(2)
Pollet, Maurice 116
Polyharpax (ch) 156*
Polyhymnia (ch) 1017(2*)
pomegranates (prs) 1330
pompae 1664
Ponet, John 294, 302
Pontefract, Yorks WR 1304
Pontisbury, John 1.297
Pool, P.A.S. 1372
Poole, Dorset 1305, 1306, 3.285
Poole, R.L. *183,* 78, 99, 102, 108, 256,